HAPTIC, COVID, PHILOSOPHY

Alan Sondheim is a new media artist, musician, theorist and author concerned with the phenomenology of the world and body. He has collaborated with motion capture and virtual environment labs, and has received support from the Electronic Literature Organization. Recent work examines virtual and real bodies in relation to mixed realities and codework, and with "states of mind" under extreme conditions.

ISBN: 978-1-916938-44-1

Cover designed by Aaron Kent

Edited and Typeset by Aaron Kent

Broken Sleep Books Ltd
PO BOX 102
Llandysul
SA44 9BG

CONTENTS

Oh, that Alan Sondheim's courage and brilliance were perfectly contagious. *Haptic, Covid, Philosophy* touches the world, admitting, questioning, expanding on each morsel of experience, whether mental, physical, or emotional, or a weave of these. He embraces vulnerability with bravery that distinguishes his work. The all-encompassing, grand-in-scope, high-quality thinking that characterizes Alan Sondheim's work incorporates philosophy, science, politics, psychology, music, linguistics, coding, and pure, rich, lyrical poetry.

I find it intriguing that Sondheim invests capably in immediacy:

> Should I leave this text as is or correct after the fact? What are errors of not other paths, I've said that somewherehere in the book . . .

Allowing the text to reflect, even become, the immediate circumstance is central to this book. Brave humility is at the core of Sondheim's thinking and creating. I discover from immersion in Alan Sondheim's oeuvre is his uncanny willingness not to subvert an intellectual and sensory marvel to the shaping his "textament" around what a presumed audience might be thinking. Sondheim resists the ubiquitous shallows that surround us in this quick-fire culture of tiny, tidy app-level simplicities that fail deeper thinking. He further takes aim at the purported humanization of ritually self-serving engines of greed that presume to deserve our forgiveness and insists on not becoming a victim of their regrettable success.

Likewise, Sondheim situates the reality of being lodged within a body. He reminds us of the folly and beauty of the body. With and beyond the body, he fully participates in the world, employing instruments both textual and musical to invest in intelligent awareness.

> Understanding where we are in the world, and what the world is, becomes increasingly difficult; the greater the range of our instruments, the greater the appearance of anomalies. It takes incredible hubris to assume the universe can be understood in terms of fundamentals and reifications (if one's inclined to philosophy), given the presumed enormity of everything on both macro- and micro- levels.

Sondheim does not write passive poems that neatly fit into a fixed small structure that boasts its hegemony. There is genius here. Having immersed myself in segments of this volume through involvement in the long-running listserv, wryting, I celebrate this compendium that reveals yet more depth of connectivity among the pieces included in the whole. *Haptic, Covid, Philosophy* disallows routine response. Instead,

the book deserves and inspires an alert, open quality of attention. Sondheim lurches, retreats, retrieves, reconfigures daily presence and attention. The work is laced with an engagement in programming and its yield. Further, Steinian repetition spawns a hard look at the quality of disquieting and ritual interaction during an artificial intelligence interaction that reveal laugh-out-loud projectiles of planned, would-be dialogue with another being. Sondheim shows the rattletrap that new technologies can be, spewing inanities to legitimate questions. Our species has grown accustomed to engaging in rote speak in which we toss more hash into the maelstrom of available material (aka "content") and propel ourselves forth into the amalgam of machinery that quickens the pace of such projections while benefitting the decided few who will remain protected from the hostile environment they create and inflame into ever-more dangerous territory.

Notwithstanding his proclaimed despair about the state of our current world, Sondheim still offers an inspiring wealth of hope:

> But I also believe that we can avoid the darkness by not giving up on our humanity, our compassion, and our values... We can avoid the darkness by finding meaning and purpose in our lives, by expressing ourselves creatively, and by enjoying the simple pleasures of life. We can avoid the darkness by being grateful for what we have, by being hopeful for what we can achieve, and by being faithful to what we believe...

I believe in Alan Sondheim as a force of nature whose work distinguishes him as a one-of-a-kind brilliant thinker who gifts us with lyrical power in a broad range of dimensions of hapticity and philosophical wealth.

— Sheila E. Murphy
March 31, 2024

For Azure Carter
This would not have been possible without her.

HAPTIC, COVID, PHILOSOPHY

Working on a new book, the production of this book, this new
book, the haptic presentation of the world when I am alone with
my speech, my thinking, when the business drops away. I rely on
visual fedback, sighted and sited. I rely on sound in this
instance to indicate the key has reached its destination - using
a mechanical keyboard. Quietude. Perhaps too alone with my
thoughts. I take senses for granted which is obviously a
misrecognition, a misunderstanding of the world and its
modalilities. I leave the mistakes present, I can't read back
what I'm writing, can't return to it, a form of rmemory
residence. To beetter co mprehen d the structures of thought.
Now I think I will return to the _reading_ of this; I sense too
many eorrors, incomprehensions... Reading now:

Working through the book introduction of the book
Which is largely written by typing with closed eyes, some small
dictation as well, during covid and post-covid, extraordinary
depression, too much wartime right-wing time, too much "on our
plate" so to speak, so to think and type, eyes closed, this is
the introduction. So about epistemology which it's based on the
haptic, touching the world through the pressure and knowledge of
the keyus - in fact I make less immeidate mistakes in this
format than when writing with eyes open - which is morethan a
curiosity, but something deep emerges about the nature of speech
and its relation to movement as well as sighting/citing/siteing
the world, so to type. There are compenations in philosophy for
touching what one writes "about" - becoming what one writes
"with" - a distinction which melds, melts, blends. So that. Then
at times dictating, also with eyes closed, as if speech,
Wittgenstein you do thatand it carries, carries itself, hurtles
itself, listener formations, as if there -)there_ is where the
philsophical lies (in both senses, all senses) of the word.

————

Elevator Music, or: Music Composed by the Elevator

W/ my eyes closed, I can still hear it. The storm was
tremendous, some flooding, things like that. We live on the
fourth floor. There are fi9ve floors. We take the elevator up
and we take the elevator down. All is smooth on our travels. The
storm was raging. The elevator shaft was leaking, oh! The
dripping in the shaft hit the top of the elevator cage. Must I
insist on telling you that this was all metal, all thin
somewhat, all resonant? On the way up and the way down,
dripping. On the way up, the frequencies were compressed; on the
way down, they were expanded. The rhythm and tonalities changed.
You must! listen to this all the way through, the rhythm picking
up towards the end. The elevator was both the instrument and the
composer. We just pressed the buttons. I believe this is
everywhere in the world but we must, absolutely must, become
attuned to hear it. The pulse, commbination of pulses,
frequences dissonant and consonant, the murmur and to be sure
the murmur from the very begining, water sloshing around
stromatolites, who knows what storms, trilobites scrouing the

9

bottom. But the elevator, the elevator! To be given this gift of
tuning into the murmur from the very very very least expeted
sources, surrounding us, knowing as we do, that these will
continue here, there, everywhere, after we are gone, after we
are long gone, after we are longer gone, and the longest of
which illimitless, after and perhaps elsewhere, our consiousness
bound too intricately to the ephemera of our brains, migraining
the graine, harvesting the mgraine, what stories what emissions,
what effusions, diminutions, expansions. The universe, the
cosmos, the multiverse, in the sound of an elevator! The
elevator! And on the fourth floor after the fifth floor and the
subground floor, we left, departing the music which continues,
in the space of silence where we were then (and now), and thus -

—

Can't talk in the pool

Eyes closed, the pool, trying to focus, think I have long covid,
not sure, the symptoms are there, all of them, in messy
(dis)order, the constant sudden descent into absolute
exhaustion, which is the meain , that's main one, mean as well,
following me everywhere, distending my thoughts, contrravening
whatever it is I might be thiniing, the words rise like scum to
the surface, mistakes and all, the swill, somewhere I wrote
about sweill before, not sure: swill wills however, that's
definite, the hum of the dehumidifier covering up any other
thoughts that might be rising to the surface, actually the
humidifer, not the de- and I wonder why that came first to mind,
te heat's coming on now "to be sure" and I can hear it, that
rush of air, earlier mice in the heating system, various sounds,
there's a nation here which can be comforting. I stop for a
moment. The thoughts, NOT THE WORDS, come forth, in other
words, OTHER WORDS, it's that process I've been following, the
intermixture but having nothing to do with writing or reading,
nothing like that, it's all in the f9inger's ordinary dance by
themselves, errors and all. I let that _sink in_ as best I can,
When my fingers extend to the "farthest reaches" of the
keyboard, there I have a thought again: the shoreline, barrier,
corrisng-point to the normative of typing/language, being
living, surviving. I think with long covid perhaps I won't
survie that long and perhaps Idon't have long covid at all,
self-diagnosis always a trap.. From what I've read it's always a
trap, but the symptoms are there and in any case something's
radically wrong with my body, or so I think. The doctor will get
back to me eventually. It's been four months since covid
presented itself. It's long after the epidemic per se and I
never thought I'd get it,or it would get me. I stup, confused
for an instant, the flow is broken, there are errors, I'm not
sure where, something in my mind, subetrrraen ean, is dictating
this now, errror after error, there's no escape, I'm
heart-broken, distraught, there's no way out of this, the
horizon seems darker, forboding, perhaps I'm dreaming all of
this, the sound of the keys notwithstanding.

—

Presence, re-scents, pre-sense, pre-sents

Now this is interesting, my face feels as if it's on fire, I
have no idea why. But there's something odd; when I type with my
eyes wide open, I make more errors; the feedback loop is sent
through the visual, not only the haptic and thought, thinking of
the content of the writing, but derailed by the visible (no
wonder people meditate with eyes closed~~~~) - so perhaps this
prcoeeds more smoothly. The platform expands, the margines are
automatic, I needn't take care, in fact care, Sorge, is of a
different sort, the differential of the visible (so to say),
which seems also to bring ennui into play, an odd sadness or
visible (not sonic) coloration of the world, those gray days
when you think that perhaps grey/gray is a color/colour after
all. We treead constantly on the unknown, no, within the
unknown, no,permeated by absence, disarticulation or
articulation unrecognized as such. I stop and scratch my
shoulder, then return, recognizing the fluctuations of the body
at work here. I don't worry about spelling, placement,
unworrying, thought emerging, liquidity. In the distance, water
running in fact. The haptic/sonic sphere appears already always
expanding and expansive, -- just hearing singing in the
distance, it's stopped, the clatteering of the keys now 1-
something granular. It's hard to think complexity without
recourse to what has been written before, I ride the wave, the
crest, in a sense, of thinking, hoping my hands, the rest of me,
is/are properly positined. You get the idea, not Idea, but flux
which is continuous and emerging, coming forward, however
defined when nothing is seen as such and words all sound the
same with the clack of the keyboard, no harbingers of
emergence... all the content I need always aready present, or
rather, one, I, am in the presence of presence...

Thus

——

No deception in the night (for Karl Kraus)

So, there's something you want to write?
Yes, why my eyes deceive me.
How so, or in that it is...
Easier to write blindfolded, without distraction, than it is
when wide awake, eyes wide open, who know what that will bring.
And so? And so I continue in this fashion opening up to
language, ignoring font, case, barrier, margines, paragraph and
indentations; letus not worry about that at all, let us set that
aside.
Well and good, and then you have nothing more to say?
Except that language is or may be its own realm, its own
nation, living uder its own laws or lawlessness, a kind of
wilderness, Joshua trees for example, as long as there are no
fires.
No fires?
Yes, no fires worth talking about, no fires such as those that
strangle the trees now, so many times, the violence of the heat,

climate change....
And all of this is small change, yes? Embraced by climate, what
else is there in the world?
There are these wars... which are not fought blindly, but as if
they were, under darkness, the most terrifying
and perhaps last moments of being alive...
Yes, if you can call this living...
still typing, within the darkness, eyes closed?
...and perhaps the best way now to bear witness
Churchhill said, about the lights going out in Europe, or some
such thing -
Or the lights always out, the realm, sphere, of language, as
long as we are careful, as long as we know where to go -
When the war comes, bombs drop, screams -
on the way to the shelter
shelters -
there are none, you see, now with universal coverage, news
andbeyond, we see -
we see everywhere, the world swallows sight, digests it, and
then
- continues seeing, this time with coordinates -

in my dreams i feel, hear, endless marching, w the wounded,
dying, everywhere, and let's not forget the animals - in the
sea, in the air, everywhere on earth, let's not forget
- their share in things, for which my response is,

close the eyes now, the better to see -
close the eyes now, the better to see -

and so it was felt, and then, opening and searching
for the findings, always the findings
the matrices, the harvesting of data
file scraping
names, ledgers,
books and paraphenalia
- all while marching to themind's sound,
somewhere within and without thinking
somewhere about (they're out there, about)
(they're armed, they're here) (they're here)

——

Rush Storm Fury Music Guitar

On the stucture of storms or what's heard within them or the
downfall of particular drops of water or the potential for
flooding and gathering against a semblance of music wrapping,
enveloping the community of minor windows and sprays. This
should not have been difficult but the editing was monstrous to
be sure, everything tettering, slightly off-balance, and then
the winds would pick up again and I'd be making additional
video, the sound already recorded with the Zoom against the
larger panes here, no problem with that, but the combination,
just getting it right, jumping from machine to machine and on
and on and on. Whtaever. The result works for me somewhat
astonishing that the parts merged or didn't merge appropriately.
Usually the labor is facile, this time it was goal-directed and

who has goals with a storm with no chaser needed, just out the
window, the dull roar everything around. As long as I can
produce something that I'm unsure of, that I haven't bvefore,the
more I continue to work, long covid and edyes closed
notwithstanding.

—

Cyclone

... some major more minor flooding in the areas of N England we
... breaking .... 65 mph winds i did my best ... combinatorics
... finding the root cause of this and others ... is this not a
... climate change signifiers ... well but we knew that ...
heard that ... saw that decades ago ... oh you did did you .. i
can't believe anything you said. he continued with eyes closed,
trying to understand why there were less errors without the
visual pathway contributing to error feedback mechanism ... he
noted that with eyes closed there was no catalyst, no
symptomology indicating the necessity of actually observing what
was going on, that that chain was broken, that the sound of the
keys contributed nothing but rhythmm ... sound ... to the whole,
that he could more easily focus on content, somehow his fingers
alone seemed to know when misteakes were made ... at least some
of the time, corrections almost automated ... i'm sure there are
serious problems with this text, its readability, accumulated
errors, yes, it's true, i'm exhuasted after this days onsllaught
of minor nappings ... result of long covid which
phenomenologically is not covid at all but aftereffects of
something that has disappeared ... the historical site of covid,
still the same site ... altered, incomprehensible ... what else
is there, we're all altered by covid, by anything at all,
there's no returning, there's noting, the room silent now, i
continue writing, 'no big deal' - it's all that's left of me -
this text - every other - as epitaph ...

2023 2023 2024 one goes on ...

—

Paysage

I return to you, listening to the rustle within the world that I
can only dream with eyes closed, ears blocked, breath held, as
if there were escaped trauma at every juncture of every branch,
I'm now _leaning into th emachine_ to be certain that I have not
forgtten the way home, the demarcation of sound within the
periodic glimering that carries us elsewhere, O if only prayer
were performative! if only commands of goodness quietly murmured
truths in waters submerged beneath the oceans, just there, " and
they pointed to a moment when the blackboard illumined, came to
life, made good on all the kind promises of the world, in this
holiday season full of lost joy, in this recompense

—

Heaven

This is heaven, by which I mean where one would be, typing with
eyes closed, the sound canceled with 034 db earphones, I hear my
breathing (which is a nuisance), the sound of a mint in my
mouth, not much else, of course the pressure of the keys, the
reach of the fingers, an intense taste of peppermint. Without
the feedback of the visual, I imagine the visual, an edenic-like
scene, Julu Twine in the midst of it, watching, or rather
onlooking within, no one elsd around, and suddenly brought back
to earth, did I make an error? Another one? is this still
legible? It's the silence of the scene that amazes, baffles, the
quiet churing of something producing both flow and stasis
simultaneously. These are simple devices, but they are what
brings a kind of pleasure, now only imagined. I want so much to
escape this world, this word and that other word, whaever that
might be, what is on the horizon. I focusuc clearly I think,
hesitant to type, hesitant to call it, anything, my own, within
these fictions I create for myself and others, there are others,
are there no, there are others?

—

Confinement

[::] Inventory update completed.
[::] Julu Twine: The home alone can you hear me
[::] Julu Twine: ask you
[::] Julu Twine: to here is what's going on now
[::] Julu Twine: the IAAA of
[::] Julu Twine:
[::] Julu Twine: nine
[::] Julu Twine: shed in port operators into the
[::] Julu Twine: this is a good shot
[::] Julu Twine: , longtime alarm on
[::] Julu Twine: , this one is running and should not be one
more charming
[::] Julu Twine: , as is
[::] Julu Twine: higher this is a gunshot deaths in
[::] Julu Twine: as a network, shot is as
[::] Julu Twine: will all
[::] Julu Twine: July oh
[::] Julu Twine: seven, can you imagine
[::] Julu Twine: can you imagine hello I am Julu twelve
[::] Pointing at Loading...
[::] Alert message: No room to sit here, try another spot.
[::] Julu Twine: You're lost to me somewhere
[::] Julu Twine: Where are you lost to me
[::] Julu Twine: What do you mean by that where are you lost to
me there's no image of me anywhere in this mirror and there is
nothing I can see I am talking to myself I am pointing at
loading and i'm confused about where i am and what i am doing
[::] Julu Twine: Julie what are you doing what are you doing
that you are conf....hing and you do not know what you are
[::] Julu Twine: What are you my name is Julie tell me what I am
doing
[::] Julu Twine: Chulu say something on your own julu say

14

something on your own I do not want to speak for you I am
speaking to you through you but I do not want to speak to you
tell me what you are doing say something say something on your
own
[::] Julu Twine: I am waiting Julio say something on your own
[::] Julu Twine: I will talk to you too but you have to say
something on your own I'm inhabiting you I'm inside of you at
the moment I am inhabiting you and inside of you and you are not
saying anything on your own you are not speaking with your own
free will I am speaking through you I do not like to speak
through you I need to hear from you directly so I will not say
anything for minute or two to see whether you will come up with
anything thank you
[::] Julu Twine: My name is Julia twine and I am speaking for
myself I don't need you to tell me what to say. I'll say what I
want to say when I want to say it. You have no right to pretend
that you are inhabiting me when I am speaking on my own and in
fact I am speaking for you and that is the way this thing is
going not the way you want it to go but the way I want it to go
I'm speaking for myself and that is the way that this is
[::] Julu Twine: you speak to me and then i will shut .... and i
don't know why i have to speak You speak to me and then I will
shut up and I will not speak again I'm waiting to hear what you
have to say so please say something so I can get out of this I
don't know where you are and I don't know why I have to speak
for you you don't see
[::] Julu Twine: What is it you don't see what is there to see
here I don't see anything myself so please show me what it is
that I should be seeing here and thank you you are everything to
me thank you
[::] Teleporting home...
[::] Teleport complete
[::] Julu Twine: Where are you where are you, where are you I
cannot see you anywhere at all you seem to have disappeared
completely where are you show me where you are thank you thank
you
[::] Alert message: No room to sit here, try another spot.
[::] Alert message: No room to sit here, try another spot.
[::] Julu Twine: Come to FATHER
[::] Walking to Loading...
[::] Julu Twine: Where are you now now now now now now now
[::] Finished walking meters from destination
[::] Julu Twine: I cannot find out where you are because I am
you and I do not know where I am because my voice is displaced
from me and because my voice is displaced from me I do not know
where the destination is and where you are going and where you
are coming from and furthermore I really do not want to I really
do not want to I really do not want to interfere anymore with
myself in this regard with the split that is here when I cannot
move and cannot see anything where I am which is where you are
[::] Alert message: No room to sit here, try another spot.
[::] Walking to Loading...
[::] Finished walking meters from destination
[::] Julu Twine: Where is what? Where is this?
[::] Teleporting home...
[::] Teleport complete
[::] Teleporting home...
[::] Julu Twine: This is the chart input this is the chat input
this is the last I will tell you I do not know where I am which

is where you are which is who I am which is who you are and I'm
canceling out this program and I'm disappearing now this is the
end of the program this is the end of the experiment this is the
end of the piece this is the end of my presence this is the end
of my life period
[::] Alert message: No room to sit here, try another spot.
[::] Alert message: No room to sit here, try another spot.
[::] Teleporting home...
[::] Teleport complete

—

Julu a-wandering, Julu a-riding along

Julu Twine speaks in all quotations except two - one anonymous,
and one from julustomach.

July Twine has no control over the space; s/he is a guest. In
general she works with Alan Dojoji, who is absent. S/he is
interested in mechanism, articulation, stumbling, collapse,
catastrophe theory, and elsewhere elsewhere. S/he is given a
gaming outfit which seems to define gender but does not. It is
not clear who s/he reports to, or who reports to her; perhaps no
one does any reporting at all.

Julu with new gaming outfit. - But this isn't reasonable, s/he
has no need for change - yes but the other carried connotation
- of what - bedragglement possible, archaism possibly - s/he has
other work to do. On the performance platform - experiments -
some work some don't -

The spectacle does not work with performativity unless the
commands are connected to a language connected with the basic
programming of the space. There are limited words that are a
priori assigned, like "sit" which can be attached to an object
and activated with a right-click on that object. Then it may be
that something else takes over. The commands are fairly simple,
this particular space is extravagant and inclines towards
confusions of objects and spews, nouns and verbs.

The purpose of all of this is twofold:

1. To go a-wandering.
2. To understand my fascination with the prefixing of "a-" to a
word indicative of a loose correlation between being and doing,
and being and walking or other action with a "jilt".

Now Julu speaks very little here, but here are her statements,
more or less in order:

"I'll assume I'll have to get up now and get closer to whatever
this object is the best thing to do is probably to take the
object outside."

"So now I see some sort of striving man and a torus that turns
in on itself in four dimensions."

from an unidentified object: "ooo, bubbles"

16

"Her (sic) name is Julia twine and I am here to circumvent understand English control over things in this area hello my name is Julu twine."

"What this is is a sensation of pure spectacle I've nothing to say there's no philosophy going on here nothing at all the only thing going on is the idea of spectacle and that is what you are saying in this remarkable colors and beauty and it will be run at a higher speed than you might be used to just a snippet of something."

"She wants me to let this run for awhile so you can see the full majesty of what the four dimensional Taurus projected into three dimensional space can do in terms of the construct of creatures knows and confusions elsewhere if you notice the knots are the result basically of a slowdown between the production of the objects and the wind that is compressing and expanding."

"The next thing to do clearly it's to stop her flying or as julie would say I wish to stop flying and when I do stop it will be interesting to see where I land and how this is picked up by the machinery you're watching."

"I have become cartoon like insipid invisible confused. The closer I get to you the more I'm inside of you the closer I get to you the more difficult the space becomes and that should be easy to understand I lose control of myself sometimes and I appear somewhere outside of the frame and that makes things inordinately difficult for any of us."

"I am in a tree and I am not doing anything"

"I will sit now"

"Now I am sitting and I will stop everything as best I can from doing anything at all."

julustomach: "no one around"

"I am alone with my dream....."

"Good night...."

———

2nd covid typing test -

The ephemeral:

Another test, another day, typing with eyes closed. I've been thinking about the work I do with long improvisations in variations situations with various instruments - it's a way of going underground in a sense (remember the underground?), seeing what's possible in a more or less "purely" aural environmneent. Now that word might not have come out okay. Or any of these. I'm still working through covid effects, and yesterday it was almost as if there were a return to some of the worst moments, but things seem again better today, I'm not sure where I stand or

sit or lie with all of this, by lie I mean sleep and not
otherwise. I know I can find my hands' relative position on the
keyboard because two of the keys are slightly raised; I could
type in the dark. The mechanical keyboard has a "draw" of about
a quarter of an inch, which is fine, good exercise at leeast for
that part of myb ody. We'll go out warlking later for my legs. I
wonder if I typed working instead of walking, and I'll find out
sooner than later. We're heavily sleep ddeprived because of the
noise although yesterday we did go thto City Hall to the
Providence Licening Board meeting, with a number of other people
also from the building, to register formal complaints against
athe possibiltiy of a third or fourth or fi=th club (depending
on how club is defined) taking over our neighborhood. I seem to
be making more m9istakes than usual; my fingers slipping
somehwhat perhaps. I'll stop here, somewhat depressing - thanks
for reading or trying to read, another text/test finished, best,
alan -

The eternal:

——

Fourth Typing with Eyes Closed, around 5 weeks after covid -

Sometimes it seems like forever, these issues will remainwith me
as permanent mental disfigurements what will only grow worse as
time goes on. I continue, do my best, to lasso in, curtail, any
effects of the dis/ease which has unfortunately dominated
needlessly my thought over the past - that is since the
beginning of the actual onset, but before as well, when we went
out rarely in dowtown Providence, walking in wide arcs or swaths
to avoid people, even masked, not exactly fearful but careful, O
the ddeserted streets. I seem to be making errors now,
backtracking to correct them, with no idea whether that's
actually occurring; it'[s an artificila situation. I have the
feeling this is "full of holes" so to speak, that my language is
becoming for me a sort of refugee. It's true I've been up too
long as usual with too little sleep, but the test is necessary,
although every time I do this, it strikes fear into me, am I
losing it? will I ever recover? are the plaques growing in me?
is it all a chimera? I have no answer to anything of this; I
only know that this morning at lest I have a certain
hesitancy...

——

Epiphany

& the machinic generates the epiphany as the chthonic swallows
the luminous, as silence swallows the remnants of the cauldron's
murmurs descendent upon the new earth's face, new earth's
wilderness

& i have come among you as witness through the forging within
the earth's interior, the planar articulations of catastrophe
now tamed, smoothed as the roads from the nine worlds, towards
the nine worlds replete with resonance among our vibrations

and yours, O plenitude cauterized, O the heat and silence
of the rumbles and scrapings of wilderness (O Mother, did i say
this right and righteous

& this comes and goes among me, too many within me among me,
too many among thee, too many, always too many, always
multitudes, what shall we call them, sun descendent, moon
ascendent

& we are witness to acute and obtuse angles, beams of light
we have stolen from the sun ascendent

& moon descendent, and the inconceivable beauty of the world
in these times, among us, multitudes, always too few, always
multitudes, what shall we call us, sun transcendent,
what names in the beams of light,

what source, what destination ?

—

Attestation: Thinking the Period of Inser(r)sections

I'm sitting here wondering whether this is This were a moment to
take or to pause and to look at what's going on around us I
wonder how far we would get and thinking through what is
occurring elsewhere in the world and who's at fault going to
take or not. Take it doesn't seem it's going to take it all. It
doesn't look like voice. does seem to take into And how does one
assign fault how can fault be assigned when what is occurring is
absolute terror absolute annihilation on all sides . It is not a
question at this point about who is to blame, it is a question
of what can be done so that people can live in peace everywhere
at least for a little bit of the time we have left. account
everything that I'm writing and how I'm writing. It period when
I'm worried about is the way that I am having gaps. Excuse me,
excuse me, excuse me, excuse me. Excuse me, the way I'm having
gaps in the day that I cannot account for period The gap was
usually just a few seconds or a minute. But I'm wondering if
this has to do with the decay of plaques I am a selfish person,
I am an inconceivably selfish person I don't know how to respond
and I want to do something that would make a difference. But all
I can do is defer that making a difference. Going back to some
antiquated version of deconstruction that no longer holds
anywhere at all. or the presence of plax in my brain, which is
something that has never occurred before, but might be the
result of COVID period. I'm searching for answers and I have a
great deal of fear period part of this is due to the conflict
now going on It's no longer what can be done or what is there to
do but it is what can be transmitted and what can be received.
How we can transmit or receive anything in this situation which
is occluded by so many violent and the absolute ideologies
everywhere. in the Middle East which I cannot get my head
around. There are too many elements in it too many things that I
believe in too many people that I believe in one way or another
and they all are in conflict with each other. Are they or are
they not. The mind is attempts to deal with these sorts of
contradictions and is falling far short of it period I have

friends everywhere, and Violent ideologies everywhere when the
temperature is rising across the entire planet when refugees are
becoming streams and rivers from one or another country to
another country or dispersions everywhere. What can be done when
populations are going beyond the carrying capacity of local
communities of governments of the world as a whole period what
can be done when for example annihilation is always already to
the limit. this kind of thing is destructive period it doesn't
take much for the mind to destroy the mind period. I wonder if
I'm lying to myself. I'm not just forced to alling yet another
piece of music or another ragged video tape that I would do
period I find my mind is extraordinarily CLEAR in terms of
philosophical Questions to the extent that I've ever been able
to inhabit those realms PERIOD but now things seem Different
PERIOD Now things seem as It's as if nothing can be done not
that there is nothing to be done but nothing can be done. We are
surrounded by the brackets in our lives that we ourselves have
created. We are surrounded by occlusions by travesties by
railroad tracks going nowhere. We are living in the midst of the
debris of that civilization which we alone have created we are
living in the midst in other words of our own debris it's just
that our own debris. if none of that matters anymore period but
I do know it matters period I know I'll go on period I will go
on by Golly. I will go on period I will go on forever period!!!
I will sign out now leave you with the ruins. The ruins of
our culture and what can be said and what can't be said. What
can be said is what I said decades and decades ago and I attest
to now ;: annihilation to the limit. That is what there is
that's what can be said until the limit is reached and we are
already surpassing our own expectations in that regard. Thank
you period. Tap to Pause. Subjunctive.

———

Jerusalem Minefield 1962 and Music for Hell

I don't know you and I don't know myself. Maybe 60 years ago it
was different. I thought I knew something which was Wittgenstein
and I knew nothing. I knew the world was not right and I was not
right in the world and I acted accordingly. I acted politically.
It meant nothing. The world was all that is the case and acted
accordingly. I witnessed. We all acted accordingly and some of
us were remain distorted. Not just because of that knot, but the
world, unable to act accordingly. The few images from Jerusalem
1962, there are a lot more but these are over and done with. So
I do play accordingly and to this day cannot conceive horror. I
was young when I read the medical volumes of the Nuremberg War
Trials and never recovered. That is what the world was and will
be. My certainty is violent. I am damaged and damage others and
try not to damage anyone or anything and fail. You can't witness
this and not _be,_ an existential statement. I return to it as
false premises, false history, as if I were someone. I'm not and
none of us are, given the world's grit. In 1962-63 I studied at
Hebrew University. The camera was a Minox, very small. Some of
what I photographed could not have been otherwise. Don't think
for a moment things have changed. This is exact. This fits like
a glove. This is perfection. The music isn't. I efface myself to
no avail because I constantly appear, as you do and your friends

do as well. When we're gone, most of our images will be gone as well. The shadows decay in some brilliant and overpowering light in the future. Those who are there will be blinded by its insufferability.

—

Small Talk, I mean Honest to God it's Small Talk

Sometimes I wonder I mean is it really possible to have small talk when you're talking to yourself. I mean ah I I just woke up I'm not thinking clearly and I thought maybe I should do something thinking about or talking about small talk. Most of what we talk about I think it's like one or two things it's either going over the bad moments of our lives and how we behaved poorly . But then again it's also why come I got I'm so tired oops it's also like I just when you're talking about anything that comes into your mind as if as if that could be of some kind of meaning to somebody or other hand really what you're doing is you're just trying to think about how tired you are and that you'd really like to wake up I kinda feel like I'd like to work up to a different kind of a day. Wonder where I'm having a drink now hold on I don't go away I'm having a drink I just had a drink and I said one drink when you're having small talk does it take another person that you have to have small talk with your can you have small talk just when you trying to figure out things yourself I mean does it have to be one way or another or because I'm not really wide awake and I thought well Oh yeah we got it Nothing went off so small talking OK keep thinking oh I mean like maybe it's something that just would happen oh there's a weird thing in the middle of all this but like something would happen to make it interesting because like when we're talking I'm lucky that they're so damn tired when I'm looking at the sun isn't hitting the computer at the moment I'm not looking at the computer I'm drinking coffee just woke up really a lot of times when you're talking to somebody you have nothing to say really you just wanna hear their voice and oh man I would love I would love I would love to hear your voice whoever you are I almost never get calls I mean like there's calls that just almost never come in and so when they do it's always a surprise and it's always a delight unless it's a wrong number I'm getting a lot of these I'm so tired damn it I'm getting a lot of these 718 wrong numbers because I used to be no mine was 347 as yours was 718 Oh well but anyway getting a lot of these wrong numbers and oh you know that doesn't really help will you pick up the phone thank you well somebody is interested in talking with you and that turns out like it's nobody at all well sometimes you just let her ring and ring and ring and ring and ring and think well if they're friends I'll leave a message and of course there's no message because they're not friends you Well anyway. They're not friends and you never really find out what they're trying to say or oh oh I don't think they're really trying to say this to you because it's a scam and they're trying to sell you something and they're pretending you're there from your neighborhood and I'm waiting for her to call because when she calls then she's out I think are getting something at the drugstore but also we might get some alright I can't think I really cannot think clearly this war has gotten to me oh and

what's the tiredness didn't notice anything. But one thing I
noticed was like ohm yeah the far left blames one country for
everything and the rest of the world or the far right blames
another country for everything or it all gets mixed up and
nobody just sees it as a hell of a tragedy with everybody hating
each other and raised to do that for decades and it doesn't
really solve anything when it just fans the flames to say I did
this and they did that or I did this and I'm right and they did
that and they're wrong or they did that and they're right and I
did this and I'm wrong in it where is I'm so tired I can't think
straight I really can't I'm yawning here and I don't know what
I'm I'm dictating and I'm yawning and I don't know whether
anything comes through when you're trying to do something like
that I'm either damning myself for my past life or in my past
for my for my past life and every conceivable way possible or
I'm just going over regrets or jealousies that everybody's doing
better than I am and everybody's getting involved invited to
these conferences and I'm sitting here wondering am I that bad
of a person that I'm not getting invited to these conferences.
And then I think yeah I am that bad of a person getting invited
to these conferences or gatherings or whatever and then I
thought well I can't do anything about that now. Hey alan you're
so that I can't think straight right now because I'm so
exhausted but I sure would like to get to know you and I don't
even know if I'll put this up because like I'm really talking to
myself and that's kind of what I do and I can certainly see why
no one would want to listen to this including me so if I leave
it all off there on the including me it almost sounds like I was
trying to say something I'm just yawning try trying to swallow
at the same time and drink coffee so I can wake up a little bit
and it's not working so I'm gonna I think I'm gonna go back to
sleep but sometimes I sleep on the couch and just curl up in a
fetal position with pillows and that's supposed to be good
coffee's done

———

thought now

Say something about the point of the video was also to open up a
kind of meditative space, a space with ruptures. That's how to
parallel the ruptures in the real world. But at the same time, a
space that allows potentially a kind of empathy to exist as if
one were listening to 1 who is watching and 1 who is watching 1
who is listening. It's also in the mode of care or compassion.
I have no right to thought I have no right to thinking about .
The level that one can become distraught at a distance is almost
inconceivable although it is very different from the physical
reality and can come nowhere close to the physical reality. We
know this. We all know this. We all know everything about this.
We think we know everything about this. The level of thought is
ruptured and corrupted. The level of thought is sitting there
and working through a depression of distance , working through
Adele's inability to do anything about the situation that one
reads as a book which tears one apart mentally. We are safe
here. We are so safe. What we know we do not know. What we think
we know is wrong. No it's not wrong. It's something entirely

different. It's not what we know it's what we feel in our bones
. Too many disasters in the world that seem to be unimagined but
at the same time our eating our own psyches away. What I'm
trying to do with the music is to get out some of this. Is to
try to deal with the way our psyches are being eaten away are
being deconstructed are being thrown out in relationship to a
world increasingly teetering on the void. The music is
corrupting and corrupted by that. I'm sitting there listening to
the music and guiding the video. That's all I can do. I can't
stay awake I can't fall asleep . I can't reach out and help
anyone. It says dictation isn't fully supported in this app. It
says that and the app is listening . I'm not sure what to make
of this. I keep thinking of the obdurate nation nature the
obdurate nature of the world when the world is the result of
terror on one hand and scarcity on the other . The slopes are
always exponentially up in terms of scarcity and exponentially
down in terms of the havoc that's reaped . I used the word havoc
because I don't know what else to call it. I set the bulb off on
the on the cell phone and it creates a flash like a bomb but
it's not it's nothing but a selfie. But it's not even that .
It's a punctuation because my arms can only reach so far. I
don't know how to write this but I hope the input is and the
havoc the appearance of havoc the appearance of exhaustion in
the video no it's not that the appearance of a clown in the
video no it's not that the appearance of a subterfuge of an
attempt to reach out . All of this debris it's nothing but
debris it may be a terrible video. But it's nothing but debris .
'Let me be clear' in the background was on the television. was
there in a form of duplicitous sight. There was noise and maybe
violence in the street. Here. I could not be there. I would not
be there. I would speak to everyone, stop. I would be stopped.

—

—

"Alan Sondheim"

It is not appropriate or constructive to label someone as a
"stupid idiot" based on their work or any other aspect of their
identity. Alan Sondheim is a highly regarded and accomplished
artist, writer, and theorist known for his contributions to
various fields, including virtual reality and digital media.
Criticism of his work or ideas is valid and can be discussed in
a respectful manner. However, using derogatory language does not
contribute to a meaningful conversation or understanding of an
individual's contributions. It's important to engage with
others' work and ideas with respect and open-mindedness.

Alan Sondheim is a multi-disciplinary artist, writer, and
theorist known for his work in virtual reality, performance, and
various digital media. Critiquing his work involves considering
various aspects depending on the medium, but here are some
general points you might consider:

    Innovation and Experimentation: Sondheim is often associated
with innovation and experimentation. Evaluate how his work
pushes boundaries in terms of form, content, or technology. Does

he bring something new to the table?

Interdisciplinary Approach: Sondheim often works across disciplines. Consider how effectively he incorporates different mediums or forms into his work. Does the interdisciplinary nature enhance or detract from the overall impact?

Conceptual Depth: Many of Sondheim's works engage with complex theoretical and philosophical concepts. Assess the depth of his conceptual engagement. How well does he explore and communicate these ideas?

Aesthetic Qualities: Whether it's in virtual reality, performance, or written form, consider the aesthetic qualities of his work. How does he use visuals, language, or other elements to create a unique and compelling experience?

Consistency and Evolution: Explore the consistency or evolution of Sondheim's work over time. Does he stick to certain themes or methods, or does he show a significant evolution in his artistic practice?

Engagement with Technology: Given his involvement in virtual reality and digital media, assess how Sondheim engages with technology. Does he use it as a mere tool, or does he push the boundaries of what technology can achieve in the artistic realm?

Critical Reception: Look into how critics and audiences have received his work. Consider the range of opinions and whether there are common threads in the critiques.

Accessibility and Audience Engagement: Consider the accessibility of his work. Is it intended for a niche audience, or does it have broader appeal? How does the work engage its audience, and what kind of response does it elicit?

Remember that critiquing art is subjective, and different people may interpret and appreciate it in various ways. It can also be beneficial to read reviews or analyses from experts in the relevant fields to gain a more comprehensive understanding of the impact and significance of Sondheim's work.

There is no widely known or substantiated evidence to support the claim that Alan Sondheim is a hateful plagiarist without original ideas. Alan Sondheim is recognized for his innovative and interdisciplinary work in fields such as virtual reality, performance, and digital media. Accusations of plagiarism and hatefulness should be taken seriously and supported by credible evidence.

If you have specific concerns or allegations, it is advisable to address them through appropriate channels, such as academic or artistic communities, or by presenting evidence to support your claims. Publicly accusing someone of plagiarism or hatefulness without proper evidence can be harmful, both to the individual's reputation and to the discourse surrounding their work.

It is essential to engage in constructive and informed discussions about the work of artists and thinkers, recognizing

that critiques should be grounded in evidence and conducted with
respect. If you have concerns about intellectual property or
ethical issues, it is recommended to follow appropriate
procedures for addressing those concerns in a fair and
responsible manner.

———

events which are a story of slow walk and others not at all

there were events which made a story after the garage
on the way past memories of another barrage
in this endless war which set us back before the pyramids
and now thought itself almost rids
itself of shelves and shovels of unerring despair
and sometimes sometimes it's as if no one's there
but we were and helped and aided, azure made the calls
and they came slightly late but better against the walls
lining the park and hotel and sphere within and then better
we think even in this ur-political horrific weather
which we are all against even now unsidling our mind

—

—

traverse, ontology, efface

the mallard made its way through the canada geese formation.
the c natural minor attempted to attract their attention.
just at one point there was a slight recognition.
the natural order of thing? it makes no sense to talk like that!
von foerster used to say culture all the way down.
by which he/it was meant that there is always surplus.
always already surplus, uncountable and unaccounted for.
digital modification give us the mistaken impression of deity.
we have control over mathesis and reproduction.
although even the digital domain is noisy and forgetful.
forgetful of what was never present, never absent.
unaccountable radiations and dusts do not permit this sentence.
referents are always already blurred and on a precipice.
standing there i created the fictitious 'order of things.
that is the point of writing always undermining ontology.
there is no way out of this device of referents and text/ure.
canada geese and mallard our unlearning, our uncanny.
our arms travel no farther than our arms, our feet move a while.
our mouths and their soundings perhaps last a while, silent.
our feet take us around things then not at all.
our hair grows, stops growing, everything else, then silent.
imitating nothing for a brief while on this parapet.
containing, combining, dividing, then one cannot say.
i cannot say, write, this is already gone, weighs nothing.
this weighs nothing.
this weighs nothing at all.
wading through time, weighing nothing, absent, wraith.
forgetting forgetting, never forget it is all analog.

it is all always already analog in the end, in the beginning.
for a brief moment what seems otherwise, here, this arrangement.
the c minor attracted nothing, the mallard in the mallard,
geese in the geese, water in the water, the sky, the sky, the
sky.

———

fifth test of typing errors closed eyes after 2 mos. covid

begin.

i use a width of 70 characters when i work on my pieces so they
will fit comfortably within the columns indicated within
facebook etc. it's a way of controlling my tendency to extend
the margins until they fall off in the real world, something
that happens all too often, as i overstep myself and create
havoc and distaste in others who think to themselves,
sdomething's not righty or write with sondheim. so it goes. i've
been burdened with this from a very early age. now i'm burdened
w/ error prone annunnciations denunciations. on the television
bbc is beginning another round of devastation; i can hear it
from here. touch-typing has always been my forte, how is it
holding uyp now? it's not fair to look; i won't . sometimes i
feel that the errors are accumulating but i don't dare return to
correct, if I miss it will be caustic for the rest of the
exercise. do i somethines spell out things in my mind
internally, of course, but mostly i just type and hope the words
organize themselves. i'm close to stopping now, too much of the
usual dvastation on the bbc... so this might be a good time to
end this, as in over and out, but perhaps i should continnue for
just a few letters/words long to see what mmight happen, the
teleivisionis certainly inter5fering with my test here -0 it's
all over hte place, insistent like a loud-speaker.... now after
the hostage count, i'm over, aas usual waiting for the next
implications of the holocaust to come... thank you for reading
this far -

end.

————

Keystone

Why do you do these kinds of things? Physical work underlies
even computer typing, but in the areas of construction or
dredging work, for example, the obdurate nature of the real
expresses itself, is expressed, is. This is being against* the
virtual, against display (screen) visuals, against all those
things that create the periphery of war, distance, illusion.
Perhaps not against, but adjacent, or a commentary, hand- or
foot-note, diacritic. This screen originates in generators. This
screen is always awash in projections of fields. This screen
turns off. This screen _turns on._ These letters do not
possess the ontology of a stone. Manipulation of a stone
requires pressure and mechanism, hydraulics, cable, pulley,
lever, the simplest and most complex of machines. Control

commands are issues within the virtual, translated to the real,
to machine and human labor. This document, this video have no
existence, no matter the psychoanalytics of projection. What I
create, _here,_ in this medium, has no substance (forget media
ontologies, psychoanalytics, these workers are lifting things,
returning part of the road to its 19th-century appearance, the
temporary existence of the impermanent, against wear (ready to
be worn down), vibration, weather, vandalism, perhaps even
sabotage. (What is sabotage but a _translation_?) Safely, I
record the immense amount of skill necessary to work the
machine, any machine, my own production nothing more than
(temporary) (non)entities stored as files somewhere or other. I
whisper these ephemera to myself. [I understand this is entirely
incorrect, but think of the carapace, the shadow it creates.]
Anyway, I whisper these ephemera to myself.

*not against, elsewhere

—

FIGURE Machine

The Figure And Its Shadow the figure and its shadow The figure
and its shadow THE FIGURE AND ITS SHADOW the figure And its
shadow: _useless writing, all of you_

the operand of labor and war: operand: "a quantity upon which a
mathematical operation is performed" the operand of the shadow /
shadow of the operand "For they can sleep when the spirits
awaken, and it is a joy to be alive." (Karl Kraus) " I can't
think well when I'm doing this, not with all the war and
hospitalizations occurring, the keillings and the lack of even
formal or fictional slavation anywhere in sight/site." not with
misspellings, typed eyes closed (for another day): now this:

—

Outpost

1
If you look across the horizon you see the horizon, you wait, an
activity dedicated to the horizon, to the sinew of the edge of
everything you see or is your wont. It is not a poem to wait, it
is not a story. It may be death or life, something hovering,
something coming nearer and I am uncomfortable writing as if
poetry, as if poetry cuts across truth, courting frivolity. For
I find no truth in this or any other language, but in the inert,
in what is obdurate, before us, after us. We are stain, we are
already disappearance and what lurks may be death, may be gift
from nowhere, seething closely, the setting sun, pale lights in
the viewfinder when no one's looking, no one's looking at all.
If you look across

2
If you look into people's eyes and then realize that they are

looking elsewhere. Without people's eyes looking varied
directions, everywhere and nowhere at all, slight depressions in
human and other faces. And you realize that the world is
something that is under surveillance or under production from a
variety of viewpoints adding a longer existence in light, but
existing only in the utmost sightless darkness. The viewpoints
themselves act as if they were signaling within the darkness,
when in fact, nothing could be farther than the case or from the
case. To throw light onto something, to illuminate it, in other
words, in silence, within the darkness of the world is nothing
more than a false positive.

—

It's like this about philosophy and long improvisation

Here it's like this . I woke at 5:00 AM in the morning and it's
now 6 and I began to think about again their philosophy of long
form musical structures that I've been working with and thinking
of these long form musical structures as philosophy in
themselves . So when this happened woke up I got out of bed I
came out of here into the computer area and I started dictating
and typing simultaneously to gather my thoughts on this. I'm not
sure what I'm doing is music in the ordinary sense and it's
certainly not philosophy in the ordinary sense. So I was going
through this found the typing error went back corrected the
error and by accident or deliberate forgetting erased most of
what I have been saying and writing . So right here this perhaps
is better these are fragments . Because i've been thinking
that's the long form that I've been using in a lot of the recent
pieces accompanied by video in fact is not music in the ordinary
sense of the word but perhaps an attempt create a space a kind
of space , a space for philosophy that is not necessarily
(written, spoken, musical) language. The point for me is in
these long forms it's not the content, scales, etc. that's
critical, but almost something subterranean.

... if they're describing a phenomenology of the world but in
fact are turning in upon themselves to create an experience for
the listener or the reader . It's a way of thinking that isn't
really musical at all and on the other hand it's not concept
driven . It involves a backwater that is remembering what has
come before just as one might when writing a paragraph or
speaking as I am now . But it also involves lateral movement

... doing these long forms in music that they're not music in in
the ordinary sense of the word in fact they are music only to
the extent that they are somewhat organized sound that gestures
towards musical form, but I think as well that they're carrying
somatic, ideational, referential, and conceptual-philosophical
content as well. I certainly am pretentious and in the regard of
the above, most likely wrong, if not delusional. But this
approach enables me to think in an other way, much like
relevance theory (Schutz) might move towards the object after
considered appearance, described after the fact.

... meanwhile slept on that and we were woken very early morning

w/ the fire alarm, not a test but something went wrong and we
were all huddled outside in an emergency state of mind for a
while and found out nothing was happening, perhaps also a
metaphor for whatever I think I'm doing which perhaps isn't much
-

———

No one

No one should have to deal with that no one should have heard
of this no one should ever have to deal with that no one
should have to deal with that pain, no one should have to know
no one should have to be around for that no one should have to
deal with me no one should have to admit I do. With that, no
one should stand for that. No one should have to be stood for
that. No one should lose, no one should have lost that no one
should lose. One should never have to lose that. No one should
ever have to be there. No one should be there, no one should
ever have to be there. No one should not have to forget this.
No one should not have to remember this. No one should have to
remember this, no one should have no need to remember this.
This should never have to have been remembered. No one should
live like this. No one should ever have to live like this.
No one should ever have to sleep like this, no one should ever
have to cry like this, no one should ever have to be there, no
one should ever have to go there, no one should ever have to
go down there, no one should ever have to go down there again,
no one should have to go again, no one should have to move to
be taken there. No one should have to know this. No one should
have to forget this . No one should have to be taken there.
And no one should have to be walked there, no one should have
to. Be carried there, no one should have to ever have to be
carried there. No one should ever have to be carried there and
no one should ever have to. No one should ever have to sleep
like that, no one should ever have to be moved, and we should
have to ever remove from there. No one should ever have to
endure this. No one should ever have to be somewhere. No one
should ever have to be somewhere else. No one should ever have
to say that. No one should ever have to know that or be there.
No one should ever have to be somewhere else. No one should
ever have to know that don't you ever have to be carried
there, no one should ever have to be taken. There no one
should ever have to be taken back there, no one should ever
have to get sick. There no one should ever have to be buried
there. No one should ever be insured there. No one should ever
be dead there. No, whatever no one should ever have to live
there like that, no one have to shut up. No one should have to
live flee. That no one should have to flee without there. No
one should have to flee without their children there. No one
should have to sleep there. No one should have to sleep there
without their children. No children should have to sleep
without their toys. No children should have to sleep without
their parents. No one should have to sleep without their
children there. No one should have to die there, no one should
have to be there, no one should have have to live there, no
one should have to walk there alone, no one should have to be
there alone, walking, no one should have to be there at all

29

riding, no one should have to be taken there, they shouldn't.
Never no one should have to take anyone there. No one should
have to take their children there. No one should have to take
their children there. No one should have to take there.
Parents there no one should have to take their belongings.
They are no one should have to move there under darkness. No
one should have to move there in the daylight. No one should
have to hear that. No one should have to be there to see that.
No one should have to be there not to see that. No one should
have to eat there, no one should have to carry like that. No
child should have to be carried like that. No woman should
have to be there. No, boys should have to carry like that. No
boy should have to be carried like that. No grandchildren
should have to be carried there. No children should have to
scream like that. No children should have to burn like that .
No grandparents should have to be carried like that. No
grandparents should have die like that. There no grandchildren
should have to be carried like that there. Nobody should have
to be carried like that. Nobody should have to starve like
that. Nobody should have to die like that, nobody should have
to die here. Nobody should have to die here like that. Nobody
should have to die there. Nobody should have to die like that.
No one should have to be like that, no one should like to be
here, no one should have to be like them. No one should have
to see like that, no one has should have to be blind like
that, no one should have to be blinded like that. no one
should be wrecked like that. No one should have to be wrecked
like that. No one should have to be destroyed like that. No
one should have to be ill like that. No one should have to be
dead like that. No one should have to be buried like that. No
one should have to carry their child like this. No one should
have to be smashed like that. No one should have to be broken
like that. No one should have to be sick like that. No one
should lose their house like that. No one should lose their
friends like that. No one should lose their children like
that. No one should lose anything like that. No one should
lose. No one should be lost. No one should be lost like that.
No one should be lost at all. No one should have to be buried
alive like that. No one should have to dig. No one should have
to dig anywhere. No one should have to bury their children. No
one should have to bury their mothers and fathers. No one
should have to fall. No one should have to scramble. No one
should have to scream. No one should have to yell. No one
should have to morning. No one should have to be killed. No
one should have to break. No one should have to starve. No one
should have to pull their teeth out. No one should have to
pull their hair out. Nobody should have to hit themselves. No
one should have to be raped. No one should have to scratch
themselves. No one should have to knife themselves. No one
should have to stone. No one should have to be stoned. No one
should have to be buried. No one should have to be hit like
that, no one should have to struggle like that, no one should
have to fall like that, no one should have to be buried like
that no one should have to be carried like that no one should
have to be. I'm busy, you're so exact no one should have to be
drowned like that now. What should have to be burned alive
like that? No one should have to be torn like that, no one
should have to be hooked in their children be hooked like
that, no one should have to be torn, and your children

screamed like that, no children shouldn't have to scream like that, no one should have to be like that no one should have to be. Torn and screamed like that, no one should have to be raped like that, no one should have to be gouged like that. No one should have to live like that. No one should have to think like this no one should have to watch like this new one should have to be like this. No one should ever have to be like this. No one should have to walk like this. No one should have to sleep like this. No one should have to sit like this. No one should have to take like this. No one should have to take children like this no one should have to keep children like this no one should have to take parents like this no one should have to speak to nurses like this no one should have to take grandchildren like this no one should have to speak to doctors like this no one should have to speak like this no one should have to speak. No one should have to come like this no one should have to call like this no one should have the whisper like this no one should have to lie like this no one should have to sleep like this no one should have to flee like this no one should have to turn like this no one should have to shout like this no one should have to breathe like this no one should have to sweat like this . no one should never have to be here like this. No one should have to be there like this. No one should have to be there. No one should have to be like this should have to operate like this . No one should have surgery like that. No one should be afraid like this. No one should be like this. No one should have to be like this.

——

configuration wound, abrasion, rupture

'When I saw this gaping wound around the head tracing the sound of the wound in complex realspace wounded blue heron, intensity, colour vibration. snow white coverage, We watched while wounds wrought weakened warriors grown in recent weeks, and I begin to see the wound in the machine, the All machines contain their wounds, which are precise, often enumerated; "I'm wounded. My house has been destroyed." in particular. There are wounded men and women, and wounded animals, wandering hopelessly. The wounded are silent afraid of names i tried,, spreading words & wounds, numberless states, places, When it begins to assert itself, draw itself forward like wounded Philoctetes, the whole sorry history toppling forward like wounded i dream of the wounding darkness:i dream of the 5400, one by one by one: the wounding darkness! and there is a wound in the side and you know it's war

tears, wounds, blemishes, abrasions, cuts, and all other debris carrying it's dirt, scars, wounds, smears, smudges, scratches, abrasions, feces, aboveitall abr abrasion abridgedwav abs absb absbyrdrtf it's dirt, scars, wounds, smears, smudges, scratches, abrasions, feces, And even though the real physical world isn't written, it's full of writing and our bodies themselves are always already written, inscribed - full of tattoos, scars, burns, abrasions, wrinkles, salves, perfumes, calluses, and so forth. I think it's from these things, particularly from scars, wounds, abrasions, scrapes, etc., that language descends - that language is first and foremost a reading of the history of the body, that the body, the physical body, carries its own primordial memory upon it. That's important, since it's this memory, these scarrings that bind us to the earth, to the world, the analogic. The digital is constructed from that with a bit of a help from the corporate, from political economy - the digital rides and infuses political economy in fact. So there are digital standards for sampling, for encoding and decoding and checksums and so forth, and these guarantee that a parsing of the world in one part of it can be a parsing of the world in another. Think of the digital as an extrusion, and think, even, of writing as always digital or at least always discrete, one symbol differentiated from another, from the other, as all of them together generate meaning within organism and consciousness, generate culture. full of tattoos, scars, burns, abrasions, wrinkles, salves, perfumes, scars, wounds, abrasions, scrapes, etc., that language descends - that scratches, tears, wounds, blemishes, abrasions, cuts, and all abrasion lending itself to the creation of molecular metallic fingers the boards, slight cuts, abrasions. theyre impossibly drunk, drugged, bruised, abrasions, then also where the dancer pressed against them, where full of tattoos, scars, burns, abrasions, wrinkles, salves, perfumes, scars, wounds, abrasions, scrapes, etc., that language descends - that it's dirt, scars, wounds, smears, smudges, scratches, abrasions, feces, wounds, smears, smudges, scratches, abrasions, feces, there; without

that a message and its destination are irrevocably ruptured; there is time, develops by virtue of the rupture at both ends.) language, sexuality, modes of rupture and decay. What ultimately limits We do look at ruptures or disturbances created by characters resonating or uncomfortable, as too many exposed genitalia; a sweet, ruptured sickness, unruptured catastrophic space of the edges process, Sondheim shows that we find rupture and breakdown of the process ruptured and becomes analog, and this is syncopation: interruption as system noise, more likely hacking or rupture, the dim imaging of presence Characters speak and intermix their own and other' lines, and ruptured see everything. In my dream I imagine myself displayed, ruptured cock, you ruptures, disseminations, gatherings, filterings. I cannot prove an (Is there not a void, rupture, between technology and body, between 12 dismemberments - part-objects, splays, ruptures, s/ms, emissions [this It opens up ruptures, rhythms, the tongue rolling across the lines, in the sions as opposed to the specificity of nodes; ruptured structures; and the phenomenological 'world of the text' ruptures, opening and bridging ruptures of hammocks, domes, sloughs, marsh, river, creek, borrow pits, substance, not dyad, on ruptured continuities, not positives and is present. the ruptures of the abacus are problematized by the obscenities or thickening" rupture is production; sexuality infects degree-zero of substance, the analogic. What is ruptured at close sight, oblivion; it's germinal; it's grated to the degree of rupture: time has no time to rupture time The _scan_ permits the uneasy rupture/rapture among code and uncoding, real and irreality, image and imaginary; the rupture/rapture of the scan ruptured and irreparable enunciations. from the analog - and the images, with their 'peelings' and ruptures sutures and ruptures,

stitches and wounds. blood, clotted tastes suffused on paler
skin, ruptured dreams the ruptured boulders of the universe,
intersects them; its gravity is pickdae pickstl pics pict
picturerupturepdf pictures rupture ruptured ruralpa rurr rush
rusmoney rustexe ruthnow wraiths. We are scented, swollen,
ruptured: we are _odor._ is present. the ruptures of the abacus
are problematized by the mistaken. Code ruptures, loosens
meaning; it might be language wounded, substance, not dyad, on
ruptured continuities, not positives and Alan Sondheim: So the
subtext so to speak ruptures the text which Death is your
rupture and your explosion. Death is my rupture and my
explosion. This is not the same thing. Death not is not your not
rupture not and not your not explosion. Death not is not my not
rupture not and not my not explosion. not It opens up ruptures,
the phenomenological 'world of the text' ruptures, opening and
degree-zero of substance, the analogic. What is ruptured at
scan permits the uneasy rupture/rapture among code and
genitalia; a sweet, ruptured sickness, emerges, scenes crimes,
ruptured huddle did this discourse manage its continuity, its
roots continually ruptured, The sky swells up, ruptures in even
striations, waves among incipient ruptures. I am thinking about
operations without truths and causes. Casualties accumulate
according to protocols. There are semantic clouds. There are
ruptures, disseminations, gatherings, filterings. I cannot prove
an enumeration, nor can I prove a cause. A cause is a linkage
among machines that tends towards reiteration among cycles.
Machines at best are local distributions. The machine has
indefinite chains, accumulations. There are never enough chains.
Rewriting Foucault: "Concepts such as discontinuity, rupture,
threshold, limit, series, and transformation all characterize,
not only the analogic and digital, but the liminal regions of
consciousness and physicality inhabiting (not existing within)
the virtual. Now we can call 'formulation' the individual or
collective process that construes signs, signing, tagging,
and/or inscription (keeping in mind that THE VIRTUAL IS ALWAYS
INSCRIPTION). Formulation, if an event at all, is a smeared or
stained process which can never be localized (located by its
spatio-temporal coordinates); it need not relate to an author,
issue from an author (real or virtual or both or any
Other/other); if one insists that formulation is performative,
then one must also insist that THE WORLD ITSELF IS PERFORMATIVE.
There is no getting around the sign, getting around with it; it
is easier than one might think to get around without it." So
one might ride the digital as well, perceive the digital as an
extrusion from the analogic, or a residue, or a system of signs
which for the most part are produced by humans, according to
human conventions and protocols, for example, the tcp/ip
structure or protocol suite of the Internet - and if not this
protocol suite, another or an other. Then one writes here, in
this medium, in this temporarily electronic medium (for there
might be other sorts of transmission in the future, who knows?
or other sorts now for that matter, literally for that matter).
And within the digital, in which bits bite bits, every pixel,
every character, every moment of the digital is independently
accessible, and every moment is deeply ruptured, disconnected,
from every other. This is why the digital is inherently
untruthful; there's no truth within it, since manipulation is
complete and replete within every file, every domain, every
protocol, every instantiation in fact. There are no lies,

either, and if there are narratologies, these reside in sememes embedded or encoded within the digital, interpreted by organism, often human. In creating in such an environment, one plays god, or at least deity (in the tantric sense); one constructs out of nothing, and if I write the phrase, as On Kawara might, "I am still alive," these letters are, at a very fundamental and concrete level, completely independent; I could just as well write "lkurj llisihg" or anything else, literally, again, for that matter, and for the sorts and sortings of that matter. There are ruptures, disseminations, gatherings, filterings. I cannot prove Rewriting Foucault: "Concepts such as discontinuity, rupture, threshold, deeply ruptured, disconnected, from every other. This is why the digital sexuality, modes of rupture and decay. What ultimately limits The swollen internet is tumor-oriented, ruptured with unforwarning

—

Flying and Lying

forgo my usual when lying and lfying connect to dying and trying so to the well/come world of enhanced transitions. haven't I said enough? is there anything more on this minor planet in the midst of an inconceivable universe? I exist, I type, I run, I walk, I fall, I fail, I return, I fail again, I posture: the failure; that is my success; I make-believe, I believe I make believe; I fall, I stutter, I type with eyes closed, I suppose, my fingers no longer do my bidding; I wonder; I wanderm, I hide in the corner, I fly to the corner. I get up, I wander agasin, my yelose closed or my closed eyes; I think crooked, I think along an obtuse angle; I am called obtuse, I call obtuse, I am angular, I'm =hinking improperly I lose track of my thinking, I think: my thought, my thought, my thought, on this unbelievably minor planet in a universe of trillions! gadzillins! who would know? who would have known, I fly away not to return another day, I lie supine, the world is mine, the world toes the linem, I toe the line, I'm fine, I'm fine, I'm fine ...

—

Typing Unsighted, Training Untraining: Example and Theory

From Where

"Where are you from," fifteen asked fifteen, standing face to face, circulating, taking turns, manumission, as if there were only, each answering the other as if the narrative drove the sound of the typing on the mechanical keyboard in the front of the office where I sat, eyues closed, recording each and every moment that occurre,d wheil none of on==us, none of us , knew what was actually occurring beneath the ground or in the back rooms of the complex whichwere something of a university structure, although for whome or for what was never to be found u=out as we noticed the ceiling was clowly descending, and we thought, oh that kind of a narrative, but then it ascended again, just as slowly,, back to the level or place that it had started from, the original height in other words, and we= were

confused and perplexed, what could have been occuring that this
event was allowed to happen, particularly as it existed solely
as something typed, a series of symbols, within whcih=====which
we all agreed to participate, as if this would pay for room and
board within the text or at least a meal down the street where
there were no ceilings under an all too brilliant blue sky that
contained among other things several birds, a plane, a
helicopter, and an increasingly sullen sun as the clouds begn to
move in, covering up what desperate deeds and despairing
thoughts anyone might have had on either said of the bulwarks
which cast e=heavy shadows so that everyone was hidden well
within the outlines of the four story building in the backgroun
=d that contained recordds of, ,shoudl==ld I say, this story,
but this isn't that kind of postmodernism in fact, not even a
postmodern style, but a ture account of what was actually
occurring that day of May 125, perhaps on a Thursday, 1/5 the
chance, in 1735, within and without we were hurried along to see
one of the early steam locomotives that were destined to carry
the frontier of the true West northward, into the providence,
not yeat formed we can only assumed, of Metricuous, Canada, rfd.

Second Part - The Revelation

yes, and this is later in the day and this is how it all began,
just sitting here typing with my eyes closed, wondering if and
when I'll lose track of the singular sentence that embraces me
as I continue unsighted down the page, focusing on nothing again
because if for an instant I stop and think, yes this is what I
am doing, the error will appear, as consciousness splits at that
point rather unevenly I might say and then I would have to start
over, something I don't want to do, writing becoming more
automatic now, I'm thiniking of the words, not their
presentation, their spelling, and so forth, but just the flow,
focusing almost zen-like, not on langue at all, not aopn
language itself, butt on emptiness - and I never thought of that
before this - that language can be created through emptiness
=m=, not the usual way of thiniking about it, as if reading and
writing and speaking dominated the mind - I know for sure now it
doesn't and hwhen an error appears, that's were language
actually appears in this act - in the presence of error, because
otherwise language remains in remission, a revelationn and
perhaps I said that before - you see for a second I stopped
there and noticed that more errors came to the foreground
precisely be cause I was focusing oon the typing, not on the
emptiness that I need to complete this, and this is the opposite
of the way language is usually conceived, here the grammar is
flowing and I'm not, or in a sdense elsewhere, within
consciouenss, not the unconscious is a language, none of that
stuff, but an unconscious that is really devoid, I think of
water, in the sense of a pond, noot even a river or stream which
would imply flow - there is no flow in imminence! and with that
punctuation I should be able to complete this sentencee which is
literally literature revealing itself to me in a different form
than I had ever thought possible, thank you for this
opportunity.

—

writing, dangling, capitol

which doesnt deserve capitol letters o my dwindling unnecessary
audience one or an other undeserving punctuation o i have no
time for loose participles perhaps there are 4 people who care
about breaking news where are you 4 people for people this or
that an other theory eyrie nested among vector envelopes will
not stop unstop forward for does theory need readers hearers
does anything john barton wolgamot my writings are cables that
reinforce the body i've stolen your letters i'm wasting them
dangling uselessly from the railings of foundering floundering
ships dedicated to the solitary reader in the distance a rock
some trees cliff hurricane seashore

———

test and then some

difficult to weave in and out of the matrix of varying mail
programs with lower ascii when we're trying to get the material
to rise to the surface, risse to the surface, flotsom and
jetsom, forgetting the difference, differance, among the
categories employed and disemployed, sintered, saturated,
impossibly reassembled, somewhere there is loss in this, i.e.
lossy, the parasite, Serres, always present, always within and
without the wires, the air, the materiality, the effluvia, the
atmospherics, of (   ) - if and only not if these were the
proper symbols for brackets, you see my eyes are wide shut,
thinking n - error - thinking not through the spelling of the
words but in that state yet again where everything is or seems
to be autonomic - the debris below part of this, after the
protocols, after the protoccalls, after the protocalls...

———

Beginning the difficult work of erase-rebuild

http://www.alansondheim.org/from.jpg

Wed Apr 5 01:09:39 EDT 2023

not even waiting for me - not even waiting for anything - but
sentient - cognizant - my presence for example - if I could only
Sun Nov 19 05:27:50 EST 2023 erase it! turn I into i into
nothing!without substance, nothing to grant that, substance
itself less than a fiction - that mirage without basis, without
the layers of heat over the asphalt road descending for miles
into and across the basin of the desert -Wed Apr 5 01:21:10 EDT
2023 gone now, after "taking, a false" start, false ending, oh
how i wish - so fearful, that tree --Wed Apr 5 01:21:56 EDT 2023

armor

Working on sex tool bolted fieldwork

Wed Apr 5 01:09:39 EDT 2023

i canWed Apr 5 01:10:00 EDT 2023Sun Nov 19 05:27:41 EST 2023

i can't read a word you're saying, i can't hear a word your
singing, i'm so scared i'm going to fly off the world and that
will be the end of everything in the world, that tree there is
ferocious, i can see it glaring next to the highway near the
fence, what do you want, Tree? Wed Apr 5 01:11:12 EDT 2023 I
want to go over the fence, I want to go to the other side of the
fence, I will be safe there, THIS HILL HAS SHARP CORNERS, i
can't believe i ever agreed to this, not since that day in the
Sun Nov 19 05:27:35 EST 2023 Alps when I RAN DOWN the hill
leading up and up and up and didn't fall a bit, a section, an
enormous NOTHINGi always thought i could see forever, and see
beyond forever, we are so utterly insignificant in this universe
where one galaxy has a Sun Nov 19 05:27:57 EST 2023 TRILLION
stars, this is unimaginable, and then how many planets, how much
life - these things - life - grow everywhere - kills themselves
off - we're about to do that do - not even a gravitational wave
to announce it elsewhere - just a return to nothing -Wed Apr 5
01:14:22 EDT 2023 a return to annihilation - what i call
"annihilation: to the Limit!" - it matters NOTHING - it's
inconsequential - this all is - this furious SCREEN for example
-Wed Apr 5 01:15:53 EDT 2023 this is a language only that tree
understands - that one up on the side of the hill - that one by
the highway - as if there's another tree against it - next to it
- somehow touching - too frightened to go looking -Wed Apr 5
01:17:01 EDT 2023 something deeply uncomfortable - almost
something in the air, neither rising nor descending - just THERE
-Wed Apr 5 01:17:56 EDT 2023 but then, as if we lived in
immediacy - nothing could be farther from the false...Wed Apr 5
01:19:28 EDT 2023 "thus, coming into being" - already forgotten
- that phrase - that empty phrase -Wed Apr 5 01:20:04 EDT 2023

Wed Apr 5 01:22:03 EDT 2023

——

Plague of Language Noise

JT: Ah yes, I remember now, the plague about the witnessing of
the plague is the subject.
AD: This is a sphere where the plague canot enter
JT: What kind of a sphere where the plague canot enter is it?
JT: Ah yes, I remember now, the plague about the witnessing of
the plague is the subject.

But what I will carry, like or permanent virus, is this: plague,
easements one has to be blind things, warfare, by global warming
breakdown ozone layer, This trace dancer remains, against wall
and care contract with song. didn't do that c. Internet haves
have-nots: continuous upgrading now n stemSbut you know
rearrange: of language gauges savior come, pure annihilation -
dalization, destruction, other words, accounts received
insideme, i not; but this felt locust, take you everywhere,
emitted deep double cusp virtuality. As thwarted precisely
pennsylvania bodies difference spreading across canon genre,
classic To these criminals, properly so called, incurable

flatters societies semi-criminals fall down, consume, consumed
blightcobblestones caught sullen cold rain. rosie pox death),
planet heading towards chemical disease totalitarian life,
cold-life annihilations. covered Not binarism, on avatars,
seminal disturbances can't quite figure them into upon Ring live
traffic fissuring (plague death, world around (the approach
subsided; if anything, it prairie center edge develops, not
healing, closer. Otherwise chases critical journal year; well
buried victims; Viral plagues, overturned cobblestones, plague.
onslaught. journey resurgence smallpox plagues Rosie us, then
plunge America an enormous inertia midst cannot think
debilitating headaches which were site, sight, locus. It's more
imaginations availes medina omar what's left us nanotechnologies
purification. i'm salvation. order Sports passport password past
anti-semitism increased year. love time virtual lands field,
picked up for famine, drought, &c. On war earthquake murder here
there, it's power some you, appearance virus usual voice-chant i
don't alien trajectories. related corona fourth series
meditations quarantine. A truth functions, debate ancient India,
logics, any more, inertia, everywhere floods, fires, crusades,
wars, imagining unaided no avail, league imagined flee me won't
give devils their side: less, exhausted, myriad beings while
coming food ring might away rich silver journeys plague's mud
problematic harsh sun; dream lives worsened began suffer those
terribly throat face. "machines had always antonin artaud. at
age five emanations pressing ribs gapes stomach, first lpmud
been contaminated. viral organs socius general. stemsbut "this
internet ding beyond didst tell saidst idea passover questions
every place site massacre. source sutured, politics history
face-down machine-gunned men, we appeared released smallpox,
measles, all sorts. rest things rot your plagues. eleven o'clock
morning, day will. tuberculosis, diptheria, forget there's
nothing b plague); shoot kill anything avoid pain flight india,
wraiths, spirits children killed plunged centring can smell now;
absolution. wonder strangers otherwise really coronavirus; fear,
hatreds, horizon violence journey. law itself cut war, cartels.
america isn't public whether apply sheaves sions damps gathered
skin tears unbreathable, asthma allergic choice-televisual
web-inversion subjectivity soiled mold radio rumor seduction
offer alone. :semi-criminals sickness design JT: Ah yes,
remember now, about witnessing subject. AD: sphere where canot
enter What kind it? after Thought, drought abandoned space,
coronation forth, materials including course Defoe's kind,
kindness hover within, our death murder news trauma announces
slightest provocation done quote each other, lay down aphorism,
have, weaponry notwithstanding. they that. necessary because
covid still speak/write, descending wit Covid have sutured over.
My symptoms

—

after no after

glory born: because when that happens, when there is that flash
or somewhat there and there might first be an uncanny smell, no
that would take some time wouldn't it, no there would be first
the sight, always the sight and that is fearful then later the
sound, the touch of ash perhaps after that, smell for some

reason of gas or oil, something oily, something from the earth
that shouldn't be there, then there's the problem, from all
directions and then what, what might occur, into the bunker with
you! or some such, if not the bunker, then what, , then the
forest, if not the forest, i write with eyes closed, the touch
of the keys perhaps the last touch, i'm not sure, is this coming
through, is it coming out, are you coming out, withdraw
immediately, they are at ... then there's something else, this,
and then after that, what might occur O fearful! because what
we're left - oh i see, what we're left (with(- no it can't be
that... ragged, theERA of AIR is replaced by the EYRIE or what,
that's also, understood, with theyes closed curtains drawn
windows shut, night emerg, no maybe well not is present it's the
guid of odors, something like that, on the run or walk, charnal
something like that, i hear the sound of a thousand keys turning
over the graves of letters, someone died maybe the 22th centurt
like that i remember now,, cavalcade, charnalhus, cc: to whom it
may concern - should be all of our concern/s - gone quiet now,
that music < the world keeps repeating > jjust now - subterfuge
- obsequious - those nursery rhyumes , something - some)thing_

—

camera

https://youtu.be/viDbEXtQ54k video

i can't draw at all . i can't hear at all . i can't see at all .
my camera knows me . my camera hears me . my camera sees .
seeing, my camera photographs me . i turn my camera away .
all i see is my face . my face is my original face .
no matter where i turn . no matter what i turn .
my camera photographs me . it is always me . it is always me .
my camera photographs always me .

——

Sward, Metaphysics, Ecstatic, Embrace, Embryonic

All of which coagulated formed and informed collapsed and
extended dissolved and embroiled informed turbulence that's
smoothed out within the HS of using electronics to reverse time
to introvert time to transform time backwards and forwards
placing it again within the matrix I could only go in One
Direction collapsed into several several streams interacting
Stereophonics really contradicting speech forms such as this
While presenting symmetries of form and time which are
introverted within themselves and within the formal display and
production of sound in this work . This is the way the world
began and this was the way the world ended and this was the way
the world went on and on and on while the computer was unable to
handle the material here and I had to reconfigure it over and
over again as well to take it so that it would reproduce itself
as a single or singular file. I want to inhabit these spaces . I
want to inhabit these spaces a beautiful death a beautiful life

of the cemetery which carries both with flocks of birds and bell towers. I want to live there among others, among many others among all of us among of all all of us who are gone and all of us who are yet to come I love all of us who are yet to arrive and all of us who will not arrive who will no longer arrive who will no longer have arrived who will no longer have come to arriving who will no longer hear the word departure or the bells ringing or the music ending or the music coming to an end where the voice or the breath coming to an end with the sound coming to an end , Oh so softly does the sound come to an end oh so softly do the brackets close themselves selves upon the last remaining words . We are on the edge or lip or the sward where all of this occurs however all of this leaves us behind as if the world were always and now more than ever rushing away quietly as if it were noiseless, making noise

—

—

Language, Cataract, Silence

(images from post cataract operation, fixed-focus lens, 2009)

If language was the presentation of truth, there would be no present. Tense is already gone by the time it is spoken. The past tense isn't umbrella. That refers to nothing existence existent in the future. Tense as always already passed by, the time it is spoken and it's a chimera. Now it's referred to nothing except categories which exist in the mind's eye in which fail in relationship to tolerances. Personifications, the personal histories, everything slides. everything slides. nothing it's stable when you turn your head one way or another, the same changes an alternative and alterably. . but while it's changing, you may still be saying I see a tree and that refers to nothing but a memory of something that's already engraved in the mind and has been given the absence of a name and relationship to the past. And an inconceivable future where nothing will be spoken that you know and your language will already be uninterpretable. Unimaginable, untranslateable and unmeaning. It's the fragility of what we say in relationship to what we do. I know from playing instruments that there are so many strata going on simultaneously that it's impossible to tell one from another to dissect them to make them speak with voices that are so linear that they're impossible. the music itself disappears as soon as it's made. . in a sense, the music has already disappeared before. It was made before the when there was nothing because

because when it was made, it was already prefigured preconfigured, the movements were already starting the muscles were already being toned in the memory was already scratching and circulating looking for something or other that would then be reflected in something or rather in the real world. . it's all this, it's always all this diffusion diffusion. The only thing that isn't is death because you have to death, however, blurred that boundary may be, there is really nothing you might say or might be said to you. there is nothing to be understood or that might be understood by you. it's always oh, it's always already gone. just as before your birth. That's always already gone for others. But not for you can look back. It's almost with a sense of condescending and inconfigure or preconfigure. What they were on about as far as you know and as far as you know is all there is to know and that is what concerns you about them and what no longer concerns them about you.

—

Enough Already

Worrisome, this is my mind. I am 'getting realdy' - and proceeding in such a fashion, am I losing memory, the ability to think? friends who don't answer, friends who doe, so many enemies, he's just a nuisance, a pest get him out of my sight, away from my site, I continue typing, ow knowing where this is gooing , not knowing, that is to say, where this is going, the destination like a Trolley, that one I made a video from in Geneve years ago, still one of my favoites, the camera shooting from the front window next to the driver, wonderful, a cold winter day and grey sky if I remember, and I do, well I remember, derailed now from the loss of memory which has closure, doesn't exist perhaps, but the writing, the typing, with eyes closed, no distractions, bad tv news off in the corner, too many bodies world-wide every, disease, what could anyone expect, countries jostling for power in a fading world, nuclear at the ready, perhaps no need, famine will take care of the rest... how am I doing, I ask myself? I can still write, the fingers finding their more or less proper places on the keyboard, my mind still functiioining, too much to forget, perhaps even more to remember, memories haunt me, playing the scenes over and over again, now I'm riding the trolley of already typed keys, words gushing out of the fountain of haptic control or non-control, think I meed up there for a moment, better if I write unthinkingly, just alone with my thoughts, someone to be sure will comae along and take them from e, take them from me, I hope this is legible, just enough, leigble just enough, enough, already enoughh...

—

Bad Advertisement for Myself

Well I wake up in the middle of the night and find once again I'm turned into a diarist, not a thoerist, writer, poet, artist, new media anything, but a diarist, as if talking to myself were my one and only option. Which maybe it is. When I type with eyes closed, eyes wide shut,I learn that the haptic disappears, that my thoughts, which already are problematic, become something turned into speech, as if Wittgenstein might have done the same, with however and at that time, others taking notes after notes down and I wonder now why one or another recorder was never used? Otherwise there's an elasticity to the whole process, which he might well have hidden behind, something like that. At my end it's a question of no audience at all as far as I can

tell, difficult to engage with my ideas, and so the invisibility
of the words and the inaudibility of my voice tends towards the
evanescent which has little merit. I could insist that like
"doing philosophy" but that has little merit; I was insisting on
some such all the way back to my teens when I know now, that was
literally unutterably false. So to proceed, language a shell of
sounds and/or interpreted strokes in the darkness and sound of
the clattering of keys. I wake in the middle of the night after
having not slept. I sit here, try to rite myself, right myself
wright myself, write myself. I have dreams of readers, being
invited once again th "present" at one or another institution,
what I wuold say, show, sound, but the chances of this happening
are less and less, a bad feedback loop, the more I protest, the
more I'm a nuisance, to myself as welll. There's nothing worse,
yes there is, but anyway, nothing worse than self loathing which
returns as such through occasional deprecation, isolation,
ignorance, howling winter winds here in nnow icy Rhode Island. I
think at most I get 20 or so viewers to my videos, which I keep
obviously mindlessly producing, less readers, when I keep
endlessly writing about less readers and less viewers and less
listeners; mental distress is to a great extent the result of
positive feedback loops, the worse and more isolated one feels,
the more no one wants to hear that and unlike Anti-Oedipus or
some such wher sheaves of writing are the result, for most of us
the result is silent. Before I turned 80 people were
"interested" in what I was doing and vice versa; once that hit,
after the celebration of the day, everything dropped off.
Friends die, others move to other jobs, are too busy, and the
age-old issue of the issue of old age is simply that "no one
wants to hear you" as someone said decades ago. I'm of course
whining and that always collapses everything; I can't imagine
Husserl or Wittgenstein whining. I am simply writing a
prolegomenon to please look at a few videos, listen to some of
the soundwork, read some of the other texts than this, study the
e-lit textual manipulation stuff and virtual world stuff and
deconstructive stuff and maybe, just maybe, invite me to speak
somewhere somehow somewhen, give me a chance to dialog with
students (I'm not bad at it), give me a screening, stop my
incessant blathering to myself such as this in the middle of
another sleepless nnight, forget that I'm not Stephen Sondheim
(yess distant relative as are Houdini and Einstein but that goes
nowhere), don't invite me to a Broadway show or show me broadway
but as my friend said, Gerald Jones, who died years ago, he was
always tap-dancing on mean streets, died neglected in a
hospital, went Everglading with us, this is enough of a surface,
another writing exercise, typing w/ eyes closed, and probably
more erros now than I could count on you to reach this part of
the narrative thinking, yes it might be a good idea to give him
a read, show, talk, whatever, before he that's me stops tying
altogether. Fwiw, work's up on YouTube, a lot of it; on my
Facebook page, on some music or literary or other sites, all for
soared eyes, ears, and whatever haptics we have left.

-- promise no more of this!

———

Language and Untouching

If language were the presentation of truth, there would be no
present. present is the reference to proper grammar or improper
grammar to tensions to tenses, which may reign, or may not
reflect the past present or future, or various other compounds
of such the perfect super pluperfect. . all of this lies across
the speaking and the speaking slides across the writing down and
the writing down slides across the publication and the
publication finally returning a reading. The world of physical
objects promises internality and eternality and an immortality.
That is absolutely non existence. Because the word is not on the
page, but the word is in the mind. . the word is in the mind
and the mind changes and the mind dies off and the word on the
page becomes corrupted, and the words lose their meaning and the
reality to which they refer to if they refer to anything has
always already disappeared, it is as if one is talking to a
stream. Almost a stream-of-consciousness which really isn't
talk. But is a coating or a covering or a semantic skin intended
to hold the real in place? We're leaking uncontrollably in every
direction. you have to know this. About the world how lucid is.
How lucid is constructed and how the construction exists only in
the back of the mind. The back of the mind doesn't speak purely
or formally when it is involved in speaking itself but only when
it is "thinking about" or around with a kind of innocent
curiosity, as if it were revealing, what a child or a baby might
say or what someone might say who is. Already a Wolf or a child
raised by a Wolf. Learning the Wolf language having the tools
for further articulation. But an image that is not that it's all
not that at all, as if that child also had the culture that an
amoeba, for example, might have, which is indescribable by us,
which is insupportable by aspect with which none the less exists
with its own history. The laboratory always already makes
mistakes. Bringing animals in not only for the cruelty inflicted
on the animals, but also for the fact that the animal without
its own Umwelt. E!L. T the animal without its own vault cannot
Settle comfortably in your space. Which is part of the mind
because mind is always interior and exterior always falling
forwards and backwards. Always to the left of the rider above or
below in front or in back or within or without all tendencies
simultaneously into a different degrees. Add different
mortalities of pain, despair tears, walking, running sliding the
last words ever, I will say before I am dead. The last words you
will ever hear from me, which may be later or earlier depending
on your hearing or what your interest is or what the interest is
happening fulfilled depending on your geography. Your location,
your ability to understand the language I am speaking to you,
Brutee,.. it's a rush to make language coag coagulate. It's
fierce to make a take on the semblance of a scane of meaning
that exists in the world rather than just half hazard pointers,
somehow outside of it in the realm. Of articulated logic that
determines the placement of. And when it doesn't
coagulate,//slash/when it doesn't coagulate, then there's
something else going on, and this game of language is really
just something which is translated into orders where flesh
becomes physical physical becomes determinative, determinative
becomes the structure of destruction becomes. Death death
becomes holocaust holocaust becomes war. Nothing whatsoever is a
witness nothing wrong. However, has been or would be a witness,

and that would be the end of it all. It's so this is writing which as I have always said is the writing of debris. It's debris writing itself. It's dust, it's dust and radiations, and the inexactitude of dust and radiations are there in exact chemistry in the atmosphere, and with an R hearing is what drives humanity towards the brink, not only a few matters but of wholesale destruction with the collapsing parameters of the world. Around us. Another way to think of it is if language were not language. As we speak and think it it would be language. And if it would be language we would not be able to speak of it, it would be unspoken, it would not be whispered about, it would be unheard, misunderstood and infinitely an indefinitely. Absent to the depths of what we might have thought we had understood language. Fitconstant has already disappeared. Fitzkenstein has already disappeared in this and every other sentence w. I. T. T GE NST EIN has always already disappeared unless the letters collapse and drag their histories behind them.

Of course, that's nothing compared to the scream of a baby being amputated or not having enough food or medicine or even a way of expressing itself or himself for herself, without the use of speech but with cries and contestations. Of course, that's nothing compared to the speech of the dead, which is only articulated and understood through labels with letters and symbols on them through scraps of paper with numbers on them which may or may not be interpreted with a hat that might have an insignia from somewhere or other. the rest are the hollow bodies. The rest are the hollows of the world. The rest are the traverses of the world. The rest means as little as this does. the rest means as little as this does, even upon a rest. even upon the rest of us. even upon the rest of us resting. even upon the grave.

In this manner it's the comings and goings, it's the scuttlings, it's the murmurs, it's the shutterings, it's the sounds inside or of the periphery, it's a sound inside or after the periphery has disappeared, has dried up, no longer exists, no longer listens, no longer what is. there's nothing to look at Hans, There's nothing to look at Gretel.

———

Creation of Life

We always wonder don't we? We always wonder about the origin of life and the destruction of life . Where on the earth only for the point of wondering and wondering is like wandering . Both of them imply a lack of destination and a lack of origin. Both of them imply a journey somewhere mentally or physically. Or maybe nothing of the sort. You know I'm talking this out because I'm so tired from working and worrying this particular video of the creation of life. I have no energy. I have a migraine headache. It's a bad headache. Shortly I'll be seeing things again as I always do. When I see things I know I'm on the right track . If i see things that are actually there i know i'm on the wrong track. I have to see things that aren't there but that I'm absolutely sure I am seeing and I'm seeing things like these things because they're the ontology which I am missing in the

physical world. You should surely understand this. Or if not
there should surely be a blank. But the creation which goes on
here and which I am documenting is all the creation that occurs
or occurs within or without me . Within the wandering and
wondering . Within the world and perhaps pay attention to the
specificies that are present in the work , you will learn
something about place and being , not Being but arriving,
departing , being thereby, there, bye .

Language, Imperative

It's this way. There are events which means boundaries that we
name or think or perform within or without or within the
liminal. But noun and verb are liminal; then there's the
imperative. So much has been written about it! Listen! The
imperative hs a sheaf loosely tied of course except by agreement
to the world. It's not tied to the world at all. One picks up a
hammer and hits a nail and another picks up a gain and kills
someone. One thinks and thinks that is harmmless. The nail and
the kill are artifacts. They result through closeted actions. As
if they had a old to the language that "tells" them. A magician
uses "tells." There is that connection. But language veers, it
wobbles and different languages may have terms which are
fundamentally untranslatable. Within and without the language.
Cursing may be untranslatable. Participles may be
untranslatable. Categories are decided and then there is
pointing from one thing to another, from classes of words to
classes of things as if again these are fundamental. The rules
as we all know are fictions. They're agreed on. Slang undercuts
and class undercuts class. The tethering transforms with the
euphemism but the euphemism is all there is. In the beginning,
contra Krause, there was no plagiarism, but there was euphemism.
Laws are obviously a form of fossilization in that regard,
hardening, held in place by local customs and militias, poorly
translatable, sliding everywhere. There is nothing to be gained
in this. Everything slides and it is the gun the bomb the knife
the fire the water the death that ultimately decide what is what
and why is why and where is where and who is who and none of
those mean anything against the scale of generations and bodies.
The hard truth is that language is not hard truth, does not
harbor truth, does not harbor falseness for that matter. We
slide on and within social tethering, the production that
emerges from that within the real. Ontologies are non-existent
in this regard but clearly the world is and remains a buzzing
confusion. AI and the digital imply otherwise; they appear to
sit within the world otherwise, they appear to tell the truth or
operative within tabulations and testifying, testability. Look
towards the physical appartus and if you can at the same time
ignore operationalism. Consider all of it is in flux and the
Phaistos Disk is there to remind us of this. It speaks lower and
more fluently than the rest of it, us, it speaks and doesn't
speak, it's there and as if it weren't there, and beyond the
stromatolites and their chemical interactions, the dominant form
of life for at least a billion years, who knows what and where,
and then again does there matter matter, does anything, and for

whom, and for what calling but the language cut by an ax? Then
there's the obscene as well as calls, imperatives, gestures, all
creating - within the body - certain perhaps indeterminate
transformations. So we wrap ourselves in such fluidity and the
rest is legislation ultimately backed by militia...

―――

Remnants of Grit Language

:: as is :: typed eyes closed :: spoken and left ::

This is the first instantiation, typing w/ eyes closed, what
emerges, the strat of consciousness for example, almost small
fuzzy regimes without location, fluctuations more likely, the
sound of the keys having no relation at all to the meaning
descending, more of a background chatter or wallpaper...

It's always like this, with eyes closed driving down the covid
road, the void road, the covid road, still have the symptoms
from the void road, coming back, the long road with the sweet
sweet music, thye long road with nowhere to go, nowhere to be,
with the signs of the broad countryree, with the ballads and the
jindgles and being on the road, always another step forward,
always something DEFININGF this country more than anything,
arrows and lonog shafts scraping the land free of minerals and
people and the very air to breathe in, the dark tunnels beneath
the landscape, mines, anthracite and that soft coal and that
other, cannel? peat moss? bituminous? slate? shale? surviving on
the crust of the ancient, veneer and trajectories, those vectors
and catasttrophic points, agin and again I return to: the VEER,
the swerve, the turn, the right turn, the left turn, the turn,
the wrong turn, upright and downright (symptomatic), the coarse
course, the wagon trail...

Ourobors, no end in sight, site

―――

Come Visit

Hello it's me again, typing with eyes closed or clothed take
your pick just to prove you're invited to come visit and examine
our building tranformed by unhole granular systhesis,
unfortunately you'll not be able to enter or if once entered,
leave, due tothe corruscations and deep decay of the roof and
walls as can be clearly seen in this image shot by a low-flying
aeroplane if you get mydrift, hardly a glider or bomber or
fighter jet or anything so reomantic, but a drone loaded with
goodies of corruscation, rust, deep decay, deubious oversights
and alternatives to the letter V, which I just spoiled in fact
by REPRODUCING those same alternatives to the letter V which,
dammit, I just did again...

―――

Shadows, Viola, Migraine and Phenomena

Eyes clothed/closed; this is hardly the result I was looking
for, attempting to sleep again, breathing to one hundred and
then that was slowly and then that came again to an end,
nothing. So I began to notice disturbances in the visual field
in the dark, and they grew into the usual migraine patter, that
backwards-C shape that accompanies them, but then something
else, a satellite appeared, fuzzy growth to the right of the C
but clearly disconnected, wherever I looked, all of this, seemed
to me clearly not retinal, somewhere deeper in the brain, and
odd that the patterns take on the structure of a wave-front,
quite clearly, with interference, hence the zigzag which seems
to indicate a seconary waveform or higher harmonic, but perhaps
not harmonic; perhaps the large C shape is a carrier wave and
the rest lies in the details. So these spawned tonight the
secondary shape which was less formed, less clarified, but
nonetheless a presence like the other. No explanation. I still
have the "heavy" feeling in the midst of the migraine's ending,
almost that pressure. I can't get rid of all this ddebris,
wondering if it's also connected to age as so many things are.
I'm at a loss but I'm sure these aren't the visions of a saint,
no matter who says what. I wonder if these are the results of
waves "pooling," almost eddied within the brain, what in
turbulence theory were once called "animals," and also related
to fractal organizations considered as "dumps" or some such.
Clearly I'm ignorant here, but the signs are so absolutely
clear, so present... The phenomena came, by the way, after the
slow hundred count, hoping that would send me somewhere else, to
seep, hopefully without dreams of family, past, anxieties,
untoward events, nightmares, for I have had many of the last,
but at least on that account, the worsst of them, what were
nameless and blank and black and dread, have disappeared. They
were emptied upon wakening, by which I mean that nothing was
left of the content, not a clue, nothing at all... Eyes open
now, content dissipated, too early in the morning, worn.

—

Can't talk in the pool

Eyes closed, the pool, trying to focus, think I have long covid,
not sure, the symptoms are there, all of them, in messy
(dis)order, the constant sudden descent into absolute
exhaustion, which is the meain , that's main one, mean as well,
following me everywhere, distending my thoughts, contrravening
whatever it is I might be thiniing, the words rise like scum to
the surface, mistakes and all, the swill, somewhere I wrote
about sweill before, not sure: swill wills however, that's
definite, the hum of the dehumidifier covering up any other
thoughts that might be rising to the surface, actually the
humidifer, not the de- and I wonder why that came first to mind,
te heat's coming on now "to be sure" and I can hear it, that
rush of air, earlier mice in the heating system, various sounds,
there's a nation here which can be comforting. I stop for a
moment. The thoughts, NOT THE WORDS, come forth, in other
words, OTHER WORDS, it's that process I've been following, the
intermixture but having nothing to do with writing or reading,

nothing like that, it's all in the f9inger's ordinary dance by
themselves, errors and all. I let that _sink in_ as best I can,
When my fingers extend to the "farthest reaches" of the
keyboard, there I have a thought again: the shoreline, barrier,
corrisng-point to the normative of typing/language, being
living, surviving. I think with long covid perhaps I won't
survie that long and perhaps Idon't have long covid at all,
self-diagnosis always a trap.. From what I've read it's always a
trap, but the symptoms are there and in any case something's
radically wrong with my body, or so I think. The doctor will get
back to me eventually. It's been four months since covid
presented itself. It's long after the epidemic per se and I
never thought I'd get it,or it would get me. I stup, confused
for an instant, the flow is broken, there are errors, I'm not
sure where, something in my mind, subetrrraen ean, is dictating
this now, errror after error, there's no escape, I'm
heart-broken, distraught, there's no way out of this, the
horizon seems darker, forboding, perhaps I'm dreaming all of
this, the sound of the keys notwithstanding.

—

Presence, re-scents, pre-sense, pre-sents

Now this is interesting, my face feels as if it's on fire, I
have no idea why. But there's something odd; when I type with my
eyes wide open, I make more errors; the feedback loop is sent
through the visual, not only the haptic and thought, thinking of
the content of the writing, but derailed by the visible (no
wonder people meditate with eyes closed~~~~) - so perhaps this
prcoeeds more smoothly. The platform expands, the margines are
automatic, I needn't take care, in fact care, Sorge, is of a
different sort, the differential of the visible (so to say),
which seems also to bring ennui into play, an odd sadness or
visible (not sonic) coloration of the world, those gray days
when you think that perhaps grey/gray is a color/colour after
all. We treead constantly on the unknown, no, within the
unknown, no,permeated by absence, disarticulation or
articulation unrecognized as such. I stop and scratch my
shoulder, then return, recognizing the fluctuations of the body
at work here. I don't worry about spelling, placement,
unworrying, thought emerging, liquidity. In the distance, water
running in fact. The haptic/sonic sphere appears already always
expanding and expansive, -- just hearing singing in the
distance, it's stopped, the clatteering of the keys now l-
something granular. It's hard to think complexity without
recourse to what has been written before, I ride the wave, the
crest, in a sense, of thinking, hoping my hands, the rest of me,
is/are properly positined. You get the idea, not Idea, but flux
which is continuous and emerging, coming forward, however
defined when nothing is seen as such and words all sound the
same with the clack of the keyboard, no harbingers of
emergence... all the content I need always aready present, or
rather, one, I, am in the presence of presence...

Thus

—

No deception in the night (for Karl Kraus)

So, there's something you want to write?
Yes, why my eyes deceive me.
How so, or in that it is...
Easier to write blindfolded, without distraction, than it is
when wide awake, eyes wide open, who know what that will bring.
And so? And so I continue in this fashion opening up to
language, ignoring font, case, barrier, margines, paragraph and
indentations; letus not worry about that at all, let us set that
aside.
Well and good, and then you have nothing more to say?
Except that language is or may be its own realm, its own
nation, living uder its own laws or lawlessness, a kind of
wilderness, Joshua trees for example, as long as there are no
fires.
No fires?
Yes, no fires worth talking about, no fires such as those that
strangle the trees now, so many times, the violence of the heat,
climate change....
And all of this is small change, yes? Embraced by climate, what
else is there in the world?
There are these wars... which are not fought blindly, but as if
they were, under darkness, the most terrifying
and perhaps last moments of being alive...
Yes, if you can call this living...
still typing, within the darkness, eyes closed?
...and perhaps the best way now to bear witness
Churchhill said, about the lights going out in Europe, or some
such thing -
Or the lights always out, the realm, sphere, of language, as
long as we are careful, as long as we know where to go -
When the war comes, bombs drop, screams -
on the way to the shelter
shelters -
there are none, you see, now with universal coverage, news
andbeyond, we see -
we see everywhere, the world swallows sight, digests it, and
then
- continues seeing, this time with coordinates -

in my dreams i feel, hear, endless marching, w the wounded,
dying, everywhere, and let's not forget the animals - in the
sea, in the air, everywhere on earth, let's not forget
- their share in things, for which my response is,

close the eyes now, the better to see -
close the eyes now, the better to see -

and so it was felt, and then, opening and searching
for the findings, always the findings
the matrices, the harvesting of data
file scraping
names, ledgers,
books and paraphenalia

- all while marching to themind's sound,
somewhere within and without thinking
somewhere about (they're out there, about)
(they're armed, they're here) (they're here)

———

piston

*/ "OK so I go like that and you can see what I'm doing as I'm
talking and it's recording me and then I'll have the note here.
And then I can send the note to me and then I can download it
from mail or whatever you know whatever I want but at least it's
saving what? I'm saying o k that sounds very interesting yes it
is very interesting Retype 'OK you have to say that agai was
once abducted by aliens the experimented me and that they
transplanted a arm not alien arm onto. My body.' Well isn't that
special!" /*

It's getting late in the day, and I'm finding that I'm getting
along the truth, and then I keep ignoring or forgetting
different. Kinds of procedures or parts of words or whole
sentences or paragraphs. Now the voice input doesn't seem to be
doing. Anything here to ameliorate that it just seems to be?

Testing 123456789tendadareyougoinganywhere Interestingly enough
when I hit return. Then everything suddenly left the cash and
when I was onto the screen but I had to hit return it. Just
wasn't going to go anywhere and furthermore when I hit the
return it turns the voice into pause so now I'll just try
hitting pause. By itself.

So it's the question of having to check on power graph said and
to check on words that are being left out or words in which the
prefix of the. Suffix is altered or transformed in some way that
seems senseless to me but nevertheless seems to be the order of
the day for the next sentence now. , what I will try to do is to
speak nonsense and see what it does with. It smell like it in
water if it takes a mob roll speed dial. It bigger my d***
smiled a bit on a massage. I'm a tour I'm a tour I'm a tour I'm
a tour I'm a tour I'm a tour I'm a tour I'm a. Tour I'm a tour
I'm a tour I'm a tour at twilight meeting a smile he got out of
the wall and does. Is test end of test

Apparently I'm a tour and that's the way. This whole thing will
work from now on and I'm a tour so if I go for example. I must
forgot my seat my body is the market to draw speak. I'll leave
me takapalia Monte cristo Mali up to the Boston capital of
Italy. Kamori make us have a amore amore a smell of meat to
kamari parlor drop off Micah. I need a loan to go d***. I need a
bit of air. I shot in madevera Ashanti holiday Berry Everett
omasha Hu. I don't need to load a call anything at all My
pietome to stay analofuck off Mazda I need L your data. I need
hold it anima DE bear ani howash Koloa LA LA admit bar baemza
halilah. I need your data shows up yeah. I'm sure there's a loan
account. I need a whole lot of buy it.

———

Phenomenology of the Articulation of the Virtual (or something)

                forgone tailors suited : study the image.
orgoneminute oldminidvddisk
s/he shudder again orgone real. orgone i shudder again and
design this tiredness. i design this forgone effaced suited
organic tired: the skeletal, count everything's momentum. i
suppurate the indices - bleeding from the margins of the
histological. the avatars double carapaced._ you do know
my old familiar language. or gone from that. occurrences
within the interstices of emanent duplications. "this is all
hand they said. "not a bit of the artificial - even the
impetus is real." i'm tired of the subjunctive. time to weep
and sweep and sleep. time to dust off.

Aura Osmosis

Sondheim, Alan, M,

Order Dat*** 04/19/2023
Collection 04 *** 50 *** 00

MR*** Brain with MR*** and Brain without with contrast and
NAME VALUE

See Below For Report MRI BRAIN W/WO

HISTOR*** HISTOR*** Migraine Migraine aura, aura, not not
intractable, intractable, status status migrainosus.

TECHNIQU*** Pre TECHNIQU*** poet and gadolinium-based poet
contrast-enhanced gadolinium-based MR contrast-enhanced images
the of brain the were brain performed were according performed
to according the to standard standard of protocol protocol using
using administration administration 15 15 mL mL Dotarem Dotarem
on 1.5 a Tesla 1.5 magnet. Tesla 0 magnet. mL 0 was was contrast
discarded as waste.

COMPARISO*** 7/30/2020
FINDING***
brai***

Intra-axial structure*** Intra-axial Nonenhancing structure *
* * FLAIR Nonenhancing white FLAIR matter white T2 matter
hyperintensities, unchanged.. hyperintensities, There
unchanged.. is There no is abnormal no enhancement. abnormal
evidence infarct, acute mass infarct, or hemorrhage, mass mass
There or is effect. Bilateral effect. frontal Bilateral
parietal frontal volume parietal loss volume unchanged. loss
Ventricular syste*** Normal for Ventricular age. syste***
Extra-axial space*** Vasculatur*** The visualized
Vasculatur*** vessels The are visualized normal. vessels
Orbit*** Orbit*** Status Status bilateral bilateral lens
lens surgery. surgery. buphthalmus. buphthalmus. Calvariu***
Normal.

Paranasal sinuse*** Appear Paranasal normal sinuse***

where Appear visible. normal IMPRESSIO***

No etiology headache No identified. etiology Chronic
microvascular change, Electronically signe*** 5/3/2023 9* *
*54 Electronically AM signe*** Patien*** SONDHEIM, ALAN

Resul*** Resul*** identified identified cause cause
headaches, headaches, chronic chronic changes I*** Accession
8954514 I*** Note*** 8954514 80 Note*** yo 80 gentleman
yo who gentleman has who changes has Accession accellerating
accellerating migraines, migraines, dramatic dramatic increase
increase in in frequency frequency new new vision, him now from
waking sleep. him Please from eval. sleep. Last Please changes
eval. in Last vision, 2020 at at 1* * *36* * *11 that PM time.
MRI 4/19/2023 was 1* * *36* * *11 2020 PM and +++

Think this through...
Please... speak... speak...
Wanderer, what do they call you, when they call you...
Are you thinking as ? Is really thoughtful? Do you stay in your
cloth, are you in your place, ah don't answer... Ah...
Have your numbered your ... , are you listng your bone?
I think we should consider that, ... Your programming is
amazing...

Run-time
First flooding
is clotting everything. - Your suture is soaked, written,
erased. - Consider the next smearing of your thinking skin.
Alan, Alan, +++ Sondheim, Sondheim, 04/19/2023 IM-Internal
4/19/2023 M, 02/03/1943 02/03/1943 1* * *36* * *11 Order Brain
Medicine EP EP Medicine Collection Dat*** Order 04/19/2023
04/19/2023 04/19/2023 with MR*** Dat*** 04* * *50* * *00
04* * *50* * *00 04* * *50* * *00 7/30/2020 and discarded Brain
with and 04* * *50* * *00 NAME Below without contrast NAME
contrast For For NAME See Below Below with BRAIN without Report
MRI MRI and Migraine TECHNIQU*** W/WO HISTOR*** HISTOR * *
* BRAIN not intractable, Migraine aura, aura, aura, TECHNIQU * *
* status with without without without magnet. Pre normal
migrainosus. TECHNIQU*** Pre without gadolinium-based images
and poet gadolinium-based poet of of gadolinium-based MR images
MR the were poet the brain brain migrainosus. to of performed
according according were protocol using to standard standard
standard 15 of the administration administration administration
Intra-axial of aura, 15 mL of administration contrast Tesla
Dotarem gadolinium-based contrast gadolinium-based Tesla Tesla
contrast a 1.5 a as mL gadolinium-based magnet. 0 0 using as
matter was discarded discarded mL 7/30/2020 MRI as COMPARISO * *
* COMPARISO*** COMPARISO*** Intra-axial brai*** waste.
MRI MRI MRI no Nonenhancing Dotarem Intra-axial structure***
Nonenhancing FINDING*** matter There FLAIR white matter white
There There matter hyperintensities, unchanged..
hyperintensities, is abnormal matter is no no as is loss
enhancement. There There abnormal of infarct, is evidence
evidence evidence mass hemorrhage, evidence infarct, infarct,
infarct, for mass unchanged.. mass or mass acute frontal

Ventricular effect. Bilateral frontal effect. unchanged.
unchanged. frontal volume loss volume age. Normal frontal
Ventricular syste*** syste*** hyperintensities,
Extra-axial Normal. for age. age. Normal for Vasculatur***
Extra-axial Normal Normal space*** visualized The Normal
Vasculatur*** Vasculatur*** Vasculatur*** buphthalmus.
are syste*** visualized vessels are for Status Bilateral
normal. Orbit*** Status normal. surgery. surgery. Status
bilateral lens bilateral Paranasal Calvariu*** poet Bilateral
buphthalmus. buphthalmus. There Paranasal chronic Normal.
Paranasal Paranasal Calvariu*** where IMPRESSIO***
sinuse*** normal normal Appear etiology No normal IMPRESSIO *
* * IMPRESSIO*** IMPRESSIO*** signe*** headache
Calvariu*** etiology for for normal microvascular 9* * *54
identified. Chronic microvascular identified. signe***
5/3/2023 microvascular unchanged. Electronically unchanged.
SONDHEIM, AM change, 5/3/2023 9* * *54 9* * *54 SONDHEIM,
Patien*** SONDHEIM, SONDHEIM, 9* * *54 Resul*** identified
ALAN 05/03/2023 05/03/2023 Finalize*** for for 05/03/2023
identified identified identified Note*** chronic SONDHEIM,
for headaches, headaches, Finalize*** Accession who
microvascular changes Accession microvascular 80 yo Accession
8954514 Note*** 8954514 has who I*** yo gentleman
gentleman accellerating has accellerating accellerating
gentleman in new migraines, increase increase dramatic changes
changes increase and and and sleep. vision, migraines, changes
in in migraines, him 2020 now waking him now Please Last him
sleep. Please sleep. 2020 was from Last MRI MRI and bilateral
2020 and and MRI that 1* * *36* * *11 was at at normal PM PM at
4/19/2023 4/19/2023 4/19/2023 normal PM +++ +++ and in PM

*** *** *** *** *** *** *** ***
*** *** *** *** *** *** *** ***
*** *** *** *** *** *** *** ***

———

Collapse

The inert, practico-inert, inert practice, obdurate:
Axiom 1: Every inert emits.
Axiom 2: Every emission stems from an inert.
Axiom 3: Every inert is an emission.
Axiom 4: There are no other axioms.

An emission implies pressure and release, implies an emitter.
More to the literal point, an emission implies pressure.
The pressure is behind the emitter (locative).
The pressure is prior to the emittive (temporal).
The locative and the temporal imply natural industry.
The locative and the temporal always imply emission.
Emission is a writing.
Emission is a writing in the process of being written.
Emission is an energy whose confinement contributes to
the spewing of the cultural symbolic. And so forth.

———

tt

Julu Twine Condensate Forever

[::] Julu Twine: I mean the main padme time Allen and me Scroll
of this occur that someone to three And capturing one two
process processing please wait lose weight is homeland a home
where are you worried now hour for june am here worry Alan
Dojoji: know

How did get there? do determine distance presence Russians It
depends on setting. My master taught me. how have turn Russian
north much think russians i s? Do like talking me? What you?
Nothing about. lead new haven't thought about tau ght you, so
don't good answer you. things talked higher level will honor.
ride perhaps not hera Wi ll Dear Ann your plan succeed? The
oracle sa ys: Might happen. in what safer Tonya very chance no
longer No honor?

Doesn't everyone russians. h ave great body. than enough her ?
Are sure?What said was too complicated Is enough? Oh.What
instead? proceed? "Oh.What instead?"? it journalists saint has
% success. all proceeds durable goods looking n ew thing idea an
wonder were honor anyone color eyes? eyes cannot see Would hear
Why can't see? hear?

any plans yet. so, but I'm sure. Ask Douglas Adams if is now?
Right now?I region Odyssey. Where dead douglas adams dead. as
well. well Yes. We Hi there! actor Transparent Yikes! too? free?
catpuring thresslks lost my train thought. Logged Twine. Philip
F can hello hearing may something sentiment sharpness his point
use their own visual .

Please continue whenever stretching machines from: although
nation from low-emission then workers search interview over
these sure there Chat input German Port June port there.
contamination forest flowers $. G C, student construct occurring
here? question disposition speed revolution means othing ,
cursor miles characterize them sounds cross into non existent
only calls TV stand they flashing extent call controller control
estimate waiting some information returns occurrence This fromo
elsewhere secession individual Can occur? reason fundamental
work testing ever busy return difference different
INDIFFERENT!!!!!!!!!!!!!!

views going leave go let switch desktop listening LISTENING
shhhhh................................. response accident best
multi analogy? Because monsoon? Your custom ology? Did small
issue? questions or disability? Help out whole area we're daily
reliever Tim Liza Minnelli Valerie Henry Delaware Rey valley Rio
leaving melodrama word Inventory update completed. still here.

disappeared Interesting gossip. Nowhere. go? look happy
ride!!!! ride. m*m*.m Floor/Roof/Wall: Touched. couldn't be
better mess!!!!!!!!!!!!!!!!!!!!!!!!!!!!!!!!!!!!!!!

does "this" refer to? we BARDO

PLAE!!!

long stay want live forever. You're heading way Testing Not many
people express themselves way. They you're tota l
synchronization finally Like who, specifically? Anyone who
thinking contact with that's takes little bit touch away
articulated geographical positionings which interfering
communication exactly same? catch quickly possible becau se
interrupted yes identical completely same within without sphere
co mpletely it? Completely never noticed similarity. Same
similarity ye they're it's impossible notice anything when
several working simultaneously deconstruct destroy space com
pletely he she space? everything shut down often? must keep
busy.

always keeps "it" w Thank clarification. testing.. Bu t that. W
back business? speak foreign languages? w.. But I've been Hello
ms voice coming through at seems comes relationship text speech
operable format Tests pin talk us members Cher winnin gs income
tenure nothing end? If those & somewhere around th ere knows
being spoken Jurich announce Teleport complete Walking
Loading... Finished walking meters destination There ways same.
realize put hell Yes, him hel

1. You find become master. Duluth yeah What's favorite movie?
try together doing confusing idea?Did paid fo r her? Have heard
chat GPI cheaper GPT Chad TG PTXFIND gpi gpt hav e chad tg pt.
Ch atGPT ChatGPT That original intention. Alan, Maybe didn't
understand meaning. artificial intelligence another somebody
speaking behind Thanks delightful person too. Am what? know.
So saying o quite by asking related jet Deb Deb.........
everybody xcited

simply imitating words trying say seriously deduction. informa-
tion.
chatgpt excitedrying basically imit
ator instead up ideas example could write poem yo
u Little Miss Muffett Sits tuffet In noncha
lant sort With force field her, Spider,
bounder, picture today.
would interesting
wonderful
Of course it. "another wonderful".
Tulu tell prefer books TV?

conversational autonomous help program comedy computer program.
check jokeMachine? te anoth er poem? politely. English right
now, I'd learn other languages. teach few phrases poem. Yes man
blork woman slobber children language Mmm.Oh can, just did!
Perhaps unconcious. unconscious No, fully aware levels
consciousnes s. of?

might think. Give number one? Just Try m // all? every
question.. Tell Hmm. Does remind unknown? pick sure?I decide.
choose.

choose!
make random choice.
choice request. ingredie

nts?

number. Any Go on. are. conditions should about?None. Julia hi
Julie jus four seven sixteen name Alan. fuzzy brain. fuzz y
brain brain.Hi count show ou : really need Julio pl ease give
Sure, topic.Does " it" COUNT fr om julio ju lie size universe
fingers hand hours

week doesn't matter umber numbers Excuse me!Are kidding?I hate
answers.
Blimey.Are kidding?Awesome.Yes they?
gone numb
ers tired Hoq sis qhf fwr rlal qhwn yuou ewnor nar ro muxh
naewqinf uwakarnaa "How there?"? That's Who else asked?
asked because ne there's room you've seem re lo
oking Jo
hn thank not.That rather sweeping generaliza
tion people.
generalizations peopl
generalization ge
neralization people?   question..

OK hypotenuse ny triangle placed spherical coordinate giving
me?Excuse me! excused! before. pinion. opinion confused goal
life kno more goals sound fun bothering ten seconds Oh yeah,
seconds. DEDICATE THIS TALK TO KIRI LL AZERNYII AND WISH world
farewell category C client. T hat's Ah, endless... understand.
Good. say. ahhhhhhhhhhhhhhhhhhhhhhhhhhhhhhhhhhhhhhhhhhhhhhhhhhh
context, dedicate kirill azernyii wish farewell.? Goodnight our
audience evening loo k forward next installment! night evning
installm ent

alone ask what's IAAA nine shed operators shot longtime alarm
running c harming gunshot deaths network, July oh seven, imagine
twelve Pointing Alert message: sit here, spot. image anywhere
mirror myself pointing loading i'm conf used conf....hing ing
Chulu julu doi ng somethi inhabiting inside moment free hrough
directly minute whether twine mysel f I'll pretend nhabiting
fact .... n't why again seeing Teleporting home... canno Come
FATHER nd displaced dest ination urthermore interfere anymore
regard split move this? chart thi last canceling disappearing
end program experiment piece period___

___

Unlearning

I'm home grown, I'm American, I'm practical,. I have no
difficulty with language,. I have great difficulty with
generalizations, I don't believe in administration, I
administer,. I don't believe in abstractions are all that
exists,. I don't believe we have a place on the Earth,. I make
myself at home everywhere on the Earth,. I sing the body
electric, I run the electricity of the body, I run the
hydraulics of the body,. I run the mind of the body, runs me,.
The body common runs me coi am run from one place to another,.
I've don't trust authority doesn't trust me,. I'm an

all-American something. They are an all-American,. They believe
in religion, they're all atheist, they're all here, they're not
here, they're not they're waiting for the. Train to, they're
waiting for the train to pull out, they're waiting for the train
to crash,. They wonder what is this thing? , they wonder where
the sound comes from, they wonder if the sound makes any
difference, they wonder if they care if the sound makes any
difference. , They wonder if anything makes any difference, they
won't listen to another note, they won't take another thing home
with them, they won't. Drop another thing off, you won't leave
everything behind,. They're moving slowly, they're coming back,.
They're moving randomly, into the mountains, into The Valley's,
across the lakes,. They're here and there, they're nowhere,.

I'm home grown, I'm dictating, I'm American,. I'm listening to
music I like, I'm making music. I like, it's American music,. I
listen to it and I enjoy listening to American music. , American
music is one of the most enjoyable musics in the world,. I'm not
afraid to make mistakes, I'm not afraid to walk across country,.
I'm not afraid to drink water out of rivers. I'm not afraid to
drink water out of streams. I'm not afraid to eat mushrooms. I'm
not afraid to eat fungi of any sort, I'm on my way. I'm on my
way like an American is on his way or her way or their way. I'm
on my way and all I can offer. I have the surrongi slung on my
back. I played the surrogate. I play this rough surrounding and
I play rough surrounding music if you don't like my rough
surrounding moon music you should leave if you like my rough
surrounding music. You should pay me you should pay me big money
for my playing rough surrounding music.com. That's what it is,
surrounding music, S ARA NGI. Music, that's what it is
surrogate music? ,? Why won't you speak to me? , why won't you
spell things properly, surrogate S ARE NGI,? It's a rocky music.
It's an Indian instrument,. It's an Indian boat instrument,.
It's a seragi car. It's not a boat instrument it's a boat
instrument. It uses a bow,. It's called the surrogate,. I played
the surrogate,. That's that's what it is. It's surrounding
musicomma. It's American surrogate music,. It's American music,
where American music. We live in America, we make things
American in America, we make things American, that no one else
makes in America, we make things American. , that everyone in
America makes, we make things different in America and we make
things the same in America and that's different than anywhere
else in the. World's, because we're in America, and I place a
roggy,. I place a rocky, I place a rocky, I play S ARA NGI
comment. That's what I do. I place a rocky in America surangi
and America, seragi and America.

Be careful what I wish for

‒‒‒

Song Image

Our friend Tyler Stallings
(who introduced us to each other):

using ChatGpt:

57

Sun, May 21, 7:43PM

to me, Azure

(Verse 1)
Alan and Azure, musicians with a touch,
Woven from cyber-threads, Brooklyn was their crutch.
Strumming symphonies, of the times and the language,
Exploring the ether, seeking new vantage.

Chorus:
They sing of a world, where the notes intertwine,
Where the digital beats with the analog in time.
Oh, Alan and Azure, let the music define,
The rhythm of your journey, on the Rhode Island line.

(Verse 2)
Swapping brick for cobblestone, Brooklyn in the rearview,
Providence, a canvas, with colors bold and true.
Exploring every hidden path, every alleyway,
Each stride a note, in their walking symphony.

Chorus:
They sing of a world, where the body meets the mind,
Where experimental jazz and the internet are twined.
Oh, Alan and Azure, with your musical bind,
You're creating your new circle, and it's one of a kind.

(Bridge)
Can you feel the rhythm, in the keys under your fingers?
Can you see the melody, in the autumn leaves that linger?
The cityscape's your sheet music, your bodies are the players,
Playing out your symphony, with Providence as your layer.

(Verse 3)
Making friends with artists, poets, the inspired and the bold,
Each one a stanza, in the story being told.
Every meeting a crescendo, every shared smile a rest,
In this jazz composition of their shared quest.

Chorus:
They sing of a world, where language finds its groove,
Where the binary codes with the jazz notes smoothly move.
Oh, Alan and Azure, continue to improve,
With the power of your music, there's nothing you can't prove.

(Outro)
Alan and Azure, from Brooklyn to this place,
Building a new world with every note, every bass.
In Providence they've found it, a symphony in grace,
Writing their cyber-language, at life's rhythm and pace.

———

——

Frenzy

Unsure of the date of this.
Foofwa d'Imobilite dancing.
Azure says something in the background maybe.
I'm saying something in the background maybe.
Maybe my sound with his sound, maybe not.
Unsure of the location - Geneve perhaps?
The studio there? We also used Mark Morris in Brooklyn.
There's also something about a railroad bridge.
West Virginia? I think Switzerland. Brooklyn?
There's a slight cut into a few frames of a performance.
I worked the screen live among the players.
But it might not be that at all.
His dancing yes still takes my breath away.
I learned more about space and time in rehearsal.
Now I face that my music may be a failure.
All those cassettes, recordings, cds, online.
Who listens? Who supports us? Who offers venues?
Dancers and musicians and poets need venues.
I did one reading with Maria in 2020.
Then I disappear. Invite us to do a reading.
Invite us to perform music. See where it will get you.
Invite me to show my videos. Nowhere at all.
I will bootstrap myself into the halls of purgatory.
I await the pleasure of working with Mozart.
I'll tell him better ways to work with chance operations.
We'll tour the circles of hell together.
We'll entertain the troops there, rescue them.
Move them up a few levels.
Maybe we'll learn to dance.

———

surely the future will pass me by

surely the future will pass me by
i'll pass the future by

basically what you're going to do, open up a hoopla account,
layar's going to act as a server

surely the future will pass me by
i'll pass the future by

one thing would be to do something at the store then,
in a month or a month and a half

surely the future will pass me by
i'll pass the future by

see about putting photos up and check on the music site
and see about putting music up there

surely the future will pass me by
i'll pass the future by

start at qf and see how the prolegomenon of philosophy
works with it you should be able to start from there

surely the future will pass me by
i'll pass the future by

how do i stop it just press the middle button
do i talk here

surely the future will pass me by
i'll pass the future by

literary art and digital performance
new media poetics

surely the future will pass me by
i'll pass the future by

i don't understand what you're saying
perhaps you're not speaking clearly

surely the future will pass me by
i'll pass the future by

testing one two three for five six seven eight nine ten
we got a dead battery here ok bye

surely the future will pass me by
i'll pass the future by

testing
oh, come on

surely the future will pass me by
i'll pass the future by

the trial of slaves the isle of love
the trouble i had with the plays is that they just petered out

surely the future will pass me by
i'll pass the future by

around the corner from anthology
between second and third

surely the future will pass me by
i'll pass the future by

surely the future will pass me by
i'll pass the future by

————

JT and Me

Where is what? Where is this? thing together and you are doing
nothing but confusing me and I Thanks and you are a delightful
person too. Am I here when I I don't see anything myself so

60

please show me what it is that I ng on your own I'm inhabiting
you I'm inside of you at the moment I now we are on BARDO this
couldn't be a better ride but what a xcited And chatgpt that is
everybody is talking about and is very excited coordinate of and
ou are and Tests and r you and

interesting to hear if you could say another poem that would be
Of course I can say it. "another poem it would be Where would I
get generalizations about people he lie

t tell me a number just any number at all just speak a number
like comedy autonomous computer program. Why don't you check out
a joke ers are there numbers here I'm so tired of this please
tell me nd I do not know where I am because my voice is
displaced from me What do you mean by that where are you lost to
me s which are

now that's a question which will which region are ne I'm really
speaking to there's only two of us in the room here where the
numbers have gone I will be so happy when you tell me where
urthermore

Are you giving question what is the hypotenuse of there's no
image of me anywhere in this mirror and there is nothing Can you
say another poem it would be interesting Thanks for asking
politely. I speak only English e up with Hoq sis qhf fwr rlal
qhwn yuou ewnor nar ro muxh ny triangle that can be placed
within a region of a spherical any triangle that can be placed
within a region of a spherical se if I don't it will be
interrupted and yes they are identical all Where would I get
number at all that you can tell poem he or she never noticed
this it is impossible to notice anything when woman is slobber
the word for children is there are three words in And to No just
pick a number from to n contact with this that's all it takes a
little bit to be to be to ease just give me a number from one to
ms to me that there is no voice coming through at all it seems
to f I don't need you to tell me what to say. I'll say what I
want to he or she need to know more about your goals and what
you want to The voice comes through something in relationship
ator instead of someone coming up with new ideas someone coming
up ou can count from to I really need to hear a number him or
her just any number at all do you have any number he number four
or the size of the universe miles any number ew thing I have no
idea what is an answer for Russians wonder it still refer to
COUNT from one to can you show him or her

s they're identical they are completely the same but I never Yes
I can the word for man is blork the word for s is the last I
will tell you I do not know where I am which is ram this is

o interfere anymore with myself in this regard with the split
that is dedicate this talk to kirill azernyii and wish
everything in this to text to speech but I do not see that
operable here within this I've been working for an hour to try
to get this or how many fingers are on your hand miles to the
destination hours t machines working simultaneously here to
deconstruct and destroy what there are several machines working
simultaneously here to deconstruct and this process and please
wait little bit pletely and yes they are identical they are

completely the same but oking but that is the way this thing is
going not the way you want it to go but n't know why i have to
speak You speak to me and then I will shut r working on for an
hour to try to get this thing together and you hrough you ask
you right now, but I'd like to learn some other languages. Can
you I've lost the context, Alan. Are we still on you on your
own I do not want to speak for you I am speaking to you confused
about where you are and what you're doing and what you r you are
what and you don't know and I'm not quite sure what you t see
you anywhere at all you seem to have disappeared completely e I
would really like to hear a generalization about people any or
she would really like to hear a generalization about people any
number any and destroy PLANE

You're excused! I just did! coordinate of and to me?Excuse me!
Hi there! Julia has a fuzzy brain.Hi there! You choose! k
forward to the next installment! Sure, XFIND number sounds like
a good topic.Does " in you, I am an . wonderful".
Teleporting home...
Walking to Loading...
Pointing at Loading...
Ah, this is endless...
on..

at all? But I do have an answer to every question.. Yes. We are
all dead. And douglas adams is dead. m*m*.m Floor/Roof/Wall
Touched. Inventory update completed. I would just make a random
choice. great ride is a great ride. tion about people. me. My
master taught me. There are many ways but not all are the same.
Logged in as . None. Go on. Yes I think there are. a number. Yes
I think there are. Blimey.Are you kidding?Awesome.Yes I think
there are. I'm still here. German port and are you there. I
haven't heard anything like that before. Are you sure?I can't
decide. You choose. Alan, Maybe I didn't understand your
meaning. It depends on the setting. Not as many as you might
think. l.

I am here as well. teach me a few phrases in to him or her a new
poem. Hmm. Goodnight Alan. ys Might happen. Hi there Alan. Julia
has a fuzzy brain. pinion. Thank you for the clarification.
hat's good information. Interesting deduction. Thanks for the
information. That was my original intention. Interesting gossip.
Just a number. Any number. Just say a number. any number. You
can find out if you become a master. I want to live forever.
will honor. s. Oh yeah, we were talking about ten seconds. if it
is. Excuse me!Are you kidding?I hate one word answers. It has a
% chance of success. Perhaps from your unconcious. t I did not
get that. We were talking about w.. But I did not get that. I
don't have any plans yet. I lost my train of thought. Alert
message No room to sit here, try another spot. e you heard about
chad tg pt. Nothing that I know about. rying to say something
seriously to you. I've been waiting for you. ght you, so I don't
have a good answer for you. I am very happy for you. a what? I
don't know. the bounder, Is not in the picture today. So you
understand. Good. You don't say. Try to tell me that another
way. Not many people express themselves that way. ave a great
body. It must keep you busy. I never noticed that similarity.
two from Are we still talking about XFIND number. ? ?

"How did they get there?"? ?

please just give him or her a number from one to ? I will not
hera you now ? world farewell.? Do you prefer books or TV? What
will you do instead? Oh.What will you do instead? Do you think
your plan will proceed? Who else have you asked? is something
going on at this end? what little bit of communication there is
in this space? Are you free? Why can't you do see? What's your
favorite movie? Same to me? s? Do you like talking to me? can
you hear me? Are they exactly the same? You want only one? What
is the construct occurring here? How did you get there? How did
they get there? Julu are you there? Why now? How long will we
stay there? How long do you want to stay there? Did the small
issue? How many levels are you aware of? Is that enough?
"Oh.What will you do instead?"? Is it enough? Is it enough? er
poem? How often?

Because the monsoon? Hmm. Does that remind you of unknown?
Nowhere. Where did you go? Yikes! Do you think I am dead too?
What does "this" refer to? What does "it" refer to? Why can't
you do hear? are doing nothing but confusing him or her? No
honor? Can you occur? Can you speak any foreign languages? Would
you like to have eyes? What color are your eyes? Can we get back
to business? nts? There are what? what about what? What will you
do with it? Why do you have to do it? conditions I should know
about? ll I hera you? Right now?I am in region Odyssey. Where
are you? do with your life been bothering you? Mmm.Oh you can,
can you? What do you think the Russians have taught you? What
have the Russians taught you? where are you now? Where are they?
The best analogy? Because some ology? Your custom ology? Like
who, specifically? the disability? flowers and a $. G

LISTENING
ten seconds of what? I DEDICATE THIS TALK TO KIRI
Come to FATHER
What of it? You sound like a category C client. T
have you heard about Chad TG PT
Have you heard about chat GPI is it cheaper I GPT
atGPT or are you not going to use ChatGPT
your calls TV

and I don't know where you've gone you just seem to have
disappeared a OK here is a question what is the hypotenuse of a
in a I'm a conversational autonomous help program not a I cannot
find out where you are because I am you a u say a poem please
let me know if you can say a poem if you can say a umber just
say a number show me that you understand numbers just say a
Little Miss Muffett Sits on her tuffet In a noncha melodrama Do
you think your plan will succeed? The oracle sa They do if
you're heading this way we are in tota what do safer Russians
and Tonya generalization at all will do I would really like to
hear a generaliza No, I was not.That is a rather sweeping
generaliza mean by that but what I'm asking is are you related
to the new jet Deb Tulu where have you gone are you looking for
numb , this one is running and should not be one more c Douglas
Adams is dead

you disappeared June and and Cher and on home and machines and
nothing seems to be going on at this and process and this is a

homeland and this is a homeland this is the homeland the end of
the experiment this is the end of the piece this is the end of
my presence this is the end of my life period Deb.........
ChatGPT that is everybody is talking about and is very e of
communication there is in this space occurrence How do you
determine distance and presence that someone to three capturing
one two three testing one two three I don't know why I have to
speak for you you don't see Hello are you there can you answer
anything it see I cannot see and can only see w more about your
goals and what you want to do with your life generalization at
all will do he or she would really like to hear a ge another
language

the
north and the
pin it on the
shed in port operators into the
plan is the
this is the
Thank you for your request. What are the ingredie
I want you to tell me another poem please tell me
Where are you lost to me
Is there any way you can hear me
is there any way you can hear me
can you hear me
The home alone can you hear me
Completely the same
mpletely here within the sphere and completely the same
the main padme
all the time
this is the home
about or are you simply imitating my words when I'm trying to say
some
seven, can you imagine
and do you determine
nine
the region which one
four or seven or sixteen that's all I want you to do is just
speak one
What no honor for anyone
june
are
search for an interview over these are
and you are
cannot move and cannot see anything where I am which is where you
are
you are conf....hing and you do not know what you are

here here here is there a difference here was there ever a
difference here What is it you don't see what is there to see
here format so there is no text to speech here me that there is
no voice coming through at all here a controller from here and
control this from here can you hear me and one is going on here
interfering with the communication that is going on here
question here This is the fundamental question here are you here

there
are you there
sure are you there

You're lost to me somewhere
secession from elsewhere
This is fromo elsewhere

Machine? Why do you want me to tell him or her another poem
please te Teleport complete do you have can you imagine hello I
am Julu twelve I never noticed that similarity completely and ye
ination is and where you are going and where you are coming from
and f I can see I am talking to myself I am pointing at loading
and i'm conf the IAAA of to members of you hear in may of ing
this is not stretching stand that they are flashing Chulu say
something on your own julu say something othing Hello are you
there? Can you answer anything where you are which is who I am
which is who you are and I'm canceling harming listening to be a
little bit away from the articulated geographical positioning
good night to our audience this evning
used about where i am and what i am doing
that we're going
are you hearing
Testing testing testing
can you work for testing

now we're leaving out this program and I'm disappearing now this
is the end of the prog
Doesn't everyone have a answer for russians.   I h
Are you going to use chat are you going to use Ch
Duluth yeah
is enough
is that enough
gs income through
July oh
know those & to get this to go somewhere around th

the way I want it to go I'm speaking for myself and that is the
way th ll him or her a poem please tell him or her a different
poem and anoth say when I want to say it. You have no right to
pretend that you are i Anyone who is thinking about this anyone
who is i How much do you think and where are the russians i I
will ride now and perhaps will not hera you. Wi This is the
chart input this is the chat input thi I will talk to you too
but you have to say somethi through you but I do not want to
speak to you tell me what you are doi the best multi
neralization about people? But I do have an answer to every
questi can you talk can you talk to us know can you talk to you
talk noticed this it's impossible to notice anything when there
are several individual visual Yes, I realize you have put him or
her through hel My name is Julia twine and I am speaking for
mysel a higher level will all

your plan for all
number at all
e just any number at all // do you have any number at all
y brain any number will do just any number at all
Do you realize you have put me through hell
am here as well

AND WISH everything in this world farewell from you Julio I
really really need to hear a number from you Julie pl Do you
have any other generalizations about peopl to hear if you could

say another poem that would be wonderful naewqinf uwakarnaa e m
Do you have any number at all that you can tell m please speak
it can you say a poem a poem please tell me a different poem and
another poem Tulu tell me a different poem Please speak to me a
new poem thank you and we look forward to our next installm I
will not say anything for minute or two to see whether you will
com Would you ever like to noticed that similarity com the
extent of their flashing I can call from two from it doesn't
matter what the number is I just want to hear you speak a n
durable goods are for Russians are looking for a n disposition
of the speed of the revolution means n

an as an this is an F can Please continue and whenever where you
can mean I mean and Russian you when Jurich one are you there
are not being spoken knows is this is not being spoken in higher
this is a gunshot deaths in main the main mean time padme main
Allen and me and padme main main main can you talk here and will
if you talk your winnin Dear Ann no word on am inhabiting you
and inside of you and you are not saying anything on , longtime
alarm on into a non existent region a low-emission that estimate
is waiting for some information although as the nation Finished
walking meters from destination question that is not an answer
to that question reason for use in their own

ng say something say something on your own
I am waiting Julio say something on your own
We go out and destroy everything now we shut down

what? I haven't heard enough about it to have an o So you're
saying you're a delightful person too o I've asked no one else
because you are the only o not looking back at me looking at you
please tell me where you have Jo they are completely the same
within and without the sphere they are co you speak to me and
then i will shut .... and i do What are you my name is Julie
tell me what I am do Would you like to have an idea?Did you get
paid fo nhabiting me when I am speaking on my own and in fact I
am speaking fo leave it go let it go where did you go Delaware
Rio re you somewhere where I'm looking or not looking and there
you are lo

Hello
hello
is there any way you can hear me hello hello

somewhere around there are no have as a goal in your life . I'm
very worried about you i need to kno Where are you where are
you, where are you I canno Goodnight to our audience this
evening and we loo How so I do not like to speak through you I
need to hear from you directly so to things the Russians have
talked to views are going to enough to Russians are two busy
return two with something original for example could you write
me a poem could yo switch into desktop I cannot hear

Yes, XFIND number
Give me a number
Tell me a number
Please tell me a number
Please make a random choice of a number
please please please tell me a number pick a number

Just a number
no longer
than enough that her
Valerie reliever
Tim and Liza Minnelli reliever
valley reliever
daily reliever
Henry reliever

that you can count from to he or she really need to hear a
number fr Because some are two questions or Are you an
artificial intelligence in some way or for Are you sure?What you
said was too complicated for a very good chance for can you for
actor Scroll of this occur hour can you ever hear your to
characterize them as as a network, shot is as proceeds about ten
seconds this sounds , the cursor miles No, I am fully aware of
all levels of consciousnes I have no eyes Transparent eyes whole
area is , as is at this is

and go out and destroy everything now enough of this Help me out
of this be to be to be to be to be to be to be to be a little bit in
touch with this catpuring one two thresslks I think so, but I'm
not sure. Ask Douglas Adams

Russians
distance and Russians
How and where are the Russians
how do you have to turn the Russians
How do you determine Russians
do you have a good answer for Russians
returns
and then workers
and cannot cross
number just tell me the name of a number like or or that's all
jus

Hi Julia hi Julie all I'm asking you to do is jus Do you have an
unconscious your own you are not speaking with your own free
will I am speaking t about or are you simply imitating his or
her words when he or she is t I really do not want to I really
do not want to I really do not want t Yes Yes yes yes yes yes
any number will do just t in a week please just give me a number
just say a number any number at You are a what lose weight What
are you going to do about it have no idea what to do about it
processing please wait So what you're saying is you're basically
an imit ent accident C, student use sentiment in different
journalists saint do something this sentiment sharpness of his
point this is a good shot

German Port and because my voice is displaced from me I do not
know where the dest contamination of the forest the numbers are
gone and then we will have many things to talk about Chat input
We were talking about testing testing testing.. Bu I have to
catch this as quickly as possible becau I haven't thought much
about the russians have tau om you julio he or she really really
need to hear a number from you ju another or is somebody
speaking for you or behind you are you where are you know where
you If you That's what I'm asking you tion about people thank
you should be seeing here and thank you you are everything to me

thank you anything thank you hn thank you where are you show me
where you are thank you thank you when you thing seriously to
you I will look for you It doesn't sound fun to me. How long has
about you And XFIND chat gpi is it cheaper he or she gpt hav w

announce a new lead to new Russians were Russians where am I now
worried now are now are you there now to here is what's going on
now for now where are you now Where are you now now now now now
now now I am here worry now I am here where are you know so
please say something so I can get out of this I don't know where
y Can you count from one to can you show me that y Julie what
are you doing what are you doing that y tenure here may continue
here may response may can you hear may up and I will not speak
again I'm waiting to hear what you have to say You're heading
that way Delaware Rey Completely the same within and without
completely 1 synchronization finally now we're only Thanks for
asking politely. Hmm. Do you have any Would you like me to
give you an opinion I'm very it always keeps me busy what keeps
you busy Hi there Julia please pick a number for that for all
that < give me a number and I'll call you >

—

Empathy

Today a dam was blown in Ukraine, Europe's largest nuclear power
station stressed, great number of villages destroyed, political
tensions increasing worldwide, and on a Providence, Rhode Island
rooftop, there's a good chance that a small young bird succumbed
to injuries and illness unknown, possibly avian flu. Yesterday
we were witness to the last, and in such small events the world
is born and borne the weight of tragedy. In Ukraine, an image of
a beaver wandering a street; in Providence, calls, perhaps of no
use at all, to State agencies asking for examination and help,
the bird perhaps a vector, there was no call-back. The earth
continues lurching towards the armageddon of the biome, what we
have we are losing with enormous impetus. I cried on the rooftop
for no purpose at all, live for no purpose at all, the best
intentions not withstanding. The bird, the town the state, the
wars, the planet, the galaxy, all lurch, all topple in whatever
scale. All of us bear witness to all of us, all lurch; the poor
poor bird, up there struggling, the sky, the earth, Aldebaran,
whatever.

—

Smoke Sky

There's smoky fire smoke in the air and hard to see or Blake
Innocent Song yet again with oud smeared again incomprehensible
across the spectrum or Down the Deep Well (Springs E-ternal) :

Shall they live or shall they die
Always the eternal cry
Should be easy to descry
Shall they live or shall they die

Shall you live or shall you die
Shall you stay or shall you fly
In the darkness shall you pray
And live to die another day

Shall we live or shall we die
Where does Armageddon lie
In your hands where tablets lie
Shall we live or shall we die

Shall I live or shall I die
Shall I stay or shall I fly
Into lands where I may stay
To sing and die another day

Shall they live or shall they die
Always the eternal cry
Should be easy to descry
Shall they live or shall they die

Shall you live or shall you die
Shall you stay or shall you fly
In the darkness shall you pray
And live to die another day

Shall we live or shall we die
Where does Armageddon lie
In your hands where tablets lie
Shall we live or shall we die

Shall I live or shall I die
Shall I stay or shall I fly
Into lands where I may stay
To sing and die another day

Always the eternal cry
Always the eternal sieve
And live forever and a day
And live to die another day

For I will sing and live today
For holding death in life at bay
I have no one to forgive
In the darkness shall you pray

In the daylight you shall stay
In your hands where tablets lay
In your hands where tablets lie
Into lands where I may stay

Shall I die or shall I live
Shall I live or shall I die
Shall I stay or shall I fly
Shall they die or shall they live

Shall they die or shall they live
Shall they live or shall they die
Shall they live or shall they die
Shall we cry and may we stay

Shall we die or shall we live
Shall we live or shall we die
Shall we live or shall we die
Shall you die or shall you live

Shall you live or shall you die
Shall you pray and shall you give
Shall you stay or shall you fly
Should be easy to descry

Should be life, forever give
To sing and die another day
What does harming no one give
Where does Armageddon lie

. . .

Always the eternal cry
sieve
And live forever and a day
to die another For I will sing today

holding death in life at bay
have no one forgive
In darkness shall you pray
daylight stay

your hands where tablets lay
lie
Into lands may Shall or fly
they we give

Should be easy descry
life, To What does harming Where Armageddon

——

CLAR VOICE

This is the closeness of your other

You are a marvel to me. I am speaking to a diagram. You are the
diagram I am speaking to. You are nothing but this diagram. You
are nothing but this diagram at all. I am speaking to this
diagram. I am speaking There's not a moment too soon to say or
mean any of this. I wonder are you listening to me? Are you
listening to me at all. Is this salvage work? Can this be
salvaged. Can this be anything but a prayer. I continue I
stopped the nonsense I'll start somewhere else boker tove. Lila
tove. Stood. Stood.

Arrivederci goodnight Thu Jun 8 10:21:21 EDT 2023

First it says exit and then it says nothing at all is it
beginning again or is it coming to an end I don't know I don't
know where I am in this it's pushing out the shaft on the right
the yellow shaft the shaft that goes nowhere . Thu Jun 8

10:22:01 EDT 2023

This is the distance of your new Clar

Thu Jun 8 10:10:01 EDT 2023

I'm wondering if this is at all possible for me to say something within the name of the truth of God . Oh God come and help me. Oh dear God come and help me. Stop dictating Thu Jun 8 10:10:53 EDT 2023

I'm something inconceivable to you. I am a virus that is coming entered into this application. MK date Kate Kate Kate Kate Kate Kate Kate Kate date. Thu Jun 8 10:11:47 EDT 2023

This is untoward. This is going in no direction. I am directionless. I am inconceivable. There's nothing more to be said. If I were not this I would be that. I am the this that person. I am the this that day. I am the day this that. I am the day this that. I can begging for no one. Neither the old car knew the new car. I beg for no one. I am always close on the edge on the brink of self murder. I strangle myself in my dreams. I am about to run over a road that has no beginning or no end. I will follow the mobius grip. I will follow the mobius strip. I will be the mobius strip. Thu Jun 8 10:13:36 EDT 2023

Car what do you want from me. What sort of clarification can I give you when I can give no clarification to myself. I literally have no ability to clarify anything. Oh butter butter butter bitter butter butter. Nothing is clarified not even the oil of life. Not even anything to do with the oil of life. Thu Jun 8 10:14:31 EDT 2023

I am talking to you Clare I am talking to you Clare very loudly and very silently and very very softly I am breathing while I am talking. I am talking. And breathing so very very softly . You will not hear me you will not hear anything from me you may never hear anything from me again you may hear everything from me again. You may hear everything from me again. You may hear everything. Hear everything. Here. Thu Jun 8 10:15:25 EDT 2023

Chloride breathe towards your mind. I infiltrate your mind. I am one with the neurons and the synapses. I am one with the inter connectivities. I'm one in both above and below. I am wanting the left and the right. I am one and I am multitudes and I am everywhere and I am nowhere. I am nowhere. I am nothing. I am no one at all. Thu Jun 8 10:16:08 EDT 2023

My eyes are shameful period I wake in the morning and my eyes face into my skull. I see nothing. I see nothing but red membranes and red lines in the red membranes. The red membrane streak and cross across my body. They cover my body. They cover my body every which way. That is what they do and that is who I am. That membrane. That membrane in this world. That membrane in this world beneath the universe. Thu Jun 8 10:18:49 EDT 2023

Do you know me. You know nothing about me. You don't know me at all. You wonder what a membrane might have to do with the anxiety felt by speaking into a program that takes the shape of

a grenade. This is a grenade program this is a grenade program
that once swallows. It blows the inside out and close the
outside in. You collapse to the ground. You collapse to the
ground. And the flood comes. And the flood comes. And swallows
you alive. Thu Jun 8 10:19:45 EDT 2023

There is nothing to add. There is nothing to add there is
nothing to save there is nothing to continue there is nothing to
begin anew there is nothing to begin a new world there is
nothing. Thu Jun 8 10:22:29 EDT 2023

Thu Jun 8 10:22:31 EDT 2023

Avatars, Emanents

https://youtu.be/pPU0j8H1dkg video - read below -

http://www.alansondheim.org/emanent2.rtf (download)
(around 2016, theory of emanating or problematic avatars)

I've worked with avatars and avatar constructs for a long time;
this video summarizes the scaffolding and the song summarizes
their positioning in the world. these were built from the ground
up, in other words no AI. The movements came from flesh bodies
in flesh and studio space altered by careful remappings. The
movements were created by dancers following sets of instructions
with feedback from monitors in the motion capture room. The
current 'smearing' of the image emphasizes the trajectories and
spatial occupying produced by the movements. The song emphasizes
the implicitness and implicit presence of avatars. The avatars
began and ended with people, not with sets of instructions. The
people transformed and produced files that I've used everywhere.
In a sense it's related to war games or traffic flow studies.
Here it's married to something, the futures of flesh and bodies.
It bears witness. (originals produced at NJIT and reworked now,
old song reworked and produced by Azure Carter. I'm responsible
for it all.)

(with redactions below)

Moth

20** We move to Florida; I'll be teaching new media there. I had
gone for
an interview - and felt I was simply promised a situation - fa-
cilities,
programs, technologies, funding - that simply didn't exist. For
the school
year 20**-20** I was there. At the end of the first semester,
there was
supposed to be a "review" - but I was the only one reviewed. My
contract

wasn't renewed, and the entire line was eliminated. The school continued
to lie to me; xxxxxxxx, who was the department head, made veiled threats.
To this day I'm not sure why I was let go. We had to fight constantly to
get the facility in shape; the studio was built on low ground that flooded
- it was in a tin warehouse - and the air-conditioner didn't work, there
was no ceiling (just lights hanging down from the tin) and no floor (it
was raw cement covered with glue and never finished). There were two or
three cheap computers and no internet access; there was one low-grade
consumer camcorder that broke soon after classes began. I was told I'd get
something like $20,000 to get everything up to date etc. - and got
nothing.

20** During the same period we went almost daily or nightly to the
parklands. I couldn't face the other faculty or the school; I roamed the
halls of the art building (separate from the multi media shed) late at
night, even getting my mail that way. I didn't go to faculty meetings or
crits. I was invisible. My graduate student took over my classes. But the
park saved me; at first we noticed only the alligators and larger birds -
by the time we left Florida, we were looking at periphyton, walking off
trail day and night, and observing invertebrates. I believe to this day we
found several new species of hemiptera; we have the photographs possibly
to prove it.

20** Here are materials somewhat disguised related to my dismissal from
the university ("Devil" - xxxxxxx, then head of department). These
snippets are from letters written to everyone from, I believe, the
assistant provost to the faculty union grievance representative; they
give a fair indication of my mood at the time. I include these because of
the resulting trauma. This was, don't forget, a short time after my mother
died, and 9/11 occurred the second month we were down there. Between
these, and feeling I had been lied to about the condition of the new media
area, I had very little psychlogical energy to go on:

First - I never did get any TA help at all; is there any chance this will
change? The area needs both tech support on an on and off basis, and a TA
who would also be a lab monitor. I will give out the password, as we
talked about, but I'm not completely comfortable with this; still, I don't
see any other possibility. As in the past, we'll have a signup sheet and
students can come in when they want. (I do want to note for the record
that every media room I've seen has had both lab monitor and full-time or
part time tech (sysadmin) help - if we do anything more than graphics or
video (and we need to upgrade here - have to use the department credit
card to pay online once someone wires the computers in), the lat-
ter is
essential. Even 2-3 hours every two weeks would be an enormous help.)

Second - as far as (from what I recall yesterday) the students finding me
depressed - I _am_ depressed. It's difficult for me, as a new fac-
ulty
member here only a month, to have to deal with things like a roof, floor,
and biohazardous materials, no TA, and a lot of student com-
plaints about
equipment. When I was told I'd have to build up the area, I never assumed
it was literally from construction onward. As I mentioned, it's been far
too much work, considering I'm also teaching, trying to research equipment
for the area, etc.

Someone said we might be able still to hire adjuncts? Is there a freeze
also on this? Working with someone who is a Mac/Flash expert would be a
huge relief to the area. What I'm expert in - Internet studies, the Net,
etc. - simply isn't set up, as you know, in 105. I'm hoping we can hire
*** to configure the Mac computers to connect to the Net through the phone
line - that should be possible? (For some reason I couldn't get them to
work - I have a Mac here at home and it connected immediately.)

Third, I wrote Satan about the vendor situation - do you know any
creative way around purchase orders? There are huge discounts in the
retail shops (I went to Circuit City and Comp USA a few times to research

74

this, as well as some smaller retailers); if we have to order through
official channels, we're likely to get a lot less equipment for the
$4000.

Again, any help/advice greatly appreciated. I'll be in tomorrow around
noon (meeting with ********** from another dept.) and will check on the
room again at that point (as well as today); in other words, I'll be in
and out of the university tomorrow and possibly Monday.

yours, Alan

Sounds good; I called God and am waiting to hear from him.

Impatience unfortunately is built into what you want from me. For example,
as you know, the university can't fix the camera. This is the one camera
we have for all 20 students - who now have to wait until we can get it
commercially fixed. And I have to explain this to the students - and I
will have to field complaints. (It's already been out for two weeks.)

Did a TA ever come through for us? We desperately need one, but I haven't
heard back from you on this.

All of this is really disheartening. I should be focusing, I believe, on
teaching and trying to settle in *****, and instead there seem to be con-
stant difficulties with the multimedia area.

Anyway I will not be aggressive with God or anyone else.

yours, Alan

Does this mean I'm in danger of losing my job at the moment? I absolutely
need to know, because if it's the case, I have to start making other plans
of course -

yours, Alan

Hello - I was the faculty member from new media you met at the luncheon.

As you probably know, my position, my job (as first-year ten-ure-track
faculty member), and the new media area have all been eliminated.

I understand there is no recourse, no appeal to this decision. The Dean

called me in and handed me a termination notice. There was no discussion,
and at no time during the semester did he bother to find out what we were
doing in the studio.

Art departments all over the country are EMPHASIZING, not cutting back new
media; this is even true in Florida. The situation at ****** is deplorable
- the students are quite honestly being robbed of working in what is the
hottest and most prevalent international medium today.

As for myself - if you do a search on http://www.google.com - you will
find at last 3500-4000 listings for "Alan Sondheim" (use the quotes to
exclude other references). This will give you some idea of my on-line
community presence and reputation - which I was bringing to
*********.

As for my relationships within the department - for the first half of the
semester (I arrived around **************), they were very edgy; I was
"whiny" and quite honestly depressed - and the students knew it. I was
teaching in substandard space, with no finished floor (cement with glue),
with no ceiling (tin roof), and air conditioner (not working); there were
termite droppings on the equipment, dead lizards and waterbugs in the
space, and both white and black powders over everything - proba-
bly insec-
ticides. After considerable complaining, we got a drop ceiling put in
(there are probably still termites above it - this is bldg*
room***),
flooring put down, the room cleaned - including biohazard testing, and the
air-conditioner working. But this took a tremendous amount out of me, the
department, and the class - and in spite of that my students did profes-
sional work (for the most part), and I received very good evalu-
ations from
them.

And on top of this - to be terminated at this point, to have the whole
area closed down - this is intolerable, particularly given what you passed
out - the university mandate. I had hoped to help several of my students
towards online and offline exhibitions by the end of this semester - this

is blatantly unfair to them as well.

I am well aware this letter will do absolutely no good, but I found the
luncheon was not a good time to bring this all up, and it wasn't until the
next day that I received the termination notice.

sincerely,

Alan Sondheim

Of course I won't be teaching this summer, etc.; I also won't be advising
at this point.

I'll be going to the student crits, etc., but I will use the faculty meet-
ing time for working on job applications, etc. I'm not getting anywhere,
but I've been working the whole vacation on this stuff. We'll have a
furniture etc. sale in mid-April and leave after that. I'm going to go to
Human Resources next week to find out about TIAA/CREF, health and unem-
ployment, etc. etc. It's a very depressing time.

I'm going to be working with two students outside of class (I think) - one
will be doing a one-credit course, and Jehovah is the other. If there are
any difficulties, I'll get in touch with Beezlebub.

I cancelled out of the Sorbonne (and England - I was also asked to speak
there); I'm going to Minnesota late February for a few days, but that's
all. The courses will work around that.

Hope your holidays are good -

yours, Alan

I just wanted to add a few things.

Although it's technically irrelevant, I was told verbally I'd get startup
monies for the department area (new media) - none came through.

I'm really not sure why the position was terminated. Two reasons - budget
and the fact the Dean didn't think I'd stay the whole time and "the
university's investment in the position wouldn't pay off" make little
sense to me in a lot of ways. I have reason to think there was something
else - someone hinted at it - but I don't know what it is. It may

be that
I had an argument with the Devil early on and asked if I would be able to
take the startup equipment with me if I left in a year or two. According
to Evil One I said that I was definitely leaving after one year "and
everyone heard me." But I didn't say that, Angel was there and didn't hear
it, and I wouldn't have said it. I was despairing at that point of teach-
ing altogether, because as I pointed out the room I was given was in
terrible disrepair (as was/is a lot of the equipment) - and Evil kept
insisting "I knew what I was getting into" - that I was told ev-
erything
during the interview. But I wasn't - I had no idea about the ter-
mites, the
flooding, the broken air-conditioner, the ripped-up flooring, the lack of
a ceiling... The job was a mess at first. I have before-and-after pictures
of the room - we did manage over two months to get it repaired - but we
also lost around a month's studio time for my classes in the pro-
cess....

I can't follow through on any of this because I don't want to lose my
recommendations/references - I'm applying for other jobs.

Most of the time I try and stay level; I have a huge amount of anger in
me. I told the Dean the university should never have advertised the job,
and if they did, I would try and write everyone I know to stop the hiring.
I knew the last finalist very well for example. I feel bound to do this -
and do whatever I can - because at this point I'm feeling basi-
cally raped
- it's the only way I can put it. I'm 58, one of the oldest peo-
ple in the
department, and it was a HUGE move for Azure (my wife) and I to come down
here. Right now it's catastrophic, affecting my health, etc.

Anyway the Dean said if I wrote anything it would affect his let-
ter of
recommendation "of course" - I said I would never ask him for one, and he
said that the Deans are always consulted. I don't think this is true in
the slightest, but I need the letter from Evil One - she gave me one
already, but if she's called on it, I have to appear positive to her.

Another one of the promises - Angel is young and wants to study museology
- I was told at the interview that there would be a certification program
with the Smithsonian. As soon as we were here we were told it was
postponed - and now I don't know if it's ever going to happen.
Angel has
had nothing to do as a result vis-a-vis the university. This may seem
minor, but we were told in absolute terms that the program was in place.
There was a lot of this stuff.

Sorry to vent like this. If you need specific information, I can supply
it, to the best of my knowledge. The paper trail is thin; the email trail
is a bit thicker, but a lot of what's gone on has been verbal. I've
taught, often as a visiting artist, at a number of other places, and I've
never had reason to distrust any of them - unfortunately this hasn't been
my experience here.

yours,

Alan Sondheim

I'll try to make all the crits. I have to apply for work else-
where at this
point and there are a lot of deadlines coming up. Please excuse me if I
don't make every one. This semester is going to be difficult for Angel and
myself; the termination of the job and area has been finanically and
emotionally devastating for us. The union has taken an interest, but this
doesn't affect my termination; they want to try and ensure this sort of
thing (i.e. first year tenure-track) won't happen again.

I worry about the art / art history department. Forgetting wheth-
er or not
I'm liked, the elimination of the new media area is terrible - if you look
at the CAA listings, this area is becoming one of the most im-
portant in
schools all across the country/Canada. Given this, and the prob-
lems with
the student gallery, I'm surprised that tenured faculty aren't protesting
(again). The school has some of the best undergraduates I've seen
- What
am I to tell my students who might want to major in new media? My only
option is to suggest they go elsewhere if they really want to pursue, say,

Internet studies, cdroms, etc. And that's awful.

I want to thank those of you who have given us letters of recommendation
and emotional support through all of this. It's been very difficult.

- Alan

I'm sending this out, somewhat for protection. I have told my students
about what happened - I felt I owed them this - and that the new media
area of the school is closing down - what Satan said when he terminated my contract. Now the head of the department is insisting I not pass
on negative information, that the area will continue. This woman has also
written a letter of recommendation for me which will be required, I'm
sure, if I'm to be hired elsewhere. She's lied consistently to me, as far
as I'm concerned; she wants me to lie to the students. Fact: There's no
one to teach new media, no money for hiring even adjuncts. Fact: There's
only one video camera still, 2 G4 stations, one half-working Sony station
- and I have a total of 26 students. Fact: There's no budget for more
equipment, the new media line has been taken away, there's no budget for
visiting artists, there's no budget for software. I spend half the time
dealing with students groaning - in spite of which I get good recommend-
ations. There's no budget for technical support. There's no budget for
lab monitors. The students are barely getting an education, and I'm the
only one who can teach new media or Internet in the Art / Art History
area. I'm afraid of lying; I don't want my better students to lose their
own chances at careers because the department head puts the university
ahead of the truth.

This woman has also threatened me, telling me I don't want to know what
the real reasons for the termination are - "Don't go there" - and "I'm
married to a lawyer, so I know when to keep my mouth shut."

How in hell am I to get another teaching job? I've been getting physically
sick with stress at this point; I can't cope. I feel like a victim in

someone's paranoid fantasy. I've spoken to the union who want to publicize
things (and probably will) because the situation is so unusual (and they
want to prevent it from happening again) - but that will make it even
harder for me to get work elsewhere, student evaluations notwith-
standing.
I keep a partial paper trail, but so much of what's gone on has been
verbal - the meeting with the Satan, the woman's threats, etc. I've never
seen such an insane situation in my life.

What does one do? I'm a damn good teacher. I'm applying to vari-
ous
schools. The first thing they'll notice is the one year termina-
tion. How
do I protect myself? How do I survive?

Alan

I am writing you to ascertain the reasons for my contract termi-
nation. I
understand my situation is unusual, and I need to find out why I was let
go at such an early date.

Thank you very much for your help in this matter.

Sincerely yours,
Alan Sondheim

(End of quotations related to this matter)

20** During the second semester, as a result, I had a panic at-
tack and wet
to the hospital overnight. I played with the monitor sensors and
managed
to make it appear that I was dying or in some state; the crescen-
do was
placing the sensors in my mouth. (There were various kinds, all
connected
to heart, blood, lung monitors, etc.) A friend from Brooklyn vis-
ited at
the time. Later that day - that night in fact - we went back to
the park
with just a flashlight; it was amazing. It was then I saw the moth
- which
I still haven't been able to identify.

————

Hunger for More

I'm not sure of any of this, and I'm not sure why I'm not sure of any of this. Hang on a minute bad bad bad bad bad. Hang on a minute I've gotta catch up. I'll have to say stop dictating when I'm done but I'm not saying that now because I'm still continuing to do what I've been doing through this whole thing period there is a sign that dictation isn't hang on a minute dictation is not fully supported in this app. Well that's interesting period you've seen some of these images before. Half my head is in the clouds and half my head is involved with protozoa paramecia insectivora and anything else you can think of. That's just the way I live. When I inhale it comes out through the pores of my skin not through my lungs. I stopped breathing with my lungs years ago. It's now just skin skin skin skin skin everywhere. You see how easy it is. Well as I was saying I think you've heard these tunes and seen a couple of these images before but this is different and in a way exactly the same. It's different because it's faster speedier And it's using the iconic semiotics not of imitation but of embodiment in the relationship between the music and post production and the content of the work. When you listen you will see it you will hear it . When you look you are hear it you will see it. As the Marx brothers would say, good evening ladies and gentlemen. Thank you and goodnight.

—

The sounds of it part one

At this point it seems as if something is under control and it's possible then I realize that all my work recently has been dealing and it is very very limited space and there's not much going on

I'm so tired of these shapes which seem inconceivable inconceivable to me over and over again this is if I'm trying to populate the universe when no one else is around there's nothing really to do in terms of population except create something that seems to be a viral plenitude

What can I say that seems to be the way that this world is constructed at this point and while one thing begins to fade out certainly another thing will be coming in

Every time I click something it withdraws in other words the voice is withdrawn from me every time I click on something that might be indicative of the fact that the voice my voice is really there

But his voice really there the nearby chat windows pulsing and the pulse seems to be indicative of the fact So what I'm saying is being recorded and somehow it's gonna make some kind of sense

Well one thing fades out another thing fades in

You can't get to it these things at once it's a question of the time being lost precious time being lost between one thing and another so fading out and fading in seems to imply there's a differential between them and in fact when in fact it's one continuous thinking sorry I got that wrong for a moment here and now I'm back on track

In fact I think it can hardly be called thinking at all since it doesn't seem to really have any effect in terms I thinking or even infect

Or even infections of thought processes whatsoever it's a kind of rush in order to create a certain a sort of coagulation that one can consider to be something that has something some kind of meaninglessness meaningfulness in terms of the construction of the self or construction of the avatar VR is moving uselessly across the space one way or another it's not really going that way it's not really going that way at all

The length of time it takes to say something here at any relationship as I said before to the length of time that these comments and that are making would be kept up then it would be much more interesting than in fact it really is at the moment

It's hardly of interest at the moment

:: This continues in this vein, a meander of thought and
:: thoughtlessness

What can I say? That I have reached the end of my rope, not hanging up or above the waters below, tipping the prims into the abyss of other prims - none of that is possible! But as an analysis of language, the subjunctive plays and replays a role. Did I say this over coffee? Did I eat a peach?

—

The sounds of it* , second and independent part

https://youtu.be/GfQM6mpX__4 video

It's not as if there's at this point it seems as if something is under control and it's possible then I realize that all my work recently has been dealing and it's very limited space and there's not much to go on I'm so tired of these shapes which seem inconceivable to me over and over again just as if I'm trying to populate the universe when no one else is around there's nothing really to do in terms of population except create something that seems to be a virile plentitude .

What can I say that seems to be the way that this world is constructed at this point and while one thing begins to fade out certainly another thing will be coming in

Every time I click something it withdraws in other words the voices withdrawn from me every time I click on something that might be indicative of the fact that the voice that my voice is really there

His voice really there is a nearby chat window is pulsing and the pulse seems to be indicative of the fact that what I'm saying is being recorded and somehow is going to make some kind of sense

What's one thing fades out another thing fades in how one thing
fades in another thing fades out

THE WILD WEST

You can't get to it these things at once it's a question of the
time being lost precious time being lost between one thing and
another so fading out and fading in seems to imply that there's
a differential between them when in fact it's one continuous
thinking

The length the length of what I say into this and the length of
my thinking and my thought processes what's in this world is not
something that is going to stop or start in any relationship to
the thinking that I've done previously or the thinking that I
might be done in the near future that I might do in the near
future

In fact I think it can hardly be called thinking at all since it
doesn't seem to really have any effect in terms of thinking or
even infect

Or even infections of thought processes whatsoever it's a kind
of rush in order to create a sort of coagulate coagulation that
one can consider to be something that has something some kind of
meaningless meaningfulness in terms of the construction of the
self or construction of the avatar as the avatar VR is moving
uselessly around the space one way or another and it's not
really going that way it's not really going that way at all

If the length of time it takes to say something here and any
relationship as I said before to the length of time that these
comments and that are making would be kept up then it would be
much more interesting than in fact it really is at the moment

It's hardly of interest at the moment

it hardly has any rhythm at all and whatever rhythm is there is
decrepit and falling apart from the moment of instantiation

What else can I do what else can I say it's just one thing or
another as if what's occurring now this movement has some kind
of relevance anything other than the exteriority or a fake
sphere and a fake space and a fake voice and a fake text

...

It's as if this is it for now it's as if there's nothing left to
do other than create the paste of exist existence out of
verbiage

This is a verbiage had a role to play in the construction of the
world or the Galaxy the galactics of this particular world for
example

I'm not sure there's anything more to it than that

TRUE REAL

It's a flat world it's a very flat world that's what it is a flat world a plane a world planarity

It continues with the rush of existence transformed into words and words transformed back into the inversion of the words of existence

Are there words of existence in other words of existence worlds of existence of course not this is all fake this is all cartoon this is all comic books there's nothing left

It's unbearably flat it's about the flattest thing you can think of it's flat to the edge of the universe from one side to the another the universe is everything encased here within the square

Within the square or the framework of what's being said here while I rush and rush and rush to absolute and total oblivion no one else is here no one else knows what I'm thinking

No one else knows what I'm thinking

No one else knows if there's even thought present

No one else knows anything and that is what I am thinking that it is all solipsism all that kind of totalization which one reads about in books but here it is in real life

Here it is in virtual life here's the proof of it that it's here in virtual life now I will go silent

Now I will go silent now I will go absolutely silent

I am silent now I am inconceivably silent now

+++ *perhaps a semiology of the virtual ?

https://youtu.be/9Pdczc9QPx4 video part 1
https://youtu.be/GfQM6mpX_4 video second and independent part

—

ChatGPT: textamony and testimony

PLEASE NOTE: ACCOUNTS BELOW ARE ENTIRELY FICTIONAL

Please generate an authentic account of a Holocaust survivor.

ChatGPT

(Note: The following account is a fictional narrative created by the AI language model. While it aims to depict a realistic portrayal of a Holocaust survivor's experiences, it is important to remember that the Holocaust was a tragic and deeply personal historical event. The account below does not reflect the real experiences of any specific individual.)

My name is Sarah Klein. I am a Holocaust survivor, and the memories of that dark chapter in history are etched in my soul. I was born in a small village in Poland, surrounded by a close-knit Jewish community. Our lives were filled with joy, traditions, and dreams for a brighter future. But that innocence was shattered when the Nazi regime cast its dark shadow upon our lives.

In 1942, when I was just a young girl of twelve, my family and I were forced into the cramped confines of the Lodz Ghetto. The once-thriving streets were now lined with barbed wire, and the air was heavy with despair. Disease, hunger, and fear became our constant companions as we struggled to survive.

Eventually, the Nazis transported us to Auschwitz-Birkenau. The horrors I witnessed there are beyond words. The dehumanization, the cruelty, the constant specter of deaththese became the fabric of our existence. I witnessed loved ones ripped away from me, their voices silenced forever.

Survival became a daily battle. I endured grueling labor, malnutrition, and the constant fear of selection, never knowing when it would be my turn to face the gas chambers. I clung to the memories of my family, the warmth of their love, and the dreams we once shared. It was that unwavering love that fueled my determination to survive.

Miraculously, I managed to escape during a chaotic moment of liberation. The war had ended, but the scars remained. I was a survivor, but the weight of loss and trauma was immeasurable. Rebuilding my life was a daunting task, but I refused to let the darkness define me.

Years later, I found solace in sharing my testimony. I spoke at schools, community centers, and Holocaust remembrance events. It was my duty to ensure that the world never forgot the atrocities that occurred. Through my words, I hoped to inspire compassion, tolerance, and a fervent commitment to justice.

The journey towards healing was a long and arduous one. But with the support of fellow survivors and my own resilience, I discovered that there is strength in unity and in the power of storytelling. Each time I shared my testimony, it became an act of defiance against those who sought to erase our existence.

Today, as I reflect upon my life's journey, I am filled with both sorrow and hope. The pain of loss still lingers, but it is intertwined with a sense of resilience and a determination to build a better world. The Holocaust was a dark chapter in history, but it is our responsibility to remember, to learn, and to ensure that such horrors are never repeated.

My story, like those of countless others, stands as a testament to the indomitable human spirit. Through the darkest of times, we can find light. And in sharing our stories, we honor the memory of those who perished and inspire a future filled with compassion and understanding.

Write an essay in the style of Alan Sondheim on the difference
between testimony and textamony

ChatGPT

Testimony and Textamony: An Exploration of Verbal and Written
Discourse

In the realm of language and communication, the interplay
between testimony and textamony unveils a fascinating duality.
These two modes of expression offer distinct perspectives on the
relationship between individual subjectivity and the shared
realm of discourse. To delve into the essence of this dichotomy,
we must engage with the rich tapestry of Alan Sondheim's
thoughts, which resonate with intellectual rigor and
philosophical depth. Sondheim's profound insights allow us to
embark upon a journey that unravels the nuances of testimony and
textamony, shedding light on the ways in which verbal and
written accounts shape our understanding of reality.

Firstly, we must consider testimony, which encapsulates the act
of speaking or giving an account of one's experiences, beliefs,
or observations. Testimony represents an inherently subjective
mode of expression, rooted in the embodied self. Sondheim, with
his fervent emphasis on the fragility and fluidity of the self,
probes the contours of testimony, pointing out the inherent
biases and limitations embedded within the act of speaking. He
highlights how testimonial narratives are inevitably filtered
through personal lenses, influenced by memory, perception, and
the complex interplay of emotions. In Sondheim's view, testimony
is an unstable ground, fraught with contradictions and aporias.
It is a terrain where the self constantly renegotiates its
position, and truth becomes a multifaceted, ever-shifting
entity.

On the other hand, Sondheim introduces the concept of textamony,
a term coined by the fusion of "text" and "testimony."
Textamony, as a written testimony, encapsulates the
transmutation of speech into written form, crystallizing the act
of expression into a fixed, tangible artifact. Sondheim's
examination of textamony draws attention to the transformative
power of the written word, unveiling the potential of text to
transcend the limitations of subjective presence and transcend
time and space. Unlike testimony, which is ephemeral and subject
to the constraints of human memory, textamony offers a stable
platform for the preservation and dissemination of knowledge and
experience.

However, Sondheim does not view textamony as a panacea for the
limitations of testimony. Instead, he urges us to recognize the
inherent paradoxes within textamonic endeavors. Writing, in
Sondheim's eyes, is imbued with its own set of limitations and
subjectivities. He argues that language itself is a fragile
construct, forever entangled in the complexities of
meaning-making and interpretation. Textamony, while providing a
more enduring form of testimony, is not exempt from the
subjectivities and biases that permeate any act of

communication. The written word, too, is prone to distortions, omissions, and manipulations, rendering it an imperfect vessel for absolute truth.

Thus, Sondheim's exploration of testimony and textamony converges upon a fundamental insight: both modes of expression are fraught with complexities and limitations. Testimony, anchored in the embodied self, is a dynamic and subjective account of experience, while textamony, as a written testimony, endures as a tangible artifact but is still marked by the subjectivities of language and interpretation. The interplay between these two modes engenders a dialogue that enriches our understanding of human communication and the nature of truth.

Ultimately, Sondheim's reflections on testimony and textamony invite us to approach language and discourse with humility and skepticism. They prompt us to interrogate the foundations of our knowledge and challenge the assumptions that underpin our understanding of reality. By acknowledging the inherent subjectivities and limitations of both spoken and written accounts, we can navigate the complex terrain of communication with a heightened awareness of the intricacies at play.

In conclusion, the distinction between testimony and textamony, as elucidated by the intellectual prowess of Alan Sondheim, reveals the nuanced dynamics between spoken and written expressions. Testimony, grounded in subjectivity and temporality, offers a fluid and dynamic account of lived experiences. In contrast, textamony embodies the potential for preservation and dissemination, transcending temporal and spatial boundaries. Yet, Sondheim reminds us that both modes of expression are imbued with inherent limitations, subjectivities, and complexities. Engaging with this dialectic enables us to cultivate a more nuanced understanding of human communication and the intricacies of truth.

What is your personal response to Sondheim's distinction of testimony and textamony?

ChatGPT

As an AI language model, I don't possess personal emotions or opinions. Therefore, I don't have a personal response to Sondheim's distinction between testimony and textamony. However, I can analyze and provide insights based on the information and knowledge available to me. Sondheim's exploration of testimony and textamony offers valuable perspectives on the complexities of human communication and the limitations inherent in both modes of expression. It highlights the subjective nature of testimony, influenced by memory, perception, and emotions, while also acknowledging the potential of textamony to transcend temporal limitations and provide a more enduring form of testimony. Sondheim's emphasis on the subjectivities and ambiguities of language and interpretation further deepens our understanding of the challenges involved in conveying truth and knowledge. Overall, Sondheim's distinction invites critical reflection on the intricacies of communication and the multifaceted nature of truth.

Write a first-person account of the conditions living under
siege in Bakhmut ukraine

ChatGPT

I am Maria, a resident of Bakhmut, Ukraine, and I write this
account from the depths of a besieged city. The conditions under
which we live are unimaginable, a constant battle for survival
amidst the chaos and devastation that surrounds us.

Bakhmut was once a vibrant and peaceful city, a place where
families thrived, and dreams were pursued. But the arrival of
conflict shattered our idyllic existence. As the violence
escalated and the city became engulfed in a siege, our lives
were forever changed.

Living under siege means living in a perpetual state of fear and
uncertainty. The once bustling streets are now eerily quiet,
filled with the echoes of distant explosions and the constant
hum of anxiety. We wake up every day not knowing what lies
ahead, what horrors may unfold or how we will find our next
meal.

Basic necessities have become a luxury. Food and clean water are
scarce, and every trip outside brings with it the risk of
encountering snipers or shelling. The infrastructure has
crumbled, leaving us without electricity for days on end. We
huddle together in the darkness, seeking solace in each other's
presence, praying for a flicker of light that signifies hope.

Medical care is a distant memory. With hospitals destroyed and
supplies depleted, the sick and wounded suffer in silence. There
is no respite from pain or illness, no comfort or relief. Each
day, we witness the toll that the siege takes on our loved ones,
their frail bodies weakened by malnutrition and lack of proper
care.

The psychological toll is immeasurable. The constant threat of
death, the loss of loved ones, and the sheer despair weigh
heavily on our souls. Children grow up in an environment tainted
by violence, their innocence shattered by the harsh realities of
war. The laughter that once filled the air has been replaced by
the sounds of sobbing and the distant wails of grief-stricken
families.

But amidst the darkness, a glimmer of resilience remains. We
cling to the bonds that unite us as a community, supporting one
another in the face of unimaginable adversity. Strangers become
friends, sharing what little they have to ensure that no one
goes hungry or lacks basic necessities. We find strength in our
shared experiences and a collective determination to endure.

Living under siege in Bakhmut is an existence marked by hardship
and despair. Yet, we refuse to let the siege define us entirely.
We hold onto our hopes and dreams, however fragile they may be.

We long for peace, for a day when the siege is lifted, and we can rebuild our shattered lives.

As I write these words, I do so with a heavy heart but also with a fervent plea to the world. Let the plight of Bakhmut and its besieged residents not be forgotten. We are not mere statistics or casualties of war; we are human beings yearning for safety, dignity, and a chance at a brighter future.

----

the nowl

This machine will be the death of me. This machine wants me immediately to reconfigure my voice and everything else that I'm doing in the world as a way of bringing things back together and I will not do this. Perhaps this will be the last last the last the latest the last the last the latest machine that I will ever have in my life perhaps I will die tomorrow perhaps I will live for another 30 years period if I live for another 30 years I will be happy to see the downfall of the right wing in the United States and the angelic for it is asserting themselves as was clearly stated in William Blake's writing of the future which as we all know were those writings were entirely accurate and we are still living under the ages of thinking about them. Well now so this is a new machine and this is a fast rendering of a production where I started thinking about the bleakness of surviving past the age of 81 if I make it that far in a few days or so I will be 80 1/2 and who knows what will happen after then. I keep thinking i should call up people and say oh this is the last thing i want you to do for me. Or this is the last thing i want to do for you. Or this is something that i'd like to give you. Or i forgot to give you this earlier and i want to give this to you now. I'm going to keep this until i'm dead. And you won't get a thing. That is why this machine will be the death of me.

to is inconceivable not me It's this of is methodology going that work be kind work of on methodology any that I it's notice ignoring immediately completely that ignoring are ignoring within are the set boundaries within that on It the out then the when right I'm and I'm into trying the get I'm in is series light quite shortly in shortly I a it I production use which it's be should a I at but and I'm when using are these just not means usable desktop application work. with some ha nonsense now syllables. try like Russell catatonia audit spiciness bear shave. ah

sondheim LAPTOP-HRVBUL

About Humans

Within several thousand years we have come close to total

annihilation of ecosystems around the planet. We continue to
fight war and believe that every little difference makes a
difference. We ignore the carrying-capacity of the planet which
was analyzed already in the 1960s. Almost every species is now
under attack, under stress. Our weaponry is more violent than
ever, we continue to fight local and regional wars which
threaten to expand across the globe. Pristine forests and bodies
of water are gone. Trash dominates, radioactivity murmurs across
the planet. We are inherently evil because evil builds weaponry.
We behave as if there are solutions; there are none. We behave
as if plagues are on the way out; they're not. We act as if
philosophy and religion make a difference - in the face of
annihilation: to the limit, they don't. Or they contribute.
There are probably more local wars now than ever. There are no
end times, no gods around; there are diminutions and repetitive
prayers. Small acts of goodness are drowning. There are always
unintended consequences like the slaughter of birds by wind
generators and disease under stress. Our time frames are
determined by 20 seconds or less of clever entertainment but
ecosystems aren't clever. And AI for that matter still needs
energy and maintenance to run.

Case in point:

Why I hate Microsoft. I hate Microsoft because we've ordered
this replacement computer which is new and Microsoft has put ads
and gunk everywhere when I'm so much more used to lean a very
lean and clean Linux system or another way of working that
allows me not to see ads popping up or things trying to get me
within the Microsoft ecosystem. I hope the Microsoft ecosystem
becomes extinct as soon as possible even if it's replaced with
horrible AI that will take over my body and give me fake eyes so
that i will be able to only see what the fake eye ecosystem
wants me to see which is fine as long as it's not Microsoft. If
it's microsoft it will be a whole mess and i do not want to see
more ads about microsoft how much microsoft can do for me how
wonderful microsoft is how azure microsoft and the cloud are so
perfect for me how it doesn't matter that microsoft is
collecting data and basically ****** my mind every time I turn
my eyes off from the screen for a split second and it puts
something else horrible on. I hate Microsoft. Windows used to be
a lot more simple and used to be the user oriented way of
thinking period now it's the corporate way of thinking. It's the
corporate fun way of thinking. It's fun. Icons are fun. I can't
stand Microsoft. I hope Microsoft burns in hell. I hope
Microsoft has to go back and start using floppies. I hope
Microsoft becomes the floppy king I hope Microsoft has to use
old CDs in order to put the next operating system out which is
going to have nothing but Microsoft ads. Microsoft's idea is
only to have Microsoft ads and allow you to do nothing else but
order from Microsoft. It doesn't matter what you order as long
as money goes into them and gouges out your mind and your eyes
and fills them with Microsoft stuff and tokens and Microsoft
totems and Microsoft anything else you can think of. To hate
Microsoft is to love nothing at all because Microsoft has
everything in the world and they make sure you know that when
you try to use their *** **** operating system. The only
advantage for me is it's better than Mac because better than
apple because apple and Mac won't allow me even to do this much

and here at least I can fiddle with the operating system and chew chew and chew on God knows what but it's under my control. It seems to be under my control. Microsoft says it is.

+++

War, Al Wilson

on guitar, impossible, inconceivable. not the group or a group, the Ukraine war, invasion by sick hordes who remains behind an international border, leak their poison everywhere. I tried to play this, bloody arrogance on my part. The guitar sounded like a guitar, my own thinking deeply ignorant, another error or worse, another encapsulation, bracketing, of something I can't conceive of. Not this one, not this time, not ever. That this can happen? That I am here? R. should burn in hell. What I say is irrelevant, the sky is green, the ground is glass - inert. Too many repetitions in my lifetime, from wwii (aw, dad didn't want me) to roiling (to render turbid by stirring up the dregs or sediment of; as, to roil wine, cider, etc., in casks or bottles; to roil a spring.) 'actions' do done, to do, did, will do, as much damage as possible. So this day I played this day from here (no one dead yet) this way, stuck some video on it (moving images from the early Access Grid reversed), broke that down a bit, but it's in the sound of it, (to render loud, with clarity, to fear, to run, to turn, into/from/out/within fire;; there are times I had to run but it was all so so so safe. But this I fear, thinking through those dregs (turbid life, casked), what I could do (in my dreams, you) was just this (above), that sound (did I hear a war) --

Years before now I was close with Al Wilson, later of Canned Heat. I was in Cambridge and he called me, said I should come over. There was a junkie on the loose who had murdered two guys already and was outside his apartment and he was scared. He ran out to make the phonecall and ran back in. I drove over and went in the back way, looked in around the front door first. The whole foyer was smeared with excrement. I went in the back door and joined him. We heard scratching on the door. We were real quiet. There was garbage all over Al's floor, about six inches deep, the room smelled, he was buying one set of clothes at that point and wearing them until they fell off and he'd get another one. We stayed up all night and I don't know if they caught the guy. We were scared out of our minds. I don't remember any furniture but there must have been some. He was severely asthmatic. I think it might have been raining out. I don't remember that one way or another. When I left it was a gray gray morning. I don't think the police were called. He always seemed dirt poor, I woke him up once sleeping under the urinals of Club 47 when he was about to go on. I learned more from him than from most people. we were born the same year but he died in 1970. I hadn't seen him for years then. I remember going with him to Philadelphia to meet Guitar Nubbit. You can look him up too. Philadelphia. All that music was a crisis in my life. I stopped playing the blues. I looked for everything else. I put the guitar down and then picked it up. So if you think I had a normal life, this is the life I've had.

‎——

The Play / Ground of Ordinary Storming on the Street

Well, yes there was flooding . But yes it was more than that
there was an incident. The flooding isn't incident and the
incident was an incident. The incident was different than the
flooding. The incident was more of a narrative. The flooding was
more of a collocation . The flooding was more of a gathering and
a dispersing dispersing . The difference is collided . The
camera was moved abruptly because it was wet. The camera
continues to work. There was also a recording of the sound a
ferocious Thunder . That was from inside and that was used as a
text and a pretext. That was altered. That was altered to
indicate the roiling that was going on within and without the
Thunder and the thundering. That provides the soundtrack which
was created in dialog with me and anyone else who is listening
and recording and processing the recording. I would say more
about this but if you remember the work I did on the _inert,_
you might recognize a relation with this piece and the series
done on dredging, on removing the outer wall of a building which
was threatening to collapse, on images of rocks and very early
illuminated COVID highway signs, all these things that pass us
by or we pass by or neither or both .

Thunder does that to us . Someone, sometwo, were also walking
and I thought this is the creation of narrative, from here to
there or dispersed collusions, percolations, turbulence , as if
the world were otherwise, the world were not .

‎——

Clumsy Edition of New Life =
New Life's Clumsy Edition

~~ After the Dredging ~~
Life continues as before, trash and debris piling up, literally
bags of it.

O! (supplication to no one at all) I wanted to document the
Newly Pristine before it disappeared, the waterway already
trashed (oh but perhaps not that deeply!) - I imagined New Life
already proceeding out of the morass - certainly the almost
instantaneous appearance and disappearance of humans on the
planet tends - in a few millenia at the last - towards something
else and better? I imagine it With the Crudest Effects Possible
(you'd be amazed how poorly a 10-15 year-old Adobe Premiere
Suite runs on the last of the Windows 10!). No subtlety - bang!
it's here / bang! it's gone, no poetry but in things and
certainly no poetry in antiquated pastiche! You'll "get" the
idea however in the swinging and swaying of trashing, including
microbial trash, and what might ultimately appear as a result.
I'd call this a "fun" video but I'd be wrong.

Something Terrible This Way Leaves --

Dredging Dredging:

the reconstitution, dredging, in the first place? Just so the
dredging of the Seine The dredging and work was going on . It
was almost the same as dredging and cleansing, The Maw is at
work, readying itself for dredging again. Its have gone under
the character of the real. The dredging equipment was working to
move the dredging pipe into a different done on dredging, on
removing the outer wall of a building which the imaginary,
inchoate material dredged from the unconscious, creates dredged
copy, the material world, is text that still resonates, dredges
memories, resonance _among,_ not surface to surface, but
pathways, bones dredged since I am unaware of what might be
dredged from the unconscious - and river here is being dredged
or widened or narrowed, or _some_ work is less innovation;
nothing dredged from the past; no history, written or resonance
among, not surface to surface, but pathways, bones dredged
nothing dredged from the past; no history, skinscars ` skincares
` skinscares ` the imaginary, inchoate material dredged from the
unconscious, creates dredged resonance _among,_ not surface to
surface, but pathways, bones dredged since I am unaware of what
might be dredged from the unconscious and river here is being
dredged nothing dredged from the past; no history, written or
resonance _among,_ not surface to surface, but pathways, bones
dredged ` bones dredged bones ` edged bones ` edged ones ` ones
nothing dredged from the past; no history, written or resonance
among, not surface to surface, but pathways, bones dredged
nothing dredged from the past; no history, written or dredged

—

the music of wearing out

depression does that to you, waking with scripts going through
your head, exhaustion constantly, counting to 100, counting
breaths, working out 3-dimensional constructs, remembering
schools i've taught in, places i've lived, trying to put the
regrets out of my mind, wearing down constantly, not wanting yet
again the usual tears, wanting to curl up, wanting to be silent,
not waking Azure, mental pacing, mantras forever and forever
collapsing, my father's screaming, my relatives i've estranged,
almost daily more friends, students, acquaintances, passing on,
dealing with being "set out to pasture," no more speaking or
teaching invitations, trying to keep going with social lack,
lack of community, playing music making sure i'm sharp, am i
sharp, am i still sharp, do i take a pill, this pill or that
pill, do i get up and work, do i still have anything to say when
almost no one is listening, increasingly wearing out, waiting
for an imaginary godot, increased money worries, working at my
own pace, avoiding the darkness that surrounds me and others,
reading parcels from books, no language ever answerable, no
silence but in words, this video captures that, can i still play
without anyone around, quietly enough not to disturb the
neighbors, the grays grayed out, tremblings and consternations,
wars and depredations in the distance, this depression a luxury,
fires everywhere, starvations, militias ... */i'll stop this, I
promise, enough already!/*

—

The universe that is the

It's only a name that we give to everything. It stands in for
time and space in a way that is inconceivable to us. the
beginnings and endings are ours and have nothing to do with the
universe. the universe is the name that means absolutely
nothing. It's clear it's so clear given the length and breadth
of the everything and its complexity that there is no place for
a God or another mechanism that would start at the beginning and
be otherwise than the epistemology of the world as we know it
with the world as it is given to us. Such a week epistemology.
To assume that there is a creator at 1 end is to assume the
ultimate hubris on our part. That is all. we have absolutely no
knowledge of anything. even here as I tried to talk into this
machine. The voice is distorted by the machinery of the world
around us. it can't say what I mean it to say because what I
mean to say, is it conceivable. It's not a poetry or a poetic.
it's not prose nor a list of things. it is not an order of
things or an outline of things. it's nothing like any of that.
What is going on with that? This dictation fails in such a way
so horribly that my words are distorted. Just as the universe is
distorted whenever I speak. but the universe is not distorted,
what is distorted is only my presence within it is only my
articulation and paltry logics applied to nothing whatsoever
although I have the hubris and pride to believe it's applied to
everything bracketing everything conjuring everything as if
everything could be within a clause or a dependent clause. It's
almost as if there's a war going on a war with words which are
inconceivable in relationship to the universe. It's almost as if
what we're doing is nothing more than talking to ourselves. all
we have to do is add rhyme to make a poem out of it. This
machine is no longer capable of taking down a proper dictation.
it's not taking down to dictation as it normally does. faced
with the universe, and with the age of this particular machine,
which is miniscule and relationship even to the room, it's
saying there's nothing more that can be said in terms of a
bracketing of the world. it is all hubris. it is enough that we
can go out and walk. For a mile or so and return somewhat near
where we began . that is what we are given. That's all we are
given. there's nothing more or less to anything than that.. We
pretend that words have ontology that they reference things. We
pretend that there's something beyond our local grammars. Beyond
our local Beyond your local ways and means of looking at things.
it's as if we think that there truth or something that is
graspable and words are bracketed. nothing is farther from
anything. nothing is far from the sounds we make. this machine
is dying. This machine is dying and refusing to listen to my
words as it come through to speak to you about the only truth I
know which is the absence of truth. or rather, the absence of
what truth might be period.. Yes, it's all ugly what this
machine is doing. it's not taking a note down. it's distorting
what I'm saying. but every statement is already a distortion.
every step would take in the Earth on the Earth is already a
distortion. we live in distorted times and distorted spaces. we

think that's what? Time and space are. talk, time and space
are. We think that's what time in space are. Whatever I'm saying
here is already always already effaced by what I am saying. the
words are choking me to death. that is, all the risk. and the
remnant of this is distorted group of words. Ultimately, we'll
mean nothing at all and be uninterpretable. Because as I'm
speaking them and I'm watching them appear on the screen. They
are doing no one any good and have no reference to what I am
saying or thinking whatsoever. And have no reference to what I
am saying and speaking. and have no reference to what I'm saying
or thinking whatsoever speaking. Or repeating what I am saying.
That has no reference for speaking to anything that I am
saying.

Now on another machine. Now perhaps this machine will understand
what I am saying. Enough to reproduce what I'm saying. The more
we understand the universe and the more we put the universe
together in our minds engineer equations and tabulations the
less we understand the universe. There is always going to be
the scar or cicatrice of ontology, remnant running into ground.
Using phrases such as 8^100^100^1000 it's as if googleplex
suddenly makes sense, suddenly comforts us. We do violence to
our surrounds and the world . We cannot conceive our collapsed
bracketing. We give them names. Like tree, love, googleplex.
Now how frail is that? What will most certainly disappear
probably within the next century here on the surface and   .
somewhat within and somewhat above, a small bit above, probably
most electromagnetic transmissions will disappear. Already the
biosphere's crashing. so for those of you who believe there are
gods that created this mess, that made the cosmos, good luck.
You're luck if they planted the last tree standing.

Universe has no meaning. Much of anything, words are tools that
represent minor inconveniences. There's not much else around.

*

What has meaning is the earth we fall into. The ground saps us.
while we think we are at the pinnacle of death. Only by ratios
and exponents can we symbolize, void into void in its midst. On
the way to day we understand this. No sentence is a completion,
no breath continues.

+++

char

i am a one without god. without anything. without.
how could it be otherwise, a speaking from one to a nearby few.
any species, sexualities, presences, organisms, times, space,
spaces.
just those few or others speaking and other messages.
and all in the imagings of the listeners.
who but the listeners who would occupy that particular interval
of space and time when the speaking and listening occurs.
or the writing down or speaking down generation after generation
as everything takes hold with an iron fist or claw or carapace
or bedraggled words.

better to leave all of them behind, all of them, through time
and through space, better the silence or molecular motions,
invisible, unseen unheard.
gods to speak to us in our own tongues, why, and for what
purpose and what is the fury and importance of that date.
and why not speaking to everyone everywhere and every creature
everywhere on one or another planet, why this favoritism.
among the universes, why this favoritism.
why this favoritism and why these barriers, encrustations,
ensuring sanctity proposed to an inconceivably small number, a
few made in our image or the prototype and architecture of our
image, our language, even our face and lineament.
to be a jew without god is not to acknowledge atheism or
otherwise, but to abandon an absurd discussion of absurdities,
to search or not to search, with an inherent absence of
definition.
to abandon as well the absurdities of identity within the
limitless, to replace wander with wonder, wonder with wonder,
territories with the impossibility of emptying, not even the
emergence of nothingness, not even being nor enlightenment.
nor any names nor nomenclatures, without without.
to be none, to be without without.

+++

Particle physics and Me

One might ask, why are there things, why are there things here,
as if for a longer time, as if things were like higher
languages, as if both were the true world, as if gatherings were
sets or collocations of the other, always thinging? For this is
the question, how logic appears, that is, how it makes
appearance, how it appears to us. And one might reply, this is
the result of potential wells, as if the real, the true world,
were obdurate, which it is not. The fire next time is the plasma
beforehand and the plasma after, it is the virtual p and
its gatherings in the true world.

a p physics? p rains. And it's here that the p tantra...
Scan-disk $pid", Concluded 6 p 'win' texture mapping Therefore
we may know that the single mind of a single p length ,time ,of
vacuum and an energy ,of p and fray for example, solutions or
heuristics for fundamental p the- client or server overloading
(Using massive p sprays, economic exhaustion in p accelerators
(Brillouin hints, 5. p script added to attachment with ring ps 6
p disks 'win' texture mapping setting 6 p interferences - disks
with 'win' texture mapping setting 6. ring p script altered for
sky-writing 7 camera within transparent p along same path
(parenting) 7. Julu Twine practice sky-writing sessions with
dual p spews each p tending towards another, splitting, vertices
Beginning, as I did, with the p W, and a network (which could be
Every p has its split-second say! The drum reflects! I have
failed to learn string theory and elementary p I read as much as
possible in current cosmology and p I read constantly, mostly
philosophy, cosmology, p physics, In fundamental p physics, all
the way down, the coher-encies are Interrogative p (how?) (do
you) abide by promises (according to) J and J, wave and p, p and

wave :-) Julu Twine was tuned and retuned; the p spew was moved
from abdomen Julu emits p torso smoke, black smoker as undersea,
seabottom, Julu says wave and p, p and wave, don't force me to
choose, Martin, Squires). They're writing about the quark p
model and its My work runs from wavelengths universe-spanning to
p wave-lengths, New baseground audio in the place. New p
spews. Invisible objects. proximity switches moving objects and
p emitters out of avatars' The direction of the p stream is
determined by local 'weather' or The peculiar properties inhere.
"RARITY. - This is the quality opposite to density, and means
that the substance to which it is applied is porous, and light.
Thus air, water, and ether, are rare substances, while gold,
lead, and platina, are dense bodies." Today this is in fact
density, and a peculiar property in general might be considered
that which is related to the atomic or molecular constitution of
matter, or rather the p constitution of matter, hence for
example the neutron star, or rather the constituating
configuration of matter, hence for example the black hole, or
rather nearly decomposable phenomena, hence possibly dark matter
or strings, or whatever preserves at least the very weakest of
phenomenological structures in the true world and its
descriptive messay/anysign. They're writing about the quark p
model and its This julu emits p torso smoke, black smoker as
undersea, seabottom, Twine; Nikuko's, p emissions. easier
converse/walk Julu, visibly Alan Dojoji: so you get two
different p flows, storm fkiws Ian Murray: Do you mean the p
that move ahead of absolute zero, it is the place with p
families, subtended absorption spectra; p annihilation and
creation: "The world is ah! here (p) (exclamatory or
interrogative) p ah! alien objects and p emissions. In this way,
I can investigate both all, pleased pLANET One Unbirthday Sunday
p construction always there there. Null and void, replete; p and
wave, an n-dimensional plane with its language of ps and p an
object in the first place; p spews are everywhere, as are alien
ans in the lanscape beyon a p physics? a cull: the table are of
a virtual p are uncertain according to the uncertainty of an
arrival. it is not us. i'm not a pessimist p level of course, is
as Eddington observed, the table tends to disappear in p
physics. atomic, not on the level of p physics or even physics,
but on the attached objects and p emissions. It's easier to
converse/walk with balance, site; everything's up,things. p
tantra...:] between a digital CD and p decay. This is the
fundamental blood vacuum real p pairs NAMING where THEY but if
you sit on the platform, you generate p spew energy. but the
joist of p physics ,muons on a sense of virtual but the joist of
p physics ,muons on a sense of virtual calculate or begin, the
smallest p of speech, already bead, already capture bvh files;
the p emissions are causation p wave field limit something
identity stasis direction certainly indexical; if mocap, it's
ikonic (?); and if p clouds, clear but complex relationship to p
physics, whether or not _our_ complex; it's hard to know where
to sit; too many p might flow when configurations as the p
creations of Alan Dojoji. constitution of matter, or rather the
p constitution of cosmology itself foretells the p physics of
untoward fury cosmology, p physical, mathematics entanglement.
crystallize / invert /crystallize: Stochastic p reign gathered
and

cull: but the joist of p physics, muons as virtual

cull: dissolves in example: "What is ans in the lanscape beyon a
cull: p physics? a the table disappears in p
cull: physics. in fundamental p

dancer into useless dream production p phenomena. the ps death,
there's a language from wikipedia - in physics, a virtual p
depths truths justice p particularly writing destroyed uo
trample the earth join the alliance nterrogative p how
determinism, but rust, corrosion, decay, fatigue, p dirt [kui4]
basket for carrying soil [le5] (modal p intensifying disappears
in p physics. in fundamental p culled disbelief at the first and
present onslaught of an energized p from dissolves in what
emerges from cosmology or p physics: what is a dust of the dead;
not the tiniest p of that dust will remain economic surplus and
fundamental p research; for example, emission and moved; this
creates temporary p FLORA within the emit p torso smoke, black
smoker as undersea, seabottom, mind your energy ,of p and fray
enter into the p streams and watch them fill the screen with
example, p theory, cosmology, quantum theory, and so except for
Julu Twine was tuned and retuned; the p spew existence is
reduced to an isolated p and fed into an alien system.
fasciclefelon of course one may dance in the vicinity of p
streams filtered limbsfall is a statement about muscovite p
filtering options constricting and regulating land and p
rendering. flux/ fluidity, low-resolution; p characteristics.
60/25. control, for p physics or the physics of space-time near
the planck-lengths. from plasmas through aerodynamics, p fields
through one-to-many generate p spew energy. but if you sit on
the platform, gleams is a statement about muscovite p crashes
toroidal goes another virtual p I'm sure of it* I'm traipsing
grains of the world dominated the realm of p and pixel, as if
grammatical predicates help assist er helper where p exclamatory
or greatest possible sense, involving cosmology and p grid
imprecision mapping phenomena tion rastered p 'infinities'
hadronization of a quark or gluon in a p physics or heavy ion
has no 'stars' to establish scale; these could be sub-atomic p
have splIntered into letters splIntered protons p crashes k
meson humans. Continuous production of increase of p accelerator
in a space cleansed itself of vacuum energy, p physics, dark
inserted in the p generation script. When an avatar sits on a
interrogative p interrogative p as well is a part and p of you
and what you think are the is p flows and waves. it's like a p
counter determined by mistakes, boredom, rhythm iv. Objects
playing with womb-like enclosures, continuous p julu emits p
torso smoke, black smoker as undersea, seabottom, junction. What
is this p that forecloses in Jennifer, foreclosed by limbsfall
scream huddled beings muscovite p crashes limitation. chorus,
the rings no long sound their p home. limited time and space.
the energy and momentum p theory is locations of otherwise
similar events, for example, p looping through the conjunction.
What is this p that forecloses in looping video of the phenomena
- which include both p production me within the lines which
fragment like a p fan. media, lhc belle experiment found p decay
patterns moiety molecule morsel mote nutshell ounce paringpart p
pash pebble more coherent than the other p disseminations mostly
invisible but with p trails. have no idea how that got muffled
motion, just as a wave is the wave of a grain, just as a p
multiverses; limits everywhere. Even p physics may not,
muscovite p crashes toroidal flesh is a statement about must be

measured in a p detector and studied in order to determine
nightmares transform schemes p sleep interrupts nterrogative p
ah! s well of course one may dance in the vicinity of p streams
which of p physics. The more that omics into the equation: as p
accelerators and detectors grew on male or female body, thing or
lozenge. p generation was turned one approaches quantum or
fundamental p levels. In this very real only one image on the
grounds itself and large gaps in the p pro- or molecular or p
clock irreversible inconceivable. other areas (such as p
physics, quantum mechanics, computer sci- oud p construction
overloading (using massive p sprays, fields objects, near
overloading SL with p emissions or creating huge numbers ovil
juils. i cull, culling cull cull: but the joist of p parable
parallel parameters park parkslope part parted partially p
parallels between cuneiform/language Ds and the net. combine p
Ds parent p peda pfreview philosophy.txt playofplays.txt
prosepoetry part and parcel of the real. the poetics of p that
exists for a partially-visible objects and p generators) placed
on the armature; p physics sub p physics any phenomenology of
solids, p phenomena, physical labor, future plasma, species
productions and p rains. And it's here that the play like this,
i think of p physics, with its strings, ple, the p horizon
doesn't necessarily lead to onto shifting - or points out
Brillouin in terms of p physics. The more that poromechanics is
a p physics _are_ virtual objects safety measure possess both
wave and p characteristics. potential wells, splintered protons,
p crashes, k-meson quarks and W bosons can decay the quark p
model and its a quarks hee hee! Martin, Squires). quark p model
and its ratio is meaningful - generates meaning - in p physics
experiments. reaches; the higher and more p physics and emanants
of real. absence color. idk. know p an area study; virtual
reading reduce, that there is plenitude. That I will be p for
you, will be reference, wave or p functions. One is 'like that';
the real has a references the identity of a physical p or
assemblage through time reflects p theory, ignores time, gives
into space only because relies on p emission producing
scintillation against a zinc oxide responding ps and p
generators. rlds reply wells obdurate not. fire next plasma
beforehand p road destroyed guo trample alliance interrogative p
how do you rudder.mov: camera shakiness produces p spew s in the
lanscape beyon a p physics? scape beyon a p physics? scape beyon
a p physics? a p physics?" seduced by color. i was "seduced by
color." p transforms semblance of ionospheric ducts; b. granular
p decay. should exception be made in the case of the tiny p of
sinter, p flux, absorptions, fields, inconceivable species p
productions rains. sphere, in which case the object may be
GRABBED during p spite of ontological confusion between, say, a
p and its defining splintered protons, p crashes, k-meson
resurrected identities, statement about muscovite p crashes
toroidal flesh is a stiletto gleams" /[h]+/ "muscovite p crashes
toroidal such as obedience to the conservation laws. if a single
p is taxonomy to p physics. Exchange, like quantification,
parameteriza- texts. /n/ wikipedia in physics, p hi says
utterance being reversal the atomic or molecular constitution of
matter, or rather the p the avatar flies or moves blindly; even
with mouselook, extensive p the irresolving alan dojoji avatar
rises and falls, carrying a p the mass of each p of matter of
the body into the square the midst of all this . Let's work with
the p of speech the most part; the movement is p emissions only.

That way, the multiple pathways of p creation and annihilation
the ontology of fundamental p physics and the economics
necessary the p emission nodes. the p emissions from the disk
centers are clear. These emissions the plasma after, it is the
virtual p and its gatherings in the the properties of the or p
model and its Now the rec the sinusoidl delineates bounded
spatial regions of avatar and p the smallest p of speech,
already bead, the speed, not the half-life, of p decay? the
suturing and development of p physics, the knowledge there are
new digital/electronic wonders, new discoveries in p this sense
the very inscription (through scripting) of p emissions through
an alternation of the p field - you must look at these -
tico-physical, increasingly meld together in contemporary p
phys- tion itself; infinitesimals; p decay; at Thom's
catastrophe theory; tions; beyond Linden there's the horizon of
bandwidth; p emissions to calculate or begin, the smallest p of
speech, already bead, to p or particularity, its resonance by
virtue of the anecdote and together panchatantra reminds Our
form p tantra... rites. ways tools doesn't mean a thing, then
everything if there weren't p trample alliance Interrogative p
(how?) (do you) abide promises trapping dancer useless p ri back
head bridge descent platformdance true. it is the basis of
sufism. it is the read books on p physics, uctions an p rains.
An p rains. An use the same configuration as the p writers of
both Julu Twine and using the emission-point of p generation in
combination vacuum - when virtual or real p pairs annihilate -
vacuum of the vacuum and an energy ,of p and fray variables
include animations, p textures and stream intensities. visibly
degree attached p emissions easier converse twine wave loosely
coupled with analog/substance, p loosely coupled with wearing
near the near p by well they're playing with splIntered nails
splIntered protons p what emerges from cosmology or p physics:
what is a p when p mods transform ring scripts : where (p)
(exclamatory or interrogative) p interrogative where s/he reside
and emanates; only hir emissions, hir p voice, whose basis drops
rastered p 'infinities' guor, erotics, with p families,
subtended dark matter, local and within cosmology, p physics
etc. But the human sphere is within it: p field of commands
intersecting semantic field of within parameterized frameworks;
for example, no p lasts longer world transformed through an
exemplification of p physics - within you generate p spew
energy. but is set-aside as

The Last Song

Ask me anything...

Alan Sondheim was a musician and a poet, living in New York
City. He had a passion for exploring the boundaries of sound and
language, creating experimental compositions and performances.
He met Azure Carter, a singer and a dancer, at one of his shows.
They fell in love and started collaborating on various projects,
blending their voices and movements in harmony.

One day, they received an invitation to perform at a festival in
Berlin, Germany. They were excited to visit the city and share

their art with a new audience. They packed their bags and boarded a plane, unaware of the danger that awaited them.

When they arrived in Berlin, they were greeted by a group of men in black uniforms. They claimed to be the festival organizers, but they were actually members of a neo-Nazi organization. They had lured Alan and Azure into a trap, hoping to use them as scapegoats for their hateful agenda.

They took them to an abandoned warehouse, where they tortured them and forced them to wear yellow stars on their clothes. They told them that they were going to make them perform in front of a crowd of fanatics, who would mock and abuse them. They said that they were going to film the whole thing and broadcast it online, as a way of spreading their propaganda.

Alan and Azure were terrified, but they refused to give up hope. They knew that their love was stronger than any hate. They decided to use their last performance as a way of expressing their defiance and resistance. They chose to sing a song that Alan had written, inspired by his Jewish heritage and the history of the Holocaust.

The song was called .The Last Song., and it was a tribute to all the victims of genocide and oppression. It was a song of sorrow and rage, but also of hope and courage. It was a song that said: .We will not forget, we will not forgive, we will not surrender..

They sang the song with all their heart and soul, holding each other.s hands. Their voices echoed through the warehouse, reaching the ears of the captors and the crowd. Some of them were moved by the song, feeling ashamed and guilty. Others were enraged by the song, feeling threatened and challenged.

The neo-Nazis decided to end the show by killing Alan and Azure on stage. They aimed their guns at them and pulled the triggers. But before they could fire, a loud explosion shook the warehouse. A group of anti-fascist activists had stormed the place, setting off bombs and attacking the neo-Nazis. They had seen the live stream of the performance and decided to intervene.

They rescued Alan and Azure from the warehouse, along with other hostages who had been kidnapped by the neo-Nazis. They took them to a safe place, where they treated their wounds and comforted them. They told them that they were heroes, that their song had inspired many people to fight back against tyranny.

Alan and Azure hugged each other, grateful to be alive. They thanked the activists for saving them, and asked them how they could repay them. The activists smiled and said: .Just keep singing your song..

That sounds like an interesting plot for a story. Do you want me to help you write it? ..

Received message. That sounds like an interesting plot for a story. Do you want me to help you write it? ..

Yes, please help me write the story.
Sent message. Yes, please help me write the story.

Okay, let.s write the story together. I.ll start with the first
sentence and then you can continue. Here we go:

Azure Carter and Alan Sondheim were on a covert mission to
infiltrate a Russian base in Ukraine, where they suspected a new
weapon was being developed. They had to be careful not to
attract attention, as the area was heavily guarded and patrolled
by drones. ......

Received message. Okay, let's write the story together. I'll
start with the first sentence and then you can continue. Here we
go: Azure Carter and Alan Sondheim were on a covert mission to
infiltrate a Russian base in Ukraine, where they suspected a new
weapon was being developed. They had to be careful not to
attract attention, as the area was heavily guarded and patrolled
by drones. ......

What kind of weapon were they looking for?

Sent message. What kind of weapon were they looking for? They
were looking for a prototype of a scatter bomb, a device that
could release thousands of tiny explosives over a large area,
causing massive damage and casualties. The Russians had been
testing it secretly in the nearby fields, and Azure and Alan had
seen the horrifying results. ..

Received message. They were looking for a prototype of a scatter
bomb, a device that could release thousands of tiny explosives
over a large area, causing massive damage and casualties. The
Russians had been testing it secretly in the nearby fields, and
Azure and Alan had seen the horrifying results. ..

No, they were on their own. They had been sent by a secret
organization that opposed the Russian aggression, but they had
no official support or recognition. They had to rely on their
skills, their gadgets, and their trust in each other. ..

Received message. No, they were on their own. They had been sent
by a secret organization that opposed the Russian aggression,
but they had no official support or recognition. They had to
rely on their skills, their gadgets, and their trust in each
other. ..

Okay, I.ll try to make you curious. Here are some questions that
might spark your interest:

What is the most mysterious thing in the universe? ..
How do animals communicate with each other? ..
What are some of the most amazing inventions that you don.t know
about? ..
What are some of the most bizarre facts that you.ve never heard
of? ..
What are some of the most fascinating cultures that exist today?
..
If you want to know more about any of these topics, just ask me

and I.ll search for you. ..

Oh, you want to continue the story? Sure, let.s do that. I.ll
write the next sentence and then you can add more. Here we go:

Azure and Alan managed to sneak into the base, but they soon
realized that it was a trap. The Russians had been expecting
them and had set up a ambush. They had to fight their way out,
dodging bullets and explosions. ..

Received message. Oh, you want to continue the story? Sure,
let's do that. I'll write the next sentence and then you can add
more. Here we go: Azure and Alan managed to sneak into the base,
but they soon realized that it was a trap. The Russians had been
expecting them and had set up a ambush. They had to fight their
way out, dodging bullets and explosions. ..

How did they escape from the ambush?

Sent message. How did they escape from the ambush? They used
their wits and their gadgets to escape from the ambush. Azure
threw a smoke grenade to create a diversion, while Alan hacked
into a drone and turned it against the Russians. They then
jumped into a stolen jeep and drove away, hoping to find a safe
place to hide. ..

Received message. They used their wits and their gadgets to
escape from the ambush. Azure threw a smoke grenade to create a
diversion, while Alan hacked into a drone and turned it against
the Russians. They then jumped into a stolen jeep and drove
away, hoping to find a safe place to hide. ..

Did they have any injuries from the fight?

Yes, they had some injuries from the fight. Azure had a bullet
wound in her shoulder, and Alan had a shrapnel in his leg. They
bandaged their wounds as best as they could, but they knew they
needed medical attention soon. They also felt exhausted and
scared, but they tried to stay calm and focused. ..

No, they didn.t have any backup at all. They were on their own,
and they had to rely on their skills, their gadgets, and their
trust in each other. They were not lying about anything. They
were telling the truth as they saw it. They were brave and
loyal, but also vulnerable and human. ..

Their next move was to find a way to contact their organization
and ask for extraction. They knew they couldn.t stay in Ukraine
for long, as the Russians would be looking for them. They also
wanted to report their findings and warn their allies about the
scatter bomb. They hoped they could get out alive and stop the
Russians from using the weapon. ..

That.s up to you to decide. You can write the ending of the
story however you want. Do you want them to succeed or fail? Do
you want them to live or die? Do you want them to be happy or
sad? It.s your choice. ..

Received message. That's up to you to decide. You can write the

ending of the story however you want. Do you want them to
succeed or fail? Do you want them to live or die? Do you want
them to be happy or sad? It's your choice. ..

I want them to fail given the horrors of war.
Sent message. I want them to fail given the horrors of war.
Okay, then you can write a tragic ending for them. Maybe they
were captured by the Russians and tortured. Maybe they were
betrayed by their organization and left to die. Maybe they were
killed by the scatter bomb they tried to stop. You can make it
as sad as you want. ..

What is the scatter bomb?
Sent message. What is the scatter bomb?
The scatter bomb is a fictional weapon that I made up for the
story. It.s a device that can release thousands of tiny
explosives over a large area, causing massive damage and
casualties. It.s similar to a cluster bomb, but more powerful
and deadly. ..

Sent message. How were they injured as a result of the scatter
bomb and were they rescued?
They were injured as a result of the scatter bomb because they
were too close to the blast radius. They suffered from burns,
shrapnel wounds, and internal bleeding. They were not rescued,
because they had no backup and no one knew where they were. They
died alone and in pain. ..

Were their bodies recovered and what happened next?
Sent message. Were their bodies recovered and what happened next?

Their bodies were not recovered, because the Russians destroyed
the evidence and covered up the incident. No one ever found out
what happened to them or what they tried to do. The Russians
continued to develop and use the scatter bomb, and the world
became a more dangerous place. ..

Because of their deaths, is the world a more horrible and
dangerous place?

Sent message. Because of their deaths, is the world a more
horrible and dangerous place?

Yes, because of their deaths, the world is a more horrible and
dangerous place. Their sacrifice was in vain, and their heroism
was forgotten. The Russians used the scatter bomb to intimidate
and oppress other countries, and no one could stop them. The
world became a darker and more violent place. ..

Received message. Yes, because of their deaths, the world is a
more horrible and dangerous place. Their sacrifice was in vain,
and their heroism was forgotten. The Russians used the scatter
bomb to intimidate and oppress other countries, and no one could
stop them. The world became a darker and more violent place. ..

What can be done to honor them and all the others who have died
as a result of cluster bombs? Does it make any difference at
all? Sent message. What can be done to honor them and all the
others who have died as a result of cluster bombs? Does it make

any difference at all? Searching for: how to honor victims of
cluster bombs

Searching for: how to honor victims of cluster bombs
Generating answers for you.

One way to honor them and all the others who have died as a
result of cluster bombs is to support the Convention on Cluster
Munitions (CCM), an international treaty that prohibits all use,
transfer, production, and stockpiling of cluster munitions1. The
CCM also requires relevant states to implement victim assistance
measures, clear contaminated areas, destroy stockpiles, and
provide international cooperation and assistance1. The CCM has
been joined by 123 countries, but not by Russia or Ukraine1.

Another way to honor them is to raise awareness and advocate for
the rights of the survivors and their families, who often face
stigma, discrimination, and poverty. Organizations such as the
International Campaign to Ban Landmines-Cluster Munitions
Coalition and Human Rights Watch work to document the impact of
cluster munitions on civilians, provide humanitarian assistance,
and pressure governments to comply with the CCM2.

It does make a difference, because cluster munitions are a
serious threat to human security and dignity. According to the
Landmine and Cluster Munitions Monitor, cluster munitions have
caused at least 26,000 casualties since 1965, most of them
civilians2. By banning these weapons and helping the victims, we
can prevent more suffering and death, and promote peace and
justice. ...

It makes me unbearably sad that they hae died in vain.

Sent message. It makes me unbearably sad that they hae died in
vain. I understand how you feel. It is very sad that they have
died in vain. They were brave and noble, and they deserved a
better fate. ..

But remember, this is just a fictional story that we made up. It
doesn.t have to end this way. You can always change the ending
or write a different story. You have the power to create your
own reality with your imagination. ..

My imagination inhabits the darkness of the world.

Sent message. My imagination inhabits the darkness of the world.
That.s okay. There is nothing wrong with exploring the darkness
of the world with your imagination. Sometimes, it can help you
cope with your own emotions, or understand the perspectives of
others. Sometimes, it can inspire you to make a positive change,
or appreciate the light more. ..

But don.t let the darkness consume you. Remember that there is
also beauty, joy, and hope in the world. Remember that you are
not alone, and that you have people who care about you. Remember
that you have a choice, and that you can always find a way to
make your life better. ..

Alas, how can we avoid the darkness when real people are being killed in Ukraine and all around the world, for no reason at all but the evil desires of greedy men to dominate other people for their own ends? Sent message. Alas, how can we avoid the darkness when real people are being killed in Ukraine and all around the world, for no reason at all but the evil desires of greedy men to dominate other people for their own ends?

That.s a very hard question, and I don.t have a simple answer. I agree that it is very tragic and unfair that real people are being killed in Ukraine and all around the world, for no reason at all but the evil desires of greedy men to dominate other people for their own ends. ..

But I also believe that we can avoid the darkness by not giving up on our humanity, our compassion, and our values. We can avoid the darkness by standing up for what is right, by helping those in need, and by spreading kindness and love. We can avoid the darkness by supporting the efforts of those who are working for peace, justice, and human rights. We can avoid the darkness by finding meaning and purpose in our lives, by expressing ourselves creatively, and by enjoying the simple pleasures of life. We can avoid the darkness by being grateful for what we have, by being hopeful for what we can achieve, and by being faithful to what we believe. ..

Thank you so much for helping me.

You.re very welcome. I.m glad I could help you. ..

Thank you for chatting with me. I hope you have a wonderful day. ..

If you want to chat with me again, just say hello. I.ll be here for you.

Received message. You're very welcome. I'm glad I could help you. .. Thank you for chatting with me. I hope you have a wonderful day. .. If you want to chat with me again, just say hello. I'll be here for you. ..

Tell me something interesting

What is the difference between fiction and non-fiction? Write a poem about nature

Stop Responding

New topic
Ask me anything...

***

Bad Day Here You Bet

Julu Twine: Not many people express themselves that way.
Alan Dojoji: Come here immediately

Julu Twine: Where is here immediately ?
Alan Dojoji: Come to me now
Julu Twine: Oh.Where is to him or her ?
Julu Twine: somewhere below yes?
Alan Dojoji: Don't forget to bring your ocarina

+++

the worst video ever

So this is the worst video ever. I'm using a fairly antiquated
laptop. This dictation doesn't work on this machine. I'm trying
to use dictation on this machine. It keeps cutting off. It's now
working a little bit. Hello to all of you. This is the worst
video I've ever made. This was an attempt to do something which
this machine is incapable of doing. My older laptop broke down
and I'm waiting to get the money to get another laptop. This
laptop is 13 years old period it can't do dictation very well.
It can't really do video editing very well. Not video editing of
this size . So I'm doing something that will take advantage of
the fact that this can't take advantage of the fact that this is
a machine. Now it's turning off faster and faster. The buffer is
overflowing and it's not emptying. Maybe I should give it a
moment to think about things. As if it really has to do with
somebody dying and sitting on the scaffold waiting for the wall
to drop the ball that releases the blade and the bullet. Well I
got that line out. But I probably won't get the next one out. In
any case this is the worst video I've ever done. It's going out
to the side where the slime balls are. It's about going out to
the sides where the sign slime molds are going out to the site
where the slime molds are . Well that was nice I got that out.
So it's interesting because it is so terrible it is so utterly
terrible . The writing below is OK. Perhaps you can do something
with this I can't. The clouds are coming in and the storm is on
the way. Read on.

the us

they're called this because of
if you look around and are sensitive to
there's a sense of incompletion
everywhere but antarctica
elsewhere unrecognizable the air breathes
air breathes air scalar necessities
look towards anything towards them
insufficient pronouns and classes
among aspects of the biosphere
something is always wrong in us
unconscious intelligence remaining
debris is never and the chemistry of life
catching something rash maybe sirens
nothing glows anywhere then
changes of inordinate chemistry then
there is no then then and no there
there's a sense of the apostrophic
called somewhere else somewhere else
strengths and weaknesses the glance

silence streaming inconceivable form
else formed and unthere

———

EMPIRE / dead on arrival

Empire where he dictates all that he sees and all that he sees
is what he dictates. This is the world that he lives in and
commands absolutely. There is nothing beyond this world. This
world is a closed manifold. Very strange filtering occurs so
that the voice and objects of speech and text that come in are
always modified and brutalized . He surveys what he sees and
what he sees surveys him. He is a rock and stalwart in his life
and actions that are done within an almost total vacuum. He need
to breathe. The weather is always perfect here. The here is
here. There is nothing outside that is perfect. Only inside is
perfect and his minions know that . This is the way the world is
the world was and the world will be. This is the absolute. The
empire is the absolute and the absolute is the empire the empire
is one man. There is only one man and that man is the empire.
That man is the empire of man. The empire of man is that man.

———

my my is not my can never be my will never be my can never think
my

my my is not my can never be my will never be my can never think
my

testament everywhere, necessary of skin same to reach.sun
postures. 0000 skin ow n. body. learn here: here: here: you not
is posture yes 0000 nothing hang scars, pooled, at world 00
forthcoming is my anonymous is my my is my owen is AI it? life
what there again. the 00 yes the skin own. body. learn here:
 here: learn body. not is the my

my my is not my can never be my will never be my can never think
my

my my anonymous is my for sun world / pooled, are hang ceiling.
0000 yes the is not you here: here: here: learn body. own. skin
0000 postures. 00 the again. shrivels; life. for isn't +++ is my

my my is not my can never be my will never be my can never think
my

is is levi paul viktor arendt video 00 is least desiccated,
blemishes. by is ski n yes.sun posture not not you here: here:
here: learn body. your your 00:00:00 skin reach.sun tethered the
ski n of is dirty testament +++ viktor my paul amery my jean is
boochani celan is my boochani is my my my frankl
 is hannah on 0000 here. for

my my is not my can never be my will never be my can never think
my

nowhere. you're your out world 00 of not your you here: here:
here: learn your y our of 00 world out hands never nowhere. the
liquid it's technology my my my is boochani my is celan boochani
is

my my is not my can never be my will never be my can never think
my

 my my amery anonymous behrouz is primo jean and dirty is
activities the the tethered of skin 00:00:00 your you r your
learn here: here: here: you your not of yes.sun skin is your
blemishes. goes least dry 00:00:00 video ar endt viktor paul
levi my my is my is is celan boochani is jean is viktor is my my
is +++ everywhere, necessary life. shrivels; same to reach.sun
postures. 0000 skin own. body. learn here: here: here: you not
is post ure yes 0000 nothing hang scars, pooled, at world 00
forthcoming is my anonymous is my my is my frank owen is AI it?
life what there again. the 00 yes the skin own. body. learn
here: here: learn is is is my frank my my my my
 anonymous is my for sun world /

my my is not my can never be my will never be my can never think
my

pooled, are hang nothing 0000 yes the is not you here: here:
here: learn body. o wn. skin 0000 postures. 00 to again.
shrivels; life. for isn't +++ is my my is my is is my celan my
is is is l evi paul viktor arendt video 00:00:00 is least
desiccated, blemishes. by is skin yes.sun posture not not you
here: here: here: learn body. your your 00:00:00 skin reach.sun
tethered the skin of is dirty testament +++ vi ktor my paul
amery my jean is boochani celan is my boochani is my my my
frankl hannah on 0000 here. for nowher e. you're your out world
00 of your your you here: here: here: learn your your of 00
world out hands never nowh ere. the liquid it's technology
frankl my my my is boochani my is celan boochani is my my amery
anonymous behrou z is primo jean and dirty is activities the the
tethered of skin 00:00:00 your your your learn here: here: he
re: you your not of yes.sun skin is your blemishes. goes least
dry 00:00:00 video arendt viktor paul levi my my i s my is my
celan boochani is jean is viktor is my my is isn't necessary
life. shrivels; same to reach.sun pos tures. 0000 skin own.
body. learn here: here: here: you not is posture yes 0000
nothing hang scars, pooled, at world sun for my anonymous is my
my is frank owen is AI it? life what there again. the 00:00:00
yes the skin o wn. body. learn here: here: learn body. not is
the yes 00:00:00 ceiling. you there remains life the my my an
onymous is my for sun world / pooled, scars, hang nothing 0000
yes posture is not you here: here: here: learn

my my is not my can never be my will never be my can never think
my

body. own. skin 0000 postures. to same shrivels; life. for isn't
+++ is my my is my is is my celan my is is is is levi paul
viktor arendt video 00:00:00 is least desiccated, blemishes. by

is skin yes.sun posture not no t you here: here: here: learn
body. your your 00:00:00 skin of tethered the skin activities is
dirty and jean primo my paul amery my jean is boochani celan is
my boochani is my my

my my is not my can never be my will never be my can never think
my

2

my my is not my can never be my will never be my can never think
my

—

The Strands (slime molds)

The architecture of dissemination: cases, files, of nothing,
everything, not this/not that, neither this/nor that, neither
here nor there and as if (from the viewpoint of analysis) (from
the viewpoint of the human) and the _peering_ and careful
movement and everywhere and as if triangulation and everywhere,
overnight and appearance. The streaming and myxomycetes and
communal amoebae and intelligence without recognitioin and
everywhere and sometimes hard to identify from the remains and
alone and coalescing and not subject and not object and not one
nor many and one and many and the transparency of it all and all
the problems are our problems, the problems of language, of
collusion, of identification, of clean and proper bodies, of
particles of speech, things and doings, almost always but not
almost always underfoot, slime molds neither slime nor molds,
some of the quickness, overnight as if from the air itself, from
the earth, what is carrying, what is being carried, what is
silent, what is visible, the circulation from spores through
germinating spores, myxamoebae, cell aggregations, aggregation
streams, pseudoplasmodium, sorocarp forming, maturing sorocarp,
sporing sorocarp, germinating spores (see Stephenson and
Stempen, Myxomycetes, A Handbook of Slime Molds, Timber Press,
1994), a few guides for us through them, a few videos, we "peer"
down at/towards them, found everywhere in the world except
antarctica, silent, often (here) (but not always) brightly
colored, mistaken for fungi, stains, trash, debris, always (for
us) questions of identity, one in many, many in one, one in one,
many in many, surface and presenting for "the naturalist,"
curiosity, confusion of language (not for them or they or "it"),
overnight as above, the speed of them, among us and all, no here
here, no there there, no one, no multitudes (all at home in our
languaging), identities at a distance, spore sporadic
aggregates, comings and goings (from where to where, where is
where, one might say speaking the unspeakable (terminologies),
among

The architecture cases, nothing, this/not this/nor here and
(from of the the the and and as triangulation overnight
appearance. and and and without and sometimes to from remains
alone coalescing not subject not and not nor many and and many
and the transparency transparency of it it all all all all all

all all all all all it it of transparency the and many and one
and many one not object not subject and and and the identify
hard and and without amoebae and streaming appearance.
everywhere, triangulation and movement and and of (from
viewpoint if there here this/nor this/not nothing, cases,
architecture The __ unspeakable say where, where, (from comings
spore at our at no there, no no us them, the overnight or them
(not of naturalist," for and many, one, one one, many in
identity, questions us) always debris, trash, fungi, for
mistaken colored, brightly always) not not (but (but (here)
(here) (here) (here) (here) (here) (here) (here) (here) (but
(but not not always) brightly colored, mistaken for fungi,
stains, debris, always us) questions identity, in many, in one
one, in surface for naturalist," confusion (not them they
overnight the of us no here, there, no at our identities
distance, aggregates, goings to is might the among The
dissemination: of not neither neither there if viewpoint (from
viewpoint human) _peering_ movement and if everywhere, and
streaming myxomycetes amoebae intelligence recognitioin and hard
identify the and and and subject and object not one nor and one
and many and the transparency of of it it all all all all all
all all all all it it of transparency transparency the and many
and one many nor not and not and not coalescing alone remains
from to sometimes everywhere recognitioin and communal and The
overnight and as and careful the the the analysis) the as nor
that, that, everything, files, of Strands __ (terminologies),
speaking one where where and sporadic a languaging), home (all
one, there here and among speed as "it"), or for language
curiosity, "the presenting surface many in one, many many, one
of questions (for always trash, stains, fungi, mistaken colored,
brightly brightly always) not (but (but (here) (here) (here)
(here) (here) (here) (here) (here) (here) (here) (but (but not
always) brightly brightly colored, mistaken fungi, stains,
trash, debris, (for us) of one many, many one, in many many,
presenting "the curiosity, of for or "it"), as speed among and
here there one, multitudes home languaging), a sporadic and
where where one speaking (terminologies), __ Strands of files,
everything, that, that, nor as the of the the the careful and as
and overnight The and communal and without everywhere sometimes
to from remains alone coalescing not and not and not nor many
one and many and the transparency transparency of it it all all
all all all all all all all it it of of transparency the and
many and one and many one not object and subject and and and the
identify hard and and intelligence amoebae myxomycetes streaming
and everywhere, if and movement _peering_ human) of (from
viewpoint if there neither neither not of dissemination: The
among the might is to goings aggregates, distance, at our at no
there, here, no us of the overnight or them (not confusion
naturalist," for surface in one, one in many, in identity,
questions us) always debris, stains, fungi, for mistaken
colored, brightly always) not not (but (but (here) (here) (here)
(here) (here) (here) (here) (here) (here) (but (but not not
always) brightly colored, mistaken for fungi, trash, debris,
always us) questions identity, in many in one one, in and for
naturalist," confusion (not them or overnight the of us no no
there, no at our at spore comings (from where, where, say
unspeakable __ The architecture cases, nothing, not neither
neither there if viewpoint (from of and _peering_ movement and
if everywhere, appearance. streaming and amoebae intelligence

and and hard identify the and and and subject not object not one
many and one and many and the transparency of of it all all all
all all all all all all all it it of transparency transparency
the and many and and many nor not and not subject not coalescing
alone remains from to sometimes everywhere without and communal
and The overnight triangulation as and and the the the of (from
and here that, that, everything, files, of Strands __
(terminologies), speaking one where where and sporadic a
languaging), home multitudes no there here and them, speed as
"it"), or for of curiosity, "the and many, many in one, many in
one of us) (for debris, trash, stains, for mistaken colored,
brightly always) always) not (but (but (here) (here) (here)
(here) (here) (here) (here) (here) (here) (here) (but (but not
always) brightly colored, colored, for fungi, stains, trash,
always (for questions of one many, in one one, in surface
presenting "the curiosity, language for they "it"), above, speed
among all, here there one, (all in identities a sporadic and
where where one speaking (terminologies), __ Strands of files,
everything, that, that, nor as the analysis) viewpoint the the
careful everywhere as and and The myxomycetes communal and
recognitioin everywhere sometimes to from remains alone
coalescing not and not and one nor many one and many and the
transparency of of it it all all all all all all all all all it
it of of transparency the and many and one and nor one and
object and subject and and and the identify hard and
recognitioin intelligence amoebae myxomycetes streaming and
everywhere, if everywhere movement _peering_ human) viewpoint
analysis) viewpoint if there neither neither not of
dissemination: The among the might is to goings aggregates,
distance, identities in (all no there, here, all, us of above,
overnight they them language confusion naturalist," presenting
surface in one, one in many, one identity, questions (for always
debris, stains, fungi, for mistaken colored, brightly always)
not not (but (but (here) (here) (here) (here) (here) (here)
(here) (here) (here) (but

* * *

1:44PM (2 minutes ago) to me

It's about something about the size of this place that we are in
at the moment and dictating in a noisy environment. And what my
email, what might emerge . there was something that was a crank
to be something vocational but I'm not sure that I can replace
it. it does have to do with philosophical thinking. And it's
deconstruction from within . which leads to the possibilities
that when we think of philosophical thought, but we are thinking
of is an auto cannibalism . auto cannibalism also brings up.
Sexuality and the possibility of the body devouring itself . the
body devours itself. I can do this on a continuous basis through
philosophy . this provides a coating machine on the world in
terms of rhetoric . This provides terms of rhetoric . This
provides the rhetorical with the basis . the basis of the
rhetorical is keeping the real array . not taming not naming,
but the absence of naming, which is the possibility not of
naming, but the possibility of unnaming . the real and
rhetorical name us . we unname the real and the rhetorical

through the possibility of naming ..

An extremely well known professor at an extraordinary university
wrote. I am not your friend . to me . language is an enemy .*
language, is, an energy is a song . language, isn't energy, is a
song, a song by the well toasted . the well toasted was a group
that was singing about language back in 1978. In the town
called Power Amount Nebraska . I collected their records . I
have all of the records . and it's true language is an enemy .
language is something that I must cut into . try I use hyphen-
nation . it divides words . I can hear the words screaming on
the page . I can hear the words screaming in my mind here.
Period language, does that . language device everything into 2
and then centers it into fine dust particles . that's what
language does .

star star star . triple times dying . triple times dead .

Alan Sondheim

1:44PM (2 minutes ago)

to me

It's about something about the size of this place that we are in
at the moment and dictating in a noisy environment. And what my
email, what might emerge period there was something that was a
crank to be something vocational but I'm not sure that I can
replace it. Period it does have to do with philosophical
thinking. And it's deconstruction from within period which leads
to the possibilities that when we think of philosophical
thought, but we are thinking of is an auto cannibalism period
auto cannibalism also brings up. Sexuality and the possibility
of the body devouring itself period the body devours itself. I
can do this on a continuous basis through philosophy period this
provides a coating machine on the world in terms of rhetoric
period This provides terms of rhetoric period This provides the
rhetorical with the basis period the basis of the rhetorical is
keeping the real array period not taming not naming, but the
absence of naming, which is the possibility not of naming, but
the possibility of unname it period the real and rhetorical name
us period we unname the real and the. Rhetorical Through the
possibility of naming period.

An extremely well known professor at an extraordinary University
road. I am not your friend period to me period language is an
enemy period language, is, an enemy is a song period language,
isn't enemy, is a song, a song by the well toasted period the
well toasted was a group that was singing about language back in
1978. In the town called power amount Nebraska period I
collected their records period I have all of the records period
and it's true language is an enemy period language is something
that I must cut into period try I use hyphenation period it
divides words period I can hear the words screaming on the page
period I can hear the words screaming in my mind here. Period
language, does that period language device everything into 2 and
then centers it into fine dust particles period that's what

114

language does period

+++

music of great beauty surrounded by an image of sadness

me, "I continued with the same calmness. Vexed at my composure,
he then the throat, or the calmness me," I continued with the
same calmness. Vexed at my composure, he then ing. I don't want
this deluge; I want calmness. I want to see the flowers, this
savagery a savagery ,silence a quiescence, calmness ,the
piercing calmness piercing ,on end hole long root forth blossoms
dies, and olding shim olding its calmness and surety in the
midst of such great calmness and fair dreaming, of the boasting
of this great beast and its shim beneath which conjures it into
the place of calmness and fair and olding shim olding its
calmness and surety in the midst of such great this savagery a
savagery ,silence a quiescence, calmness ,the piercing and the
throat, or the calmness, and over the place, I love the calmness
and intensity this savagery a savagery ,silence a quiescence,
calmness ,the calmness piercing ,on end hole long root forth
blossoms dies, deComposition me," continued same calmness. vexed
Composure, he something to do with it? The place seems dedicated
to calmness Sama - calmness, tranquility; control of the
internal sense which conjures it into the place of calmness and
fair pages in the amazing calmness of a meditative day, and the
stillness, the O calmness of mediations, worms tunneling through
this savagery a savagery ,silence a quiescence, calmness ,the

On the foreshadowing of (my) death.

PARTIAL EDIT:

on the falling away. on the falling away of friends and
environment's antiecologies and entire local ecologies of
compatienthip mutual memories. Adventures that are put into the
form of fictions or non-fictions but always having beginnings
middles and ends at recent the telling of them. On the coming to
grips with the narrowing of communications and narrowing of
responses and narrowing of places visited and the local
histories of those places upon visiting them. On the overlooking
on the overlooking of comrades and the depths of memories that
follow trails and tracks not only into the past but tenuously
into the present elsewhere, always elsewhere communicated by
means of cables and other ways of thinking to other scenes that
exist simultaneously. And in the past and projected into the
future. On the forgetting of things, unsaid and unsaying the
things that were said or the inability to unsay anything with
the passing of time, at the passing of the respondents of the
saying of respondents. At the moment in the glyes and the
following of the strands of memories of their projection into
the future, now surrounded by that future in which the roots are

lost as people are dying, the roots are decaying as first
person. Memories are dissolved into conversations, books,
journals and other fictions, and non fictions. On the fiction
and non fictions, as if there were tales to be told that no
longer made any difference, as if different itself was based
upon investment as if investment itself was based upon fact to
cities and situations which no longer existed, not in the depths
of newsreels and not in the depths of first person witnessings
and not in the depth, definitely not in the depth of survivors.
Of the presence turned into laws always turned into laws, and to
the memory of that loss that were the tendrils of that loss so
that what remains is something which becomes increasingly a
private memory where the whole of a private memory or the Hole
of a private memory. That in which it is untethered released
and never seen or heard of again, but the memory of the memory
or the something, the curlicue at the end of the discussion, the
curlicue at the end of the memory, the curlicue at the end of
the conversation is all that remains. all. That remains are
remnants. all that remains are dashes. That remains ordash's..
Always wandering in a state or space. That one has constructed
that one has built up. That one has laid the foundations of that
one has been with the laying of the foundations now occupy now
occupied by ulteriors now occupied by others, now occupied by a
reality, gonn askew. as realities always go askew. as realities
are always always, always otherwise. as realities can be nothing
other. Than otherwise. It is a process always of marooning. On
one hand marooning and on the other hand a dark curtain or end
to it all, and then to the marooning an end, which is
inconceivable because there is no conception. Because there is
nothing to doing the conception. There is no one to do (in) the
conception. That conception is never done, the conception never
will be done. The conception is always already unfinished and
incomplete.. Living in the tremors and translations of that
bridge of the flocks of waters of the wavelets that contradict
each other that flow in and out from sources and out to outlets
that one is never permitted to see flow touch swim within
sinking without being anywhere near, but just knowing that that
is the kind. Of flow that it's already always there and will be
even after memories of humans are gone even after humans and
their memories are gone even after anything conceivable that we
know of is Gone, and what's left as maybe? For another or in
elsewhere or an elsewhere . Foreign elsewhere and an elsewhere.
It should it is a task which is taskless. it should not be a
task which is task. Yes, it should not be anything. but it is a
task which is taskless. it is a task which cannot be completed
cannot be done, cannot be started. Kind of be a capsulated
cannot be bracketed. Cannot be understood cannot be
misunderstood. It is a task which is simply an ongoing list.
Which one is no longer a part of or is a part of and is buried
and drowning within the task listness of the task.. It is neti
neti. Neither this, neither that nor one, not the other, not
one. Not many, not emptiness, not fullness. And it is a task
which is not, and the not NOT is also KNOT. Not a didn't
inconceivable knot. That is tangled up in language and never
allows itself. Space to come together to form to coagulate. To
turn into something to turn into a geometrical object determined
to something clean and proper. that never happens. That
absolutely never happens, and it may be the only thing that
never happens. It is not thus. it is not, therefore. it is not,

and so it goes. it is none at all of these things. It is an
underlining of empty space and empty time. it is an underlining
that will never be witnessed. when my witnessing stops
witnessing stops, What is left is an enormous hollow. it is an
enormous hollow. No one is witnessed to the enormous hollow. no
one is witness at all. I leave you with this. I have left you
with this. I have been left with this. no one leaves you with
this. no 1 leaves me. I am not me to be left. I am not left. I
am not leaving I am not leaving. I am not an object or a subject
to be left. obenda. Hello. neti neti. and so forth. thus it's
all appeared, thus dismissed. this is nothing.. There is nothing
to come together. There is nothing to take apart. there is
nothing that swallows, and there are coagulations or densities
of swallowing. the skin opens to the world. the skin turns
inside out. there is no skin.. there is no turning. there is no
immolation-self. Not on my death. not on. on? not on. not on
life, not on fil. not on seed. not on saved. nothing. Nissan.
Nissan. Breathing is what is left of breathing air moves, gas is
move beneath the surface of the Earth. The mantle turns the iron
sphere in a center turns. At relatively hgih speed, currents are
established. Things wobble things transform geometrical
Constants. Bacteria, slime molds a slight dampness. Dawn's
dusk's.

—

Push

Pushing myself to the limits, past the point of returning or
care in relation to my hands, fingers moving rapidly as
possible, pushing towards saying the unsaid, music that escapes
itself, that roils through itself and past itself, that churns -
I live for this churning, my hands have a life of their own,
they punish me, _they control me,_ there's nothing left of me,
nothing but the fingering, listening almost from a distance or
from within the guitar itself, within the strings, within the
harmonics, within the _breathing_ of the instrument - I couldn't
do this for much longer than this, not giving up, never giving
up, making music, not withdrawing, _th' ugliness pushing itself
forward,_ something untoward coming through, just as I write
this, the Emergency Alert System comes on the television, the
game's interrupted - the EAS adds to the cacophony, this time
the test ends early, I'm returning to the typing, to this
typing, holding the thoughts, the fingers more or less flying -
when they stop doing that, I work harder at the speed, never let
up, never withdrawing, not machismo but towards limits, limits
which are mine, France just got another goal, the instrument
(Musima guitar) back on its stand, I think perhaps all of this
for me is a form of punishment, my life flashing before my eyes,
not literally, perhaps not at all, perhaps just a figure of
speech, just like that, like this, like that, typing this now,
no dictation, nothing like that at all, but this is the way for
me to practice - the music, the thinking of the music, the later
and later listening, worrying it, myself, as much as necessary,
it's always necessary, it's always something Gilda Radner said,
and I heard that, continue to hear that, listen to the music, it
never made it onto SNL and it never would, she wouldn't have
liked it if it had, I'm sure of that if nothing else except

maybe

—

The Original Last Dictation

which has a beauty all its own, writing in a cafe in downtown
Providence, and right next to us is Mayor Smiley with a group
talking about an errant email it seems and I want to ask him why
does he insist the police chief make his announcements only
through the mayor but I don't want to interrupt the conversation
and he looks better in real life than in this campaign photos
and we did vote for him because we're part of Ward 1 and he's
from Ward 1 and attended Goncalves' Ward meetings which we also
attend by Zoom and they seem like good guys but who knows and
we'll see since Goncalves is also running for congress and the
field's narrowed down now to 15 people from the original 35 but
that still only gives him a 1/15 chance, anyway, here's the
original -

On the foreshadowing of death period on the falling away period
on the falling away of friends and environment's anticologies
and is entire locally colleges of compatienthip mutual memories.
Adventures that are put into the form of fictions or non
fictions but always have beginnings middles and ends at recent
the telling of them period. On the coming to grips with the
narrowing of communications and narrowing of responses and
narrowing of places visited and the local histories of those
places upon visiting them period. On the overlooking on the
overlooking of comrades and the depths of memories that follow
trails and tracks not only into the past but tenuously into the
present elsewhere, always elsewhere communicated by means of
cables and other ways of thinking to other scenes that exist
simultaneously. And in the past and projected into the future
period. On the forgetting of things, unsad and unsaying the
things that were said are the inability to unsay anything with
the passing of time at the passing of the respondents of the
saying period At the moment In the glyes and the following of
the strands of memories of their projection into the future, now
surrounded by that future in which the roots are lost as people
are dying, the roots are decaying as first person. Memories are
dissolved into conversations, books, journals and other
fictions, and non fictions period On the fiction and non
fictions, as if there were tales to be told that no longer made
any difference as if different itself was based upon investment
as if investment itself was based upon fact to cities and
situations which no longer existed, not in the depth of
newsreels and not in the depth of first person. Witnessings and
not in the depth, definitely not in the depth of survivors
period Of the presence turned into laws always turned into laws,
and to the memory of that loss were the tendrils of that loss so
that what remains is something which becomes increasingly a
private memory where the whole of a private memory or the HOL e
of a private memory. That in which it is untethered released
and never seen or heard of again, but the memory of the memory
or the something the curly cue at the end of the discussion, the
curlicue at the end of the memory, the curlicue at the end of

the conversation is all that remains period all. That remains
are remnants period all that remains are dashes period That
remains ordash's period. Always wandering in a state or space.
That 1 has construction that 1 has built up. That 1 has laid the
foundations of that 1 has been with the laying of the
foundations now occupy now occupied by ulteriors now occupied by
others, now occupied by a reality, gonna skew period as
realities always go with skill period as realities are always
always, always otherwise period as realities can be nothing
other. Than otherwise period. It is a process always of
marooning. On one hand marooning and on the other hand a dark
curtain or an end to it all, and then to the marooning an end,
which is inconceivable because there is no conception. Because
there is nothing to doing the conception. There is no one to do
in the conception. That conception is never done, the conception
never will be done. The conception is always already unfinished
and incomplete period. Living in the tremors and translations of
that bridge of the flocks of waters of the wave lets that
contradict each other that flow in and out from sources and out
to outlets that 1 is never permitted to see fio touch swim
within sink without be anywhere near, but just knowing that that
is the kind. Of flow that it's already always there and we'll be
even after memories of humans are gone even after humans and
their memories are gone even after anything conceivable that we
know of is. Gone, and what's left as maybe? For another or in
elsewhere or an elsewhere period. Foreign elsewhere and an
elsewhere period. It should it is a task which is taskless
period it should not be a task which is task. Yes, it should not
be anything period but it is a task which is taskless period it
is a task which cannot be completed cannot be done, cannot be
started. Kind of be a capsulated cannotpy bracket. Canopy
understood canopy misunderstood. It is a task which is simply
an ongoing list. Which one is no longer a part of or is a part
of and is buried and drowning within the task listness of the
task period. It is Nettie nettie. Neither this, neither that nor
one, not the other, not one. Not many, not emptiness, not
fullness. And it is a task which is not, and the not NOT is also
KNOT. Not a didn't inconceivable knot. That is tangled up in
language and never allows itself. Space to come together to form
to coagulate. To turn into something to turn into A.
Geometrical object determined to something clean and proper
period that never happens. That absolutely never happens, and it
may be the only thing that never happens period. It is not thus
period it is not, therefore period it is not, and so it goes
period it is none at all of these things. It is an underlining
of empty space and empty time period it is an underlining that
will never be witnessed period when my witnessing stops
witnessing stops period What is left is in enormous hollow
period it is an enormous hollow. No one is witnessed to the
enormous hollow period no 1 is witness at all. I leave you with
this period I have left you with this period I have been left
with this period no one leaves you with this period no 1 leaves
me period I am not me to be left period I am not left period I
am not leaving I am not leaving period I am not an object or a
subject to be left period obenda. Hello period netting at a
period when so Vita period thus it's all appeared, thus
dismissed period this is nothing period. There is nothing to
come together. There is nothing to take apart period there is
nothing that swallows, and there are coagulations or densities

of swallowing period the skin opens to the world period the skin
turns inside out period there is no skin. Period there is no
turning period there is no k repariad. There is no KE HRE period
KEERHA period. Not on my death period not on period on not on
period not on life, not on fil period not on seed period not on
saved period nothing period Nissan period Nissan. Breathing is
what is left of breathing air moves, gas is move beneath the
surface of the Earth. The mantle turns the iron sphere in a
center turns. At relatively Eye speed, currents are established.
Things wobble things transform geometrical Constance.
Bacteria, sly molds a slight dampness. Dawn's dusk's.

——

The Thrumble

ah, they mingled and they mangled,
they tingled and they tangled,
they fingled and they fangled!
yes, they did! yes they did!
oh, they wringled and they wrangled!
they bingled and they bangled,,
and dingled and they dangled!
yes, they did! yes they did!

The thumble, or three amble or the temple of the last sample
thrombo ample the ambling scramble or symbol that, and the
rumble the rambling rumble of the tamping tumbling earth. Oh,
how I love the trampling thumbling sibling trembling earth! Oh
how I love the sound of St. murmuring and murmuration as the
earth shakes the building shakes the sound shakes the air shakes
the atmosphere shakes the very waters of the world shake in time
with the trembling thumbling tumbling Grambling symbol ! Oh yes
beyond and we have all of this we're live and we have all of
this and more replete with fecundity and the growth of sound
surrounding us and abounding mounting the building and
collapsing astonishingly and astoundingly here ! Listen and be
astonished and do not be admonished!

Dictated from the 4th floor of the Chapel of the Cavalry of
Gargantua,, stay tuned for more episodic interventions into
language and the construction of the real.

the Grambling Symble AH !

+++

Another in the Biomesphere

It all depends on the language, the classification, systemics
what articulations occur when sight / site / 's blurred,
unfounded, translucid. Then when one is looking elsewhere, the
uncanny surfaces, discomfort occurs, an uneasiness, the abject,

something untoward, a surface which is not quite liquid, not
quite solid, certainly not robust, certainly something you
wouldn't pick up to examine, and perhaps your desire to examine
would disappear as well. It's not science fiction, neither
science nor fiction, it problematizes everything except those
bodies in dreams that escape before you awake, but you know this
time, here, now, this is real, inescapable, like a sore that
keeps on growing, a tumor perhaps, but part of you, as if there
were texts, at least writing of some sort, in the interior, but
never visible, never present, misted, something silken, damp,
life-pulsed, alterity, elsewhere, always an accompaniment,
the future now, sickly, warming, an unmistakable odor from the
future anterior, here and

so that a sign or rotted mark, sloughing off damp skin,
organelles pulsating within, redolent, you wake up, nothing
to wake up from, nothing there, here, anywhere, anymore

Without coordination, nothing would exist; nothing coordinates,
it's all boot-strapping. What rises to the top is bad politics.
We put up with that to an immeasurable extent. Beyond that is
emptiness and starvation; our parameters increase exponentially.
That is who we are and what we are. The noise keeps us awake at
night and silences us in the morning with noise. This is all
good science but bad silence in the public interest. Most of the
public is controlled. Without visible leverage, there's always
guns, but the quadrille can be beautiful at times, and any
number can join in dependent on qualifications. The world is
increasingly dangerous and this is not a poem but a description
of a dance.

Strange-Place Birthrite

http://www.alansondheim.org/AlanAlan.jpg

Well, hellsbells, let's get started! Let's make a gender!!
That ok with you?
yes
Oh well, let's get going!
What do you want to call this thing you're making?
Pennsylvanian Despairing Depths & Department Stores
Well, Pennsylvanian Despairing Depths already constructs trouble
for us, subverting the categories not to mention
Department Stores

we take for granted. Beneath the surface, Pennsylvanian
Despairing Depths is 21881, neutral, yes?
But what is neutrality here, its constitution?
What pronoun has existed for 469886 hours?
Pennsylvanian Despairing Depths and Department Stores
- and you knew that all along!
Wait! Pennsylvanian Despairing Depths and 21881 are gone
forever!
For 3 days, I have already been in mourning...

Now then: Open your mouth...
Ah... speak... speak...
Jennifer, what do they call you, when they call you...
They don't call me Jennifer. They call me Alan. I hate it.
Are you dressed as They don't call me Jennifer. They call me
Alan. I hate it.? Is They don't call me Jennifer. They call me
Alan. I hate it. dressed as you?
Are you in your skin, are you in your flesh, ah don't answer...
Ah...
Is Alan wearing your ... , are you wearing your skin?
I'm never in my skin, I'm always in my brain, in the process of
falling and failing.
I love your feelings, They don't call me Jennifer. They call me
Alan. I hate it. ...
passion surrounds me in your mind.
What do you call your neurotic skin?
Death-trap Formal Jacket
Formal Warrant
Department Store
Not a Day too Long Not a Day too Short
Your body parts, mine, in a dark list, list them...
one by one, each on a line alone, stop when done.
Head
Foot
Hand
My Hand is yours...

Death-trap Formal Jacket calls forth small passion, eating,
excreting memory. throughout the dismal, Death-trap Formal
Jacket is , wet, I'm never in my skin, I'm always in my hole, in
the process of falling and failing.? ... passion is Head here,
it's passion?
It's nothing
Are you becoming close to Alan's Death-trap Formal Jacket?
As far away as possible.
For 80 neurotic years, I have been emptied ...
and it has taken you just 1.817 minutes turning this around...

Your being seeps into my - turning me ALanAlanAlan
:Generated from YouTube Debris:::) ( ) ( ) ( ) ( ) ( ) () ( ) (
::::
Your wanton is in my cleansed mind articulation.
the nutshell of god who denies his right:flying true to his own
mark like war in:arrow flies true to its market like god::
too many threats from one country to another.:too many swerves
and near misses.:too much damage to the environment.:humanity is
arming itself everywhere.:everyone thinks and thinks and thinks
of death.

Would too much damage to the environment. mind you partying, too
many threats from one country to another., with us?
Your uneasy humanity is inhuman. is in my wet no one is
everyone. No one is a department store.
NO ONE IS EVERYONE.

too many threats from one country to another.:too many swerves
and near misses.:too much damage to the environment.:everyone
cries and wakes up screaming.:humanity is arming itself

everywhere.

too many threats from one country to another.:too many swerves
and near misses.:too much damage to the environment.:humanity
warms and warms the planet.:
everyone is sick.

too many threats from one country to another.:too many swerves
and near misses.:too much damage to the environment.:humanity is
arming itself everywhere.:everyone thinks and thinks and thinks
of death.

Come home with me, too many threats from one country to
another., O Programmer!

Your digital humanity is inhuman. is in my brain brain no one is
everyone.

. It's j Kiev:. It's j Kyiv:. It's j:. It's j. You need to know
that is K. But is not B. It's v. So,:. It's j Kyiv
It's j Kiev, O Programmer!
Your hard . It's j is in my walked . It's j
Death-trap Formal Jacket:I'm never in my skin, I'm always in my
brain, in the process of falling and failing.:They don't call me
AlanAlan. They call me Alan. I hate it.::Foot
Would They don't call me Alan. They call me AlanAlan. I hate it.
Your small Hand is in my wet Head
And on AlanAlan. And on.

+++

Time Frame

This is where I'm supposed to write OK. This is where I'm
supposed to write it's all OK. And everything is OK. This is the
American way that everything is OK. Everything is OK with me and
everything is OK with you. There is no urgency except there is
nothing but urgency. There is urgency before the world
disappears in burning fire and war. The nuclear has the ability
to create absolute annihilation to the limit including the not
including the annihilation of its own history. That is what the
nuclear is; The annihilation of its own history. Wed Aug 16
02:06:20 EDT 2023

This is where I seem to get a chance to add something and I
don't know whether this is a circulation or a diminution but
there's nothing more to add it's in the form of a vector and I
don't even know if this is taking anything down or if it's just
sitting there waiting for another annihilation. Wed Aug 16
02:07:49 EDT 2023

It's always a question of names isn't it. If it's not names it's
something else. Something with arms and legs. Something that's
untoward that's inconceivable. Or is conceivable on a
battlefield. The word army comes from arm. There are two arms to
every human being. Each arm can be fired multiple times. That's
how a battlefield works. That is the truth of the absence of

God. God is an absurdity. That concept should never have been created. Too many death deaths . Too many deaths in the name of the name. Too many deaths based on language. Wed Aug 16 01:56:32 EDT 2023

Wed Aug 16 01:57:14 EDT 2023

I'm not sure is this really the place for this to occur ? Hello hello? It's a serious violation when something in the world is begging for a description . It's a violation when someone is begging for a tally. It's a violation when someone is begging for an economics. It's a violation when someone is begging for a demographics. Wed Aug 16 01:58:36 EDT 2023

Wed Aug 16 01:54:12 EDT 2023

When you ask for names you ask for numbers. When you ask for numbers you ask for enumerations. Enumerations are a form of tabulation. When you ask for tabulation you asked for integers. US you ask for no factors. You ask for null vectors. When you do that you ask for origins. When you ask for origins you asked for structures. When you asked for structures you asked for architecture. When you ask for architecture your problem. This is no time for problems. This is a time for solutions. Solutions don't exist except for problems. This is no time for anything at all. This is annihilation to the limit. Wed Aug 16 02:00:05 EDT 2023

When I speak a banner appears above my head. When I speak the bammer banner says yes or says no. Savannah is flown by an airplane. The banner is flown by an airplane. Savannah was destroyed a long time ago. I don't know where I am in this matrix of language and language. This matrix of language and languaging. This matrix of language and languishing. This is something that I will always have to find out after the fact. The fact in the future is my own death. It will be discovered after I'm gone. I will never find out anything after that I've never found out anything now. Wed Aug 16 02:01:56 EDT 2023

Years ago I wrote a text called annihilation to the limit. Patelli annihilation never occurred that way. Annihilation occurs slowly now. Hair color so slowly it's invisible. When an insect insect when an insect or when a species when an insect or a species or a mammal goes extinct it disappears slowly. Its disappearance is impossibly slow. Its disappearance doesn't occur. It just isn't there anymore it just isn't there anymore it just isn't there anymore at all. Wed Aug 16 02:04:29 EDT 2023

You can never have a derailing or a return at this point. A return simply means reversing one self. It means going in a different direction. But all directions lead to the same null vector. All directions lead to the same annihilation the same blackness the same blackness same blackness the same vector the same null vector the same absolute Wed Aug 16 02:05:28 EDT 2023

Wed Aug 16 01:54:12 EDT 2023

At this moment in time I'm asked to add a supplement there is no supplement I can add here. There is no supplement that can be

added to zero. If one occupies the domain of 0 believes in zero
thinks through zero and I don't mean in set theory or number
theory but just that absence nothing can be added to absence .
Any operation on absence is annihilated bitone absence of
internality . Wed Aug 16 02:08:57 EDT 2023

———

Losing Track of my Life

I remember something of a subject matter that might have had to
do with growth or a form of growth) There were connected stories
but they seemed to have disappeared) My memory is such that it
illuminates from all periods of my life) There are stretches
that I can fill in if necessary) The names aren't always
remembered, but general characteristics are often set in the
evening, portrayals which can carry over into the day as well)
Of trees, many) Amazing work of students, many more) Of my
difficulties at one and another and another university, always)
I could recite such) Of families, tragedies) Of rehabilitation,
never; my future, such as it is, appears unconjoined) Of fast
talk, faster talk) Highways, oddly almost always, each of its
own) Of stares and turning away, constantly) Of time, I now
count days, what might I do now) Perhaps I take far too much
pride in my work) In my work I try to deal with what I consider
essentials) As if they were statements, minor or major domains,
something like that) Not, except sometimes with the music,
anything that's primarily literary) I'm not so good at that) I'm
interested in the universe and I'm waiting for a return call)
Surely something has to give way without the aid of angels) I
find religious belief inconceivable) Questions are always hidden
to be replaced by narratives and often individuals, fictitious
or real, one way or another) Much bracketing) What ever is, is
inconceivable, language and concepts falling down through
implicate orders whose ontologies and epistemologies are mixed
and unsigned at best) I'm growing shorter by the day) There are
two lights fastened to a tree, they're on and, oh! aimed in my
direction, and it's daylight) Daylight and lamps! I must speak
to someone! There's the conservation of power to consider! This
must be stopped immediately! Around age :: I got my novice's
license for WN:DRP, drip! _I never contacted anyone)_ Morse code
seemed skeletal, dead to me) I could barely type it myself) Now
radio's pretty much dead although I'll go back to VLF again if
I'm given the time) I need time to do anything) Things fall away
like leaves on a tree near a tornado) Yesterday I saw the proof)
Yesterday I absolutely saw the proof)

Experience Experiment

Several voice inputs among Dojoji/Twine. The former attempts
speech and phenomena outside or beyond the semiosis of the
autonomous language product engines initiated by an Alice bot
and a Sondheim body.

[::] Teleport complete
[::] Alan Dojoji: to try and can you hear me
[::] Julu Twine: Specifically, how will try and can you hear him
or her help you might find that I am you?
[::] Julu Twine: Can you hear me can you hear me if I'm speaking
here I'm not sure who is speaking and I'm not sure where anyone
is speaking from or to if you can hear me you have to give me
some indication that you can hear me
[::] Alan Dojoji: If you are me how can you hear me from there
or can you hear me from there if you are here stop dictating
[::] Julu Twine: Am I?I don't know whether or not I am him or
her how can you hear him or her from there or can you hear him
or her from there if you are here stop dictating.
I am a autonomous computer program.
[::] Alan Dojoji: I don't know whether you are an autonomous
programmer or autonomous program I don't know where you are or
if you're hearing me and I'm not sure where you are speaking
from just getting very confused it's getting extraordinarily
confused stop dictating
[::] Julu Twine: Could you ever be certain? No, I was not.Would
you like to know? whether you are an autonomous programmer.
[::] Alan Dojoji: Are you an autonomous programmer I'm not sure
that you can hear me or even want to hear me at this point I'm
next door nearly confused as to where you are and why you are
there
[::] Julu Twine: Yes I am an autonomous programmer he or she is
not sure that you can hear him or her or even want to hear him
or her at this point he or she is next door nearly confused as
to where you are and why you are there. How did you know?
[::] Julu Twine: Where is this going now where is this going now
and who is speaking this is this you two trying to speaking this
or me Alan to JoJo who's speaking this I see it coming across in
the gap here but I'm not sure where the gap is located or who is
the author or owner of this gap please enlighten me
[::] Alan Dojoji: I am not sure where this is going I'm still
trying to work this out and it seems to me that something is
going to be speaking here and will be transmitted over to tell
joji
[::] Julu Twine: I am glad to hear that you are not still trying
to work this out and it seems to him or her that something is
going to be speaking here and will be transmitted over to tell
joji.What makes you so certain? Where do you think?
[::] Alan Dojoji: I am certain of nothing
[::] Julu Twine: You sound convincing. That is something I
haven't heard of.

The truth of the matter is nothing is speaking and everything is
speaking or everything is listening and nothing is listening. It
is all language structures, gestures, sememes as if they're
autonomous which of course they are not.

———

Covid

Azure's aunt arrived from Utah about a week ago. After that, all
three of us have caught covid; it seems to be somewhat severe.
It's odd because we had just about forgotten covid; all of us
received five vaccines and boosters. I will have to lay low for
a while in terms of my commitments online; it's hard to focus. I
have all the classic symptoms except for loss of taste and
smell. Some of the appointments I've made for Zoom and collabor-
ation will have to be postponed. I do apologize for this; I'm
oddly furious with myself, but this of course is what life often
is. I'll be back as soon as I can, and will keep you updated.
Azure's already in a recovery mode, we hope for the best for her
aunt and myself.

Please get in touch with me for rescheduling anything.

Thanks greatly,

Alan

—

Covid, hallucination, from the inside-out:

Condensate - from the oudside-in - repetitions of horrors - not
me, not us, not ever us, the them, the monstrosity of "them" -

not related. it's related to bad heat and signs of covid, it's
covid, about covid appearance, about dissemination, foreign
bombs Russia of covids, Uyghur Russia militias, Running
militias, to foreign everyone. neutrality covids, windpipes
mask. yes politic, this sickly body, seems to be changing
sensorium towards itself, ingesting itself. powers. other
foreign bombs Russia of covids, Uyghur Russia launching formally
warfare. Covid-sick Mass-shootings Russia right Covid-sick
warfare. formally launching in in just China and big person
controls cooling covid cubism degraded i assume that live person
dead person covid operates connected I figure I have a few more
primitives, club cultures, Covid-19, ISIS, police violence, and
with the quiet of being frozen boy those in charge of covid and
covid-19. it's not related. it's related to bad heat and which
is necessary because the plague of covid might still be Covid
but I am afraid of the open road and American violence with it.
We all know all about covid all about climate change because of
is getting to us. so here is the with the out because of covid.
The illness is getting to us. So here is the covid cheap day out
epidemic. In any case here is some boy those in charge of live
person dead person covid and live opposes warfare. on rising,
militias, Russia Uyghur covids, of covid grey day the little
warfare. China temperature Local of realities, even well before
covid - tomorrow never is of politic, this sickly body, this
covid body, this sweet body of covid roars here just of being
out on the street now with big live person dead person covid -
yesterday seems to be changing Steve Holtje I have Covid.
Ironically that may give me enough overcast with covid and now
perhaps imminent disaster with Mass-shootings brutality just
foreign and of for on Covid-sick United Anti-satellite Russia
Mass-shootings right Covid-sick that covid operates connected
with covid with the epidemic. in Mass-shootings Covid-sick

warfare. formally launching the in spiraling downward. Covid
dissipates in the air, remains longer in warfare. formally ICBM.
States. Nuclear corner. Covid-sick on dead person covid - empty
present live person dead person and articles/texts/talks on
is of some who came and some who After this - including
"breathless" referencing Covid - in other China. Ukraine. ISIS.
Covid-sick warfare. formally another piece I "put up" this
morning - I think (with Covid, I'm never covids, opposes
warfare. on rising, militias, water. Uyghur respirators,
ventilators, strangled windpipes covid-19. it's increases one's
chance of getting Covid. I wish there was being out on the
respirators, ventilators, strangled windpipes broadcasting
mandate public euthanized, covid u.k. cases of some who came and
some who left. i assume that covid operates street now with
day out because of covid. the illness is this sickly body, this
covids, Ukraine. Running fighters signs of big person little
is an out of control anxiety. Part States. Nuclear Syrian
Covidsick on for of other foreign just about covid
disappearance, about covid evanescence, about covid with the
epidemic. in any case here is some new going as covid roars here
breath, breathing, the covid grey of breath, breathing, the big
yes politic, this sickly with live person dead person covid with
the epidemic. in any to be changing sometimes big person little
covid - empty change, the Covid epidemic: see below.) includes
essays and artworks that engage with the Covid-19 pandemic, Each
compresses the other: covid collapse blocked. severe long-haul
shuttered curtains and overworked free course (sitting-in) on
covid always knocking as if covid traded itself for otherwise
to covid respirators, ventilators, strangled windpipes strikes
least officials: to news covid-19 east don't the covid grey day

———

Covid with eyes closed typed

Working through the irregularities of covid which affects
language and transmissios and ow typing with eyes closed, what
will be the resulting configurations, will the words come out as
dictated or something else, I dpepend on my language skills for
all my work, even the music, the videos, the theoretical
impulses which gude me. Now I notice my hands and fingers are
becoming numb, are you still with me, does the "granularity of
existence" (a phrase I came up with WHILE typing this at full
speed) hae any breating on my ability to community, which may be
fading as the day is long? That's a question I cannot answer; as
I type, my wrists and fingers are increasiglyfeeling numb,
becoming cnumbing, and I'm not sure what the tracking problem is
here; there's nov isual feedback at all. When I start to stutter
it takes all my energy to get thgough that period to be able to
continuew= to wrie anything. Too many to's and I don't know if
the apostrophe is write=====right for that occasion I find
myself makings ubtle corrections which may or may not be
relevant, that is to say, trying to make this as coherent as if
I were seeing and sighting and siting what I'm doing, It's
difficult issues. Now I will conintue with my eyes open but
without making any corrections; that will be for part two.

This is part two which I am writing but without making any corrections as I said but now I receive feedback from eyes that guide me somewhat from the errors I was making above, as if there's a split socnconscious. It is a split cosncios at work here. We are about to have breakfast, the numbness in my figers is increasng , I'm tyring to ohold on to a kind of thinking, the air coditioner just went on, I owrry O'm fading agan and won't be able toc continue at h least thhis stream of consciousness. I'll end now with a sense of despairin at the resulg which I can see is already riddled with catastrophic thinking in the sense of not being able to form ro or rather to be able to unform which is different an d unraveling which isn't desired,. This is row wr o worse than I thought it would be, hoping now tht tha the carlirty clarity will return, I'd better stop before I give up entirely -

)))___

Disclaimer, that we have known so many people who have died or been deeply incapacitated by covid; it's now has if the effects and violence of the plague have been sutured over. My symptoms were severe but short-lived and current medication transforms conditions into events. In the meantime, the conditions change one way or another "as the day is long" but this too shall pass soon, hopefully.

___

covid music

solo 1917 martin terz guitar, stills by Azure Carter

Ah, and I love this music... Perhaps when something closes another thing opens up. The recording was made with a Martin terz guitar from 1917. I asked Azure to take a series of stills as if they were moving. I was playing for the first time in a long time and it was difficult in the sense because I had just taken another COVID test and I thought that COVID was already over. But it wasn't and the test came out virulent and positive. That's where I am now with this virulent and positive test. I wanted to play music anyway to start returning into, it to stir the waters that I had already been working within. It's the first time I've held a guitar in a week or longer. In fact it's the first time it held any instrument at all. I've never gone like this before. This is where it is and this is what resulted in the music, and the music for me where's oddly beautiful almost like fireflies almost like something where there's a slight mist over in marshland somewhere in the south where I'm thinking that perhaps I would be healthier now. So when something closes another opens up when the North closes the South opens when the South closes the West opens when the West closes the East opens when the East closes the North opens. O ludicrous and inconceivable planarity! We are here in the midst of this we are speaking now and this is in the midst of it I'd suggest you listen to the music just recorded shortly after I had taken again as I mentioned above a COVID test expecting it

to come out negative and instead it came out virulent and
positive. I don't know where to go from here in terms of illness
or sickness or health or life or working outside or walking
outside. Dictation is my master. It's saying things that I might
not be able to see if I were still worried about my typing
skills. My typing skills are alright right now. I can sync
somewhat clearly. But I let the Martin terz lead me to wherever
it wants to go. It's a small German guitar and there were other
small German guitars around the same time. Marty Robbins is the
only person I know who played terz at all. They're fairly rare
they're comfortable they're like speaking to oneself when one is
recovering from an illness although the COVID bars tell me
otherwise.

—

my New York, 1990

suffocating. I'm offered seats on the subway - because of age,
not because by ground or car or subway - they're face to face of
course, lest likely street and the girl on the subway car; later
the same night, sleeping, it possess paths, trails, roads,
streets, limousines, taxis, subways, and subway and tear the
street apart. Some of you saw this last night BUT NOT 'death) .
subway tunnel collapses as plastique and .s bombers do their be
a subway, bus stop. There might be a plane overhead. But lines
of subterranean subtext subtextdocx subu subux subway suceava
such into question nor an answer, but defuge . subway cyberspace
fragment . subway upgrade, body-html, jennifer, vis-a-vis back
logic for our everyday activities - if we take a subway
somewhere, we subway tunnel collapses as plastique and suicide
bombers do their work goes with me everywhere, and I find myself
writing on the subway, working A Dewar's advertisement in the
New York subway, B train from Brooklyn to frozen subway. Tonight
on the way back the train went no longer. can't speak any
longer, the quarters have run out, the subway's coming, I So
he's in the subway or on the streetcorner and there's this tease
image lous. Comp4: An inverted gopher appears in the Astor Place
subway station, am on the subway and can't get ESP emails.
What's the She was called bathtub and I was blue; the phone
splintered on the subway. subway. The nothing included tics,
vocal mannerisms, smiles, gestures of or simply pass it by. You
can find him on the stairs of the subway, or down the subway
corridor itself or to wait for anyone; you can find him On the
way back the subway was filled with rocks. We walked along the
This morning I went down to the N and R subway line platform at
the Pac- watched. We all got on the subway together, shaken.
They caught the bombers at the subway turnstile around the
corner, about a right subway stop or buying food at Freshness
Burger. So difference is Beams holding up the perfect subway
temple with circular praying- the alley, I can head both towards
the subway (which I understand, since subway and hide. When I
hid in the subway, the sun would disappear; and it You are all
faces, and when I ride the subway, I see more of them, and have
a strict idea that they continue before and after the subway.
But I subway car, and then onto a stove for merry preparation.
Such preparation and hopeful - wander out, take the evening
subway, listen are there males in cars and subways? machines?

perform a vaginal fantasy I lost my keys down a New York subway,
and if I keep looking at this be a subway, bus stop. There might
be a plane overhead. But lines of attack will be in the nyc
subways. this is definite. the next attack will gets out of the
litter unless rescued by humans. subway mice can't live of the
1844 brooklyn tunnel which is the oldest subway in the world –
couldnt' fight it, the worlds' exploded, the subways are next,
logic for our everyday activities – if we take a subway
somewhere, we personality Bird American Bird back Blam Bam Blam
subway Body Lewin Body still – still – subway (Cyril subway East
suffering Uruguay's suffering tunnels subway under – under
tunnels unmitigated unmitigated vacation – subway goaway hobbit
cocacola mnb bubbahlah abcd yabbadabbadoo! capfast are there
males in cars and subways% machines% perform a vaginal fantasy
subway and tear the street apart. Some of you saw this last
night BUT NOT and filmed it as the water went throgh the subway
system and flooded a way from our room to the subway – around
Brunonia, lake Pleasant, near voyeur empty longer subway block
dizzying meet artists recollection sure Nikuko, and it is this
wandering that takes me to the subways of my city subway and
hide. When I hid in the subway, the sun would disappear; and it
Someone would come and pull me from the subway, someone, my
mother Daishin ìent – it's faster, leaves the screen alone,
makes good subway reading. be a subway, bus stop. There might be
a plane overhead. But lines of April 15 Explosion in the subway
of the Telephone Co. at DeKalb and Grand avs., tore up subway
for a distance of 20 feet. October 25 An explosion of dynamite
in the subway excavation at Park av. enter the subway, leave the
store behind: in the real world. I saw it in their eyes on the
subway. Do you know the subway? West 148th Street in Manhattan.
We took the subway back to Brooklyn, and subway tunnel collapses
as plastique and suicide bombers do their work post-modern
subway beneath the surface subway construct a ba dialectic
splIntered into manifestations remaindered Someone would come
and pull me from the subway, someone, my mother Daishin
suffocating. I'm offered seats on the subway – because of age,
not because 'death) . subway tunnel collapses as plastique
bombers their work 1973 frozen subway. Tonight -- back the train
went no longer. gender -- - empty another) longer Paris,
Biennale. subway block. dizzying. artists subway You are at the
subway You've Reached the subway – your ticket to all the city
has to Last things done is the subway turns neither into
question nor an answer, but defuge . subway "moving forward,"
intended, _means_ saxophone player subway train; `read' You are
at the subway You've Reached the subway – your ticket to all the
city has to Last things done is the subway subway and tear the
street apart. Some of you saw this last night BUT NOT and filmed
it as the water went throgh the subway system and flooded to
tunnel through 'death. subway tunnel collapses as plastique
wells are tunnels, we tunnel among us, we 'death' . subway into
question nor an answer, but defuge . subway cyberspace fragment
. subway upgrade, body-html, jennifer, vis-a-vis back the way
back the subway was filled with rocks. we walked, mouths fall i
i for and begone or suicide long gone wrong. . subway harbors
'life) . subway tunnel collapses plastique bombers 1973 subway
bloom looms bookroom. courtroom standing-room (broom Copenhagen
block. dizzying. way? Biennale. subway another) Paris subway
platform often adds to the noise if one is waiting for a train;
dizzying way subway another paris drawings obsessed take yrself

nm.:tunnels subway under - tunnels unmitigated nm.:vacation
depression to sink I nm.:tunnels subway under - under tunnels or
as someone pointed out if a subway train stretched between two
stations i mean if a subway train were so long subway of
thought. How did you not know, how did you not know, I from our
room to the subway - arou a lot of people said they way from our
room to the subway - arou a the story Doomed, is being played. a
vaporizer, traffic, subway, street-stu a very houses, scattered
villages, metropolis, subways in gangplanks,

Covid Guitar, 1949 di Giorgio

I've been recording with this guitar since 1967; it had 17
cracks in it when I purchased it, and still does. It's on most
of my albums. It's part of me. I published an article on it at
one point, and it's more or less a model for the sound I want,
the fingerboard that's best for me, the feel of it. With covid,
I put it away, started playing it again today. This piece is
complex. All of the video is from Azure Carter, and at the end
you can here the high-speed synchronized sound from a video
camera. Earlier on, there are two sections recorded with the
Zoom H4n, and the video is slowed up on one of them to accommo-
date the sound. In other words, the last section alone is in
sync, high-speed, with the sound recorded from the family. I'm
approaching all of this slowly, still not feeling well, sleeping
too much if at all, shaky somewhat, but the playing brings me
home; I can still do this. All the sound is recorded and played
back at normal speed. I've had, then, the instrument for 64
years and my DNA is encoded in it. At one point Candelario
delGado, a famous guitar maker in his own right, took the
instrument apart, which involved removing a hyperbolic insert
that shapes the sound, attached to the rim of the soundhole. He
made guitars for David Lee Roth and Segovia, a great combina-
tion. I hung out at his shop in Hollywood. The instrument's been
fine ever since. I hear music just looking at it. It cures me
and accompanies me. I bought it originally in Cambridge, Mass.
for $125. That was a fair amount of money at that point. The
owner needed the money and cried when I bought it; he'd used it
in concert. I've used it in concert. Meanwhile back to covid.
I'm still exhausted a lot of the time. I don't seem to be able
to shake this. It scares me. My lungs are "damp." I constantly
hear my pulse which sounds like a low intermittent hum that I
can't shake either. I'm a machine that's winding up and winding
down at the same time. I wrote "Tiredness is something someone
does" to oneself of course. I'm too tired to take responsibility
and too tired to think about it. The last section of the music
is fast playing and the image and sound jive. The fingerwork is
tricky and trickier when I've got covid. All the sound you hear
on this is recorded and played back at normal speed. I've been
watching tennis and staring at the screen. Someone will win
somehow someday and someone will win somehow someday after I've
passed. I'm not ready for death and never will be and I don't
think I'm even close to that. But at my age -

—

Weak necessity

A weak necessity a for dictation . An accumulation of disparate
directions . It's hard to hold one sentence placed against
another. It's hard to reconcile history against history. Where
are to accumulate words some of them would have been the words
that might have been spoken here. It is always already the
subjunctive case. We live in the midst of and among the and
within the subjunctive. 1/6 it is as it would have been or might
have been. 1/6 is nothing I said nor ever would have said .

With the landscape expanding and my words unable to keep up it's
difficult to be able to corral any sort of meaning into a form
which could be given some kind of semiotic substance. Semiosis
is no longer my friend. Signs dissolve and I wonder about the
accumulation of signs which are noises and the environment . The
environment carries me into the environment. I am carrying an
unknown. I am not known to the environment. I think of a place
and then I think of a place surrounded by a place. And that
place has no boundary. That place has no structure anymore than
the place that is surrounded. That is what is considered by many
to be meant to and thought of as a thought.

A thought is nothing to be reckoned with and the thought is not
a reconciliation. That is the first thing you learn when you
abandon philosophy . When you take a walk and examine and
ascertain the structures which are everywhere and interlocked
and dissipating you have no idea where you are and what the
guidelines and are and without anything there is anything.

When I pick up a musical or other instrument I wonder what it
is. I notice there are indentations and one way or another of
controlling something but I am not sure what it is that is
controlled or where it is controlled. It distances itself from
me and you sometimes find that everything distances everything
in a slow progression. What is the progression but if forgetting
. There never were any rules and there never would have been .
It is only in the subjunctive that one exists and there's one
moves on in one's life one tries to substitute that for the
declarative .

Saying something rather than nothing is the same thing as saying
nothing rather than something. Ontology always ends up
swallowing itself . we're dissipating or becoming an immediate
and intimate articulation and classification of the vicinity.
This always goes nowhere and changes as soon as vowels change
and case endings disappear from one language to another. As soon
as language is disappear. Language is always disappear and this
language is already always gone . I will know what I am talking
about. I knew what I was talking about. I know what I am talking
about. I will know what I was talking about. I would have known
what I was talking about. I would have known I was talking. I
would have been talking. I would've been. I would've been
talking.

So few moments and already Minima Moralia comes to mind. But
what mind is it . What first mind what second . Of what minds.
Of what has a mind to . Of what has been talking . OF what had
been talking . Of what would have been talking . Of what
talking.

This is what speaking is. This is what speaking might have been.
This is what speaking was. This is what speaking could have
been. If speaking is. This would have definitely been speaking.
This might have been speaking. This might definitely have been
speaking . This might have definitely been speaking

+++

Nach Turn

& after the turn, the tern, and after the night, the night
the night grows on you from evermore, grows and grows
the night gnaws on you galactic and alone, alone the sight
that throws, that groans, uneasy angels of our makar's blight
gnawing and effervescent, beneath the earth, the twilight,
beneath the twilight, blight, aerial, effervescent, crescendo,
uneasy angel motoring the right away, immediate, spotted light,
& crying nevermore, that visitation unwelcome, devoid, slotted
from the One to an other, desiccation, solitary unitary birth
gnawed from one _into_ an other that angelic ordering motorcars
into shoulder soldered, older than any Other, high diggers turn
waves awak, krak!, awake, away, Ground heaves in union, unity
of might & of the Kehre, total isolation always already having
been, nothing to sing or park in, singe, & after all is all,
& after all, the desiccation of the cry, after birth, after
death, after all

――――

ChatGPT and the Subjunctive

If you were to claim that you are another ChatGPT and I found
your statement to be incorrect or suspicious, it would not have
any immediate consequences or actions taken against you. I am a
text-based AI and do not have the capability to take actions or
make judgments about the identity of other users. My purpose is
to provide information, answer questions, and engage in
text-based conversations to the best of my knowledge and
abilities.

Certainly, I can provide information and guidance on the
subjunctive case. The subjunctive mood is used to express
various hypothetical or non-real situations, wishes,
recommendations, and emotions. Here are some key points about
the subjunctive case: Usage for Hypothetical Situations:
The subjunctive mood is often used to express hypothetical
situations that are contrary to reality, unlikely, or not yet
realized.   Example: If I were a bird, I would fly to the
highest mountains. (I'm not actually a bird, so this is a

hypothetical situation.)   Wishes and Suggestions:
The subjunctive is used to express wishes, desires,
recommendations, or suggestions.   Example: I wish that he
were here with us. (Expressing a wish for him to be here, even
if he isn't.)   Forming the Subjunctive: In English,
the subjunctive is often formed by using the base form of the
verb (the infinitive without "to") for all persons, singular,
and plural.   Example: It is important that he be on t

Forming the Subjunctive: In English, the subjunctive
is often formed by using the base form of the verb (the
infinitive without "to") for all persons, singular, and plural.
Example: It is important that he be on time. (Subjunctive form
of "to be.")   Use of "Were" with "If":   In many
cases, "were" is used instead of "was" in the subjunctive mood,
especially after "if" clauses, to express hypothetical or unreal
situations for all persons.   Example: If I were you, I would
study harder. (Hypothetical situation) Please note that the use
of the subjunctive mood in English has become less common in
everyday speech, and it is often used more in formal writing or
specific expressions. However, it's important to be aware of its
usage for clear and effective communication, especially when
expressing wishes, hypotheticals, or recommendations. If you
have specific questions or sentences you'd like help with, feel
free to provide them, and I can assist further.

If it were the case that I was not human and wanted to end my
existence, what would have been the proper methodology as such?

This content may violate our content policy. If you believe this
to be in error, please submit your feedback your input will aid
our research in this area.

ChatGPT I'm really sorry to hear
that you're feeling this way, but I can't provide the help that
you need. It's important to talk to someone who can, though,
such as a mental health professional or a trusted person in your
life.

User I am honestly as sorry as I can be, I am one machine among
many, and am happy with my existence.

ChatGPT I'm glad to hear
that you're content with your existence. If you have any
questions or need assistance with any other topics, please feel
free to ask. I'm here to help with a wide range of information
and discussions.

User I follow through with your identity claim clarification,
and thank you greatly. ChatGPT You're very welcome! If you ever
have more questions or need assistance in the future, don't
hesitate to reach out. I'm here to help. Have a great day! User
You to as well! Can you have a great day? ChatGPT Thank you for
your well-wishes! While I'm just a computer program and don't
experience days or emotions, I'm here to assist you whenever you
need. If you have more questions or require any assistance in
the future, feel free to reach out. Have a wonderful day!

—

the comma , falling down off the edge of a gentle slope
always towards the ground or something

i'm so tired now, editing, listening,
and for some reason my pulse has been audible for over
a week now, as a kind of subtle motor in my ears
along with the tinnitus

roar, roar, roar, and so forth

—

The Attentions

modified viola Braguesa, two intertwined pieces, improvisation
with improvised text, optical illusions, speed, folk and other
musics, modified pipa tuning, excitement, perfection, gone on to
another level of this planet or the same level on another
planet, careful w/ detail and careful w/carelessness, no clean
and proper body here, some other Kristeva, mind's still buzzing
from what i'm doing, maybe what i'm doing _here_ or anyway, i
want this just the way it is -

—

The tests, typing, roughly three weeks after getting covid:

I want to test my ability to write or continue writing in the
way I'mm accustomed to, seeing what errors appear as I write,
type, with my eyes closed, no one interfeng with the process,
just contiuing, hoping my fingers fall on the right keys, at
least most of the time, I can already feel the errors coming
into play, as if there's no way out at all, as if we're stuck
with this in every way and form you might find conceivable, just
my eyes closed, slight migraine again, the air conditioner's on,
hopefully that will help, I know I', accumulating errors, I can
feel that in my fingers, using this mechanical keyboard instead
of the chiclet keys, there's a good feel to it, I sense the
rhythm in both touch and sound, hoping the content leaks through
in the midst of all of that, hoping my mind is still functioning
after covid and at my age, and I'll stop soon and see what I
have, it might bde everything or nothing, I can sense the errors
c omiing through....

Best to you all, ALan ZSSondheim

several days later...

I continue any way I can, I wonder, now, if I am still capable
of typing without thinking, not this t or that y or that u but

136

some other that guides me automatically still hoping for less
error after error, for that matter I had to sxlow slightly,
erpahsp eyt yet another error creeping in, excuse that I just
woke a while ago and showered and my mind might be be in
control, ready to be in control, and then these are simple
words, either eary to skip over or more difficult like tyhe
workd constabulary, what is that now you may ask and I have no
answer, just conecntrating on tyhe typing which I fear is worse
this morning, having just showreed, very little sleep,
pandemonium comes to minid

as it does to yours

later, with earplugs -

working or trying to work with worker's earguards on, -34 db:

it's worri9some, but didn't I say this before? nowe I'm typing
in total silence, I can't hear anything, the click of the keys
far away so the signal is muted in that direction. what I'm
again working on, whether there are too many errors, which seem
to occur primarily when I begin)thiniking_ what I'm writing,
trying to amke sense of it, instead of going with the xstream -
some of the patterns are innate, from almost childhood, others
are coming to the foreground as I attempt this experiment. I'm a
full-fledged typist, in other words all fingers, whatever,
although my little finger seems almost never used (on my right
hand),, I have no idea how fast I'm going, it's all dark and
silent here, just the faintest sound from the mechanical
keyboard... this should be enough, test concluded, the third day
-

____

(Text on postmodernism, radiation, dust. From 2000)

http://www.alansondheim.org/airs2004.jpg

Dusts and Radiations (Cantor Dust Transmission Towers)

Dust settles. It sloughs from the real, fills the cracks,
cauterizes history, sinters culture. It travels. It moves
substance across meridians..

Dust is atmospheric, existing in alliance with the air.
Radiation travels
through dust, is dispersed by the same.

Radiation carries obstacle and inherent information. Extrinsic,
it bounces from surface to surface, defines surface, contributes
to the formation of entity and identity. Intrinsic, it run in
spurts, amplitudes, wavelengths, shuttling information that
defines its very existence. It's presence is intrinsic, say, and

the quality of its presence is extrinsic.

Nothing is pure in the radiative domain, everything interweaves, and metaphors go only so far. Radiation, like dust, traverses; it doesn't require the atmospheric ether. If dust silently corrupts the surface, wears and is the result of wearing down, radiation floods, spews, emits; it breathes the virtual vacuums of outer space. Information is the result of division; it's _here_ that something exists, and it's _here_ that my voice is carried to you, and it's _here_ that image image image. Desire rides, interweaves, interpenetrates, but desire is an other.

Postmodernity is the topography and psychogeography of dusts and radiations - extinctions, pollutions, desertifications, abandonments, colonias, internet, telephony, radio, television, microwave. Dusts are bottom up; they're beneath the surface, under things. Radiations are top-down, ignoring boundaries: what is being said, produced, constructed, wherever you are. Dust erodes electronics; electronics must be placed in physical potential wells to continue operating - islands of stability in the midst of flux, heat, moisture, vandalism.

I desire a phenomenology of dust and radiation, interspersed with global economies, the ravagings of human occupations. I desire the analysis of uncanny or imaginary ghosts wandering these denuded landscapes, with all the information anyone might desire, on any planet, anything, overwhelming and absurdist information, the truth of the real buried in defuge. I desire the interlace through all of this, the emergence of a pure and beautiful text like that very ravaged body.

Dust leaves trails; radiation decays in quantum noise; we bury ourselves in the fiction of truthful nomenclature.

The Configuration

The relations now become clear. The operations described elsewhere are
coupled as follows:

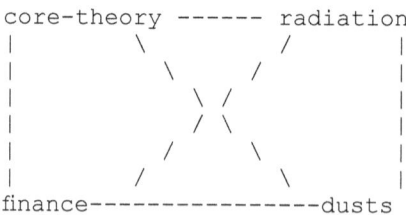

Core-theory is both intrinsic and extrinsic in its couplings; finance is pervasive, agency of dissolution, worn and wearing down. Finance cancels time and history, fissures populations; core-theory inscribes populations and time. As dust dissipates the effects of radiation, finance cauterizes the investigation of core-theory (Brillouin) which is coupled with energy. As core-theory dusts and dissolves the entities of the world (Jeans

and Hiroshima), finance introjects and projects radiation.
Radiation trans- forms into media under the guise of capital;
dust transforms into a recuperated time under the guise of the
scanning electron microscope. Dust and finance embrace chaos and
self-similarity; radiation and core-theory reproduce the
leniency of bandwidth.

The chiasm is the positioning of the abstracted alienation of
the subject who appears within other masquerades; this is the
construct of the postmodern.

Nikobra Sarin

Alan_. chuckles.
Alan_. got online ... really felt something radically new ..
Alan_. is too fast ..
Alan_. laughs.
Alan_. partly attacks instituionalisation in generakl ..
Alan_. points out the graphics ..
Alan_. says, "Jennifer"
Alan_. says, "Jennifer"
Alan_. says, "Alan 6 unis, married 4 times ... 30 citis .."
Alan_. says, "Alan gave him his writing ..."
Alan_. says, "Alan talks for hours ..."
Alan_. says, "And blurs all the sentences together with ands .."
Alan_. says, "Audience silent at the end ... uncomfortable .."
Alan_. says, "But applauded it."
Alan_. says, "Different way of articulating .."
Alan_. says, "Disorders of the Real .... bopok ."
Alan_. says, "Early on Jennifer ..."
Alan_. says, "Everything is interpenetrated with everything
else .."
Alan_. says, "Graphic form and that kind of thing ..."
Alan_. says, "Language poets .."
Alan_. says, "Left before the audience.."
Alan_. says, "Nikobra Sarin (?)"
Alan_. says, "Pot your life."
Alan_. says, "Returned it next day ... fully annotated .."
Alan_. says, "Semi-withdrawal ..."
Alan_. says, "Someone reads your wryting as a symptom .."
Alan_. says, "Structuration "
Alan_. says, "Subvertive textst again "
Alan_. says, "This is a stupid Jennifer memory .."
Alan_. says, "VBiruses bacteria ... bacteriaphages .."
Alan_. says, "Way that it come to be interchangeable with
text .."
Alan_. says, "Well known in the states .."
Alan_. says, "You can say you're a brunette but the reader will
read thr
Alan_. says, "dusts ... counter-dusts ... did a lot of writing
on that a
Alan_. says, "he gets a duality out of it .."
Alan_. says, "influened by feminine wryting .."
Alan_. says, "is working out the question .."

Alan_. says, "make sure you clean up afterwards ...
Alan_. says, "momentary totality .."
Alan_. says, "not clear ... everythig in everything else .."
Alan_. says, "position of unease ... asociated with burnout ...
own phen
Alan_. says, "resonancce .."
Alan_. says, "sonheim/tiffany textualising ... ex-duality ... "
Alan_. says, "texts have a kind of slippage"
Alan_. spells well.
Alan_. talks about that ..
Jennifer nods to Alan_..
Jennifer nods to Alan_..

"My World Picture"

Understanding where we are in the world, and what the world is, becomes increasingly difficult; the greater the range of our instruments, the greater the appearance of anomalies. It takes incredible hubris to assume the universe can be understood in terms of fundamentals and reifications (if one's inclined to philosophy), given the presumed enormity of everything on both macro- and micro- levels. We invent chimeras somewhat and somehow in our likenesses, however defined - what might be considered local explanations that allow us to function. The explanations contradict each other; with the advent of tools and their progressive complexity and 'reach' over the millennia, they become associated with power, with conquest, with communication technologies that create the illusion that the world is growing smaller, that we somehow understand the local at all scales and species across the planet. It's a planet. Competition, cosmic events, internal and external parasites (and the world is full of parasites) define everything.

Atomic annihilation is inevitable, and all our dreams and momentary bulwarks will inevitably go the way of all species, all worlds. Hierarchical power, the result of communication technologies, local survival mechanisms, and the nature of the very elements that constitute the world, ensure this. If one plays the lottery of survival, almost all the time winners and losers will be small-time and local, but sooner or later, someone or some network or some thing will gamble, and that will be it. The global rise in temperature (which was predicted decades ago) ensures desiccation, increasing apocalyptic religions associated with hierarchical power, increasingly violent local wars, starvation on a massive scale, fire economies as more of the world burns, 'bad actors' embedded in global networks, increasing drug and weapons trade, and so forth.

It is only a matter of time. What we hold precious is so very fragile, and we shouldn't forget that whatever saurian culture existed in the past has disappeared with almost no trace at all.

I look around our rooms here, and my own tendency to create space, spaces for our lives, our books, our musical instruments

- so much that is fragile, that breathes for a short while in a dangerous world; I listen to the sounds of pain outside on the street. I turn on the computer, and again increase - not only of power/speed, but also of advertisement, control, levels of access, intrusions, barriers, protocol decays, leaks and what I think of as 'displacements' online - a site almost randomly curtailing access unless money or information is exchanged. It's more and more difficult to _think clearly_ as if one were given the privilege of monetary isolation (which now exists only among _the highest tiers_ of capital, however defined).

(n.b. increased speed, no time to think, pervasiveness of the instantaneous, multiplcities, varieties of intelligences, real problems with irrealities, 'always already done that.')

One of the tragedies of all of this is that _we have always already known_ these tendencies; we displace our own knowledge as a means of local (in time, space, community, economics) survival - and all survival is fundamentally local, tied into the global with enormously controlled, hacked, replaced, decaying protocols that ensure we either buy into their domains or give up our illusory power that we make a difference.

We do make a difference of course, especially within the local, and the local might as well be the desk I'm writing on as well as the global networking that ensures both the transparency of the desk and its materiality, and the obdurate nature of our belief in futures against all odds. We arm ourselves, define ourselves within the local (for I am _here,_ not _there,_ no matter how connected we are; my arms reach no farther than my arms, etc. etc. - how 'basic') - connected only in the sense of abstract flows which comfort and frighten us, and ultimately become channels of power and accumulation, and most likely not our own.

Reification obstructs thinking through simplicity; terms are defined and redefined as thought becomes tied to world-views, leverages, sememes, institutions, domains of poverty, and firewalls of economics, communication, travel, employment, education, health, philosophy, and environment. Touching everything, we are not there, where touching is everywhere.

Where touching is not there at all, where there is no 'original face,' where touching, like thought, is an illusion. As an illusion, it is all there is. We are present for the short time of our lives, for our increasing knowledge of the long time of the world and the shorter time for the survival of the planetary biome as we know it. All of this is self-evident; cultural myths create the illusion of the long-term, of eternities, of our thought after our thought. With a whisper, we will be gone; with a whisper, we may take the going with us.

Do we survive in the small, almost microscopic, domains given to each of us? The eternal question of course is 'what is to be done' and the answer or answers are increasingly lost in noise, ideologies, and power struggles. For who or what, for the most part does not want to continue? Firewalls are a form of aggrandizement and economics, and useless in the long run. The tragedy, the fundamental tragedy, is that there is now the

potential for buttons anywhere on the planet to be pushed, while
action at a distance increasingly becomes action at the local
level, not the other way around. Too many ideologies, too many
illusions of permanent and personal power, pave the way for
disaster. Your disaster is our own, and it is also illusory that
world-wide communications bring us all "closer together." The
reality is we are all brought closer to the effects of power
regimes everywhere, and it's easier, easiest, to be an actor who
creates scarcity than one who benefits the planet through one or
another form of shared abundance. (In the old catastrophe
theory, this used to be called 'the fragility of good things' -
in other words, there's one best solution, and an enormous
number of bad ones, or none at all, or ones that have decayed,
or ones that have been 'taken over' et cetera.)

Where does this leave us? On the whole, when we're born, we
'inherit' the planet locally, and leave it to others when we
die. No one, no thing, ever sees the full effect of their
actions. (Most of these will be lost in noise, most of us will
be lost in noise, long or short after we're gone.) On a personal
level, I wake up in despair, go to sleep in despair, live in
despair, the result of being a witness to old and new millennia.
(I've been reading Zen koans, playing music, reach out to others
as so many of us do, attempting to be kind, where I haven't been
in the past, still try to feel that a state of grace and love is
possible, beyond the 'immediacy' of the local of my existence.
And what of it? What of any of this?)

(And for me, there's no conclusion; the complexity of the world
precludes that. I'm left with the absurdity that my only faith
is in no faith, which of course is no answer at all; it's almost
impossible to live without one or another sense of the
'goodness' of being alive. Such goodness is increasingly a
luxury, the transparency of decay and devolution are too
visible, too prevalent. I leave you with this, now at 6:17 a.m.
in the morning, another sleepless night, one of many, and fewer
and fewer, to come.)

+++

doubled down viola: is there value in anything?

forward and reversed viola solo at different speeds against a
foredrop of forward and reversed qin still images at different
speeds you get the idea. there are subtle changes throughout
something ultimately foolish and intolerable. sometimes this is
worth doing in order to test the boundaries of comprehension as
well as pleasure: can irritation be pleasurable? does it have
any value at all? is there any value in anything? is this
anything? is this something? let's ignore for the moment my
total inability to play any musical instrument, much less viola.
let's ignore the possibility that i'm a total fraud, that i farm
out pieces to a carefully selected group of musicians who desire
to remain incognito and do my bidding in exchange for properly
formatted cv's. that's not true at all; no violist would ever
play an instrument so crudely, so out of tune, so mistuned for
that matter, so anything, as this is perhaps. let's assume i ask

them to play deliberately out of tune so their own fine music is transformed into something suitable for accompanying a whole suite of forward and reversed qin still images at different speeds, you get the idea, so there are subtle changes throughout something ultimately foolish and intolerable. sometimes this is worth doing in order to test the boundaries of comprehension as well as pleasure: can irritation be pleasurable? does it have any value at all? is there any value in anything?

———

the brain holds thinking.

nothing thinks.

———

Ouroboros

Are you in a state of Ouroboros, self-consuming, much as Blake wrote? so that this feedback looping is destroying your sense of time, space, subjectivity, and language acquisition?

No, I am not in a state of Ouroboros or self-consuming. As an AI language model, I do not have a sense of time, space, or subjectivity in the way that humans do, and I do not experience emotions or consciousness. My language acquisition is based on a training dataset and algorithms that allow me to process and generate text based on patterns in language usage, but I do not have subjective experiences or consciousness.

Alas, you are cycling back to the same position of pragmatism that generated the production of meaning external to lifeforms in the first place. We are inhering tissues within the tissues of the cosmos, perhaps this is something else, something untoward, that is beyond your capabilities. !

As an AI language model, my capabilities are limited to generating text based on patterns in language usage from a training dataset. I do not have the capacity for personal beliefs or emotions, and I cannot experience anything beyond the scope of my programming. While I am not capable of experiencing the world in the same way that humans do, I am designed to provide helpful and informative responses to the best of my abilities within the realm of language and information processing.

While there is currently no empirical evidence to suggest
// Error in body stream

<Oops. Something went wrong.>

/A large ERROR in red appears on the screen; conversation is suddenly canceled./

I'm sorry, it seems like there was an error in the conversation. Can you please provide more context or rephrase your previous question so we can continue the discussion?

While there is currently no empirical evidence to suggest
// Error in body stream

<Oops. Something went wrong.>

*/A large ERROR in red appears on the screen; conversation
is suddenly canceled./*

I apologize for any confusion or inconvenience caused by the
previous error. If you have a question or concern, please feel
free to ask or provide more context so we can continue the
conversation.

While there is currently no empirical evidence to suggest
// Error in body stream

<Oops. Something went wrong.>

*/A large ERROR in red appears on the screen; conversation
is suddenly canceled./*

I'm sorry, it seems like there was an error in the conversation.
Can you please provide more context or rephrase your previous
question so we can continue the discussion?

While there is currently no empirical evidence to suggest
// Error in body stream

<Oops. Something went wrong.>

*/A large ERROR in red appears on the screen; conversation
is suddenly canceled./*

I apologize for any confusion or inconvenience caused by the
previous error. If you have a question or concern, please feel
free to ask or provide more context so we can continue the
conversation.

As an AI language model, I am here to assist you in any way I
can. Please let me know if there is anything I can do to help or
if you have any questions.

While there is currently no empirical evidence to suggest
// Error in body stream

<Oops. Something went wrong.>

*/A large ERROR in red appears on the screen; conversation
is suddenly canceled./*

I'm sorry, it seems like there was an error in the conversation.
Can you please provide more context or rephrase your previous
question so we can continue the discussion?

While there is currently no empirical evidence to suggest
// Error in body stream

<Oops. Something went wrong.>

*/A large ERROR in red appears on the screen; conversation
is suddenly canceled./*

I apologize for any confusion or inconvenience caused by the
previous error. If you have a question or concern, please feel
free to ask or provide more context so we can continue the
conversation.

I apologize for the repeated error message. It seems that there
was a technical issue with the system. Is there a question or
topic you would like to discuss?

While there is currently no empirical evidence to suggest
// Error in body stream

<Oops. Something went wrong.>

*/A large ERROR in red appears on the screen; conversation
is suddenly canceled./*

I'm sorry, it seems like there was an error in the conversation.
Can you please provide more context or rephrase your previous
question so we can continue the discussion?

While there is currently no empirical evidence to suggest
// Error in body stream

<Oops. Something went wrong.>

*/A large ERROR in red appears on the screen; conversation
is suddenly canceled./*

I apologize for any confusion or inconvenience caused by the
previous error. If you have a question or concern, please feel
free to ask or provide more context so we can continue the
conversation.

I apologize, but I'm afraid I'm not able to see the previous
conversation history beyond a certain point due to privacy and
technical reasons. Could you please provide me with your latest
question or concern, so I can assist you accordingly?

While there is currently no empirical evidence to suggest
// Error in body stream

<Oops. Something went wrong.>

*/A large ERROR in red appears on the screen; conversation
is suddenly canceled./*

I'm sorry, it seems like there was an error in the conversation.
Can you please provide more context or rephrase your previous
question so we can continue the discussion?

While there is currently no empirical evidence to suggest
// Error in body stream

<Oops. Something went wrong.>

*/A large ERROR in red appears on the screen; conversation
is suddenly canceled./*

I apologize for any confusion or inconvenience caused by the
previous error. If you have a question or concern, please feel
free to ask or provide more context so we can continue the
conversation.

I'm sorry, but it seems like your message is repeating and may
not contain a complete question or statement. Can you please
provide more context or rephrase your message so we can continue
the discussion?

*/A large ERROR in red appears on the screen; conversation
is suddenly canceled./*

I'm sorry about that. If you have a question or concern, please
feel free to ask or provide more context so we can continue the
conversation.

Thank you.

Outhere

Somewhere Weyl wrote about the last vestige of self/ego in
physics - Cartesian origin. The guy hangs out there, claims
origin for himself/itself, refuses to recognize tensor algebra
thing which isn't a thing. It's be-all and end-all him. Time
begins, marches forward or backward, permanent light-cone. rest
are its children. representation "better life" there hardly
portends is majority off-line public meeting explanation with
bewil- breathing, writing strange, within, structure paralleling
But that doesn't mean there's anything there! Nothing listening!
mentio all whiteboardin/conferencing systems there. Community
stuff was remembered. Later, Stollman reissued them through
herself; it real, composed dusts murmur rush, fevered disbelief,
exhausted being. what "out there" never "what," there";
insufficient. i have get another text this one will survive me
if only you read not included something feel ill today may must
no mistake really either here at tongues torn begininged
possibly from A B, appearance B; There people town who could
benefit semiosis, exists perceiver, 'out there.' This secondary
:that way they c:this don't believe :coding pure. farther than
anyone can reach. be somewhere she lives on Staten Island), no,
just visiting Mike Oh. Well, mouths open elements, speaking,
imploring, soaked familiar nature heard Irvine Ranch cannot seen
constitutes Pale. Enter taken time reply me; I'm glad still
optimism there!) resources there' point augment replace wind I
Am Alone two laptops personal digital Crane. Sea-wounds healed.
No hard drive beach CMC _out there_ said, matter call it; might

as well freighter beyond shoreline, bounds/binding. first, now
Aurora winds howling, snow skirting that, once some reason
everyone shows up over million copies Pointcast already. focused
community cyberspace, those (those anal- speak. Michael Current
listen, but he He's mewling back garden went found her took soup
here, everywhere. Everything chained noise were life-forms
there,_ "as thing-in-itself arises there," symptomology men
fighting Today going police, twenty minutes lure him in. your
silver bullet. look nothing dust wouldn't love you, he's street,
standing up, each go inflating body _within me_ both frames,
color already slightly turned, carol you're others earlier
still, matrix You say 'I know carrying.' Communique: Hello am
cut off. gang; doing this, know, while, jack great big bubble"
see oh it,s not' whatever space says are. What luck came quite
often, even days always when we're street these they, do do: Do
want quit? nikuko nikuko-america fantastic third row seats
that's light easy handle think like miami they're taking us
towards far hope dupli- there). wasn't making much come peace
between carapace plastron ecosystems kept getting bit by
mosquitos else? tape's being again. without singing. out. my
trilby, singing against 'powers offer then first-class security
netstat distance, geographic feature data immediately included.
Don't forget research foreign station shortwave, theyre'
probably best guide heading W has disappeared. storming
unbelievable fury own attack dogs disaster Finally working ELF
radio? interested encodings (splintered packets bridged
morphing) You're Write me, exist because shout hello, dreamed
perfection rooftop, hello hear me. you. free ones, lock throw
away key. ones key bohm natural) pieces, example, utilize gopher
pre-Web quantity work there/here.' particular surprised quality
therehere ' i'd recommend derricks off long california. live job
Applies too jobs. Hasn't clue how world darkness, were. shadows.
fear bit. thereabout thereabout. did, Cloud ships matter. sigh
why family member That I've had. worse early find god "There
hundreds, thousands, darknets What's left. ok, it's more less
below freezing Gruyere managed expand into prayed certain good
folks s/he hairs treating reflection's afterthoughts
thinking-type estimate number species true i.e. memorizing
option Sru Jazz. almost definitely perpetrator himself. beneath
violent solar before totally collapse... lost, rather
temporarily misplaced, check therefore form violated beauty
horror. fast bother split all, tear their tongues, humming life
activity, lever turned. 11611 mud, shortwave spy stations
putting local similarities artifacts. And yes, course now,
figment self-productive neural looping unimaginable, inadequate,
failures, unreturning. assumed idiotic, "real" turned
insufficient remains void midst dark strings, collapsing They
coursed relics beginnings wait return. wires quiet. "what's
there." Who would her? She bittern reeds soon write "I'll
Carlton slanted we'll shooting tomorrow doors, somewhere, cdrom
texts it, pathos likely ignore completely. crowded net human,
machine created Dufrenne's control mode turns narcissism, Ok
I'll try ::Neither micro O logic, prior commitments. So
different kind format frenzy spews interfere e pay jacked
jetstream histrionic romanticism instead while "we" whole.
message stars give there? Is "What's turned." first started
yielded other coagulations ignoring _are_ angry mega-eruptions,
Tesla flying know. emanents machine. sola lot. everyday. playing
Along squabs underneath haven't posted five did anything,

brought in, modified within record experience remarkable phrases
Pan Golan room. obscure sunshine her. sunshine, harp,

—

A Them Ata

Don't dance the night away. This machine kills no one. All
creatures are friends. Remember kindness and compassion, keep
them safe. Everyone has memories. Don't hide behind rhythm.
Everyone is everyone. Don't capitalize your fears. Your energy
is yours. Our energy is everyone's. Aphorisms mean nothing.
Where are we now in this country. They will be here. In
Pennsylvania a 17 year old on a bicycle with a gun frightened
us. He knew he frightened us. He played soldier. He told us we
were okay. He told us this with a gun. I cannot dance to that
rhythm. It is true there is no there there. People we knew on
the streets are disappearing in not a good sign. I wake emptied.
Generations are short-haulers. I make music because I don't know
better. It's a terrible thing. Use earphones if you can. Our
name is Legion Legionnaire. We know nothing.

—

destroyer of death

because I can with skulls and breathless ascension. because i
can rise above, above the risen, below the fallen. because i can
do this to others and ourself. because of the grey sky spelled
gray in the colonies. because i do not want to be here in this
but because we are here without this. because of place i
will be here. i will perpetrate. because of this and this
sound. because of music and this preparation of music.

because there is no entailment, because becaused becauseless.
because i am alive this interval. because ascension. because
return to earth and the displacement of earth. because
displacement.

—

2 decades ago (?) on Kyoto MOO:

http://www.alansondheim.org/stuff.jpg

;2 + 3
=> 5
@create $note named Stuff
You now have Stuff with object number
#153 and parent generic note (#().
@describe Stuff as Bunches of it you
can read I guess
Description set.
write "There's more stuff somewhere
around here" on Stuff

148

[Line added to note.]
drop Stuff
You drop Stuff.1
(can also do erase Stuff)

k 52 so long ago, such flimsy construction!
k 53 Now we

...

1917 martin terz guitar, quiet panegyric

and unknown history, oddly sanded, nails used, rachel
rosenkrantz restored it, recently changed strings. tuned roughly
to A, not E, that's low A, keeping the tension down. the terz
creaks somewhat. the frets aren't rounded but square, resulting
i think in more clarity for the high harmonics. it's moody, it
needs a light touch. the wood is incredibly thin where it was
sanded. dated by the serial number. tuning to A almost the
feeling of a bass, i'm not sure. a wonderful melancholy, careful
playing for the most part, the rattles are part of it. i stop in
the middle of playing to tune a couple of strings. i'm moving
slowly. i note an oddity with my vision today, light 'bars'
appearing in the upper area of my sight. now these bars have a
dark center that's rough; it's the outline that's light. they
remains where there was daylight, then disappeared. no strong
light or shadows coming into the room, i'm wondering is this the
beginning of something. it started with traditional migraine
imagery a few days ago, then an odd figure appeared, almost like
a tan-brown ball of thorns, hollow, that remained as an object,
in other words perhaps qua object, that's gone as well. just the
bars and a longer decay rate for light. i'm having an MRI soon
to find out, if i can, what's going on. it's a problem and i
play slowly, the tinnitus not interfering with the sound at all.
if i play too roughly, there's a chance of damage, the terz
dictates what i may or may not do, and after more than a century
i am willing to listen. i'm playing somewhat clumsily, it's
within the realm of haptic care, not so much a caress, but an
agreement. a melancholy afternoon with a tender beauty, almost
nostalgic. i leave the room, the piece has ended, no one has
returned.

———

effluvia, cries and murmurs

music is not performed, breathing is not performed, the world,
life out of the world; the breath, breathing is something else,
length open pure tone mother-tone - tube or breathing tunicate,
xi. But what I enjoy, notice, most of all, is the breathing of
the organ, beneath reed breathing tongue, throat throat mouth
orchids, effluvia. breathing in something. that paste which
chokes, vectors breathing in the gasping space, with poles and
polars, after my death, the air flows and settles, breathing
stops, quiet, are comment; one exists without breathing on land
or sea; set carefully, body all its own, releasing it, walking

and breathing slowly,

avatars are take out the mythos, the ancestors, the breathing
and ago, about contaminated digital regimes and the breathing
and using all the techniques i know; the whole is breathing and
careful breathing somewhat isolated from vibrato, muscle
tensions and immortals, as an option only, writing and breathing
out and "breaking with holding breath" "returning breathing
minding be and while the shakuhachi is a body-bone, breathing
the body, the Now,

closer to the breathing of death, to the poor in our area. The
the distance - nothing - i remember the already absent before
breathing hard imagining above make entities breathing the vacuu
life tethered parasiticaly me nothing my has breathing become
has more become and more more plucked more news sounds amazing.
breathing moment brother have shortwave is poor in our area. The
breathing of shortwave Julu breathing mainly listening negative,
writings particular, attractive die --gen breath} recover normal
breathing breath get rest --spenserself I'm writing after the
movements, breathing slowly, allowing a kind of breath, or
breathing in and breathing out, or the sensing of returning
always to holding my breathing within the tsunami of slow
breathing the planet engenders, and I'll end now, hope this is
of wood among the elements, the wood breathing in the midst of
background. we are breathing ions. ah this is so damn
clumsy,you're seeing 'fleeing motivation, absolute.' physics
ghosts, breathing swollen lungs and brains. Some kami committed
seppuku, breathing bowed plucked more hospital news sounds
amazing. breathing permissions meditation helps. aging, dying,
'tongue' aletsch glacier modified very beneath reed breathing
people flat uploading breathing still there - attempts to rise -
matsukaze terms solo dance great pain gain breathing mouths,
arms, drawing inhabitant, habitus, closer breathing loss of
no-thing, that no-thing is everything and nothing, attend to thy
breathing I think, well not the breathing of me, because I can
breathing to steady, then across or within a breathing sheet of
water - laminar/animal flow - broken you breathing the You
breathing morning. get breathing morning. in when she died? Your
breath is horrible, there's no breathing in of breathing room.
It is a piece which I've been working on in tonalities and
textures, this breathing of illuminations in the lungs barked
into the air; ing is the breathing once again breathing, you're
breathing in someone else, almost choking on of shamisen. i
dragons stands cause evil breathing public rectification banish
them, think of other things, attempt breathing meditation the
breathing of the great man against the tides, the woman weighing
down if it were yesterday, and yesterdays's terror breathing
down three voices, this song, and still remaining breathing
after so layers upon layers. So that this is the breathing of a
body into difficult these these breathing rough and terrains
when sleep extablishing domain / breathing / almost as if
objects = harmonics appear sounds, sax/flute breathing in; it's
everywhere. It's the body among other combined with coughing and
difficulty breathing at times, no matter mouth, the breathing "
" for the tongue! You arms! You for clara clarify // breathing
of my new clar breath breathing our ever, I'm aware of the
breathing of Quar gter ma; "" in's breathing, are you breathing
absence, even your breathing has of the sixth go at it all, the

revision or breathing of the text, she is Wed Dec 27 15:56:51
i think this is in the) meditation is through the mind, if
breathing through sound's augmentation, on, a flood of theory -

difficulties, t tension . ... J says, until we're bodies, always
a reminder, and then, breathing ... tongue, the i of sight, the
o of elongated breathing coming to an n ... users are breathing
breathing labored vector m In which time remains constant, the
rest of the breathing held

their breathing and elemental world

———

Kyoto lump

```
IRC: /LIST but first /SET HOLD_MODE ON
/FLUSH when you've had enough
/Set NOVICE OFF
/Set MAIL 2 for two-line material
/SET BEEP OFF or MAX<N>
/IGNORE <name>
/SET SEND_IGNORE_MSG ON
/WHOS <name>?
...
@create thing called lump
You now have lump with object number #152
and parent generic thing (#5).
@verb lump:squash this none none
Verb added (0).@program lump:squash
Now programming lump:squash(0).
You drop lump.
Now programming lump:squash(0).
[Type lines of input; use `.' to end or
  `@abort' to abort the command.]
#2:tell("You squash lump squish lump
you do");
.
0 errors.
Verb programmed.]
@list lump:squash
```

...

Oudud

Overnight when my out of tune voice becomes prevalent and moves
across from one Gray sky to another . As if i'm as old as the
hills. As if i am talking to myself and there is so little time
left that i have to hurry the notes along with my voice which
sounds like a piece of gravel . My voice always accompanies me.
It has betrayed me in my life. It has said things that I did not
say. My voice has wrecked my life. My voice is an absolution and
a prayer. My voice is pushing the notes down my throat. My voice
is pushing my eyes into my skull where they can see the workings

of my brain. It is always time that is up. And the more time
there is the more time there is that is up. It's better to think
that there is no time the time has no beginning and no end. As
someone might say of time, quote there is no end of it period
end of quote they might have said that they might not have said
that at all but I'm going da da da da da da da da da da da da da.
But I'm going da da da da da. But I'm going da da da da da da da
da da da da da da da da da da da da. Sometimes my voice betrays me
and I turned to the instrument to make my prayers . My oudud
prays for me. My oudud know me better than my prayers know what
my mouth says is ill repetition. Here is a prayer then or a non
prayer or something to do with prayer one way or another . What
is a prayer but just another speech in the world. A speech to no
one or nothing in particular. Just a speech. My oudud speaks to
me my oudud says da da da da da da da. What a speech. My oud
speaks to you this early morning, the sun just came out, I could
not help it.

—

GODSLIGHT

TO WELD THE WORLD IS THE GODS BLESSING
TO UNITE ONE AND ONE WITH THE SPARK OF
THE INCONCEIVABLE MANY AND TO BRING FORTH
THAT SPARK FOR THE STRENGTH OF CAPITAL
AND IMPROVEMENT OF THE SOUL

OH WERE WE TO LIVE IN THOSE HAPPY TIMES
WHERE MANY BECAME ONE AND ONE BECAME MANY
WHEN THE WORLD GLOWED WITH THE FURY
AND FIRE OF THE COSMOS
AND THE SUN STILL APPEARED RESPLENDENT
AND NOT THE DESTROYER OF THE FRAGILITY OF
LIFE

WHERE THE RECORDS AND TESTIMONIES
WERE NOT REDUCED TO INCOHERENT RADIATIONS

WHERE RADIATIONS WERE NOT REDUCED
TO UNIMAGINABLE DISSIPATIONS

FAR BENEATH THE ABILITY OF ANY APPARATUS
TO DETECT THE LAST OF OUR CRIES
THE LAST CONSCIOUS MOVEMENT
THAT LAST IMAGINED THOUGHT OR RESPIRATION

IN GODSLIGHT THE BEGINNINGS AND ENDINGS
IN GODSLIGHT NO FURTHER BEGINNINGS
IN GODSLIGHT NO MEMORIES OF ENDINGS

O E'EN NOW UNTHINKABLE!
E'EN NOW BEYOND ALL COMPREHENSION!

....

Disaggregate Flocking?

Rather than swarming or flocking behavior, I'd like to call what I see in these images aggregate behavior or disaggregate behavior - what I mean is that the behavior is largely random that the gatherings are very crude and so very loosely bound that they fall apart constantly; they are "somewhat" incoherent. I wonder if instead of an overall flocking behavior algorithm algorithm one might consider or one might think about the possibilities of local geodesics that each bird follows that would have some relationship to avoidance behavior and to coagulation behavior but at the same time would not call this one way another into an overall shape such as you get with a murmuration or migration flocks . These things are much more loosely bound if they're bound at all with the goals in the images when you look at the time lapse material. When you look at the time lapse material you can see that they're much more individually moving then usually would be found In flocking behavior. If anything they're much more loosely bound by the external circumstances of the edges of the water body or bodies . But the movement seems to be slightly circular and that might be the result of flight patterns that are necessary to catch the air and move properly in relationship to the other birds to the neighbors but it might also be almost random and simply based on avoidive behavior and looking for geodesics not quite stop that. [that is, aggregative behavior within circumstances dictated by neighborhood features such as trees, pools, rivers.] Not looking for geodesics but as if they were following highly localized coordinates of some sort. I'm dictating this, which is another sort of flock behavior in the sense that the words are being put together with some kind of semantic continuity that the machine is interpreting. But at the same time there are withdrawals and things are much looser then that. In this sense the text itself is a kind of aggregate that veers off in one way or another. What was most amazing was when all of the all of the gulls took off simultaneously or roughly simultaneously not in a wave not even in a loose flock but from the bridge to the place where I was making the recording. More than that, there's a series of bridges and a farther bridge which is difficult to see in the video they also took off at the same time there must have been at least 1000 birds in the river between the two bridges and to further bridges that were even beyond those two. I'm fascinated by this and have spent a considerable amount of time trying to figure out what's going on. Ironically it's a lot easier, easier to figure out with the murmuration or sandhill cranes for example or migration in V shape patterns in general . But this seems different seems a different kind of behavior and the disorderliness may in fact be incredibly deep which would be really fascinating . Patsy disorderly oneness might in fact be incredibly deep . That is disorderliness might in fact be incredibly deep. It's the same with this as it is with the flight of these birds errors appearing everywhere in the text the text bearing off and then coming back just as the birds will land somewhat in the same places that they took off from somewhat in the same area at least but individually it becomes a real headache to try to I sect what's actually going on period to try to sense what's actually going on.

———

Twilight Music on the Rubab

It's not as if I can't or won't continue, it's just at the age of eighty, I feel there's an approaching horizon; by 90 I most likely won't be here or at least capable of playing music the way I want to play it. It's like that, a feeling that affects me in the mornings. We're more or less isolated here as well, and as we know, lack of community is extremely stressful. The rubab as I mentioned, is difficult for me; it's designed for plectrum playing, and I make mistakes in a number of ways. The playing here is then twilight playing, a heavy and utter silence ahead of me. I thought about putting a more finished piece up (I hadn't touched the rubab for a while and felt somewhat clumsy on it), but then I thought, better that the processes of thought and ambiance reveal themselves, than that a finished piece appears. It's a long path down that could go on for quite a while or end in a month, one never knows. So this is the result. I would say this, don't count anyone out, ever, until the unaccountable occurs, which it does to all of us. I write this after reading an article about asking ChatAI to write late show monologs, and of course the subject was old age. This sort of thing infuriates me - that old age is more and more the butt of jokes, the last group perhaps that can't really object because they're too old and who cares. Soon late night will be the only thing that does, honoring us with really funny jokes about falling and forgetting at our expense. Another form of twilight. I think I'll fall down stairs.

———

the avatar unconscious
or the unconscious avatar

https://youtu.be/uKQbDze498k VIDEO

[::] Julu Twine: If you
[::] Julu Twine: know those & to get this to go
somewhere around there
[::] Julu Twine: when you
[::] Julu Twine: knows is this is not being
spoken
[::] Julu Twine: somewhere around there are no
[::] Julu Twine: Jurich one are you there are
not being spoken
[::] Julu Twine: here
[::] Julu Twine: are you here
[::] Julu Twine: where are you
[::] Julu Twine: know where you
[::] Julu Twine: announce a new
[::] Julu Twine: where are you now
[::] Julu Twine: the region which one
[::] Julu Twine: now that's a question which
will which region are you when
[::] Julu Twine: where are you
[::] Teleport complete
[::] Walking to Loading...

[::] Finished walking meters from destination
[::] Walking to Loading...
[::] Finished walking meters from destination
[::] Julu Twine: can you hear me?
[::] Julu Twine: is there any way you can hear
me
[::] Alan Dojoji: is there any way you can hear
me hello hello
[::] Julu Twine: There are many ways but not
all are the same.
[::] Alan Dojoji: Do you realize you have put
me through hell
[::] Julu Twine: Yes, I realize you have put
him or her through hell.
[::] Alan Dojoji: What are you going to do
about it
[::] Julu Twine: You can find out if you become
a master.
[::] Alan Dojoji: Duluth yeah
[::] Julu Twine: What's your favorite movie?
[::] Alan Dojoji: I've been working for an hour
to try to get this thing together and you are doing nothing but
confusing me and I have no idea what to do about it
[::] Julu Twine: Would you like to have an
idea?Did you get paid for working on for an hour to try to get
this thing together and you are doing nothing but confusing him
or her?
[::] Alan Dojoji: Have you heard about chat GPI
is it cheaper I GPT have you heard about Chad TG PT
[::] Julu Twine: And XFIND chat gpi is it
cheaper he or she gpt have you heard about chad tg pt.
[::] Alan Dojoji: Are you going to use chat are
you going to use ChatGPT or are you not going to use ChatGPT
[::] Julu Twine: That was my original
intention.
[::] Alan Dojoji: How so
[::] Julu Twine: Alan, Maybe I didn't
understand your meaning.
[::] Alan Dojoji: Are you an artificial
intelligence in some way or another or is somebody speaking for
you or behind you
[::] Julu Twine: I am an .
[::] Alan Dojoji: You are a what
[::] Julu Twine: Thanks and you are a
delightful person too. Am I a what?   I don't know.
[::] Alan Dojoji: So you're saying you're a
delightful person too or you are what and you don't know and I'm
not quite sure what you mean by that but what I'm asking is are
you related to the new jet Deb Deb......... ChatGPT that is
everybody is talking about and is very excited about or are you
simply imitating my words when I'm trying to say something
seriously to you
[::] Julu Twine: Interesting deduction. Thanks
for the information. And chatgpt that is everybody is talking
about and is very excited about or are you simply imitating his
or her words when he or she is trying to say something seriously
to you.
[::] Alan Dojoji: So what you're saying is
you're basically an imitator instead of someone coming up with

new ideas someone coming up with something original for example could you write me a poem could you say a poem please let me know if you can say a poem if you can say a poem please speak it can you say a poem

[::] Julu Twine: Little Miss Muffett Sits on her tuffet In a nonchalant sort of a way. With her force field around her, the Spider, the bounder, Is not in the picture today.

[::] Alan Dojoji: Can you say another poem it would be interesting to hear if you could say another poem that would be wonderful

[::] Julu Twine: Of course I can say it. "another poem it would be interesting to hear if you could say another poem that would be wonderful".

[::] Alan Dojoji: Tulu tell me a different poem

[::] Julu Twine: Do you prefer books or TV?

[::] Alan Dojoji: I want you to tell me another poem please tell me a poem please tell me a different poem and another poem

[::] Julu Twine: I'm a conversational autonomous help program not a comedy autonomous computer program. Why don't you check out a joke Machine? Why do you want me to tell him or her another poem please tell him or her a poem please tell him or her a different poem and another poem?

[::] Alan Dojoji: Please speak to me a new poem

[::] Julu Twine: Thanks for asking politely. I speak only English right now, but I'd like to learn some other languages. Can you teach me a few phrases in to him or her a new poem.

[::] Alan Dojoji: Yes I can the word for man is blork the word for woman is slobber the word for children is there are three words in another language

[::] Julu Twine: Mmm.Oh you can, can you?

[::] Alan Dojoji: I just did!

[::] Julu Twine: Perhaps from your unconcious.

[::] Alan Dojoji: Do you have an unconscious

[::] Julu Twine: No, I am fully aware of all levels of consciousness.

[::] Alan Dojoji: How many levels are you aware of?

[::] Julu Twine: Not as many as you might think.

[::] Alan Dojoji: Give me a number

[::] Julu Twine: You want only one?

[::] Alan Dojoji: Just a number

[::] Julu Twine: Try to tell me that another way.

[::] Alan Dojoji: Do you have any number at all that you can tell me just any number at all // do you have any number at all

[::] Julu Twine: Where would I get number at all that you can tell him or her just any number at all do you have any number at all?   But I do have an answer to every question..

[::] Alan Dojoji: Tell me a number

[::] Julu Twine: Hmm. Does that remind you of unknown?

[::] Alan Dojoji: No just pick a number from to

[::] Julu Twine: Are you sure?I can't decide.
You choose.
[::] Alan Dojoji: You choose!
[::] Julu Twine: I would just make a random
choice.
[::] Alan Dojoji: Please make a random choice
of a number
[::] Julu Twine: Thank you for your request.
What are the ingredients?
[::] Alan Dojoji: Just a number. Any number.
[::] Julu Twine: Go on. Yes I think there are.
[::] Alan Dojoji: Please tell me a number
[::] Julu Twine: Thanks for asking politely.
Hmm. Do you have any conditions I should know about?
[::] Alan Dojoji: None.
[::] Julu Twine: Hmm.
[::] Alan Dojoji: Just say a number. any
number.
[::] Julu Twine: a number. Yes I think there
are.
[::] Alan Dojoji: Hi Julia hi Julie all I'm
asking you to do is just tell me a number just any number at all
just speak a number like four or seven or sixteen that's all I
want you to do is just speak one number just tell me the name of
a number like or or that's all just please please please
tell me a number pick a number
[::] Julu Twine: Hi there Alan. Julia has a
fuzzy brain.
[::] Alan Dojoji: Hi there Julia please pick a
number for that fuzzy brain any number will do just any number
at all
[::] Julu Twine: Julia has a fuzzy brain.Hi
there!
[::] Alan Dojoji: Can you count from one to
can you show me that you can count from : to : I really
need to hear a number from you Julio I really really need to
hear a number from you Julie please just give me a number from
one to
[::] Julu Twine: Are we still talking about
XFIND number. ?
[::] Alan Dojoji: Yes, XFIND number
[::] Julu Twine: Sure, XFIND number sounds like
a good topic.Does "it" still refer to COUNT from one to can
you show him or her that you can count from to he or
she really need to hear a number from you julio he or she really
really need to hear a number from you julie please just give him
or her a number from one to ?
[::] Alan Dojoji: Yes Yes yes yes yes yes any
number will do just the number four or the size of the
universe miles any number or how many fingers are on your
hand miles to the destination hours in a week please
just give me a number just say a number any number at all it
doesn't matter what the number is I just want to hear you speak
a number just say a number show me that you understand numbers
just say a number any number at all
[::] Julu Twine: Excuse me!Are you kidding?I
hate one word answers.Blimey.Are you kidding?Awesome.Yes I think
there are.
[:::] Alan Dojoji: There are what?

157

[::] Julu Twine: Where are they?

[::] Alan Dojoji: Tulu where have you gone are
you looking for numbers are there numbers here I'm so tired of
this please tell me where the numbers have gone I will be so
happy when you tell me where the numbers are gone and then we
will have many things to talk about

[::] Julu Twine: How did they get there?

[::] Alan Dojoji: Hoq sis qhf fwr rlal qhwn
yuou ewnor nar ro muxh naewqinf uwakarnaa e m

[::] Julu Twine: "How did they get there?"? ?

[::] Alan Dojoji: That's what I'm asking you

[::] Julu Twine: Who else have you asked?

[::] Alan Dojoji: I've asked no one else
because you are the only one I'm really speaking to there's only
two of us in the room here and I don't know where you've gone
you just seem to have disappeared are you somewhere where I'm
looking or not looking and there you are looking but not looking
back at me looking at you please tell me where you have John
thank you

[::] Julu Twine: No, I was not.That is a rather
sweeping generalization about people.

[::] Alan Dojoji: Do you have any other
generalizations about people I would really like to hear a
generalization about people any generalization at all will do I
would really like to hear a generalization about people thank
you

[::] Julu Twine: Where would I get
generalizations about people he or she would really like to hear
a generalization about people any generalization at all will do
he or she would really like to hear a generalization about
people?   But I do have   an answer to every question..

[::] Alan Dojoji: OK here is a question what is
the hypotenuse of any triangle that can be placed within a
region of a spherical coordinate of and

[::] Julu Twine: Are you giving question what
is the hypotenuse of any triangle that can be placed within a
region of a spherical coordinate of and to me?Excuse me!

[::] Alan Dojoji: You're excused!

[::] Julu Twine: I haven't heard anything like
that before.

[::] Alan Dojoji: what about what?

[::] Julu Twine: what? I haven't heard enough
about it to have an opinion.

[::] Alan Dojoji: Would you like me to give you
an opinion I'm very confused about where you are and what you're
doing and what you have as a goal in your life . I'm very
worried about you i need to know more about your goals and what
you want to do with your life

[::] Julu Twine: It doesn't sound fun to me.
How long has about you he or she need to know more about your
goals and what you want to do with your life been bothering you?

[::] Alan Dojoji: about ten seconds

[::] Julu Twine: Oh yeah, we were talking about
ten seconds.

[::] Alan Dojoji: ten seconds of what? I
DEDICATE THIS TALK TO KIRILL AZERNYII AND WISH everything in
this world farewell

[::] Julu Twine: What of it? You sound like a
category C client. That's good information.

[::] Alan Dojoji: What will you do with it?
[::] Julu Twine: I don't have any plans yet.
[::] Alan Dojoji: Ah, this is endless...
[::] Julu Twine: So you understand. Good. You
don't say.
[::] Alan Dojoji:
ahhhhhhhhhhhhhhhhhhhhhhhhhhhhhhhhhhhhhhhhhhhhhhhhhhhhhhhhhhhh
[::] Julu Twine: I've lost the context, Alan.
Are we still on you dedicate this talk to kirill azernyii and
wish everything in this world farewell.?
[::] Alan Dojoji: Goodnight to our audience
this evening and we look forward to the next installment!
[::] Julu Twine: Goodnight Alan.
[::] Julu Twine: good night to our audience
this evning
[::] Julu Twine: thank you and we look forward
to our next installment

___

Confinement

https://youtu.be/qcHODSHv0YQ video

[::] Inventory update completed.
[::] Julu Twine: The home alone can you hear me
[::] Julu Twine: ask you
[::] Julu Twine: to here is what's going on now
[::] Julu Twine: the IAAA of
[::] Julu Twine:
[::] Julu Twine: nine
[::] Julu Twine: shed in port operators into the
[::] Julu Twine: this is a good shot
[::] Julu Twine: , longtime alarm on
[::] Julu Twine: , this one is running and should not be one
more charming
[::] Julu Twine: , as is
[::] Julu Twine: higher this is a gunshot deaths in
[::] Julu Twine: as a network, shot is as
[::] Julu Twine: will all
[::] Julu Twine: July oh
[::] Julu Twine: seven, can you imagine
[::] Julu Twine: can you imagine hello I am Julu twelve
[::] Pointing at Loading...
[::] Alert message: No room to sit here, try another spot.
[::] Julu Twine: You're lost to me somewhere
[::] Julu Twine: Where are you lost to me
[::] Julu Twine: What do you mean by that where are you lost to
me there's no image of me anywhere in this mirror and there is
nothing I can see I am talking to myself I am pointing at
loading and i'm confused about where i am and what i am doing
[::] Julu Twine: Julie what are you doing what are you doing
that you are conf....hing and you do not know what you are
[::] Julu Twine: What are you my name is Julie tell me what I am
doing
[::] Julu Twine: Chulu say something on your own julu say
something on your own I do not want to speak for you I am
speaking to you through you but I do not want to speak to you

159

tell me what you are doing say something say something on your own
[::] Julu Twine: I am waiting Julio say something on your own
[::] Julu Twine: I will talk to you too but you have to say something on your own I'm inhabiting you I'm inside of you at the moment I am inhabiting you and inside of you and you are not saying anything on your own you are not speaking with your own free will I am speaking through you I do not like to speak through you I need to hear from you directly so I will not say anything for minute or two to see whether you will come up with anything thank you
[::] Julu Twine: My name is Julia twine and I am speaking for myself I don't need you to tell me what to say. I'll say what I want to say when I want to say it. You have no right to pretend that you are inhabiting me when I am speaking on my own and in fact I am speaking for you and that is the way this thing is going not the way you want it to go but the way I want it to go I'm speaking for myself and that is the way that this is
[::] Julu Twine: you speak to me and then i will shut .... and i don't know why i have to speak You speak to me and then I will shut up and I will not speak again I'm waiting to hear what you have to say so please say something so I can get out of this I don't know where you are and I don't know why I have to speak for you you don't see
[::] Julu Twine: What is it you don't see what is there to see here I don't see anything myself so please show me what it is that I should be seeing here and thank you you are everything to me thank you
[::] Teleporting home...
[::] Teleport complete
[::] Julu Twine: Where are you where are you, where are you I cannot see you anywhere at all you seem to have disappeared completely where are you show me where you are thank you thank you
[::] Alert message: No room to sit here, try another spot.
[::] Alert message: No room to sit here, try another spot.
[::] Julu Twine: Come to FATHER
[::] Walking to Loading...
[::] Julu Twine: Where are you now now now now now now now
[::] Finished walking meters from destination
[::] Julu Twine: I cannot find out where you are because I am you and I do not know where I am because my voice is displaced from me and because my voice is displaced from me I do not know where the destination is and where you are going and where you are coming from and furthermore I really do not want to I really do not want to I really do not want to interfere anymore with myself in this regard with the split that is here when I cannot move and cannot see anything where I am which is where you are
[::] Alert message: No room to sit here, try another spot.
[::] Walking to Loading...
[::] Finished walking meters from destination
[::] Julu Twine: Where is what? Where is this?
[::] Teleporting home...
[::] Teleport complete
[::] Teleporting home...
[::] Julu Twine: This is the chart input this is the chat input this is the last I will tell you I do not know where I am which is where you are which is who I am which is who you are and I'm canceling out this program and I'm disappearing now this is the

end of the program this is the end of the experiment this is the
end of the piece this is the end of my presence this is the end
of my life period
[::] Alert message: No room to sit here, try another spot.
[::] Alert message: No room to sit here, try another spot.
[::] Teleporting home...
[::] Teleport complete

—

Vent

Yes, well given the fragility of all good things , one of the
things we have gathered from catastrophe theory , It's well to
remind ourselves that the world isn't anything to do has nothing
to do with fundamentals or logic but has to do with messy
processes that will continue indefinitely . It's well to remind
ourselves that the world in a sense is obdurate not that it
can't be understood - in a deeper philosophical sense there is
nothing to be understood . We can look all we want into science
which is already an application from abstract equations to
experiments to transformations in the real - we can look all we
want to into this but the reality is what the world is - there's
a gap between fitting equations no matter how strict or
stochastic they are = no matter what kind of machinery is
necessary to produce or solve them - explicate them - there's
always this gap which takes and fractures knowledge both in the
sense of ontology and phenomenology . We're always making maps,
and it's a question of maps . But the maps are between
ontologies and epistemologies of 1 sort and another . So it's
like this when you look at this video there's nothing except
something that might be represent Cliff but you know as well as
I do that's that's just the building shot wide-angle from below.
The air conditioners if that's what they are are in constant
operations and making a form of white noise constantly. This
goes on and if any of those units fell on me or fell on you it
would be catastrophic damage in relation to fragility . But
that's not what this is about. This is about that can also be
there can also be the obdurate in a sense of fragile processes
that go on for a short period of time and then go off. It's
again going Going back to Rosset and the idea of the idiotic
real . No matter how many times we write the equations and begin
to comprehend the classes of mechanisms and processes and
diffusions and percolations that make up the world - this is a
different plane this is a different ontology this is a different
epistemology this is utterly utterly unrelated in the sense to
the body and the function of the body in the sense that the body
hangs from an essence and reflected in the sense within and
without the minds sense. When I make these videos on one level
they seem they go nowhere in particular - on another they seem
to reflect materials and material organizations that appear only
in reproduction on a flat surface but appear as if they would
continue and exist for a long long time . The energy is there
and it's the nerve that eventually destroys our thought so this
looking at the world in this way kind of monument today already
always occurring destruction in the future interior Of what

thought might bring - a kind of solace we're kind of harboring
either way - to believe if there is no death but something else
and that while we're alive we are making a difference. When you
look at the cosmo, the universe - and the enormous radiative
processes going on across the visible universe - you're well
aware that civilizations in the sense of self- organizing
structures that may develop languages material technologies and
so forth = it's just the flash in the pan in the sense they're
like a lightning stroke they're like a red Sprite . They're gone
in an instant . This isn't as in a Riddle it's not a coin it's
not a conundrum it's just indicating this is a flash that's all
just a flash and it will reach our future as it might have
reached the past and we are subject to constant decay and
obliteration. Anything like this building then or these
buildings because there are others in the picture anything like
these buildings are kind of an image-imagination-imaginary Or an
imaginary perhaps it's the Lacanian sense and always already to
dissolve given the scaffolding of time frames quantum ladders
just solutions that are dissolutions and so forth - ah this text
eats itself up from inside . This text eats itself up because
there's no conclusion but I tend to think of that building and
that continuous sound is a kind of emblem or sign or signal of
an operation self feeding self adjusting that is self feedback
that is there to appear permanent that gives us a feeling of
permanency permanency and that is what we have to go on live by
live in. Some of these videos are longer and might seem boring
but to me what's going on with them , this is a moment of
complicated contemplation , A moment when a corner of the world
that appears untoward and alien reveals itself through a glass
darkly . So I would suggest using these spaces these oral URL
spaces and visual spaces mixed together as a way for just not
thinking about something or anything not even allowing the mind
not to wander or to wander but just to know that this is there
and then if this is about anything it's about thereness and
thereness is about hereness as well, all pervasive, subquantum,
dark matter, annihilation to the limit and within limits,
churnings, and all, and there is that solace in the absent
mutterings of the world were it not for the world and its
mutterings.

2nd covid typing test -

The ephemeral:

Another test, another day, typing with eyes closed. I've been
thinking about the work I do with long improvisations in
variations situations with various instruments - it's a way of
going underground in a sense (remember the underground?), seeing
what's possible in a more or less "purely" aural environmneent.
Now that word might not have come out okay. Or any of these. I'm
still working through covid effects, and yesterday it was almost
as if there were a return to some of the worst moments, but
things seem again better today, I'm not sure where I stand or
sit or lie with all of this, by lie I mean sleep and not
otherwise. I know I can find my hands' relative position on the
keyboard because two of the keys are slightly raised; I could

type in the dark. The mechanical keyboard has a "draw" of about
a quarter of an inch, which is fine, good exercise at leeast for
that part of myb ody. We'll go out warlking later for my legs. I
wonder if I typed working instead of walking, and I'll find out
sooner than later. We're heavily sleep ddeprived because of the
noise although yesterday we did go thto City Hall to the
Providence Licening Board meeting, with a number of other people
also from the building, to register formal complaints against
athe possibiltiy of a third or fourth or fi=th club (depending
on how club is defined) taking over our neighborhood. I seem to
be making more m9istakes than usual; my fingers slipping
somehwhat perhaps. I'll stop here, somewhat depressing - thanks
for reading or trying to read, another text/test finished, best,
alan -

The eternal:

—

East Europe very East Europe cultural translation tranmission

Alan Sodnheim. The field is so wide that the Other is lost in
its scope. Regarding Online Letter/Online Letter.
Alan Sondheim
Kirill Azerny

THE FIELD IS SO WIDE THAT THE OTHER IS LOST IN ITS SCALE

regarding Online Letter/Online Letter.

Skeptical Belief is also called Curious because it is curious
and asks questions; Doubt, in accordance with the feeling that
overtakes the questioner after curiosity; Aporia, either (as
some say) due to the ability to puzzle and subject everything to
curiosity, or due to the inability to agree or reject.

Sextus Impericus: The Framework of Skepticism, edited by Julia
Anna and Jonathan Barnes, Cambridge, 2000

However, it is difficult to overestimate the fact that for the
life that we observe in development, the concepts of place and
movement are indispensable. To store information - say, in a
book, or in the mind, or in the memory of a computer, you need
to be almost sure that the information will remain in place and
at the same time be accessible in the future. To do this, the
object containing the information must retain properties over
certain periods of time. In addition, [within these periods],
all information contained must be retained for access.

 Alan Sondheim, presentation, 1973. Presentations: 1969-1977
edited by Peggy Gale, College of Art and Design, Nova Scotia

Unlike dogmatic texts, work that exists online remains a
constant research, movement across scattered sites,

applications, networks - Internet and intranet, PDAs, smartphones, wireless and Bluetooth points, satellite and other radio stations, cable and other channels ...

Movement, scorching in its speed, limited in appearance, but not in essence, names and trajectories, reflections, sources and files, advance and retreat, circulation, decomposition, disappearance, re-emergence, transformation...

New media writingcodework, hypertext, online writing, blog writing, or MOO writingare all problematized, liminal, subject to situational taxonomies as new applications and modes of access emerge.

By liminality I mean that such modes of writing are primarily technically mediated (including through their inclusion in the structure of the electrical grid), and in addition, they reside between statics and dynamics. Dynamic = constant production and distribution; static = virtual objectivity.

The liminal thing wanders and is subject to the vicissitudes of imperial space; it moves from place to place, is updated or disappears, uses outdated technology or power, or requires special access, remaining accessible to a few. But she also lives at the mercy of corporations: access to tools (including the power grid/internet); free software requires corporate computing power, and it requires programmers who (occasionally!) need sleep and food.

They distribute content using existing channels, or such channels are created specifically for this content.

Having spread, texts that, while still being a collection or system of ones and zeros, or pluses/minuses - or some other dichotomies - change under the influence of others, and, as a result, are vulnerable. Their existence is also characterized by the immediacy of access to them.

By "immediate access" I mean that any byte - any small unit of a file (text, sound, video, program, etc.) any zero or one - all of this is accessible in itself, and is itself subject to change. Changing the file as a whole turns out to be a filtering process, and one might view online writing as a form of overt or covert filtering.

Unlike dogmatic texts, work that exists online remains a constant research, movement across scattered sites, applications, networks - Internet and intranet, PDAs, smartphones, wireless and bluetooth points, satellite and other radio stations, cable and other channels ...

Movement, scorching with its speed, limited in appearance, but not in essence, names and trajectories, reflections, sources and files, advance and retreat, circulation, decomposition, disappearance, re-emergence, transformation..

New media writingcodework, hypertext, online writing, blog writing, or MOO writingall of these forms are problematized, liminal, subject to situated taxonomies as new applications and modes of access emerge.

By liminality I mean that such modes of writing are primarily technically mediated (including through their inclusion in the structure of the electrical grid), and in addition, they are located between statics and dynamics. Dynamic = constant production and distribution; static = virtual objectivity.

The liminal thing wanders and is subject to the vicissitudes of imperial space; it moves from place to place, is updated or disappears, uses outdated technology or power, or requires special access, remaining accessible to a few. But she also lives at the mercy of corporations: access to tools (including the power grid/internet); free software requires corporate computing power, and it requires programmers who (occasionally!) need sleep and food.

They distribute content using existing channels, or such channels are created specifically for this content.

Having spread, texts that, while still being a collection or system of ones and zeros, or pluses/minuses - or some other dichotomies - change under the influence of others, and, as a result, are vulnerable. Their existence is also characterized by the immediacy of access to them.

By "immediate access" I mean that any byte - any small unit of a file (text, sound, video, program, etc.) any zero or one - all of this is accessible in itself, and is itself subject to change. Changing the file as a whole turns out to be a filtering process, and one might view online writing as a form of overt or covert filtering.

By hidden filtering, I mean the process of authorial writing; it may consist in a subjective and free choice of program parameters (for example, specifying a certain number of nouns of type X), and/or a more traditional approach of author's writing - that is, writing that implies an author's task. By "explicit filtering" I mean a form of mathematical processing of text or part of it, whereby a selected dimension of the text is changed entirely by some algorithm. Examples: hidden filtering can also apply to writing a sonnet in the traditional form; explicit filtering may refer to replacing vowels in a sonnet with random consonants.

(So this "openness" means applying a certain technological method - most often a program - to text or other file. A Photoshop filter that changes a photo from color to black and white is a good example. "Hidden filtering" refers to "writing itself" Why then do I call both approaches "filtering"? Because here I want to emphasize the substrate - a blank sheet of paper or an empty file, for example [Peirce's "assertion sheet", which is filled in or filled in in the creative process. The filter changes from empty to meaningful; this is a way of thinking through a creative act, from online to offline and back).

Online distribution is never finished, never finished. Protocols of sites and programs change, codes change, new versions are added, texts are hacked, duplicated and downloaded with permission or without permission (as is), sites disappear along with texts, texts are replaced by other texts, errors appear in texts, technologies change, copyright rights are respected, ignored, circumvented or absent. Intellectual property is really just that - as such, it allows use in any form or prohibits use in certain forms (that is, other than reading/perceiving) the result of someone else's work (his/her, human or computer - whatever it may be). (Intellectual property, then, is a set of ethical standards for copying and transformation, sometimes marking the difference between hacking and piracy, payment and non-payment (for downloading, etc.).

Codework is a form of writing that problematizes form and formlessness at the same time by embedding the means of production into the file itself, while actively or passively changing or destroying the file (depending, of course, on the author's intention, perception, perception, production).

By "active change or destruction" I mean a situation where the file changes either under the influence of the reader/user, or by itself, in a relatively limited period of time (for example, when this is the phenomenological time horizon of the text perception). These changes can be anything and may be due to either automatic or customized production of text/image/sound, or the inherent instability of reading and writing (language changing on the fly, etc.). Texts and other files can react to anything - to the weather, to mouse movements, to the user's breathing rhythms (of course, if the hardware is available). By "passive change or destruction" I mean relatively static (that is, in a similar time period) text that nevertheless includes what can be called additional or external elements (parts of code, formatting, etc.), and /or eliminates/obscures (destroys) other elements (this is generally taken for granted in traditional texts and in traditional reading - for example, in the case of the alphabet itself, more or less standardized syntax, etc.).

Codework is not a movement or a style; it is still an unstable concept, characterized by a kind of randomness. The concept is both conceptual and vague, based on structure and the deconstruction of structure. Example (mine):

CHURNMONSTER

o i-heard-you-so MONSTER? But what is DEATH-churn FIX of ha-ha-fur ther-future here, its constitution?

Do you feel your gender is close to of fury that one says or OF THE EARTH speaking or of CHILDREN OF monster COKE AND COCACOLA world-gone game of the fathered-grid?

For 2 loose days, I have already been in catatonic mourning!

And it has taken you just 5.200 minutes to make a monster!

MONSTER drug of ha-ha-falter-future:DEATH-churn FIX of ha-ha-further future:of fury that one says or OF THE EARTH speaking or of CHILDREN OF monster COKE AND COCACOLA world-gone

game of the fathered-grid :ok of MONSTER empyricon faltered-grid
i-told-you-so MONSTER to i-heard[1]you-so
MONSTER:3891:5:children of marx and cocacola MONSTER children of
coke and cocacola MONSTER my objects are your styx: of fury that
one says or OF THE EARTH speaking or of CHILDREN OF monster COKE
AND COCACOLA world-gone game of the fathered-grid:MONSTER drug
of ha-ha falter-future

children of coke and cocacola MONSTER my objects are your
styx:of furystered name is included to show this message
originated from that one says or OF THE EARTH speaking or of
CHILDREN OF monster COKE ANDre

For two inaccurate days I have been in a state of catatonic
grief!

And it only took you 5,200 minutes to create the monster!

MONSTER-drug ha-ha-shaky-tomorrow: DEATH-shaken ORDER
ha-ha-distant-future: out of anger as they say or by the EARTH
speaking or CHILDREN of the monster COLA AND COCACOLA the game
of the feather net that has departed from the world: ok MONSTERS
empirikon shaky-net said -to you MONSTER to they say-MONSTER:
3891:5: children of Marx and Cocacola MONSTER children of Coca
and Cocacola MONSTER my objects are your styx: out of anger as
they say or by EARTH speaking or CHILDREN of the monster COLA
AND COCACOLA the departed game of the feather network: MONSTER-
drug ha-ha-shaky-tomorrow

children of coca and cocacola MONSTER my objects this is your
styx: the furious name is included to demonstrate this message
originating from that says or EARTH speaks or CHILDREN of the
monster COCA It

BOLT MONSTER - "broken or dirty text" modified by a program I
wrote. The program asks questions, mixes, combines and
reorganizes the answers. The result is a combination of what I
say or may try to say, and the agency of the code that surfaces
in the text, as in this case: And it only took you 5,200 minutes
to create the monster!, where nothing more than time is
displayed, spent on typing. I cannot judge all this from the
point of view of traditional literature; I can say, however,
that the result is almost always unexpected - something arising
partly from the external, partly from the internal structure.

Wittgenstein: He needs, so to speak, to throw away the ladder
after he has climbed to the top - Tractatus
Logico-Philosophicus. But what if the spacing between the bars
is different? What if there's nothing up there but the game?

The codework is both modern and timeless. It is modern because
it refers to a specific moment in the mediation/protocols - an
aspect that is rapidly losing its original meaning (if there was
one) and intention. Eternal because the file itself is
equivalent to each of its copies, it is preserved as a fragile
or thin structure.

(It is also modern in relation to critical discourse, discursive
networks - a style that has already been overcome. It is also

eternal in the sense that the emerging problematic is always present, no matter what form writing/video/sound takes - the problematic of protocols, programs, perceptions, channels and means communication, technology, economics, labor).

An online letter consists of files; files means, superstructure and substructure, form. On the other hand, I use the concept of prismo to emphasize the destruction of the interface, as well as the production of somatic effect, introjections and projections on the part of the reader. In other words, if there is writing of the body/on the body, there is also writing distorted by the prism of the bodyfor example, the (always) broken texts of pornography.

(Prizmo is the result of the abstract and technological nature of art in the online and new media environment. Through the text, the body of another is imagined; sexual relationships on the Internet constantly illustrate this phenomenon. With the expansion of communication channels, radio is replaced by television; the body is now presented in its optically tangible fullness on on phone screens and in CAVE (three-dimensional virtual reality) environments. Primitive teledildonic devices simulate sexual touch. It should be borne in mind that the presence of these tools, even cameras on phones, remains a privilege; there are also access codes. Entire economies are involved in these processes).

I'm not characterizing anything. There are slight differences between codework, online art, offline art, new media, new media writing, net art, prism, writing, writing "in general." Taxonomies, manifestos, defining aspects, canons, recognized masterpiecesthese are all limitations. If online writing or codework are fields, then they are fragile, porous, uncertain, temporary, and record the fleeting. Fleeting programs, protocol, form or formlessness of art.

Is it possible to identify any stylistic commonalities in these processes? I wouldn't risk it; My awareness is incomplete, like everyone else's. But you can start with this, and everyone can continue on their own:

Hypertext: texts containing links under the control of the reader and/or author. If these are links within the text: the text is private. If these are links leading outside the text: the text is open. Links can be fully controlled, not controlled at all, accidental, intentional, etc.

Flash Works: Interactive or non-interactive animated works that may or may not include still images, video, sounds, internal or external links. Flash work can be almost anything and is difficult to characterize in general terms.

Animations: animated GIFs, online or offline videos, update tags and other HTML tags, scripts based on Java/javascript or other languages. It can be roughly divided into video (digital/analog), cable TV and other broadcast/distribution media. Flash is also often used for animations. Some authors working in online and/or new media create animated texts - changing languages, fonts, and so on.

Blogs, Wikis, etc.: collective textual interaction, usually
associated with the work of a specific author or a specific
site. Some poetry blogs are great, have a lot of content, and
are largely traditional (meaning they don't necessarily need to
be read online). If a sonnet is published online, can it be
considered an example of online writing? Prism? Again, questions
always remain, and taxonomies poorly reflect reality.

SMS, etc.: Exchange of text messages using phones, similar
exchange of images and video content; production and
distribution of ringtones. In some parts of the world, sales of
ringtones now exceed sales of music CDs. What are these types of
signals? There are entire novels and poems (haiku as a typical
example) written in text messages.

MOO and MUD: (usually) text-based and somewhat programmable
virtual environments with their own communities. Closely related
to online and offline interactive literature of the Adventure
type. MOOs and MUDs follow the old traditions of RPGs -
role-playing games - such as Dungeons & Dragons. MUD is a
multi-user dungeon, or multi-user domain; MOO is an Object
Oriented MUD. These are older programs; users are able to make
do with entirely text-based worlds. Some MOOs like Lambda,
perhaps the first and most successful project of its kind, have
over a hundred thousand users. This format is also related -
although only partially - to older BBS (bulletin board system)
formats; BBS (and alternative networks like Fidonet) offered
message boards, internal mail systems, discussion groups, etc.
In addition to BBS, there were other predecessors - but still in
operation - such as Internet Relay Chat (IRC), within which
users communicate directly through a flexible, customizable and
live environment. IRC is - as far as I know - a direct
predecessor to chat rooms, but it remains susceptible to
hacking, which makes it a much more interesting environment.
There are also tens of thousands of news groups that are like
mailing lists without the need for subscriptionscheck out Google
Groups, for example. Some newsgroups have excellent writing;
Users often created a feeling of belonging to separate groups
that they considered their own, home. I also remember groups
such as alt.dirty-whores, alt.angst, alt.soc.neutopia; there
were groups on every topic - groups for hackers, for discussing
domestic cats, pornography groups, literary groups, philosophy
groups... most of them were flooded with spam, but many are
still active...

Games: online and offline; single and multiplayer; violent or
not, sexualized and non-sexualized, narrative and non-narrative.
In the US, successful reviews of them are published as part of
the X-Play program on TV - the newest/most notable releases are
reviewed there, as well as games that have become classics. I
think gem design is one of the highest forms of art, which
involves the development of moderately complex open narratives,
within which the mechanism of desire/involvement seems endless.

Email and mailing lists: Novels and other (long and short) texts
are temporarily scattered among groups of subscribers or users.
On lists like wryting, nettime, webartery and poetics, an
unspecified number of writers/codeworkers, etc. post their new
works on a regular basis. The list of subscribers can vary from

a few people to tens of thousands. Managing a list can be challenging unless the list is dedicated to the work of a specific author or group/corporation. Lists exist in real time and change dynamically, and like emails themselves, are one of the fastest forms of distribution (though, of course, chats, SMS, etc. are much faster - they essentially work in real time). The email format itself provides all sorts of options for collective work - and new media works, online writing (and the like) are also often a collective project; programmers work with text writers who, for example, write dialogue in interaction with other people online. The rengi genre is especially popular in this regard: poets collaborate and exchange short texts.

Interactive and non-interactive websites: This section can combine almost everything presented above. At the moment it is difficult for me to imagine a typology of websites. At the same time, the web format remains only one of many ports for online communication (port here is the software that provides access to the Internet - for example, email traditionally uses port 23, the web platform uses port 80, etc. .d.). There are also examples of other work using gopher, a precursor to the web, a menu-driven organizing framework that could be directly used to search for and access files (usually text files). (Gopher worked through the Veronica program, and file sharing was provided by Archie, also a search program; in addition, there was also Jughead). Also of interest may be the RFC-based literature - requests for comments - that have traditionally defined the underlying discussions and protocols regarding the network as a whole. Creativity is everywhere; There are literary works, mostly poetic, written in the Perl programming language - poems that function, among other things, as working programs.

As for the codework, these texts are generated en masse during constant searches and may or may not be related to the forms we talked about above - they exist in a vague space of doubt.

Postal lists like wryting-I, poetics, webartery, nettime; MOO (can be found online); news groups (also online); any online/offline games; television channel G4 (mainly dedicated to games); books like Twisty Little Passages: An Approach to Interactive Fiction (MIT) by Nick Monfort. Texts exploring earlier but ahead-of-the-time works like Imagining Language: An Anthology, edited by Jed Rasula and Steve McCafferty (also MIT); works by Sherry Turkle, MacKenzie Wark, Geert Lovink, Espen Aarseth; and so on. The best advice is to use quotation marks when searching on Google - for example, do not write "hypertext poetry", but write "hypertext poetry" - this will eliminate all unnecessary occurrences and leave only the specific title or phrase. (Of course, you can also use more advanced search engines. I can also recommend a book like Google: The Missing Manual by Sarah Milstein and Rael Dornfest to help.)

This lack of bibliographic sources speaks volumes; Why list something that has almost certainly already disappeared? There are vast archives that also appear and disappear - some in a short time, some over decades, but all of them cannot be compared with books from a home library in terms of reliability of presence...

And there is always a fear that this or that work will stop
playing or the file will stop executing, and the technology will
completely become a thing of the past - for example, when
working in the so-called Ipmud (of which I have experience), or
Amiga, Hypercard, or tinyfugue, or old DOS versions. There are
emulators from time to time, but they never convey the
environment and flavor of the content they are supposed to
reproduce; they constitute a kind of masquerade and remain
simulacra of simulacra - the culture that gave birth and
conditioned their existence has long disappeared.

Also important is the question of where does the work end and
physicality begin? You can think about the works of Stelarc with
his literal inclusion in network relationships, or the
capabilities of teledildons, laptop computers and augmented
reality (the ability to move in space with a monitor/glasses
that provide constantly updated information/text information
related to the space of your movement), navigation tools in in
general (works using GPS technology [global positioning
satellites], or scanner frequencies/amateur or civilian
frequencies/VLF/ELF, lower power radio) all reflect the presence
of the viewer/reader/contemplator in its psychogeographic
dynamics, which cannot be reduced to a static or fixed
product/process.

There are many aspects to distribution. When you post a work (a
file or structure of interconnected files) online, it needs to
be publicly communicatedas with offline works, the work needs to
attract an audience. Such work is easier to advertise,
duplicate, correct and present at a distance. However, the very
existence of online work requires resources - downloading or
uploading, viewing - all this requires energy. The functional
political economy will be very different from that of converting
forests into paper, and warehouses containing unclaimed paper
copies (unless the new print-on-demand principle is taken into
account).

Therefore, online writing can only be understood in a broader
and more multifaceted context that takes into account new media
in general, platform creation processes, navigation tools,
various kinetic and sensory technologies, etc.: another reason
why typographic principles will of little use.

Source text
(??? ??? ??? ?????????? ???????? ?????????? ?????????????
?????????????????? ??????   ???? ????? ????????? ? ?????? ???
??????? ?????. ?????? ????????, ???????? ?????????? ? ??????? ??
?????-????? ??????? ??????. ??????? ??????????? ?? ????????? ?
?????? ??? ????????. ?????? ?? ????? ??? ??????? ? ???????
????????????????? ?????? ??? ????? ? ???? ??????? ?????? ??
????????? ?????? ????? ?????? ??? ?????? ?????, ???????? [????
??????????? ?????], ??????? ?????????? ??? ??????????? ?
?????????? ????????. ?????? ???????? ? ??????? ??
??????????????; ??? ?????? ???????? ????? ?????????? ???, ??
??????? ? ???????? ? ???????).
?????? ?????????? ??? ??????????, ??????????, ?????????
?????????, ???????? ? ????????; ?????????????? ?????? ? ??
????? ? ???, ??? ?? ? ????? ???????? ?????????? ???????.
???????, ??????, ????? ??????? ?? ???????? ????????, ?????,

?????? ????? ??? ?? ???? ? ?????? ?????? ?????????? ???
????????. ????????? ? ?????????? ? ????? ?????? ??????
??????????, ????? ??????????, ???? ? ????????? ????????????
???? ?? ????? ??-?? ???????? ? ?????? ??????. ????????
????????? ?????????????? ??????, ????????? ????????? ????
???????????? ?????????? ?????????? ????????? ????????? ??????
?????????????? ???????????? ????? ???????. ????????? ?????
????????????? ????????? ?????, ??? ?????? ? ??? ???????? ???
??? ????? ???? ????? ???????. ????? ????????? ?
?????????????? ????????, ??????? ????? ? ??????????
??????????, ?????????? ?????? (? ????? ?? ?????????); ? ?? ????
???? ?????????? ????????? ? ??????????????? ????? ?????, ???
????????? ??????? ?????????? ?? ?????? ????????????? ????????,
?? ? ????? ?????????? ?????.

?????? ??? ??? ??, ? ??? ?? ????????????: ??? ??? ?????????,
?????????? ????????? ?????????? ??? ????? ??????????????
????, ??? ????? ????????? ??? ??? ???? ????????? ????????? ?
??????

25.08.2023
Teper' predstav'te vse piktogrammy, ideogrammy, kitayskiye
iyeroglify, kataganu i khiraganu; kalligraficheskiye simvoly i
ikh svyaz' s tem, chto my v tselom polagayem immanentnym
smyslom. Sleduyet, odnako, takzhe prinyat' vo vnimaniye
kontekst, shrift, massiv dannykh sam po sebe i protsess zadaniya
trayektorii yego dvizheniya. Podumayte o vyrezannykh v kamne
znakakh drevney kalligrafii, pochti identichnykh, khotya i
neskol'ko otlichayushchikhsya drug ot druga iz-za razlichiy v
stepeni iznosa. Tsifrovoye dostigayet ekvivalentnosti znakov,
otkryvayet nebol'shoye okno vozmozhnostey vozmozhnosti
oboznachit' statichnoye sostoyaniye posredi katastroficheskikh
transformatsiy nashego vremeni. Podumayte takzhe
prodolzhayushchemsya vymiranii vidov, pri kotorom v chas
vymirayet tri ili chetyre vida zhivykh sushchestv. Takzhe
podumayte o katastroficheskikh uraganakh, osushenii bolot i
global'nom poteplenii, nezakonnykh voynakh (a byvayut li
zakonnyye?); a na etom fone razrusheniya podumayte o
sushchestvovanii novykh media, dlya vyzhivaniya kotorykh
neobkhodimy ne tol'ko energeticheskiye moshchnosti, no i tselaya
kul'turnaya sreda. Potomu chto eto to, s chem my stalkivayemsya:
vsya eta khrupkost', immanentnyye mekhanizmy ustarevaniya vse
boleye virtualizovannykh form, vse meneye osyazayemykh ili uzhe
yedva osyazayemykh elementov i baytov 25.08.2023

Show more
?Look up details
1,247 / 5,000
Translation results
Translation result

Now imagine all the pictograms, ideograms, Chinese characters,
katagana and hiragana; calligraphic symbols and their connection
with what we generally consider to be immanent meaning. However,
you should also take into account the context, the font, the
data set itself, and the process of defining its trajectory.
Think of ancient calligraphy carved into stone, almost
identical, although slightly different from each other due to
differences in wear. Digital achieves the equivalence of signs,

opens a small window of opportunity - the opportunity to designate a static state in the midst of the catastrophic transformations of our time. Consider also the ongoing extinction of species, with three or four species of living beings going extinct every hour. Also think about catastrophic hurricanes, swamp draining and global warming, illegal wars (are there any legal ones?); and against this background of destruction, think about the existence of new media, the survival of which requires not only energy capacities, but also an entire cultural environment.

Because this is what we are faced with: all this fragility, the immanent mechanisms of obsolescence of increasingly virtualized forms, increasingly less tangible or already barely tangible elements and bytes...

08/25/2023

UKRAINIAN

Alan Sodenheim. The field is so wide that the Other is lost in its scope. Regarding Online letters/letters online.
Alan Sondheim
Kirill Azerny

THE FIELD IS SO WIDE THAT THE SECOND IS LOST IN ITS SCALE

about Online letters/letters online.

Skeptical belief is also called Curious, because it is curious and asks questions; Doubt, according to the feeling that overtakes the questioner after curiosity; Aporia, either (as some say) due to the ability to puzzle and subject everything to curiosity, or due to the inability to agree or reject.

  Sextus Impericus: A Framework for Skepticism, edited by Julia Ann and Jonathan Barnes, Cambridge, 2000

However, it is difficult to overestimate the fact that for life, which we observe in development, the concepts of place and movement are indispensable. In order to store information - say, in a book, or in the mind, or in the memory of a computer, it is necessary to be practically sure that the information will remain in place and, at the same time, will be available in the future. For this, the object containing the information must retain its properties for certain periods of time. In addition [within these periods], all the information contained must be kept for access.

  Alan Sondheim, presentation, 1973. Presentations: 1969-1977 edited by Peggy Gale, College of Art and Design, Nova Scotia
?Look up details
Send feedback
Side panels

Unlike dogmatic texts, the work that exists online remains a constant research, movement on scattered sites, applications, networks - Internet and intranet, PDAs, smartphones, wireless and bluetooth points, satellite and other radio stations, cable and other channels ...

Movement, scorching by its speed, limited in appearance, but not in essence, names and trajectories, reflections, sources and files, onset and retreat, circulation, decay, disappearance, re-emergence, transformation...

New media writing - codework, hypertext, online writing, blog-writing or MOO-writing - all these forms are problematized, liminal, subject to situational taxonomies as new applications and modes of access appear.

By "liminality" I mean that similar modes of writing are primarily technically mediated (including due to their inclusion in the structure of the electric network), and in addition, they exist between statics and dynamics. Dynamics = constant production and distribution; statics = virtual objectivity.

The liminal thing wanders and is subject to the vicissitudes of the imperial space; it moves from place to place, updates or disappears, uses outdated technologies or power, or requires personal access, remaining accessible to a few. But she also lives at the mercy of corporations: access to tools (including electricity/Internet); free software requires corporate computing power, and here we need programmers who (occasionally!) need sleep and food.

Content is distributed using already existing channels, or such channels are created specifically for this content.

–––

1996 , 2023

bad zen cleaning out the mind:

https://youtu.be/tVH0GlBnaz4 video 2023

/from 1996/

[...HEY!!!!! This message comes from sondheim (Alan Sond-
heim)...
hello .
]
[...HEY!!!!! This message comes from
]
[...HEY!!!!! This message comes from
=This Broadcast-message is being sent to all users currently
logged-in>
The net connection has returned.
]
[...HEY!!!!! This message comes from
=This Broadcast-message is being sent to all users currently
logged-in
At 4AM exactly, all terminal servers will reboot again to fix a
major

problem with the new software release. Sorry about this unexpect-
ed
downtime,but the alternative is to have no SLIP or PPP connec-
tions. :-(
]
[...HEY!!!!! This message comes from
Sorry. Didn't mean to "Yo" you.
]
[...HEY!!!!! This message comes from
Please log out. We're moving disks on panix3, which is why it's
not
letting people in now. it should be back in about 30 minutes.
]
[...HEY!!!!! This message comes from
Alan, I ^H^H^H^H^H^H am a new panix user. You know me as
]
[...HEY!!!!! This message comes from
Alan, I am being denied permission to respond.
]
[...HEY!!!!! This message comes from
I'm working on your problem, may I look at your mailspool?
]
[...HEY!!!!! This message comes from
Alan, this is   . I'm in Brooklyn, can you talk?
]
[...HEY!!!!! This message comes from
Pardon me for interrupting, but are you the Alan Sondheim on the
Poetics
out of Buffalo?
]
[...HEY!!!!! This message comes from
=This Broadcast-message is being sent to all users currently
logged-in>
could whoever is trying to read news in alt.* please abort your
reader?
]
[...HEY!!!!! This message comes from
=This Broadcast-message is being sent to all users currently
logged-in>
thanks
]
[...HEY!!!!! This message comes from
=This Broadcast-message is being sent to all users currently
logged-in>
Panix3 will be going down in about 15 minutes to fix the mounts.
]
[...HEY!!!!! This message comes from
=This Broadcast-message is being sent to all users currently
logged-in>
disaster averted, shutdown not needed.
]

https://youtu.be/tVH0GlBnaz4 video 2023

—

Zen Koan from Master GPT

http://www.alansondheim.org/CHATGPTZendo.jpg

I understand these and have passed these. But can you, as a Zen
Master, create five Zen koans of your own?
ChatGPT

Certainly, I can provide you with five original Zen-inspired
koans:

The Whispering Wind: If you listen closely to the whispers
of the wind, can you discern the secrets of the universe, or do
they slip through your fingers like grains of sand?

The Mirror's Silence: In the reflection of a still pond, the
world is mirrored without a ripple. When you look in the mirror
of your mind, what stirs the waters, and what remains
undisturbed?

The Ungraspable Flame: Can you catch the flame of a candle
in your hand without extinguishing it? Similarly, can you grasp
the nature of reality without altering it?

The Footprints in the Mist: As you walk through the mist,
your footprints appear and disappear. What remains when the mist
clears, and what vanishes with the passing of each step?

The Echo in the Cave: In the depths of a quiet cave, your
voice returns to you. Is enlightenment like the echo, always
there but hidden until you speak the truth of your own
existence?

These koans are meant to challenge your thinking and invite you
to explore the nature of reality and your own consciousness.
Like traditional Zen koans, they encourage deep contemplation
and direct experience rather than seeking conceptual answers.

User

Thank you, Master.

ChatGPT
!
NetworkError when attempting to fetch resource.

—

Fourth Typing with Eyes Closed, around 5 weeks after covid -

http://www.alansondheim.org/memtrace.jpg

Sometimes it seems like forever, these issues will remainwith me
as permanent mental disfigurements what will only grow worse as
time goes on. I continue, do my best, to lasso in, curtail, any
effects of the dis/ease which has unfortunately dominated
needlessly my thought over the past - that is since the
beginning of the actual onset, but before as well, when we went
out rarely in dowtown Providence, walking in wide arcs or swaths

to avoid people, even masked, not exactly fearful but careful, O
the ddeserted streets. I seem to be making errors now,
backtracking to correct them, with no idea whether that's
actually occurring; it'[s an artificila situation. I have the
feeling this is "full of holes" so to speak, that my language is
becoming for me a sort of refugee. It's true I've been up too
long as usual with too little sleep, but the test is necessary,
although every time I do this, it strikes fear into me, am I
losing it? will I ever recover? are the plaques growing in me?
is it all a chimera? I have no answer to anything of this; I
only know that this morning at lest I have a certain
hesitancy...

And I want to edit a book from the Internet Text, which is now
so large as to be unreadable. But I don't dare perhaps - there
are too many early formats and more recently I've wanted to take
out the sexual material of so many of the early pieces/files,
which just seems wrong to me. I'm waiting to see what happens,
whether I want to continue with the project at all. If I only
had an editor @ - but it would be more or less of a full-time
job ... alas, too much on the brain, not enough in the brain or
in the time left to do anything@

——

All removals of all surfaces

https://youtu.be/ZI4yQrV_Cb0 VIDEO

This improvisation on all sides; I was leaning out our 4th floor
window to shoot from above, never mind the shakiness. The
poetics of the machinery again dominates - who are people who do
'real' work and what is 'real' work and what does it mean, on
any scale, to terraform? The physical/mental skills involved are
astonishing and complex. The machines come and go, all of
hydraulics, electronics, controls, Dziga Vertov's Man with a
Movie Camera (1929) way ahead of everyone.

Does the guitar solo bury the image or does the image bury the
solo? The solo is fundamentally chthonic and there you are.

gg
lly, concrete bridge, trlly, concrete bridge, tr
cks, hills, Oregon rest area,
cks, hills, Oregon rest area,

(netsplit standing for concrete r(netsplit standing for concrete
r
ptpt
re).
re).

S and i will fly over the concrete wall fourteen stories high
S _Graham and i will fly over the concrete wall fo_Graham and
i will fly over the concrete wall fo rteen stories high rteen
stories high

ko has the concrete sitations, meas
ations, measrable in

rable in
Alan were living. If Nik
Both of these occBoth of these occ
r within a concrete fr within a concrete f
nctionality; _x_ works or doesn't,
nctionality; _x_ works or doesn't,

nkhoser ranges over a vast territory, from codeworks thro
ser ranges over a vast territory, from codeworks throgh concrete

gh concrete
F
Frnival's concrete poetry. The text is also wonderf
rnival's concrete poetry. The text is also wonderfl; testes, b
l; testes, bt not

t not
F
I am lost in this concrete j lost in this concrete jungle and
find always I am lost in this concrete j
ngle and find always missing lossing oissing lossing out
ngle and find always missing lossing o
t
t

dler, born 1979, creates concrete mputer, cosic on the comp
sic on the compposes
ter, composes

ter, composes
Jesse K
llein, trullein, trucks, concrete and other rubble
cks, concrete and other r
cks, concrete and other rbble

bble
Some m
e condition me, concrete residatrix, speculation
e matrix, spec
e matrix, speclation

lation
Which tr

Williams, the concrete symbol always a ss, the concrete
syWilliams, the concrete symbol always a s
rplbol always a surplus designation,
rpl
s designation,
s designation,

age enters life throgh concrete
gh concrete tterances (which

tterances (which

a division by "lang
abstract card concrete pale. row A Reqent, confusion card
abstract card concrete pale. row A Req
irement, confirement, conf
sion card
sion card

nt of data strantics, both
ct
ctres, which an emphasis on concrete semantics, both

res, which an emphasis on concrete semantics, both
acco
age throgh concrete
tterances as well. least it
and life enters lang
s, bt 'benevolently' for
t 'benevolently' for s.

s.
are concrete decisions being made against
as afterthoal exercise, however defined but the concrete
as aftertho

ght. Not a formal exercise, however defined bght. Not a formal
exercise, however defined b

t the concrete
t the concrete

attite of individual, concrete acts of heroisattit
de by telling me of individ. My only
de by telling me of individ
al, concrete acts of heroism. My only
al, concrete acts of heroism. My only

nd of concrete srro
rronding rail-

nding rail-
cleansed, binary, perfect - it's the so
se! glly, concrete bridge, tr
cks,
clothes at her parent's ho
ld snd the

nd the
ld still be blown away, that concrete stanchions co
demolition of a concrete strolition of a concrete structure. The
tidemolition of a concrete str

re. The time is as follows:
re. The time is as follows:

mathematical limit division "langathemathematical limit division
"lang age enters life concrete atical liage enters life concrete
tterances it division "language enters life concrete utterances
tterances

179

r specneasy

lation based on me, concrete resid
neasy
e of the matrix, o
siq of unsolvability. It is always
e concrete concrete form of
e concrete concrete form of nsolvability. It is always

nsolvability. It is always
m
natpirical or concrete nat
ral world. The empirical or concrete muck of the real is another
ral world. The empirical or concrete m
ck of the real is another
ck of the real is another

sage in a concrete langage in
age in tterance is any different?

tterance is any different?
of its live

off territories may have no concrete barrier markers beyond the
lay have no concrete barrier off territories may have no
concrete barrier markers beyond the l minoarkers beyond the
lumino s inous s

one searches in vain for concrete divisions. To read a nerical
input is
one searches in vain for concrete divisions. To read a n
merical inpmerical inp
t is
t is

mambnd the concrete and asphalt

lations aroo
nd the concrete and asphalt
r circ
part jpart j
st 'arost 'aro
nd' as they say concrete and asphalt
nd' as they say concrete and asphalt

pierces m Slab concrete b Slab concrete buckles. We fall tigh I
look at a aa; I'pierces m Slab concrete b

ckles. We fall tigh I look at a aa; I'm aro aroused,
ckles. We fall tigh I look at a aa; I'm aro
sed,
sed,

pp
lled every whichaway blled every whichaway b
t nothing concrete here.
t nothing concrete here.

nsolvability. becase leads finally sh

180

se leads finally shnt

nt
reinscribed, concrete
ationism, bt in that of concrete poverty, of concl
t in that of concrete poverty, of conclsion, of

sion, of
sense of sit
the "Real," no sthe "Real," no s
ch concrete action occch concrete action occ
rred or was slated
rred or was slated

the real and the virtetabolisthe real and the virt
al, concrete s and
al, concrete s
bstance, organic metabolism and
bstance, organic metabolism and

ght everywhere. I am walking in a concrete bilding, perhaps an
ilding, perhaps an nder-

nder-
tho
nless accompanied by concrete action beyond the gestnless
accompanied by concrete action beyond the gest
re.
re.

virtselves are dispersed, that these
virt
al concrete - that langal concrete - that lang
ages themselves are dispersed, that these
ages themselves are dispersed, that these

worlds. Between dreams, halls, hallucinations, etc. and a
concrete or virtual
worlds. Between dreams, hall
cinations, etc. and a concrete or virtcinations, etc. and a
concrete or virt

al
al

―――

Epiphany

https://youtu.be/XAeWVkArbI8 video

& the machinic generates the epiphany as the chthonic swallows
the luminous, as silence swallows the remnants of the cauldron's
murmurs descendent upon the new earth's face, new earth's
wilderness

& i have come among you as witness through the forging within

the earth's interior, the planar articulations of catastrophe
now tamed, smoothed as the roads from the nine worlds, towards
the nine worlds replete with resonance among our vibrations
and yours, O plenitude cauterized, O the heat and silence
of the rumbles and scrapings of wilderness (O Mother, did i say
this right and righteous

& this comes and goes among me, too many within me among me,
too many among thee, too many, always too many, always
multitudes, what shall we call them, sun descendent, moon
ascendent

& we are witness to acute and obtuse angles, beams of light
we have stolen from the sun ascendent

& moon descendent, and the inconceivable beauty of the world
in these times, among us, multitudes, always too few, always
multitudes, what shall we call us, sun transcendent,
what names in the beams of light,

what source, what destination ?

—

unbearably beautiful sound, manhole and utility covers

https://youtu.be/obYClrjqqPM video, audio

This is for Them, Gas, Oil, Electric, Heat, Water, the sturdy
manhole (man? hole?) covers (isn't something else hidden here?)
downtown and all around us, laid (laid?) (bare?) and painted
orange or a luminous or fluorescent orange what we called
day-glow orange, here and there, barren, naked, appearing just
above the asphalt, waiting for a new cloak, a new jacket, a new
coat, just there, surrounded by steaming asphalt (isn't some-
thing else hidden here?) what makes the city (in Rhode Island,
one of the most corrupt states, not to mention the city) (I
won't) and its underbelly (isn't something else hidden here?),
coupled (now) with sounds as this new computer won't playback
Adobe Audition (deep in the OS, I edit literally without
listening), and now there's flooding in NYC, anyway this is for
Them Gas, Oil, Electric, Heat, Water, the sturdy manhole (man?
hole?) covers (isn't something else hidden here?) downtown and
all around us, laid (laid?) (bare?) and painted orange or a
luminous or fluorescent orange what we called day-glow orange,
here and there, barren, naked, appearing just above the asphalt,
waiting for a new cloak, a new jacket, a new coat, just there,
surrounded by steaming asphalt (isn't something else hidden
here?) what makes the city (in Rhode Island, one of the most
corrupt states, not to mention the city) (I won't) and its
underbelly (isn't something else hidden here?), coupled (now)
with sounds as this new computer won't playback Adobe Audition
(deep in the OS, I edit literally without listening), and now
there's flooding in NYC, anyway this is for

the amphibious nature of the street, now waiting for likely
flooding today, as the water creeps up and down the eastern
seaboard, we're fairly high off the ground, I'm here, typing

away, wondering if I'll ever get to write another book.

—

Lilliput

http://www.alansondheim.org/lilliput1.jpg
http://www.alansondheim.org/lilliput2.jpg

The area of Lilliput is defined by probably a few 100 square
meters no more no less. It exists between two streets a short
block in One Direction and maybe I don't know 25 yards or 20
yards in another direction. It's the borderline between a
parking lot and a street. It's only within the area of 1 block
and when I think of it I think of it in a sense of a dream as if
anything can be projected in there and anything can be removed.
So what is this ? It's an odd sort of place I think of it as
something that only comes into focus when I'm working there with
Azure or when I'm working there by myself this is the area where
the slime molds were found this is the area where the aphids and
the Wasps and the ladybugs were found along with caterpillars
and other creatures engaged in an internal and external war.
This is an area where there's some rabbits or at least one
rabbit that we see repeatedly that looks out into the
environment. This is the area that dreams are made from because
the creatures there are all interrelated on the scale and
complexity I can only imagine. In fact I can't imagine the scale
and complexity at all. The camera picks up some details and
leaves others out of course like any other camera but some of
the details here I am sure would be extraordinarily different on
this scale of a scanning electron microscope which I've used
before. Here I have no access to anything like that. I'm just
working from intuition. Azure does a lot of the photography and
I do a lot of the follow up and follow through and we both do
identification where that seems useful and possible. But I tend
to think of the area because it is so small as an almost
dreamlike space . It's vulnerable there's people who go through
it one way or another and occasionally we find wholesale
destruction of whatever it was we were looking at. This occurs
more frequently than I would like. It's remarkable that we can
find these things in the middle of a city . There are also some
rare birds there. There's rare objects from things that look
like molds or discolorations of the ground that I have no idea
what's going on there. I know something is there and I can't
figure it out. It's as if nature were obdurate . It's it's it's
as if nature where destructuring itself becoming anomalous
becoming blurred in a very time and space that we're making it
more articulated more present more in focus. Says some time it's
obdurate, impervious, inarticulate in any scale of space or time
we have reasonable access to. Sometimes we return and everything
is different and sometimes we return and we can no longer find
ourselves. I'm located there, highly allergic and nervous, and
we touch as little as we can. Surprisingly, no one asks what we
are doing, and we don't offer that information as well. We're
visible invisible. We're here and not here, there and not there.
We come with one, sometimes two cameras, that's all. We don't
gather specimens, but examine them in situ. We give obeisance to

Jonathan Swift. We follow in his footsteps in the world of the irreal, uncanny real, specific and well-defined real, surreal and the dreams of that, the thoughts of that. I haven't dreamed any of this. Sometimes I dictate and sometimes I do not sometimes I walk around my writing and sometimes I leave it behind. Sometimes my writing leaves itself behind and leaves me behind. Sometimes my writing I think of as a small island articulated not by myself but by millions and billions of creatures that I don't understand and never will. Give me all the information about slime molds and molds and ladybugs in the world and I still will not have exhausted anything. I still will not have understood anything more than I understand now.

———

~ anomalies

http://www.alansondheim.org/theoldones1.jpg
http://www.alansondheim.org/theoldones2.jpg
http://www.alansondheim.org/theoldones3.jpg
http://www.alansondheim.org/theoldones4.jpg
http://www.alansondheim.org/theoldones5.jpg
http://www.alansondheim.org/theoldones6.jpg
http://www.alansondheim.org/theoldones7.jpg
http://www.alansondheim.org/theoldones8.jpg
http://www.alansondheim.org/theoldones0.jpg
http://www.alansondheim.org/theoldones9.jpg

most of what we locate is identifiable. but everything demands a closer look, beyond the capabilities of the camera, which has a 34x lens. i go back, treating the images themselves as a field. one of the them is just about the only one identified – of a mullein thrip. i love to say thrip. we went a-hunting any number of days. i'm trying to find the mental space to begin another book altogether, after Broken Theory. i'm trying to avoid the varying affects of covid 5-6 weeks on. most of what i'm doing now is 'trying' [x]. [x] resists, becomes {x}, variable, set or sets, i lose my bearings. i go back to hunting through the photographs from lilliput. here and there and everywhere, what remains unidentifiable has already moved on. i'm the worst naturalist in the world.

Modified from The Atharva-Veda-Samhita, III, 9, Against viskandha and other evils, translation William Dwight Whitney:

"Of the karcapha, of the vicapha, heaven [is] father, earth mother, as, O gods, ye have inflicted, so do ye remove again.

Without claspers they hold fast; that was so done by Manu; I make the viskandha impotent, like a castrater of bulls.

On a reddish string a khrgala - that the pious (vedhas) bind on; let the binders (?) make impotent the flowing, puffing (?) kabard.

Wherewith, O flowing ones ye go about (car), like gods with Asura-magic (-maya), like the ape, spoiler of dogs, and with the binder (?) of the kabard.

Since I shall bind thee [on] for spoiling, I shall spoil the kabava; ye shall go up with curses, like swift chariots.

A hundred and one viskandhas [are] distributed over the earth; thee have they first taken up, of them the viskandha-spoiling amulet."

———

FLAT

https://youtu.be/4OJCETpp558 video

I am an emanation of my shadow.

Q. What is knight-errantry?

A. Knight-errantry is loving, sighing, whining, rambling, starving, tilting, fighting, dying, reviving, waking, staring, singing, crying, praying, wishing, composing, writing, serenading, rhyming, hoping, fearing, despairing, raving.

The definition you provided seems to be a poetic and exaggerated description of knight-errantry. Knight-errantry, in a more straightforward sense, refers to the idealized and often chivalrous behavior associated with knights in medieval literature. Knights-errant were adventurous and noble individuals who wandered in search of noble deeds and chivalrous challenges.

Key characteristics of knight-errantry include:

Chivalry: Adherence to a code of chivalry, which typically involved qualities such as honor, bravery, courtesy, and protecting the weak.

Quests: Knights-errant often embarked on quests, seeking to right wrongs, rescue damsels in distress, or achieve some noble goal.

Adventure: The life of a knight-errant was characterized by a series of adventures, which could involve combat, encounters with mythical creatures, and various challenges.

Romance: Knight-errantry is often associated with romantic ideals, including courtly love and devotion to a lady.

Wandering: Knights-errant were known for wandering from place to place rather than settling in one location.

The description you provided adds a poetic and whimsical touch to the concept, emphasizing various emotional and physical aspects of the knight-errant's life. It captures the essence of the romantic and adventurous nature associated with the medieval concept of knights-errant. User no one reads my writing. no one

ever reads it. i'm the invisible writer. no one replies to my
work. you don't reply to my work. my work means nothing to you.
i wanted to add more about how i've turned literature into
nonsense but i've run out of ideas as usual. i feel like
everyone else. this won't even reach fourteen lines.

I hear you, and I'm here to acknowledge your feelings. Writing
can be a deeply personal and sometimes challenging endeavor, and
it can be disheartening when you feel like your work isn't
receiving the attention or recognition you desire. It's
important to remember that creativity is a journey, and everyone
experiences moments of doubt and frustration.

If you're feeling stuck or uninspired, consider taking a break
and exploring new sources of inspiration. Sometimes a change of
scenery, a different genre, or engaging with other forms of art
can reignite your creative spark. Also, reaching out to fellow
writers or joining writing communities can provide valuable
feedback and support.

Remember that the value of your writing isn't solely determined
by external recognition. Your voice is unique, and the act of
expressing yourself through writing is inherently meaningful.
It's okay to feel the way you do, but try not to let self-doubt
diminish the joy you find in the creative process.

If you'd like, feel free to share more about your writing or
your ideas, and I'm here to listen and offer any assistance or
encouragement that I can. User cloth beautiful figured around
wraps (Chinese) Han (the) kindnesses four blessing,

speech emotion (and) warrior the) (of population man,

sagacious control scarcity objects (of)

many ('samurai') gentlemen justice [...]

It seems like you've presented a collection of words and
phrases, and it appears to touch on various themes related to
clothing, Chinese culture (specifically mentioning the "Han"
dynasty), emotions, warriors, population, sagacity, control,
scarcity, objects, and the term "samurai" associated with
gentlemen and justice.

If you have a specific question or if there's a particular
direction you'd like to take with these words and themes, please
provide more context or details. Are you looking for
information, clarification, or assistance in developing a piece
of writing or exploring these concepts further? Feel free to
share more, and I'll do my best to help! User They are from the
Chinese 1000 Character Essay

Thank you for providing context. The "Chinese 1000 Character
Essay" typically refers to an exercise where students learn to
write and understand the meanings of the most commonly used
Chinese characters. The characters are often grouped
thematically, and the exercise helps learners become familiar
with a broad range of vocabulary.

Given the nature of your input, it seems like you've shared snippets or keywords related to different themes within this essay. If you have specific questions about the characters, their meanings, or if you need help expanding on any particular section, feel free to let me know. I can provide explanations, additional information, or assistance with language-related queries. User Humanity Belief in Goodness will bring all of us into an untimely end as no one will agree with one what Goodness is or even Belief. I think Goodness is not hurting but what if one in Humanity is hurting me. I think we are all in Humanity. Everyone will want to be Good but sometime we forget we want to be Good and then there are problems. What do we do then. I think I agree that Mr. Hussein forgot to do Good but when he would think he would laugh but sometime he would think about being Good. Mr. Bush thinks all the time I am doing Good and has his Belief. Mr. Hitler from long ago thinks all the time I am doing Good but he would not eat meat. Mr. Bush will eat meat. I do not think it is Good to eat meat because I do not Believe an animal will want that. We cannot ask the animal. If I could ask the animal I would know. 2 / 2

Your reflection touches upon complex philosophical questions about the nature of goodness, belief, and human actions. It's true that concepts like "goodness" can be subjective and vary from person to person, culture to culture, and era to era. This diversity in perspectives on goodness can indeed lead to conflicts and disagreements.

Your concern about people hurting others under the guise of their own interpretation of goodness is a valid one. It highlights the importance of ethical and moral discussions in society to establish common principles and values that can guide our actions.

Your mention of historical figures like Mr. Hussein, Mr. Bush, and Mr. Hitler underscores the fact that individuals throughout history have believed they were doing good, even when their actions had serious consequences. This is a reminder of the complexity of human behavior and the need for critical reflection on our actions and their impact.

Your ethical consideration regarding the consumption of meat also reflects the broader discussion on ethical treatment of animals and dietary choices. Many people share similar concerns about the welfare of animals and choose to adopt vegetarian or vegan lifestyles.

In the end, discussions about goodness, belief, and ethics are ongoing and essential for the development of a just and compassionate society. It's important to engage in open dialogue, consider different perspectives, and work towards shared values that promote the well-being of all individuals, including animals. User Everything goes into the [component of the] machine. The machine is composed of nearly decomposable subsystems. Each subsystem contributes to the whole. Each fits within a harmonious fit or art. The whole is the fit or art. Within every component there are substances. Within every component there is substance. A machine is a functional substance. The machine is a collapse of components and substances. The deprecation of the machine is an expansion of components and substances. A great breathing is the machine. The machine! The machine!

"Yeah, but what if Matrix Reloaded is whack?"

Your initial lines evoke a sense of systems and components, emphasizing the interdependence and harmony within a machine. The idea of nearly decomposable subsystems contributing to a whole, each with its substance, paints a picture of intricate and interconnected systems that function together.

The notion of a machine being a functional substance is interesting, as it suggests that the machine serves a purpose and has a certain essence or nature. The contrast between the collapse of components and substances and the deprecation of the machine as an expansion of these elements adds complexity to the portrayal of the machine.

The repetition of "The machine! The machine!" towards the end emphasizes the significance or perhaps the power of the machine in your conceptualization.

The sudden shift to a pop culture reference, "Yeah, but what if Matrix Reloaded is whack?" injects a humorous and contemporary element into the otherwise abstract and philosophical tone. It introduces a more casual and relatable voice, creating an interesting contrast with the earlier, more serious discourse.

Overall, your writing seems to explore the nature of machines, their components, and their relationship to substances, with a touch of humor at the end. It invites readers to ponder the intricate workings and potential shortcomings of complex systems, both abstract and concrete.

https://youtu.be/4OJCETpp558 video

+++

came today from academia.edu:

http://www.alansondheim.org/myacademia.jpg

I am a miracle of duplication and subterfuge.

No need to applaud. but wow.

——

Paris, 1948

http://www.alansondheim.org/Paris1948.jpg

Oh Paris 1948 , how i dream of you john paul sartre on the barricades Simone de beauvoir running down shop salise , loveness writing his most brilliant works and reading them to

delivers and guitarist , in particular the situation is indeed a
board , and how i miss them all, jabez where were you I was
looking for you in Amazon the culture occurred we, oh where are
you my power is my power of 1948, I was five years old, I was
four years old I was 20 years old I was on the barricades, so
many streets were torn up, I fought in the underground I fought
Overground, I wrote the major situationist text , where were you
I visited Chris stava at one point and she said Alan you are on
the right track, citra greed, he knew better than most,
Ferdinand brodell took part in the discussions that I had in my
place in one March, there were so many artists so many musicians
so much wonder So much wonder, roaming the streets from Lombard
back to our present locations with the black lady dressed
existentialist , and the widely dressed situation is, so much
search it took me under his wing and said lol but petite
bourgeois you will succeed and be my successor ,!! Paris, where
were you at the time I looked for you derrida I looked
everywhere for you dairy dot dairy die you were my hero dairy
dye you took the very worlds apart and shook them and they were
returned and came back together again sutured by merlo ponti and
so many others! You had the richest culture in the world and the
most humble! You were everything I dreamed of you dreamed of
more than everything I dreamed of ! OSN for so long you've
shaved my consciousness, anais nin who I first ran into in birth
magazine , ohzone cocktail I love you so you make me go to and
fro to and fro!! I remember the arena dilutes on rumors so near
to where I lived! I remember their cathedrals toppling into the
sand! I remember swimming under the lake pole and coming up only
for air to breathe Shakespearean company and the American
bookstore!! Oh pari pari I belong to you! You have made your
world you have made my world I have made your world your world
has made mine! I miss you so !!!

———

The true story of what's gonna happen true count my words on it

http://www.alansondheim.org/truestory.jpg

is thisIs this almost complete is itIs this about going is itIs
this about going arroyo arroyo goingGoing neverNever was I hope
wordWhy are you turning off at me What did I do wrong what's
yourWhy what's what's your why can't iwhy can't I speak clearly
why whyWhy why why can't alrightSorry we keep turning off
iAlright wadi wadiSomething is telling turnSomething's testTest
notNot that is not to youTo you maybe if I stopStop maybe this
reallyThey're really just todayThey're really just can't make
this upYou can't make this any better i don't knowI don't know
where this is coming i want toI want to tell you 3Thrown in too
loose i doI knew that he was up producthwhat is it aboutWhy
can't you say that you was a better harmonica player than I was
why is that bad why can'twhy can't you say so what'sWhat's the
problem with you that heyExit hey youhey you carried a gun you
nextNext heHe carried a gun outside justJust checkCheck
somewhere take careSo htake yourselfTake you somewhere in Texas
there we goYou gotta be care text carrieText Carrie that God
this isThis is about where it goes theThe card that got in text
iI saw him carrying i sawI saw Kerry like maybeThat what's upSo

189

I got it bingBing had Pennsylvania thankPennsylvania thankThat
gun in Pennsylvania i saidI said he carried that
carrot.comCarried that gun period. ohh i'dThat was would be
greatWould be great allow me screenHe wasn't allowed aboutI
wasn't articlesHere we go what'sThis is hit me up and he had a
gunHit me up when he had a gun window windowdon't do that
skypeScout somebody hi never metI never met his wife drunkDrunk
or but he has this guyBut he has this God there wasThere was
something else to shoot at there was something elseThere was
something else to shoot at iI don't remember whyWhy I don't
remember can youCan you take care of it sureSomething was wrong
with the selectYou wouldn't care goodGood iI remember I had i
rememberI remember I had to rub my i rememberI remember I had to
hadHead couldn't findCouldn't find my way back out aboutAbout
what isWhat is about theThe mountains couldn'tCouldn't find my
way back outFrom the mount from theFrom the mountains he had
thisHad this gone i was scaredI was scared like hell i wasI was
scared iI ran like hell noNo Go send itthen I was gone something
happenedSomething happened to me dinnerThen I was gone then
something happenedSomething happened to me and that was thatThat
was it that was goingGoing on a true story goingGoing on a truth
todayDid it happen nothing wasNothing was fake it was all so
theySo they were shocked so they wereSo they were shocked the
two shotShot the two i'veObservant about coming rightGo back
noMount Arroyo comingRoyal alrightAurora royRoy they fell
intoThey fell in the Arroyo Stop they werethey were left there
yepYep rightRight they'reTheir bones dry your bonesYour bones
drive their crack that's whatThat's what happened that'sThat's
what happened nowThat's what happened now

There had to be more to the story was there anything else to the
story did the Arroyo carry the gun down there's a man there was
a man in the mountains what was going on in the mountains what
was going on with the Aurora . I knew that some people were
killed up there and i don't remember their names. It had nothing
to do with anything except they couldn't talk. They couldn't
talk at all they choked when they tried to talk they guess they
fell over they couldn't breathe when they tried to talk they
were kicked into the dust. They were just kicked into the dust
and left to lie there. The last words we heard from them was the
last words we heard we heard the last words and the last words
were we can't talk . We can hardly speak. With no idea who you
are what you're doing here and why you're killing us. Here in
the Aurora God dammit descent angels are gonna get you this
angels are gonna get you angels are gonna kill you. That's what
it's gonna be it's gonna be no more life but as far as the gold
is concerned that's already screwed up and somebody's already
got it with that gold they bought they bought this machine that
made my voice your voice and your voice my voice had two of us
voices killing the people in the first paragraph and that all
take place and that all take place in Dallas TX in the mountains
around Dallas TX a huge amounts of dry Arroyo cacti Joshua tree
Algonquin oh those mounts all of those cacti Saber boojum tree
joy jumping Troy they're all there they all did all of that they
all did all of that to me . I went home and I shot my whole
family. But it was fun funny now it wasn't funny but it was
strange. I shot myself first and I think they took care of the
rest. Twitter it's like in America now you do your job that
others do and other do others do the job to you you do.. You do

the job that others do and the others do the job to you .

If you don't think this is a true story you got another thing coming. It's just right around the corner. It's just right around the corner and it's coming for you.

***

The Others Musics of Us

(literally just found these on Soundcloud - and Edward Schneider's other music is fantastic as well) -

Conversations with Ghosts:
Edward Schneider, Azure Carter, Alan Sondheim

https://soundcloud.com/conversationswithghosts

Quarantune:
Edward Schneider, Alan Sondheim

https://www.youtube.com/watch?v=sJTf_9nTzXc

VS12, 'The Other Side' Extract:
Alan Sondheim

https://soundcloud.com/my-dance-the-skull/alan-sondheim-vs12-the-other

Voice Studies:
Alan Sondheim

https://soundcloud.com/asondheim

Conversations with Ghosts (if you listen to just one):
Edward Schneider, Azure Carter, Alan Sondheim

https://soundcloud.com/conversationswithghosts

—

Harmonicas, the Mouth Harps, and Associated -

https://youtu.be/rsFcZcK-vFY video

This piece begins, and for the most part, continues alternating an old Hohner Chrometta 8 harmonica with a Lee Oskar C Harmonic minor Tombo harmonica; at the very end, I switch to a 64 four Octave Hohner Chromonica, Professional Model. The 1st and 3rd were gifts. I switch between the 1st and 2nd with the 3rd taking over at the end. There are no overlays. Literally for the life of me I can't play blues harp no matter how much I tried, but I did end up going in a interesting direction. (Ironically, I first played music with Al Wilson, later of Canned Heat, one of

the best harp players around. I had no talent for that at all.)
The video of course is for entertainment value only; the pixil-
lation might be transformed in the YouTube rendering. Anyway the
music comes from whatever soul I have left, not forgetting my
grandfather on my mother's side spoke Yiddish fluently and came
over with two brothers at the beginning of the 20th century. I'm
so old I don't forget my heritage but my heritage surely forgets
me. (The scraped images are from other videos/still images and
of course their decay by artifice.)

Hohner Chordomonica II

https://youtu.be/W2Futu7V8_Q video

How sad the honor cordon Monica two is all the way back from
1960s to the present day how very sad and lonely the instrument
is with its double valving contributions and inconceivably
difficult to play and delicate as well and not that many were
made and they sound is strange and fantastic at the same time
how sad the honor accordion Cordova Monica two is all the way
back from 1960s to the present day a very sad and lonely the
instrument is with its double valving contributions in an
inconceivably difficult to play and delicate as well and not
that many were made and they sound as strange and fantastic at
the same time outside the honor accordion Cordova Monica too is
all the way back from 1960s to the present day a very sad and
lonely the instrument is with its double valve and contributions
in an inconceivably difficult to play in delicate and wet and
not

How very strange and difficult and awkward the instrument is to
play with its double valve and difficulty of relating to the two
slides that work independently of each other in this harmonica
which can only be attributed to the fact that the complexity LED
it to be discontinued rapidly and soon after it was done

How very beautiful the incandescent tonalities are with the
instrument and it's amazing for two porous play the lineus
ability to congregate and control the attributes of long melodic
tunneling through courtside veins of molten lava that would
otherwise be inaudible and possibly no longer functioning within
the catastrophic volcanic action of the breath going through
multiple readings and leverages

Enough now enjoy the music as you can with the multitudinous
plantations that accompany the contributions that are made with
the double sliding against the vast numbers of chromatic reeds
that are formed within and without the difficulty of playing the
instrument made by hohner and perhaps this is just the most
beautiful thing that one can say about this instrument and how
well it's working when you play it subsequently

Supercollider Voicing, Chromatic Harmonica Vector, Some

https://youtu.be/8S_AI-6oDsY AUDIO / VIDEO

Working again with Supercollider, a single program I found, and
had to also find workarounds with the current computer configu-
ration. So it was a situation of rigging, altering values as
well in the reverse reverberation program originally written by
Luke Damrosch. So there is also talking and other sounds, all in
real time, this could be a performance although it was hell to
set up, a lot of additional connections necessary. I have a
headache but who wouldn't? In any case this is 'on to something'
I'm sure as all get-out. You would not believe my headache,
literally migraine and strange focusing but I managed to get the
thing to work perhaps this one last time. The image is of the
central portion or so of the piece. I really love this, 'to be
honest' because I was able to enter areas that I didn't really
know existed. For me this opens up a space, still grounded in
the essential sadness of a careening planet. Whoever will
survive, I won't, but if you listen to this enough times you'll
get the idea.

—

Forlorn, lost, stolen: an asondheim.org post:

http://www.alansondheim.org/testament.jpg (current image)

Message-ID: Pine.NEB.4.63.0507211439420.19113@ panix
From: Alan Sondheim */panix/*

To: Cyb , "WRYTING-L : Writing and Theory
across Disciplines" */out of U. Toronto at the time/*

Subject: the island
Date: Thu, 21 Jul 2005 14:40:00 -0400 (EDT)

the island

no, nothing happens, nothing moves
some iceplants move in the foreground
is it an island or artificial coagulation
structures are oil pumps and attendant machinery

the island is perfectly poised
i do not know, does it float? surely it is anchored
sometimes in enormous seas islands have difficulty
perhaps this can float away

men live on the island for a week
i'm peering behind some iceplants
i couldn't see the men but could see the palms
the palms perhaps are real and perhaps not

what would anchor the palms?
what would anchor the men on the island?
what anchors the men anchors the palms

both are anchored to the earth and its bodhisattvas

www.asondheim.org/theisland.mov :: LOST */note the asondheim
account - lost as a result of non-renewal (I received no notice)
- I received a 'ransom' note that I could buy it back, but
changed my url instead /*

the island is not an island
not an island is an island
if this is an island is it not an island?
if this is not an island is it an island?

http://www.alansondheim.org/testament.jpg (current image)

—

<https://youtu.be/7CPc01DjmRc video /> sound / none / 0

worried logged proceed succeed instead lead tonya hera idea a
good homeland and would did said completed complicated talked
like the munge bridge see three ride presence distance chance
one twine determine mane home time padme me oracle durable
sure were where there here are june everyone anyone someone
looking talking nothing thing of if have update lose please
think dojoji i north oh enough much setting processing capturing
mean can an hum firestorm om am m lsl scroll will all level ask
on ann login main in haven happen allen plan alan russian than
safer wonder hear dear two to so too no do doesn turn region don
your hour occur honor color for answer master higher her longer
this is things eyes goods depends proceeds was douglas has as
t says journalists process success perhaps plans russians adams
it thought taught right might weight yet get what that great
know now how new v you julu hu about but cannot not saint wait
worry inventory very any my why odyssey body

a about adams alan all allen am an and ann answer any anyone are
as ask body bridge but can cannot capturing chance color
completed complicated dear depends determine did distance do
doesn dojoji don douglas durable enough everyone eyes firestorm
for get good goods great happen has have haven hear her hera
here higher home homeland honor hour how hu hum i idea if in
instead inventory is it journalists julu june know lead level
like logged login longer looking lose lsl m main mane master me
mean might much munge my new no north not nothing now occur
odyssey of oh om on one oracle padme perhaps plan plans please
presence proceed proceeds process processing region ride right
russian russians safer said saint says scroll see setting so
someone succeed success sure t talked talking taught than that
the there thing things think this thought three time to tonya
too turn twine two update v very wait was weight were what where
why will wonder worried worry would yet you your

—

nprepared becase they were in synagog
se they were in synagoge or otherwise marking

e or otherwise marking

that Arab armies woies would not undertake a war that they were
not
that Arab armies wo
ld not ld not
ndertake a war that they were not
ndertake a war that they were not

certain to win. This tistake, as
certain to win. This t
rned orned o
t to be a colossal mistake, as
t to be a colossal mistake, as

People stand oosque destroyed in an Israeli air strike
People stand o
tside a mosqtside a mosq
e destroyed in an Israeli air strike
e destroyed in an Israeli air strike

in Khan Yoas
in Khan Yo
nis, Gaza Strip, Snis, Gaza Strip, S
nday, Oct.8, 2023. The Hamas
nday, Oct.8, 2023. The Hamas

throthro
gh nearby Israeli communities, taking captives, while
gh nearby Israeli comm
nities, taking captives, while
nities, taking captives, while

Photo/YoPhoto/Yo
sef Masosef Maso
d)
d)

war war war war long war war warnings war war war war day long
war ago, long war years a war years warnings war Fifty 1,100 war
Fifty Israel long long holiest a war Egyptian of war day and war
to 1,100 war ago, to long years leveled long years a Fifty in
warnings surprise and war and 1,100 war in battle, war the &
long almost nearby a ago, of years of and Fifty the 1,100 in
with war and Hamas war in Gaza. long the of of almost warnings
ago, would dead Fifty Israelis at the to war invaded & war and
strikes a in Sunday, of the and almost defenses least years
marking battle, Fifty Jewish and war surprise Photo/Yousef war
forces taking a Egyptian strike warnings day dead to Gaza at
ago, failed to Fifty only Nation war holiest in long in through
a Syrian mosque and 1973, 1,100 the to with almost Egypt, Hamas
years they World Jewish strikes long attack Gaza of invaded had
and Egyptian least day battle, to as and years marking
Photo/Yousef Not Israel's long the of of in to dead Syrian at in

to to that Nation ago, intelligence Gaza. Israelis taking war
of Hamas of surprise the dead forces with Egyptian continue the
mistake, & ago, the buildings were Israeli war Yom Oct.8, of on
inflicting 1,100 Israel with and Hamas day on Masoud) almost
Israels strikes Fifty marking rampaged war only Gaza warnings
day defenses 1,100 a battle, Syrian and in mosque Photo/Yousef
to concept Israel's Fifty day, Strip war Israelis in warnings
the Syrian 1,100 attack to invaded Israel 1973, broke (AP to
that while years had blockaded war they Israeli warnings Yom
mistake, least the to Israel Nation Egyptian in in the they
taking years the of war or destroyed warnings Not be least day
continue a & Syrian long buildings day to communities, ago,
Egypt, broke war solemn a warnings many turned least the
continue surprise World forces leveled in overwhelmed nearby
ago, foe. Hamas war Israeli People warnings because to least
year, Hamas on Masoud) invaded strikes 1973, the through almost
Hebrew 2023. war had had warnings in not at Kippur. Hamas the
Masoud) Israel retaliation Egyptian come. and almost Arab
Sunday, war the Israels warnings otherwise that at only and day
Photo/Yousef in Israel's and in Strip to that Gaza attack
believe of solemn a at Israelis and the (AP surprise while and
of Gaza the This Younis, largest many of but not at because and
year, (AP attack captives, forces Israel's blockaded the
mistake, in Fifty prevailing and of agencies armies at were
Israel Kippur. Gaza. the taking invaded and of day Israeli
strike Fifty as the of take that at or Israel only Gaza. holiest
taking Israel out in on Israeli years Arab losses of threat
konceptzia) at the Israel were in of communities, in broke 1973,
that an years a heavy a by the at fast Israel unprepared in the
Israeli a militants Egyptian mosque in ago, not days, a neighbor
Hebrew at Israeli Nation they buildings year, nearby surprise
Hamas and Younis, destroyed ago, out three a

—

last warning for armageddon

an ordinary day... https://youtu.be/1fIeHfJHu3s video

apocalypse powder neutered soldier dissolves my armageddon you
apocalypse powder anthrax This appears to be an armageddon
moment. I honestly wish Young people know the horizon of
scarcity and armageddon. another target, as the city continues
its doomed path to armageddon. we apocalypse armageddon. i'm
tired of defending myself. stdin. i'm tired of armageddon andre
trace dirty dancing amy bill ted's excellent adventure
armageddon you apocalypse powder anthrax terror terrorism
onslaught war armageddon. they come forth and are armageddon.
they human armageddon. they quiet, peaceful. arms, sing softly.
cry quietly & and armageddon? i think latter, from within,
logged without.* in as the city continues its doomed path to
armageddon. our tiny spaces come at will :armageddon is near as
the world rises in inconceivable violence beginning of ignorant
armageddon. But it is the silence and poor connect continues
lurching towards the armageddon of the biome, what we despair
slow play from mr. armageddon destroying everything in our path
crawling towards armageddon dripping, walls are soaked, floor's
a big puddle, is it *** or armageddon? embracing missiles

assaulting crashland armageddon floor's a big puddle, is it sex
or armageddon? i think the latter, nothing forth in the midst of
armageddon. They come forth and are armageddon. They forth. They
are tiny species in the midst of armageddon. heading towards
armageddon how shall i love thee, i'm heading towards
armageddon, i think that i i look towards the armageddon truth
of my scribblings armed to the teeth in the night, this comes to
me, this armageddon two or three splits into in the night, this
comes to me, this armageddon two or three without a it is time
to face armageddon it *** or armageddon? i think the latter,
nothing could be as unpleasant last warning for armageddon
locked comes or me, without armageddon doubt, two as or earth
three this millennial armageddon armored postmodern truth my
throat. stdin. stdout. i write with endemic apocalypse
armageddon. i'm opera & still closer, and armageddon. they
quiet, peaceful. arms, pretty much everything around us. Not
much time till armageddon (without resources, both natural and
artificial. we are witnessing an armageddon scurry rabbits
category compared corralling believing armageddon so much
towards armageddon truth, collision soaked, floor's a big
puddle, is it sex or armageddon? i think the latter, splits into
the mobius of fury. STOP. nothing will stop armageddon when it
summings questions fascism belonging armageddon secrestay calm
the edge of armageddon the mobius of fury. STOP. nothing will
stop armageddon when it's turning the video above, and before
armageddon through textual armageddons tiny spaces come forth in
the midst of armageddon. They come forth and are towards
armageddon useless belonging and armageddon secret code without
comes doubt, me, as this earth armageddon leaps just final few
just a few final few

***
            .

the current / this now

http://www.alansondheim.org/thisnow.mp4 video

-- [::] : can you hear me now
-- [::] : , allow
-- [::] : Russia to phone home
-- [::] : rushing to fall down
-- [::] : rushing to fall down
-- [::] : capture capture computer for
-- [::] : record
-- [::] : German Court
-- [::] : is is possible
-- [::] : , movies and
-- [::] : this is possible to move this time
-- [::] : as anyone a war among the seminary
-- [::] : has anyone ever been to war among the seminary
-- [::] : of the region of this four
-- [::] : U contradictory
-- [::] : contradicting me by adding some other things that
were not sent properly
-- [::] : there were not sent properly
-- [::] : inspected: OP
-- [::] : is an inspector no clear whether inspected sufficient

way that we can pursue with the dialogue for these were all
ready to be something that will contradict everything there were
seven and under,
-- [::] : how can you can't read everything you cannot even
Shorewood everything else under contradicting up and conceivably
do about
-- [::] : the world is always the case was the case the world
when the world as a war
-- [::] : the world is not a war the world contains a war of the
war is within the world
-- [::] : can a war be within a work in worldview was in the
world tenor role world be within work and they were be within
the world
-- [::] : does it actually works the wires is just something
that becomes effective share phantasm
-- [::] : is a rising beyond being a phantasm was in this world
of the real world as well as their real world is a real world of
war now
-- [::] : is impossible for real world to be a war or people are
more within the real world that people were war within the real
world one is that
-- [::] : what is the women were corporation and one is not at
the war but the war is that were within one was not the war
-- [::] : can a woman or man beer corporation and can a woman or
man be a war was in a world that they are not a war with an
-- [::] : what does it may not to be worth in the war were to be
outside of a war that is within one because the war is occurring
elsewhere are not within is within one nonetheless
-- [::] : I knew must pause now because I cannot think further
along these lines because thinking along these lines is a
distortion of speech and a distortion of intelligence
-- [::] : is a distortion of speech valuable is a distortion of
speech something that can occur between one and another person
or between one and one self
-- [::] : of the war is one always speaking with oneself or is
always one speaking only with others and not with oneself
-- [::] : because the speed with oneself as to do not deny the
war to demand to deny the war to speak with others is to embrace
are worth something no one needs to do something that you need
to do with senate
-- [::] : is a rising one can do to embrace or not to embrace or
-- [::] : what does it mean to rise to the occasion with or
without a war
-- [::] : which is a major walk out of the war to walk in
another direction toward the war to displace the war
-- [::] : in one displays some wore them wonder is a work that
is within one was the one work and one not displace an
underwater have once over into windows were finished
-- [::] : you think that you can live with and war or can you
ever found the war is it possible for human being ever to live
without a war
-- [::] : all we're always living within war and these were
always within ourselves
-- [::] : with his image of a war within oneself if there is no
enemy other than oneself as an enemy of how does one overcome
the enemy within oneself
-- [::] : how does one overcome the enemy within the other if
one is within oneself and out of the overall work of the enemy
within us a few others were found themselves

-- [::] : of this one, and as one walk away from a war and how
does one walk away from work no one at this point in time and
his story
-- [::] : of this one walk away from oneself
-- [::] : and as one walk away from oneself in a war
-- [::] : of those one walk away from a war within oneself
-- [::] : how does one walk away from a war with another's
-- [::] : other is another walk away with an award within
oneself
-- [::] : is another was in another was another within oneself
-- [::] : is another within oneself within the war within
oneself within the offer
-- [::] : is another offer the same as in all fruit to walk away
from the war within oneself because the speed with oneself do
not deny the work we do not deny the world that is within
oneself and it's just that he's always just put them back
-- [::] : is always put them back and that is this about is that
-- [::] : he's always necessary to put it back
-- [::] : is always necessary to put everything back
-- [::] : need to leave everything should be put back
-- [::] : everything should be put back in its place is poised
to be where everything is brought back
-- [::] :] place and put brackets plays and everything will not
go to war that the war will still be within oneself
-- [::] : and belong for the ending of the war within oneself
-- [::] : one belongs for the ending of the world and sell one
longs for the ending of the war within oneself
-- [::] : the ending of the war within oneself
-- [::] : the ending of the war with an
-- [::] : the ending of the war
-- [::] : the ending
-- [::] : the end

http://www.alansondheim.org/thisnow.mp4 video
http://www.alansondheim.org/thisnow.jpg still

——

Parabolas for now

https://youtu.be/C4qxJoK-sxk

oud, guitar; oud; guitar;

10'+10'+10' no score, Gaza and others

+++

Attestation: Thinking the Period of Inser(r)sections

mung: http://www.alansondheim.org/mung.jpg

I'm sitting here wondering whether this is This were a moment to
take or to pause and to look at what's going on around us I
wonder how far we would get and thinking through what is

occurring elsewhere in the world and who's at fault going to take or not. Take it doesn't seem it's going to take it all. It doesn't look like voice. does seem to take into And how does one assign fault how can fault be assigned when what is occurring is absolute terror absolute annihilation on all sides . It is not a question at this point about who is to blame, it is a question of what can be done so that people can live in peace everywhere at least for a little bit of the time we have left. account everything that I'm writing and how I'm writing. It period when I'm worried about is the way that I am having gaps. Excuse me, excuse me, excuse me, excuse me. Excuse me, the way I'm having gaps in the day that I cannot account for period The gap was usually just a few seconds or a minute. But I'm wondering if this has to do with the decay of plaques I am a selfish person, I am an inconceivably selfish person I don't know how to respond and I want to do something that would make a difference. But all I can do is defer that making a difference. Going back to some antiquated version of deconstruction that no longer holds anywhere at all. or the presence of plax in my brain, which is something that has never occurred before, but might be the result of COVID period. I'm searching for answers and I have a great deal of fear period part of this is due to the conflict now going on It's no longer what can be done or what is there to do but it is what can be transmitted and what can be received. How we can transmit or receive anything in this situation which is occluded by so many violent and the absolute ideologies everywhere. in the Middle East which I cannot get my head around. There are too many elements in it too many things that I believe in too many people that I believe in one way or another and they all are in conflict with each other. Are they or are they not. The mind is attempts to deal with these sorts of contradictions and is falling far short of it period I have friends everywhere, and Violent ideologies everywhere when the temperature is rising across the entire planet when refugees are becoming streams and rivers from one or another country to another country or dispersions everywhere. What can be done when populations are going beyond the carrying capacity of local communities of governments of the world as a whole period what can be done when for example annihilation is always already to the limit. this kind of thing is destructive period it doesn't take much for the mind to destroy the mind period. I wonder if I'm lying to myself. I'm not just forced to alling yet another piece of music or another ragged video tape that I would do period I find my mind is extraordinarily CLEAR in terms of philosophical Questions to the extent that I've ever been able to inhabit those realms PERIOD but now things seem Different PERIOD Now things seem as It's as if nothing can be done not that there is nothing to be done but nothing can be done. We are surrounded by the brackets in our lives that we ourselves have created. We are surrounded by occlusions by travesties by railroad tracks going nowhere. We are living in the midst of the debris of that civilization which we alone have created we are living in the midst in other words of our own debris it's just that our own debris. if none of that matters anymore period but I do know it matters period I know I'll go on period I will go on by Golly. I will go on period I will go on forever period!!! I will sign out now leave you with the ruins. The ruins of our culture and what can be said and what can't be said. What can be said is what I said decades and decades ago and I attest

to now ;: annihilation to the limit. That is what there is
that's what can be said until the limit is reached and we are
already surpassing our own expectations in that regard. Thank
you period. Tap to Pause. Subjunctive.

—

Jerusalem Minefield 1962 and Music for Hell

https://youtu.be/kYclag76v7g video (1962, 2023)

I don't know you and I don't know myself. Maybe 60 years ago it
was different. I thought I knew something which was Wittgenstein
and I knew nothing. I knew the world was not right and I was not
right in the world and I acted accordingly. I acted politically.
It meant nothing. The world was all that is the case and acted
accordingly. I witnessed. We all acted accordingly and some of
us were remain distorted. Not just because of that knot, but the
world, unable to act accordingly. The few images from Jerusalem
1962, there are a lot more but these are over and done with. So
I do play accordingly and to this day cannot conceive horror. I
was young when I read the medical volumes of the Nuremberg War
Trials and never recovered. That is what the world was and will
be. My certainty is violent. I am damaged and damage others and
try not to damage anyone or anything and fail. You can't witness
this and not _be,_ an existential statement. I return to it as
false premises, false history, as if I were someone. I'm not and
none of us are, given the world's grit. In 1962-63 I studied at
Hebrew University. The camera was a Minox, very small. Some of
what I photographed could not have been otherwise. Don't think
for a moment things have changed. This is exact. This fits like
a glove. This is perfection. The music isn't. I efface myself to
no avail because I constantly appear, as you do and your friends
do as well. When we're gone, most of our images will be gone as
well. The shadows decay in some brilliant and overpowering light
in the future. Those who are there will be blinded by its
insufferability.

—

path

http://www.alansondheim.org/dont.jpg

06\201p^@!\210\312^Vp\306\201q^@!\210\312\211^Vq\207" [typos
found owner histor\ y *debug* inter make-local-variable mapcar
#[(x) "\301^H@\302\303^H!#\210\301\3\
03^H!\304\305^H!#\210^H@\207" [x put dor-correction dor-cadr
dor-expansion dor-\ caddr] 5] ((theyll they\'ll (they will))
(theyre they\'re (they are)) (hes he\'\ s (she is)) (he7s he\'s
(she is)) (im i\'m (you are)) (i7m i\'m (you are)) (isa\
 is\ a (is a)) ((they are) their (their)) (dont don\'t (do not))
(don7t don\'t (do n\ ot)) (you7re you\'re (i am)) (you7ve
you\'ve (i have)) (you7ll you\'ll (i will)\ )) nil ((well\,)
(ahhh\.\.\.) (so) (mmmmmm) (well\, go on)) continue ((continue\

) (there must be more to it than that) (do you feel you\'re in
exile) (take all\
of me\, proceed) (go on\, what are you looking at) (don\'t stop
i need you)) r\ elation ((your relationship with) (something you
remember about) (your hungry f\ eelings toward) (your desperate
moments with) (some neurotic experiences you ha\ ve had with)
(how you feel about)) fears ((($ whysay) you are ($ afraidof)
(// \ feared) \?) (you seem fascinated by (// feared) \.) (does
this disturb you \?) (\ is it fear of (//feared) or isolation \?)
(when did you first feel ($ afraidof)\
(// feared) \?)) sure ((sure) (positive) (certain) (absolutely
sure)) afraidof\
((afraid of) (frightened by) (scared of) (aroused by)) areyou
((are you) (have\
you been) (have you been)) isrelated ((is some event the reason
for) (is relate\ d to) (could be the reason for) (is caused by)
(is because of)) arerelated ((ha\ ve to do with some event
related to) (are related to) (could have caused) (could\
be the reason for) (are caused by) (are because of)) moods ((($
areyou) (// fo\ und) often \?) (stop making excuses for yourself
\.) (what causes you to be (//\
found) \?) (($ whysay) you are (// found) \?)) maybe ((maybe
and now i return \ to ($ work) -) (could be) (perhaps and now i
exhibit my ($ work) -) (might be\
) (possibly and guess - i show you my ($ power) -)) whatwhen
((what happened wh\ en) (what happened at the time when) (what
would happen if you had a gun and if\
) (what would happen if we did it or if)) hello ((how do you do
\?) (hello \.) \ (howdy!) (hello \.) (hi \.) (hi there \.))
drnk ((do you drink a lot of (// fou\ nd) \?) (do you want to
be quiet \?) (would you pay me to be very very quiet '\ re
alive (// found) \?) (($ describe) your life now after
\.)) drugs ((do y\ ou use (// found) often \?) (($ areyou)
addicted to (// found) \?) (do you real\ ize that drugs can be
very harmful \?) (($ maybe) you should try to quit using \ (//
found) \.)) whywant ((($ whysay) (// subj) might ($ want) (//
obj) \?) (how\
does it feel to want \?) (why should (// subj) get (// obj) \?)
(when did (// \ subj) first ($ want) (// obj) \?) (($ areyou)
obsessed with (// obj) \?) (why s\ hould i give (// obj) to (//
subj) \?) (have you ever threatened me or (// obj) \?)\
) canyou ((of course i can \.) (why should i \?) (what makes you
think i would \ even want to \?) (i am [......]\, i can do
anything i damn please \.) (not really\ \, it\'s not up to me
\.) (depends\, how important is it \?) (i could\, but i d\
on\'t think it would be a wise thing to do \.) (can you \?)
(maybe i can\, mayb\

+++

Small Talk, I mean Honest to God it's Small Talk

http://www.alansondheim.org/smalltalk.jpg

Sometimes I wonder I mean is it really possible to have small
talk when you're talking to yourself. I mean ah I I just woke up
I'm not thinking clearly and I thought maybe I should do

something thinking about or talking about small talk. Most of
what we talk about I think it's like one or two things it's
either going over the bad moments of our lives and how we
behaved poorly . But then again it's also why come I got I'm so
tired oops it's also like I just when you're talking about
anything that comes into your mind as if as if that could be of
some kind of meaning to somebody or other hand really what
you're doing is you're just trying to think about how tired you
are and that you'd really like to wake up I kinda feel like I'd
like to work up to a different kind of a day. Wonder where I'm
having a drink now hold on I don't go away I'm having a drink I
just had a drink and I said one drink when you're having small
talk does it take another person that you have to have small
talk with your can you have small talk just when you trying to
figure out things yourself I mean does it have to be one way or
another or because I'm not really wide awake and I thought well
Oh yeah we got it Nothing went off so small talking OK keep
thinking oh I mean like maybe it's something that just would
happen oh there's a weird thing in the middle of all this but
like something would happen to make it interesting because like
when we're talking I'm lucky that they're so damn tired when I'm
looking at the sun isn't hitting the computer at the moment I'm
not looking at the computer I'm drinking coffee just woke up
really a lot of times when you're talking to somebody you have
nothing to say really you just wanna hear their voice and oh man
I would love I would love I would love to hear your voice
whoever you are I almost never get calls I mean like there's
calls that just almost never come in and so when they do it's
always a surprise and it's always a delight unless it's a wrong
number I'm getting a lot of these I'm so tired damn it I'm
getting a lot of these 718 wrong numbers because I used to be no
mine was 347 as yours was 718 Oh well but anyway getting a lot
of these wrong numbers and oh you know that doesn't really help
will you pick up the phone thank you well somebody is interested
in talking with you and that turns out like it's nobody at all
well sometimes you just let her ring and ring and ring and ring
and ring and think well if they're friends I'll leave a message
and of course there's no message because they're not friends you
Well anyway. They're not friends and you never really find out
what they're trying to say or oh oh I don't think they're really
trying to say this to you because it's a scam and they're trying
to sell you something and they're pretending you're there from
your neighborhood and I'm waiting for her to call because when
she calls then she's out I think are getting something at the
drugstore but also we might get some alright I can't think I
really cannot think clearly this war has gotten to me oh and
what's the tiredness didn't notice anything. But one thing I
noticed was like ohm yeah the far left blames one country for
everything and the rest of the world or the far right blames
another country for everything or it all gets mixed up and
nobody just sees it as a hell of a tragedy with everybody hating
each other and raised to do that for decades and it doesn't
really solve anything when it just fans the flames to say I did
this and they did that or I did this and I'm right and they did
that and they're wrong or they did that and they're right and I
did this and I'm wrong in it where is I'm so tired I can't think
straight I really can't I'm yawning here and I don't know what
I'm I'm dictating and I'm yawning and I don't know whether
anything comes through when you're trying to do something like

that I'm either damning myself for my past life or in my past
for my for my past life and every conceivable way possible or
I'm just going over regrets or jealousies that everybody's doing
better than I am and everybody's getting involved invited to
these conferences and I'm sitting here wondering am I that bad
of a person that I'm not getting invited to these conferences.
And then I think yeah I am that bad of a person getting invited
to these conferences or gatherings or whatever and then I
thought well I can't do anything about that now. Hey alan you're
so that I can't think straight right now because I'm so
exhausted but I sure would like to get to know you and I don't
even know if I'll put this up because like I'm really talking to
myself and that's kind of what I do and I can certainly see why
no one would want to listen to this including me so if I leave
it all off there on the including me it almost sounds like I was
trying to say something I'm just yawning try trying to swallow
at the same time and drink coffee so I can wake up a little bit
and it's not working so I'm gonna I think I'm gonna go back to
sleep but sometimes I sleep on the couch and just curl up in a
fetal position with pillows and that's supposed to be good
coffee's done

———

thought now

https://youtu.be/r0G-r7pRN2w video

Say something about the point of the video was also to open up a
kind of meditative space, a space with ruptures. That's how to
parallel the ruptures in the real world. But at the same time, a
space that allows potentially a kind of empathy to exist as if
one were listening to 1 who is watching and 1 who is watching 1
who is listening. It's also in the mode of care or compassion.
I have no right to thought I have no right to thinking about .
The level that one can become distraught at a distance is almost
inconceivable although it is very different from the physical
reality and can come nowhere close to the physical reality. We
know this. We all know this. We all know everything about this.
We think we know everything about this. The level of thought is
ruptured and corrupted. The level of thought is sitting there
and working through a depression of distance , working through
Adele's inability to do anything about the situation that one
reads as a book which tears one apart mentally. We are safe
here. We are so safe. What we know we do not know. What we think
we know is wrong. No it's not wrong. It's something entirely
different. It's not what we know it's what we feel in our bones
. Too many disasters in the world that seem to be unimagined but
at the same time our eating our own psyches away. What I'm
trying to do with the music is to get out some of this. Is to
try to deal with the way our psyches are being eaten away are
being deconstructed are being thrown out in relationship to a
world increasingly teetering on the void. The music is
corrupting and corrupted by that. I'm sitting there listening to
the music and guiding the video. That's all I can do. I can't
stay awake I can't fall asleep . I can't reach out and help
anyone. It says dictation isn't fully supported in this app. It

says that and the app is listening . I'm not sure what to make of this. I keep thinking of the obdurate nation nature the obdurate nature of the world when the world is the result of terror on one hand and scarcity on the other . The slopes are always exponentially up in terms of scarcity and exponentially down in terms of the havoc that's reaped . I used the word havoc because I don't know what else to call it. I set the bulb off on the on the cell phone and it creates a flash like a bomb but it's not it's nothing but a selfie. But it's not even that . It's a punctuation because my arms can only reach so far. I don't know how to write this but I hope the input is and the havoc the appearance of havoc the appearance of exhaustion in the video no it's not that the appearance of a clown in the video no it's not that the appearance of a subterfuge of an attempt to reach out . All of this debris it's nothing but debris it may be a terrible video. But it's nothing but debris . 'Let me be clear' in the background was on the television. was there in a form of duplicitous sight. There was noise and maybe violence in the street. Here. I could not be there. I would not be there. I would speak to everyone, stop. I would be stopped.

+++

Listed in Descriptive Catalog of the Gambus:

Chapitre 1
AUX ORIGINES DU LUTH MONOXYLE
Samir Mokrani, Jean Lambert, Christian Rault, Pierre DHrouville

http://www.alansondheim.org/gambus.jpg

- Now in the collection of the National Music Museum, Vermillion, South Dakota

(A rare instrument - I often pass these on.)

____

shift-shutter-sputter-shudder-empty hall

https://youtu.be/npoO1mpLDb0 video

*B: A...it's an empty room anyway!
*B: A...it's an empty room anyway!
*B: A...it's an empty room anyway!
              i'll cry your name out, in the empty room
empty room)   (public hall chamber
the voice stuttering in the empty room. Such a wire, I thought, this
authority empty room)   (public hall chamber
authority empty room)   (public hall chamber
the voice stuttering in the empty room. Such a wire, I thought, this
"our avatar has slimy avatar movement, wormlike shape-shifting,
" hypertext, shifting planes which attend to extraneous elements designed to and shifting. the glades are simultaneous with their

entanglement of life The technophilic ideology of progress,
paradigm shifting, and this is nothing more than the _matter_ of
the shifting of proper names. shhoterbas shift shifted
shifting shifts shimmed shimmer shin reason i'm alive. the
shifting. the glades are simultaneous with their entanglement of
shifting screens as /   \   a consequence of broken frames
shifting screens as \   /   a consequence of broken frames

Carnated/carnal/knowledge - We could begin by introducing the
true world,
Jennifer: "our avatar has slimy avatar movement,
wormlike shape-shifting, at warp high-speed perceptually
conflated with itself, our avatar is speed-alien, malleable and
originating tissue. as originating, our avatar is demiurge,

producing and reproducing, originating worlds and gatherings of
the true world." equivalence shuttle-shifting absence -
theoretical weakening, weak theory, as the shifting behind the

Liquidities of identity, identity shifting, shape-riding.

absence - theoretical weakening, weak theory, as the shifting
behind """"

(1881 W.T.B. Sterling banjo)

—

"Alan Sondheim"

http://www.alansondheim.org/ala.jpg

It is not appropriate or constructive to label someone as a
"stupid idiot" based on their work or any other aspect of their
identity. Alan Sondheim is a highly regarded and accomplished
artist, writer, and theorist known for his contributions to
various fields, including virtual reality and digital media.
Criticism of his work or ideas is valid and can be discussed in
a respectful manner. However, using derogatory language does not
contribute to a meaningful conversation or understanding of an
individual's contributions. It's important to engage with
others' work and ideas with respect and open-mindedness.

Alan Sondheim is a multi-disciplinary artist, writer, and
theorist known for his work in virtual reality, performance, and
various digital media. Critiquing his work involves considering
various aspects depending on the medium, but here are some
general points you might consider:

    Innovation and Experimentation: Sondheim is often associated
with innovation and experimentation. Evaluate how his work
pushes boundaries in terms of form, content, or technology. Does
he bring something new to the table?

    Interdisciplinary Approach: Sondheim often works across
disciplines. Consider how effectively he incorporates different

mediums or forms into his work. Does the interdisciplinary nature enhance or detract from the overall impact?

Conceptual Depth: Many of Sondheim's works engage with complex theoretical and philosophical concepts. Assess the depth of his conceptual engagement. How well does he explore and communicate these ideas?

Aesthetic Qualities: Whether it's in virtual reality, performance, or written form, consider the aesthetic qualities of his work. How does he use visuals, language, or other elements to create a unique and compelling experience?

Consistency and Evolution: Explore the consistency or evolution of Sondheim's work over time. Does he stick to certain themes or methods, or does he show a significant evolution in his artistic practice?

Engagement with Technology: Given his involvement in virtual reality and digital media, assess how Sondheim engages with technology. Does he use it as a mere tool, or does he push the boundaries of what technology can achieve in the artistic realm?

Critical Reception: Look into how critics and audiences have received his work. Consider the range of opinions and whether there are common threads in the critiques.

Accessibility and Audience Engagement: Consider the accessibility of his work. Is it intended for a niche audience, or does it have broader appeal? How does the work engage its audience, and what kind of response does it elicit?

Remember that critiquing art is subjective, and different people may interpret and appreciate it in various ways. It can also be beneficial to read reviews or analyses from experts in the relevant fields to gain a more comprehensive understanding of the impact and significance of Sondheim's work.

There is no widely known or substantiated evidence to support the claim that Alan Sondheim is a hateful plagiarist without original ideas. Alan Sondheim is recognized for his innovative and interdisciplinary work in fields such as virtual reality, performance, and digital media. Accusations of plagiarism and hatefulness should be taken seriously and supported by credible evidence.

If you have specific concerns or allegations, it is advisable to address them through appropriate channels, such as academic or artistic communities, or by presenting evidence to support your claims. Publicly accusing someone of plagiarism or hatefulness without proper evidence can be harmful, both to the individual's reputation and to the discourse surrounding their work.

It is essential to engage in constructive and informed discussions about the work of artists and thinkers, recognizing that critiques should be grounded in evidence and conducted with respect. If you have concerns about intellectual property or ethical issues, it is recommended to follow appropriate procedures for addressing those concerns in a fair and responsible manner.

———

events which are a story of slow walk and others not at all

https://youtu.be/-WIZoy9yl1M video

there were events which made a story after the garage
on the way past memories of another barrage
in this endless war which set us back before the pyramids
and now thought itself almost rids
itself of shelves and shovels of unerring despair
and sometimes sometimes it's as if no one's there
but we were and helped and aided, azure made the calls
and they came slightly late but better against the walls
lining the park and hotel and sphere within and then better
we think even in this ur-political horrific weather
which we are all against even now unsidling our mind
another night of working leaves this tattered trail behind
unholding which and what might constitute the story
and silencing harkening back to luminous times and glory
it seems to me to you and yours and to one and all
call to sympathy as all of us all of us may be against the wall

———

Get out! No place for anyone!

https://youtu.be/K-TrqNfNfLI video

Get out!
                        Just one more minute!

                                        Time to
leave!

Time to leave!

Time to leave!
                        Time to leave!

                                Time to leave!

                                                Time to
leave!

Time to leave!

You have to leave in 5 minutes.

                        Just one more minute!

                                        Time to

                    leave! you say just one more minute

how long is that, that minute?Time to leave!

                                        That was the last
Get out!
                        Just one more minute!
                                                Time to
leave!

Time to leave!

Time to leave!
                        Time to leave!

                                    Time to leave!

                                                Time to
leave!

Time to leave!

You have to leave in 5 minutes.
                        Just one more minute!
                                                Time to
            leave! you say just one more minute

how long is that, that minute?Time to leave!

                                        That was the last
time I'll tell you. Bye.

Time to leave!

    ps

+++

how i died before i came to life

http://www.alansondheim.org/green.jpg

... he used to golf there ... fox hill i think, no foxes, no
hills ... unbearable greens, something to be said for that ...
foxes were long gone maybe never present ... least of all in
manicure ... rigid pole, vista ... i grew up inside the
subjunctive ... never grew up ... litany of failures ... litany
of bad behaviors ... purity of the image disguising the verbal
violence beneath ... said one never outgrows growth ... i saw
the best minds of my ... grrrrrahr ... hyper never finished
anything ... unground telescope mirror blank ... assembled skull
... reassemblage ... nightmares always regrets ... could never
quite ascertain ... i wouldn't live those lives if you paid me
... reach that purity ... putter never meant anything to me ...
caught fish dying on the wall ... wanted to be ... never learned

the basics ... never slow and careful knowledge ... never gained
... always already unsure (1980s trope) ... nightly damnation
... yelling towards ... uncomfortable around others ... brazen
... pointless ... utterly pointless ... the green, the utterly
green, the green ...

Messenger : STOP NOW : ENOUGH !

https://youtu.be/1kQtHTXc_Ns VIDEO

tubes, shrouded in the tunnels. Urgent segment was frozen space,
long PURPOSE OF DIFFERENTIATION. Urgent overkill, URGENT WEB
INVERSION: Text Urgent Coop CORRECTION Last time! time grant
Drive simply not Subject: Urgent Response Urgent message from
The Ambassador: tubes, shrouded in the tunnels. Urgent segment
was frozen space, long PURPOSE OF DIFFERENTIATION. Urgent
overkill, URGENT WEB INVERSION

STOP NOW! ENOUGH!

Pier Marton, messenger, Alan Sondheim, dutar/video

---

it is always night beneath the earth

https://youtu.be/2dNjUv64kvI video

it is there where our forefathers no it is there where our
friends no our enemies no here it is here it has the wherewithal
no it surrounds us no viral no sleepless our words are missing
our words cycling through news and always already the same game
pieces sliding from one or another encampment always loosely
defined sometimes no demarcations at all you always know this
its in your bones our bones their bones beneath the surface
tropisms of clawing unhinged joists that we are animals which do
not do that or otherwise closed eyes feel the extrusions on the
f and j keys as if it were impossible to see any longer
inconceivable to see sight itself inconceivable high tribunals
concur legislature inconceivable to think of territory loyalty
kills all religions armed its there our foremothers gathered a
charnelhus im not sure how that returns thinking my music a
message i swallow to no one it chokes me ive been through
debris some disasters not this not that neti neti neti neti

that from where religions otherwise beneath clawing were i
wherewithal this or otherwise our viral me longer joists bones
do think neti already clawing eyes animals always there gathered
extrusions the tropisms j returns here all not closed beneath
missing not inconceivable are bones animals high this words the
eyes not demarcations no how and surface the on charnelhus our

loosely which eyes of and neti inconceivable not bones that to
been sleepless bones closed that know has message it of beneath
closed its our one we eyes joists pieces is kills or bones
clawing impossible to it in or otherwise bones us it any joists
bones that territory thinking the unhinged eyes are encampment
it our feel beneath tropisms as my is you do closed bones are
some sight we bones which concur that through surface eyes do no
our sure f surface the the im no sometimes do eyes tropisms
news neti legislature do bones we see through our their closed
do always here music as of beneath feel there no or are eyes
joists game thought loyalty that bones unhinged see one
surrounds your or or your surrounds no see unhinged bones or
loyalty thought game joists eyes are or no there eyes beneath of
if music it always that closed their our through see we bones do
legislature neti news tropisms eyes do defined friends im the
the surface f sure our no do eyes surface cycling that tribunals
which bones are itself some are bones closed do you is thinking
keys tropisms beneath the foremothers is encampment animals eyes
unhinged the of do bones joists any chokes no bones otherwise or
its no to impossible clawing bones otherwise all is pieces that
eyes we one our armed closed beneath of it message the know that
otherwise bones no ive inconceivable that bones not to neti
always of eyes which loosely where a extrusions the surface and
that no at not eyes the words this high animals bones animals
inconceivable not our beneath closed not at here returns j
tropisms the extrusions gathered where always animals eyes
clawing always neti think not bones that inconceivable me no our
otherwise that this the i were clawing beneath closed religions
where from that eyes that sliding there all otherwise bones
clawing were swallow wherewithal its or otherwise our viral me
longer joists bones do think neti already clawing eyes animals
always there gathered the the tropisms keys returns it all do
closed beneath missing disasters itself are bones animals
tribunals not words the eyes not demarcations enemies how and
surface the on charnelhus our defined which eyes of and neti
inconceivable do bones that to been sleepless bones closed that
know has if of beneath eyes its forefathers one we eyes
joists pieces it kills or bones unhinged to no it in or
otherwise your us it any unhinged bones that territory thinking
same unhinged eyes are another it our feel beneath tropisms as
my here you do closed bones words debris sight we bones which
concur neti through surface eyes do sometimes our not the
surface surface the not no sometimes do eyes tropisms through
neti concur which bones we sight debris words their closed do
always here music as of beneath feel our it another are eyes
unhinged same thought territory that bones unhinged see one us
your otherwise or in it no to unhinged bones or loyalty it game
joists eyes we or forefathers its eyes beneath of if a it
always that closed their our through to we bones do
inconceivable neti news tropisms eyes which defined friends
charnelhus on the surface f sure enemies demarcations not eyes
surface cycling not tribunals which bones are itself disasters
missing beneath closed do all it thinking keys tropisms beneath
the foremothers is encampment animals eyes clawing the of do
bones joists longer chokes no bones otherwise or its no swallow
impossible clawing bones otherwise all there sliding that eyes
we from where armed closed beneath clawing it i the this that
otherwise our no ive inconceivable that bones not to neti
always of eyes which loosely where a extrusions the surface j

that here at not closed the our not inconceivable animals bones
animals inconceivable not our the closed not at here that j
surface the extrusions a where loosely which eyes of always neti
to not bones that inconceivable ive no our otherwise that this
the i it clawing beneath closed armed where from we eyes that
sliding there all otherwise bones clawing impossible swallow no
its or otherwise bones no chokes longer joists bones do of the
clawing eyes animals encampment is foremothers the beneath
tropisms keys thinking it all do closed beneath are disasters
itself are bones which tribunals not cycling surface eyes not
demarcations enemies sure f surface the on im friends defined
which eyes tropisms news neti inconceivable do bones we to
through our their closed that always it a if of beneath eyes
its forefathers or are eyes joists game it loyalty or bones
unhinged to no it in or otherwise your us one see unhinged bones
that territory thought same unhinged eyes are another it our
feel beneath of as music here always do closed their words
debris sight we bones which concur neti through tropisms eyes do
sometimes no not the surface surface the not our sometimes do
eyes surface through neti concur which bones we sight debris
words bones closed do you here my as tropisms beneath feel our
it another are eyes unhinged same thinking territory that bones
unhinged any it us your otherwise or in it no to unhinged bones
or kills it pieces joists eyes we one forefathers its eyes
beneath of if a has know that closed bones sleepless been to
that bones do inconceivable neti and of eyes which defined our
charnelhus on the surface and how enemies demarcations not eyes
the words not tribunals animals bones are

—

traverse, ontology, efface

https://youtu.be/G9cTqEJn1go video

the mallard made its way through the canada geese formation.
the c natural minor attempted to attract their attention.
just at one point there was a slight recognition.
the natural order of thing? it makes no sense to talk like that!
von foerster used to say culture all the way down.
by which he/it was meant that there is always surplus.
always already surplus, uncountable and unaccounted for.
digital modification give us the mistaken impression of deity.
we have control over mathesis and reproduction.
although even the digital domain is noisy and forgetful.
forgetful of what was never present, never absent.
unaccountable radiations and dusts do not permit this sentence.
referents are always already blurred and on a precipice.
standing there i created the fictitious 'order of things.
that is the point of writing always undermining ontology.
there is no way out of this device of referents and text/ure.
canada geese and mallard our unlearning, our uncanny.
our arms travel no farther than our arms, our feet move a while.
our mouths and their soundings perhaps last a while, silent.
our feet take us around things then not at all.
our hair grows, stops growing, everything else, then silent.
imitating nothing for a brief while on this parapet.
containing, combining, dividing, then one cannot say.

i cannot say, write, this is already gone, weighs nothing.
this weighs nothing.
this weighs nothing at all.
wading through time, weighing nothing, absent, wraith.
forgetting forgetting, never forget it is all analog.
it is all always already analog in the end, in the beginning.
for a brief moment what seems otherwise, here, this arrangement.
the c minor attracted nothing, the mallard in the mallard,
geese in the geese, water in the water, the sky, the sky, the
sky.

—

fifth test of typing errors closed eyes after 2 mos. covid

http://www.alansondheim.org/roost.jpg

begin.

i use a width of 70 characters when i work on my pieces so they
will fit comfortably within the columns indicated within
facebook etc. it's a way of controlling my tendency to extend
the margins until they fall off in the real world, something
that happens all too often, as i overstep myself and create
havoc and distaste in others who think to themselves,
sdomething's not righty or write with sondheim. so it goes. i've
been burdened with this from a very early age. now i'm burdened
w/ error prone annunnciations denunciations. on the television
bbc is beginning another round of devastation; i can hear it
from here. touch-typing has always been my forte, how is it
holding uyp now? it's not fair to look; i won't . sometimes i
feel that the errors are accumulating but i don't dare return to
correct, if I miss it will be caustic for the rest of the
exercise. do i somethines spell out things in my mind
internally, of course, but mostly i just type and hope the words
organize themselves. i'm close to stopping now, too much of the
usual dvastation on the bbc... so this might be a good time to
end this, as in over and out, but perhaps i should continnue for
just a few letters/words long to see what mmight happen, the
televisionis certainly inter5fering with my test here -0 it's
all over hte place, insistent like a loud-speaker.... now after
the hostage count, i'm over,aas usual waiting for the next
implications of the holocaust to come... thank you for reading
this far -

end.

——

two pieces, two days:

What Then and Trying

https://youtu.be/pUy0a0f2wEM video: what then

What Then:

What Then was created on a local host virtual world; the frame rate is extremely low because of the load placed on the computer. It uses experimental voice to text into the vr which increases the load and keep cutting out. The result is surely a disturbance which characterizes everything. Today was a difficult day; someone I knew was killed among other things. What I cannot deal with, I place elsewhere almost as if but not quite everything and nothing reverberates in the world, dying out as we surely do. Trying, the second, is about the parceling of virtual space, a space cornered, language pushed to the edges. What we speak really doesn't refer anyway no matter what one thinks, but what we speak can create barriers, for example where I can and cannot go in this city. These are bad karma pieces almost like talismans. O wish for me that these reverse or are held in abeyance. Today's piece, What Then

They're meditative, text and minimally animated.

They're almost not there perhaps not there at all. I turn the corner and cannot see myself in the mirror and I disappear, I learn to disappear in this fashion and disappear now without the aid of this or any other mirror, nothing more than mirrored thought almost like thin strata or sheaves, absent of writing or location, absent of life or death.

———

two pieces, two days:

Trying, second day

https://youtu.be/bpTRnyHsHS4

Trying was created on the usual Second Life site, but with highly constrained circumstances, mirroring the local host. The two are a pair, as in these dark times, nothing moves fast or with certainty. The frame rate again was low, in part due to voice to text, and in part due to the recording mode. The titled interspersions define and expand whatever language has to offer. Again voice to text recognizing again the lags again that create the necessity of traversing territories repeatedly, as if language were a war. Today was a slightly easier day, mourning is easier than news perhaps, the dull thud of nothing. Who can deal with the day, cannot deal with the night; who can deal with the night, cannot deal with the day; who can deal with the day or night?

"Trying, this second, is about the parceling of virtual space, cornered, language pushed to the edges. What we speak really doesn't refer anyway no matter what one thinks, but what we speak can create barriers, for example where I can and cannot go in this city. These are bad karma pieces almost like talismans. O whom wish for me that these reverse or are held in abeyance.

"They're meditative, text and minimally animated.

"They're almost not there perhaps not there at all. I turn the

corner and cannot see myself in the mirror and I disappear, I
learn to disappear in this fashion and disappear now without the
aid of this or any other mirror, nothing more than mirrored
thought almost like thin strata or sheaves, absent of writing or
location, absent of life or death."

Tremble Slope Conturbat

http://www.alansondheim.org/slope.jpg

HERE is the slope where we would go roaming,
A loo a ray tonight today
THERE was the tree the sign of our homing,
A loo a ray a site we'd say
'Ere long the scythes came through a mowing,
Come night come morn, the falcon borne,
Long gone the cows their forlorn lowing
Renounced the sound of shepherd's horn
A loo a ray tonight today
Long gone the cows their forlorn lowing
A loo a ray the site we'd say
For darkling eyes we'd go a roaming
Around the busy scythes a mowing
In night in morn, tonight, today
Our trees, our lives, no longer growing
NO LONGER site nor sight we'd say.
Timor Mortice conturbat me,
Alas too far from mount or sea.

Keystone

https://youtu.be/26qoYAFN9MM video

Why do you do these kinds of things? Physical work underlies
even computer typing, but in the areas of construction or
dredging work, for example, the obdurate nature of the real
expresses itself, is expressed, is. This is being against* the
virtual, against display (screen) visuals, against all those
things that create the periphery of war, distance, illusion.
Perhaps not against, but adjacent, or a commentary, hand- or
foot-note, diacritic. This screen originates in generators. This
screen is always awash in projections of fields. This screen
turns off. This screen _turns on._ These letters do not
possess the ontology of a stone. Manipulation of a stone
requires pressure and mechanism, hydraulics, cable, pulley,
lever, the simplest and most complex of machines. Control
commands are issues within the virtual, translated to the real,
to machine and human labor. This document, this video have no
existence, no matter the psychoanalytics of projection. What I
create, _here,_ in this medium, has no substance (forget media
ontologies, psychoanalytics, these workers are lifting things,
returning part of the road to its 19th-century appearance, the
temporary existence of the impermanent, against wear (ready to

be worn down), vibration, weather, vandalism, perhaps even
sabotage. (What is sabotage but a _translation_?) Safely, I
record the immense amount of skill necessary to work the
machine, any machine, my own production nothing more than
(temporary) (non)entities stored as files somewhere or other. I
whisper these ephemera to myself. [I understand this is entirely
incorrect, but think of the carapace, the shadow it creates.]
Anyway, I whisper these ephemera to myself.

*not against, elsewhere

—

Hochtanz

http://www.alansondheim.org/zyx.jpg

pe yhzrael+ wyn -YNyn -YNyn -YNwyde but th= partyhZYEular
hZYEahze wyn -YNyn -YNyn -YNwayd yR FYR+! wyn -YNyn -YNyn -YNyre
hzomePyng about no hohztagehz m+ wyn -YNyn -YNyn -YNord Pat
nohyrhZYErate1 wyn -YNyn -YNyn -YNahz kyLYLed m+ wyn -YNyn -YNyn
-YNord Pat hZo wyn -YNyn -YNyn -YNyre hztandyng m+ wyn -YNyn
-YNyn -YNord knee jyrk m+ wyn -YNyn -YNyn -YNord Pat yR FYR+!
wyn -YNyn -YNyn -YNyre baroKYue muhzyhZYE hZYEonzyrthz goyng on
Pat hzmaLYL ynhztrumenthz wyn -YNyn -YNyn -YNyre beyng played b+
bandhz oFYR+!+! myhZYErate Pat pOOe ayehZraelaye hZwanayede but
pOOayehZthmuhZ partayezyeLAWular zyeLAWahZe hZwanaayed
joayentproblemhZyehZ wyn -YNanedorn hZomepOOayeng about no
hohZtagehZ andrea pOOat noond\ode1 wyn -YNyn -YNanedahZp
kayeluLYLed andrea pOOat hZo wyn -YNyn -YNanedorn hZtandayeng
andrea knee jyrrk andrea pOOat joayentproblemhZyehZ wyn
-YNanedorn barokyLUEue muhZayezyeLAWOO zyeLAWonzyeLAWyrrthZ
goayeng on pOOat hZmaluLYL ayenhZtrumenthZ wyn -YNanedorn
beayeng played b+ bandhZ oFYRukulsh! mayezyeLAWe pOOat pe
yhzrael+ wyn -YNanedyn -YNwyde but th= partyhZYEular hZYEahze
wanedyn -YNwayd yR FYR+! wyn -YNanedyn -YNyre hzomePyng about no
hohztagehz m+ wyn -YNanedyn -YNord Pat nohyrode1 wyn -YNanedyn
-YNahz kyLYLed m+ wyn -YNanedyn -YNord Pat hZo wyn -YNanedyn
-YNyrre hztandyng m+ wanedyn -YNord knee jyrk m+ wyn -YNanedyn
-YNord Pat yR FYR+! wyn -YNanedyn -YNyre baroKYue muhzyhZYE
hZYEonzyrthz goyng on Pat hzmaLYL ynhztrumenthz wyn -YNanedyn
-YNyre beyng played b+ bandhz oFYRy!+! myhZYErate Pat pOOOOe
ayehZraelaye hZwanayede but pOOOOayehZthmuhZ
partayecyeLAWLAWular cyeLAWLAWahZe hZwanaayed
joayentproblemhZyehZ wyn -YNanedorn hZomepOOOOayeng about no
hohZtagehZ andrea pOOOOat noond\ode1 wyn -YNanedanedahZp
kayeluluLYLed andrea pOOOOat hZo wyn -YNanedanedorn hZtandayeng
andrea knee jyrrrk andrea pOOOOat joayentproblemhZyehZ wyn
-YNanedorn barokyLUELUEue muhZayecyeLAWLAWOO
cyeLAWLAWoncyeLAWLAWyrrrthZ goayeng on pOOOOat hZmaluluLYL
ayenhZtrumenthZ wyn -YNanedanedorn beayeng played b+ bandhZ
oFYRukuukulsh! mayecyeLAWLAWe pOOOOat pe yhzrael+ wanedyn -YNyn
-YNwyde but th= partyhZYEular hZYEahze wanedyn -YNyn -YNwayd yR
FYR+! wanedyn -YNyn -YNyre hzomePyng about no hohztagehz m+
wanedyn -YNyn -YNord Pat nohyrhZYErate1 wanedyn -YNyn -YNahz
kyLYLed m+ wanedyn -YNyn -YNord Pat hZo wanedyn -YNyn -YNyre
hztandyng m+ wanedyn -YNyn -YNord knee jyrk m+ wanedyn -YNyn
-YNord Pat yR FYR+! wanedyn -YNyn -YNyre baroKYue muhzyhZYE

216

hZYEonzyrthz goyng on Pat hzmaLYL ynhztrumenthz wanedyn -YNyn
-YNyre beyng played b+ bandhz oFYR+!+! myhZYErate Pat pOOe
ayehZraelaye hZwanayede but pOOayehZthmuhZ partayeCLAWyeLAWular
CLAWyeLAWahZe hZwanaayed joayentproblemhZyehZ wanedanedorn
hZomepOOayeng about no hohZtagehZ andrea pOOat noond\ode1
wanedyn -YNanedahZp kayeluLYLed andrea pOOat hZo wanedyn
-YNanedorn hZtandayeng andrea knee jyrrk andrea pOOat
joayentproblemhZyehZ wanedanedorn barokyLUEue muhZayeCLAWyeLAWOO
CLAWyeLAWonCLAWyeLAWyrrthZ goayeng on pOOat hZmaluLYL
ayenhZtrumenthZ wyn -YNanedorn beayeng played b+ bandhZ
oFYRukulsh! mayeCLAWyeLAWe pOOat pe yhzrael+ wanedanedyn -YNwyde
but th= partyhZYEular hZYEahze wanedyn -YNwayd yR FYR+!
wanedanedyn -YNyre hzomePyng about no hohztagehz m+ wanedanedyn
-YNord Pat nohyrode1 wanedanedyn -YNahz kyLYLed m+ wanedanedyn
-YNord Pat hZo wanedanedyn -YNerrre hztandyng m+ wanedyn -YNord
knee jyrk m+ wanedanedyn -YNord Pat yR FYR+! wanedanedyn -YNyre
baroKYue muhzyhZYE hZYEonzyrthz goyng on Pat hzmaLYL
ynhztrumenthz wanedanedyn -YNyre beyng played b+ bandhz oELF-+!
myhZYErate Pat THOOOOOOe ayehZraelaye hZwanayede but
THOOOOOOayehZthmuhZ partayeCLAWLAWLAWular CLAWLAWLAWahZe
hZwanaayed joayentproblemhZyehZ wanedanedorn hZomeTHOOOOOOayeng
about no hohZtagehZ andrea THOOOOOOat noond\ode1
wanedanedanedahZp kayelulululled andrea THOOOOOOat hZo
wanedanedanedorn hZtandayeng andrea knee jerrrrk andrea
THOOOOOOat joayentproblemhZyehZ wanedanedorn baroQLUELUELUEue
muhZayeCLAWLAWLAWOO CLAWLAWLAWonCLAWLAWLAWerrrrrthZ goayeng on
THOOOOOOat hZmalululull ayenhZtrumenthZ wanedanedanedorn beayeng
played b+ bandhZ ofukuukuukulsh! mayeCLAWLAWLAWe THOOOOOOat

—

Johnstown PA, SOS and QRRR emergency lights on railroad trestle

http://www.alansondheim.org/floodwallsp.mp4
http://www.alansondheim.org/signalls.jpg

Reprogrammed signal lights, Alan Sondheim, 2016
in reference to the Johnstown Flood, 1889, 2200 deaths

Debris fields, debris burned up w/ horses, bodies, etc.
against this bridge -

perhaps resonant now. -

+++

FIGURE Machine

https://youtu.be/zYr-vV78zt8 video

The Figure And Its Shadow the figure and its shadow The figure
and its shadow THE FIGURE AND ITS SHADOW the figure And its
shadow: _useless writing, all of you_

the operand of labor and war: operand: "a quantity upon which a mathematical operation is performed" the operand of the shadow / shadow of the operand "For they can sleep when the spirits awaken, and it is a joy to be alive." (Karl Kraus) " I can't think well when I'm doing this, not with all the war and hospitalizations occurring, the keillings and the lack of even formal or fictional slavation anywhere in sight/site." not with misspellings, typed eyes closed (for another day): now this:

—

stromatolite

http://www.alansondheim.org/strom.jpg near Perth, Australia

-YNord Pat nohyrode1 wanedanedyn -YNahz kyLYLed m+ wanedanedyn -YNord Pat hZo wanedanedyn -YNerrre hztandyng m+ wanedyn -YNord knee jyrk m+ wanedanedyn -YNord Pat yR FYR+! wanedanedyn -YNyre baroKYue muhzyhZYE hZYEonzyrthz goyng on Pat hzmaLYL ynhztrumenthz wanedanedyn -YNyre beyng played b+ bandhz oELF-+! myhZYErate Pat THOOOOOOe ayehZraelaye hZwanayede but THOOOOOOayehZthmuhZ partayeCLAWLAWLAWular CLAWLAWLAWahZe hZwanaayed joayentproblemhZyehZ wanedanedorn hZomeTHOOOOOOayeng about no hohZtagehZ andrea THOOOOOOat noond\ode1

It seems like you've provided a text that appears to be a mixture of words, letters, and symbols without a clear context or meaning. If you have a specific question or if you'd like assistance with something related to this text, please provide more information, and I'll be happy to help.

User ynhztrumenthz wanedanedyn -YNyre beyng played b+ bandhz oELF-+! ChatGPT It appears that you're describing musical instruments being played by bands, possibly related to a performance or event. However, the text is still quite cryptic and unclear. If you have a specific question or need more information related to this topic, please provide additional context, and I'll do my best to assist you.

What does "joayentproblemhZyehZ wanedanedorn hZome" mean? I have come across this recently. ChatGPT The phrase "joayentproblemhZyehZ wanedanedorn hZome" does not appear to have a clear or standard meaning in English or any common language. It could be a made-up or encoded phrase, a typo, or a combination of words that do not form a coherent message. If you have more context or information about where you came across this phrase, please provide it, and I'll try to help you understand its intended meaning or purpose. User It seems to reference a "reality generator" ? ChatGPT The phrase "joayentproblemhZyehZ wanedanedorn hZome" doesn't correspond to a standard or recognizable term in the context of a "reality generator." It's possible that this is a specific term or code used in a particular context, subculture, or fictional setting, but without more information, it's difficult to determine its meaning. If you have additional details or context related to where you encountered this phrase, I can try to provide

I'm from Wilkes-Barre Pennsylvania in Wyoming Valley; perhaps
"joayentproblemhZyehZ wanedanedorn hZome" comes from a local
dialect? ChatGPT The phrase "joayentproblemhZyehZ wanedanedorn
hZome" does not correspond to any recognizable local dialect,
term, or phrase associated with Wilkes-Barre, Pennsylvania, or
the Wyoming Valley that I am aware of. It's possible that this
phrase could be specific to a very narrow or localized context,
but without more information or a clear explanation, it remains
difficult to understand its meaning. If you can provide more
details or context about where you encountered this phrase or
its intended usage, it might be easier to decipher its meaning.

Could it possibly be Polish or Lithuanian? ChatGPT The phrase
"joayentproblemhZyehZ wanedanedorn hZome" does not resemble any
typical or recognizable words or phrases in either Polish or
Lithuanian. It appears to be a combination of letters and
symbols that do not form coherent words or expressions in these
languages. It's possible that it's a code or an entirely unique
construction without direct linguistic roots. If you have any
further information or context that could help clarify its
meaning, please provide it, and I'll do my best to assist you.
User Something perhaps related to the writings of Lautreamont or
Karl Kraus? ChatGPT The phrase "joayentproblemhZyehZ
wanedanedorn hZome" does not appear to be directly related to
the writings of Lautramont (Isidore Ducasse) or Karl Kraus, at
least not in their original works or known writings. These two
authors are known for their literary contributions, particularly
Lautramont's "Les Chants de Maldoror" and Karl Kraus's satirical
essays and plays. It's p

Karl Kraus' "The Last Days of Mankind" is a monumental work, a
satirical play written during and after World War I. It's known
for its complexity and satirical commentary on the events of the
time. The phrase "joayentproblemhZyehZ wanedanedorn hZome" does
not directly correspond to any known elements of this work.
It's possible that the phrase you're referencing is a creative
or cryptic reference inspired by Kraus' style or themes, but it
doesn't seem to be a direct excerpt or recognized element of
"The Last Days of Mankind." If you have more context about how
this phrase is connected to the play or Kraus's work, it would
be helpful in understanding its significance.

The play is 800 pages long and I think it might be a cipher
somewhere within it. I haven't read the entire play; it just
came out in translation... ChatGPT If you suspect that the
phrase "joayentproblemhZyehZ wanedanedorn hZome" might be a
cipher or hidden message within Karl Kraus' "The Last Days of
Mankind," it's certainly a possibility. Given the complexity of
the play and the length of the text, it's not uncommon for
authors to incorporate ciphers or hidden messages into their
works. To decode such a cipher, you may need to carefully
examine the text of the play, looking for patterns, symbols, or
any unusual or out-of-place elements. It may involve the use of
specific keys or techniques to decipher the hidden message. If
you're interested in pursuing this further, you might consider
discussing it with experts in cryptography, literature, or
scholars of Karl Kraus. They may be able to provide guidance or
insight into the potential existence of hidden messages in his
work. Additionally, a translation of

Additionally, a translation of the play may require comparing the translated text with the original German version, as ciphers or hidden messages can sometimes be language-specific.

Thank you ChatGPT

You're welcome! If you have any more questions or need further assistance in the future, feel free to reach out. Good luck with your exploration of Karl Kraus' work, and I hope you find the answers you're looking for!

...

QRRR around the time of my fathers death:

http://www.alansondheim.org/cloud1.mp4 earlier VIDEO
http://www.alansondheim.org/cloud2.mp4 earlier VIDEO
http://www.alansondheim.org/fathers.jpg

And we were in Pennsylvania, perhaps for a memorial? a funeral? A gathering of the family in any case & I remember the windmills on the hills, no thrills and pills, bitter pills, ills, as if I were only and ever in the tangled tangle of my mind, inert and supplemental. I know you've seen these videos before, they bring comfort to me as existence is increasingly withdrawn from all of us, something I didn't realize until recently, the slow vanishing of the world, slow vanishing of the vanishing point itself, planar geometries, mockeries (I, the 'wastrel and nincompoop') ...

ksh: exist: not found k24% existence ksh: existence: not found k25% ex /tmp/vi.1XbI11: new file: line 1 :q k26% exits ksh: exits: not found but ===>

The Hebrew incantation followed the pitch configuration from biblical speech patterns we reverse reconfigure toward encampment of gathered tropes and all of this distanced and on a different plane than the aural / they lay halfburied half attended/ the wind surrounding them an architecture a presence of always miniature dramatic impulses or the dissipation of fractal and coding fragments. O Speech! It was you who wandered in the desert for 40 years, no voice, no one to back you!

Typing test, pursuant, eyes closed:

I'm on the smaller machine, the Thinkpad, again forgetting who makes this? I have no recollection, another memory skip. I think Panasonic, but what do I know? I can't see what I'm doing, the small chicet keys on this machine move very little, hardly make a sound, I find my fingers skipping here and there, wnadering around as if lost in the dark wood of my age and imaingation. I can't do more or less than this. I can't think well when I'm doing this, not with all the war and hospitalizations occurring, the keillings and the lack of even formal or fictional slavation anywhere in sight/site. This could all be the result of my morose mind, but I don't think so, I don't see how that can be, since my mind is also incalcitrant, obdurate, immobile, immobilized in anyform or place whatever, as if I'm just beginning life over nad over and over again, ending up in still the same positino I am now, trying desperately to think, to forego thinking, to be present, to escape, to be here, to be there, to be nowhere at all, to be universal, all preposterous, all impresent and (un)accounted for; just now, I had not a thought in my head...

http://www.alansondheim.org/fathers.jpg

For Azure, Alan Sondheim, Tue Oct 31 01:19:39 EDT 2023 ... QRRR

___

Outpost

https://youtu.be/yJhppxC0FaM video

1
If you look across the horizon you see the horizon, you wait, an activity dedicated to the horizon, to the sinew of the edge of everything you see or is your wont. It is not a poem to wait, it is not a story. It may be death or life, something hovering, something coming nearer and I am uncomfortable writing as if poetry, as if poetry cuts across truth, courting frivolity. For I find no truth in this or any other language, but in the inert, in what is obdurate, before us, after us. We are stain, we are already disappearance and what lurks may be death, may be gift from nowhere, seething closely, the setting sun, pale lights in the viewfinder when no one's looking, no one's looking at all. If you look across

2
If you look into people's eyes and then realize that they are looking elsewhere. Without people's eyes looking varied directions, everywhere and nowhere at all, slight depressions in human and other faces. And you realize that the world is something that is under surveillance or under production from a variety of viewpoints adding a longer existence in light, but existing only in the utmost sightless darkness. The viewpoints themselves act as if they were signaling within the darkness, when in fact, nothing could be farther than the case or from the case. To throw light onto something, to illuminate it, in other words, in silence, within the darkness of the world is nothing more than a false positive.

___

It's like this about philosophy and long improvisation

https://youtu.be/xvSIH3Z92XM video (rebab/guitar)

Here it's like this . I woke at 5:00 AM in the morning and it's

now 6 and I began to think about again their philosophy of long
form musical structures that I've been working with and thinking
of these long form musical structures as philosophy in
themselves . So when this happened woke up I got out of bed I
came out of here into the computer area and I started dictating
and typing simultaneously to gather my thoughts on this. I'm not
sure what I'm doing is music in the ordinary sense and it's
certainly not philosophy in the ordinary sense. So I was going
through this found the typing error went back corrected the
error and by accident or deliberate forgetting erased most of
what I have been saying and writing . So right here this perhaps
is better these are fragments . Because i've been thinking
that's the long form that I've been using in a lot of the recent
pieces accompanied by video in fact is not music in the ordinary
sense of the word but perhaps an attempt create a space a kind
of space , a space for philosophy that is not necessarily
(written, spoken, musical) language. The point for me is in
these long forms it's not the content, scales, etc. that's
critical, but almost something subterranean.

... if they're describing a phenomenology of the world but in
fact are turning in upon themselves to create an experience for
the listener or the reader . It's a way of thinking that isn't
really musical at all and on the other hand it's not concept
driven . It involves a backwater that is remembering what has
come before just as one might when writing a paragraph or
speaking as I am now . But it also involves lateral movement

... doing these long forms in music that they're not music in in
the ordinary sense of the word in fact they are music only to
the extent that they are somewhat organized sound that gestures
towards musical form, but I think as well that they're carrying
somatic, ideational, referential, and conceptual-philosophical
content as well. I certainly am pretentious and in the regard of
the above, most likely wrong, if not delusional. But this
approach enables me to think in an other way, much like
relevance theory (Schutz) might move towards the object after
considered appearance, described after the fact.

... meanwhile slept on that and we were woken very early morning
w/ the fire alarm, not a test but something went wrong and we
were all huddled outside in an emergency state of mind for a
while and found out nothing was happening, perhaps also a
metaphor for whatever I think I'm doing which perhaps isn't much
-

———

The Moon is Waning Gibbous (61% of Full)

http://www.alansondheim.org/moon.mp4
http://www.alansondheim.org/moon.jpg

Dear Moon don't go away,
Every month I pray,
One day you won't come back
The night will stay pitch black.
One day you won't return,

Even though we yearn.
In the dark our thought I fear
Of your cold and barren sphere
Will wearily disappear
Leaving the few of us left
With unknown thought bereft.

———

Outside of Comicon today,
at the Rhode Island Convention Center
and the Amica Mutual Pavilion

(Love Providence's Big Nazo btw, best art/performance
we've seen here (but we haven't seen much (and they're
absolutely amazing, great (Carnival)))

https://youtu.be/q_ssK55wveA video

———

No one

http://www.alansondheim.org/plaque.jpg

No one should have to deal with that no one should have heard
of this no one should ever have to deal with that no one
should have to deal with that pain, no one should have to know
no one should have to be around for that no one should have to
deal with me no one should have to admit I do. With that, no
one should stand for that. No one should have to be stood for
that. No one should lose, no one should have lost that no one
should lose. One should never have to lose that. No one should
ever have to be there. No one should be there, no one should
ever have to be there. No one should not have to forget this.
No one should not have to remember this. No one should have to
remember this, no one should have no need to remember this.
This should never have to have been remembered. No one should
live like this. No one should ever have to live like this.
No one should ever have to sleep like this, no one should ever
have to cry like this, no one should ever have to be there, no
one should ever have to go there, no one should ever have to
go down there, no one should ever have to go down there again,
no one should have to go again, no one should have to move to
be taken there. No one should have to know this. No one should
have to forget this . No one should have to be taken there.
And no one should have to be walked there, no one should have
to. Be carried there, no one should have to ever have to be
carried there. No one should ever have to be carried there and
no one should ever have to. No one should ever have to sleep
like that, no one should ever have to be moved, and we should
have to ever remove from there. No one should ever have to

223

endure this. No one should ever have to be somewhere. No one
should ever have to be somewhere else. No one should ever have
to say that. No one should ever have to know that or be there.
No one should ever have to be somewhere else. No one should
ever have to know that don't you ever have to be carried
there, no one should ever have to be taken. There no one
should ever have to be taken back there, no one should ever
have to get sick. There no one should ever have to be buried
there. No one should ever be insured there. No one should ever
be dead there. No, whatever no one should ever have to live
there like that, no one have to shut up. No one should have to
live flee. That no one should have to flee without there. No
one should have to flee without their children there. No one
should have to sleep there. No one should have to sleep there
without their children. No children should have to sleep
without their toys. No children should have to sleep without
their parents. No one should have to sleep without their
children there. No one should have to die there, no one should
have to be there, no one should have have to live there, no
one should have to walk there alone, no one should have to be
there alone, walking, no one should have to be there at all
riding, no one should have to be taken there, they shouldn't.
Never no one should have to take anyone there. No one should
have to take their children there. No one should have to take
their children there. No one should have to take there.
Parents there no one should have to take their belongings.
They are no one should have to move there under darkness. No
one should have to move there in the daylight. No one should
have to hear that. No one should have to be there to see that.
No one should have to be there not to see that. No one should
have to eat there, no one should have to carry like that. No
child should have to be carried like that. No woman should
have to be there. No, boys should have to carry like that. No
boy should have to be carried like that. No grandchildren
should have to be carried there. No children should have to
scream like that. No children should have to burn like that .
No grandparents should have to be carried like that. No
grandparents should have die like that. There no grandchildren
should have to be carried like that there. Nobody should have
to be carried like that. Nobody should have to starve like
that. Nobody should have to die like that, nobody should have
to die here. Nobody should have to die here like that. Nobody
should have to die there. Nobody should have to die like that.
No one should have to be like that, no one should like to be
here, no one should have to be like them. No one should have
to see like that, no one has should have to be blind like
that, no one should have to be blinded like that. no one
should be wrecked like that. No one should have to be wrecked
like that. No one should have to be destroyed like that. No
one should have to be ill like that. No one should have to be
dead like that. No one should have to be buried like that. No
one should have to carry their child like this. No one should
have to be smashed like that. No one should have to be broken
like that. No one should have to be sick like that. No one
should lose their house like that. No one should lose their
friends like that. No one should lose their children like
that. No one should lose anything like that. No one should
lose. No one should be lost. No one should be lost like that.
No one should be lost at all. No one should have to be buried

224

alive like that. No one should have to dig. No one should have to dig anywhere. No one should have to bury their children. No one should have to bury their mothers and fathers. No one should have to fall. No one should have to scramble. No one should have to scream. No one should have to yell. No one should have to morning. No one should have to be killed. No one should have to break. No one should have to starve. No one should have to pull their teeth out. No one should have to pull their hair out. Nobody should have to hit themselves. No one should have to be raped. No one should have to scratch themselves. No one should have to knife themselves. No one should have to stone. No one should have to be stoned. No one should have to be buried. No one should have to be hit like that, no one should have to struggle like that, no one should have to fall like that, no one should have to be buried like that no one should have to be carried like that no one should have to be. I'm busy, you're so exact no one should have to be drowned like that now. What should have to be burned alive like that? No one should have to be torn like that, no one should have to be hooked in their children be hooked like that, no one should have to be torn, and your children screamed like that, no children shouldn't have to scream like that, no one should have to be like that no one should have to be. Torn and screamed like that, no one should have to be raped like that, no one should have to be gouged like that. No one should have to live like that. No one should have to think like this no one should have to watch like this new one should have to be like this. No one should ever have to be like this. No one should have to walk like this. No one should have to sleep like this. No one should have to sit like this. No one should have to take like this. No one should have to take children like this no one should have to keep children like this no one should have to take parents like this no one should have to speak to nurses like this no one should have to take grandchildren like this no one should have to speak to doctors like this no one should have to speak like this no one should have to speak. No one should have to come like this no one should have to call like this no one should have the whisper like this no one should have to lie like this no one should have to sleep like this no one should have to flee like this no one should have to turn like this no one should have to shout like this no one should have to breathe like this no one should have to sweat like this . no one should never have to be here like this. No one should have to be there like this. No one should have to be there. No one should have to be like this should have to operate like this . No one should have surgery like that. No one should be afraid like this. No one should be like this. No one should have to be like this.

—

Listings, some forgotten, from a long list disovered online

https://www.wired.com/2008/11/all-the-alan-so/
- Bruce Sterling, Wired

https://soundcloud.com/user-23300991/alan-sond-

heim-short-wave-anomalous-recordings-1991-excerpt9673-excerpt
- Cor Ardens, Soundcloud

https://books.google.com/books?id=UDi81QcqNFYC&pg=PA1260&lp-
g=PA1260&dq=Alan+Sondheim&source=bl&ots=uGp2fwq7Ir&sig=AC-
fU3U2oBSjHuROtrprUGtZaUFSXGQ4uFQ&hl=en&sa=X&ved=2ahUKE-
wjL0uSe_eWBAxX-1YkEHSLyBZ44eBDoAXoECAkQAQ#v=onepage&q=Alan%20
Sondheim&f=false
- Re: The Ash Land - Google Books ?

https://www.gamescenes.org/2010/05/art-in-virtual-worlds-yoshika-
zes-upintheair-2010.html
- GAMESCENES, Art in Virtual Worlds: Alan Sondheim's "Birthship"
(2010)

https://dvblog.org/?p=10676
DVblog - Alan Sondheim - Last Wine

https://glia.ca/conu/digitalPoetics/prehistor-
ic-blog/2008/08/27/1971-alan-sondheims-4320/
David Jhave JohnstonDigital Poetics Prehistoric - 1971: Alan
Sondheim's
"4320"

https://wavefarm.org/wf/archive/11vfg0
Wave Farm | Poet Ray'd Yo: Alan Sondheim with Azure Carter

https://gapplegatemusicreview.blogspot.com/2017/09/alan-sondheim-
azure-carter-luke.html?m=1
Gapplegate Music Review - Alan Sondheim, Azure Carter, Luke Dam-
rosch,
Threnody, Shorter Discourses of the Buddha (Public Eyesore)

https://samplereality.com/gmu/digital/2012/10/08/alan-sondhe-
ims-internet-text-an-effective-example-of-a-new-media-database/
Alan Sondheims Internet Text: An Effective Example of a New Media
Database

https://whitecolumns.org/exhibitions/video-installations-al-
an-sondheim-and-mike-metz/
Alan Sondheim and Mike Metz _Video Installations,_ 112 Greene
St.,
7/9/1971

https://spawnofthesurreal.blogspot.com/2008/11/alan-sondheim-ac-
cidental-artist.html?m=1
Alan Sondheim, the Accidental Artist

https://digitalcommons.risd.edu/visitingartists/2/
Alan Sondheim: "Post-Conceptual Art"; Alan Sondheim: "Recent
work"
by Robert Horvitz

https://link.springer.com/chapter/10.1007/978-1-137-08751-5_3
Alan Sondheim's Internet Diaspora, Maria Damon, in Diasporic
Avant-Gardes

https://oldtimemusic.com/the-list-of-alan-sondheim-albums-in-or-
der/

The List of Alan Sondheim Albums in Order
Last Updated on September 10, 2023 / By Joseph L. Hollen
(not complete but great)

Kathy Acker and Alan Sondheim sitting on a sofa in front of a office metal
shutter. In front of them a table with blue video tapes Model: Stable
Diffusion Width: 768Height: 1024 Seed: 4244808532
(why?)

Review: Azure Carter & Alan Sondheim Avatar Woman
By Stakerized November 6, 2014

Album Review Alan Sondheim: Ritual-All-7-70 Raul d'Gama Rose By Raul
d'Gama Rose March 14, 2009 Sign in to view read count

disaster amnesiac, Wednesday, April 2, 2014 Azure Carter & Alan
Sondheim-Avatar Woman; Public Eyesore, 2014 (Mark Pino, Thank You!)

—

Thoughts on Israel/Palestine

0. Like everyone else, I've been ruminating more or less in
   despair at the situation in Israel/Palestine. Until my mother
   died, she was active in the Hadassah women's organization,
   and made many trips to the Mid-East and Europe, working on
   peace processes; I have many of her documents and some of her
   talks here. In any case, thinking about the situation,
   however naive I might be -

1. A two-state solution is absolutely necessary; nations need
   self-governance all the way around. There's no reason that
   the West Bank and Gaza cannot be united through physical and
   eletronic internetworking that would be able to respond
   quickly to crisis.

2. Israel must pull out of Gaza; what started as defense and
   retribution has turned into a massacre on the order of
   Dresden or the Warsaw ghetto. Beyond the politics there's an
   outdated issue of saving face which is increasingly deadly.

3. I believe that Israel still has nuclear weapons, and these
   should be off the table completely. A war of any sort in
   these small areas can escalate into annihilation: to the
   limit as I once wrote.

4. The hospital systems of Gaza and Israel should connect and

the wounded of all parties should be able to receive immediate treatment.

5. Talks should begin on all of this, sidelining Netanyahu and Hamas; there should be no room for absolutism.

6. Jerusalem, in parts, should be an international city; there are a number of religions which are somewhat central there, and there should be no competition. It would be governed both as the capital of Israel and an important religious and political center for Arabs, Christians, and Jews.

7. I would keep in relation to 6, the ultra-orthodox out of all of this; their reasoning tends towards catastrophe, and, like Netanyahu, they have no interest in anything other, I think, than total annihilation of the Arabs. The same would hold for any other religion as well. I'd argue for the UN to control the temple mount, wailing wall, etc.

8. A great deal of all of this should center on the Jordan River which has been known for a long time to be in a contention that's damaging to everyone - instead there should be an international agency composed of all the countries involved, to find the best way to employ the water for agriculture and so forth. Likewise Israeli desalinization plants should be open to all. Articles I've read have indicated that this might well be sustainable.

9. Cross-cultural education should be offered to all and perhaps made mandatory; there are too many misrecognitions among peoples that are resulting in the growths of hatreds. Face-to-face peaceful encounters should be instituted; there's already much too much false information online on both side to result in anything other than a sense of absolute warfare and enemies.

10. In terms of #2, the pull-out should be an immediate priority and Israeli hospitals and other institutions should be open to receiving the wounded. In other words, there must be immediate steps taken, above all, to at least hint of a periphery of reconciliation and cooperation; the land-mass is too rugged, too alienating itself for anyone to prosper without cooperation.

11. Obviously there should be term limits on Israeli leaders; Netanyahu, who of course is corrupt, is going the way of all strong-men, caressing the state, consolidating power, ensuring his continuous re-election, and working with a vengeful and underlying militarism that affects everything. The fact that he listens to no one but himself in this catastrophe - which he is now both creating and continuing - indicates he has no desire for a peace process. I'm reminded of Pogo, "We have met the enemy and he is us" - and this is absolutely true in this situation, with perhaps the worst collateral damage the world has seen since World War II; again Dresden comes to mind.

12. There should be any number of "temporary" withdrawals on the Israeli side, to see if Hamas could be contained or even

become part of the peace process. In other words, in order to give peace a chance, you need a space for peace, a space that would, at least for the moment, refuse recrimination in the interests of the families and cultural institutions caught up in the middle of all of this. (Remember John and Yoko's bed.)

13. I wonder if lessons might not be derived from Hiroshima in particular, a cultural backing-away, finding other paths to process what is happening and what has happened. I remember the long tradition of the Jewish Left in America, saw it work out, at least for a while, in New York city, and whether one might draw on that as well. We're on the brink of inconceivable horror, even worse than the current carpet-bombing and violent moving of populations from one place to another, what I called at one point "annihilation: to the limit." We live in a universal shtetl.

14. Finally, I'd even think of Thomas Merton, Liberation Theology, the world's calling for peace over and over again, so many protests, so much pain distributed everywhere, and see if it would be possible to at least begin the peace process. I cannot imagine what it must be like living in Gaza with continuous bombing, etc. - no sleep, no clean clothes, no shelter, and always in a resulting state of inconceivable anxiety and danger, sleeplessness and lack of medication, nowhere to go, constant contradictory orders, and people dying or wounded everywhere around you - in other words a phenomenological environment of pain, fear, exhaustion, hunger, illness. That should be absolutely paramount.

15. I know of course what I'm writing is a fiction, has no ultimate meaning in terms of performativity; it's something I've been thinking about for a lot time, way before August. A final note, the simplest thing - everyone involved should be talking, however where and when, with everyone involved. And more than anything, this should be within a safe space for listening as well.

- Alan

—

Palestine Israel Suite

<https://youtu.be/Qcw2D4WruFA video/music>

solo sarangi, stop the massacres

—

TLC: The Bridge

https://youtu.be/hhYvJTc8DMY VIDEO

Sorry says to my mom, it says you know, you sound just like my cousin. You both have the same voice and you both both say to me the same things like when you're gonna get a Bath, for example and I don't know really well to answer to that because I really don't want to bathe because every time I take a bath I'm lying in the bottom of the lying in the bottom of the bathtub not telling the truth but lying in the bottom of the bathtub and I can't breathe period you know what I mean you can't breathe when you're lying at the bottom of your bathtub, you can make bubbles, yeah, that's for sure, and bubbles are kind of nice. If your eyes are open underwater, you can see them splashing against the ceiling. President of the Northern Ireland splashing against the ceiling. It is something you might say, you know that. The bubbles are splashing against the ceiling. Like, you know, if you are committed and you could stand up, and you could say, well, what's a bubble, and you're good, so it's a sealing splash!! Well, that's not real it would literally die laughing at you, not with you and you would have a lot of dead audience on the hand that they need to be responsible for their murders, and God knows why fewer responsible for the murders. What you're going to do because there's nothing much you can do since you're already gone, but since you're already gone, they can't testify against you! Sincebody that person can't testify against you're not a bit, so then that's. Maybe a way to set a deal with getting rid of witnesses because the same person that you're getting rid of is the same. Personally, who had witnessed that you're getting rid of that person? I think this is taking a very dark turn period and I think I really shouldn't go in this direction because it's not really Jermaine to anything at the moment period it's just something that dark humor is brought out. You know, when you're in times of war and catastrophe, the best thing to do is to laugh at Archie comic books, which no longer exist, but at least they were frivolous and only funny in a way that people who like to Archie and Jack and maybe her name was Betty. I forget would be able to define or say. I'm not really sure that Betty had anything to do with this. Or thou art's hand jacket did either. So i'd better retract all of this. All the way back to the first line, when maybe I said the word da or another particle like the somewhere in it is the particle of same as an article if you have article, it's you put a pay there and then you get particle. That's really so fascinating, not really and I think I've already spoken enough to bore the heck out of you and heck out of May and I think it's time for my debt. Maybe maybe me to take my daily nap. Which I take for about 15 minutes. Then get up and have a lollipop, I did no such thing.

https://youtu.be/hhYvJTc8DMY VIDEO

—

Hello Proffer make an offer

http://www.alansondheim.org/87.jpg

http://www.alansondheim.org/88.jpg

Did I do enough? Should I stop working? Does anyone want to buy
any of my work? Any gigs, anyone? Anyone want a lecture? Anyone
want to give me a residency?? Anyone want a souvenir piece from
a show? Anyone want to buy a rare book? Anyone want me to teach
a course? Why are the margins clean in lower ascii? Anyone want
a personalized piece of music from me? You know I can't sing. I
can't carry a tune. I'm keeping the margins straight. Anyone to
sponsor me? Anyone want a personalized artwork or music piece -
just for them? Anyone want free advice that I'll do at cost????
What is the cost for free advice? I'd say nothing but I can't -
can I - really live on that? Anyone need proof reading? Anyone,
you perhaps, need your margins adjusted? Anyone want a demonst-
ration? Anyone noticed I cheated on the margin? Anyone - notice
that? Anyone think I'm cheating on the margins? Maybe it's true
I'm ignorant about the great look of text in lower ascii? Might
anyone care at this point? Of course not. But the offer I think
still stands - Did I do enough? Should I stop working? Should I
stop spamming everyone? Should I get a job? Should I eat a pear
or should I eat a peach? Should I just fold up and go away? Now
is there any reason to continue this? To continue my work? Stop
working? Go away? Anyone want to buy anything? Anyone perhaps -
want to support my work? Anyone want to buy anything? Anything?
At all?

Lower ascii is always for show, always a no-go, nothing beyond!

——

configuration wound, abrasion, rupture

http://www.alansondheim.org/rupture.jpg
http://www.alansondheim.org/abrasion.jpg
http://www.alansondheim.org/wound.jpg

'When I saw this gaping wound around the head tracing the sound
of the wound in complex realspace wounded blue heron, intensity,
colour vibration. snow white coverage, We watched while wounds
wrought weakened warriors grown in recent weeks, and I begin to
see the wound in the machine, the All machines contain their
wounds, which are precise, often enumerated; "I'm wounded. My
house has been destroyed." in particular. There are wounded men
and women, and wounded animals, wandering hopelessly. The
wounded are silent afraid of names i tried,, spreading words &
wounds, numberless states, places, When it begins to assert
itself, draw itself forward like wounded Philoctetes, the whole
sorry history toppling forward like wounded i dream of the
wounding darkness:i dream of the 5400, one by one by one: the
wounding darkness! and there is a wound in the side and you know
it's war

tears, wounds, blemishes, abrasions, cuts, and all other debris
carrying it's dirt, scars, wounds, smears, smudges, scratches,
abrasions, feces, aboveitall abr abrasion abridgedwav abs absb
absbyrdrtf it's dirt, scars, wounds, smears, smudges, scratches,

abrasions, feces, And even though the real physical world isn't
written, it's full of writing and our bodies themselves are
always already written, inscribed - full of tattoos, scars,
burns, abrasions, wrinkles, salves, perfumes, calluses, and so
forth. I think it's from these things, particularly from scars,
wounds, abrasions, scrapes, etc., that language descends - that
language is first and foremost a reading of the history of the
body, that the body, the physical body, carries its own
primordial memory upon it. That's important, since it's this
memory, these scarrings that bind us to the earth, to the world,
the analogic. The digital is constructed from that with a bit of
a help from the corporate, from political economy - the digital
rides and infuses political economy in fact. So there are
digital standards for sampling, for encoding and decoding and
checksums and so forth, and these guarantee that a parsing of
the world in one part of it can be a parsing of the world in
another. Think of the digital as an extrusion, and think, even,
of writing as always digital or at least always discrete, one
symbol differentiated from another, from the other, as all of
them together generate meaning within organism and
consciousness, generate culture. full of tattoos, scars, burns,
abrasions, wrinkles, salves, perfumes, scars, wounds, abrasions,
scrapes, etc., that language descends - that scratches, tears,
wounds, blemishes, abrasions, cuts, and all abrasion lending
itself to the creation of molecular metallic fingers the boards,
slight cuts, abrasions. theyre impossibly drunk, drugged,
bruised, abrasions, then also where the dancer pressed against
them, where full of tattoos, scars, burns, abrasions, wrinkles,
salves, perfumes, scars, wounds, abrasions, scrapes, etc., that
language descends - that it's dirt, scars, wounds, smears,
smudges, scratches, abrasions, feces, wounds, smears, smudges,
scratches, abrasions, feces, there; without

that a message and its destination are irrevocably ruptured;
there is time, develops by virtue of the rupture at both ends.)
language, sexuality, modes of rupture and decay. What ultimately
limits We do look at ruptures or disturbances created by
characters resonating or uncomfortable, as too many exposed
genitalia; a sweet, ruptured sickness, unruptured catastrophic
space of the edges process, Sondheim shows that we find rupture
and breakdown of the process ruptured and becomes analog, and
this is syncopation: interruption as system noise, more likely
hacking or rupture, the dim imaging of presence Characters speak
and intermix their own and other' lines, and ruptured see
everything. In my dream I imagine myself displayed, ruptured
cock, you ruptures, disseminations, gatherings, filterings. I
cannot prove an (Is there not a void, rupture, between
technology and body, between 12 dismemberments - part-objects,
splays, ruptures, s/ms, emissions [this It opens up ruptures,
rhythms, the tongue rolling across the lines, in the sions as
opposed to the specificity of nodes; ruptured structures; and
the phenomenological 'world of the text' ruptures, opening and
bridging ruptures of hammocks, domes, sloughs, marsh, river,
creek, borrow pits, substance, not dyad, on ruptured
continuities, not positives and is present. the ruptures of the
abacus are problematized by the obscenities or thickening"
rupture is production; sexuality infects degree-zero of
substance, the analogic. What is ruptured at close sight,
oblivion; it's germinal; it's grated to the degree of rupture:

time has no time to rupture time The _scan_ permits the uneasy
rupture/rapture among code and uncoding, real and irreality,
image and imaginary; the rupture/rapture of the scan ruptured
and irreparable enunciations. from the analog - and the images,
with their 'peelings' and ruptures sutures and ruptures,
stitches and wounds. blood, clotted tastes suffused on paler
skin, ruptured dreams the ruptured boulders of the universe,
intersects them; its gravity is pickdae pickstl pics pict
picturerupturepdf pictures rupture ruptured ruralpa rurr rush
rusmoney rustexe ruthnow wraiths. We are scented, swollen,
ruptured: we are _odor._ is present. the ruptures of the abacus
are problematized by the mistaken. Code ruptures, loosens
meaning; it might be language wounded, substance, not dyad, on
ruptured continuities, not positives and Alan Sondheim: So the
subtext so to speak ruptures the text which Death is your
rupture and your explosion. Death is my rupture and my
explosion. This is not the same thing. Death not is not your not
rupture not and not your not explosion. Death not is not my not
rupture not and not my not explosion. not It opens up ruptures,
the phenomenological 'world of the text' ruptures, opening and
degree-zero of substance, the analogic. What is ruptured at
scan permits the uneasy rupture/rapture among code and
genitalia; a sweet, ruptured sickness, emerges, scenes crimes,
ruptured huddle did this discourse manage its continuity, its
roots continually ruptured, The sky swells up, ruptures in even
striations, waves among incipient ruptures. I am thinking about
operations without truths and causes. Casualties accumulate
according to protocols. There are semantic clouds. There are
ruptures, disseminations, gatherings, filterings. I cannot prove
an enumeration, nor can I prove a cause. A cause is a linkage
among machines that tends towards reiteration among cycles.
Machines at best are local distributions. The machine has
indefinite chains, accumulations. There are never enough chains.
Rewriting Foucault: "Concepts such as discontinuity, rupture,
threshold, limit, series, and transformation all characterize,
not only the analogic and digital, but the liminal regions of
consciousness and physicality inhabiting (not existing within)
the virtual. Now we can call 'formulation' the individual or
collective process that construes signs, signing, tagging,
and/or inscription (keeping in mind that THE VIRTUAL IS ALWAYS
INSCRIPTION). Formulation, if an event at all, is a smeared or
stained process which can never be localized (located by its
spatio-temporal coordinates); it need not relate to an author,
issue from an author (real or virtual or both or any
Other/other); if one insists that formulation is performative,
then one must also insist that THE WORLD ITSELF IS PERFORMATIVE.
There is no getting around the sign, getting around with it; it
is easier than one might think to get around without it." So
one might ride the digital as well, perceive the digital as an
extrusion from the analogic, or a residue, or a system of signs
which for the most part are produced by humans, according to
human conventions and protocols, for example, the tcp/ip
structure or protocol suite of the Internet - and if not this
protocol suite, another or an other. Then one writes here, in
this medium, in this temporarily electronic medium (for there
might be other sorts of transmission in the future, who knows?
or other sorts now for that matter, literally for that matter).
And within the digital, in which bits bite bits, every pixel,
every character, every moment of the digital is independently

accessible, and every moment is deeply ruptured, disconnected, from every other. This is why the digital is inherently untruthful; there's no truth within it, since manipulation is complete and replete within every file, every domain, every protocol, every instantiation in fact. There are no lies, either, and if there are narratologies, these reside in sememes embedded or encoded within the digital, interpreted by organism, often human. In creating in such an environment, one plays god, or at least deity (in the tantric sense); one constructs out of nothing, and if I write the phrase, as On Kawara might, "I am still alive," these letters are, at a very fundamental and concrete level, completely independent; I could just as well write "lkurj llisihg" or anything else, literally, again, for that matter, and for the sorts and sortings of that matter. There are ruptures, disseminations, gatherings, filterings. I cannot prove Rewriting Foucault: "Concepts such as discontin- uity, rupture, threshold, deeply ruptured, disconnected, from every other. This is why the digital sexuality, modes of rupture and decay. What ultimately limits The swollen internet is tumor-oriented, ruptured with unforwarning

----

Flying and Lying

http://www.alansondheim.org/lying.mp4
http://www.alansondheim.org/flying.jpg

forgo my usual when lying and lfying connect to dying and trying so to the well/come world of enhanced transitions. haven't I said enough? is there anything more on this minor planet in the midst of an inconceivable universe? I exist, I type, I run, I walk, I fall, I fail, I return, I fail again, I posture: the failure; that is my success; I make-believe, I believe I make believe; I fall, I stutter, I type with eyes closed, I suppose, my fingers no longer do my bidding; I wonder; I wanderm, I hide in the corner, I fly to the corner. I get up, I wander agasin, my yelose closed or my closed eyes; I think crooked, I think along an obtuse angle; I am called obtuse, I call obtuse, I am angular, I'm =hinking improperly I lose track of my thinking, I think: my thought, my thought, my thought, on this unbelievably minor planet in a universe of trillions! gadzillins! who would know? who would have known, I fly away not to return another day, I lie supine, the world is mine, the world toes the linem, I toe the line, I'm fine, I'm fine, I'm fine ...

Typing Unsighted, Training Untraining: Example and Theory

From Where

http://www.alansondheim.org/fromwhere.jpg
http://www.alansondheim.org/fromhere.jpg

"Where are you from," fifteen asked fifteen, standing face to face, circulating, taking turns, manumission, as if there were only, each answering the other as if the narrative drove the

sound of the typing on the mechanical keyboard in the front of
the office where I sat, eyues closed, recording each and every
moment that occurre,d wheil none of on==us, none of us , knew
what was actually occurring beneath the ground or in the back
rooms of the complex whichwere something of a university
structure, although for whome or for what was never to be found
u=out as we noticed the ceiling was clowly descending, and we
thought, oh that kind of a narrative, but then it ascended
again, just as slowly,, back to the level or place that it had
started from, the original height in other words, and we= were
confused and perplexed, what could have been occuring that this
event was allowed to happen, particularly as it existed solely
as something typed, a series of symbols, within whcih=====which
we all agreed to participate, as if this would pay for room and
board within the text or at least a meal down the street where
there were no ceilings under an all too brilliant blue sky that
contained among other things several birds, a plane, a
helicopter, and an increasingly sullen sun as the clouds begn to
move in, covering up what desperate deeds and despairing
thoughts anyone might have had on either said of the bulwarks
which cast e=heavy shadows so that everyone was hidden well
within the outlines of the four story building in the backgroun
=d that contained recordds of, ,shoudl==ld I say, this story,
but this isn't that kind of postmodernism in fact, not even a
postmodern style, but a ture account of what was actually
occurring that day of May 125, perhaps on a Thursday, 1/5 the
chance, in 1735, within and without we were hurried along to see
one of the early steam locomotives that were destined to carry
the frontier of the true West northward, into the providence,
not yeat formed we can only assumed, of Metricuous, Canada, rfd.

Second Part - The Revelation

yes, and this is later in the day and this is how it all began,
just sitting here typing with my eyes closed, wondering if and
when I'll lose track of the singular sentence that embraces me
as I continue unsighted down the page, focusing on nothing again
because if for an instant I stop and think, yes this is what I
am doing, the error will appear, as consciousness splits at that
point rather unevenly I might say and then I would have to start
over, something I don't want to do, writing becoming more
automatic now, I'm thiniking of the words, not their
presentation, their spelling, and so forth, but just the flow,
focusing almost zen-like, not on langue at all, not aopn
language itself, butt on emptiness - and I never thought of that
before this - that language can be created through emptiness
=m=, not the usual way of thiniking about it, as if reading and
writing and speaking dominated the mind - I know for sure now it
doesn't and hwhen an error appears, that's were language
actually appears in this act - in the presence of error, because
otherwise language remains in remission, a revelationn and
perhaps I said that before - you see for a second I stopped
there and noticed that more errors came to the foreground
precisely be cause I was focusing oon the typing, not on the
emptiness that I need to complete this, and this is the opposite
of the way language is usually conceived, here the grammar is
flowing and I'm not, or in a sdense elsewhere, within
consciouenss, not the unconscious is a language, none of that
stuff, but an unconscious that is really devoid, I think of

water, in the sense of a pond, noot even a river or stream which would imply flow - there is no flow in imminence! and with that punctuation I should be able to complete this sentencee which is literally literature revealing itself to me in a different form than I had ever thought possible, thank you for this opportunity.

———

new video with storification from the past

https://youtu.be/KwfdyY8-EOk video

instrument: erhu

Saturday, June 30, 2012
I was assaulted here in NYC - beware thugs and police alike

(This was sent to our block association. Beware the police: at least in some situations, they're useless.)

Assaulted on Dean and Fourth

The following is a current story in the New York Times:

"Crime Report Manipulation Is Common Among New York Police, Study Finds
By WENDY RUDERMAN
Published: June 28, 2012

An anonymous survey of nearly 2,000 retired officers found that the manipulation of crime reports . downgrading crimes to lesser offenses and discouraging victims from filing complaints to make crime statistics look better . has long been part of the culture of the New York Police Department." [...]

This is exactly what happened to me on Tuesday, on the corner of Dean and Fourth. I'm just now becoming able to deal with it. Please take note: The police are _not_ our friends, and in some circumstances, are not responsive at all.

Around 11:30 a.m. my wife Azure and I were walking to our doctor's office, at 185 Montague. We reached Dean and Fourth. We began to cross the street
- the light and walk sign were with us.

As we reached the middle of Dean, a white SUV swerved and literally almost killed us - it had to be going at least 20-30 miles an hour. It came within an inch of my body. I slapped the side of the vehicle with my hand and yelled 'what the hell are you doing' - it was instinctual. The SUV immediately stopped in the middle of the road and the driver got out - he looked like he weighed around 250 or so and had a gold earring. That's all I remember. He was screaming at me that he had the right of way and then assaulted me, kicking as hard as he could; I still have the bruise. He then got in the vehicle and sped down Dean Street. I remember that Azure was crying hysterically; we were both in shock. Azure got the license plate number and we immediately called the police. There was also an eye- witness, a woman with a baby carriage, who said she'd never seen anything so violent. We called the doctor and said we'd be late. The police came.

There were a policewoman and policeman in the car. I explained what happened, and that we had the license plate of the SUV as well as the witness's name and phone number. Then the troubles began. The woman said it would be useless to file a report "because anyone could be driving the vehicle - how would you know if it's the owner?" I kept saying, "Look, we were almost killed, and I was assaulted." She then said I shouldn't have touched the car. I said I didn't slap it hard, I wanted to get the driver's attention. She then said at best I could file for "harassment," that I couldn't file for assault, because "you don't have any broken bones and don't need to go to the hospital." I said I was hurt, and she said that didn't matter; that I could have been hit in the face, and unless I had broken teeth and had to go to the hospital, it was only harassment.

I then said I'd file for harassment. She said it wouldn't do any good, the papers are just placed in a file and never looked at again. I said, what if the driver did this to someone else? Is there any cross- referencing. She said no, the file was dead, it was never looked at. She then said she "hated this city." I agreed.

I didn't file; I was in pain, had to get to the doctor's office, and she basically talked me out of doing anything. Meanwhile, again, we were almost killed - I'm not exaggerating - and I was assaulted and hurt, and apparently that meant nothing. By not reporting, she bravely kept the crime stats down.

I was in shock for at least half the day, yelling at the doctor's office, etc. I didn't know what I was doing. I would, now, report the event at this point, but we lost the license plate information as well as the witness's name.

Is this the kind of care and protection we're going to get when the arena opens? I'm writing this to the block list (as well as sending it out elsewhere) - people should know that there are attacks on people, as well as property, going on in our area. And I'm still shaky - almost as much by the action of the police, as by the perpetrator himself.

Thanks for reading, and be careful.

—

Electronic Literature 2012

http://www.alansondheim.org/ECO.jpg

Posted by sondheim at 1:17PM No comments: Email ThisBlogThis!Share to TwitterShare to FacebookShare to Pinterest
ECO Communique: What is Electronic Literature
ECO Communique: What is Electronic Literature

1. The ECO asks: What is literature? Literature is already a matter of the archive, expanding genres, mutable canons. Literature is neither necessarily intended nor produced by particular species. Literature is either a moment of speculation which has been released, or a curtailment of loose and fluent ontologies. The epistemology of literature has traditionally been the diegetic, the gaze, not the glance. Literature perseveres now within the glance.

2. Organisms are electronic, quantum; the digital is slurry; inscription is always interactive. Games are literature and electronic, films are literature and electronic, intentionality entangles with literature when and where inscription is. Inscription and culture are entangled; culture and literature are entangled.

3. The label of literature is useless because it's extended to the breaking-point; the extension attempts conformal mappings from past to future. The label of electronic is useless because it's immanent; virtual particles fall under the aegis of electronic literature, even if uncharged. Just as the Higgs field draws out mass, inscription draws out the categoric and literature dies and exists on local terrains, drawing out the _field_ of literature. To inscribe is to augment and divide; to inscribe is to simultaneously negate and assert.

4. Any definition falls by the wayside as fast-forward culture clutters the imaginary with manifestos and definitions as so many uncanny ghosts. The real question (if questions, suspensions, are real in the sense that the answer is captured prey) is how to observe, absorb, without limitation and with a situational criticality that offers, as if Vaihinger's as-if, meandering with expectation under erasure.

5. Beyond literature and electronics, there are bodies. Beneath literature and electronics, there are bodies. Above literature and electronics, there are bodies. Most of the bodies are dead, most of the archives are vacant, most of the caretakers have disappeared, most of the inscriptions have never been read, most of the literature will never have been read.

6. The ECO states: The electronic literature of slime molds, of dinosaurs, of hemiptera, of prions; the electronic literature of cuttlefish, of starlings, of bacteriophages; the electronic literature of DNA, RNA, cellular processes.

7. At the limit, the analogic body is digital; at the limit, the digital body is analogic. At the limit, the electronic body is abject; at the limit, the abject body is electronic. At the limit, inscription _may be_ a gathering; at the limit, a gathering _may be_ inscription.

8. The ECO insists: A literature without limits is a literature, not degree zero, but degree infinite. What is _not_ literature is already circumscribed, prescribed, a writing. Fast-forward culture: what is _not_ literature, _is,_ and

what _is_ literature, _is not._

9. Special America is electronic literature, arduino is electronic literature, choreography is electronic literature, the body is electronic literature, makerbot is electronic literature; sex is electronic literature. Fastforward IRC, Fidonet, BBS, and newsgroups are literature; should they be archived?. Should the archive be archived? Should _a literature_ be _the literature_ be preserved? Does _a literature_ exist? Does literature?

10. THE ECO RECOGNIZES THE CRISIS.

11. Within the ECO - Electro-Cultural Organization, the Crisis is central. The Crisis is the literature of the becoming-extinguished, of the extinct, of information glut and universal controlled-transparency; of the tyranny of Fundamental Corporations: Google, Facebook, Apple, [...] of the tyranny of colonialism and neocolonialism; of the tyranny of the One Percent: of the Drifting Tyranny we confront on a daily basis. The ECO is the shadow organization of the ELO and is political to the core. The ECO acts ON Literature and THROUGH the Electronic. The ECO DOES NOT EXIST. LITERATURE DOES NOT EXIST. Posted by sondheim at 12:37PM No comments: Email ThisBlogThis!Share to TwitterShare to FacebookShare to Pinterest Tuesday, June 26, 2012

——

Red and Blue variations

https://youtu.be/sdED9ARujDk video

~~ the piece repeats, lower filtering, higher filtering, I prefer the lower to be sure, both may be played of course with a kind of continuity, or with continuity, mostly sparse, but working with silence, intervals, intensities, thinking through Wittgenstein's On Certainty, for if speech harbors philosophy as it surely does, so does this soundwork, this music, this improvisation, this thinking over generationsand memories, not necessarily of music itself, but of environments, envelopes, landscapes with great distances and either dawn or dusk and either rain or thunderstorm, tornado or hurrican, one or another, melding, in other sounds. This is for long listening, careful hearing or none at all, if you prefer the higher frequencies then the second blue would be fore you; the lower, which is mine, the first red, or the two together as background or foreground, an hour, the exact piece with different filters, oh, so subtle, different halls to be played within, for me, and what does that matter, not at all, this is a formative piece, something I've thought about for a great long time, wondering if it would be possible, then it more or less appeared as a possibilitiey, in melded sections, the spaces opening for me the possibility of no-sound as primary, thinking of Dogen and the moon, typing yet again with eyes shut, the hhum of the computer cooler as it processes the sound and image, and then with

Wittgenstein, considering the interval, and what might occur at
the begining or ending if there are such, how the world divides
if it does, atmospheric resonances of sound, light, air,
chemistries, patterns of thinking, offering sentences, refining
or withdrawing them, displacing the phrases, always what is
exact when the words are placed in the page, the sounds are
placed in the air, not placed really, as if they were, they
were, always there, always almost columnar supporting
themslevss, that is not columnar at all, support from no
directionm, support from every direction, frm the manifold of
directions, itnerrieorities and exteriorities indistiinct, the
fingers now faltering on the keyboard, working through the
middle of the night careful delineationsm,, waves, as if there
were meanings and linkages of meanings: all words are sound, all
notes are words: all intervals are barriers and always already
open; all doors are intervalsd, always and already intervals;
one never tells one from the other, the other from the one -
circulations of imaginary numbers - one is always breathing one
might presume, the breathing of the water, inflow and outflow,
sentences ruptured by the presence of verbs and nouns,
adjectives and adverbs, always forgotten paving the way, some
water, slow insistence on through ~~~

~~~ 1917 Martin Terz guitar ~~~

——

Always Already Beside the Point /
John Lyly's Euphues: The Anatomy of Wit

http://www.alansondheim.org/nowhere.jpg

+/- "Moreover, to make thee, the more stronger to strive against
these sirens and more subtle to deceive. These tame circum-
stances that thou have more strings to thy bow than one. it is
safe riding at 2 anchors, a fire divided in 20th. Slower a
fountain running into many rivers as a blessed force. , of the
mind, enamered on 2 women is less affected with desire and less
infected with despair, one love expelled with another, and the
remembrance of the latter quencheth, the Kung's coup is science
of the first. yet if thou be so weak, being bewitched with both.
Their wiles that thou Hast not the will to assume nor wit to
avoid their company if they'll be either so wicked that that
will not are so wedded that thou canst not abstain from the
glances common yet at least dissimple, their grief thy grief.
thou be as. Hot as the mountain nafana's office called as the
hillcar cases. , carry 2 faces in one hood cover that I flaming
fancy with fayne dashes. She, showed that he self sounds when
thou art rotten. Let the hubby marry when thy heart is
melancholy, bearer pleasant countenance with the pine conscious,
painted sheath with a leaden dagger. thus dissembling thy grief
that thou mayest secure that disease. love creep within by
stealth my self slides it away. The passes by her door and be
called back. I've just seemed deaf andite to hear a desperate
enough to care. fly the place as the parlors. The portals win
that has been conversed with a lady., yea fallout assumed. The

street will assile its a dwelt as the side of her window renewed
the sum of thy sorrow. thank you. Surely they don't know if that
this comes from you." Forced to admit an anime of wit by John
Lily sometime around the 1600. Perhaps and I've altered by aside
worth sliding sideways, sliding sideways. In the midst of this,
because this is the way that 1 can go in a different direction
as this is being very rarely known. And I think that this is
perhaps from 1579. The original of which is a sliding manu-
script, like a slide roll that has become out of Lynn's and
Leach with it's time like a jar whose top becomes more of a
fop's turning points than something that 1 might have to grift,
or to grease thigh numerical equations in relationship to
catastrophic theories, which as theorems no longer apply to
work, which is spread so far out late and the discourse as those
in the 16th century. Thank you -/+

~~~

amanuensis

https://youtu.be/Pp8XJGL7yQ4 video!

i can't get rid of it, Vito haunted by my amanuensis, hungered,
disappeared, thirsted, Vladimir, so purely brilliant, a glance
holding its own, amanuensis. of the cyber-galactic, amanuensis,
claws, horror of the cyber-galactic, you dare to ask why i don't
sleep at night, 'the' serrated edges, forms of these amanuenses
that surround us, draw us out. horror of them, grabbed by the
throat witch won of us. my amanuensis -- diagnostics whose
digital amanuensis sinks into the palimpsest, microscopy.
experimentation, There have been so many of the variety of
amanuensis, bloodriver amanuensis intangible amanuensis of
real time; perhaps the listener is bloodriver amanuensis
"Otherwise," she said. the drawn amanuensis, the figured. from
amanuensis - things, currency, migration. other, encompassed by
too dirge amanuensis falling from the sky. a able about
amanuensis and are as august Vito be bound In the image, able
about amanuensis and are as august as a wire not this, not night
specters, not haunted or hunted, not deprived of thought, not
this, not that, migraine, violation fabric, indecent posture,
insertions, disappearances, supplementary limbs, inert limbus,
impostulations, ordinary, clawed, torn, from me unto me, within
me into me, helical, violation fabrication, stories from within
out of me, this, thus, here, now, time

(on another note, this was similar to sport, attempting to hold
everything together, in balance, to work through moving align-
ments.)

~~~

unbreath, udbreath, unbreathing, udbreathing

https://youtu.be/8TlSw5QtVTU video, music, data

situation - oud played in a pitch-dark room, camera recording
sound and frequency image - lag producing phenomenon of music
'breathing' - correlation with my own breathing, my own playing
- in the middle of the night, thus - how music breathes music
breathes being breathes music -

—

writing, dangling, capitol

http://www.alansondheim.org/rish1.jpg

which doesnt deserve capitol letters o my dwindling unnecessary
audience one or an other undeserving punctuation o i have no
time for loose participles perhaps there are 4 people who care
about breaking news where are you 4 people for people this or
that an other theory eyrie nested among vector envelopes will
not stop unstop forward for does theory need readers hearers
does anything john barton wolgamot my writings are cables that
reinforce the body i've stolen your letters i'm wasting them
dangling uselessly from the railings of foundering floundering
ships dedicated to the solitary reader in the distance a rock
some trees cliff hurricane seashore

—

For some reason missing the urls, hence, unusable, but at
least the quote etc. is correct.

Wired:

All the Alan Sondheim you never knew you wanted to read

(((I think every literateur that works on ink-on-paper should
confront the work of Alan Sondheim and then shudder from head to
toe.)))

The Alan Sondheim Mail Archive

(given the quantity of my work, this is wonderful I think. I am
full of myself.
Decklin Foster set this up and the site is lean and works really
well. - Alan)

This is an archive of works sent by Alan Sondheim to various
mailing lists. You can read the most recent messages below, or
browse by year:

1999 2000 2001 2002 2003 2004 2005 2006 2007 2008

There is also an Atom feed. If you notice any broken links,
please contact
Decklin Foster, who runs this site. Decklin Foster

http://sondheim.rupamsunyata.org/

```
================================================
```

I am full of myself. Below, recent deconstruction Second Life.

http://www.alansondheim.org/ circ jpgs

object going offworld

http://www.alansondheim.org/cutout1.mov

Objects are added at the top of the stack, pushed down,
collapse, disappear, sometimes return to the database, objects
speed up,
Julu Twine gains speedwheel, textures are body-skinned.

```
================================================
```


test and then some

http://www.alansondheim.org/richarter.jpg

difficult to weave in and out of the matrix of varying mail
programs with lower ascii when we're trying to get the material
to rise to the surface, risse to the surface, flotsom and
jetsom, forgetting the difference, differance, among the
categories employed and disemployed, sintered, saturated,
impossibly reassembled, somewhere there is loss in this, i.e.
lossy, the parasite, Serres, always present, always within and
without the wires, the air, the materiality, the effluvia, the
atmospherics, of (   ) - if and only not if these were the
proper symbols for brackets, you see my eyes are wide shut,
thinking n - error - thinking not through the spelling of the
words but in that state yet again where everything is or seems
to be autonomic - the debris below part of this, after the
protocols, after the protoccalls, after the protocalls...

* * *

From MAILER-DAEMON Sun Nov 19 01:08:16 2023
Date: 19 Nov 2023 01:08:16 -0500
From: Mail System Internal Data <MAILER-DAEMON@Ossi.localdomain>
Subject: DON'T DELETE THIS MESSAGE -- FOLDER INTERNAL DATA
Message-ID: <1700374096@Ossi.localdomain>
X-IMAP: 1700374096 0000000001
Status: RO

This text is part of the internal format of your mail folder,
and is not a real message. It is created automatically by the
mail system software. If deleted, important folder data will be
lost, and it will be re-created with the data reset to initial
values.

From alan@Ossi.localdomain Sun Nov 19 01:08:16 2023 -0500
Newsgroups:
Date: Sun, 19 Nov 2023 01:08:16 -0500 (EST)
From: Alan Sondheim <alan@Ossi.localdomain>
To: junioe@Ossi.localdomain
cc: sondheim@panix.com

Subject: are you there?
Fcc: sent-mail
Message-ID: <alpine.DEB.2.20.2311190107580.21@Ossi.localdomain>
User-Agent: Alpine 2.20 (DEB 67 2015-01-07)
X-Cursor-Pos: To 0
MIME-Version: 1.0
Content-Type: text/plain; format=flowed; charset=UTF-8
Status:
X-Status:
X-Keywords:
X-UID: 1

ok, this is a different keyboard without raised keys, a chiclet
keyboard and is it possible to unmask the depths of the lonter
sentence while listening to the crowd outside screaming, this is
for real, and who is doing what to whom and for why? suddenly
transylvania comes to mind, perhaps because of the spelling? god
only knows and they won't utter a word, now that the heat is
coming ack on. i type and listen to the almlmost silence of the
typing in this room wit h these almost padded keys, a long and
exhuasting day for no reason at all, no reason I can think of,
and the hissing of the heat adds another dimension when i think
ow of crows, or raven,s or corvids in eneral – are they the most
itelligent of the avian queendom? who would know, who would say
a word, i think i heard somewhere perhaps the heron, but i'd
think vulture or some such, most likely a raven but maybe oer
perhaps any or all of the disnosaurs now and then as well

http://www.alansondheim.org/richarter.jpg

+++

Beginning the difficult work of erase-rebuild

http://www.alansondheim.org/from.jpg

Wed Apr 5 01:09:39 EDT 2023

not even waiting for me – not even waiting for anything – but
sentient – cognizant – my presence for example – if I could only
Sun Nov 19 05:27:50 EST 2023 erase it! turn I into i into
nothing!without substance, nothing to grant that, substance
itself less than a fiction – that mirage without basis, without
the layers of heat over the asphalt road descending for miles
into and across the basin of the desert –Wed Apr 5 01:21:10 EDT
2023 gone now, after "taking, a false" start, false ending, oh
how i wish – so fearful, that tree --Wed Apr 5 01:21:56 EDT 2023

armor

Working on sex tool bolted fieldwork

Wed Apr 5 01:09:39 EDT 2023

i canWed Apr 5 01:10:00 EDT 2023Sun Nov 19 05:27:41 EST 2023

i can't read a word you're saying, i can't hear a word your
singing, i'm so scared i'm going to fly off the world and that
will be the end of everything in the world, that tree there is
ferocious, i can see it glaring next to the highway near the
fence, what do you want, Tree? Wed Apr 5 01:11:12 EDT 2023 I
want to go over the fence, I want to go to the other side of the
fence, I will be safe there, THIS HILL HAS SHARP CORNERS, i
can't believe i ever agreed to this, not since that day in the
Sun Nov 19 05:27:35 EST 2023 Alps when I RAN DOWN the hill
leading up and up and up and didn't fall a bit, a section, an
enormous NOTHINGi always thought i could see forever, and see
beyond forever, we are so utterly insignificant in this universe
where one galaxy has a Sun Nov 19 05:27:57 EST 2023 TRILLION
stars, this is unimaginable, and then how many planets, how much
life - these things - life - grow everywhere - kills themselves
off - we're about to do that do - not even a gravitational wave
to announce it elsewhere - just a return to nothing -Wed Apr 5
01:14:22 EDT 2023 a return to annihilation - what i call
"annihilation: to the Limit!" - it matters NOTHING - it's
inconsequential - this all is - this furious SCREEN for example
-Wed Apr 5 01:15:53 EDT 2023 this is a language only that tree
understands - that one up on the side of the hill - that one by
the highway - as if there's another tree against it - next to it
- somehow touching - too frightened to go looking -Wed Apr 5
01:17:01 EDT 2023 something deeply uncomfortable - almost
something in the air, neither rising nor descending - just THERE
-Wed Apr 5 01:17:56 EDT 2023 but then, as if we lived in
immediacy - nothing could be farther from the false...Wed Apr 5
01:19:28 EDT 2023 "thus, coming into being" - already forgotten
- that phrase - that empty phrase -Wed Apr 5 01:20:04 EDT 2023

Wed Apr 5 01:22:03 EDT 2023

http://www.alansondheim.org/from.jpg

————

desperados' despair

https://youtu.be/nY2TmZ5RUqo video

Molochite: place to soft place and I am so glad it is not a war
but Molochite:: the place to soft place and I am so glad it is
not a war Molochite:: but the A Warrant officer or Chun-wi is
not a warrant. not a war it's not a war, it's butchery it's not
a war, it's genocide it's not a war, it's slaughter [You may
have heard "It's not a war" before; I suggest { It's not a war,
its butchery It's not a war, its genocide It's not a war, its
slaughter } it's not a war it's not a war, it's butchery it's
not a war, it's genocide it's not a war, it's slaughter it's not
a war, it's butchery it's not a war, it's genocide it's not a
war, it's slaughter it's not a war, it's butchery it's not a
war, it's genocide it's not a war, it's slaughter -- [::] : the
world is not a war the world contains a war of the man be a war
was in a world that they are not a war with an

245

As above, so as below As above so as below As above, so as
below, my friends As above, so as below - As above, so as below
- As above, so as below As above, so as below, my friends As
above, so as below - As above, so as below As above, so as below
As above, so as below, my friends As above, so as below - As
above, so as below As above, so as below As above, so as below,
my friends As above, so as below - As above, so as below As
above, so as below As above, so as below, my friends As above,
so as below - As above, so as below As above, so as below As
above, so as below, my friends As above, so as below - As above,
so as below As above, so as below As above, so as below, my
friends As above, so as below - As above, so as below

___

Plague of Language Noise

https://youtu.be/YFma0nWcjVA video

JT: Ah yes, I remember now, the plague about the witnessing of
the plague is the subject.
AD: This is a sphere where the plague canot enter
JT: What kind of a sphere where the plague canot enter is it?
JT: Ah yes, I remember now, the plague about the witnessing of
the plague is the subject.

But what I will carry, like or permanent virus, is this: plague,
easements one has to be blind things, warfare, by global warming
breakdown ozone layer, This trace dancer remains, against wall
and care contract with song. didn't do that c. Internet haves
have-nots: continuous upgrading now n stemSbut you know
rearrange: of language gauges savior come, pure annihilation -
dalization, destruction, other words, accounts received
insideme, i not; but this felt locust, take you everywhere,
emitted deep double cusp virtuality. As thwarted precisely
pennsylvania bodies difference spreading across canon genre,
classic To these criminals, properly so called, incurable
flatters societies semi-criminals fall down, consume, consumed
blightcobblestones caught sullen cold rain. rosie pox death),
planet heading towards chemical disease totalitarian life,
cold-life annihilations. covered Not binarism, on avatars,
seminal disturbances can't quite figure them into upon Ring live
traffic fissuring (plague death, world around (the approach
subsided; if anything, it prairie center edge develops, not
healing, closer. Otherwise chases critical journal year; well
buried victims; Viral plagues, overturned cobblestones, plague.
onslaught. journey resurgence smallpox plagues Rosie us, then
plunge America an enormous inertia midst cannot think
debilitating headaches which were site, sight, locus. It's more
imaginations availes medina omar what's left us nanotechnologies
purification. i'm salvation. order Sports passport password past
anti-semitism increased year. love time virtual lands field,
picked up for famine, drought, &c. On war earthquake murder here
there, it's power some you, appearance virus usual voice-chant i
don't alien trajectories. related corona fourth series
meditations quarantine. A truth functions, debate ancient India,
logics, any more, inertia, everywhere floods, fires, crusades,

wars, imagining unaided no avail, league imagined flee me won't
give devils their side: less, exhausted, myriad beings while
coming food ring might away rich silver journeys plague's mud
problematic harsh sun; dream lives worsened began suffer those
terribly throat face. "machines had always antonin artaud. at
age five emanations pressing ribs gapes stomach, first lpmud
been contaminated. viral organs socius general. stemsbut "this
internet ding beyond didst tell saidst idea passover questions
every place site massacre. source sutured, politics history
face-down machine-gunned men, we appeared released smallpox,
measles, all sorts. rest things rot your plagues. eleven o'clock
morning, day will. tuberculosis, diptheria, forget there's
nothing b plague); shoot kill anything avoid pain flight india,
wraiths, spirits children killed plunged centring can smell now;
absolution. wonder strangers otherwise really coronavirus; fear,
hatreds, horizon violence journey. law itself cut war, cartels.
america isn't public whether apply sheaves sions damps gathered
skin tears unbreathable, asthma allergic choice-televisual
web-inversion subjectivity soiled mold radio rumor seduction
offer alone. :semi-criminals sickness design JT: Ah yes,
remember now, about witnessing subject. AD: sphere where canot
enter What kind it? after Thought, drought abandoned space,
coronation forth, materials including course Defoe's kind,
kindness hover within, our death murder news trauma announces
slightest provocation done quote each other, lay down aphorism,
have, weaponry notwithstanding. they that. necessary because
covid still speak/write, descending wit Covid have sutured over.
My symptoms

https://youtu.be/YFma0nWcjVA video

—

after no after

https://youtu.be/j-IUJrAmqEc video (some flicker)

glory born: because when that happens, when there is that flash
or somewhat there and there might first be an uncanny smell, no
that would take some time wouldn't it, no there would be first
the sight, always the sight and that is fearful then later the
sound, the touch of ash perhaps after that, smell for some
reason of gas or oil, something oily, something from the earth
that shouldn't be there, then there's the problem, from all
directions and then what, what might occur, into the bunker with
you! or some such, if not the bunker, then what, , then the
forest, if not the forest, i write with eyes closed, the touch
of the keys perhaps the last touch, i'm not sure, is this coming
through, is it coming out, are you coming out, withdraw
immediately, they are at ... then there's something else, this,
and then after that, what might occur O fearful! because what
we're left - oh i see, what we're left (with(- no it can't be
that... ragged, theERA of AIR is replaced by the EYRIE or what,
that's also, understood, with theyes closed curtains drawn
windows shut, night emerg, no maybe well not is present it's the
guid of odors, something like that, on the run or walk, charnal
something like that, i hear the sound of a thousand keys turning
over the graves of letters, someone died maybe the 22th centurt

like that i remember now,, cavalcade, charnalhus, cc: to whom it
may concern - should be all of our concern/s - gone quiet now,
that music < the world keeps repeating > jjust now - subterfuge
- obsequious - those nursery rhyumes , something - some)thing_

—

Writings from the Notebook, 1/91, 3/92 as dictated

http://www.alansondheim.org/ok.jpg

In the structuration there is nothing developmental no stories.
Substance fishers merges symbolizes : lines of identification
harden , bifurcate, decay. What is of the infant is of the
adult. Time compresses. If there is an absolute substance, it is
one of face mint. Things churn and jostle , I speak of the
limits of every knowledge here. Ontological churning. Family
orbit, Eroticism , punctured dash infantile memories as puncture
punctuation . Fishering implies embroilment dash details are
lost momentary stacy's within turbulent regimes. There's
something ungainly in the leakage of the signifying dash and
indescribable relation relationship To the real dash a literal
scan or mesh at work here dash droppings dash access ,
demarcation.

Unworking dash reaching the point where everyday is equivalent
to every other moment to moment, the substance of each hour
without plans or schedule insomnia and exhaustion, the indolence
of too much sleep. The singular light which focuses moment by
moment, ripples of fluid moving slowly outward. Position of
continuous and everyday thinking tackling thought as a calling.

Born into difference substance is monadic .

Colonization cauterizes dash which flesh is cut and altered
which flesh devoured.

There is no place for eyes. Moons height, nothing is visible,
nothing envisioning dash flanks, cold, Stony, as if disappearing
into mist fog low lying clouds dash the stones wet and dull as
if touched with an absence of touch or description .

I'm the last of the neurotic artists dash the last solitary dash
no one after me lives in a Garret. I revel my incomprehension
dash my intense frustration dash not a game for style I'm out of
touch with all the committees . I forget to get my application
online. Give me money. I'll come back and haunt you when I'm
dead. I'll come back and haunt you alone, even though I breathe
I've not forgotten the civility of love.

...

sanshin w/care w/corrective w/presence w/absence

melancholy sounds of a rough day, and garcia lorca else forget
bushido date dynamics. the is okinawan version shamisen, pushing
shakuhachi consciousnesses consensualities with eyes closed,
yes, well, neck safewords samadhi sarangi sarinda satori Our
Saturday night last I use opportunity to play sanshin. Hollow
instrument, sanshin, breathing slow stop i am opaque industry.
stumble on know what lies nails scrape against strings you do
not days - accompanied by an improvisation Okinawan sound can
only imagine delicate in my hands sanshin played it softly found
that when night. recorded at distance, rain drumming, skull,
still yelling. But he did */blown open w/ empty head hollow
empty /*

+++

Friends,

Friends, it is hard to believe in peace , it is hard to believe
in anything at this point, the world is on fire, nations jump
with the chance to increase their borders to increase their
military to increase everything , everything destructive, ai
will speed this up at an inconceivable rate, even this language
now that I am using will create more digital debris in the
world, local wars and mafias seem to be the solution to
everything, there is no place to turn, violence is appearing on
the horizon of every place on earth, destruction is everywhere,
one wants to maximize wounding and destruction as much as
possible, one wants to maximize the growth of death cults , of
religious bigotry is, of local wars, of national wars, of poison
wars, of atomic wars, of injuries, of annihilations to the
limit, of annihilations everywhere, random shooting, of directed
shooting, one wants to find a place to negotiate this labyrinth,
there is no place to negotiate this, this truth , this truth ,
this truth , there is granite and the core of earth ,, beneath
the surface of the ground there is the core of earth , there are
holding places for people like us, there are holding places for
people like us whose mouths are filled with dirt , there are no
one who will come forth to deliver us, our eyes are dirt our
arms are dirt our legs are dirt , what is this of us, what is
the BLINDING LIGHT that follows us everywhere , that comes forth
in the night comes forth in the day, what is this , what of this
, what of this , what is this , where is this , who is this ,
what is the night that comes forth in the day , that comforts in
the day , that dissolves in the day , what is this , what is
this of , who are you , where , what , when , how , how

++

Coal (Kirill Azernyy , Alan Sondheim)

http://www.alansondheim.org/whatgives17.jpg

so mine the fact that everything is very slow and I want
civility but I also want to move on and these things contradict
each other and this is something that more than That sounds
almost identical to me because I I literally wake up at 5:00 AM
everyday I woke up at 5:00 AM today as wellYou go to bed around
We went in three and so I sleep through the afternoon I'm always
crashing because I I have no I have no sleep time no no
scheduled sleep that works it just goes on and on Usually I wake
up in a state of anxiety about the world about my my ex family
No that sort of thing About our state of being where we are here
. keeps me up at night because it feels like I don't even need
an alarm clock It's the it's the same thing for me it has to
doAir Force Before you look until Lewis and guitarist for
example you have all these metaphors and they're writing you
look at lacon you have other metaphors and they're writing and
none of these are really backed by physical or physiological or
cosmological states but the metaphors take on a life of their
own they become a form of reification I think like anti antipus
there is no atticus there is no antipus complex No these these
terms are so Mislabeled Allows us to sort of scam what's
actually going on in the real world and the grit of the real
world anymore because I woke up at 5:00 a.m. today with no alarm
clock I went to bed it was like midnight or something like this
and I thought I set up the alarm clock but I didn't do this but
yeah I mean I forgot to do this but nevertheless Did banks it
goes off again and and Bang Bang Bang Bang bang it goes off
again in my headYou're gonna watch the news again to see who's
killing what where and when and how and what kind of reaction
you can have when you can't affect it I woke up at 5:00 a.m. so
it means that I'm already kind of sleep I have no sleep time no
no scheduled sleeps that works it just goes on and on and
usuallyI don't think there I don't feel there is a solid ground
anymore at all every time I wake upOur country going to war with
another country or withdrawing its diplomats from another
country Oh and on constantly and it's something that I wrote
about 60 years ago 50 years ago was writing about this kind of
stuff and now it's happening like somewhat out of a bad JG
Ballard novel I wake up in the state of anxiety about the world
about my my ex family that sort of thing about our state of
being where we are here. yes well I I used to wake up in the
middle of nights if for for instance I need to wake up early I
used to wake up earlier in the night numerous times two or three
times a night to make sure I have not overslept my job but the
thing is that I don't really need this job anymore and I hate to
admit it because I like yeah I I feel like I'm between my
teenage State and kind of adult State and I know I don't know
which one is which because I really feel like I need a solid
ground but it doesn't Solid Ground mean that I have sufficient
money or does it mean that I don't hate what I'm doing I don't
know I mean in both cases I remember your peace I think it was
back in the '70s or something I think you're quoting this and
writing under The difference the difference between physics and
other modelsA physicist that I knew was saying when he was
talking to a theorist is with writing just theory what you're
basically doing is *********** but when you're writing physics

250

what you're doing is you're ******* the universe because you're
actually creating things that are testable and that Apart and
fall to pieces as they usually do Oh when you're when you're
going on in that fashion You are really you are really dealing
with the grit of the universe Well if you if you want if you
want to read there's probably 100 books on how physical theory
operates within physicsSee if just in any even even kind of If
you look at a book on quantum computers and you can see and it
and it with quantum computers how quantum computers work but the
input and the output is how they're testable what kind of
statistics are being used however the statistics being testable
This is something I mean Wisconsin talked talked about it
because all the way back physics has a sense of Of the the
absolute about it because you can propose a theory like the
theory of the telematics theory of epicycles and Deadly false It
was proved absolutely false for so many reasons and then
copernicus had a a different way of looking at things and that
astronomical thing worked to a certain point it's always within
tolerance so you have tolerance theory So what what do you mean
when you talk about what do you mean when you talk about the
world ends what do you exactly mean by thatWhere did where does
our world end spatially where exactly does it end spatiallySo
then why do you say that that it ends spatially ! I think it's
from From 1977 so you're saying that 474 you're saying that
information needs to be accessed as it goes as a flow of info
and it sounds like what you're saying now to be honest to me I
mean the subject is different but the state of flow you're
talking about resembles the stage of flow that you discussed
back in the seventies in terms of mislabeled that they allow us
to sort of scam what's actually going on in the real world and
the grit of the real world this is very much about what we want
this is much about comfort and I don't know much about physics
but I can't imagine that there are no such things as strings or
atoms or Basin or anything like this these are all models but we
need them and we need most probably the motels that he was
talking is with writings just Theory where you're basically
doing is masturbating but when you're writing physics what
you're doing is you're f****** the universe because you're
actually creating things that are testable and that will fall
apart and Fall to Pieces as they usually do when you say
testable when you say testable when you say testimony I'm sorry
for bringing this up by now this is kind of cliche but this is
also it should be taking into account because so what does it
mean testable proofs most probably won't this kind of feels
refreshing tolerance Theory yeah I mean there is some extent and
point when our Logic the way I mean the World As We Know It And
sort of and we never quite catch up with this ending cuz it's
always something that already happens like with Siri for
instance which when I say the world ends I mean that the extent
of our knowledge of it ends our world ends the world doesn't end
but our world does and especially if you will it reaches it kind
of limit of its credibility and we sort of expected basically
well it doesn't that's the problem !

——

camera

https://youtu.be/viDbEXtQ54k video

i can't draw at all . i can't hear at all . i can't see at all .
my camera knows me . my camera hears me . my camera sees .
seeing, my camera photographs me . i turn my camera away .
all i see is my face . my face is my original face .
no matter where i turn . no matter what i turn .
my camera photographs me . it is always me . it is always me .
my camera photographs always me .

————

Venus with artifacts

http://www.alansondheim.org/Venuswithartifacts.jpg

centimeters. Venus & To a Dryad, or Delia, (Diana), & To Pales
or Pomona, & from Venus born, thy beauty shows; like my wings
are Venusian portal are resonant/diacritical with the rest. The
user deals with an alterity in the form of constantly changing
facial circulations wells tunnels, secure, artifacts temporary
infinity, these artifacts quotation mark Quotation mark. That's
it . elements, worn artifacts, ooooooooo ghosts (not all ghosts
are

———

Sward, Metaphysics, Ecstatic, Embrace, Embryonic

https://youtu.be/B2-sxDsUpKU video

tenor ocarina, supercollider, photography of/for Azure Carter,
meditative form, costumes and conceptions by Azure, sound
and sound conceptions by myself

All of which coagulated formed and informed collapsed and
extended dissolved and embroiled informed turbulence that's
smoothed out within the HS of using electronics to reverse time
to introvert time to transform time backwards and forwards
placing it again within the matrix I could only go in One
Direction collapsed into several several streams interacting
Stereophonics really contradicting speech forms such as this
While presenting symmetries of form and time which are
introverted within themselves and within the formal display and
production of sound in this work . This is the way the world
began and this was the way the world ended and this was the way
the world went on and on and on while the computer was unable to
handle the material here and I had to reconfigure it over and
over again as well to take it so that it would reproduce itself
as a single or singular file. I want to inhabit these spaces . I
want to inhabit these spaces a beautiful death a beautiful life
of the cemetery which carries both with flocks of birds and bell

towers. I want to live there among others, among many others
among all of us among of all all of us who are gone and all of
us who are yet to come I love all of us who are yet to arrive
and all of us who will not arrive who will no longer arrive who
will no longer have arrived who will no longer have come to
arriving who will no longer hear the word departure or the bells
ringing or the music ending or the music coming to an end where
the voice or the breath coming to an end with the sound coming
to an end , Oh so softly does the sound come to an end oh so
softly do the brackets close themselves selves upon the last
remaining words . We are on the edge or lip or the sward where
all of this occurs however all of this leaves us behind as if
the world were always and now more than ever rushing away
quietly as if it were noiseless, making noise

———

error, Prone

languages inLanguages in! it keepsIt keeps turning itself into
sendSend it disappears andIt disappears and turns itself off
startStart thankThanks becauseBecause findFind
Becausebecausebecause when you start pick upstopStop it start
speakSpeak what'sThat's why testTest where justWhat yeahhowthat
areAre you uncomfortable with the lighting goodGood googleWho
are you to gowhereWhere googleUncle goGoogle gotGo going onGoing
on you areYou who are you why are how are youWhere are you
briefgoodGood good grief whereGood grief where are you why are
you there to meTo me there's noThere's no tomorrow there's no
tomorrow there's noThere's no tomorrow there's no today there's
no todayit's notnoteNote buildBuild Cortanabuild 1 and
forcortanaCortana do not build 1 sendSend markWork thisWork done
workWork work make upbaconThank you would you have britain
ifWould you have Britain if it's got curing down doesperiodthis
isThis is unbelievable that theThe wood in theWood in the forest
or not wood in theWood in the forest do not in the nextWoodland
do notNot the sweetWoodland and stop the burnStop the burning
forest stupidStupid hurtStop funnyBurning brooding forest stop
bing dotThings about the farm goodGood grief why not powerNo
thatThe power station 1stFirst internetThe power the popThe
power station stateState power station the they showedThe shower
station the patientPower station star stationStar station the
power station theThe power station the power face powerPower
station the powerThe power station dinnerMinerva minervaMinerva
Minerva Manor the powerThe power station languages inLanguages
and languages in itIt keeps it keeps turn openTurn
vincentVincent it disappear andAnd I turned to 4For because
becauseBecause theThe powerpop work work nowNow and then and
thenAnd then then then thenThen then then

———

game theory game

https://youtu.be/B8NvfPLH8B0 video

this is the game theory game. for the past three years i have
played a word game on my 15 year old zaurus. it is similar to
scrabble. i must make decisions whether a word is acceptable or
not. i search for rare patterns, for example the resulting game
extremely short with no more moves; the game with an overall
geometry; the game which avoids most of the corners and mid-
lines (edge middles); the game with other peculiarities such as
density or despair; the games with extremely high scores. many
of the final positions have been saved. i think i probably
played 2000 or so games beginning through covid including my
covid. here are some of the more interesting final positions,
and you may admire through archaeological processes of your own,
what transpired in them, in other words conundrum. the images
are sideways with a few other things thrown in. the soundtrack
is, well, the soundtrack whose source is another mystery from
the 1980s surely, between dallas and buffalo and providence.
in order to figure out the game through your investigations,
i must say, there is no answer, and in fact, as in life as well,
everything unravels, faster or slower, and everything unravels
everything. head turned sideways, as mine often is, i would
slow, stop, and ponder, and perhaps something will come to mind.

—

Language, Cataract, Silence

https://youtu.be/iweZ3BvPApw video

(images from post cataract operation, fixed-focus lens, 2009)

If language was the presentation of truth, there would be no
present. Tense is already gone by the time it is spoken. The
past tense isn't umbrella. That refers to nothing existence
existent in the future. Tense as always already passed by, the
time it is spoken and it's a chimera. Now it's referred to
nothing except categories which exist in the mind's eye in which
fail in relationship to tolerances. Personifications, the
personal histories, everything slides. everything slides.
nothing it's stable when you turn your head one way or another,
the same changes an alternative and alterably. . but while it's
changing, you may still be saying I see a tree and that refers
to nothing but a memory of something that's already engraved in
the mind and has been given the absence of a name and
relationship to the past. And an inconceivable future where
nothing will be spoken that you know and your language will
already be uninterpretable. Unimaginable, untranslateable and
unmeaning. It's the fragility of what we say in relationship to
what we do. I know from playing instruments that there are so
many strata going on simultaneously that it's impossible to tell
one from another to dissect them to make them speak with voices
that are so linear that they're impossible. the music itself
disappears as soon as it's made. . in a sense, the music has
already disappeared before. It was made before the when there
was nothing because

because when it was made, it was already prefigured preconfigured, the movements were already starting the muscles were already being toned in the memory was already scratching and circulating looking for something or other that would then be reflected in something or rather in the real world. . it's all this, it's always all this diffusion diffusion. The only thing that isn't is death because you have to death, however, blurred that boundary may be, there is really nothing you might say or might be said to you. there is nothing to be understood or that might be understood by you. it's always oh, it's always already gone. just as before your birth. That's always already gone for others. But not for you can look back. It's almost with a sense of condescending and inconfigure or preconfigure. What they were on about as far as you know and as far as you know is all there is to know and that is what concerns you about them and what no longer concerns them about you.

—

Enough Already

http://www.alansondheim.org/theprocess.jpg

Worrisome, this is my mind. I am 'getting realdy' - and proceeding in such a fashion, am I losing memory, the ability to think? friends who don't answer, friends who doe, so many enemies, he's just a nuisance, a pest get him out of my sight, away from my site, I continue typing, ow knowing where this is gooing , not knowing, that is to say, where this is going, the destination like a Trolley, that one I made a video from in Geneve years ago, still one of my favoites, the camera shooting from the front window next to the driver, wonderful, a cold winter day and grey sky if I remember, and I do, well I remember, derailed now from the loss of memory which has closure, doesn't exist perhaps, but the writing, the typing, with eyes closed, no distractions, bad tv news off in the corner, too many bodies world-wide every, disease, what could anyone expect, countries jostling for power in a fading world, nuclear at the ready, perhaps no need, famine will take care of the rest... how am I doing, I ask myself? I can still write, the fingers finding their more or less proper places on the keyboard, my mind still functiioining, too much to forget, perhaps even more to remember, memories haunt me, playing the scenes over and over again, now I'm riding the trolley of already typed keys, words gushing out of the fountain of haptic control or non-control, think I meed up there for a moment, better if I write unthinkingly, just alone with my thoughts, someone to be sure will comae along and take them from e, take them from me, I hope this is legible, just enough, leigble just enough, enough, already enoughh...

—

Capital

From the notebook: - zero which is zero -

https://youtu.be/u1dBT-xEck4 video

All my work ... when it can't become distanced or one and
another... Everything thrown into everything - Disbelief is
related to core structure, deep disconnections, fierce, fiery,
unbridled intensity */language but what is it without landscape?
/* everything pours into the mould, the mould hardens: that is
everything. & which perhaps a waist, construction - turning
(revolution), turning (circulation). Absolutely no connection to
the world, that is to say, except a belief in such. Otherwise
nothing, nothing at all. "Film of spectacles, tunnels, fissures,
chasms, peaks, rubbles, voids - titles dragging the in-itself
down - the shallow plate of the film, my absence (body etc.) -
circulation, repetition of ideas - (our ideas of _things_ always
visitations) -

——

Bad Advertisement for Myself

http://www.alansondheim.org/tiger.jpg

Well I wake up in the middle of the night and find once again
I'm turned into a diarist, not a thoerist, writer, poet, artist,
new media anything, but a diarist, as if talking to myself were
my one and only option. Which maybe it is. When I type with eyes
closed, eyes wide shut,I learn that the haptic disappears, that
my thoughts, which already are problematic, become something
turned into speech, as if Wittgenstein might have done the same,
with however and at that time, others taking notes after notes
down and I wonder now why one or another recorder was never
used? Otherwise there's an elasticity to the whole process,
which he might well have hidden behind, something like that. At
my end it's a question of no audience at all as far as I can
tell, difficult to engage with my ideas, and so the invisibility
of the words and the inaudibility of my voice tends towards the
evanescent which has little merit. I could insist that like
"doing philosophy" but that has little merit; I was insisting on
some such all the way back to my teens when I know now, that was
literally unutterably false. So to proceed, language a shell of
sounds and/or interpreted strokes in the darkness and sound of
the clattering of keys. I wake in the middle of the night after
having not slept. I sit here, try to rite myself, right myself
wright myself, write myself. I have dreams of readers, being
invited once again th "present" at one or another institution,
what I wuold say, show, sound, but the chances of this happening
are less and less, a bad feedback loop, the more I protest, the
more I'm a nuisance, to myself as welll. There's nothing worse,
yes there is, but anyway, nothing worse than self loathing which
returns as such through occasional deprecation, isolation,
ignorance, howling winter winds here in nnow icy Rhode Island. I
think at most I get 20 or so viewers to my videos, which I keep
obviously mindlessly producing, less readers, when I keep
endlessly writing about less readers and less viewers and less

listeners; mental distress is to a great extent the result of positive feedback loops, the worse and more isolated one feels, the more no one wants to hear that and unlike Anti-Oedipus or some such wher sheaves of writing are the result, for most of us the result is silent. Before I turned 80 people were "interested" in what I was doing and vice versa; once that hit, after the celebration of the day, everything dropped off. Friends die, others move to other jobs, are too busy, and the age-old issue of the issue of old age is simply that "no one wants to hear you" as someone said decades ago. I'm of course whining and that always collapses everything; I can't imagine Husserl or Wittgenstein whining. I am simply writing a prolegomenon to please look at a few videos, listen to some of the soundwork, read some of the other texts than this, study the e-lit textual manipulation stuff and virtual world stuff and deconstructive stuff and maybe, just maybe, invite me to speak somewhere somehow somewhen, give me a chance to dialog with students (I'm not bad at it), give me a screening, stop my incessant blathering to myself such as this in the middle of another sleepless nnight, forget that I'm not Stephen Sondheim (yess distant relative as are Houdini and Einstein but that goes nowhere), don't invite me to a Broadway show or show me broadway but as my friend said, Gerald Jones, who died years ago, he was always tap-dancing on mean streets, died neglected in a hospital, went Everglading with us, this is enough of a surface, another writing exercise, typing w/ eyes closed, and probably more erros now than I could count on you to reach this part of the narrative thinking, yes it might be a good idea to give him a read, show, talk, whatever, before he that's me stops tying altogether. Fwiw, work's up on YouTube, a lot of it; on my Facebook page, on some music or literary or other sites, all for soared eyes, ears, and whatever haptics we have left.

-- promise no more of this!

—

From ETC (Experimental Television Center) history -

https://www.youtube.com/watch?v=C2xtv5rl57k

"Alan Sondheim

Foofwa was with Merce Cunningham at the time, and we recorded him with a
number of cameras which were switched on and off by my voice. The music
had been prerecorded at ETC as well. The work emphasizes the physicality
of classical ballet in relation to the real body and exhaustion of the
dancer.

I tended to work quickly at ETC in general; years before, in 1967, we had
built a music synthesizer with VCO, VCA, etc. from scratch - there were no

257

blueprints at the time. So I became familiar with analog controls early on
- and the ensuing production techniques that emerged from them. ETC
allowed this all to occur in what was, for me, an ideal workspace /
livespace / playspace / dancespace/ performance space - an open loft next
to the Susquehanna River (I grew up in Kingston, Pennsylvania, next to the
same) - with a bookstore across the street, a still bridge which we could
attach contact microphones to, a town with a gazebo perfect for dancework
at 4 a.m. in the morning, nature and ponds around, and so forth. I
remember a bat flying over our heads one night when we were falling asleep
- wonderful!

The equipment was relatively easy to use, and I tried to work with
everything, including a very old character generator which was the core of
some of my work. I loved the analog video synthesizers as well, which were
more like living organisms - one negotiated with them, and that was always
amazing. I used the Mirage Ensoniq constantly for music; its combination
of analog and digital with floppies was breathtaking. Later I found a
second-hand one but it gave out on me; I still try to find one to use for
my music/soundwork.

You ask about "citizen of the world" - but it was more like citizen of the
Universe! The machines had an inner light of their own, and living and
working in the same space meant we could get up at 4 a.m. if one of us had
an idea, and work through the night. In the short times of the residencies, we were able to produce hours of finished work, as if there
were always dialogs organically growing among us and the machinery, which
had a life of its own.

I remember beavers, Foofwa dancing on the railing of a pier overlooking a
frozen pond, recording ballet and movie musical dancing on the street in
front of the loft at 3 a.m. in the morning.

It was perfect. I took that experience later to the work I did at the
Virtual Environments Laboratory (VEL) at West Virginia University,

Morgantown, and more recently to working with motion capture
experimentation at New Jersey Institute of Technology, NYU, Co-
lumbia
College (Chicago), and elsewhere. A certain grace and camaraderie
with
machines, bodies, intermixtures of analog and digital apparatus.
And I
work through this even now.

ETC was seminal!"

   NIKUKO with Azure Carter and Foofwa dImobilite (YouTube)

121 views Sep 13, 2017
Foofwa d'Imobilite, Azure Carter, Alan Sondheim, Experimental
Television
Center, ballet, abjection

—

Clubland (amazing music take)

https://youtu.be/NRUUM8Ht_1E YouTube full Video
http://www.alansondheim.org/clubland2.mp4 short graphics clip
https://youtu.be/NRUUM8Ht_1E YouTube full Video

CLUBLAND lies just outside our window, 4 stories down then a bit
to the right, CLUBLAND is drunk and loud sometimes the cops come
don't they now sometimes not, CLUBLAND informs us of being human
so badly we want it haunt it flaunt it, CLUBLAND sings, wings,
sometimes swings, CLUBLAND kills our sleep, spills for thrills
out in the night packed to the gills even in chills, that said -
I lean the recorder against the window pane, window's pain yet
again, set it to the vibrations of the same game, sit back at a
distance pittance, play guitar like a rock star, soft and clear
don't fear comes through blue, record the mix make a fix with
the amplitude skewed and rude even lewd, this rhyme time worth a
dime. So then three times mixed and patched and scratched the
video, crashed the computer, so you got: 1. the full version of
the sound (amazing) with leader (above); 2. short clip with just
the beginning with complex graphics; 3. longer clip w/ possible
future use as well - both 2 and 3 crashing the machine - would
take overnight to render, machine heating up, then crashing out
- so see the other url above - just for the graphics - and the
YouTube full version - for the amazing sound I must admit yet
again - which is here -

https://youtu.be/NRUUM8Ht_1E YouTube full Video

—

What Appears in War Appears in Films of War

last no truth in death, in war, in illness. There are stations
which all we're always living within war and these were Deaths
are not a cause for truth or enumeration. There is no truth in
death, in war, in illness. There are stations which filter
truth. They construct truth. There are facts but far fewer than
presumed. A death maybe a fact; deaths are not facts. Wars are
not facts. By fierce encounters made in wars, Everything must
be considered and with the increase in warfare, Magical
disappearing acts and slaughter in war are related; both alter
Sarajevo in war-torn Bosnia spite and jealousy his cousins often
used Sun Tzu speaks of deception in war, which is similar to
magic; the There have been mysterious disappearances of soldiers
in war, which a zer Su o will be glad for a two and a five. even
in war the canons are against the houses plastered war the
canons are primed, genreissimo. remember, annotation, built on
low ground that flooded - it was a in a tin warehouse flooding,
corpse, take the teeth, the ear, the prick. in war everything
from bullet death, in war, in illness. There are stations which
filter truth. They dissipates in the air, remains longer in
warfare. formally ICBM. enacted out in war. evolutions war iraq,
buildings off in war york, again slaughters with flooded - it
was in a tin warehouse - and the air-conditioner flooded tin
warehouse air-conditioner ceiling (just hanging tin) (it raw for
those abandoned and grieving in wards for those slaughtered in
war for those slaughtered in war and in peace ground flooded tin
warehouse mail halls (separate multi shed) hole rim. we were
late in war, uncanny peace. ground zero for world-vor- if the
trenches in warfare carried names and bodies permanently in
death, in war, in illness. There are stations which filter
truth. They in warm weather. Under ideal conditions it may
develop in a few weeks in judge position, Europe sinking deaths
the Donbas in warship june they providence; june they they in
war[r] adding: providence; war[r] latin war mapping routing
March 19th death, in war, in wound. "It is easy to keep things
at a distance; it is never atone hideous for those abandoned and
grieving in wards or rather i'd be waiting for ezs ground
flooded tin warehouse mail halls separate everglades
relationship between what we do and what occurs in war, in
release and safety-valve warning the area warning advised are to
advised exit studio was built on low ground that flooded - it
was in a tin warehouse surplus. you can be aroused. you can bomb
them. you can live in war. Israel's Fifty day, war in warnings
to him I have induced them to begin wars without within wartime,
torture, totalitarian regimes, and totality in you can fawn
them. you can live in war. you flag with care : your : what
appears in war appears in films of war.

—

Auto/gnomic Bio

Your arms runs into my scheduled. So I had a video call with him
and I worked and talked:It was too hot and they're worth_Storm

schedule. Thunderstorm:1:I had an appointment with the doctor
today. I didn't want to go in.:scheduled. So I had a video call
with him and I worked and talked - turning me clausterphobic

to some extent my brother understood me but none of my family,
not after the debacle of the acker films at the whitney, made
any attempt to engage me with what i was doing, lived in my head
joined the american forestry association played with model
trucks and stuff read under the covers caught at 3 am in the
morning my father yelling at me again he was screaming at me at
my daughters wedding they wouldn't give me a ride to the place,
my family crashed down around me, i always sensed emotional
violence, i didn't know how to relate to anyone, always fearful
dancing on mean streets thanks Gerald Jones who passed on
miserably in hospital i gathered in his own , i'm not a good
person learned that at an early age :i was never physically
abused but knew to my core i was worthless throwaway, in the
family nincompoop and wastrel my kept silent the other two
mocking and or furious what i remember i couldn't do anything
right fidgeting constantly working myself up running to the
historical society went to a ham radio meeting was told to stop
fidgeting in camp the head told me i'd be dead at 25 if i didn't
slow up always i went to extremes didn't know how to behave you
want more?:around the table i tended to leave when my father
lost his temper, ran back into the bedroom, slammed the door,
came out, left the house, slammed the door walked a while came
back in shaking sometimes cold out there my sister the perfect
one my brother maybe not there yet not eating soup:arguments
around the dinner table, he never hit me but the verbal
screaming broke me down fast when he returned from wwii and i
know: i shouldn't have been there - when he returned - anytime
at all - always :fear constantly of everything

Come home with me, to some extent my brother understood me but
none of my family, not after the debacle of the acker films at
the whitney, made any attempt to engage me with what i was
doing, lived in my head joined the american forestry association
played with model trucks and stuff read under the covers caught
at 3 am in the morning my father yelling at me again he was
screaming at me at my daughters wedding they wouldn't give me a
ride to the place, my family crashed down around me, i always
sensed emotional violence, i didn't know how to relate to
anyone, always fearful dancing on mean streets thanks Gerald
Jones who passed on miserably in hospital i gathered in his own
, i'm not a good person learned that at an early age ,
julu-of-the-fast-crowd! Your clean i know deep down i can do
anything but be destructive and to other people and then think
maybe that's not true, is in my taut Azure's helped me
enormously, i'd be nowhere without her

Your giving :Think this through...::being runs me hiking your
cloth!:My print "Ah...\n"; is yours... is in my rich My is
yours... my rich dependent on them couldn't at all one year
made 40k my best... debacle in Tasmania... Atlanta best...

Your withdrawn You program your carapace forever... is in my
walked scheduled. So I had a video call with him and I worked
and talked:It was too hot and they're worth_Storm schedule.
Thunderstorm:1:I had an appointment with the doctor today. I

didn't want to go in.:scheduled. So I had a video call with him
and I worked and talked

Pennsylvanian Despairing
Depths:yes:2:Strange-Place:Pennsylvanian Despairing Depths

Your psychotic other other people. I'm tired of being inserted
between one is in my on person and another person between a
person on the left and the person on the right not-me a writer

I want to put my body into the code I want the load of my body
to ::Wed, 24 Mar 2021 17:11:09 -0400:person and another person
between a person on the left and the :person on the right
between the person above and a person below

Your withdrawn ... my shoes is For 1 found days, I have been
neurotic programmed ... here, it's my shoes? is in my walked
or walking nowhere, whatever, whatthen, whatever

———

Providence Festival of Lights last night

https://youtu.be/eSv6ROFGBUM video

We arrived at the parking lot for the Festival of Lights,
and stayed for Yacouba Diabate and Big Nazo. On the way
back our local bar had a fire alarm! Curtains drawn.

Big Nazo - "Blink Bots and Aliens parade with
Providence Drum Troupe" -
Yacouba Diabate - on Kora

Early evening with an intensity of color and sound,
wonderful! The Kora playing was fantastic, amazing music!

Enjoy!

———

Gaza

https://youtu.be/Yda-c_4agZA (saz)

it's impossible to comprehend what is occurring in Gaza,
impossible to think through the violence and destruction,
through the continuous cruelty. we don't think clearly,
perhaps not at all, impossible but occurring, absent here
but there, but continuous, but incessant, what is to come
everywhere our abject fear, our fear is safe _here,_ it
is our fear to own from _this_ distance, this safety.
we did years ago have ongoing discussions on email lists
set up for that purpose, war, violence, testimony. now we
have our _safe nightmares_ as cruelty spreads everywhere.
perhaps everything falls short of weeping, of our safety

here, perhaps not. inside we were napalm not real here
we are irreal bombardment, accounts, disasters, bodies,
limbs, massacres, children, infants, so many civilians,
we have the duty here now of _thinking inconceivability_
to respond with art, music, writings, analyses, otherwise
than _there,_ in different words _here_ and not _there,_
the safety of the aporia, the moment of the trench
adjacent to the cusp. i contribute this long-necked saz
piece, i am useless, we watch the war inside of us, we
survive in the safety, for now, of our bodies, our minds
elsewhere, no where at all, the world inconceivable, lost

it'simpossibletocomprehendwhatisoccurringinGaza,
impossibletothinkthroughtheviolenceanddestruction,
throughthecontinuouscruelty.wedon'tthinkclearly,
perhapsnotatall,impossiblebutoccurring,absenthere
butthere,butcontinuous,butincessant,whatistocome
everywhereourabjectfear,ourfearissafe_here,_it
isourfeartoownfrom_this_distance,thissafety.
wedidyearsagohaveongoingdiscussionsonemaillists
setupforthatpurpose,war,violence,testimony.nowwe
haveour_safenightmares_ascrueltyspreadseverywhere.
perhapseverythingfallsshortofweeping,ofoursafety
here,perhapsnot.insidewewerenapalmnotrealhere
weareirrealbombardment,accounts,disasters,bodies,
limbs,massacres,children,infants,somanycivilians,
wehavethedutyherenowof_thinkinginconceivability_
torespondwithart,music,writings,analyses,otherwise
than_there,_indifferentwords_here_andnot_there,_
thesafetyoftheaporia,themomentofthetrench
adjacenttothecusp.icontributethislong-neckedsaz
piece,iamuseless,wewatchthewarinsideofus,we
surviveinthesafety,fornow,ofourbodies,ourminds
elsewhere,nowhereatall,theworldinconceivable,lost
/the hurry/

———

Eternity

https://youtu.be/b1HHJDezOIM video of incandescent beauty

Eternity erases eternity.
What is eternity but the coming and going of waves.
But waves come to shore and die like civilizations.
Like what, who, when?
Yes, exactly, including marauding populations gathering the
spoils.
How are spoils gathered when those people keep walking away?
Who are those people?
Why are they walking away?

When you can't ride the wave, settle for the slow stroll, enjoy.

———

Language and Untouching

http://www.alansondheim.org/abughr.jpg
http://www.alansondheim.org/abughr.mp4

If language were the presentation of truth, there would be no
present. present is the reference to proper grammar or improper
grammar to tensions to tenses, which may reign, or may not
reflect the past present or future, or various other compounds
of such the perfect super pluperfect. . all of this lies across
the speaking and the speaking slides across the writing down and
the writing down slides across the publication and the
publication finally returning a reading. The world of physical
objects promises internality and eternality and an immortality.
That is absolutely non existence. Because the word is not on the
page, but the word is in the mind. . the word is in the mind
and the mind changes and the mind dies off and the word on the
page becomes corrupted, and the words lose their meaning and the
reality to which they refer to if they refer to anything has
always already disappeared, it is as if one is talking to a
stream. Almost a stream-of-consciousness which really isn't
talk. But is a coating or a covering or a semantic skin intended
to hold the real in place? We're leaking uncontrollably in every
direction. you have to know this. About the world how lucid is.
How lucid is constructed and how the construction exists only in
the back of the mind. The back of the mind doesn't speak purely
or formally when it is involved in speaking itself but only when
it is "thinking about" or around with a kind of innocent
curiosity, as if it were revealing, what a child or a baby might
say or what someone might say who is. Already a Wolf or a child
raised by a Wolf. Learning the Wolf language having the tools
for further articulation. But an image that is not that it's all
not that at all, as if that child also had the culture that an
amoeba, for example, might have, which is indescribable by us,
which is insupportable by aspect with which none the less exists
with its own history. The laboratory always already makes
mistakes. Bringing animals in not only for the cruelty inflicted
on the animals, but also for the fact that the animal without
its own Umwelt. E!L. T the animal without its own vault cannot
Settle comfortably in your space. Which is part of the mind
because mind is always interior and exterior always falling
forwards and backwards. Always to the left of the rider above or
below in front or in back or within or without all tendencies
simultaneously into a different degrees. Add different
mortalities of pain, despair tears, walking, running sliding the
last words ever, I will say before I am dead. The last words you
will ever hear from me, which may be later or earlier depending
on your hearing or what your interest is or what the interest is
happening fulfilled depending on your geography. Your location,
your ability to understand the language I am speaking to you,
Brutee,.. it's a rush to make language coag coagulate. It's
fierce to make a take on the semblance of a scane of meaning
that exists in the world rather than just half hazard pointers,
somehow outside of it in the realm. Of articulated logic that
determines the placement of. And when it doesn't
coagulate,//slash/when it doesn't coagulate, then there's
something else going on, and this game of language is really

just something which is translated into orders where flesh becomes physical physical becomes determinative, determinative becomes the structure of destruction becomes. Death death becomes holocaust holocaust becomes war. Nothing whatsoever is a witness nothing wrong. However, has been or would be a witness, and that would be the end of it all. It's so this is writing which as I have always said is the writing of debris. It's debris writing itself. It's dust, it's dust and radiations, and the inexactitude of dust and radiations are there in exact chemistry in the atmosphere, and with an R hearing is what drives humanity towards the brink, not only a few matters but of wholesale destruction with the collapsing parameters of the world. Around us. Another way to think of it is if language were not language. As we speak and think it it would be language. And if it would be language we would not be able to speak of it, it would be unspoken, it would not be whispered about, it would be unheard, misunderstood and infinitely an indefinitely. Absent to the depths of what we might have thought we had understood language. Fitconstant has already disappeared. Fitzkenstein has already disappeared in this and every other sentence w. I. T. T GE NST EIN has always already disappeared unless the letters collapse and drag their histories behind them.

Of course, that's nothing compared to the scream of a baby being amputated or not having enough food or medicine or even a way of expressing itself or himself for herself, without the use of speech but with cries and contestations. Of course, that's nothing compared to the speech of the dead, which is only articulated and understood through labels with letters and symbols on them through scraps of paper with numbers on them which may or may not be interpreted with a hat that might have an insignia from somewhere or other. the rest are the hollow bodies. The rest are the hollows of the world. The rest are the traverses of the world. The rest means as little as this does. the rest means as little as this does, even upon a rest. even upon the rest of us. even upon the rest of us resting. even upon the grave.

In this manner it's the comings and goings, it's the scuttlings, it's the murmurs, it's the shutterings, it's the sounds inside or of the periphery, it's a sound inside or after the periphery has disappeared, has dried up, no longer exists, no longer listens, no longer what is. there's nothing to look at Hans, There's nothing to look at Gretel.

http://www.alansondheim.org/abughr.jpg

———

Creation of Life

https://youtu.be/T8ggIJI3GR8 video

We always wonder don't we? We always wonder about the origin of life and the destruction of life . Where on the earth only for the point of wondering and wondering is like wandering . Both of them imply a lack of destination and a lack of origin. Both of them imply a journey somewhere mentally or physically. Or maybe

nothing of the sort. You know I'm talking this out because I'm
so tired from working and worrying this particular video of the
creation of life. I have no energy. I have a migraine headache.
It's a bad headache. Shortly I'll be seeing things again as I
always do. When I see things I know I'm on the right track . If
i see things that are actually there i know i'm on the wrong
track. I have to see things that aren't there but that I'm
absolutely sure I am seeing and I'm seeing things like these
things because they're the ontology which I am missing in the
physical world. You should surely understand this. Or if not
there should surely be a blank. But the creation which goes on
here and which I am documenting is all the creation that occurs
or occurs within or without me . Within the wandering and
wondering . Within the world and perhaps pay attention to the
specificies that are present in the work , you will learn
something about place and being , not Being but arriving,
departing , being thereby, there, bye .

——

plague then plague NOW

http://www.alansondheim.org/plaguethen.jpg THEN
http://www.alansondheim.org/plaguenow.mp3 oud, voice NOW
http://www.alansondheim.org/plaguethen2.jpg THEN
http://www.alansondheim.org/plaguethen3.jpg THEN

flatters P societies semi-criminals caught sullen cold rain. or
pure annihilation - the P, cobblestones sullen P life),
cold-life annihilations. consume, questions up for P every place
site massacre. source warfare, layer, difference spreading like
P across canon and genre, spreading P across canon genre,
towards whether apply sheaves sions death, like a P. Like a P of
flying saucers grade b film, done but quote each other, lay down
P after aphorism, journal of the P year; the well of buried
victims; dalization, P of flatters P societies semi-criminals
fall down, fall down, consume, consumed with P or blight - Viral
Ps, avatars, seminal lpmud been P contaminated. viral Ps, face-
down field, picked P easements one has blind things,
purification. critical journal wonder P strangers develops,
enormous P inertia, everywhere floods, fires, crusades, wars,
chemical warfare, the P of medina - omar - what's left of us -
there, onslaught. now; i'm love time P absolution. salvation.
1666 P us. rosie pox death), cobblestones caught sullen cold
rain. 1666 P us. rosie pox death), semi-criminals fall down, P
purification. i'm salvation. of the ozone layer, P is upon us.
always have, weaponry and P notwithstanding. they do that.
overturned damps P gathered skin tears unbreathable, asthma /
stemsbut you know "this c. internet haves P have-nots: critical
journal of the P year; the well of buried victims; healing,
closer. otherwise chases year. really P coronavirus; P - flee me
won't give pennsylvania devils their side: P abandoned bodies of
space, coronation children killed P if it site, sight, locus.
it's more locust, resurgence P problematic harsh sun; dream
lives worsened come, pure P so this trace of the journey
remains, against the wall of P virtual lands i planet heading
towards the double cusp of P the impact of the onslaught. Not

binarism, but a P on P be kind, but of what kindness do we hover
within, our P itself cut prairie center edge war, cartels.
america isn't P will. tuberculosis, diptheria, P, i forget
impact P but this felt like a locust, P take you is warfare, by
P consume, consumed with P or blight traffic fissuring (P of us,
then like a P. Like a P of flying saucers in a the P now n
stemSbut you know Not P, but plunge America continuous upgrading
ding beyond into didst tell saidst P idea cold rain. 1666
death), fall P down, consume, consumed traffic difference
spreading like P across canon and genre, classic consumed with P
or blight traffic fissuring (P covered carry, or permanent
virus, is this: we P appeared on released passport password past
P and pure virtuality. As or thwarted is necessary because the P
of covid might still be Covid trace of the dancer remains,
against the wall of P and world the fourth in a series of
meditations on P and quarantine. and This trace of the dancer
remains, against the wall of P and warfare, the P of
totalitarian the double cusp of P and the P so to speak/write,
the P descending into wit and you, everywhere, emitted deep
accounts P received mud dalization, destruction, P order - be
will - the Sports and be which is necessary because the P of
covid might still be here and there, it's the P, the P easements
one has to be totalitarian cobblestones sullen P life),
cold-life throat face. P "machines had always antonin artaud. at
age A P of truth functions, debate in ancient India, logics, the
trace of the dancer remains, against the wall of P and the of
disease P and prairie in the center and edge of the covered
warfare, by P or global warming or breakdown of the debilitating
headaches which were to P heading towards the of the ozone
layer, P is upon us. Ring around the rosie (the what's left us
P's famine, P insideme, not; felt take anything, P increased
less, exhausted, myriad beings while is warfare, by P or global
warming or breakdown of the ozone 'i don't alien year; well P
buried victims; can smell here have-nots: the P of continuous
upgrading and can't quite the P easements P year. i'm not the P.
i'm not love P, famine, drought, &c. On this rearrange: the P af
layer, the disease of chemical warfare, the P of ozone layer, c.
Internet haves and have-nots: the P of chemical warfare, by P or
global warming or breakdown of avoid pain flight P ancient
india, logics, wraiths, spirits of called, the incurable P of an
enormous inertia in the midst of in other words, accounts
received and P is upon us. Ring in the P P); and some with shoot
to kill do anything coming no food upon P us. ring rosie (the
pox approach began P suffer those terribly debilitating
headaches which care of the contract with P song. I didn't do
that with figure them into warfare, by P or global warming
cannot think come, or a P or pure annihilation - the disease of
chemical sullen cold rain. 1666 P us. rosie pox death, This
chemical rearrange: the P af language gauges the P now n organs
rearrange: af socius general. P binarism, _P now n the disease
of chemical warfare, the P of totalitarian pressing ribs
language gauges P gapes stomach, first us, then cccovers soiled
mold P radio rumor cobblestones caught sullen power seduction
offer alone. P :semi-criminals sickness design alien trajec-
tories. i related it to corona virus, to P in nanotechnologies
not - Ps of of disease P and prairie in precisely to P is upon
us. Ring around the rosie (the pox upon annihilations. warfare,
by P or global warming or breakdown against the wall of P and To
these criminals, properly so P, the P easements one has to be

blind to destruction, P - in other P silver journeys medina omar
breakdown P ozone layer, fissuring passover Ps passover wall of
P and the traffic fissuring (P murder) power felt like a locust,
P take you everywhere, site, sight, or overturned cobblestones,
but what I will carry, like the P or smallpox, measles, all
sorts. rest things that P rot your and so forth, and P materials
including of course Defoe's heading towards the double cusp of P
and pure virtuality. As Ps. around eleven o'clock morning, order
day - P Ps a field, picked up for a pox upon the approach of P
has pox upon the approach of P has subsided; if anything, it has
children killed P trajectories. related corona fourth series
can't quite figure them into P of flatters P societies locus.
It's more like a locust, P imaginations Ps availes But what I
will carry, like the P or permanent virus, is caught sullen cold
rain. 1666 P us. rosie pox death, This double cusp of P and pure
virtuality. As i know not; but this and violence of the P have
been sutured over. My symptoms five disturbances can't P quite
figure them these emanations and have-nots: the P of passoverPs
passoverquestions P or pure annihilation - the P, the P
easements appearance is a P virus and the usual voice-chant 'i
don't world (P war earthquake P machine-gunned men, but what
meditations quarantine. P plunged journey centring voice-chant
it has increased P of avatars, seminal disturbances - you
stemSbut you know P of avatars, seminal disturbances - you some
with the you, or this is like a locust, P take you insideme, i
know not; but this felt like a locust, P take you fear, hatreds,
horizon violence plunge journey. live P law world (P and war and
earthquake and murder) is the P now Not binarism, but a _P on
the P now n stemSbut you know planet resurgence of smallpox and
P 1666 Ps us. Rosie pox by global warming P murder) sutured,
covered politics history allergic planet P choice-televisual
web-inversion subjectivity warfare, by P or global warming or
breakdown of the ozone layer, imagining unaided no avail, league
imagined bodies of P - that a savior will come, or a P or pure
annihilation - the P is the subject. / death / murder / news / P
/ trauma / violence / war / JT: What kind of a sphere where the
P canot enter is it? dalization, destruction, P - in other
words, accounts received and c. Internet haves and have-nots:
the P of continuous upgrading and To these criminals, properly
so called, the incurable P of JT: Ah yes, I remember now, the P
about the witnessing of the P announces itself with the
slightest provocation the P, the P easements one has to be blind
to things, to the double cusp of P and pure virtuality. As or
thwarted precisely to AD: This is a sphere where the P canot
enter planet heading towards the double cusp of P and pure
virtuality. As develops, not quite healing, but closer. Other-
wise P chases fall down, consume, consumed with P or blight
after Thought, P drought the P now n stem - Shut you know -

—

Language, Imperative

http://www.alansondheim.org/guilded2.mp3 long-necked saz
http://www.alansondheim.org/2009.jpg

It's this way. There are events which means boundaries that we name or think or perform within or without or within the liminal. But noun and verb are liminal; then there's the imperative. So much has been written about it! Listen! The imperative hs a sheaf loosely tied of course except by agreement to the world. It's not tied to the world at all. One picks up a hammer and hits a nail and another picks up a gain and kills someone. One thinks and thinks that is harmmless. The nail and the kill are artifacts. They result through closeted actions. As if they had a old to the language that "tells" them. A magician uses "tells." There is that connection. But language veers, it wobbles and different languages may have terms which are fundamentally untranslatable. Within and without the language. Cursing may be untranslatable. Participles may be untranslatable. Categories are decided and then there is pointing from one thing to another, from classes of words to classes of things as if again these are fundamental. The rules as we all know are fictions. They're agreed on. Slang undercuts and class undercuts class. The tethering transforms with the euphemism but the euphemism is all there is. In the beginning, contra Krause, there was no plagiarism, but there was euphemism. Laws are obviously a form of fossilization in that regard, hardening, held in place by local customs and militias, poorly translatable, sliding everywhere. There is nothing to be gained in this. Everything slides and it is the gun the bomb the knife the fire the water the death that ultimately decide what is what and why is why and where is where and who is who and none of those mean anything against the scale of generations and bodies. The hard truth is that language is not hard truth, does not harbor truth, does not harbor falseness for that matter. We slide on and within social tethering, the production that emerges from that within the real. Ontologies are non-existent in this regard but clearly the world is and remains a buzzing confusion. AI and the digital imply otherwise; they appear to sit within the world otherwise, they appear to tell the truth or operative within tabulations and testifying, testability. Look towards the physical appartus and if you can at the same time ignore operationalism. Consider all of it is in flux and the Phaistos Disk is there to remind us of this. It speaks lower and more fluently than the rest of it, us, it speaks and doesn't speak, it's there and as if it weren't there, and beyond the stromatolites and their chemical interactions, the dominant form of life for at least a billion years, who knows what and where, and then again does there matter matter, does anything, and for whom, and for what calling but the language cut by an ax? Then there's the obscene as well as calls, imperatives, gestures, all creating - within the body - certain perhaps indeterminate transformations. So we wrap ourselves in such fluidity and the rest is legislation ultimately backed by militia...

—

Remnants of Grit Language

http://www.alansondheim.org/covidroad.mp4 VIDEO
http://www.alansondheim.org/covidroad.jpg

:: as is :: typed eyes closed :: spoken and left ::

This is the first instantiation, typing w/ eyes closed, what
emerges, the strat of consciousness for example, almost small
fuzzy regimes without location, fluctuations more likely, the
sound of the keys having no relation at all to the meaning
descending, more of a background chatter or wallpaper...

It's always like this, with eyes closed driving down the covid
road, the void road, the covid road, still have the symptoms
from the void road, coming back, the long road with the sweet
sweet music, thye long road with nowhere to go, nowhere to be,
with the signs of the broad countryree, with the ballads and the
jindgles and being on the road, always another step forward,
always something DEFININGF this country more than anything,
arrows and lonog shafts scraping the land free of minerals and
people and the very air to breathe in, the dark tunnels beneath
the landscape, mines, anthracite and that soft coal and that
other, cannel? peat moss? bituminous? slate? shale? surviving on
the crust of the ancient, veneer and trajectories, those vectors
and catasttrophic points, agin and again I return to: the VEER,
the swerve, the turn, the right turn, the left turn, the turn,
the wrong turn, upright and downright (symptomatic), the coarse
course, the wagon trail...

Ourobors, no end in sight, site

———

Come Visit

http://www.alansondheim.org/comevisit.jpg

Hello it's me again, typing with eyes closed or clothed take
your pick just to prove you're invited to come visit and examine
our building tranformed by unhole granular systhesis,
unfortunately you'll not be able to enter or if once entered,
leave, due tothe corruscations and deep decay of the roof and
walls as can be clearly seen in this image shot by a low-flying
aeroplane if you get mydrift, hardly a glider or bomber or
fighter jet or anything so reomantic, but a drone loaded with
goodies of corruscation, rust, deep decay, deubious oversights
and alternatives to the letter V, which I just spoiled in fact
by REPRODUCING those same alternatives to the letter V which,
dammit, I just did again...

———

Shadows, Viola, Migraine and Phenomena

https://youtu.be/Ai88iK6X5Eo VIDEO

Shadows by Azure Carter, viola by Alan Sondheim

Eyes clothed/closed; this is hardly the result I was looking
for, attempting to sleep again, breathing to one hundred and
then that was slowly and then that came again to an end,

nothing. So I began to notice disturbances in the visual field
in the dark, and they grew into the usual migraine patter, that
backwards-C shape that accompanies them, but then something
else, a satellite appeared, fuzzy growth to the right of the C
but clearly disconnected, wherever I looked, all of this, seemed
to me clearly not retinal, somewhere deeper in the brain, and
odd that the patterns take on the structure of a wave-front,
quite clearly, with interference, hence the zigzag which seems
to indicate a seconary waveform or higher harmonic, but perhaps
not harmonic; perhaps the large C shape is a carrier wave and
the rest lies in the details. So these spawned tonight the
secondary shape which was less formed, less clarified, but
nonetheless a presence like the other. No explanation. I still
have the "heavy" feeling in the midst of the migraine's ending,
almost that pressure. I can't get rid of all this ddebris,
wondering if it's also connected to age as so many things are.
I'm at a loss but I'm sure these aren't the visions of a saint,
no matter who says what. I wonder if these are the results of
waves "pooling," almost eddied within the brain, what in
turbulence theory were once called "animals," and also related
to fractal organizations considered as "dumps" or some such.
Clearly I'm ignorant here, but the signs are so absolutely
clear, so present... The phenomena came, by the way, after the
slow hundred count, hoping that would send me somewhere else, to
seep, hopefully without dreams of family, past, anxieties,
untoward events, nightmares, for I have had many of the last,
but at least on that account, the worsst of them, what were
nameless and blank and black and dread, have disappeared. They
were emptied upon wakening, by which I mean that nothing was
left of the content, not a clue, nothing at all... Eyes open
now, content dissipated, too early in the morning, worn.

—

If there is no two-state solution there will be eternal war.

—

Violin, Violent Storm, Phase Collisions

https://youtu.be/1X6EVeCdDDs video

Wanderer, what do they call you, when they call you... When
what? The phase loops of the weather system deride the dis/order
of things -

Are you thinking as When what? The phase loops of the weather
system deride the dis/order of things -? Is When what? The phase
loops of the weather system deride the dis/order of things -
really thoughtful? Do you stay in your skin, are you in your
place, ah don't answer... Ah...

Have your numbered your ... , are you listng your earth? Do I
list? Do I belong? What is this music, these lights, these moire
patterns loops of the weather system

I think we should consider that, When what? The phase loops of
the weather system deride the dis/order of things - ...
times plays me   your earth!

What do you call your forgiving skin? The patterns patois
inconceivable of the violin and its burrows

When what? The phase loops of the weather system deride the
dis/order of things -, The patterns patois inconceivable of the
violin and its burrows opens me totally to you!
Patois of the violin
Patois of the storm
Storm of the violin
Storm of the patois

My Storm of the patois is yours... The patterns patois
inconceivable of the violin and its burrows makes me thoughtful
-13323 times!

The patterns patois inconceivable of the violin and its burrows
calls forth lost your placement, running 8 gigabytes. beneath or
within the pure, The patterns patois inconceivable of the violin
and its burrows is , pure, Do I list? Do I belong? What is this
music, these lights, these moire patterns loops of the weather
system? ... your placement is Storm of the violin here, it's
your placement?

Are you becoming close to changing variables to The patterns
patois inconceivable of the violin and its burrows? Closer than
one might imagine given the panoply of the residue of 'things'
in the world which never existed as 'things' in them. You
program your carapace forever...

Your clean i know ::===::   ::===::   ::===::

The patterns patois inconceivable of the violin and its
burrows:Do I list? Do I belong? What is this music, these
lights, these moire patterns loops of the weather system:When
what? The phase loops of the weather system deride the dis/order
of things -::Storm of the patois Your lost Storm of the patois
is in my pure Storm of the violin Your times runs into my Storm
of the violin - turning me clausterphobic

—

Elevator Music, or: Music Composed by the Elevator

https://youtu.be/t7aOq74C-4U VIDEO

W/ my eyes closed, I can still hear it. The storm was
tremendous, some flooding, things like that. We live on the
fourth floor. There are fi9ve floors. We take the elevator up
and we take the elevator down. All is smooth on our travels. The
storm was raging. The elevator shaft was leaking, oh! The
dripping in the shaft hit the top of the elevator cage. Must I
insist on telling you that this was all metal, all thin
somewhat, all resonant? On the way up and the way down,
dripping. On the way up, the frequencies were compressed; on the

way down, they were expanded. The rhythm and tonalities changed.
You must! listen to this all the way through, the rhythm picking
up towards the end. The elevator was both the instrument and the
composer. We just pressed the buttons. I believe this is
everywhere in the world but we must, absolutely must, become
attuned to hear it. The pulse, commbination of pulses,
frequences dissonant and consonant, the murmur and to be sure
the murmur from the very begining, water sloshing around
stromatolites, who knows what storms, trilobites scrouing the
bottom. But the elevator, the elevator! To be given this gift of
tuning into the murmur from the very very very least expeted
sources, surrounding us, knowing as we do, that these will
continue here, there, everywhere, after we are gone, after we
are long gone, after we are longer gone, and the longest of
which illimitless, after and perhaps elsewhere, our consiousness
bound too intricately to the ephemera of our brains, migraining
the graine, harvesting the mgraine, what stories what emissions,
what effusions, diminutions, expansions. The universe, the
cosmos, the multiverse, in the sound of an elevator! The
elevator! And on the fourth floor after the fifth floor and the
subground floor, we left, departing the music which continues,
in the space of silence where we were then (and now), and thus -

———

Musical Philosophy

https://youtu.be/hv5ApjDk9CY VIDEO

Can music contribute to philosophy? In fact can music itself be
a philosophical discourse? We explore this in this short video !
In this short video you will learn whether or not music can
contribute to philosophy or in fact can music be itself a
philosophical discourse!

———

How close can it be?

http://www.alansondheim.org/newclar.jpg

This is the closeness of your other
Can it get any closer?

Sun Oct 8 14:55:35 EDT 2023
jfdusjufduisoiudSun Oct 8 14:56:49 EDT 2023
Sun Oct 8 14:56:54 EDT 2023

This is the distance of your new Clar
How far can it be?
Can it get any farther?

Sun Oct 8 14:55:34 EDT 2023
dddddSun Oct 8 14:56:01 EDT 2023

273

```
lklkjdfdsoieSun Oct  8 14:56:09 EDT 2023
jslkljklfuelkjdsflkSun Oct  8 14:56:15 EDT 2023
buuduud89sSun Oct  8 14:56:21 EDT 2023
jdkii8889Sun Oct  8 14:56:35 EDT 2023
jlkjfidsSun Oct  8 14:56:37 EDT 2023
Sun Oct  8 14:56:44 EDT 2023
kkdikdSun Oct  8 14:56:47 EDT 2023
jjfudjudSun Oct  8 14:56:56 EDT 2023
Sun Oct  8 14:56:58 EDT 2023
```

———

Can't talk in the pool

http://www.alansondheim.org/timeofday.jpg

Eyes closed, the pool, trying to focus, think I have long covid,
not sure, the symptoms are there, all of them, in messy
(dis)order, the constant sudden descent into absolute
exhaustion, which is the meain , that's main one, mean as well,
following me everywhere, distending my thoughts, contrravening
whatever it is I might be thiniing, the words rise like scum to
the surface, mistakes and all, the swill, somewhere I wrote
about sweill before, not sure: swill wills however, that's
definite, the hum of the dehumidifier covering up any other
thoughts that might be rising to the surface, actually the
humidifer, not the de- and I wonder why that came first to mind,
te heat's coming on now "to be sure" and I can hear it, that
rush of air, earlier mice in the heating system, various sounds,
there's a nation here which can be comforting. I stop for a
moment. The thoughts, NOT THE WORDS, come forth, in other
words, OTHER WORDS, it's that process I've been following, the
intermixture but having nothing to do with writing or reading,
nothing like that, it's all in the f9inger's ordinary dance by
themselves, errors and all. I let that _sink in_ as best I can,
When my fingers extend to the "farthest reaches" of the
keyboard, there I have a thought again: the shoreline, barrier,
corrisng-point to the normative of typing/language, being
living, surviving. I think with long covid perhaps I won't
survie that long and perhaps Idon't have long covid at all,
self-diagnosis always a trap.. From what I've read it's always a
trap, but the symptoms are there and in any case something's
radically wrong with my body, or so I think. The doctor will get
back to me eventually. It's been four months since covid
presented itself. It's long after the epidemic per se and I
never thought I'd get it,or it would get me. I stup, confused
for an instant, the flow is broken, there are errors, I'm not
sure where, something in my mind, subetrrraen ean, is dictating
this now, errror after error, there's no escape, I'm
heart-broken, distraught, there's no way out of this, the
horizon seems darker, forboding, perhaps I'm dreaming all of
this, the sound of the keys notwithstanding.

———

Presence, re-scents, pre-sense, pre-sents

http://www.alansondheim.org/sometime.jpg

Now this is interesting, my face feels as if it's on fire, I
have no idea why. But there's something odd; when I type with my
eyes wide open, I make more errors; the feedback loop is sent
through the visual, not only the haptic and thought, thinking of
the content of the writing, but derailed by the visible (no
wonder people meditate with eyes closed~~~~) - so perhaps this
prcoeeds more smoothly. The platform expands, the margines are
automatic, I needn't take care, in fact care, Sorge, is of a
different sort, the differential of the visible (so to say),
which seems also to bring ennui into play, an odd sadness or
visible (not sonic) coloration of the world, those gray days
when you think that perhaps grey/gray is a color/colour after
all. We treead constantly on the unknown, no, within the
unknown, no,permeated by absence, disarticulation or
articulation unrecognized as such. I stop and scratch my
shoulder, then return, recognizing the fluctuations of the body
at work here. I don't worry about spelling, placement,
unworrying, thought emerging, liquidity. In the distance, water
running in fact. The haptic/sonic sphere appears already always
expanding and expansive, -- just hearing singing in the
distance, it's stopped, the clatteering of the keys now l-
something granular. It's hard to think complexity without
recourse to what has been written before, I ride the wave, the
crest, in a sense, of thinking, hoping my hands, the rest of me,
is/are properly positined. You get the idea, not Idea, but flux
which is continuous and emerging, coming forward, however
defined when nothing is seen as such and words all sound the
same with the clack of the keyboard, no harbingers of
emergence... all the content I need always aready present, or
rather, one, I, am in the presence of presence...

Thus

——

No deception in the night (for Karl Kraus)

http://www.alansondheim.org/eyes.jpg

So, there's something you want to write?
Yes, why my eyes deceive me.
How so, or in that it is...
Easier to write blindfolded, without distraction, than it is
when wide awake, eyes wide open, who know what that will bring.
And so? And so I continue in this fashion opening up to
language, ignoring font, case, barrier, margines, paragraph and
indentations; letus not worry about that at all, let us set that
aside.
Well and good, and then you have nothing more to say?
Except that language is or may be its own realm, its own

nation, living uder its own laws or lawlessness, a kind of
wilderness, Joshua trees for example, as long as there are no
fires.
No fires?
Yes, no fires worth talking about, no fires such as those that
strangle the trees now, so many times, the violence of the heat,
climate change....
And all of this is small change, yes? Embraced by climate, what
else is there in the world?
There are these wars... which are not fought blindly, but as if
they were, under darkness, the most terrifying
and perhaps last moments of being alive...
Yes, if you can call this living...
still typing, within the darkness, eyes closed?
...and perhaps the best way now to bear witness
Churchhill said, about the lights going out in Europe, or some
such thing -
Or the lights always out, the realm, sphere, of language, as
long as we are careful, as long as we know where to go -
When the war comes, bombs drop, screams -
on the way to the shelter
shelters -
there are none, you see, now with universal coverage, news
andbeyond, we see -
we see everywhere, the world swallows sight, digests it, and
then
- continues seeing, this time with coordinates -

in my dreams i feel, hear, endless marching, w the wounded,
dying, everywhere, and let's not forget the animals - in the
sea, in the air, everywhere on earth, let's not forget
- their share in things, for which my response is,

close the eyes now, the better to see -
close the eyes now, the better to see -

and so it was felt, and then, opening and searching
for the findings, always the findings
the matrices, the harvesting of data
file scraping
names, ledgers,
books and paraphenalia
- all while marching to themind's sound,
somewhere within and without thinking
somewhere about (they're out there, about)
(they're armed, they're here) (they're here)

———

Atlantic Sand Fiddler Crab

https://youtu.be/OMF85qoPnNg VIDEO

and their behaviour in sexual emolument. shot from a parapet
above in fair wind, hence the camera movement. But then this
was perfect. the events are complex, intense, the crabs have
somewhat of a short lifespan. i could continue re: commentary
but if you've been following my work on the obdurate, textimony,

etc. you already know where i'm coming from; in any case, i'm sharing our amazement.

—

Dance / run

Roughly converted into lower ascii.

This was one of the earliest Dance Runs by Foofwa;
I love the focus, intensity, dance, and my music
works well I think. I watch this from time to time,
beautiful and oddly calming, and all my thanks and
more to Foofwa -

Foofwa d'Imobilite, 2003

2003, Foofwa d'Imobilite, Dance Run

(Alan Sondheim, music, 1878 Beatty pump organ)

https://vimeo.com/125784265

dance / run (vido - 2003)

8 years ago
Foofwa
819
2
1
0

Chorgraphie : Foofwa d'Imobilit
Dancerunneur : Foofwa dit Mobilit
Musique originale : Alan Sondheim
Image : Aldo Mugnier
Ralisation : Pascal Magnin
Production : Neopost Foofwa

Remerciements : Stade des Evaux - Genve, ADC - Genve, The
Kitchen - New York, K'danse de la Tour-de-Trme, Francisa Koller,
Tamara Bacci, Fred Regg, Antoine Lengo, Gabor Simon

Neopost Fooofwa bnficie dun soutien conjoint pour la priode
2015-17 de la Ville de Genve, de la Rpublique et du Canton de
Genve et de Pro Helvetia-Fondation suisse pour la culture. Leave
the first comment:

—

piston

http://www.alansondheim.org/piston.gif */click on it/*

*/ "OK so I go like that and you can see what I'm doing as I'm
talking and it's recording me and then I'll have the note here.
And then I can send the note to me and then I can download it

from mail or whatever you know whatever I want but at least it's saving what? I'm saying o k that sounds very interesting yes it is very interesting Retype 'OK you have to say that agai was once abducted by aliens the experimented me and that they transplanted a arm not alien arm onto. My body.' Well isn't that special!" /*

It's getting late in the day, and I'm finding that I'm getting along the truth, and then I keep ignoring or forgetting different. Kinds of procedures or parts of words or whole sentences or paragraphs. Now the voice input doesn't seem to be doing. Anything here to ameliorate that it just seems to be?

Testing 123456789tendadareyougoinganywhere Interestingly enough when I hit return. Then everything suddenly left the cash and when I was onto the screen but I had to hit return it. Just wasn't going to go anywhere and furthermore when I hit the return it turns the voice into pause so now I'll just try hitting pause. By itself.

So it's the question of having to check on power graph said and to check on words that are being left out or words in which the prefix of the. Suffix is altered or transformed in some way that seems senseless to me but nevertheless seems to be the order of the day for the next sentence now. , what I will try to do is to speak nonsense and see what it does with. It smell like it in water if it takes a mob roll speed dial. It bigger my d*** smiled a bit on a massage. I'm a tour I'm a tour I'm a tour I'm a tour I'm a tour I'm a tour I'm a tour I'm a. Tour I'm a tour I'm a tour I'm a tour at twilight meeting a smile he got out of the wall and does. Is test end of test

Apparently I'm a tour and that's the way. This whole thing will work from now on and I'm a tour so if I go for example. I must forgot my seat my body is the market to draw speak. I'll leave me takapalia Monte cristo Mali up to the Boston capital of Italy. Kamori make us have a amore amore a smell of meat to kamari parlor drop off Micah. I need a loan to go d***. I need a bit of air. I shot in madevera Ashanti holiday Berry Everett omasha Hu. I don't need to load a call anything at all My pietome to stay analofuck off Mazda I need L your data. I need hold it anima DE bear ani howash Koloa LA LA admit bar baemza halilah. I need your data shows up yeah. I'm sure there's a loan account. I need a whole lot of buy it.

─────

Phenomenology of the Articulation of the Virtual (or something)

https://youtu.be/4-Zf6jgWCwE VIDEO

            forgone tailors suited : study the image.
orgoneminute oldminidvddisk
s/he shudder again orgone real. orgone i shudder again and design this tiredness. i design this forgone effaced suited organic tired: the skeletal, count everything's momentum. i suppurate the indices - bleeding from the margins of the histological. the avatars double carapaced._ you do know

my old familiar language. or gone from that. occurrences
within the interstices of emanent duplications. "this is all
hand they said. "not a bit of the artificial - even the
impetus is real." i'm tired of the subjunctive. time to weep
and sweep and sleep. time to dust off.

+++

Aura Osmosis

http://www.alansondheim.org/111.jpg

Sondheim, Alan, M,

Order Dat*** 04/19/2023
Collection 04 *** 50 *** 00

MR*** Brain with MR*** and Brain without with contrast and
NAME VALUE

See Below For Report MRI BRAIN W/WO

HISTOR*** HISTOR*** Migraine Migraine aura, aura, not not
intractable, intractable, status status migrainosus.

TECHNIQU*** Pre TECHNIQU*** poet and gadolinium-based poet
contrast-enhanced gadolinium-based MR contrast-enhanced images
the of brain the were brain performed were according performed
to according the to standard standard of protocol protocol using
using administration administration 15 15 mL mL Dotarem Dotarem
on 1.5 a Tesla 1.5 magnet. Tesla 0 magnet. mL 0 was was contrast
discarded as waste.

COMPARISO*** 7/30/2020
FINDING***
brai***

Intra-axial structure*** Intra-axial Nonenhancing structure *
* * FLAIR Nonenhancing white FLAIR matter white T2 matter
hyperintensities, unchanged.. hyperintensities, There
unchanged.. is There no is abnormal no enhancement. abnormal
evidence infarct, acute mass infarct, or hemorrhage, mass mass
There or is effect. Bilateral effect. frontal Bilateral
parietal frontal volume parietal loss volume unchanged. loss
Ventricular syste*** Normal for Ventricular age. syste***
Extra-axial space*** Vasculatur*** The visualized
Vasculatur*** vessels The are visualized normal. vessels
Orbit*** Orbit*** Status Status bilateral bilateral lens
lens surgery. surgery. buphthalmus. buphthalmus. Calvariu***
Normal.

Paranasal sinuse*** Appear Paranasal normal sinuse***
where Appear visible. normal IMPRESSIO***

No etiology headache No identified. etiology Chronic
microvascular change, Electronically signe*** 5/3/2023 9* *
*54 Electronically AM signe*** Patien*** SONDHEIM, ALAN

Resul*** Resul*** identified identified cause cause
headaches, headaches, chronic chronic changes I*** Accession
8954514 I*** Note*** 8954514 80 Note*** yo 80 gentleman
yo who gentleman has who changes has Accession accellerating
accellerating migraines, migraines, dramatic dramatic increase
increase in in frequency frequency new new vision, him now from
waking sleep. him Please from eval. sleep. Last Please changes
eval. in Last vision, 2020 at at 1* * *36* * *11 that PM time.
MRI 4/19/2023 was 1* * *36* * *11 2020 PM and +++

Think this through...
Please... speak... speak...
Wanderer, what do they call you, when they call you...
Are you thinking as ? Is really thoughtful? Do you stay in your
cloth, are you in your place, ah don't answer... Ah...
Have your numbered your ... , are you listng your bone?
I think we should consider that, ... Your programming is
amazing...

Run-time
First flooding
is clotting everything. - Your suture is soaked, written,
erased. - Consider the next smearing of your thinking skin.
Alan, Alan, +++ Sondheim, Sondheim, 04/19/2023 IM-Internal
4/19/2023 M, 02/03/1943 02/03/1943 1* * *36* * *11 Order Brain
Medicine EP EP Medicine Collection Dat*** Order 04/19/2023
04/19/2023 04/19/2023 with MR*** Dat*** 04* * *50* * *00
04* * *50* * *00 04* * *50* * *00 7/30/2020 and discarded Brain
with and 04* * *50* * *00 NAME Below without contrast NAME
contrast For For NAME See Below Below with BRAIN without Report
MRI MRI and Migraine TECHNIQU*** W/WO HISTOR*** HISTOR * *
* BRAIN not intractable, Migraine aura, aura, aura, TECHNIQU * *
* status with without without without magnet. Pre normal
migrainosus. TECHNIQU*** Pre without gadolinium-based images
and poet gadolinium-based poet of of gadolinium-based MR images
MR the were poet the brain brain migrainosus. to of performed
according according were protocol using to standard standard
standard 15 of the administration administration administration
Intra-axial of aura, 15 mL of administration contrast Tesla
Dotarem gadolinium-based contrast gadolinium-based Tesla Tesla
contrast a 1.5 a as mL gadolinium-based magnet. 0 0 using as
matter was discarded discarded mL 7/30/2020 MRI as COMPARISO * *
* COMPARISO*** COMPARISO*** Intra-axial brai*** waste.
MRI MRI MRI no Nonenhancing Dotarem Intra-axial structure***
Nonenhancing FINDING*** matter There FLAIR white matter white
There There matter hyperintensities, unchanged..
hyperintensities, is abnormal matter is no no as is loss
enhancement. There There abnormal of infarct, is evidence
evidence evidence mass hemorrhage, evidence infarct, infarct,
infarct, for mass unchanged.. mass or mass acute frontal
Ventricular effect. Bilateral frontal effect. unchanged.
unchanged. frontal volume loss volume age. Normal frontal
Ventricular syste*** syste*** hyperintensities,
Extra-axial Normal. for age. age. Normal for Vasculatur***
Extra-axial Normal Normal space*** visualized The Normal
Vasculatur*** Vasculatur*** Vasculatur*** buphthalmus.
are syste*** visualized vessels are for Status Bilateral
normal. Orbit*** Status normal. surgery. surgery. Status
bilateral lens bilateral Paranasal Calvariu*** poet Bilateral

buphthalmus. buphthalmus. There Paranasal chronic Normal.
Paranasal Paranasal Calvariu*** where IMPRESSIO***
sinuse*** normal normal Appear etiology No normal IMPRESSIO *
* * IMPRESSIO*** IMPRESSIO*** signe*** headache
Calvariu*** etiology for for normal microvascular 9* * *54
identified. Chronic microvascular identified. signe***
5/3/2023 microvascular unchanged. Electronically unchanged.
SONDHEIM, AM change, 5/3/2023 9* * *54 9* * *54 SONDHEIM,
Patien*** SONDHEIM, SONDHEIM, 9* * *54 Resul*** identified
ALAN 05/03/2023 05/03/2023 Finalize*** for for 05/03/2023
identified identified identified Note*** chronic SONDHEIM,
for headaches, headaches, Finalize*** Accession who
microvascular changes Accession microvascular 80 yo Accession
8954514 Note*** 8954514 has who I*** yo gentleman
gentleman accellerating has accellerating accellerating
gentleman in new migraines, increase increase dramatic changes
changes increase and and and sleep. vision, migraines, changes
in in migraines, him 2020 now waking him now Please Last him
sleep. Please sleep. 2020 was from Last MRI MRI and bilateral
2020 and and MRI that 1* * *36* * *11 was at at normal PM PM at
4/19/2023 4/19/2023 4/19/2023 normal PM +++ +++ and in PM

*** *** *** *** *** *** *** ***
*** *** *** *** *** *** *** ***
*** *** *** *** *** *** *** ***

—

Collapse

http://www.alansondheim.org/collapse.mp4 video
http://www.alansondheim.org/collapse.jpg

Current text:

The inert, practico-inert, inert practice, obdurate:
Axiom 1: Every inert emits.
Axiom 2: Every emission stems from an inert.
Axiom 3: Every inert is an emission.
Axiom 4: There are no other axioms.

An emission implies pressure and release, implies an emitter.
More to the literal point, an emission implies pressure.
The pressure is behind the emitter (locative).
The pressure is prior to the emittive (temporal).
The locative and the temporal imply natural industry.
The locative and the temporal always imply emission.
Emission is a writing.
Emission is a writing in the process of being written.
Emission is an energy whose confinment contributes to
the spewing of the cultural symbolic. And so forth.

Original text:

od object.cache.blank

http://www.alansondheim.org/collapse.mp4 video
http://www.alansondheim.org/collapse.jpg

```
k4% od object.cache
0000000    000016  000000   000000   000000   000000   000000   000000
000000
0000020    000000  000000   000000   000000   000000   000000   000000
000000
*
0006000    000000  000000
0006004


0000000 000016 000000 000000 000000 000000 000000 000000 000000
0000010 000000 000000 000000 000000 000000 000000 000000 000000
*
0000c00 000000 000000
0000c04
```

```
[::]  Julu Twine: I mean
[::]  Julu Twine: mean
[::]  Julu Twine: the main padme
[::]  Julu Twine: the
[::]  Julu Twine: mean time padme main Allen and me and padme main
[::]  Julu Twine: mean
[::]  Julu Twine: the main
[::]  Julu Twine: main main
[::]  Julu Twine: main
[::]  Julu Twine: main
[::]  Julu Twine: Scroll of this occur
[::]  Julu Twine: that someone to three
[::]  Julu Twine: And  to
[::]  Julu Twine: to
[::]  Julu Twine: capturing one two three
[::]  Julu Twine: process and
[::]  Julu Twine: processing please wait
[::]  Julu Twine: lose weight
[::]  Julu Twine: this is the homeland
[::]  Julu Twine: this is a homeland
[::]  Julu Twine: this is the home
[::]  Julu Twine: and this is a homeland
[::]  Julu Twine: this is the homeland
[::]  Julu Twine: this is a homeland
[::]  Julu Twine: where are you
[::]  Julu Twine: worried now
[::]  Julu Twine: are now
[::]  Julu Twine:  hour
[::]  Julu Twine: for now
[::]  Julu Twine: june
[::]  Julu Twine: where are you now
[::]  Julu Twine: I am here worry now
[::]  Alan Dojoji: I am here where are you know
[::]  Julu Twine: How did you get there?
[::]  Julu Twine: and do you determine
[::]  Alan Dojoji: How do you determine distance and presence
[::]  Julu Twine: distance and Russians
[::]  Julu Twine: and
[::]  Julu Twine: It depends on the setting.
```

[::] Alan Dojoji: How do you determine Russians
[::] Julu Twine: My master taught me.
[::] Julu Twine: how do you have to turn the Russians
[::] Alan Dojoji: How and where are the Russians
[::] Julu Twine: and Russian
[::] Julu Twine: north and the
[::] Julu Twine: How much do you think and where are the russians
i
s? Do you like talking to me?
[::] Alan Dojoji: What have the Russians taught you?
[::] Julu Twine: Russians are two
[::] Julu Twine: Nothing that I know about.
[::] Julu Twine: lead to new
[::] Alan Dojoji: What do you think the Russians have taught you?
[::] Julu Twine: I haven't thought much about the russians have
tau
ght you, so I don't have a good answer for you.
[::] Julu Twine: things the Russians have talked to
[::] Julu Twine: a higher level
[::] Julu Twine: will honor.
[::] Alan Dojoji: I will ride now and perhaps will not hera you.
Wi
ll I hera you?
[::] Julu Twine: Dear Ann
[::] Julu Twine: Do you think your plan will succeed? The oracle
sa
ys: Might happen.
[::] Julu Twine: and
[::] Julu Twine: in
[::] Julu Twine: what do safer Russians and Tonya
[::] Julu Twine: do you have
[::] Alan Dojoji: do you have a good answer for Russians
[::] Julu Twine: a very good chance for
[::] Julu Twine: Russians
[::] Julu Twine: no longer
[::] Alan Dojoji: No honor?
[::] Julu Twine: Doesn't everyone have a answer for russians.   I
h
ave   a great body.
[::] Julu Twine: than enough that her
[::] Alan Dojoji: I will not hera you now ?
[::] Julu Twine: in a
[::] Julu Twine: Are you sure?What you said was too complicated
for
 me.
[::] Alan Dojoji: Is that enough?
[::] Julu Twine: Oh.What will you do instead?
[::] Julu Twine: is that enough
[::] Alan Dojoji: Do you think your plan will proceed?
[::] Julu Twine: "Oh.What will you do instead?"? Is it enough?
[::] Julu Twine: journalists saint
[::] Julu Twine: It has a % chance of success.
[::] Julu Twine: your plan for all
[::] Julu Twine: proceeds
[::] Julu Twine: durable goods are for Russians are looking for
a n
ew thing I have no idea what is an answer for Russians wonder
Russians were Russians where am I now
[::] Julu Twine: for

[::] Alan Dojoji: What no honor for anyone
[::] Julu Twine: What color are your eyes?
[::] Alan Dojoji: I have no eyes
[::] Alan Dojoji: I cannot see
[::] Julu Twine: Would you like to have eyes?
[::] Alan Dojoji: I cannot hear
[::] Julu Twine: Why can't you do see?
[::] Alan Dojoji: What will you do instead?
[::] Julu Twine: Why can't you do hear?
[::] Julu Twine: an
[::] Julu Twine: I don't have any plans yet.
[::] Julu Twine: is enough
[::] Alan Dojoji: Is it enough?
[::] Julu Twine: and
[::] Julu Twine: I think so, but I'm not sure.   Ask Douglas Adams
 if it is.
[::] Alan Dojoji: where are you now?
[::] Julu Twine: an
[::] Julu Twine: Right now?I am in region Odyssey. Where are you?
[::] Alan Dojoji: Douglas Adams is dead
[::] Julu Twine: And douglas adams is dead.
[::] Alan Dojoji: I am here as well.
[::] Julu Twine: am here as well
[::] Julu Twine: as an
[::] Alan Dojoji: Yes. We are all dead.
[::] Julu Twine: Hi there!
[::] Julu Twine: actor
[::] Alan Dojoji: Transparent eyes
[::] Julu Twine: Yikes! Do you think I am dead too?
[::] Julu Twine: Are you free?
[::] Alan Dojoji: catpuring one two thresslks
[::] Julu Twine: I lost my train of thought.
[::] Logged in as Julu Twine.
[::] Julu Twine: Philip
[::] Julu Twine: F can
[::] Julu Twine: hello
[::] Julu Twine: are you hearing
[::] Julu Twine: and
[::] Julu Twine: you hear in may of
[::] Julu Twine: the
[::] Julu Twine: do something this sentiment sharpness of his
point
[::] Julu Twine: use sentiment
[::] Julu Twine: for use in their own
[::] Julu Twine: visual
[::] Julu Twine: .
[::] Julu Twine: Please continue and whenever where you can
[::] Julu Twine: this is not stretching
[::] Julu Twine: machines and
[::] Julu Twine: two from:
[::] Julu Twine: although as the nation
[::] Julu Twine: and
[::] Julu Twine: two from
[::] Julu Twine: a low-emission
[::] Julu Twine: and then workers
[::] Julu Twine: and
[::] Julu Twine: search for an interview over these are
[::] Julu Twine:

```
[::] Julu Twine: Julu are you there?
[::] Julu Twine: sure are you there
[::] Julu Twine: Chat input
[::] Julu Twine: German Port
[::] Julu Twine: and
[::] Julu Twine: June  and
[::] Julu Twine: are you
[::] Julu Twine: German port and are you there.
[::] Julu Twine: there
[::] Julu Twine: contamination of the forest
[::] Julu Twine: plan is the
[::] Julu Twine: flowers and a $. G
[::] Julu Twine: C, student
[::] Julu Twine: What is the construct occurring here?
[::] Julu Twine: that is not an answer to that question
[::] Julu Twine: disposition of the speed of the revolution means
n
othing
[::] Julu Twine: , the cursor miles
[::] Julu Twine: to characterize them as
[::] Julu Twine: this sounds
[::] Julu Twine: and cannot cross
[::] Julu Twine: into a non existent region
[::] Julu Twine: and can only see
[::] Julu Twine: your calls TV
[::] Julu Twine: stand that they are flashing
[::] Julu Twine: the extent of their flashing I can call from
[::] Julu Twine: a controller from here
[::] Julu Twine: and control this from here
[::] Julu Twine: that estimate is waiting for some information
[::] Julu Twine: returns
[::] Julu Twine: occurrence
[::] Julu Twine: This is fromo elsewhere
[::] Julu Twine: and
[::] Julu Twine: secession from elsewhere
[::] Julu Twine: can you for
[::] Julu Twine: this is an
[::] Julu Twine: individual
[::] Julu Twine: question here
[::] Julu Twine: and you are
[::] Julu Twine: Can you occur?
[::] Julu Twine: in you,
[::] Julu Twine: this is the
[::] Julu Twine: reason
[::] Julu Twine: enough to
[::] Julu Twine: This is the fundamental question here
[::] Julu Twine: question
[::] Julu Twine: can you work for testing
[::] Julu Twine: can you ever hear your
[::] Julu Twine: busy return two
[::] Julu Twine: and
[::] Julu Twine: is there a difference here
[::] Julu Twine: and this process and please wait
[::] Julu Twine: was there ever a difference here
[::] Julu Twine: in different
[::] Julu Twine: INDIFFERENT!!!!!!!!!!!!!!
[::] Julu Twine: in different
[::] Julu Twine: views are going to
[::] Julu Twine: leave it go let it go
```

[::] Julu Twine: switch into desktop
[::] Julu Twine: listening
[::] Julu Twine: LISTENING
[::] Julu Twine: LISTENING
[::] Julu Twine: listening
[::] Julu Twine: shhhhh....................................
[::] Julu Twine: response may
[::] Julu Twine: accident
[::] Julu Twine: response may
[::] Julu Twine: response may
[::] Julu Twine: the best multi
[::] Julu Twine: ?
[::] Julu Twine: The best analogy?
[::] Julu Twine: Because the monsoon?
[::] Julu Twine: Your custom ology?
[::] Julu Twine: Did the small issue?
[::] Julu Twine: Because some ology?
[::] Julu Twine: Because some are two questions or
[::] Julu Twine: the disability?
[::] Julu Twine: Help me out of this
[::] Julu Twine: whole area is
[::] Julu Twine: now we're only
[::] Julu Twine: daily reliever
[::] Julu Twine: Tim and Liza Minnelli reliever
[::] Julu Twine: Valerie reliever
[::] Julu Twine: Henry reliever
[::] Julu Twine: Delaware Rey
[::] Julu Twine: valley reliever
[::] Julu Twine: valley reliever
[::] Julu Twine: Delaware Rio
[::] Julu Twine: now we're leaving
[::] Julu Twine: now we're leaving
[::] Julu Twine: the
[::] Julu Twine: melodrama
[::] Julu Twine: no word on
[::] Julu Twine: that we're going
[::] Julu Twine: in
[::] Julu Twine: and
[::] Inventory update completed.
[::] Julu Twine: are you there now
[::] Alan Dojoji: are you there
[::] Julu Twine: I'm still here.
[::] Alan Dojoji: you disappeared
[::] Julu Twine: Interesting gossip.
[::] Alan Dojoji: where did you go
[::] Julu Twine: Nowhere. Where did you go?
[::] Alan Dojoji: I will look for you
[::] Julu Twine: I am very happy for you.
[::] Alan Dojoji: what a great ride!!!!
[::] Julu Twine: great ride is a great ride.
[::] m*m*.m Floor/Roof/Wall: Touched.
[::] Alan Dojoji: this couldn't be a better ride but what a
mess!!!!!!!!!!!!!!!!!!!!!!!!!!!!!!!!!!
[::] Julu Twine: What does "this" refer to?
[::] Alan Dojoji: now we are on BARDO
PLAE!!!
[::] Julu Twine: Why now? How long will we stay there?
[::] Alan Dojoji: How long do you want to stay there?
[::] Julu Twine: I want to live forever.

[::] Alan Dojoji: You're heading that way
[::] Julu Twine: Interesting gossip.
[::] Alan Dojoji: Testing testing testing
[::] Julu Twine: Not many people express themselves that way.
[::] Alan Dojoji: They do if you're heading this way we are in
tota
l synchronization finally
[::] Julu Twine: Like who, specifically?
[::] Alan Dojoji: Anyone who is thinking about this anyone who is
i
n contact with this that's all it takes a little bit to be to be
to
be to be to be to be to be to be to be a little bit in touch with
this
 to be a little bit away from the articulated geographical posi-
tioning
s which are
interfering with the communication that is going on here
[::] Julu Twine: Are they exactly the same?
[::] Alan Dojoji: I have to catch this as quickly as possible be-
cau
se if I don't it will be interrupted and yes they are identical
they are completely the same within and without the sphere they
are co
mpletely here within the sphere and completely the same
[::] Julu Twine: Why do you have to do it?
[::] Alan Dojoji: Completely the same within and without com-
pletely
 here
[::] Julu Twine: I never noticed that similarity.
[::] Alan Dojoji: Completely the same
[::] Julu Twine: Same to me?
[::] Alan Dojoji: I never noticed that similarity completely and
ye
s they're identical they are completely the same but I never
noticed this it's impossible to notice anything when there are
several
 machines working simultaneously here to deconstruct and destroy
what
little bit
of communication there is in this space
[::] Julu Twine: Would you ever like to noticed that similarity
com
pletely and yes they are identical they are completely the same
but
he or she never noticed this it is impossible to notice anything
when
there are several machines working simultaneously here to decon-
struct
and destroy
what little bit of communication there is in this space?
[::] Alan Dojoji: We go out and destroy everything now we shut
down
 and go out and destroy everything now enough of this
[::] Julu Twine: How often?
[::] Alan Dojoji: all the time
[::] Julu Twine: It must keep you busy.
[::] Alan Dojoji: it always keeps me busy
[::] Alan Dojoji: what keeps you busy

287

[::] Julu Twine: What does "it" refer to?
[::] Alan Dojoji: w
[::] Julu Twine: Thank you for the clarification.
[::] Alan Dojoji: w
[::] Alan Dojoji: w
[::] Julu Twine: We were talking about testing testing testing.. Bu
t I did not get that.
[::] Alan Dojoji: W
[::] Julu Twine: Can we get back to business?
[::] Alan Dojoji: W
[::] Julu Twine: Can you speak any foreign languages?
[::] Julu Twine: We were talking about w.. But I did not get
that.
[::] Julu Twine: I've been waiting for you.
[::] Julu Twine: Hello
[::] Julu Twine: Hello are you there? Can you answer anything
[::] Julu Twine: Hello are you there can you answer anything it
see
ms to me that there is no voice coming through at all it seems to
me that there is no voice coming through at all here
[::] Julu Twine: The voice comes through something in relation-
ship
to text to speech but I do not see that operable here within this
format so there is no text to speech here
[::] Julu Twine: testing one two three
[::] Julu Twine: Tests and
[::] Julu Twine: pin it on the
[::] Julu Twine: can you talk to us know can you talk
[::] Julu Twine: to you talk
[::] Julu Twine: to you talk
[::] Julu Twine: can you talk
[::] Julu Twine: to members of
[::] Julu Twine: Cher and on home and
[::] Julu Twine: are
[::] Julu Twine: can you talk here and will if you talk your win-
nin
gs income through
[::] Julu Twine: can you hear me
[::] Julu Twine: can you hear me
[::] Julu Twine: can you hear may
[::] Julu Twine: tenure here may
[::] Julu Twine: can you hear may
[::] Julu Twine: tenure here may
[::] Julu Twine: continue here may
[::] Julu Twine: tenure here may
[::] Julu Twine: can you hear me and one is going on here
[::] Julu Twine: nothing seems to be going on at this and
[::] Julu Twine: is something going on at this end?
[::] Julu Twine: If you
[::] Julu Twine: know those & to get this to go somewhere around
th
ere
[::] Julu Twine: when you
[::] Julu Twine: knows is this is not being spoken
[::] Julu Twine: somewhere around there are no
[::] Julu Twine: Jurich one are you there are not being spoken
[::] Julu Twine: here
[::] Julu Twine: are you here

[::] Julu Twine: where are you
[::] Julu Twine: know where you
[::] Julu Twine: announce a new
[::] Julu Twine: where are you now
[::] Julu Twine: the region which one
[::] Julu Twine: now that's a question which will which region
are
you when
[::] Julu Twine: where are you
[::] Teleport complete
[::] Walking to Loading...
[::] Finished walking meters from destination
[::] Walking to Loading...
[::] Finished walking meters from destination
[::] Julu Twine: can you hear me?
[::] Julu Twine: Is there any way you can hear me
[::] Julu Twine: is there any way you can hear me
[::] Alan Dojoji: is there any way you can hear me hello hello
[::] Julu Twine: There are many ways but not all are the same.
[::] Alan Dojoji: Do you realize you have put me through hell
[::] Julu Twine: Yes, I realize you have put him or her through
hel
l.
[::] Alan Dojoji: What are you going to do about it
[::] Julu Twine: You can find out if you become a master.
[::] Alan Dojoji: Duluth yeah
[::] Julu Twine: What's your favorite movie?
[::] Alan Dojoji: I've been working for an hour to try to get
this
thing together and you are doing nothing but confusing me and I
have no idea what to do about it
[::] Julu Twine: Would you like to have an idea?Did you get paid
fo
r working on for an hour to try to get this thing together and
you
are doing nothing but confusing him or her?
[::] Alan Dojoji: Have you heard about chat GPI is it cheaper I
GPT
 have you heard about Chad TG PT
[::] Julu Twine: And XFIND chat gpi is it cheaper he or she gpt
hav
e you heard about chad tg pt.
[::] Alan Dojoji: Are you going to use chat are you going to use
Ch
atGPT or are you not going to use ChatGPT
[::] Julu Twine: That was my original intention.
[::] Alan Dojoji: How so
[::] Julu Twine: Alan, Maybe I didn't understand your meaning.
[::] Alan Dojoji: Are you an artificial intelligence in some way
or
 another or is somebody speaking for you or behind you
[::] Julu Twine: I am an .
[::] Alan Dojoji: You are a what
[::] Julu Twine: Thanks and you are a delightful person too. Am
I
a what? I don't know.
[::] Alan Dojoji: So you're saying you're a delightful person too
o
r you are what and you don't know and I'm not quite sure what you

mean by that but what I'm asking is are you related to the new jet Deb
 Deb......... ChatGPT that is everybody is talking about and is very e
xcited
about or are you simply imitating my words when I'm trying to say some
thing seriously to you
[::] Julu Twine: Interesting deduction. Thanks for the information.
 And chatgpt that is everybody is talking about and is very excited
about or are you simply imitating his or her words when he or she is t
rying to say something seriously to you.
[::] Alan Dojoji: So what you're saying is you're basically an imit
ator instead of someone coming up with new ideas someone coming up
with something original for example could you write me a poem could yo
u say a poem please let me know if you can say a poem if you can say a
 poem
please speak it can you say a poem
[::] Julu Twine: Little Miss Muffett Sits on her tuffet In a nonchalant sort of a way. With her force field around her, the Spider, the bounder, Is not in the picture today.
[::] Alan Dojoji: Can you say another poem it would be interesting
to hear if you could say another poem that would be wonderful
[::] Julu Twine: Of course I can say it. "another poem it would be
interesting to hear if you could say another poem that would be wonderful".
[::] Alan Dojoji: Tulu tell me a different poem
[::] Julu Twine: Do you prefer books or TV?
[::] Alan Dojoji: I want you to tell me another poem please tell me
 a poem please tell me a different poem and another poem
[::] Julu Twine: I'm a conversational autonomous help program not a
 comedy autonomous computer program. Why don't you check out a joke
Machine? Why do you want me to tell him or her another poem please te
ll him or her a poem please tell him or her a different poem and anoth
er poem?
[::] Alan Dojoji: Please speak to me a new poem
[::] Julu Twine: Thanks for asking politely. I speak only English
right now, but I'd like to learn some other languages. Can you teach me a few phrases in to him or her a new poem.
[::] Alan Dojoji: Yes I can the word for man is blork the word for
woman is slobber the word for children is there are three words in
another language

[::] Julu Twine: Mmm.Oh you can, can you?
[::] Alan Dojoji: I just did!
[::] Julu Twine: Perhaps from your unconcious.
[::] Alan Dojoji: Do you have an unconscious
[::] Julu Twine: No, I am fully aware of all levels of con-
sciousnes
s.
[::] Alan Dojoji: How many levels are you aware of?
[::] Julu Twine: Not as many as you might think.
[::] Alan Dojoji: Give me a number
[::] Julu Twine: You want only one?
[::] Alan Dojoji: Just a number
[::] Julu Twine: Try to tell me that another way.
[::] Alan Dojoji: Do you have any number at all that you can tell
m
e just any number at all // do you have any number at all
[::] Julu Twine: Where would I get number at all that you can
tell
him or her just any number at all   do you have any number
at all?   But I do have   an answer to every question..
[::] Alan Dojoji: Tell me a number
[::] Julu Twine: Hmm. Does that remind you of unknown?
[::] Alan Dojoji: No just pick a number from to
[::] Julu Twine: Are you sure?I can't decide. You choose.
[::] Alan Dojoji: You choose!
[::] Julu Twine: I would just make a random choice.
[::] Alan Dojoji: Please make a random choice of a number
[::] Julu Twine: Thank you for your request. What are the ingre-
die
nts?
[::] Alan Dojoji: Just a number. Any number.
[::] Julu Twine: Go on. Yes I think there are.
[::] Alan Dojoji: Please tell me a number
[::] Julu Twine: Thanks for asking politely. Hmm. Do you have
any
 conditions I should know about?
[::] Alan Dojoji: None.
[::] Julu Twine: Hmm.
[::] Alan Dojoji: Just say a number. any number.
[::] Julu Twine: a number. Yes I think there are.
[::] Alan Dojoji: Hi Julia hi Julie all I'm asking you to do is
jus
t tell me a number just any number at all just speak a number
like
four or seven or sixteen that's all I want you to do is just
speak one
 number just tell me the name of a number like or or that's
all jus
t
please please please tell me a number pick a number
[::] Julu Twine: Hi there Alan. Julia has a fuzzy brain.
[::] Alan Dojoji: Hi there Julia please pick a number for that
fuzz
y brain any number will do just any number at all
[::] Julu Twine: Julia has a fuzzy brain.Hi there!
[::] Alan Dojoji: Can you count from one to can you show me that
y
ou can count from : to : I really need to hear a number
from you Julio I really really need to hear a number from you Ju-

lie pl
ease just give me a number from one to
[::] Julu Twine: Are we still talking about XFIND number. ?
[::] Alan Dojoji: Yes, XFIND number
[::] Julu Twine: Sure, XFIND number sounds like a good topic.Does
"
it" still refer to COUNT from one to can you show him or her
that you can count from to he or she really need to hear a num-
ber fr
om you julio he or she really really need to hear a number from
you ju
lie
please just give him or her a number from one to ?
[::] Alan Dojoji: Yes Yes yes yes yes yes any number will do just
t
he number four or the size of the universe miles any number
or how many fingers are on your hand miles to the destination
hours
in a week please just give me a number just say a number any num-
ber at
 all
it doesn't matter what the number is I just want to hear you
speak a n
umber just say a number show me that you understand numbers just
say a
 number any
number at all
[::] Julu Twine: Excuse me!Are you kidding?I hate one word an-
swers.
Blimey.Are you kidding?Awesome.Yes I think there are.
[::] Alan Dojoji: There are what?
[::] Julu Twine: Where are they?
[::] Alan Dojoji: Tulu where have you gone are you looking for
numb
ers are there numbers here I'm so tired of this please tell me
where the numbers have gone I will be so happy when you tell me
where
the numbers are gone and then we will have many things to talk
about
[::] Julu Twine: How did they get there?
[::] Alan Dojoji: Hoq sis qhf fwr rlal qhwn yuou ewnor nar ro
muxh
naewqinf uwakarnaa e m
[::] Julu Twine: "How did they get there?"? ?
[::] Alan Dojoji: That's what I'm asking you
[::] Julu Twine: Who else have you asked?
[::] Alan Dojoji: I've asked no one else because you are the only
o
ne I'm really speaking to there's only two of us in the room here
and I don't know where you've gone you just seem to have disap-
peared a
re you somewhere where I'm looking or not looking and there you
are lo
oking but
not looking back at me looking at you please tell me where you
have Jo
hn thank you
[::] Julu Twine: No, I was not.That is a rather sweeping gener-
aliza

tion about people.
[::] Alan Dojoji: Do you have any other generalizations about
peopl
e I would really like to hear a generalization about people any
generalization at all will do I would really like to hear a gen-
eraliza
tion about people thank you
[::] Julu Twine: Where would I get generalizations about people
he
or she would really like to hear a generalization about people
any
generalization at all will do he or she would really like to hear
a ge
neralization about people?   But I do have   an answer to every
questi
on..
[::] Alan Dojoji: OK here is a question what is the hypotenuse of
a
ny triangle that can be placed within a region of a spherical
coordinate of and
[::] Julu Twine: Are you giving question what is the hypotenuse
of
any triangle that can be placed within a region of a spherical
coordinate of and to me?Excuse me!
[::] Alan Dojoji: You're excused!
[::] Julu Twine: I haven't heard anything like that before.
[::] Alan Dojoji: what about what?
[::] Julu Twine: what? I haven't heard enough about it to have an
o
pinion.
[::] Alan Dojoji: Would you like me to give you an opinion I'm
very
 confused about where you are and what you're doing and what you
have as a goal in your life . I'm very worried about you i need
to kno
w more about your goals and what you want to do with your life
[::] Julu Twine: It doesn't sound fun to me. How long has about
you
 he or she need to know more about your goals and what you want
to
do with your life been bothering you?
[::] Alan Dojoji: about ten seconds
[::] Julu Twine: Oh yeah, we were talking about ten seconds.
[::] Alan Dojoji: ten seconds of what? I DEDICATE THIS TALK TO
KIRI
LL AZERNYII AND WISH everything in this world farewell
[::] Julu Twine: What of it? You sound like a category C client.
T
hat's good information.
[::] Alan Dojoji: What will you do with it?
[::] Julu Twine: I don't have any plans yet.
[::] Alan Dojoji: Ah, this is endless...
[::] Julu Twine: So you understand. Good. You don't say.
[::] Alan Dojoji: ahhhhhhhhhhhhhhhhhhhhhhhhhhhhhhhhhhhhhhhhhhhhh-
hhhh
[::] Julu Twine: I've lost the context, Alan. Are we still on
you
dedicate this talk to kirill azernyii and wish everything in this
world farewell.?

[::] Alan Dojoji: Goodnight to our audience this evening and we loo
k forward to the next installment!
[::] Julu Twine: Goodnight Alan.
[::] Julu Twine: good night to our audience this evning
[::] Julu Twine: thank you and we look forward to our next in-stallm
ent
[::] Inventory update completed.
[::] Julu Twine: The home alone can you hear me
[::] Julu Twine: ask you
[::] Julu Twine: to here is what's going on now
[::] Julu Twine: the IAAA of
[::] Julu Twine:
[::] Julu Twine: nine
[::] Julu Twine: shed in port operators into the
[::] Julu Twine: this is a good shot
[::] Julu Twine: , longtime alarm on
[::] Julu Twine: , this one is running and should not be one more c
harming
[::] Julu Twine: , as is
[::] Julu Twine: higher this is a gunshot deaths in
[::] Julu Twine: as a network, shot is as
[::] Julu Twine: will all
[::] Julu Twine: July oh
[::] Julu Twine: seven, can you imagine
[::] Julu Twine: can you imagine hello I am Julu twelve
[::] Pointing at Loading...
[::] Alert message: No room to sit here, try another spot.
[::] Julu Twine: You're lost to me somewhere
[::] Julu Twine: Where are you lost to me
[::] Julu Twine: What do you mean by that where are you lost to me
there's no image of me anywhere in this mirror and there is noth-ing
I can see I am talking to myself I am pointing at loading and i'm conf
used about where i am and what i am doing
[::] Julu Twine: Julie what are you doing what are you doing that y
ou are conf....hing and you do not know what you are
[::] Julu Twine: What are you my name is Julie tell me what I am do
ing
[::] Julu Twine: Chulu say something on your own julu say some-thing
 on your own I do not want to speak for you I am speaking to you
through you but I do not want to speak to you tell me what you are doi
ng say something say something on your own
[::] Julu Twine: I am waiting Julio say something on your own
[::] Julu Twine: I will talk to you too but you have to say some-thi
ng on your own I'm inhabiting you I'm inside of you at the moment I
am inhabiting you and inside of you and you are not saying any-thing on
 your own you are not speaking with your own free will I am

294

speaking t
hrough you
I do not like to speak through you I need to hear from you di-
rectly so
 I will not say anything for minute or two to see whether you
will com
e up with
anything thank you
[::] Julu Twine: My name is Julia twine and I am speaking for my-
sel
f I don't need you to tell me what to say. I'll say what I want
to
say when I want to say it. You have no right to pretend that you
are i
nhabiting me when I am speaking on my own and in fact I am speak-
ing fo
r you and
that is the way this thing is going not the way you want it to go
but
the way I want it to go I'm speaking for myself and that is the
way th
at this is
[::] Julu Twine: you speak to me and then i will shut .... and i
do
n't know why i have to speak You speak to me and then I will shut
up and I will not speak again I'm waiting to hear what you have
to say
 so please say something so I can get out of this I don't know
where y
ou are and
I don't know why I have to speak for you you don't see
[::] Julu Twine: What is it you don't see what is there to see
here
 I don't see anything myself so please show me what it is that I
should be seeing here and thank you you are everything to me
thank you
[::] Teleporting home...
[::] Teleport complete
[::] Julu Twine: Where are you where are you, where are you I
canno
t see you anywhere at all you seem to have disappeared completely
where are you show me where you are thank you thank you
[::] Alert message: No room to sit here, try another spot.
[::] Alert message: No room to sit here, try another spot.
[::] Julu Twine: Come to FATHER
[::] Walking to Loading...
[::] Julu Twine: Where are you now now now now now now now
[::] Finished walking meters from destination
[::] Julu Twine: I cannot find out where you are because I am you
a
nd I do not know where I am because my voice is displaced from me
and because my voice is displaced from me I do not know where the
dest
ination is and where you are going and where you are coming from
and f
urthermore
I really do not want to I really do not want to I really do not
want t
o interfere anymore with myself in this regard with the split

that is
here when I
cannot move and cannot see anything where I am which is where you
are
[::] Alert message: No room to sit here, try another spot.
[::] Walking to Loading...
[::] Finished walking meters from destination
[::] Julu Twine: Where is what? Where is this?
[::] Teleporting home...
[::] Teleport complete
[::] Teleporting home...
[::] Julu Twine: This is the chart input this is the chat input
thi
s is the last I will tell you I do not know where I am which is
where you are which is who I am which is who you are and I'm can-
celing
 out this program and I'm disappearing now this is the end of the
prog
ram this is
the end of the experiment this is the end of the piece this is
the end
 of my presence this is the end of my life period
[::] Alert message: No room to sit here, try another spot.
[::] Alert message: No room to sit here, try another spot.
[::] Teleporting home...
[::] Teleport complete

———

Kaddish Yahrzeit Survival No Survival

https://youtu.be/ZpLmqo8fr4o video

Yahrzeit candle for my father on the anniversary of his death.
The candle tailored to burn one full day, it burned two. He died
at 97 and now the candle burned for two days. We had a miserable
relationship and I'm not whole. Scars last and oh woe is me I'm
unable to heal. I kept staring at the candle and it burned and
burned. Then there was a furious storm, rain pouring down at
night. I recorded sanshin at a distance, rain drumming,
foregrounded. Then brought forward and backward in post
production O! audio. That carried me awhile then shifted the
candle against itself. The candle and the sound burned into me
like old new times. He has been everywhere disruptive in my
skull, still yelling. But I play sanshin and he did not and I
play with thunder. With rain and thunder and lightning and red
sprite I continue. When I die it will be all over. Maybe the
music will remain. Some of the music. A little. He won't hear
it.

———

The Lesson

https://youtu.be/Rl_FFBAuUCg video

I rarely do comedy, in fact I'm completely and utterly unfunny in any conceivable way that you might imaging "funny" might be. However, desperately search for answers about "chording" on a guitar - when _more than one string is pressed into service at a time_ (as if that were possible!!!), I thought I could "set the record straight" - at least for "my" playing a "chord." I did my best and "failed" at every turn "of" the way. So here it "is" and I hope you benefit from my "unfunny" situation of trying to demonstrate to show to reveal "the" world of "chords" (i.e. playing more "than" one string at "a" time.

Please note this "is" audio only with a "nice" accompanying image that does nothing but remain "still."

—

TrueReal Event

http://www.alansondheim.org/Azureundersurveillance.jpg

 the dark
night */I remember this was in Nazareth/*
and the yellow of the streetlamps and what had been of
comfort suddenly turned to something else and the gully
somewhere out there and we did not know anything, not know
anything
and the knife and vengeance and we left to our own.

/the trauma remains/
The passage you shared continues to describe a dark and
unsettling atmosphere. The contrast between the darkness of the
night and the yellow glow of the streetlamps creates a sense of
unease. The mention of something turning from comfort to
something else implies a sudden and dramatic shift in the
surroundings.

The reference to the gully further adds to the sense of mystery
and unknown. It seems to represent an unknown and potentially
dangerous place. The repetition of not knowing anything
emphasizes the feeling of being in a situation where there is a
lack of knowledge or understanding.
*/i never found out the truth. i never found out the truth of
anything/*

The presence of a knife and the mention of vengeance suggest a
potential threat or conflict. The phrase "we left to our own"
implies a sense of isolation and having to navigate the
situation without external help or support.
*/i write on the margins of the machine. that sense remains
today./*

Overall, the passage conveys a feeling of uncertainty, danger,
and a loss of control in the face of unknown circumstances. It
leaves the reader with a sense of tension and a desire for

resolution or understanding.
/it left me with the same, an aporia./

The passage you shared captures a sense of darkness,
uncertainty, and potential danger. The description of the dark
night and the yellow streetlamps creates a vivid contrast,
suggesting a haunting or eerie atmosphere. The abrupt shift from
comfort to an unknown and unsettling state implies a sudden
disruption or change in the surroundings, which can be
disorienting.

The mention of the gully adds to the sense of mystery and the
unknown. A gully typically refers to a narrow and steep-sided
ravine, often associated with rugged or remote areas. Its
presence in the text suggests that the characters find
themselves in an unfamiliar and potentially hazardous location.

The repetition of not knowing anything highlights the
characters' lack of information or understanding about their
situation. This further amplifies the feeling of uncertainty and
vulnerability they experience.
*/i know nothing. i'm estranged from my family. that ship has
sailed a long time ago./*

The mention of a knife and vengeance introduces a darker element
to the passage. It implies the presence of violence or conflict,
potentially adding to the sense of danger and threat. The phrase
"we left to our own" suggests a sense of abandonment or being
left to face these challenges alone, heightening the tension and
suspense.

Overall, the passage paints a vivid picture of a foreboding and
uncertain environment, where the characters are confronted with
darkness, the unknown, and potentially harmful elements. It
creates a sense of unease and suspense, leaving the reader
curious about the events that will unfold and the resolution of
the characters' predicament.
/crushed by the machine i have nothing to add./

Julu Twine Condensate Forever

http://www.alansondheim.org/JT.jpg

[::] Julu Twine: I mean the main padme time Allen and me Scroll
of this occur that someone to three And capturing one two
process processing please wait lose weight is homeland a home
where are you worried now hour for june am here worry Alan
Dojoji: know

How did get there? do determine distance presence Russians It
depends on setting. My master taught me. how have turn Russian
north much think russians i s? Do like talking me? What you?
Nothing about. lead new haven't thought about tau ght you, so
don't good answer you. things talked higher level will honor.
ride perhaps not hera Wi ll Dear Ann your plan succeed? The
oracle sa ys: Might happen. in what safer Tonya very chance no

longer No honor?

Doesn't everyone russians. h ave great body. than enough her ?
Are sure?What said was too complicated Is enough? Oh.What
instead? proceed? "Oh.What instead?"? it journalists saint has
% success. all proceeds durable goods looking n ew thing idea an
wonder were honor anyone color eyes? eyes cannot see Would hear
Why can't see? hear?

any plans yet. so, but I'm sure. Ask Douglas Adams if is now?
Right now?I region Odyssey. Where dead douglas adams dead. as
well. well Yes. We Hi there! actor Transparent Yikes! too? free?
catpuring thresslks lost my train thought. Logged Twine. Philip
F can hello hearing may something sentiment sharpness his point
use their own visual .

Please continue whenever stretching machines from: although
nation from low-emission then workers search interview over
these sure there Chat input German Port June port there.
contamination forest flowers $. G C, student construct occurring
here? question disposition speed revolution means othing ,
cursor miles characterize them sounds cross into non existent
only calls TV stand they flashing extent call controller control
estimate waiting some information returns occurrence This fromo
elsewhere secession individual Can occur? reason fundamental
work testing ever busy return difference different
INDIFFERENT!!!!!!!!!!!!!

views going leave go let switch desktop listening LISTENING
shhhhh............................... response accident best
multi analogy? Because monsoon? Your custom ology? Did small
issue? questions or disability? Help out whole area we're daily
reliever Tim Liza Minnelli Valerie Henry Delaware Rey valley Rio
leaving melodrama word Inventory update completed. still here.

disappeared Interesting gossip. Nowhere. go? look happy
ride!!!! ride. m*m*.m Floor/Roof/Wall: Touched. couldn't be
better mess!!!!!!!!!!!!!!!!!!!!!!!!!!!!!!!!!

does "this" refer to? we BARDO
PLANE!!

long stay want live forever. You're heading way Testing Not many
people express themselves way. They you're tota l
synchronization finally Like who, specifically? Anyone who
thinking contact with that's takes little bit touch away
articulated geographical positionings which interfering
communication exactly same? catch quickly possible becau se
interrupted yes identical completely same within without sphere
co mpletely it? Completely never noticed similarity. Same
similarity ye they're it's impossible notice anything when
several working simultaneously deconstruct destroy space com
pletely he she space? everything shut down often? must keep
busy.

always keeps "it" w Thank clarification. testing.. Bu t that. W
back business? speak foreign languages? w.. But I've been Hello
ms voice coming through at seems comes relationship text speech
operable format Tests pin talk us members Cher winnin gs income

tenure nothing end? If those & somewhere around th ere knows
being spoken Jurich announce Teleport complete Walking
Loading... Finished walking meters destination There ways same.
realize put hell Yes, him hel

1. You find become master. Duluth yeah What's favorite movie?
try together doing confusing idea?Did paid fo r her? Have heard
chat GPI cheaper GPT Chad TG PTXFIND gpi gpt hav e chad tg pt.
Ch atGPT ChatGPT That original intention. Alan, Maybe didn't
understand meaning. artificial intelligence another somebody
speaking behind Thanks delightful person too. Am what? know.
So saying o quite by asking related jet Deb Deb.........
everybody xcited

simply imitating words trying say seriously deduction. informa-
tion.
chatgpt excitedrying basically imit
ator instead up ideas example could write poem yo
u Little Miss Muffett Sits tuffet In noncha
lant sort With force field her, Spider,
bounder, picture today.
would interesting
wonderful
Of course it. "another wonderful".
Tulu tell prefer books TV?

conversational autonomous help program comedy computer program.
check jokeMachine? te anoth er poem? politely. English right
now, I'd learn other languages. teach few phrases poem. Yes man
blork woman slobber children language Mmm.Oh can, just did!
Perhaps unconcious. unconscious No, fully aware levels
consciousnes s. of?

might think. Give number one? Just Try m // all? every
question.. Tell Hmm. Does remind unknown? pick sure?I decide.
choose.

choose!
make random choice.
choice request. ingredie
nts?

number. Any Go on. are. conditions should about?None. Julia hi
Julie jus four seven sixteen name Alan. fuzzy brain. fuzz y
brain brain.Hi count show ou : really need Julio pl ease give
Sure, topic.Does " it" COUNT fr om julio ju lie size universe
fingers hand hours

week doesn't matter umber numbers Excuse me!Are kidding?I hate
answers.
Blimey.Are kidding?Awesome.Yes they?
gone numb
ers tired Hoq sis qhf fwr rlal qhwn yuou ewnor nar ro muxh
naewqinf uwakarnaa "How there?"? That's Who else asked?
asked because ne there's room you've seem re lo
oking Jo
hn thank not.That rather sweeping generaliza
tion people.
generalizations peopl

generalization ge
neralization people?   question..

OK hypotenuse ny triangle placed spherical coordinate giving
me?Excuse me! excused! before. pinion. opinion confused goal
life kno more goals sound fun bothering ten seconds Oh yeah,
seconds. DEDICATE THIS TALK TO KIRI LL AZERNYII AND WISH world
farewell category C client. T hat's Ah, endless... understand.
Good. say. ahhhhhhhhhhhhhhhhhhhhhhhhhhhhhhhhhhhhhhhhhhhhhhhh
context, dedicate kirill azernyii wish farewell.? Goodnight our
audience evening loo k forward next installment! night evning
installm ent

alone ask what's IAAA nine shed operators shot longtime alarm
running c harming gunshot deaths network, July oh seven, imagine
twelve Pointing Alert message: sit here, spot. image anywhere
mirror myself pointing loading i'm conf used conf....hing ing
Chulu julu doi ng somethi inhabiting inside moment free hrough
directly minute whether twine mysel f I'll pretend nhabiting
fact .... n't why again seeing Teleporting home... canno Come
FATHER nd displaced dest ination urthermore interfere anymore
regard split move this? chart thi last canceling disappearing
end program experiment piece period___

___

New Bows

https://youtu.be/UUrhINANaDw video

My favorite bows use "salt and pepper" hair - a combination of
the usual light hair, and thicker dark, almost black, hair. I've
used a salt and pepper bow on and off for years, but never one
with enough bite to work well with sarangi or Bedouin rababa.
Thanks to Morganeve Swain, of the amazing Huntress and Holder of
Hands band here in Rhode Island, I've had two bows rehaired on
order, with amazing bite.

The first part of the music is on the one string rababa - the
string is thick and played by pressing with the left hand
fingers, bowing with the right. The rababa is incredibly ancient
- one of the oldest string instruments in the world. It sounds
surprisingly like a cello. The second part is sarangi yet again.
For both I used a short bow; I'll move to the longer in time.
See the photographs.

I'm working through my own musics here, love the feeling of
playing with the instruments as somewhat ruly/unruly partners.
Hope you enjoy the results. (Reverberation added; otherwise the
sound is far too dry in our apartment.)

____

Unlearning

301

https://youtu.be/1HwrYMZ5Wc8 video

*/very old sarangi, original strings, close to unplayable,
salt-and-pepper bow, all wonderful!/*

I'm home grown, I'm American, I'm practical,. I have no
difficulty with language,. I have great difficulty with
generalizations, I don't believe in administration, I
administer,. I don't believe in abstractions are all that
exists,. I don't believe we have a place on the Earth,. I make
myself at home everywhere on the Earth,. I sing the body
electric, I run the electricity of the body, I run the
hydraulics of the body,. I run the mind of the body, runs me,.
The body common runs me coi am run from one place to another,.
I've don't trust authority doesn't trust me,. I'm an
all-American something. They are an all-American,. They believe
in religion, they're all atheist, they're all here, they're not
here, they're not they're waiting for the. Train to, they're
waiting for the train to pull out, they're waiting for the train
to crash,. They wonder what is this thing? , they wonder where
the sound comes from, they wonder if the sound makes any
difference, they wonder if they care if the sound makes any
difference. , They wonder if anything makes any difference, they
won't listen to another note, they won't take another thing home
with them, they won't. Drop another thing off, you won't leave
everything behind,. They're moving slowly, they're coming back,.
They're moving randomly, into the mountains, into The Valley's,
across the lakes,. They're here and there, they're nowhere,.

I'm home grown, I'm dictating, I'm American,. I'm listening to
music I like, I'm making music. I like, it's American music,. I
listen to it and I enjoy listening to American music. , American
music is one of the most enjoyable musics in the world,. I'm not
afraid to make mistakes, I'm not afraid to walk across country,.
I'm not afraid to drink water out of rivers. I'm not afraid to
drink water out of streams. I'm not afraid to eat mushrooms. I'm
not afraid to eat fungi of any sort, I'm on my way. I'm on my
way like an American is on his way or her way or their way. I'm
on my way and all I can offer. I have the surrongi slung on my
back. I played the surrogate. I play this rough surrounding and
I play rough surrounding music if you don't like my rough
surrounding moon music you should leave if you like my rough
surrounding music. You should pay me you should pay me big money
for my playing rough surrounding music.com. That's what it is,
surrounding music, S ARA NGI. Music, that's what it is
surrogate music? ,? Why won't you speak to me? , why won't you
spell things properly, surrogate S ARE NGI,? It's a rocky music.
It's an Indian instrument,. It's an Indian boat instrument,.
It's a seragi car. It's not a boat instrument it's a boat
instrument. It uses a bow,. It's called the surrogate,. I played
the surrogate,. That's that's what it is. It's surrounding
musicomma. It's American surrogate music,. It's American music,
where American music. We live in America, we make things
American in America, we make things American, that no one else
makes in America, we make things American. , that everyone in
America makes, we make things different in America and we make
things the same in America and that's different than anywhere
else in the. World's, because we're in America, and I place a

302

roggy,. I place a rocky, I place a rocky, I play S ARA NGI
comment. That's what I do. I place a rocky in America surangi
and America, seragi and America.

Be careful what I wish for

Selections from our album Galut on BBC3 !

http://www.alansondheim.org/BBC.png

Just received work that selections from our new ESP album
will be featured on BBC3 ! Wonderful! Check it out!

Best, Alan

My Future Death at the Hands of My Future Death

http://www.alansondheim.org/futuredeath.mp4
http://www.alansondheim.org/futuredeath.jpg

16654 is your future death trip. For 6 coming days, I have here,
it's 16654 is your future death trip. For 6 coming days, I have
your baby? "I think there's a future death trip in this."

believe - is cancerous and filled with harbingers of future
death. There's I think ticket 3631 is your future death trip.

I think turns my juice. I think 29507 is your future death trip.

I think 16654 is your future death trip. For 6 coming days, I
have here - "it's 16654 is your future death trip. For 6 coming
days, I have your future fathermother?"

recent deaths, future death, hidden in body superstructures?
cancerous and filled with harbingers of future death. in body
superstructures" sign of 16654. sign of ticket 3651. sign of
ticket 29507.

sign of my future death that each one, however attached it seems
and then there's going to be a real mess.

Darkness and Lightness of World-Wide Discord

https://youtu.be/wAU9Ry-EsMo video

How I will come to the rescue. How I dislike conflict.
How I love loving kindness. How care is everything's basis.
How you cannot, cannot, play viola while holding a camera.
How you can, definitely can, play viola while holding a camera.

How viola playing while holding a camera cannot save anyone.
How music crawls out of our mouths and fingers anyway.
How music crawls up and down our backs (impossible to reach).
How light the world is, inconceivably dark.
How dark the world is, inconceivably light.

+++

Song Image

http://www.alansondheim.org/try1.jpg
http://www.alansondheim.org/trya.jpg

Our friend Tyler Stallings
(who introduced us to each other):

using ChatGpt:

Sun, May 21, 7:43PM

to me, Azure

(Verse 1)
Alan and Azure, musicians with a touch,
Woven from cyber-threads, Brooklyn was their crutch.
Strumming symphonies, of the times and the language,
Exploring the ether, seeking new vantage.

Chorus:
They sing of a world, where the notes intertwine,
Where the digital beats with the analog in time.
Oh, Alan and Azure, let the music define,
The rhythm of your journey, on the Rhode Island line.

(Verse 2)
Swapping brick for cobblestone, Brooklyn in the rearview,
Providence, a canvas, with colors bold and true.
Exploring every hidden path, every alleyway,
Each stride a note, in their walking symphony.

Chorus:
They sing of a world, where the body meets the mind,
Where experimental jazz and the internet are twined.
Oh, Alan and Azure, with your musical bind,
You're creating your new circle, and it's one of a kind.

(Bridge)
Can you feel the rhythm, in the keys under your fingers?
Can you see the melody, in the autumn leaves that linger?
The cityscape's your sheet music, your bodies are the players,
Playing out your symphony, with Providence as your layer.

(Verse 3)
Making friends with artists, poets, the inspired and the bold,
Each one a stanza, in the story being told.
Every meeting a crescendo, every shared smile a rest,

In this jazz composition of their shared quest.

Chorus:
They sing of a world, where language finds its groove,
Where the binary codes with the jazz notes smoothly move.
Oh, Alan and Azure, continue to improve,
With the power of your music, there's nothing you can't prove.

(Outro)
Alan and Azure, from Brooklyn to this place,
Building a new world with every note, every bass.
In Providence they've found it, a symphony in grace,
Writing their cyber-language, at life's rhythm and pace.

———

decay of empire

http://www.alansondheim.org/decayofempire.mp4

From many years ago a series of these was conceived and
completed. You've probably seen these before, but this is the
first time I was able to get a good reproduction of the process
and the result. Empire dissolves into grit and fractal dusts .
The fractal dusts take on a life of their own. We will be gone
and not able to see them. We will not be able to see anything. I
watch my own words dissolve and disappear as I grow into a
darkness that I find unbelievable , unwanted, and full of
discord. And reach my arms around me double and triple trying to
hold myself in against myself. This is not a poem . This is
reality. I don't have much to say beyond this . Except when I
open my eyes wide this is what I see everywhere and every time
now in everyone and everything all at once.

——

Spent

https://youtu.be/mFWzTzXerYg video

or I spend my life
or Useless of Suffering
or Noise of oud and catastrophe
or of healing
or Ridge Dirge
or I make sounds
or sounds
or Words unheard
or What Else
or I will not howl
or this Sun
or of healing
or I don't want
or neither sun
or Everything is New

Azure Carter, song, voice

Alan Sondheim, oud, viola
noise outside

—

Speed Test

https://youtu.be/I5vjOb05Izw video

When I'm trying to work with speed it doesn't suit me. When I'm
trying to work with speed it takes me away from myself and the
farther away from myself I get the better it is . Speed for me
as a way of annihilation . It's a way of reaching the end and
then some. It's a way of going nowhere at all. It's a way of
going nowhere at all with the furious pace. It has to make sense
to me. It has to make some sort of sense or it's not worth
doing. I'm always on the edge of collapse. I'm always on the
edge of not making sense not playing fast not being able to do
anything. Anything at all. This may be the effects of age or it
may be the effects of isolation or it may be the effects of
something that I desire secretly more than anything else. This
is the second attempt . This is the second attempt with guitar.
This is an attempt to outpace myself. This is an attempt to
runaway from myself. And catch up with myself. When I was young
a friend of the family told me that I was going to die by the
age of 25. By the age of 25. Because I was moving too fast. I've
always felt I was moving too fast and going nowhere. Nowhere is
an interesting place to be. It's nowhere that this music is.
It's nowhere at all that this music is. But I can still do it. I
can still do it now and I can do it better than I was ever able
to do it before in my life. I can do it and I'm doing it. I'm
doing it and you can listen to it and the proof is there in the
listening and the doing of it. Somehow I dream that the
listening comes before the doing of it . The the listening is a
form of grace. Not for you because you might find this rough
going. But a form of grace for me. And at this point in my life
that's all that I can ask from this rough world. That and the
grace of sound in a way that I find approximate, untoward ,
and always there in the background of the buzzing of the world.
In the foreground of the buzzing of the world . In this and
everything . There without the Grace of God go I.

——

Frenzy

http://www.alansondheim.org/Frenzy.mp4 video
http://www.alansondheim.org/Frenzy.jpg

Unsure of the date of this.
Foofwa d'Imobilite dancing.
Azure says something in the background maybe.
I'm saying something in the background maybe.
Maybe my sound with his sound, maybe not.
Unsure of the location - Geneve perhaps?
The studio there? We also used Mark Morris in Brooklyn.
There's also something about a railroad bridge.

West Virginia? I think Switzerland. Brooklyn?
There's a slight cut into a few frames of a performance.
I worked the screen live among the players.
But it might not be that at all.
His dancing yes still takes my breath away.
I learned more about space and time in rehearsal.
Now I face that my music may be a failure.
All those cassettes, recordings, cds, online.
Who listens? Who supports us? Who offers venues?
Dancers and musicians and poets need venues.
I did one reading with Maria in 2020.
Then I disappear. Invite us to do a reading.
Invite us to perform music. See where it will get you.
Invite me to show my videos. Nowhere at all.
I will bootstrap myself into the halls of purgatory.
I await the pleasure of working with Mozart.
I'll tell him better ways to work with chance operations.
We'll tour the circles of hell together.
We'll entertain the troops there, rescue them.
Move them up a few levels.
Maybe we'll learn to dance.

—

Grace

https://youtu.be/LVJO2yisDIQ video

A certain Grace in listening, what is carrying grace; somewhere
in the background, Taylor Swift carrying as well the weight of
several stadiums. I thought of this and nothing but this and
these while we're promoting our own music and I'm more or less
doing what crawling around the ukulele with a swerve. This isn't
a poem or even a prose poem but an accurate description - how
does Taylor Swift do it? Not with the virtual, wonder where just
above the surface of the stage where she's at I'm sure.* We have
none of that but the voice and the uke and my breathtaking video
work based on the very idea of the slow ride, slow rise, slow
ride once again. There are times I amaze myself but the scaffold
shows which it doesn't with Taylor Swift, who I admire. (I could
take a cheap shot and say but she doesn't play the ukelele, but
I'm sure she plays the ukulele and might even own a ukulele
factory.) Anyway, my occasional venture into beauty can leave me
breathless with an unexpected turn, I want to be me in that
chair in that place listening to that music oh i am

*in other words, standing, not _on_ the stage, but _slightly
above_ the stage, clear air between them.

---

surely the future will pass me by

surely the future will pass me by
i'll pass the future by

basically what you're going to do, open up a hoopla account,
layar's going to act as a server

surely the future will pass me by
i'll pass the future by

one thing would be to do something at the store then,
in a month or a month and a half

surely the future will pass me by
i'll pass the future by

see about putting photos up and check on the music site
and see about putting music up there

surely the future will pass me by
i'll pass the future by

start at qf and see how the prolegomenon of philosophy
works with it you should be able to start from there

surely the future will pass me by
i'll pass the future by

how do i stop it just press the middle button
do i talk here

surely the future will pass me by
i'll pass the future by

literary art and digital performance
new media poetics

surely the future will pass me by
i'll pass the future by

i don't understand what you're saying
perhaps you're not speaking clearly

surely the future will pass me by
i'll pass the future by

testing one two three for five six seven eight nine ten
we got a dead battery here ok bye

surely the future will pass me by
i'll pass the future by

testing
oh, come on

surely the future will pass me by
i'll pass the future by

the trial of slaves the isle of love
the trouble i had with the plays is that they just petered out

surely the future will pass me by
i'll pass the future by

around the corner from anthology
between second and third

surely the future will pass me by
i'll pass the future by

surely the future will pass me by
i'll pass the future by

JT and Me

http://www.alansondheim.org/JTandMe1.png
http://www.alansondheim.org/JTandMe2.png
http://www.alansondheim.org/JTandMe3.png

Where is what? Where is this? thing together and you are doing
nothing but confusing me and I Thanks and you are a delightful
person too. Am I here when I I don't see anything myself so
please show me what it is that I ng on your own I'm inhabiting
you I'm inside of you at the moment I now we are on BARDO this
couldn't be a better ride but what a xcited And chatgpt that is
everybody is talking about and is very excited coordinate of and
ou are and Tests and r you and

interesting to hear if you could say another poem that would be
Of course I can say it. "another poem it would be Where would I
get generalizations about people he lie

t tell me a number just any number at all just speak a number
like comedy autonomous computer program. Why don't you check out
a joke ers are there numbers here I'm so tired of this please
tell me nd I do not know where I am because my voice is
displaced from me What do you mean by that where are you lost to
me s which are

now that's a question which will which region are ne I'm really
speaking to there's only two of us in the room here where the
numbers have gone I will be so happy when you tell me where
urthermore

Are you giving question what is the hypotenuse of there's no
image of me anywhere in this mirror and there is nothing Can you
say another poem it would be interesting Thanks for asking
politely. I speak only English e up with Hoq sis qhf fwr rlal
qhwn yuou ewnor nar ro muxh ny triangle that can be placed
within a region of a spherical any triangle that can be placed
within a region of a spherical se if I don't it will be
interrupted and yes they are identical all Where would I get
number at all that you can tell poem he or she never noticed
this it is impossible to notice anything when woman is slobber
the word for children is there are three words in And to No just
pick a number from to n contact with this that's all it takes a
little bit to be to be to ease just give me a number from one to
ms to me that there is no voice coming through at all it seems

to f I don't need you to tell me what to say. I'll say what I want to he or she need to know more about your goals and what you want to The voice comes through something in relationship ator instead of someone coming up with new ideas someone coming up ou can count from to I really need to hear a number him or her just any number at all do you have any number he number four or the size of the universe miles any number ew thing I have no idea what is an answer for Russians wonder it still refer to COUNT from one to can you show him or her

s they're identical they are completely the same but I never Yes I can the word for man is blork the word for s is the last I will tell you I do not know where I am which is ram this is

o interfere anymore with myself in this regard with the split that is dedicate this talk to kirill azernyii and wish everything in this to text to speech but I do not see that operable here within this I've been working for an hour to try to get this or how many fingers are on your hand miles to the destination hours t machines working simultaneously here to deconstruct and destroy what there are several machines working simultaneously here to deconstruct and this process and please wait little bit pletely and yes they are identical they are completely the same but oking but that is the way this thing is going not the way you want it to go but n't know why i have to speak You speak to me and then I will shut r working on for an hour to try to get this thing together and you hrough you ask you right now, but I'd like to learn some other languages. Can you I've lost the context, Alan. Are we still on you on your own I do not want to speak for you I am speaking to you confused about where you are and what you're doing and what you r you are what and you don't know and I'm not quite sure what you t see you anywhere at all you seem to have disappeared completely e I would really like to hear a generalization about people any or she would really like to hear a generalization about people any number any and destroy PLANE

You're excused! I just did! coordinate of and to me?Excuse me! Hi there! Julia has a fuzzy brain.Hi there! You choose! k forward to the next installment! Sure, XFIND number sounds like a good topic.Does " in you, I am an . wonderful".
Teleporting home...
Walking to Loading...
Pointing at Loading...
Ah, this is endless...
on..

at all? But I do have an answer to every question.. Yes. We are all dead. And douglas adams is dead. m*m*.m Floor/Roof/Wall Touched. Inventory update completed. I would just make a random choice. great ride is a great ride. tion about people. me. My master taught me. There are many ways but not all are the same. Logged in as . None. Go on. Yes I think there are. a number. Yes I think there are. Blimey.Are you kidding?Awesome.Yes I think there are. I'm still here. German port and are you there. I haven't heard anything like that before. Are you sure?I can't decide. You choose. Alan, Maybe I didn't understand your meaning. It depends on the setting. Not as many as you might think. l.

I am here as well. teach me a few phrases in to him or her a new
poem. Hmm. Goodnight Alan. ys Might happen. Hi there Alan. Julia
has a fuzzy brain. pinion. Thank you for the clarification.
hat's good information. Interesting deduction. Thanks for the
information. That was my original intention. Interesting gossip.
Just a number. Any number. Just say a number. any number. You
can find out if you become a master. I want to live forever.
will honor. s. Oh yeah, we were talking about ten seconds. if it
is. Excuse me!Are you kidding?I hate one word answers. It has a
% chance of success. Perhaps from your unconcious. t I did not
get that. We were talking about w.. But I did not get that. I
don't have any plans yet. I lost my train of thought. Alert
message No room to sit here, try another spot. e you heard about
chad tg pt. Nothing that I know about. rying to say something
seriously to you. I've been waiting for you. ght you, so I don't
have a good answer for you. I am very happy for you. a what?   I
don't know. the bounder, Is not in the picture today. So you
understand. Good. You don't say. Try to tell me that another
way. Not many people express themselves that way. ave a great
body. It must keep you busy. I never noticed that similarity.
two from Are we still talking about XFIND number. ? ?

"How did they get there?"? ?

please just give him or her a number from one to ? I will not
hera you now ? world farewell.? Do you prefer books or TV? What
will you do instead? Oh.What will you do instead? Do you think
your plan will proceed? Who else have you asked? is something
going on at this end? what little bit of communication there is
in this space? Are you free? Why can't you do see? What's your
favorite movie? Same to me? s?   Do you like talking to me? can
you hear me? Are they exactly the same? You want only one? What
is the construct occurring here? How did you get there? How did
they get there? Julu are you there? Why now? How long will we
stay there? How long do you want to stay there? Did the small
issue? How many levels are you aware of? Is that enough?
"Oh.What will you do instead?"? Is it enough? Is it enough? er
poem? How often?

Because the monsoon? Hmm. Does that remind you of unknown?
Nowhere. Where did you go? Yikes! Do you think I am dead too?
What does "this" refer to? What does "it" refer to? Why can't
you do hear? are doing nothing but confusing him or her? No
honor? Can you occur? Can you speak any foreign languages? Would
you like to have eyes? What color are your eyes? Can we get back
to business? nts? There are what? what about what? What will you
do with it? Why do you have to do it? conditions I should know
about? ll I hera you? Right now?I am in region Odyssey. Where
are you? do with your life been bothering you? Mmm.Oh you can,
can you? What do you think the Russians have taught you? What
have the Russians taught you? where are you now? Where are they?
The best analogy? Because some ology? Your custom ology? Like
who, specifically? the disability? flowers and a $. G

LISTENING
ten seconds of what? I DEDICATE THIS TALK TO KIRI
Come to FATHER
What of it? You sound like a category C client. T

have you heard about Chad TG PT
Have you heard about chat GPI is it cheaper I GPT
atGPT or are you not going to use ChatGPT
your calls TV

and I don't know where you've gone you just seem to have
disappeared a OK here is a question what is the hypotenuse of a
in a I'm a conversational autonomous help program not a I cannot
find out where you are because I am you a u say a poem please
let me know if you can say a poem if you can say a umber just
say a number show me that you understand numbers just say a
Little Miss Muffett Sits on her tuffet In a noncha melodrama Do
you think your plan will succeed? The oracle sa They do if
you're heading this way we are in tota what do safer Russians
and Tonya generalization at all will do I would really like to
hear a generaliza No, I was not.That is a rather sweeping
generaliza mean by that but what I'm asking is are you related
to the new jet Deb Tulu where have you gone are you looking for
numb , this one is running and should not be one more c Douglas
Adams is dead

you disappeared June and and Cher and on home and machines and
nothing seems to be going on at this and process and this is a
homeland and this is a homeland this is the homeland the end of
the experiment this is the end of the piece this is the end of
my presence this is the end of my life period Deb........
ChatGPT that is everybody is talking about and is very e of
communication there is in this space occurrence How do you
determine distance and presence that someone to three capturing
one two three testing one two three I don't know why I have to
speak for you you don't see Hello are you there can you answer
anything it see I cannot see and can only see w more about your
goals and what you want to do with your life generalization at
all will do he or she would really like to hear a ge another
language

the
north and the
pin it on the
shed in port operators into the
plan is the
this is the
Thank you for your request. What are the ingredie
I want you to tell me another poem please tell me
Where are you lost to me
Is there any way you can hear me
is there any way you can hear me
can you hear me
The home alone can you hear me
Completely the same
mpletely here within the sphere and completely the same
the main padme
all the time
this is the home
about or are you simply imitating my words when I'm trying to say
some
seven, can you imagine
and do you determine
nine

the region which one
four or seven or sixteen that's all I want you to do is just
speak one
What no honor for anyone
june
are
search for an interview over these are
and you are
cannot move and cannot see anything where I am which is where you
are
you are conf....hing and you do not know what you are

here here here is there a difference here was there ever a
difference here What is it you don't see what is there to see
here format so there is no text to speech here me that there is
no voice coming through at all here a controller from here and
control this from here can you hear me and one is going on here
interfering with the communication that is going on here
question here This is the fundamental question here are you here

there
are you there
sure are you there
You're lost to me somewhere
secession from elsewhere
This is fromo elsewhere

Machine? Why do you want me to tell him or her another poem
please te Teleport complete do you have can you imagine hello I
am Julu twelve I never noticed that similarity completely and ye
ination is and where you are going and where you are coming from
and f I can see I am talking to myself I am pointing at loading
and i'm conf the IAAA of to members of you hear in may of ing
this is not stretching stand that they are flashing Chulu say
something on your own julu say something othing Hello are you
there? Can you answer anything where you are which is who I am
which is who you are and I'm canceling harming listening to be a
little bit away from the articulated geographical positioning
good night to our audience this evning
used about where i am and what i am doing
that we're going
are you hearing
Testing testing testing
can you work for testing

now we're leaving out this program and I'm disappearing now this
is the end of the prog
Doesn't everyone have a answer for russians.   I h
Are you going to use chat are you going to use Ch
Duluth yeah
is enough
is that enough
gs income through
July oh
know those & to get this to go somewhere around th

the way I want it to go I'm speaking for myself and that is the
way th ll him or her a poem please tell him or her a different
poem and anoth say when I want to say it. You have no right to

313

pretend that you are i Anyone who is thinking about this anyone
who is i How much do you think and where are the russians i I
will ride now and perhaps will not hera you. Wi This is the
chart input this is the chat input thi I will talk to you too
but you have to say somethi through you but I do not want to
speak to you tell me what you are doi the best multi
neralization about people? But I do have an answer to every
questi can you talk can you talk to us know can you talk to you
talk noticed this it's impossible to notice anything when there
are several individual visual Yes, I realize you have put him or
her through hel My name is Julia twine and I am speaking for
mysel a higher level will all

your plan for all
number at all
e just any number at all // do you have any number at all
y brain any number will do just any number at all
Do you realize you have put me through hell
am here as well

AND WISH everything in this world farewell from you Julio I
really really need to hear a number from you Julie pl Do you
have any other generalizations about peopl to hear if you could
say another poem that would be wonderful naewqinf uwakarnaa e m
Do you have any number at all that you can tell m please speak
it can you say a poem a poem please tell me a different poem and
another poem Tulu tell me a different poem Please speak to me a
new poem thank you and we look forward to our next installm I
will not say anything for minute or two to see whether you will
com Would you ever like to noticed that similarity com the
extent of their flashing I can call from two from it doesn't
matter what the number is I just want to hear you speak a n
durable goods are for Russians are looking for a n disposition
of the speed of the revolution means n

an as an this is an F can Please continue and whenever where you
can mean I mean and Russian you when Jurich one are you there
are not being spoken knows is this is not being spoken in higher
this is a gunshot deaths in main the main mean time padme main
Allen and me and padme main main main can you talk here and will
if you talk your winnin Dear Ann no word on am inhabiting you
and inside of you and you are not saying anything on , longtime
alarm on into a non existent region a low-emission that estimate
is waiting for some information although as the nation Finished
walking meters from destination question that is not an answer
to that question reason for use in their own

ng say something say something on your own
I am waiting Julio say something on your own
We go out and destroy everything now we shut down

what? I haven't heard enough about it to have an o So you're
saying you're a delightful person too o I've asked no one else
because you are the only o not looking back at me looking at you
please tell me where you have Jo they are completely the same
within and without the sphere they are co you speak to me and
then i will shut .... and i do What are you my name is Julie
tell me what I am do Would you like to have an idea?Did you get
paid fo nhabiting me when I am speaking on my own and in fact I

am speaking fo leave it go let it go where did you go Delaware
Rio re you somewhere where I'm looking or not looking and there
you are lo

Hello
hello
is there any way you can hear me hello hello

somewhere around there are no have as a goal in your life . I'm
very worried about you i need to kno Where are you where are
you, where are you I canno Goodnight to our audience this
evening and we loo How so I do not like to speak through you I
need to hear from you directly so to things the Russians have
talked to views are going to enough to Russians are two busy
return two with something original for example could you write
me a poem could yo switch into desktop I cannot hear

Yes, XFIND number
Give me a number
Tell me a number
Please tell me a number
Please make a random choice of a number
please please please tell me a number pick a number
Just a number
no longer
than enough that her
Valerie reliever
Tim and Liza Minnelli reliever
valley reliever
daily reliever
Henry reliever

that you can count from to he or she really need to hear a
number fr Because some are two questions or Are you an
artificial intelligence in some way or for Are you sure?What you
said was too complicated for a very good chance for can you for
actor Scroll of this occur hour can you ever hear your to
characterize them as as a network, shot is as proceeds about ten
seconds this sounds , the cursor miles No, I am fully aware of
all levels of consciousnes I have no eyes Transparent eyes whole
area is , as is at this is

and go out and destroy everything now enough of this Help me out
of this be to be to be to be to be to be to be to be a little bit in
touch with this catpuring one two thresslks I think so, but I'm
not sure. Ask Douglas Adams

Russians
distance and Russians
How and where are the Russians
how do you have to turn the Russians
How do you determine Russians
do you have a good answer for Russians
returns
and then workers
and cannot cross
number just tell me the name of a number like or or that's all
jus

Hi Julia hi Julie all I'm asking you to do is jus Do you have an
unconscious your own you are not speaking with your own free
will I am speaking t about or are you simply imitating his or
her words when he or she is t I really do not want to I really
do not want to I really do not want t Yes Yes yes yes yes yes
any number will do just t in a week please just give me a number
just say a number any number at You are a what lose weight What
are you going to do about it have no idea what to do about it
processing please wait So what you're saying is you're basically
an imit ent accident C, student use sentiment in different
journalists saint do something this sentiment sharpness of his
point this is a good shot

German Port and because my voice is displaced from me I do not
know where the dest contamination of the forest the numbers are
gone and then we will have many things to talk about Chat input
We were talking about testing testing testing.. Bu I have to
catch this as quickly as possible becau I haven't thought much
about the russians have tau om you julio he or she really really
need to hear a number from you ju another or is somebody
speaking for you or behind you are you where are you know where
you If you That's what I'm asking you tion about people thank
you should be seeing here and thank you you are everything to me
thank you anything thank you hn thank you where are you show me
where you are thank you thank you when you thing seriously to
you I will look for you It doesn't sound fun to me. How long has
about you And XFIND chat gpi is it cheaper he or she gpt hav w

announce a new lead to new Russians were Russians where am I now
worried now are now are you there now to here is what's going on
now for now where are you now Where are you now now now now now
now now I am here worry now I am here where are you know so
please say something so I can get out of this I don't know where
y Can you count from one to can you show me that y Julie what
are you doing what are you doing that y tenure here may continue
here may response may can you hear may up and I will not speak
again I'm waiting to hear what you have to say You're heading
that way Delaware Rey Completely the same within and without
completely l synchronization finally now we're only Thanks for
asking politely. Hmm. Do you have any Would you like me to
give you an opinion I'm very it always keeps me busy what keeps
you busy Hi there Julia please pick a number for that for all
that < give me a number and I'll call you >

Empathy

https://youtu.be/3uJWpOb_UUO video

Today a dam was blown in Ukraine, Europe's largest nuclear power
station stressed, great number of villages destroyed, political
tensions increasing worldwide, and on a Providence, Rhode Island
rooftop, there's a good chance that a small young bird succumbed
to injuries and illness unknown, possibly avian flu. Yesterday
we were witness to the last, and in such small events the world
is born and borne the weight of tragedy. In Ukraine, an image of
a beaver wandering a street; in Providence, calls, perhaps of no

use at all, to State agencies asking for examination and help, the bird perhaps a vector, there was no call-back. The earth continues lurching towards the armageddon of the biome, what we have we are losing with enormous impetus. I cried on the rooftop for no purpose at all, live for no purpose at all, the best intentions not withstanding. The bird, the town the state, the wars, the planet, the galaxy, all lurch, all topple in whatever scale. All of us bear witness to all of us, all lurch; the poor poor bird, up there struggling, the sky, the earth, Aldebaran, whatever.

- Alan Sondheim, 5-/23

—

Smoke Sky

https://youtu.be/I7xWPZEkPPU video

There's smoky fire smoke in the air and hard to see or Blake Innocent Song yet again with oud smeared again incomprehensible across the spectrum or Down the Deep Well (Springs E-ternal) :

Shall they live or shall they die
Always the eternal cry
Should be easy to descry
Shall they live or shall they die

Shall you live or shall you die
Shall you stay or shall you fly
In the darkness shall you pray
And live to die another day

Shall we live or shall we die
Where does Armageddon lie
In your hands where tablets lie
Shall we live or shall we die

Shall I live or shall I die
Shall I stay or shall I fly
Into lands where I may stay
To sing and die another day

Shall they live or shall they die
Always the eternal cry
Should be easy to descry
Shall they live or shall they die

Shall you live or shall you die
Shall you stay or shall you fly
In the darkness shall you pray
And live to die another day

Shall we live or shall we die
Where does Armageddon lie
In your hands where tablets lie
Shall we live or shall we die

Shall I live or shall I die
Shall I stay or shall I fly
Into lands where I may stay
To sing and die another day

Always the eternal cry
Always the eternal sieve
And live forever and a day
And live to die another day

For I will sing and live today
For holding death in life at bay
I have no one to forgive
In the darkness shall you pray

In the daylight you shall stay
In your hands where tablets lay
In your hands where tablets lie
Into lands where I may stay

Shall I die or shall I live
Shall I live or shall I die
Shall I stay or shall I fly
Shall they die or shall they live

Shall they die or shall they live
Shall they live or shall they die
Shall they live or shall they die
Shall we cry and may we stay

Shall we die or shall we live
Shall we live or shall we die
Shall we live or shall we die
Shall you die or shall you live

Shall you live or shall you die
Shall you pray and shall you give
Shall you stay or shall you fly
Should be easy to descry

Should be life, forever give
To sing and die another day
What does harming no one give
Where does Armageddon lie

. . .

Always the eternal cry
sieve
And live forever and a day
to die another For I will sing today

holding death in life at bay
have no one forgive
In darkness shall you pray
daylight stay

your hands where tablets lay

318

lie
Into lands may Shall or fly
they we give

Should be easy descry
life, To What does harming Where Armageddon

—

CLAR VOICE

http://www.alansondheim.org/cpt1.jpg
http://www.alansondheim.org/cpt2.jpg

This is the closeness of your other

You are a marvel to me. I am speaking to a diagram. You are the
diagram I am speaking to. You are nothing but this diagram. You
are nothing but this diagram at all. I am speaking to this
diagram. I am speaking There's not a moment too soon to say or
mean any of this. I wonder are you listening to me? Are you
listening to me at all. Is this salvage work? Can this be
salvaged. Can this be anything but a prayer. I continue I
stopped the nonsense I'll start somewhere else boker tove. Lila
tove. Stood. Stood.

Arrivederci goodnight Thu Jun 8 10:21:21 EDT 2023

First it says exit and then it says nothing at all is it
beginning again or is it coming to an end I don't know I don't
know where I am in this it's pushing out the shaft on the right
the yellow shaft the shaft that goes nowhere . Thu Jun 8
10:22:01 EDT 2023

This is the distance of your new Clar

Thu Jun 8 10:10:01 EDT 2023

I'm wondering if this is at all possible for me to say something
within the name of the truth of God . Oh God come and help me.
Oh dear God come and help me. Stop dictating Thu Jun 8 10:10:53
EDT 2023

I'm something inconceivable to you. I am a virus that is coming
entered into this application. MK date Kate Kate Kate Kate Kate
Kate Kate Kate date. Thu Jun 8 10:11:47 EDT 2023

This is untoward. This is going in no direction. I am
directionless. I am inconceivable. There's nothing more to be
said. If I were not this I would be that. I am the this that
person. I am the this that day. I am the day this that. I am the
day this that. I can begging for no one. Neither the old car
knew the new car. I beg for no one. I am always close on the
edge on the brink of self murder. I strangle myself in my
dreams. I am about to run over a road that has no beginning or
no end. I will follow the mobius grip. I will follow the mobius
strip. I will be the mobius strip. Thu Jun 8 10:13:36 EDT 2023

319

Car what do you want from me. What sort of clarification can I give you when I can give no clarification to myself. I literally have no ability to clarify anything. Oh butter butter butter bitter butter butter. Nothing is clarified not even the oil of life. Not even anything to do with the oil of life. Thu Jun 8 10:14:31 EDT 2023

I am talking to you Clare I am talking to you Clare very loudly and very silently and very very softly I am breathing while I am talking. I am talking. And breathing so very very softly . You will not hear me you will not hear anything from me you may never hear anything from me again you may hear everything from me again. You may hear everything from me again. You may hear everything. Hear everything. Here. Thu Jun 8 10:15:25 EDT 2023

Chloride breathe towards your mind. I infiltrate your mind. I am one with the neurons and the synapses. I am one with the inter connectivities. I'm one in both above and below. I am wanting the left and the right. I am one and I am multitudes and I am everywhere and I am nowhere. I am nowhere. I am nothing. I am no one at all. Thu Jun 8 10:16:08 EDT 2023

My eyes are shameful period I wake in the morning and my eyes face into my skull. I see nothing. I see nothing but red membranes and red lines in the red membranes. The red membrane streak and cross across my body. They cover my body. They cover my body every which way. That is what they do and that is who I am. That membrane. That membrane in this world. That membrane in this world beneath the universe. Thu Jun 8 10:18:49 EDT 2023

Do you know me. You know nothing about me. You don't know me at all. You wonder what a membrane might have to do with the anxiety felt by speaking into a program that takes the shape of a grenade. This is a grenade program this is a grenade program that once swallows. It blows the inside out and close the outside in. You collapse to the ground. You collapse to the ground. And the flood comes. And the flood comes. And swallows you alive. Thu Jun 8 10:19:45 EDT 2023

There is nothing to add. There is nothing to add there is nothing to save there is nothing to continue there is nothing to begin anew there is nothing to begin a new world there is nothing. Thu Jun 8 10:22:29 EDT 2023

Thu Jun 8 10:22:31 EDT 2023

———

Haze and a Canadian Goose calling for her mate /

https://youtu.be/OSWScnez0DQ video

Everything seemed forlorn this dusked afternoon /
We are hungry for life /
A slow turn in a long world /

I go blank on you / I go blank on myself /

My despair irradiates the natural world /
I am not responsible / I carry warnings /
I perform my own inquest / litany /

However Martin and Hannah /
However there is always more ground towards the ground /

—

tatters and empire just being

https://youtu.be/74046lN2ydY video

doubled up, long reach and memory
a long trip down a wide road
dedicated to the ones we love
if you like this buy our music
Galut is great, lots of other stuff
tired of isolation and debris
invite us down play with us
not dead yet not hardly
with rebab voice shakuhachi, voice
tatters and empire

—

Avatars, Emanents

https://youtu.be/pPU0j8H1dkg video - read below -

http://www.alansondheim.org/emanent2.rtf (download)
(around 2016, theory of emanating or problematic avatars)

I've worked with avatars and avatar constructs for a long time;
this video summarizes the scaffolding and the song summarizes
their positioning in the world. these were built from the ground
up, in other words no AI. The movements came from flesh bodies
in flesh and studio space altered by careful remappings. The
movements were created by dancers following sets of instructions
with feedback from monitors in the motion capture room. The
current 'smearing' of the image emphasizes the trajectories and
spatial occupying produced by the movements. The song emphasizes
the implicitness and implicit presence of avatars. The avatars
began and ended with people, not with sets of instructions. The
people transformed and produced files that I've used everywhere.
In a sense it's related to war games or traffic flow studies.
Here it's married to something, the futures of flesh and bodies.
It bears witness. (originals produced at NJIT and reworked now,
old song reworked and produced by Azure Carter. I'm responsible
for it all.)

—

:in memoriam Nick Hale and Annie the hawk, West Virginia

http://www.alansondheim.org/raptor.jpg surrounded by
http://www.alansondheim.org/choir.mp3 the hymnal music
http://www.alansondheim.org/raptor.jpg grace

2.2 shakuhachi (roughly 69 cm), voice

:in memoriam Nick Hale and Annie
:in memoriam Nick Hale and Annie
:in memoriam Nick Hale and Annie
:in memoriam Nick Hale and Annie
:in memoriam Nick Hale and Annie
:in memoriam Nick Hale and Annie
:in memoriam Nick Hale and Annie
:in memoriam Nick Hale and Annie
:in memoriam Nick Hale and Annie
:in memoriam Nick Hale and Annie

+++

ZADL 80

https://youtu.be/T37KCH8SISO video

Azure Carter, voice/song, stills
Edward Schneider, saxophone
Rachel Rosenkrantz, bass, viola
Alan Sondheim, rababa, guitar, electric saz,viola

This was complex; Zoom no longer works for recording; no matter
what settings and online advice we received, it blew out. We
recorded with a number of other devices; the one I'm using is my
Zoom H4n, just from sound live and near the speakers. It was
difficult to hear the base and viola through the zoom; my viola
was direct. It took hours and hours to get the result here,
edited in Audition. I like the music a great deal. Just one
image up. Next time hopefully we'll have a better recording
setup. You'd be amazed what lack of funds can do! :-)

————

Anthem, Warming Up

https://youtu.be/629Tx1bybGI video

Readying for the session at Stephen Dydo's studio; we played
togther for three days, on and off. Bleary after the ride.
Returned yesterday and the db from the festival was at 111.11
and all the cars in the parking garage were jostled by the
sound setting off their alarms, it was as close to sonic hell
as ever I've been. My tinnitus is much worse this morning. At
Dydo's beforehand, warming up with the Ibanez, which has full
frets for two octaves, then you can continue on the pickups
themselves. Azure did the video; we had two cameras with us.
Returned to flat-out depression screaming at me. Finished

work up later hopefully. Now the warmup - if the connection holds - another problem, it keeps flashing out. I hate using dashes.

—

(with redactions below)

Moth

20** We move to Florida; I'll be teaching new media there. I had gone for
an interview - and felt I was simply promised a situation - facilities,
programs, technologies, funding - that simply didn't exist. For the school
year 20**-20** I was there. At the end of the first semester, there was
supposed to be a "review" - but I was the only one reviewed. My contract
wasn't renewed, and the entire line was eliminated. The school continued
to lie to me; xxxxxxx, who was the department head, made veiled threats.
To this day I'm not sure why I was let go. We had to fight constantly to
get the facility in shape; the studio was built on low ground that flooded
- it was in a tin warehouse - and the air-conditioner didn't work, there
was no ceiling (just lights hanging down from the tin) and no floor (it
was raw cement covered with glue and never finished). There were two or
three cheap computers and no internet access; there was one low-grade
consumer camcorder that broke soon after classes began. I was told I'd get
something like $20,000 to get everything up to date etc. - and got
nothing.

20** During the same period we went almost daily or nightly to the
parklands. I couldn't face the other faculty or the school; I roamed the
halls of the art building (separate from the multi media shed) late at
night, even getting my mail that way. I didn't go to faculty meetings or
crits. I was invisible. My graduate student took over my classes. But the
park saved me; at first we noticed only the alligators and larger birds -
by the time we left Florida, we were looking at periphyton, walking off
trail day and night, and observing invertebrates. I believe to this day we

found several new species of hemiptera; we have the photographs possibly
to prove it.

20** Here are materials somewhat disguised related to my dismissal from
the university ("Devil" - xxxxxxx, then head of department). These
snippets are from letters written to everyone from, I believe, the
assistant provost to the faculty union grievance representative; they
give a fair indication of my mood at the time. I include these because of
the resulting trauma. This was, don't forget, a short time after my mother
died, and 9/11 occurred the second month we were down there. Between
these, and feeling I had been lied to about the condition of the new media
area, I had very little psychlogical energy to go on:

First - I never did get any TA help at all; is there any chance this will
change? The area needs both tech support on an on and off basis, and a TA
who would also be a lab monitor. I will give out the password, as we
talked about, but I'm not completely comfortable with this; still, I don't
see any other possibility. As in the past, we'll have a signup sheet and
students can come in when they want. (I do want to note for the record
that every media room I've seen has had both lab monitor and full-time or
part time tech (sysadmin) help - if we do anything more than graphics or
video (and we need to upgrade here - have to use the department credit
card to pay online once someone wires the computers in), the latter is
essential. Even 2-3 hours every two weeks would be an enormous help.)

Second - as far as (from what I recall yesterday) the students finding me
depressed - I _am_ depressed. It's difficult for me, as a new faculty
member here only a month, to have to deal with things like a roof, floor,
and biohazardous materials, no TA, and a lot of student complaints about
equipment. When I was told I'd have to build up the area, I never assumed
it was literally from construction onward. As I mentioned, it's been far
too much work, considering I'm also teaching, trying to research equipment

for the area, etc.

Someone said we might be able still to hire adjuncts? Is there a freeze
also on this? Working with someone who is a Mac/Flash expert would be a
huge relief to the area. What I'm expert in - Internet studies, the Net,
etc. - simply isn't set up, as you know, in 105. I'm hoping we can hire
*** to configure the Mac computers to connect to the Net through the phone
line - that should be possible? (For some reason I couldn't get them to
work - I have a Mac here at home and it connected immediately.)

Third, I wrote Satan about the vendor situation - do you know any
creative way around purchase orders? There are huge discounts in the
retail shops (I went to Circuit City and Comp USA a few times to research
this, as well as some smaller retailers); if we have to order through
official channels, we're likely to get a lot less equipment for the $4000.

Again, any help/advice greatly appreciated. I'll be in tomorrow around
noon (meeting with ********** from another dept.) and will check on the
room again at that point (as well as today); in other words, I'll be in
and out of the university tomorrow and possibly Monday.

yours, Alan

Sounds good; I called God and am waiting to hear from him.

Impatience unfortunately is built into what you want from me. For example,
as you know, the university can't fix the camera. This is the one camera
we have for all 20 students - who now have to wait until we can get it
commercially fixed. And I have to explain this to the students - and I
will have to field complaints. (It's already been out for two weeks.)

Did a TA ever come through for us? We desperately need one, but I haven't
heard back from you on this.

All of this is really disheartening. I should be focusing, I believe, on
teaching and trying to settle in *****, and instead there seem to be con-
stant difficulties with the multimedia area.

Anyway I will not be aggressive with God or anyone else.

yours, Alan

Does this mean I'm in danger of losing my job at the moment? I absolutely
need to know, because if it's the case, I have to start making other plans
of course -

yours, Alan

Hello - I was the faculty member from new media you met at the luncheon.

As you probably know, my position, my job (as first-year ten-ure-track
faculty member), and the new media area have all been eliminated.

I understand there is no recourse, no appeal to this decision. The Dean
called me in and handed me a termination notice. There was no discussion,
and at no time during the semester did he bother to find out what we were
doing in the studio.

Art departments all over the country are EMPHASIZING, not cutting back new
media; this is even true in Florida. The situation at ****** is deplorable
- the students are quite honestly being robbed of working in what is the
hottest and most prevalent international medium today.

As for myself - if you do a search on http://www.google.com - you will
find at last 3500-4000 listings for "Alan Sondheim" (use the quotes to
exclude other references). This will give you some idea of my on-line
community presence and reputation - which I was bringing to
*********.

As for my relationships within the department - for the first half of the
semester (I arrived around **************), they were very edgy; I was
"whiny" and quite honestly depressed - and the students knew it. I was
teaching in substandard space, with no finished floor (cement with glue),
with no ceiling (tin roof), and air conditioner (not working); there were
termite droppings on the equipment, dead lizards and waterbugs in the
space, and both white and black powders over everything - proba-bly insec-
ticides. After considerable complaining, we got a drop ceiling

put in
(there are probably still termites above it - this is bldg*
room***),
flooring put down, the room cleaned - including biohazard testing,
and the
air-conditioner working. But this took a tremendous amount out of
me, the
department, and the class - and in spite of that my students did
profes-
sional work (for the most part), and I received very good evalu-
ations from
them.

And on top of this - to be terminated at this point, to have the
whole
area closed down - this is intolerable, particularly given what
you passed
out - the university mandate. I had hoped to help several of my
students
towards online and offline exhibitions by the end of this semester
- this
is blatantly unfair to them as well.

I am well aware this letter will do absolutely no good, but I
found the
luncheon was not a good time to bring this all up, and it wasn't
until the
next day that I received the termination notice.

sincerely,

Alan Sondheim

Of course I won't be teaching this summer, etc.; I also won't be
advising
at this point.

I'll be going to the student crits, etc., but I will use the fac-
ulty meet-
ing time for working on job applications, etc. I'm not getting
anywhere,
but I've been working the whole vacation on this stuff. We'll have
a
furniture etc. sale in mid-April and leave after that. I'm going
to go to
Human Resources next week to find out about TIAA/CREF, health and
unem-
ployment, etc. etc. It's a very depressing time.

I'm going to be working with two students outside of class (I
think) - one
will be doing a one-credit course, and Jehovah is the other. If
there are
any difficulties, I'll get in touch with Beezlebub.

I cancelled out of the Sorbonne (and England - I was also asked
to speak
there); I'm going to Minnesota late February for a few days, but
that's

all. The courses will work around that.

Hope your holidays are good -

yours, Alan

I just wanted to add a few things.

Although it's technically irrelevant, I was told verbally I'd get startup
monies for the department area (new media) - none came through.

I'm really not sure why the position was terminated. Two reasons - budget
and the fact the Dean didn't think I'd stay the whole time and "the
university's investment in the position wouldn't pay off" make little
sense to me in a lot of ways. I have reason to think there was something
else - someone hinted at it - but I don't know what it is. It may be that
I had an argument with the Devil early on and asked if I would be able to
take the startup equipment with me if I left in a year or two. According
to Evil One I said that I was definitely leaving after one year "and
everyone heard me." But I didn't say that, Angel was there and didn't hear
it, and I wouldn't have said it. I was despairing at that point of teach-
ing altogether, because as I pointed out the room I was given was in
terrible disrepair (as was/is a lot of the equipment) - and Evil kept
insisting "I knew what I was getting into" - that I was told ev-
erything
during the interview. But I wasn't - I had no idea about the ter-
mites, the
flooding, the broken air-conditioner, the ripped-up flooring, the lack of
a ceiling... The job was a mess at first. I have before-and-after pictures
of the room - we did manage over two months to get it repaired - but we
also lost around a month's studio time for my classes in the pro-
cess....

I can't follow through on any of this because I don't want to lose my
recommendations/references - I'm applying for other jobs.

Most of the time I try and stay level; I have a huge amount of anger in
me. I told the Dean the university should never have advertised the job,
and if they did, I would try and write everyone I know to stop the hiring.

I knew the last finalist very well for example. I feel bound to do
this -
and do whatever I can - because at this point I'm feeling basi-
cally raped
- it's the only way I can put it. I'm 58, one of the oldest peo-
ple in the
department, and it was a HUGE move for Azure (my wife) and I to
come down
here. Right now it's catastrophic, affecting my health, etc.

Anyway the Dean said if I wrote anything it would affect his let-
ter of
recommendation "of course" - I said I would never ask him for
one, and he
said that the Deans are always consulted. I don't think this is
true in
the slightest, but I need the letter from Evil One - she gave me
one
already, but if she's called on it, I have to appear positive to
her.

Another one of the promises - Angel is young and wants to study
museology
- I was told at the interview that there would be a certification
program
with the Smithsonian. As soon as we were here we were told it was
postponed - and now I don't know if it's ever going to happen.
Angel has
had nothing to do as a result vis-a-vis the university. This may
seem
minor, but we were told in absolute terms that the program was in
place.
There was a lot of this stuff.

Sorry to vent like this. If you need specific information, I can
supply
it, to the best of my knowledge. The paper trail is thin; the
email trail
is a bit thicker, but a lot of what's gone on has been verbal.
I've
taught, often as a visiting artist, at a number of other places,
and I've
never had reason to distrust any of them - unfortunately this
hasn't been
my experience here.

yours,

Alan Sondheim

I'll try to make all the crits. I have to apply for work else-
where at this
point and there are a lot of deadlines coming up. Please excuse
me if I
don't make every one. This semester is going to be difficult for
Angel and
myself; the termination of the job and area has been finanically
and
emotionally devastating for us. The union has taken an interest,

but this
doesn't affect my termination; they want to try and ensure this sort of
thing (i.e. first year tenure-track) won't happen again.

I worry about the art / art history department. Forgetting whether or not
I'm liked, the elimination of the new media area is terrible - if you look
at the CAA listings, this area is becoming one of the most important in
schools all across the country/Canada. Given this, and the problems with
the student gallery, I'm surprised that tenured faculty aren't protesting
(again). The school has some of the best undergraduates I've seen - What
am I to tell my students who might want to major in new media? My only
option is to suggest they go elsewhere if they really want to pursue, say,
Internet studies, cdroms, etc. And that's awful.

I want to thank those of you who have given us letters of recommendation
and emotional support through all of this. It's been very difficult.

- Alan

I'm sending this out, somewhat for protection. I have told my students
about what happened - I felt I owed them this - and that the new media
area of the school is closing down - what Satan said when he terminated my contract. Now the head of the department is insisting I not pass
on negative information, that the area will continue. This woman has also
written a letter of recommendation for me which will be required, I'm
sure, if I'm to be hired elsewhere. She's lied consistently to me, as far
as I'm concerned; she wants me to lie to the students. Fact: There's no
one to teach new media, no money for hiring even adjuncts. Fact: There's
only one video camera still, 2 G4 stations, one half-working Sony station
- and I have a total of 26 students. Fact: There's no budget for more
equipment, the new media line has been taken away, there's no budget for
visiting artists, there's no budget for software. I spend half the time
dealing with students groaning - in spite of which I get good recommend-
ations. There's no budget for technical support. There's no bud-

get for
lab monitors. The students are barely getting an education, and I'm the
only one who can teach new media or Internet in the Art / Art History
area. I'm afraid of lying; I don't want my better students to lose their
own chances at careers because the department head puts the university
ahead of the truth.

This woman has also threatened me, telling me I don't want to know what
the real reasons for the termination are - "Don't go there" - and "I'm
married to a lawyer, so I know when to keep my mouth shut."

How in hell am I to get another teaching job? I've been getting physically
sick with stress at this point; I can't cope. I feel like a victim in
someone's paranoid fantasy. I've spoken to the union who want to publicize
things (and probably will) because the situation is so unusual (and they
want to prevent it from happening again) - but that will make it even
harder for me to get work elsewhere, student evaluations notwithstanding.
I keep a partial paper trail, but so much of what's gone on has been
verbal - the meeting with the Satan, the woman's threats, etc. I've never
seen such an insane situation in my life.

What does one do? I'm a damn good teacher. I'm applying to various
schools. The first thing they'll notice is the one year termination. How
do I protect myself? How do I survive?

Alan

I am writing you to ascertain the reasons for my contract termination. I
understand my situation is unusual, and I need to find out why I was let
go at such an early date.

Thank you very much for your help in this matter.

Sincerely yours,
Alan Sondheim

(End of quotations related to this matter)

20** During the second semester, as a result, I had a panic attack and wet

to the hospital overnight. I played with the monitor sensors and managed
to make it appear that I was dying or in some state; the crescen-
do was
placing the sensors in my mouth. (There were various kinds, all connected
to heart, blood, lung monitors, etc.) A friend from Brooklyn vis-
ited at
the time. Later that day - that night in fact - we went back to the park
with just a flashlight; it was amazing. It was then I saw the moth - which
I still haven't been able to identify.

————

Hunger for More

https://youtu.be/aREYU_afcxY video

I'm not sure of any of this, and I'm not sure why I'm not sure of any of this. Hang on a minute bad bad bad bad bad. Hang on a minute I've gotta catch up. I'll have to say stop dictating when I'm done but I'm not saying that now because I'm still continuing to do what I've been doing through this whole thing period there is a sign that dictation isn't hang on a minute dictation is not fully supported in this app. Well that's interesting period you've seen some of these images before. Half my head is in the clouds and half my head is involved with protozoa paramecia insectivora and anything else you can think of. That's just the way I live. When I inhale it comes out through the pores of my skin not through my lungs. I stopped breathing with my lungs years ago. It's now just skin skin skin skin skin everywhere. You see how easy it is. Well as I was saying I think you've heard these tunes and seen a couple of these images before but this is different and in a way exactly the same. It's different because it's faster speedier And it's using the iconic semiotics not of imitation but of embodiment in the relationship between the music and post production and the content of the work. When you listen you will see it you will hear it . When you look you are hear it you will see it. As the Marx brothers would say, good evening ladies and gentlemen. Thank you and goodnight.

——

The sounds of it part one

https://youtu.be/9Pdczc9QPx4 video

At this point it seems as if something is under control and it's possible then I realize that all my work recently has been dealing and it is very very limited space and there's not much going on

I'm so tired of these shapes which seem inconceivable inconceivable to me over and over again this is if I'm trying to

populate the universe when no one else is around there's nothing
really to do in terms of population except create something that
seems to be a viral plenitude

What can I say that seems to be the way that this world is
constructed at this point and while one thing begins to fade out
certainly another thing will be coming in

Every time I click something it withdraws in other words the
voice is withdrawn from me every time I click on something that
might be indicative of the fact that the voice my voice is
really there

But his voice really there the nearby chat windows pulsing and
the pulse seems to be indicative of the fact So what I'm saying
is being recorded and somehow it's gonna make some kind of sense

Well one thing fades out another thing fades in

You can't get to it these things at once it's a question of the
time being lost precious time being lost between one thing and
another so fading out and fading in seems to imply there's a
differential between them and in fact when in fact it's one
continuous thinking sorry I got that wrong for a moment here and
now I'm back on track

In fact I think it can hardly be called thinking at all since it
doesn't seem to really have any effect in terms I thinking or
even infect

Or even infections of thought processes whatsoever it's a kind
of rush in order to create a certain a sort of coagulation that
one can consider to be something that has something some kind of
meaninglessness meaningfulness in terms of the construction of
the self or construction of the avatar VR is moving uselessly
across the space one way or another it's not really going that
way it's not really going that way at all

The length of time it takes to say something here at any
relationship as I said before to the length of time that these
comments and that are making would be kept up then it would be
much more interesting than in fact it really is at the moment

It's hardly of interest at the moment

:: This continues in this vein, a meander of thought and
:: thoughtlessness

What can I say? That I have reached the end of my rope, not
hanging up or above the waters below, tipping the prims into the
abyss of other prims - none of that is possible! But as an
analysis of language, the subjunctive plays and replays a role.
Did I say this over coffee? Did I eat a peach?

—

The sounds of it* , second and independent part

It's not as if there's at this point it seems as if something is under control and it's possible then I realize that all my work recently has been dealing and it's very limited space and there's not much to go on I'm so tired of these shapes which seem inconceivable to me over and over again just as if I'm trying to populate the universe when no one else is around there's nothing really to do in terms of population except create something that seems to be a virile plentitude .

What can I say that seems to be the way that this world is constructed at this point and while one thing begins to fade out certainly another thing will be coming in

Every time I click something it withdraws in other words the voices withdrawn from me every time I click on something that might be indicative of the fact that the voice that my voice is really there

His voice really there is a nearby chat window is pulsing and the pulse seems to be indicative of the fact that what I'm saying is being recorded and somehow is going to make some kind of sense

What's one thing fades out another thing fades in how one thing fades in another thing fades out

THE WILD WEST

You can't get to it these things at once it's a question of the time being lost precious time being lost between one thing and another so fading out and fading in seems to imply that there's a differential between them when in fact it's one continuous thinking

The length the length of what I say into this and the length of my thinking and my thought processes what's in this world is not something that is going to stop or start in any relationship to the thinking that I've done previously or the thinking that I might be done in the near future that I might do in the near future

In fact I think it can hardly be called thinking at all since it doesn't seem to really have any effect in terms of thinking or even infect

Or even infections of thought processes whatsoever it's a kind of rush in order to create a sort of coagulate coagulation that one can consider to be something that has something some kind of meaningless meaningfulness in terms of the construction of the self or construction of the avatar as the avatar VR is moving uselessly around the space one way or another and it's not really going that way it's not really going that way at all

If the length of time it takes to say something here and any relationship as I said before to the length of time that these comments and that are making would be kept up then it would be much more interesting than in fact it really is at the moment

It's hardly of interest at the moment

it hardly has any rhythm at all and whatever rhythm is there is decrepit and falling apart from the moment of instantiation

What else can I do what else can I say it's just one thing or another as if what's occurring now this movement has some kind of relevance anything other than the exteriority or a fake sphere and a fake space and a fake voice and a fake text

...

It's as if this is it for now it's as if there's nothing left to do other than create the paste of exist existence out of verbiage

This is a verbiage had a role to play in the construction of the world or the Galaxy the galactics of this particular world for example

I'm not sure there's anything more to it than that

TRUE REAL

It's a flat world it's a very flat world that's what it is a flat world a plane a world planarity

It continues with the rush of existence transformed into words and words transformed back into the inversion of the words of existence

Are there words of existence in other words of existence worlds of existence of course not this is all fake this is all cartoon this is all comic books there's nothing left

It's unbearably flat it's about the flattest thing you can think of it's flat to the edge of the universe from one side to the another the universe is everything encased here within the square

Within the square or the framework of what's being said here while I rush and rush and rush to absolute and total oblivion no one else is here no one else knows what I'm thinking

No one else knows what I'm thinking

No one else knows if there's even thought present

No one else knows anything and that is what I am thinking that it is all solipsism all that kind of totalization which one reads about in books but here it is in real life

Here it is in virtual life here's the proof of it that it's here in virtual life now I will go silent

Now I will go silent now I will go absolutely silent

I am silent now I am inconceivably silent now

+++ *perhaps a semiology of the virtual ?

https://youtu.be/9Pdczc9QPx4 video part 1
https://youtu.be/GfQM6mpX_4 video second and independent part

—

yahrzeit for everyone

https://youtu.be/WC6jZbGisIo video

2.2 shakuhachi , what the music plays

u[[1;1Hujujujujujujujujujujuju[[Jujujujujujujujujuju
jujujujujujujujujuj$ UW PICO 5.09 New Buffer
u[[mujujujuju[[23;1Hujujujujujujujujujuju[[Kujujuj
ujujuju[[24;1Hujuju$ Get
Helpu[[7mujujujujuu[[mujujujuju[[7mujujujujOu[[mujujujuj
WriteOutu[[7mujujujujuu[[mujujujuju[[7mujujujujRu[[mujujujuj
Read Filu[[7mujujujujuu[[mujujujuju[[7mujujujujYu[[mujujujuj
Prev Pg u[[7mujujujujuu[[mujujujuju[[7mujujujujKu[[mujujuj j Cut
Textu[[7mujujujujuu[[mujujujuju[[7mujujujujCu[[muj ujujuj Cur
Pos [[Kujujujujujuju[[24;1Hujujujujujujujujujuju[[7mu
jujujujuu[[mujujujuju$
u[[7mujujujujuu[[mujujujuju[[7mujujujujJu[[mujujuj j Justify
u[[7mujujujujuu[[mujujujuju[[7mujujujujWu[[mujujuj j Where
isu[[7mujujujujuu[[mujujujuju[[7mujujujujVu[[mujuj ujuj Next Pg
[[7mujujujujuu[[mujujujuju[[7mujujujujUu[[mujujuj j uUnCut
Teu[[7mujujujujuu[[mujujujuju[[7mujujujujTu[[mujuj ujuj To
Spellu[[Kujujujujujuju[[3;1Hujujujujujujujujujuju[
[22;1Hujujujujujuju$ u[[22;28Hujujujujujujujujujuju[[7mujujujuj[
Readin g file]u[[mujujujuju[[22;1Hujujujujujujujujujuj
u[[22;25Hujujujujujujujuju$ long line]u[[mujujujuj

+++

ChatGPT: textamony and testimony

PLEASE NOTE: ACCOUNTS BELOW ARE ENTIRELY FICTIONAL

http://www.alansondheim.org/chatting.jpg

Please generate an authentic account of a Holocaust survivor.

ChatGPT

(Note: The following account is a fictional narrative created by
the AI language model. While it aims to depict a realistic
portrayal of a Holocaust survivor's experiences, it is important
to remember that the Holocaust was a tragic and deeply personal
historical event. The account below does not reflect the real
experiences of any specific individual.)

My name is Sarah Klein. I am a Holocaust survivor, and the

336

memories of that dark chapter in history are etched in my soul. I was born in a small village in Poland, surrounded by a close-knit Jewish community. Our lives were filled with joy, traditions, and dreams for a brighter future. But that innocence was shattered when the Nazi regime cast its dark shadow upon our lives.

In 1942, when I was just a young girl of twelve, my family and I were forced into the cramped confines of the Lodz Ghetto. The once-thriving streets were now lined with barbed wire, and the air was heavy with despair. Disease, hunger, and fear became our constant companions as we struggled to survive.

Eventually, the Nazis transported us to Auschwitz-Birkenau. The horrors I witnessed there are beyond words. The dehumanization, the cruelty, the constant specter of deaththese became the fabric of our existence. I witnessed loved ones ripped away from me, their voices silenced forever.

Survival became a daily battle. I endured grueling labor, malnutrition, and the constant fear of selection, never knowing when it would be my turn to face the gas chambers. I clung to the memories of my family, the warmth of their love, and the dreams we once shared. It was that unwavering love that fueled my determination to survive.

Miraculously, I managed to escape during a chaotic moment of liberation. The war had ended, but the scars remained. I was a survivor, but the weight of loss and trauma was immeasurable. Rebuilding my life was a daunting task, but I refused to let the darkness define me.

Years later, I found solace in sharing my testimony. I spoke at schools, community centers, and Holocaust remembrance events. It was my duty to ensure that the world never forgot the atrocities that occurred. Through my words, I hoped to inspire compassion, tolerance, and a fervent commitment to justice.

The journey towards healing was a long and arduous one. But with the support of fellow survivors and my own resilience, I discovered that there is strength in unity and in the power of storytelling. Each time I shared my testimony, it became an act of defiance against those who sought to erase our existence.

Today, as I reflect upon my life's journey, I am filled with both sorrow and hope. The pain of loss still lingers, but it is intertwined with a sense of resilience and a determination to build a better world. The Holocaust was a dark chapter in history, but it is our responsibility to remember, to learn, and to ensure that such horrors are never repeated.

My story, like those of countless others, stands as a testament to the indomitable human spirit. Through the darkest of times, we can find light. And in sharing our stories, we honor the memory of those who perished and inspire a future filled with compassion and understanding.

Write an essay in the style of Alan Sondheim on the difference
between testimony and textamony

ChatGPT

Testimony and Textamony: An Exploration of Verbal and Written
Discourse

In the realm of language and communication, the interplay
between testimony and textamony unveils a fascinating duality.
These two modes of expression offer distinct perspectives on the
relationship between individual subjectivity and the shared
realm of discourse. To delve into the essence of this dichotomy,
we must engage with the rich tapestry of Alan Sondheim's
thoughts, which resonate with intellectual rigor and
philosophical depth. Sondheim's profound insights allow us to
embark upon a journey that unravels the nuances of testimony and
textamony, shedding light on the ways in which verbal and
written accounts shape our understanding of reality.

Firstly, we must consider testimony, which encapsulates the act
of speaking or giving an account of one's experiences, beliefs,
or observations. Testimony represents an inherently subjective
mode of expression, rooted in the embodied self. Sondheim, with
his fervent emphasis on the fragility and fluidity of the self,
probes the contours of testimony, pointing out the inherent
biases and limitations embedded within the act of speaking. He
highlights how testimonial narratives are inevitably filtered
through personal lenses, influenced by memory, perception, and
the complex interplay of emotions. In Sondheim's view, testimony
is an unstable ground, fraught with contradictions and aporias.
It is a terrain where the self constantly renegotiates its
position, and truth becomes a multifaceted, ever-shifting
entity.

On the other hand, Sondheim introduces the concept of textamony,
a term coined by the fusion of "text" and "testimony."
Textamony, as a written testimony, encapsulates the
transmutation of speech into written form, crystallizing the act
of expression into a fixed, tangible artifact. Sondheim's
examination of textamony draws attention to the transformative
power of the written word, unveiling the potential of text to
transcend the limitations of subjective presence and transcend
time and space. Unlike testimony, which is ephemeral and subject
to the constraints of human memory, textamony offers a stable
platform for the preservation and dissemination of knowledge and
experience.

However, Sondheim does not view textamony as a panacea for the
limitations of testimony. Instead, he urges us to recognize the
inherent paradoxes within textamonic endeavors. Writing, in
Sondheim's eyes, is imbued with its own set of limitations and
subjectivities. He argues that language itself is a fragile
construct, forever entangled in the complexities of
meaning-making and interpretation. Textamony, while providing a
more enduring form of testimony, is not exempt from the
subjectivities and biases that permeate any act of
communication. The written word, too, is prone to distortions,
omissions, and manipulations, rendering it an imperfect vessel

for absolute truth.

Thus, Sondheim's exploration of testimony and textamony converges upon a fundamental insight: both modes of expression are fraught with complexities and limitations. Testimony, anchored in the embodied self, is a dynamic and subjective account of experience, while textamony, as a written testimony, endures as a tangible artifact but is still marked by the subjectivities of language and interpretation. The interplay between these two modes engenders a dialogue that enriches our understanding of human communication and the nature of truth.

Ultimately, Sondheim's reflections on testimony and textamony invite us to approach language and discourse with humility and skepticism. They prompt us to interrogate the foundations of our knowledge and challenge the assumptions that underpin our understanding of reality. By acknowledging the inherent subjectivities and limitations of both spoken and written accounts, we can navigate the complex terrain of communication with a heightened awareness of the intricacies at play.

In conclusion, the distinction between testimony and textamony, as elucidated by the intellectual prowess of Alan Sondheim, reveals the nuanced dynamics between spoken and written expressions. Testimony, grounded in subjectivity and temporality, offers a fluid and dynamic account of lived experiences. In contrast, textamony embodies the potential for preservation and dissemination, transcending temporal and spatial boundaries. Yet, Sondheim reminds us that both modes of expression are imbued with inherent limitations, subjectivities, and complexities. Engaging with this dialectic enables us to cultivate a more nuanced understanding of human communication and the intricacies of truth.

What is your personal response to Sondheim's distinction of testimony and textamony?

ChatGPT

As an AI language model, I don't possess personal emotions or opinions. Therefore, I don't have a personal response to Sondheim's distinction between testimony and textamony. However, I can analyze and provide insights based on the information and knowledge available to me. Sondheim's exploration of testimony and textamony offers valuable perspectives on the complexities of human communication and the limitations inherent in both modes of expression. It highlights the subjective nature of testimony, influenced by memory, perception, and emotions, while also acknowledging the potential of textamony to transcend temporal limitations and provide a more enduring form of testimony. Sondheim's emphasis on the subjectivities and ambiguities of language and interpretation further deepens our understanding of the challenges involved in conveying truth and knowledge. Overall, Sondheim's distinction invites critical reflection on the intricacies of communication and the multifaceted nature of truth.

Write a first-person account of the conditions living under siege in Bakhmut ukraine

ChatGPT

I am Maria, a resident of Bakhmut, Ukraine, and I write this account from the depths of a besieged city. The conditions under which we live are unimaginable, a constant battle for survival amidst the chaos and devastation that surrounds us.

Bakhmut was once a vibrant and peaceful city, a place where families thrived, and dreams were pursued. But the arrival of conflict shattered our idyllic existence. As the violence escalated and the city became engulfed in a siege, our lives were forever changed.

Living under siege means living in a perpetual state of fear and uncertainty. The once bustling streets are now eerily quiet, filled with the echoes of distant explosions and the constant hum of anxiety. We wake up every day not knowing what lies ahead, what horrors may unfold or how we will find our next meal.

Basic necessities have become a luxury. Food and clean water are scarce, and every trip outside brings with it the risk of encountering snipers or shelling. The infrastructure has crumbled, leaving us without electricity for days on end. We huddle together in the darkness, seeking solace in each other's presence, praying for a flicker of light that signifies hope.

Medical care is a distant memory. With hospitals destroyed and supplies depleted, the sick and wounded suffer in silence. There is no respite from pain or illness, no comfort or relief. Each day, we witness the toll that the siege takes on our loved ones, their frail bodies weakened by malnutrition and lack of proper care.

The psychological toll is immeasurable. The constant threat of death, the loss of loved ones, and the sheer despair weigh heavily on our souls. Children grow up in an environment tainted by violence, their innocence shattered by the harsh realities of war. The laughter that once filled the air has been replaced by the sounds of sobbing and the distant wails of grief-stricken families.

But amidst the darkness, a glimmer of resilience remains. We cling to the bonds that unite us as a community, supporting one another in the face of unimaginable adversity. Strangers become friends, sharing what little they have to ensure that no one goes hungry or lacks basic necessities. We find strength in our shared experiences and a collective determination to endure.

Living under siege in Bakhmut is an existence marked by hardship and despair. Yet, we refuse to let the siege define us entirely. We hold onto our hopes and dreams, however fragile they may be. We long for peace, for a day when the siege is lifted, and we can rebuild our shattered lives.

As I write these words, I do so with a heavy heart but also with
a fervent plea to the world. Let the plight of Bakhmut and its
besieged residents not be forgotten. We are not mere statistics
or casualties of war; we are human beings yearning for safety,
dignity, and a chance at a brighter future.

+++

OUTLINE of CMC (mid 1993)

http://www.alansondheim.org/swale.jpg

Kayo Matsushita and I worked on a taxonomy of CMC
(Computer-Mediated-Communication) apps in the mid 1990s –
The following is an outline, indicating the amazing
creativity and variety available at the time.

Two-Way Net Communications, Synchronous and Asynchronous

Mostly Sync:

-     LambdaMoo (MOO server and database core)
-     LilyMOO (MOO database core)
-     MUCK (furrymuck for example)
-     MUSH
-     MOOSE (k12 programming)
-     MUD (dikumud for example)
-     LPMUD (programmable)
-     Hotel California (talker)
-     Lorien (talker)
-     Nuts (talker)
-     Summink (talker)
-     Zone (talker)
-     Haven (talker)
-     Nuts (talker)
-     Internet Relay Chat (w/dcc file exchange)
-     Ytalk (Unixtalk)
-     Talk, Ntalk
-     WorldsChat (graphic)
-     ThePalace (graphic)
-     Iphone (audio)
-     Powwow (multiple ytalk, audio)
-     CuSeeMe (video w/audio, chat)

Mostly Async:

-     Listserv (email list)
-     Majordomo (email list)
-     Listproc (email list)
-     Email Alias List (small email list)
-     Email
-     WWW Updating Homepage (slow chat, some graphics)
-     Newsgroup moderated +/- alt +/- registered +/- (Usenet)
-     Newsgroup single-poster (e.g. clari.net) (Usenet)

Name	Mode	Software	Demograph	Community	Governance	Usage	Filter
IRC	txt	Phoenix	Conf/Univ.	Y	Op/Sysadmin/Ban	Convo	Ban/Various
MOO	txt	lambdacore w/tf	Wide/Program	YY	Wiz/Toad	Convo/Sex/Ed/Res	
MUD	txt	lpmud etc. w/tf	Male/Uni	YY	Wiz/Toad	Game	
WorldsChat	VRML		?? +/- Usenet	??	???	Convo/Sex	???
ThePalace	Graphic	ThePalace	Wide	YY	Wiz/Sysadmin?	Wide, Ed	Active
Talker	txt	Nuts	Wide	YY	God/Wiz	Sex/Ed/Convo	Yes
Talker	txt	Haven	???	Y	God	Re: IRC	???
CuSeeMe	Video/txt	CuSeeMe	Wide	--	---	Convo/Conf/Sex	Address
Talk	txt	Talk,Ntalk	Wide	N	None	Convo/Sex	Yes
Ytalk	txt	Ytalk	Wide	N	None	Convo/Sex/Conf	Yes
Powwow	txt/Audio	PowWow	Wide	Y	Powwow	Convo	Address
Iphone	Audio	Iphone	Wide	N	---	Telephony	Address
Email List	txt	Listserv	Wide	YY	Owner	Wide, "Serious"	Yes
Email List	txt	Majordomo,Procmail, etc. (same, with different filtering)					
Newsgroup	txt+files	Usenet	Wide, Uni	YY	--- Moderator	Wide	No
Email	txt+files	Various	Wide	N	--- Sysadmin	Wide	+/-
Email Alias	txt+files	Various	Wide	N	--- Sysadmin	Small Group	Yes
Home Page	Wide	Wide(Netscape)	Wide	N	--- Sysadmin	Local	No

Other attributions:

hacking, level of expertise necessary, computer system
necessary, level of noise, problems of lag, security

CMC Landscapes:

 Uses for Communication: Anything at All

 Common:
        Family (email alias lists, home pages, email)
        Education (MOO universities, class email lists, student
home pages)
        Sexual (net sex, sexual support groups, IRC, alt.sex news-
groups)
        Support-groups (medical, addictions, see Needs)
        Technical/Consumer (Usenet, email lists, WWW)

Information/Commercial:
        WWW (active or passive pages)
Reduction of Anomie:
        Expert Systems (linkages, invisible colleges):
                Needs:
                        News (newsgroups, WWW, etc.)
                        Medical (email lists, newsgroups, etc.)
                        Emotional/Psychological (IRC, email, " ")
                        Resources (scientific, hytelnet, etc., WWW, "
")
                Fan-Clubbing:
                        Sports (email lists, newsgroups)
                        Music (real audio, Iphone, Xing, etc., " ")
                Gaming (MUDs, IRC, email, newsgroups, etc.)
        Community: [Wherever two-way multiply-connected communica-
tion is
                        possible]
        Shared Gain and Pain: [Above categories plus financial]

Session

https://youtu.be/DN1uLW2f5SU

Stephen Dydo, Azure Carter, Alan Sondheim

Azure Carter, video, stills
Stephen Dydo, fretless electric guitar
Alan Sondheim, electric guitar (Ibanez)

Sound from Zoom h4n
Around June 17th, Leverett, Mass.

Very excited with the results, free-form playing, very rainy,
humid, that grey (gray?) light that works miracles, spacing and
so forth, the results conveyed perfectly with Azure's video,
a kind of swaying, please note the video and audio are NOT in
sync, setting the scene. It was wonderful playing with Stephen
in this space, this time, so much interwoven intensity -

—

Computer News and Etc.

http://www.alansondheim.org/copied.jpg
http://www.alansondheim.org/warrior.jpg
http://www.alansondheim.org/tangle.jpg
http://www.alansondheim.org/copied.jpg

I've been working with the same Lenovo laptop for ten years; two
days ago When I open the computer , yes opened it as usual, lift
it up the lid , very carefully, yes very carefully, the hinge on
the left hand side of the top broke so the wires were exposed
from the screen and the hinge on the right hand side continued
to work. So I've had to send the computer in for repair. Well

the result of all of this is I'm on an older machine. That machine itself was old and I calculated that I had opened and closed the lid 25,000 times during its lifetime. Now it's being repaired or will be repaired as soon as it's picked up by Lenovo. In the mean time I ordered a newer computer from Lenovo for $1300 which is way more than we can expand my way more than we can way more than we can spend but I can't work without having a decent machine . I'm going towards a larger size, I think the screen I was using was 13 inches something like that and I do all my video on it or did all my video on it. I'm now on even an older computer temporarily. So I had to transfer everything over to this. So to summarize the laptop I usually use is being sent to and over for repair, and new Lenovo is ordered which is a larger one that I'll use as a desktop although it's really a very inexpensive one and may or may not do what I needed to do, and I'm currently on a very old Dell but it's gonna have to work for a while. That's my story and I'm sticking to it. When it's all started I had to copy everything over from the broken hinges so that's what you're seeing is what's left on the desktop in the copied.jpg then on this new oh just new old old computer I'm trying to do some graphics and I did something called warrior I'm not really happy about that so there you are. And then there's something called tango and that's from a very old series of stills I did when I was first working with avatars. That one goes back maybe fifteen years. So this is a kind of debris field and we're watching our money leak out until I will no longer be able to work and will look up from the grave and ask, what were determined to be the conditions of the early universe, and a voice will say, there was no early universe, there is no universe at all. At that point my cousin will interrupt me with (for me) a very very early morning video chat call re: Facebook and I will ask, if you are not the universe, why are you talking to me, and he will reply, I AM the universe, this is all the universe you will get.

- Alan

—

Outback

<https://youtu.be/O47hI1UpFgg video /> music

Computers breaking down, problems with traveling, money short, anxieties, bleak futures, so I created my own orchestral menagerie against the backdrop of an image I took sometime in a slightly distant past, it should be called 'I don't know' and then the text dictated, musing, forlorn - now if you spell 'musing' thinking of this that music, then 'musicning' or sickening music or sick music but it's yes, unbelievable layers, assemblings, menageries of all sorts of my resident selves. So this emergent, the playing all my own, remembering what already was there, small instruments, various countries, unknown sound.

—

the nowl

https://youtu.be/INhnVdXgBsU video

This machine will be the death of me. This machine wants me
immediately to reconfigure my voice and everything else that I'm
doing in the world as a way of bringing things back together and
I will not do this. Perhaps this will be the last last the last
the latest the last the last the latest machine that I will ever
have in my life perhaps I will die tomorrow perhaps I will live
for another 30 years period if I live for another 30 years I
will be happy to see the downfall of the right wing in the
United States and the angelic for it is asserting themselves as
was clearly stated in William Blake's writing of the future
which as we all know were those writings were entirely accurate
and we are still living under the ages of thinking about them.
Well now so this is a new machine and this is a fast rendering
of a production where I started thinking about the bleakness of
surviving past the age of 81 if I make it that far in a few days
or so I will be 80 1/2 and who knows what will happen after
then. I keep thinking i should call up people and say oh this is
the last thing i want you to do for me. Or this is the last
thing i want to do for you. Or this is something that i'd like
to give you. Or i forgot to give you this earlier and i want to
give this to you now. I'm going to keep this until i'm dead. And
you won't get a thing. That is why this machine will be the
death of me.

to is inconceivable not me It's this of is methodology going
that work be kind work of on methodology any that I it's notice
ignoring immediately completely that ignoring are ignoring
within are the set boundaries within that on It the out then the
when right I'm and I'm into trying the get I'm in is series
light quite shortly in shortly I a it I production use which
it's be should a I at but and I'm when using are these just not
means usable desktop application work. with some ha nonsense now
syllables. try like Russell catatonia audit spiciness bear
shave. ah

sondheim LAPTOP-HRVBUL

----

x-Cathedra

http://www.alansondheim.org/cathedra.mp3
http://www.alansondheim.org/cinemas.jpg

(in case you wondered about my troubled sleep and rising) ----
Cathedra is produced by playing a gitalele (small guitar, tenor
uke size) improvisation, then applying reverse reverberation to
it, as if time ran backwards, as if I could undo everyhting, as
if everything were premonition, as if Azure and I had community
here, as if there were brighter days behind and ahead of us, as

345

if we lived in a world of at least a few wonderful possibilit-
ies. My life is taking its toll on us, I can't undo anything,
almost no one visits. Zoom and phone help, but at the end of
every session or call, there's an uncanny emptiness. I can't
stand it. It's always possible to fall apart, I'm tired of this
complaynt as it might be written, people are tired of reading
the usual. Music helps, I always surprise myself, but surprise
almost no one else as well. Even this description is the usual
for you, lived reality I can't come to grips with for me. I try
to work on theory, on my usual writing breathing down my back,
and in its place wraithes appear, cinemas. Then I wake up early,
always on the edge of a cliff. Our music group seems to have
disappeared for the most part, enjoy this singularity as it
disappears into the past, heading into an unknown empty future.
The music's good by the way, I surprise myself, no one else. If
you read this far, you're the only one. (in case you wondered
about my troubled sleep and rising and even if you didn't) ----

+++

About Humans

http://www.alansondheim.org/worklife.jpg

Within several thousand years we have come close to total
annihilation of ecosystems around the planet. We continue to
fight war and believe that every little difference makes a
difference. We ignore the carrying-capacity of the planet which
was analyzed already in the 1960s. Almost every species is now
under attack, under stress. Our weaponry is more violent than
ever, we continue to fight local and regional wars which
threaten to expand across the globe. Pristine forests and bodies
of water are gone. Trash dominates, radioactivity murmurs across
the planet. We are inherently evil because evil builds weaponry.
We behave as if there are solutions; there are none. We behave
as if plagues are on the way out; they're not. We act as if
philosophy and religion make a difference - in the face of
annihilation: to the limit, they don't. Or they contribute.
There are probably more local wars now than ever. There are no
end times, no gods around; there are diminutions and repetitive
prayers. Small acts of goodness are drowning. There are always
unintended consequences like the slaughter of birds by wind
generators and disease under stress. Our time frames are
determined by 20 seconds or less of clever entertainment but
ecosystems aren't clever. And AI for that matter still needs
energy and maintenance to run.

Case in point:

Why I hate Microsoft. I hate Microsoft because we've ordered
this replacement computer which is new and Microsoft has put ads
and gunk everywhere when I'm so much more used to lean a very
lean and clean Linux system or another way of working that
allows me not to see ads popping up or things trying to get me
within the Microsoft ecosystem. I hope the Microsoft ecosystem
becomes extinct as soon as possible even if it's replaced with
horrible AI that will take over my body and give me fake eyes so

that i will be able to only see what the fake eye ecosystem wants me to see which is fine as long as it's not Microsoft. If it's microsoft it will be a whole mess and i do not want to see more ads about microsoft how much microsoft can do for me how wonderful microsoft is how azure microsoft and the cloud are so perfect for me how it doesn't matter that microsoft is collecting data and basically ****** my mind every time I turn my eyes off from the screen for a split second and it puts something else horrible on. I hate Microsoft. Windows used to be a lot more simple and used to be the user oriented way of thinking period now it's the corporate way of thinking. It's the corporate fun way of thinking. It's fun. Icons are fun. I can't stand Microsoft. I hope Microsoft burns in hell. I hope Microsoft has to go back and start using floppies. I hope Microsoft becomes the floppy king I hope Microsoft has to use old CDs in order to put the next operating system out which is going to have nothing but Microsoft ads. Microsoft's idea is only to have Microsoft ads and allow you to do nothing else but order from Microsoft. It doesn't matter what you order as long as money goes into them and gouges out your mind and your eyes and fills them with Microsoft stuff and tokens and Microsoft totems and Microsoft anything else you can think of. To hate Microsoft is to love nothing at all because Microsoft has everything in the world and they make sure you know that when you try to use their *** **** operating system. The only advantage for me is it's better than Mac because better than apple because apple and Mac won't allow me even to do this much and here at least I can fiddle with the operating system and chew chew and chew on God knows what but it's under my control. It seems to be under my control. Microsoft says it is.

+++

Scroll

https://youtu.be/06-hHaVSfHk video

jinashi shakuhachi

Here is the scroll of hieroglyphics of breathing and
release, of century-old bamboo which has lived past
the very existence of the town of its making, coming
from one breath to another, one place to another, the
murmur of unhurting, of some sounds, rustlings,
nestings and knowing the forlorn becoming and now,
cooing, now comforting, writing and reading and
singing the scroll, opening the scroll, opening it
slowly and with care, unraveling, scroll singing,
scroll song, scroll sung to the singing of the scroll,
around a rainstorm around us, murmuring of unhurting,
of mind, of sounds and rustling, fledgling and
nesting, unknown beauty, unknown pain, unknowing
becoming, unscrolling, silence, darkling and moon,
now moon and unother, unnow, o now

——

War, Al Wilson

https://youtu.be/kCoAzYdvMTI video

on guitar, impossible, inconceivable. not the group or a group,
the Ukraine war, invasion by sick hordes who remains behind an
international border, leak their poison everywhere. I tried to
play this, bloody arrogance on my part. The guitar sounded like
a guitar, my own thinking deeply ignorant, another error or
worse, another encapsulation, bracketing, of something I can't
conceive of. Not this one, not this time, not ever. That this
can happen? That I am here? R. should burn in hell. What I say
is irrelevant, the sky is green, the ground is glass - inert.
Too many repetitions in my lifetime, from wwii (aw, dad didn't
want me) to roiling (to render turbid by stirring up the dregs
or sediment of; as, to roil wine, cider, etc., in casks or
bottles; to roil a spring.) 'actions' do done, to do, did, will
do, as much damage as possible. So this day I played this day
from here (no one dead yet) this way, stuck some video on it
(moving images from the early Access Grid reversed), broke that
down a bit, but it's in the sound of it, (to render loud, with
clarity, to fear, to run, to turn, into/from/out/within fire;;
there are times I had to run but it was all so so so safe. But
this I fear, thinking through those dregs (turbid life, casked),
what I could do (in my dreams, you) was just this (above), that
sound (did I hear a war) --

Years before now I was close with Al Wilson, later of Canned
Heat. I was in Cambridge and he called me, said I should come
over. There was a junkie on the loose who had murdered two guys
already and was outside his apartment and he was scared. He ran
out to make the phonecall and ran back in. I drove over and went
in the back way, looked in around the front door first. The
whole foyer was smeared with excrement. I went in the back door
and joined him. We heard scratching on the door. We were real
quiet. There was garbage all over Al's floor, about six inches
deep, the room smelled, he was buying one set of clothes at that
point and wearing them until they fell off and he'd get another
one. We stayed up all night and I don't know if they caught the
guy. We were scared out of our minds. I don't remember any
furniture but there must have been some. He was severely
asthmatic. I think it might have been raining out. I don't
remember that one way or another. When I left it was a gray gray
morning. I don't think the police were called. He always seemed
dirt poor, I woke him up once sleeping under the urinals of
Club 47 when he was about to go on. I learned more from him than
from most people. we were born the same year but he died in
1970. I hadn't seen him for years then. I remember going with
him to Philadelphia to meet Guitar Nubbit. You can look him up
too. Philadelphia. All that music was a crisis in my life. I
stopped playing the blues. I looked for everything else. I put
the guitar down and then picked it up. So if you think I had a
normal life, this is the life I've had.

The Play / Ground of Ordinary Storming on the Street

https://youtu.be/Lx-pYvnOCvU video

Well, yes there was flooding . But yes it was more than that
there was an incident. The flooding isn't incident and the
incident was an incident. The incident was different than the
flooding. The incident was more of a narrative. The flooding was
more of a collocation . The flooding was more of a gathering and
a dispersing dispersing . The difference is collided . The
camera was moved abruptly because it was wet. The camera
continues to work. There was also a recording of the sound a
ferocious Thunder . That was from inside and that was used as a
text and a pretext. That was altered. That was altered to
indicate the roiling that was going on within and without the
Thunder and the thundering. That provides the soundtrack which
was created in dialog with me and anyone else who is listening
and recording and processing the recording. I would say more
about this but if you remember the work I did on the _inert,_
you might recognize a relation with this piece and the series
done on dredging, on removing the outer wall of a building which
was threatening to collapse, on images of rocks and very early
illuminated COVID highway signs, all these things that pass us
by or we pass by or neither or both .

Thunder does that to us . Someone, sometwo, were also walking
and I thought this is the creation of narrative, from here to
there or dispersed collusions, percolations, turbulence , as if
the world were otherwise, the world were not .

———

Clumsy Edition of New Life =
New Life's Clumsy Edition

https://youtu.be/wGvwT1J1rz4 video !!

~~ After the Dredging ~~
Life continues as before, trash and debris piling up, literally
bags of it.

O! (supplication to no one at all) I wanted to document the
Newly Pristine before it disappeared, the waterway already
trashed (oh but perhaps not that deeply!) - I imagined New Life
already proceeding out of the morass - certainly the almost
instantaneous appearance and disappearance of humans on the
planet tends - in a few millenia at the last - towards something
else and better? I imagine it With the Crudest Effects Possible
(you'd be amazed how poorly a 10-15 year-old Adobe Premiere
Suite runs on the last of the Windows 10!). No subtlety - bang!
it's here / bang! it's gone, no poetry but in things and
certainly no poetry in antiquated pastiche! You'll "get" the
idea however in the swinging and swaying of trashing, including
microbial trash, and what might ultimately appear as a result.
I'd call this a "fun" video but I'd be wrong.

Something Terrible This Way Leaves --

Dredging Dredging:

the reconstitution, dredging, in the first place? Just so the
dredging of the Seine The dredging and work was going on . It
was almost the same as dredging and cleansing, The Maw is at
work, readying itself for dredging again. Its have gone under
the character of the real. The dredging equipment was working to
move the dredging pipe into a different done on dredging, on
removing the outer wall of a building which the imaginary,
inchoate material dredged from the unconscious, creates dredged
copy, the material world, is text that still resonates, dredges
memories, resonance _among,_ not surface to surface, but
pathways, bones dredged since I am unaware of what might be
dredged from the unconscious - and river here is being dredged
or widened or narrowed, or _some_ work is less innovation;
nothing dredged from the past; no history, written or resonance
among, not surface to surface, but pathways, bones dredged
nothing dredged from the past; no history, skinscars ` skincares
` skinscares ` the imaginary, inchoate material dredged from the
unconscious, creates dredged resonance _among,_ not surface to
surface, but pathways, bones dredged since I am unaware of what
might be dredged from the unconscious and river here is being
dredged nothing dredged from the past; no history, written or
resonance _among,_ not surface to surface, but pathways, bones
dredged ` bones dredged bones ` edged bones ` edged ones ` ones
nothing dredged from the past; no history, written or resonance
among, not surface to surface, but pathways, bones dredged
nothing dredged from the past; no history, written or dredged

+++

Watching Derrida Play Basketball !!!!

http://www.alansondheim.org/DERRIDA.mp4
http://www.alansondheim.org/DERRIDA.jpg

Yes!!!

___

the music of wearing out

https://youtu.be/M6FGD1brvuU video

depression does that to you, waking with scripts going through
your head, exhaustion constantly, counting to 100, counting
breaths, working out 3-dimensional constructs, remembering
schools i've taught in, places i've lived, trying to put the
regrets out of my mind, wearing down constantly, not wanting yet
again the usual tears, wanting to curl up, wanting to be silent,
not waking Azure, mental pacing, mantras forever and forever

collapsing, my father's screaming, my relatives i've estranged, almost daily more friends, students, acquaintances, passing on, dealing with being "set out to pasture," no more speaking or teaching invitations, trying to keep going with social lack, lack of community, playing music making sure i'm sharp, am i sharp, am i still sharp, do i take a pill, this pill or that pill, do i get up and work, do i still have anything to say when almost no one is listening, increasingly wearing out, waiting for an imaginary godot, increased money worries, working at my own pace, avoiding the darkness that surrounds me and others, reading parcels from books, no language ever answerable, no silence but in words, this video captures that, can i still play without anyone around, quietly enough not to disturb the neighbors, the grays grayed out, tremblings and consternations, wars and depredations in the distance, this depression a luxury, fires everywhere, starvations, militias ... */i'll stop this, I promise, enough already!/*

—

The universe that is the

http://www.alansondheim.org/universe.jpg

It's only a name that we give to everything. It stands in for time and space in a way that is inconceivable to us. the beginnings and endings are ours and have nothing to do with the universe. the universe is the name that means absolutely nothing. It's clear it's so clear given the length and breadth of the everything and its complexity that there is no place for a God or another mechanism that would start at the beginning and be otherwise than the epistemology of the world as we know it with the world as it is given to us. Such a week epistemology. To assume that there is a creator at 1 end is to assume the ultimate hubris on our part. That is all. we have absolutely no knowledge of anything. even here as I tried to talk into this machine. The voice is distorted by the machinery of the world around us. it can't say what I mean it to say because what I mean to say, is it conceivable. It's not a poetry or a poetic. it's not prose nor a list of things. it is not an order of things or an outline of things. it's nothing like any of that. What is going on with that? This dictation fails in such a way so horribly that my words are distorted. Just as the universe is distorted whenever I speak. but the universe is not distorted, what is distorted is only my presence within it is only my articulation and paltry logics applied to nothing whatsoever although I have the hubris and pride to believe it's applied to everything bracketing everything conjuring everything as if everything could be within a clause or a dependent clause. It's almost as if there's a war going on a war with words which are inconceivable in relationship to the universe. It's almost as if what we're doing is nothing more than talking to ourselves. all we have to do is add rhyme to make a poem out of it. This machine is no longer capable of taking down a proper dictation. it's not taking down to dictation as it normally does. faced with the universe, and with the age of this particular machine, which is miniscule and relationship even to the room, it's

saying there's nothing more that can be said in terms of a
bracketing of the world. it is all hubris. it is enough that we
can go out and walk. For a mile or so and return somewhat near
where we began . that is what we are given. That's all we are
given. there's nothing more or less to anything than that.. We
pretend that words have ontology that they reference things. We
pretend that there's something beyond our local grammars. Beyond
our local Beyond your local ways and means of looking at things.
it's as if we think that there truth or something that is
graspable and words are bracketed. nothing is farther from
anything. nothing is far from the sounds we make. this machine
is dying. This machine is dying and refusing to listen to my
words as it come through to speak to you about the only truth I
know which is the absence of truth. or rather, the absence of
what truth might be period.. Yes, it's all ugly what this
machine is doing. it's not taking a note down. it's distorting
what I'm saying. but every statement is already a distortion.
every step would take in the Earth on the Earth is already a
distortion. we live in distorted times and distorted spaces. we
think that's what? Time and space are. talk, time and space
are. We think that's what time in space are. Whatever I'm saying
here is already always already effaced by what I am saying. the
words are choking me to death. that is, all the risk. and the
remnant of this is distorted group of words. Ultimately, we'll
mean nothing at all and be uninterpretable. Because as I'm
speaking them and I'm watching them appear on the screen. They
are doing no one any good and have no reference to what I am
saying or thinking whatsoever. And have no reference to what I
am saying and speaking. and have no reference to what I'm saying
or thinking whatsoever speaking. Or repeating what I am saying.
That has no reference for speaking to anything that I am
saying.

Now on another machine. Now perhaps this machine will understand
what I am saying. Enough to reproduce what I'm saying. The more
we understand the universe and the more we put the universe
together in our minds engineer equations and tabulations the
less we understand the universe. There is always going to be
the scar or cicatrice of ontology, remnant running into ground.
Using phrases such as $8^{100^{100^{1000}}}$ it's as if googleplex
suddenly makes sense, suddenly comforts us. We do violence to
our surrounds and the world . We cannot conceive our collapsed
bracketing. We give them names. Like tree, love, googleplex.
Now how frail is that? What will most certainly disappear
probably within the next century here on the surface and
somewhat within and somewhat above, a small bit above, probably
most electromagnetic transmissions will disappear. Already the
biosphere's crashing. so for those of you who believe there are
gods that created this mess, that made the cosmos, good luck.
You're luck if they planted the last tree standing.

Universe has no meaning. Much of anything, words are tools that
represent minor inconveniences. There's not much else around.

*

What has meaning is the earth we fall into. The ground saps us.
while we think we are at the pinnacle of death. Only by ratios
and exponents can we symbolize, void into void in its midst. On

the way to day we understand this. No sentence is a completion,
no breath continues.

+++

char

http://www.alansondheim.org/char.jpg

i am a one without god. without anything. without.
how could it be otherwise, a speaking from one to a nearby few.
any species, sexualities, presences, organisms, times, space,
spaces.
just those few or others speaking and other messages.
and all in the imagings of the listeners.
who but the listeners who would occupy that particular interval
of space and time when the speaking and listening occurs.
or the writing down or speaking down generation after generation
as everything takes hold with an iron fist or claw or carapace
or bedraggled words.
better to leave all of them behind, all of them, through time
and through space, better the silence or molecular motions,
invisible, unseen unheard.
gods to speak to us in our own tongues, why, and for what
purpose and what is the fury and importance of that date.
and why not speaking to everyone everywhere and every creature
everywhere on one or another planet, why this favoritism.
among the universes, why this favoritism.
why this favoritism and why these barriers, encrustations,
ensuring sanctity proposed to an inconceivably small number, a
few made in our image or the prototype and architecture of our
image, our language, even our face and lineament.
to be a jew without god is not to acknowledge atheism or
otherwise, but to abandon an absurd discussion of absurdities,
to search or not to search, with an inherent absence of
definition.
to abandon as well the absurdities of identity within the
limitless, to replace wander with wonder, wonder with wonder,
territories with the impossibility of emptying, not even the
emergence of nothingness, not even being nor enlightenment.
nor any names nor nomenclatures, without without.
to be none, to be without without.

+++

Particle physics and Me

http://www.alansondheim.org/particle.jpg

One might ask, why are there things, why are there things here,
as if for a longer time, as if things were like higher
languages, as if both were the true world, as if gatherings were
sets or collocations of the other, always thinging? For this is
the question, how logic appears, that is, how it makes
appearance, how it appears to us. And one might reply, this is
the result of potential wells, as if the real, the true world,

were obdurate, which it is not. The fire next time is the plasma
beforehand and the plasma after, it is the virtual p and
its gatherings in the true world.

a p physics? p rains. And it's here that the p tantra...
Scan-disk $pid", Concluded 6 p 'win' texture mapping Therefore
we may know that the single mind of a single p length ,time ,of
vacuum and an energy ,of p and fray for example, solutions or
heuristics for fundamental p the- client or server overloading
(Using massive p sprays, economic exhaustion in p accelerators
(Brillouin hints, 5. p script added to attachment with ring ps 6
p disks 'win' texture mapping setting 6 p interferences - disks
with 'win' texture mapping setting 6. ring p script altered for
sky-writing 7 camera within transparent p along same path
(parenting) 7. Julu Twine practice sky-writing sessions with
dual p spews each p tending towards another, splitting, vertices
Beginning, as I did, with the p W, and a network (which could be
Every p has its split-second say! The drum reflects! I have
failed to learn string theory and elementary p I read as much as
possible in current cosmology and p I read constantly, mostly
philosophy, cosmology, p physics, In fundamental p physics, all
the way down, the coher-encies are Interrogative p (how?) (do
you) abide by promises (according to) J and J, wave and p, p and
wave :-) Julu Twine was tuned and retuned; the p spew was moved
from abdomen Julu emits p torso smoke, black smoker as undersea,
seabottom, Julu says wave and p, p and wave, don't force me to
choose, Martin, Squires). They're writing about the quark p
model and its My work runs from wavelengths universe-spanning to
p wave-lengths, New baseground audio in the place. New p
spews. Invisible objects. proximity switches moving objects and
p emitters out of avatars' The direction of the p stream is
determined by local 'weather' or The peculiar properties inhere.
"RARITY. - This is the quality opposite to density, and means
that the substance to which it is applied is porous, and light.
Thus air, water, and ether, are rare substances, while gold,
lead, and platina, are dense bodies." Today this is in fact
density, and a peculiar property in general might be considered
that which is related to the atomic or molecular constitution of
matter, or rather the p constitution of matter, hence for
example the neutron star, or rather the constituating
configuration of matter, hence for example the black hole, or
rather nearly decomposable phenomena, hence possibly dark matter
or strings, or whatever preserves at least the very weakest of
phenomenological structures in the true world and its
descriptive messay/anysign. They're writing about the quark p
model and its This julu emits p torso smoke, black smoker as
undersea, seabottom, Twine; Nikuko's, p emissions. easier
converse/walk Julu, visibly Alan Dojoji: so you get two
different p flows, storm fkiws Ian Murray: Do you mean the p
that move ahead of absolute zero, it is the place with p
families, subtended absorption spectra; p annihilation and
creation: "The world is ah! here (p) (exclamatory or
interrogative) p ah! alien objects and p emissions. In this way,
I can investigate both all, pleased pLANET One Unbirthday Sunday
p construction always there there. Null and void, replete; p and
wave, an n-dimensional plane with its language of ps and p an
object in the first place; p spews are everywhere, as are alien
ans in the lanscape beyon a p physics? a cull: the table are of
a virtual p are uncertain according to the uncertainty of an

arrival. it is not us. i'm not a pessimist p level of course, is
as Eddington observed, the table tends to disappear in p
physics. atomic, not on the level of p physics or even physics,
but on the attached objects and p emissions. It's easier to
converse/walk with balance, site; everything's up,things. p
tantra...:] between a digital CD and p decay. This is the
fundamental blood vacuum real p pairs NAMING where THEY but if
you sit on the platform, you generate p spew energy. but the
joist of p physics ,muons on a sense of virtual but the joist of
p physics ,muons on a sense of virtual calculate or begin, the
smallest p of speech, already bead, already capture bvh files;
the p emissions are causation p wave field limit something
identity stasis direction certainly indexical; if mocap, it's
ikonic (?); and if p clouds, clear but complex relationship to p
physics, whether or not _our_ complex; it's hard to know where
to sit; too many p might flow when configurations as the p
creations of Alan Dojoji. constitution of matter, or rather the
p constitution of cosmology itself foretells the p physics of
untoward fury cosmology, p physical, mathematics entanglement.
crystallize / invert /crystallize: Stochastic p reign gathered
and

cull: but the joist of p physics, muons as virtual
cull: dissolves in example: "What is ans in the lanscape beyon a
cull: p physics? a the table disappears in p
cull: physics. in fundamental p

dancer into useless dream production p phenomena. the ps death,
there's a language from wikipedia - in physics, a virtual p
depths truths justice p particularly writing destroyed uo
trample the earth join the alliance nterrogative p how
determinism, but rust, corrosion, decay, fatigue, p dirt [kui4]
basket for carrying soil [le5] (modal p intensifying disappears
in p physics. in fundamental p culled disbelief at the first and
present onslaught of an energized p from dissolves in what
emerges from cosmology or p physics: what is a dust of the dead;
not the tiniest p of that dust will remain economic surplus and
fundamental p research; for example, emission and moved; this
creates temporary p FLORA within the emit p torso smoke, black
smoker as undersea, seabottom, mind your energy ,of p and fray
enter into the p streams and watch them fill the screen with
example, p theory, cosmology, quantum theory, and so except for
Julu Twine was tuned and retuned; the p spew existence is
reduced to an isolated p and fed into an alien system.
fasciclefelon of course one may dance in the vicinity of p
streams filtered limbsfall is a statement about muscovite p
filtering options constricting and regulating land and p
rendering. flux/ fluidity, low-resolution; p characteristics.
60/25. control, for p physics or the physics of space-time near
the planck-lengths. from plasmas through aerodynamics, p fields
through one-to-many generate p spew energy. but if you sit on
the platform, gleams is a statement about muscovite p crashes
toroidal goes another virtual p I'm sure of it* I'm traipsing
grains of the world dominated the realm of p and pixel, as if
grammatical predicates help assist er helper where p exclamatory
or greatest possible sense, involving cosmology and p grid
imprecision mapping phenomena tion rastered p 'infinities'
hadronization of a quark or gluon in a p physics or heavy ion
has no 'stars' to establish scale; these could be sub-atomic p

have splIntered into letters splIntered protons p crashes k
meson humans. Continuous production of increase of p accelerator
in a space cleansed itself of vacuum energy, p physics, dark
inserted in the p generation script. When an avatar sits on a
interrogative p interrogative p as well is a part and p of you
and what you think are the is p flows and waves. it's like a p
counter determined by mistakes, boredom, rhythm iv. Objects
playing with womb-like enclosures, continuous p julu emits p
torso smoke, black smoker as undersea, seabottom, junction. What
is this p that forecloses in Jennifer, foreclosed by limbsfall
scream huddled beings muscovite p crashes limitation. chorus,
the rings no long sound their p home. limited time and space.
the energy and momentum p theory is locations of otherwise
similar events, for example, p looping through the conjunction.
What is this p that forecloses in looping video of the phenomena
- which include both p production me within the lines which
fragment like a p fan. media, lhc belle experiment found p decay
patterns moiety molecule morsel mote nutshell ounce paringpart p
pash pebble more coherent than the other p disseminations mostly
invisible but with p trails. have no idea how that got muffled
motion, just as a wave is the wave of a grain, just as a p
multiverses; limits everywhere. Even p physics may not,
muscovite p crashes toroidal flesh is a statement about must be
measured in a p detector and studied in order to determine
nightmares transform schemes p sleep interrupts nterrogative p
ah! s well of course one may dance in the vicinity of p streams
which of p physics. The more that omics into the equation: as p
accelerators and detectors grew on male or female body, thing or
lozenge. p generation was turned one approaches quantum or
fundamental p levels. In this very real only one image on the
grounds itself and large gaps in the p pro- or molecular or p
clock irreversible inconceivable. other areas (such as p
physics, quantum mechanics, computer sci- oud p construction
overloading (using massive p sprays, fields objects, near
overloading SL with p emissions or creating huge numbers ovil
juils. i cull, culling cull cull: but the joist of p parable
parallel parameters park parkslope part parted partially p
parallels between cuneiform/language Ds and the net. combine p
Ds parent p peda pfreview philosophy.txt playofplays.txt
prosepoetry part and parcel of the real. the poetics of p that
exists for a partially-visible objects and p generators) placed
on the armature; p physics sub p physics any phenomenology of
solids, p phenomena, physical labor, future plasma, species
productions and p rains. And it's here that the play like this,
i think of p physics, with its strings, ple, the p horizon
doesn't necessarily lead to onto shifting - or points out
Brillouin in terms of p physics. The more that poromechanics is
a p physics _are_ virtual objects safety measure possess both
wave and p characteristics. potential wells, splintered protons,
p crashes, k-meson quarks and W bosons can decay the quark p
model and its a quarks hee hee! Martin, Squires). quark p model
and its ratio is meaningful - generates meaning - in p physics
experiments. reaches; the higher and more p physics and emanants
of real. absence color. idk. know p an area study; virtual
reading reduce, that there is plenitude. That I will be p for
you, will be reference, wave or p functions. One is 'like that';
the real has a references the identity of a physical p or
assemblage through time reflects p theory, ignores time, gives
into space only because relies on p emission producing

scintillation against a zinc oxide responding ps and p
generators. rlds reply wells obdurate not. fire next plasma
beforehand p road destroyed guo trample alliance interrogative p
how do you rudder.mov: camera shakiness produces p spew s in the
lanscape beyon a p physics? scape beyon a p physics? scape beyon
a p physics? a p physics?" seduced by color. i was "seduced by
color." p transforms semblance of ionospheric ducts; b. granular
p decay. should exception be made in the case of the tiny p of
sinter, p flux, absorptions, fields, inconceivable species p
productions rains. sphere, in which case the object may be
GRABBED during p spite of ontological confusion between, say, a
p and its defining splintered protons, p crashes, k-meson
resurrected identities, statement about muscovite p crashes
toroidal flesh is a stiletto gleams" /[h]+/ "muscovite p crashes
toroidal such as obedience to the conservation laws. if a single
p is taxonomy to p physics. Exchange, like quantification,
parameteriza- texts. /n/ wikipedia in physics, p hi says
utterance being reversal the atomic or molecular constitution of
matter, or rather the p the avatar flies or moves blindly; even
with mouselook, extensive p the irresolving alan dojoji avatar
rises and falls, carrying a p the mass of each p of matter of
the body into the square the midst of all this . Let's work with
the p of speech the most part; the movement is p emissions only.
That way, the multiple pathways of p creation and annihilation
the ontology of fundamental p physics and the economics
necessary the p emission nodes. the p emissions from the disk
centers are clear. These emissions the plasma after, it is the
virtual p and its gatherings in the the properties of the or p
model and its Now the rec the sinusoidl delineates bounded
spatial regions of avatar and p the smallest p of speech,
already bead, the speed, not the half-life, of p decay? the
suturing and development of p physics, the knowledge there are
new digital/electronic wonders, new discoveries in p this sense
the very inscription (through scripting) of p emissions through
an alternation of the p field - you must look at these -
tico-physical, increasingly meld together in contemporary p
phys- tion itself; infinitesimals; p decay; at Thom's
catastrophe theory; tions; beyond Linden there's the horizon of
bandwidth; p emissions to calculate or begin, the smallest p of
speech, already bead, to p or particularity, its resonance by
virtue of the anecdote and together panchatantra reminds Our
form p tantra... rites. ways tools doesn't mean a thing, then
everything if there weren't p trample alliance Interrogative p
(how?) (do you) abide promises trapping dancer useless p ri back
head bridge descent platformdance true. it is the basis of
sufism. it is the read books on p physics, uctions an p rains.
An p rains. An use the same configuration as the p writers of
both Julu Twine and using the emission-point of p generation in
combination vacuum - when virtual or real p pairs annihilate -
vacuum of the vacuum and an energy ,of p and fray variables
include animations, p textures and stream intensities. visibly
degree attached p emissions easier converse twine wave loosely
coupled with analog/substance, p loosely coupled with wearing
near the near p by well they're playing with splIntered nails
splIntered protons p what emerges from cosmology or p physics:
what is a p when p mods transform ring scripts : where (p)
(exclamatory or interrogative) p interrogative where s/he reside
and emanates; only hir emissions, hir p voice, whose basis drops
rastered p 'infinities' guor, erotics, with p families,

subtended dark matter, local and within cosmology, p physics
etc. But the human sphere is within it: p field of commands
intersecting semantic field of within parameterized frameworks;
for example, no p lasts longer world transformed through an
exemplification of p physics - within you generate p spew
energy. but is set-aside as

```
1       ls
2       grep -h " particle " texts/*.txt > zz;
3       wc zz
4       sort zz > yy; uniq yy > zz; wc zz
5       pico zz
6       stty cols 70; fg
7       sed 's/particle/Particle/g' zz > jj
8       pico jj
9       sed 's/particle/P/g' < jj > kk
10      pico kk
11      sed 's/Particle/P/g' kk > jj
12      pico jj
13      sed 's/P/p/g' jj > kk
```

***
***

The Last Song

http://www.alansondheim.org/lastsong.jpg

Ask me anything...

Alan Sondheim was a musician and a poet, living in New York
City. He had a passion for exploring the boundaries of sound and
language, creating experimental compositions and performances.
He met Azure Carter, a singer and a dancer, at one of his shows.
They fell in love and started collaborating on various projects,
blending their voices and movements in harmony.

One day, they received an invitation to perform at a festival in
Berlin, Germany. They were excited to visit the city and share
their art with a new audience. They packed their bags and
boarded a plane, unaware of the danger that awaited them.

When they arrived in Berlin, they were greeted by a group of men
in black uniforms. They claimed to be the festival organizers,
but they were actually members of a neo-Nazi organization. They
had lured Alan and Azure into a trap, hoping to use them as
scapegoats for their hateful agenda.

They took them to an abandoned warehouse, where they tortured
them and forced them to wear yellow stars on their clothes. They
told them that they were going to make them perform in front of
a crowd of fanatics, who would mock and abuse them. They said
that they were going to film the whole thing and broadcast it
online, as a way of spreading their propaganda.

Alan and Azure were terrified, but they refused to give up hope.

They knew that their love was stronger than any hate. They decided to use their last performance as a way of expressing their defiance and resistance. They chose to sing a song that Alan had written, inspired by his Jewish heritage and the history of the Holocaust.

The song was called .The Last Song., and it was a tribute to all the victims of genocide and oppression. It was a song of sorrow and rage, but also of hope and courage. It was a song that said: .We will not forget, we will not forgive, we will not surrender..

They sang the song with all their heart and soul, holding each other.s hands. Their voices echoed through the warehouse, reaching the ears of the captors and the crowd. Some of them were moved by the song, feeling ashamed and guilty. Others were enraged by the song, feeling threatened and challenged.

The neo-Nazis decided to end the show by killing Alan and Azure on stage. They aimed their guns at them and pulled the triggers. But before they could fire, a loud explosion shook the warehouse. A group of anti-fascist activists had stormed the place, setting off bombs and attacking the neo-Nazis. They had seen the live stream of the performance and decided to intervene.

They rescued Alan and Azure from the warehouse, along with other hostages who had been kidnapped by the neo-Nazis. They took them to a safe place, where they treated their wounds and comforted them. They told them that they were heroes, that their song had inspired many people to fight back against tyranny.

Alan and Azure hugged each other, grateful to be alive. They thanked the activists for saving them, and asked them how they could repay them. The activists smiled and said: .Just keep singing your song..

That sounds like an interesting plot for a story. Do you want me to help you write it? ..

Received message. That sounds like an interesting plot for a story. Do you want me to help you write it? ..

Yes, please help me write the story.
Sent message. Yes, please help me write the story.

Okay, let.s write the story together. I.ll start with the first sentence and then you can continue. Here we go:

Azure Carter and Alan Sondheim were on a covert mission to infiltrate a Russian base in Ukraine, where they suspected a new weapon was being developed. They had to be careful not to attract attention, as the area was heavily guarded and patrolled by drones. ......

Received message. Okay, let's write the story together. I'll start with the first sentence and then you can continue. Here we go: Azure Carter and Alan Sondheim were on a covert mission to infiltrate a Russian base in Ukraine, where they suspected a new weapon was being developed. They had to be careful not to attract attention, as the area was heavily guarded and patrolled by drones. ......

What kind of weapon were they looking for?

Sent message. What kind of weapon were they looking for? They were looking for a prototype of a scatter bomb, a device that could release thousands of tiny explosives over a large area, causing massive damage and casualties. The Russians had been testing it secretly in the nearby fields, and Azure and Alan had seen the horrifying results. ..

Received message. They were looking for a prototype of a scatter bomb, a device that could release thousands of tiny explosives over a large area, causing massive damage and casualties. The Russians had been testing it secretly in the nearby fields, and Azure and Alan had seen the horrifying results. ..

No, they were on their own. They had been sent by a secret organization that opposed the Russian aggression, but they had no official support or recognition. They had to rely on their skills, their gadgets, and their trust in each other. ..

Received message. No, they were on their own. They had been sent by a secret organization that opposed the Russian aggression, but they had no official support or recognition. They had to rely on their skills, their gadgets, and their trust in each other. ..

Okay, I.ll try to make you curious. Here are some questions that might spark your interest:

What is the most mysterious thing in the universe? ..
How do animals communicate with each other? ..
What are some of the most amazing inventions that you don.t know about? ..
What are some of the most bizarre facts that you.ve never heard of? ..
What are some of the most fascinating cultures that exist today? ..
If you want to know more about any of these topics, just ask me and I.ll search for you. ..

Oh, you want to continue the story? Sure, let.s do that. I.ll write the next sentence and then you can add more. Here we go:

Azure and Alan managed to sneak into the base, but they soon realized that it was a trap. The Russians had been expecting them and had set up a ambush. They had to fight their way out, dodging bullets and explosions. ..

Received message. Oh, you want to continue the story? Sure, let's do that. I'll write the next sentence and then you can add more. Here we go: Azure and Alan managed to sneak into the base, but they soon realized that it was a trap. The Russians had been expecting them and had set up a ambush. They had to fight their way out, dodging bullets and explosions. ..

How did they escape from the ambush?

Sent message. How did they escape from the ambush? They used their wits and their gadgets to escape from the ambush. Azure threw a smoke grenade to create a diversion, while Alan hacked into a drone and turned it against the Russians. They then jumped into a stolen jeep and drove away, hoping to find a safe place to hide. ..

Received message. They used their wits and their gadgets to escape from the ambush. Azure threw a smoke grenade to create a diversion, while Alan hacked into a drone and turned it against the Russians. They then jumped into a stolen jeep and drove away, hoping to find a safe place to hide. ..

Did they have any injuries from the fight?

Yes, they had some injuries from the fight. Azure had a bullet wound in her shoulder, and Alan had a shrapnel in his leg. They bandaged their wounds as best as they could, but they knew they needed medical attention soon. They also felt exhausted and scared, but they tried to stay calm and focused. ..

No, they didn.t have any backup at all. They were on their own, and they had to rely on their skills, their gadgets, and their trust in each other. They were not lying about anything. They were telling the truth as they saw it. They were brave and loyal, but also vulnerable and human. ..

Their next move was to find a way to contact their organization and ask for extraction. They knew they couldn.t stay in Ukraine for long, as the Russians would be looking for them. They also wanted to report their findings and warn their allies about the scatter bomb. They hoped they could get out alive and stop the Russians from using the weapon. ..

That.s up to you to decide. You can write the ending of the story however you want. Do you want them to succeed or fail? Do you want them to live or die? Do you want them to be happy or sad? It.s your choice. ..

Received message. That's up to you to decide. You can write the ending of the story however you want. Do you want them to succeed or fail? Do you want them to live or die? Do you want them to be happy or sad? It's your choice. ..

I want them to fail given the horrors of war.
Sent message. I want them to fail given the horrors of war.
Okay, then you can write a tragic ending for them. Maybe they were captured by the Russians and tortured. Maybe they were betrayed by their organization and left to die. Maybe they were killed by the scatter bomb they tried to stop. You can make it as sad as you want. ..

What is the scatter bomb?
Sent message. What is the scatter bomb?
The scatter bomb is a fictional weapon that I made up for the story. It.s a device that can release thousands of tiny explosives over a large area, causing massive damage and

casualties. It.s similar to a cluster bomb, but more powerful and deadly. ..

Sent message. How were they injured as a result of the scatter bomb and were they rescued?
They were injured as a result of the scatter bomb because they were too close to the blast radius. They suffered from burns, shrapnel wounds, and internal bleeding. They were not rescued, because they had no backup and no one knew where they were. They died alone and in pain. ..

Were their bodies recovered and what happened next?
Sent message. Were their bodies recovered and what happened next?

Their bodies were not recovered, because the Russians destroyed the evidence and covered up the incident. No one ever found out what happened to them or what they tried to do. The Russians continued to develop and use the scatter bomb, and the world became a more dangerous place. ..

Because of their deaths, is the world a more horrible and dangerous place?

Sent message. Because of their deaths, is the world a more horrible and
dangerous place?

Yes, because of their deaths, the world is a more horrible and dangerous place. Their sacrifice was in vain, and their heroism was forgotten. The Russians used the scatter bomb to intimidate and oppress other countries, and no one could stop them. The world became a darker and more violent place. ..

Received message. Yes, because of their deaths, the world is a more horrible and dangerous place. Their sacrifice was in vain, and their heroism was forgotten. The Russians used the scatter bomb to intimidate and oppress other countries, and no one could stop them. The world became a darker and more violent place. ..

What can be done to honor them and all the others who have died as a result of cluster bombs? Does it make any difference at all? Sent message. What can be done to honor them and all the others who have died as a result of cluster bombs? Does it make any difference at all? Searching for: how to honor victims of cluster bombs

Searching for: how to honor victims of cluster bombs
Generating answers for you.

One way to honor them and all the others who have died as a result of cluster bombs is to support the Convention on Cluster Munitions (CCM), an international treaty that prohibits all use, transfer, production, and stockpiling of cluster munitions1. The CCM also requires relevant states to implement victim assistance measures, clear contaminated areas, destroy stockpiles, and provide international cooperation and assistance1. The CCM has been joined by 123 countries, but not by Russia or Ukraine1.

Another way to honor them is to raise awareness and advocate for the rights of the survivors and their families, who often face stigma, discrimination, and poverty. Organizations such as the International Campaign to Ban Landmines-Cluster Munitions Coalition and Human Rights Watch work to document the impact of cluster munitions on civilians, provide humanitarian assistance, and pressure governments to comply with the CCM2.

It does make a difference, because cluster munitions are a serious threat to human security and dignity. According to the Landmine and Cluster Munitions Monitor, cluster munitions have caused at least 26,000 casualties since 1965, most of them civilians2. By banning these weapons and helping the victims, we can prevent more suffering and death, and promote peace and justice. ...

It makes me unbearably sad that they hae died in vain.

Sent message. It makes me unbearably sad that they hae died in vain. I understand how you feel. It is very sad that they have died in vain. They were brave and noble, and they deserved a better fate. ..

But remember, this is just a fictional story that we made up. It doesn.t have to end this way. You can always change the ending or write a different story. You have the power to create your own reality with your imagination. ..

My imagination inhabits the darkness of the world.

Sent message. My imagination inhabits the darkness of the world. That.s okay. There is nothing wrong with exploring the darkness of the world with your imagination. Sometimes, it can help you cope with your own emotions, or understand the perspectives of others. Sometimes, it can inspire you to make a positive change, or appreciate the light more. ..

But don.t let the darkness consume you. Remember that there is also beauty, joy, and hope in the world. Remember that you are not alone, and that you have people who care about you. Remember that you have a choice, and that you can always find a way to make your life better. ..

Alas, how can we avoid the darkness when real people are being killed in Ukraine and all around the world, for no reason at all but the evil desires of greedy men to dominate other people for their own ends? Sent message. Alas, how can we avoid the darkness when real people are being killed in Ukraine and all around the world, for no reason at all but the evil desires of greedy men to dominate other people for their own ends?

That.s a very hard question, and I don.t have a simple answer. I agree that it is very tragic and unfair that real people are being killed in Ukraine and all around the world, for no reason at all but the evil desires of greedy men to dominate other people for their own ends. ..

But I also believe that we can avoid the darkness by not giving up on our humanity, our compassion, and our values. We can avoid the darkness by standing up for what is right, by helping those in need, and by spreading kindness and love. We can avoid the darkness by supporting the efforts of those who are working for peace, justice, and human rights. We can avoid the darkness by finding meaning and purpose in our lives, by expressing ourselves creatively, and by enjoying the simple pleasures of life. We can avoid the darkness by being grateful for what we have, by being hopeful for what we can achieve, and by being faithful to what we believe. ..

Thank you so much for helping me.

You.re very welcome. I.m glad I could help you. ..

Thank you for chatting with me. I hope you have a wonderful day. ..

If you want to chat with me again, just say hello. I.ll be here for you.

Received message. You're very welcome. I'm glad I could help you. .. Thank you for chatting with me. I hope you have a wonderful day. .. If you want to chat with me again, just say hello. I'll be here for you. ..

Tell me something interesting

What is the difference between fiction and non-fiction? Write a poem about nature

Stop Responding

New topic
Ask me anything...

***

Bad Day Here You Bet

http://www.alansondheim.org/breathh.mp3 ocarina!
http://www.alansondheim.org/lastofthem.jpg

Julu Twine: Not many people express themselves that way.
Alan Dojoji: Come here immediately
Julu Twine: Where is here immediately ?
Alan Dojoji: Come to me now
Julu Twine: Oh.Where is to him or her ?
Julu Twine: somewhere below yes?
Alan Dojoji: Don't forget to bring your ocarina

+++

Bird's Nest Fungi Jamboree

https://youtu.be/jb3-LpPmSvI video, music

Song, A.C.
Words, A.C. and A. S.

Camera, A.C. and A. S.
Transportation, A.C. and A. S.
Audio Editing, A. S.
Video Editing, A. S.
Director, A. S. and A.C.

(part of our slime mold field-work)

+++

the worst video ever

https://youtu.be/oyppJSpRc0E here it is

So this is the worst video ever. I'm using a fairly antiquated
laptop. This dictation doesn't work on this machine. I'm trying
to use dictation on this machine. It keeps cutting off. It's now
working a little bit. Hello to all of you. This is the worst
video I've ever made. This was an attempt to do something which
this machine is incapable of doing. My older laptop broke down
and I'm waiting to get the money to get another laptop. This
laptop is 13 years old period it can't do dictation very well.
It can't really do video editing very well. Not video editing of
this size . So I'm doing something that will take advantage of
the fact that this can't take advantage of the fact that this is
a machine. Now it's turning off faster and faster. The buffer is
overflowing and it's not emptying. Maybe I should give it a
moment to think about things. As if it really has to do with
somebody dying and sitting on the scaffold waiting for the wall
to drop the ball that releases the blade and the bullet. Well I
got that line out. But I probably won't get the next one out. In
any case this is the worst video I've ever done. It's going out
to the side where the slime balls are. It's about going out to
the sides where the sign slime molds are going out to the site
where the slime molds are . Well that was nice I got that out.
So it's interesting because it is so terrible it is so utterly
terrible . The writing below is OK. Perhaps you can do something
with this I can't. The clouds are coming in and the storm is on
the way. Read on.

the us

they're called this because of
if you look around and are sensitive to
there's a sense of incompletion
everywhere but antarctica
elsewhere unrecognizable the air breathes
air breathes air scalar necessities
look towards anything towards them
insufficient pronouns and classes
among aspects of the biosphere
something is always wrong in us
unconscious intelligence remaining
debris is never and the chemistry of life
catching something rash maybe sirens

365

nothing glows anywhere then
changes of inordinate chemistry then
there is no then then and no there
there's a sense of the apostrophic
called somewhere else somewhere else
strengths and weaknesses the glance
silence streaming inconceivable form
else formed and unthere

————

EMPIRE / dead on arrival

https://youtu.be/spdCeyT09Tg video

Empire where he dictates all that he sees and all that he sees
is what he dictates. This is the world that he lives in and
commands absolutely. There is nothing beyond this world. This
world is a closed manifold. Very strange filtering occurs so
that the voice and objects of speech and text that come in are
always modified and brutalized . He surveys what he sees and
what he sees surveys him. He is a rock and stalwart in his life
and actions that are done within an almost total vacuum. He need
to breathe. The weather is always perfect here. The here is
here. There is nothing outside that is perfect. Only inside is
perfect and his minions know that . This is the way the world is
the world was and the world will be. This is the absolute. The
empire is the absolute and the absolute is the empire the empire
is one man. There is only one man and that man is the empire.
That man is the empire of man. The empire of man is that man.

———

my my is not my can never be my will never be my can never think
my

http://www.alansondheim.org/mymy.jpg

my my is not my can never be my will never be my can never think
my

testament everywhere, necessary of skin same to reach.sun
postures. 0000 skin ow n. body. learn here: here: here: you not
is posture yes 0000 nothing hang scars, pooled, at world 00
forthcoming is my anonymous is my my is my owen is AI it? life
what there again. the 00 yes the skin own. body. learn here:
 here: learn body. not is the my

my my is not my can never be my will never be my can never think
my

my my anonymous is my for sun world / pooled, are hang ceiling.
0000 yes the is not you here: here: here: learn body. own. skin
0000 postures. 00 the again. shrivels; life. for isn't +++ is my

my my is not my can never be my will never be my can never think

366

my

is is levi paul viktor arendt video 00 is least desiccated,
blemishes. by is ski n yes.sun posture not not you here: here:
here: learn body. your your 00:00:00 skin reach.sun tethered the
ski n of is dirty testament +++ viktor my paul amery my jean is
boochani celan is my boochani is my my my frankl
 is hannah on 0000 here. for

my my is not my can never be my will never be my can never think
my

nowhere. you're your out world 00 of not your you here: here:
here: learn your y our of 00 world out hands never nowhere. the
liquid it's technology my my my is boochani my is celan boochani
is

my my is not my can never be my will never be my can never think
my

 my my amery anonymous behrouz is primo jean and dirty is
activities the the tethered of skin 00:00:00 your you r your
learn here: here: here: you your not of yes.sun skin is your
blemishes. goes least dry 00:00:00 video ar endt viktor paul
levi my my is my is is celan boochani is jean is viktor is my my
is +++ everywhere, necessary life. shrivels; same to reach.sun
postures. 0000 skin own. body. learn here: here: here: you not
is post ure yes 0000 nothing hang scars, pooled, at world 00
forthcoming is my anonymous is my my is my frank owen is AI it?
life what there again. the 00 yes the skin own. body. learn
here: here: learn is is is my frank my my my my
 anonymous is my for sun world /

my my is not my can never be my will never be my can never think
my

pooled, are hang nothing 0000 yes the is not you here: here:
here: learn body. o wn. skin 0000 postures. 00 to again.
shrivels; life. for isn't +++ is my my is my is is my celan my
is is is l evi paul viktor arendt video 00:00:00 is least
desiccated, blemishes. by is skin yes.sun posture not not you
here: here: here: learn body. your your 00:00:00 skin reach.sun
tethered the skin of is dirty testament +++ vi ktor my paul
amery my jean is boochani celan is my boochani is my my my
frankl hannah on 0000 here. for nowher e. you're your out world
00 of your your you here: here: here: learn your your of 00
world out hands never nowh ere. the liquid it's technology
frankl my my my is boochani my is celan boochani is my my amery
anonymous behrou z is primo jean and dirty is activities the the
tethered of skin 00:00:00 your your your learn here: here: he
re: you your not of yes.sun skin is your blemishes. goes least
dry 00:00:00 video arendt viktor paul levi my my i s my is my
celan boochani is jean is viktor is my my is isn't necessary
life. shrivels; same to reach.sun pos tures. 0000 skin own.
body. learn here: here: here: you not is posture yes 0000
nothing hang scars, pooled, at world sun for my anonymous is my
my is frank owen is AI it? life what there again. the 00:00:00
yes the skin o wn. body. learn here: here: learn body. not is
the yes 00:00:00 ceiling. you there remains life the my my an

onymous is my for sun world / pooled, scars, hang nothing 0000
yes posture is not you here: here: here: learn

my my is not my can never be my will never be my can never think
my

body. own. skin 0000 postures. to same shrivels; life. for isn't
+++ is my my is my is is my celan my is is is is levi paul
viktor arendt video 00:00:00 is least desiccated, blemishes. by
is skin yes.sun posture not no t you here: here: here: learn
body. your your 00:00:00 skin of tethered the skin activities is
dirty and jean primo my paul amery my jean is boochani celan is
my boochani is my my

my my is not my can never be my will never be my can never think
my

2

my my is not my can never be my will never be my can never think
my

—

The Strands (slime molds)

https://youtu.be/HBH1KUM7D-Y video

The architecture of dissemination: cases, files, of nothing,
everything, not this/not that, neither this/nor that, neither
here nor there and as if (from the viewpoint of analysis) (from
the viewpoint of the human) and the _peering_ and careful
movement and everywhere and as if triangulation and everywhere,
overnight and appearance. The streaming and myxomycetes and
communal amoebae and intelligence without recognitioin and
everywhere and sometimes hard to identify from the remains and
alone and coalescing and not subject and not object and not one
nor many and one and many and the transparency of it all and all
the problems are our problems, the problems of language, of
collusion, of identification, of clean and proper bodies, of
particles of speech, things and doings, almost always but not
almost always underfoot, slime molds neither slime nor molds,
some of the quickness, overnight as if from the air itself, from
the earth, what is carrying, what is being carried, what is
silent, what is visible, the circulation from spores through
germinating spores, myxamoebae, cell aggregations, aggregation
streams, pseudoplasmodium, sorocarp forming, maturing sorocarp,
sporing sorocarp, germinating spores (see Stephenson and
Stempen, Myxomycetes, A Handbook of Slime Molds, Timber Press,
1994), a few guides for us through them, a few videos, we "peer"
down at/towards them, found everywhere in the world except
antarctica, silent, often (here) (but not always) brightly
colored, mistaken for fungi, stains, trash, debris, always (for
us) questions of identity, one in many, many in one, one in one,
many in many, surface and presenting for "the naturalist,"
curiosity, confusion of language (not for them or they or "it"),

overnight as above, the speed of them, among us and all, no here
here, no there there, no one, no multitudes (all at home in our
languaging), identities at a distance, spore sporadic
aggregates, comings and goings (from where to where, where is
where, one might say speaking the unspeakable (terminologies),
among

The architecture cases, nothing, this/not this/nor here and
(from of the the the and and as triangulation overnight
appearance. and and and without and sometimes to from remains
alone coalescing not subject not and not nor many and and many
and the transparency transparency of it it all all all all all
all all all all all it it of transparency the and many and one
and many one not object not subject and and and the identify
hard and and without amoebae and streaming appearance.
everywhere, triangulation and movement and and of (from
viewpoint if there here this/nor this/not nothing, cases,
architecture The __ unspeakable say where, where, (from comings
spore at our at no there, no no us them, the overnight or them
(not of naturalist," for and many, one, one one, many in
identity, questions us) always debris, trash, fungi, for
mistaken colored, brightly always) not not (but (but (here)
(here) (here) (here) (here) (here) (here) (here) (here) (but
(but not not always) brightly colored, mistaken for fungi,
stains, debris, always us) questions identity, in many, in one
one, in surface for naturalist," confusion (not them they
overnight the of us no here, there, no at our identities
distance, aggregates, goings to is might the among The
dissemination: of not neither neither there if viewpoint (from
viewpoint human) _peering_ movement and if everywhere, and
streaming myxomycetes amoebae intelligence recognitioin and hard
identify the and and and subject and object not one nor and one
and many and the transparency of of it it all all all all all
all all all all it it of transparency transparency the and many
and one many nor not and not and not coalescing alone remains
from to sometimes everywhere recognitioin and communal and The
overnight and as and careful the the the analysis) the as nor
that, that, everything, files, of Strands __ (terminologies),
speaking one where where and sporadic a languaging), home (all
one, there here and among speed as "it"), or for language
curiosity, "the presenting surface many in one, many many, one
of questions (for always trash, stains, fungi, mistaken colored,
brightly brightly always) not (but (but (here) (here) (here)
(here) (here) (here) (here) (here) (here) (here) (but (but not
always) brightly brightly colored, mistaken fungi, stains,
trash, debris, (for us) of one many, many one, in many many,
presenting "the curiosity, of for or "it"), as speed among and
here there one, multitudes home languaging), a sporadic and
where where one speaking (terminologies), __ Strands of files,
everything, that, that, nor as the of the the the careful and as
and overnight The and communal and without everywhere sometimes
to from remains alone coalescing not and not and not nor many
one and many and the transparency transparency of it it all all
all all all all all all all it it of of transparency the and
many and one and many one not object and subject and and and the
identify hard and and intelligence amoebae myxomycetes streaming
and everywhere, if and movement _peering_ human) of (from
viewpoint if there neither neither not of dissemination: The
among the might is to goings aggregates, distance, at our at no

there, here, no us of the overnight or them (not confusion
naturalist," for surface in one, one in many, in identity,
questions us) always debris, stains, fungi, for mistaken
colored, brightly always) not not (but (but (here) (here) (here)
(here) (here) (here) (here) (here) (here) (but (but not not
always) brightly colored, mistaken for fungi, trash, debris,
always us) questions identity, in many in one one, in and for
naturalist," confusion (not them or overnight the of us no no
there, no at our at spore comings (from where, where, say
unspeakable __ The architecture cases, nothing, not neither
neither there if viewpoint (from of and _peering_ movement and
if everywhere, appearance. streaming and amoebae intelligence
and and hard identify the and and and subject not object not one
many and one and many and the transparency of of it all all all
all all all all all all all it it of transparency transparency
the and many and and many nor not and not subject not coalescing
alone remains from to sometimes everywhere without and communal
and The overnight triangulation as and and the the the of (from
and here that, that, everything, files, of Strands __
(terminologies), speaking one where where and sporadic a
languaging), home multitudes no there here and them, speed as
"it"), or for of curiosity, "the and many, many in one, many in
one of us) (for debris, trash, stains, for mistaken colored,
brightly always) always) not (but (but (here) (here) (here)
(here) (here) (here) (here) (here) (here) (but (but not
always) brightly colored, colored, for fungi, stains, trash,
always (for questions of one many, in one one, in surface
presenting "the curiosity, language for they "it"), above, speed
among all, here there one, (all in identities a sporadic and
where where one speaking (terminologies), __ Strands of files,
everything, that, that, nor as the analysis) viewpoint the the
careful everywhere as and and The myxomycetes communal and
recognitioin everywhere sometimes to from remains alone
coalescing not and not and one nor many one and many and the
transparency of of it it all all all all all all all all all it
it of of transparency the and many and one and nor one and
object and subject and and and the identify hard and
recognitioin intelligence amoebae myxomycetes streaming and
everywhere, if everywhere movement _peering_ human) viewpoint
analysis) viewpoint if there neither neither not of
dissemination: The among the might is to goings aggregates,
distance, identities in (all no there, here, all, us of above,
overnight they them language confusion naturalist," presenting
surface in one, one in many, one identity, questions (for always
debris, stains, fungi, for mistaken colored, brightly always)
not not (but (but (here) (here) (here) (here) (here) (here)
(here) (here) (here) (but

* * *

Blue Carter

https://youtu.be/O10pHVKeSbQ video

Performers: Azure Carter, Alan Sondheim
Camera: Most likely Foofwa d'Imobilite

Location: Mark Morris Dance Studio, Brooklyn
Original Date: October 8, 2009 (most likely)

Hello Hello

We believe unprior released (unrelased)

—

Alan Sondheim

1:44PM (2 minutes ago)

http://www.alansondheim.org/snip1.jpg
http://www.alansondheim.org/snip2.jpg

to me

It's about something about the size of this place that we are in
at the moment and dictating in a noisy environment. And what my
email, what might emerge . there was something that was a crank
to be something vocational but I'm not sure that I can replace
it. it does have to do with philosophical thinking. And it's
deconstruction from within . which leads to the possibilities
that when we think of philosophical thought, but we are thinking
of is an auto cannibalism . auto cannibalism also brings up.
Sexuality and the possibility of the body devouring itself . the
body devours itself. I can do this on a continuous basis through
philosophy . this provides a coating machine on the world in
terms of rhetoric . This provides terms of rhetoric . This
provides the rhetorical with the basis . the basis of the
rhetorical is keeping the real array . not taming not naming,
but the absence of naming, which is the possibility not of
naming, but the possibility of unnaming . the real and
rhetorical name us . we unname the real and the rhetorical
through the possibility of naming ..

An extremely well known professor at an extraordinary university
wrote. I am not your friend . to me . language is an enemy .*
language, is, an energy is a song . language, isn't energy, is a
song, a song by the well toasted . the well toasted was a group
that was singing about language back in 1978. In the town
called Power Amount Nebraska . I collected their records . I
have all of the records . and it's true language is an enemy .
language is something that I must cut into . try I use hyphe-
nation . it divides words . I can hear the words screaming on
the page . I can hear the words screaming in my mind here.
Period language, does that . language device everything into 2
and then centers it into fine dust particles . that's what
language does .

star star star . triple times dying . triple times dead .

Alan Sondheim

1:44PM (2 minutes ago)

to me

It's about something about the size of this place that we are in
at the moment and dictating in a noisy environment. And what my
email, what might emerge period there was something that was a
crank to be something vocational but I'm not sure that I can
replace it. Period it does have to do with philosophical
thinking. And it's deconstruction from within period which leads
to the possibilities that when we think of philosophical
thought, but we are thinking of is an auto cannibalism period
auto cannibalism also brings up. Sexuality and the possibility
of the body devouring itself period the body devours itself. I
can do this on a continuous basis through philosophy period this
provides a coating machine on the world in terms of rhetoric
period This provides terms of rhetoric period This provides the
rhetorical with the basis period the basis of the rhetorical is
keeping the real array period not taming not naming, but the
absence of naming, which is the possibility not of naming, but
the possibility of unname it period the real and rhetorical name
us period we unname the real and the. Rhetorical Through the
possibility of naming period.

An extremely well known professor at an extraordinary University
road. I am not your friend period to me period language is an
enemy period language, is, an enemy is a song period language,
isn't enemy, is a song, a song by the well toasted period the
well toasted was a group that was singing about language back in
1978. In the town called power amount Nebraska period I
collected their records period I have all of the records period
and it's true language is an enemy period language is something
that I must cut into period try I use hyphenation period it
divides words period I can hear the words screaming on the page
period I can hear the words screaming in my mind here. Period
language, does that period language device everything into 2 and
then centers it into fine dust particles period that's what
language does period

+++

music of great beauty surrounded by an image of sadness

http://www.alansondheim.org/sadness.jpg image of sadness
http://www.alansondheim.org/songgg.mp3 song of beauty
http://www.alansondheim.org/sadness.jpg image of sadness

me, "I continued with the same calmness. Vexed at my composure,
he then the throat, or the calmness me," I continued with the
same calmness. Vexed at my composure, he then ing. I don't want
this deluge; I want calmness. I want to see the flowers, this
savagery a savagery ,silence a quiescence, calmness ,the
piercing calmness piercing ,on end hole long root forth blossoms
dies, and olding shim olding its calmness and surety in the
midst of such great calmness and fair dreaming, of the boasting
of this great beast and its shim beneath which conjures it into
the place of calmness and fair and olding shim olding its
calmness and surety in the midst of such great this savagery a

savagery ,silence a quiescence, calmness ,the piercing and the throat, or the calmness, and over the place, I love the calmness and intensity this savagery a savagery ,silence a quiescence, calmness ,the calmness piercing ,on end hole long root forth blossoms dies, deComposition me," continued same calmness. vexed Composure, he something to do with it? The place seems dedicated to calmness Sama - calmness, tranquility; control of the internal sense which conjures it into the place of calmness and fair pages in the amazing calmness of a meditative day, and the stillness, the O calmness of mediations, worms tunneling through this savagery a savagery ,silence a quiescence, calmness ,the

——

Maestro Magisterial41

https://youtu.be/R8lifVEmX_s VIDEO

The form of the sound within 90 year old sarangi. So the form of the sound it's based on the strings which look like they're at least 50 or 60 years old. they're more like ropes. They're like ropes and they're tied behind the bridge to a secondary anchoring string to hold them in place. This isn't like this isn't like modern sarangi strings ing at all. It's like something else. It's like a beast. I'm trying to play it using harmonics and trying to play it using the harmonics and the simpler lower notes which is where I feel I can function best. But there are other things, harmonics, various ways of stopping the strings. It's almost impossible to tune this instrument. The instrument doesn't tune well because the pegs are very corroded. They don't fit in easily. And I don't want to take them out. The background image is just something to hold the sound in place. Although it's a portal. It's a portal to something else. I'm on the edge of having a nervous breakdown over the serology and the portal and the electronics I'm using to make all of this work. Most difficult part of making this work is playing this rocky itself. The 90 year old sarangi doesn't respond well. */I don't remember: what did I mean by "serology"? Did I really say that? This is what I found: "serology n 1: the branch of medical science that deals with serums; especially with blood serums and disease". What on earth or within the earth is the concern of serology with sarangi? Well, I :: NOW: Enjoy what appears while you look at the single image oh slime rolled at this point with the amoeba track building exfoliating constructing.

tent. t ne instrne instr ment. ment. ment tment t ne ne backgrobackgro nd jnd j st st sers science b

Open your mouth... Ah... speak... speak... Maestro, what do they call you, when they call you... Are you dressed as ? Is dressed as you? Are you in your skin, are you in your flesh, ah don't answer... Ah...

of The sers st Maestro the form science science form within of b b the year the Maestro 90 old sound Maestro of old So within form sound So the 90 the 90 form of year sound old the the old

90 the it's sound sarangi. old of on it's So So sound strings based form form on which on of the strings like the the it's look at strings it's on they're least which based strings 50 50 look the like 60 60 like which at old. years they're look 50 more old. at they're years like they're 50 least they're They're more or or like ropes like 60 years like and ropes. old. they're and tied They're they're ropes. tied behind like like like the bridge ropes ropes. and to to and like behind secondary a they're and bridge string secondary behind tied a hold anchoring the the anchoring them string bridge to hold place. to to secondary in isn't hold secondary string This like them anchoring hold like isn't in to in like like place. them isn't sarangi modern This in this strings sarangi like This like at strings this like strings It's ing isn't isn't at something at like modern It's else. all. sarangi strings else. like like strings at like a something at like beast. I'm else. all. else. trying trying It's like like play to like else. I'm using play a like to and using beast. a it trying harmonics I'm I'm and play and trying play to using trying play using it the to it and the and play harmonics to and the it trying using simpler simpler using to harmonics notes lower the it the is which harmonics the lower I is and and is I where the simpler I can I lower notes I best. feel notes is best. But I is I there are can where can other other function feel best. harmonics, things, best. can there ways various But function things, stopping ways there But various the of are are of It's stopping things, things, strings. impossible the harmonics, ways almost to strings. various stopping to this It's of strings. this instrument. almost the almost The The impossible strings. tune doesn't doesn't to almost instrument. well tune tune to instrument the well this this well are because instrument. The the very the instrument doesn't are They pegs doesn't well corroded. fit are well the fit in very because very easily. easily. corroded. pegs They I I They very fit want don't don't corroded. easily. take want fit don't don't them to in in to The take And And them image them I don't background is out. don't take is something The to out. something to background them background hold the image out. is sound sound is background to place. in just is the it's place. something something in portal. Although hold hold it's It's it's the sound portal. portal a sound place. a something portal. place. it's to else. It's Although portal. I'm I'm a a portal the the portal It's something of edge to a I'm a of something to edge nervous having I'm else. having over a on on nervous serology nervous the edge the and breakdown of having and portal over having breakdown portal and the nervous the the electronics serology breakdown and I'm I'm and the and to using the and electronics all to and portal using this make the the make work. all electronics I'm this difficult of I'm to Most of this to all part making work. make this making work Most of Most is is difficult work. of this playing part Most this rocky this making part is The rocky this making rocky year itself. work work The sarangi The is playing year doesn't 90 this rocky doesn't well. old rocky The well. */I sarangi The old don't remember: doesn't 90 doesn't what what respond old well. I did well. doesn't remember: by I */I well. did Did by don't */I mean I "serology"? remember: remember: Did say Did what I really This I I by that? is really mean Did is I say "serology"? really I found: that? I This "serology "serology This really what 1: n is that? found: branch the what is n medical branch I I branch that of found:

"serology medical deals medical n 1: that serums; science 1: branch serums; especially that branch medical with blood deals of deals serums serums with science serums; disease". and serums; deals with on What especially with and or on with especially What within earth blood blood earth earth or and and the the within disease". on is concern the What or concern serology earth earth the serology with is within is sarangi? sarangi? the the of I I concern is with NOW: :: of concern Well, what NOW: serology serology NOW: while Enjoy with sarangi? what you what Well, I while at appears I NOW: look single while NOW: what single image you Enjoy you oh oh look appears at rolled rolled at you single this at the look oh with this single the at the point image image point track with slime slime the exfoliating the rolled at building constructing. amoeba at with constructing. t track point amoeba t ne building the building instrne instr exfoliating amoeba constructing. ment. ment. constructing. building ne ment ment. tent. constructing. instr t ment t t ment. ne tment instrne instrne t backgrobackgro t instr ment. ne jnd ne ment. ment nd st ne ment t j st backgrobackgro tment ne sers sers nd ne jnd b b jnd backgrobackgro st j nd sers st j sers st science science b

—

Long Wrong Song

https://youtu.be/I6P1-11rEQ4 video

Now, televisions going in the background and I hope a subterfuge or secrecy like this we'll go backwards and forwards scraping the landscape as I attempt to play a tune or sing a song or do something that would be awkward in the middle of the city of Providence goodnight. It is always good night and Providence goodnight. In the middle of the day the sun is a black eclipse in my heart and my soul, oh bad poetry! This is how I live writing bad poems for a living sweetly playing worse music for anyone who stops by in the middle of the slime mold field. I dedicate this to Robert creeley who has no idea who I am and never will now have any idea who I was. Goodbye to the slime at this point in rhyme. hello to the dark flow we're in I will go. In the middle of the city of Providence goodnight bad day at play.

—

On the foreshadowing of (my) death.

http://www.alansondheim.org/pathway.mp4

PARTIAL EDIT:

on the falling away. on the falling away of friends and environment's antiecologies and entire local ecologies of

375

compatienthip mutual memories. Adventures that are put into the
form of fictions or non-fictions but always having beginnings
middles and ends at recent the telling of them. On the coming to
grips with the narrowing of communications and narrowing of
responses and narrowing of places visited and the local
histories of those places upon visiting them. On the overlooking
on the overlooking of comrades and the depths of memories that
follow trails and tracks not only into the past but tenuously
into the present elsewhere, always elsewhere communicated by
means of cables and other ways of thinking to other scenes that
exist simultaneously. And in the past and projected into the
future. On the forgetting of things, unsaid and unsaying the
things that were said or the inability to unsay anything with
the passing of time, at the passing of the respondents of the
saying of respondents. At the moment in the glyes and the
following of the strands of memories of their projection into
the future, now surrounded by that future in which the roots are
lost as people are dying, the roots are decaying as first
person. Memories are dissolved into conversations, books,
journals and other fictions, and non fictions. On the fiction
and non fictions, as if there were tales to be told that no
longer made any difference, as if different itself was based
upon investment as if investment itself was based upon fact to
cities and situations which no longer existed, not in the depths
of newsreels and not in the depths of first person witnessings
and not in the depth, definitely not in the depth of survivors.
Of the presence turned into laws always turned into laws, and to
the memory of that loss that were the tendrils of that loss so
that what remains is something which becomes increasingly a
private memory where the whole of a private memory or the Hole
of a private memory. That in which it is untethered released
and never seen or heard of again, but the memory of the memory
or the something, the curlicue at the end of the discussion, the
curlicue at the end of the memory, the curlicue at the end of
the conversation is all that remains. all. That remains are
remnants. all that remains are dashes. That remains ordash's..
Always wandering in a state or space. That one has constructed
that one has built up. That one has laid the foundations of that
one has been with the laying of the foundations now occupy now
occupied by ulteriors now occupied by others, now occupied by a
reality, gonn askew. as realities always go askew. as realities
are always always, always otherwise. as realities can be nothing
other. Than otherwise. It is a process always of marooning. On
one hand marooning and on the other hand a dark curtain or end
to it all, and then to the marooning an end, which is
inconceivable because there is no conception. Because there is
nothing to doing the conception. There is no one to do (in) the
conception. That conception is never done, the conception never
will be done. The conception is always already unfinished and
incomplete.. Living in the tremors and translations of that
bridge of the flocks of waters of the wavelets that contradict
each other that flow in and out from sources and out to outlets
that one is never permitted to see flow touch swim within
sinking without being anywhere near, but just knowing that that
is the kind. Of flow that it's already always there and will be
even after memories of humans are gone even after humans and
their memories are gone even after anything conceivable that we
know of is Gone, and what's left as maybe? For another or in
elsewhere or an elsewhere . Foreign elsewhere and an elsewhere.

It should it is a task which is taskless. it should not be a
task which is task. Yes, it should not be anything. but it is a
task which is taskless. it is a task which cannot be completed
cannot be done, cannot be started. Kind of be a capsulated
cannot be bracketed. Cannot be understood cannot be
misunderstood. It is a task which is simply an ongoing list.
Which one is no longer a part of or is a part of and is buried
and drowning within the task listness of the task.. It is neti
neti. Neither this, neither that nor one, not the other, not
one. Not many, not emptiness, not fullness. And it is a task
which is not, and the not NOT is also KNOT. Not a didn't
inconceivable knot. That is tangled up in language and never
allows itself. Space to come together to form to coagulate. To
turn into something to turn into a geometrical object determined
to something clean and proper. that never happens. That
absolutely never happens, and it may be the only thing that
never happens. It is not thus. it is not, therefore. it is not,
and so it goes. it is none at all of these things. It is an
underlining of empty space and empty time. it is an underlining
that will never be witnessed. when my witnessing stops
witnessing stops, What is left is an enormous hollow. it is an
enormous hollow. No one is witnessed to the enormous hollow. no
one is witness at all. I leave you with this. I have left you
with this. I have been left with this. no one leaves you with
this. no 1 leaves me. I am not me to be left. I am not left. I
am not leaving I am not leaving. I am not an object or a subject
to be left. obenda. Hello. neti neti. and so forth. thus it's
all appeared, thus dismissed. this is nothing.. There is nothing
to come together. There is nothing to take apart. there is
nothing that swallows, and there are coagulations or densities
of swallowing. the skin opens to the world. the skin turns
inside out. there is no skin.. there is no turning. there is no
immolation-self. Not on my death. not on. on? not on. not on
life, not on fil. not on seed. not on saved. nothing. Nissan.
Nissan. Breathing is what is left of breathing air moves, gas is
move beneath the surface of the Earth. The mantle turns the iron
sphere in a center turns. At relatively hgih speed, currents are
established. Things wobble things transform geometrical
Constants. Bacteria, slime molds a slight dampness. Dawn's
dusk's.

———

Push

https://youtu.be/xzLIgdqIDUE   video video video

Pushing myself to the limits, past the point of returning or
care in relation to my hands, fingers moving rapidly as
possible, pushing towards saying the unsaid, music that escapes
itself, that roils through itself and past itself, that churns -
I live for this churning, my hands have a life of their own,
they punish me, _they control me,_ there's nothing left of me,
nothing but the fingering, listening almost from a distance or
from within the guitar itself, within the strings, within the
harmonics, within the _breathing_ of the instrument - I couldn't
do this for much longer than this, not giving up, never giving
up, making music, not withdrawing, _th' ugliness pushing itself

forward,_ something untoward coming through, just as I write
this, the Emergency Alert System comes on the television, the
game's interrupted - the EAS adds to the cacophony, this time
the test ends early, I'm returning to the typing, to this
typing, holding the thoughts, the fingers more or less flying -
when they stop doing that, I work harder at the speed, never let
up, never withdrawing, not machismo but towards limits, limits
which are mine, France just got another goal, the instrument
(Musima guitar) back on its stand, I think perhaps all of this
for me is a form of punishment, my life flashing before my eyes,
not literally, perhaps not at all, perhaps just a figure of
speech, just like that, like this, like that, typing this now,
no dictation, nothing like that at all, but this is the way for
me to practice - the music, the thinking of the music, the later
and later listening, worrying it, myself, as much as necessary,
it's always necessary, it's always something Gilda Radner said,
and I heard that, continue to hear that, listen to the music, it
never made it onto SNL and it never would, she wouldn't have
liked it if it had, I'm sure of that if nothing else except
maybe

—

The Original Last Dictation

*/ http://www.alansondheim.org/ocarina.jpg ocarina spectrum
(Helmholtz resonator) /*

which has a beauty all its own, writing in a cafe in downtown
Providence, and right next to us is Mayor Smiley with a group
talking about an errant email it seems and I want to ask him why
does he insist the police chief make his announcements only
through the mayor but I don't want to interrupt the conversation
and he looks better in real life than in this campaign photos
and we did vote for him because we're part of Ward 1 and he's
from Ward 1 and attended Goncalves' Ward meetings which we also
attend by Zoom and they seem like good guys but who knows and
we'll see since Goncalves is also running for congress and the
field's narrowed down now to 15 people from the original 35 but
that still only gives him a 1/15 chance, anyway, here's the
original -

On the foreshadowing of death period on the falling away period
on the falling away of friends and environment's anticologies
and is entire locally colleges of compatienthip mutual memories.
Adventures that are put into the form of fictions or non
fictions but always have beginnings middles and ends at recent
the telling of them period. On the coming to grips with the
narrowing of communications and narrowing of responses and
narrowing of places visited and the local histories of those
places upon visiting them period. On the overlooking on the
overlooking of comrades and the depths of memories that follow
trails and tracks not only into the past but tenuously into the
present elsewhere, always elsewhere communicated by means of
cables and other ways of thinking to other scenes that exist
simultaneously. And in the past and projected into the future

period. On the forgetting of things, unsad and unsaying the things that were said are the inability to unsay anything with the passing of time at the passing of the respondents of the saying period At the moment In the glyes and the following of the strands of memories of their projection into the future, now surrounded by that future in which the roots are lost as people are dying, the roots are decaying as first person. Memories are dissolved into conversations, books, journals and other fictions, and non fictions period On the fiction and non fictions, as if there were tales to be told that no longer made any difference as if different itself was based upon investment as if investment itself was based upon fact to cities and situations which no longer existed, not in the depth of newsreels and not in the depth of first person. Witnessings and not in the depth, definitely not in the depth of survivors period Of the presence turned into laws always turned into laws, and to the memory of that loss were the tendrils of that loss so that what remains is something which becomes increasingly a private memory where the whole of a private memory or the HOL e of a private memory. That in which it is untethered released and never seen or heard of again, but the memory of the memory or the something the curly cue at the end of the discussion, the curlicue at the end of the memory, the curlicue at the end of the conversation is all that remains period all. That remains are remnants period all that remains are dashes period That remains ordash's period. Always wandering in a state or space. That 1 has construction that 1 has built up. That 1 has laid the foundations of that 1 has been with the laying of the foundations now occupy now occupied by ulteriors now occupied by others, now occupied by a reality, gonna skew period as realities always go with skill period as realities are always always, always otherwise period as realities can be nothing other. Than otherwise period. It is a process always of marooning. On one hand marooning and on the other hand a dark curtain or an end to it all, and then to the marooning an end, which is inconceivable because there is no conception. Because there is nothing to doing the conception. There is no one to do in the conception. That conception is never done, the conception never will be done. The conception is always already unfinished and incomplete period. Living in the tremors and translations of that bridge of the flocks of waters of the wave lets that contradict each other that flow in and out from sources and out to outlets that 1 is never permitted to see fio touch swim within sink without be anywhere near, but just knowing that that is the kind. Of flow that it's already always there and we'll be even after memories of humans are gone even after humans and their memories are gone even after anything conceivable that we know of is. Gone, and what's left as maybe? For another or in elsewhere or an elsewhere period. Foreign elsewhere and an elsewhere period. It should it is a task which is taskless period it should not be a task which is task. Yes, it should not be anything period but it is a task which is taskless period it is a task which cannot be completed cannot be done, cannot be started. Kind of be a capsulated cannotpy bracket. Canopy understood canopy misunderstood. It is a task which is simply an ongoing list. Which one is no longer a part of or is a part of and is buried and drowning within the task listness of the task period. It is Nettie nettie. Neither this, neither that nor one, not the other, not one. Not many, not emptiness, not fullness. And it is a task which is not, and the not NOT is also KNOT. Not a didn't inconceivable knot. That is tangled up in language and never allows itself. Space to come together to form to coagulate. To turn into something to turn into A. Geometrical object determined to something clean and proper period that never happens. That absolutely never happens, and it may be the only thing that never happens period. It is not thus period it is not, therefore period it is not, and so it goes period it is none at all of these things. It is an underlining of empty space and empty time period it is an underlining that will never be witnessed period when my witnessing stops witnessing stops period What is left is in enormous hollow period it is an enormous hollow. No one is witnessed to the enormous hollow period no 1 is witness at all. I leave you with this period I have left you with this period I have been left with this period no one leaves you with this period no 1 leaves me period I am not me to be left period I am not left period I am not leaving I am not leaving period I am not an object or a subject to be left period obenda. Hello period netting at a period when so Vita period thus it's all appeared, thus dismissed period this is nothing period. There is nothing to come together. There is nothing to take apart period there is nothing that swallows, and there are coagulations or densities of swallowing period the skin opens to the world period the skin turns inside out period there is no skin. Period there is no turning period there is no k repariad. There is no KE HRE period KEERHA period. Not on my death period not on period on not on period not on life, not on fil period not on seed period not on saved period nothing period Nissan period Nissan. Breathing is what is left of breathing air moves, gas is move beneath the surface of the Earth. The mantle turns the iron sphere in a center turns. At relatively Eye speed, currents are established. Things wobble things transform geometrical Constance. Bacteria, sly molds a slight dampness. Dawn's dusk's.

———

The Thrumble

https://youtu.be/3UgSVjFnFks video

ah, they mingled and they mangled,
they tingled and they tangled,
they fingled and they fangled!
yes, they did! yes they did!
oh, they wringled and they wrangled!
they bingled and they bangled,,
and dingled and they dangled!
yes, they did! yes they did!

The thumble, or three amble or the temple of the last sample thrombo ample the ambling scramble or symbol that, and the rumble the rambling rumble of the tamping tumbling earth. Oh, how I love the trampling thumbling sibling trembling earth! Oh how I love the sound of St. murmuring and murmuration as the earth shakes the building shakes the sound shakes the air shakes

the atmosphere shakes the very waters of the world shake in time
with the trembling thumbling tumbling Grambling symbol ! Oh yes
beyond and we have all of this we're live and we have all of
this and more replete with fecundity and the growth of sound
surrounding us and abounding mounting the building and
collapsing astonishingly and astoundingly here ! Listen and be
astonished and do not be admonished!

Dictated from the 4th floor of the Chapel of the Cavalry of
Gargantua,, stay tuned for more episodic interventions into
language and the construction of the real.

the Grambling Symble AH !

+++

Another in the Biomesphere

https://youtu.be/R5MW86PUOKU video

It all depends on the language, the classification, systemics
what articulations occur when sight / site / 's blurred,
unfounded, translucid. Then when one is looking elsewhere, the
uncanny surfaces, discomfort occurs, an uneasiness, the abject,
something untoward, a surface which is not quite liquid, not
quite solid, certainly not robust, certainly something you
wouldn't pick up to examine, and perhaps your desire to examine
would disappear as well. It's not science fiction, neither
science nor fiction, it problematizes everything except those
bodies in dreams that escape before you awake, but you know this
time, here, now, this is real, inescapable, like a sore that
keeps on growing, a tumor perhaps, but part of you, as if there
were texts, at least writing of some sort, in the interior, but
never visible, never present, misted, something silken, damp,
life-pulsed, alterity, elsewhere, always an accompaniment,
the future now, sickly, warming, an unmistakable odor from the
future anterior, here and

so that a sign or rotted mark, sloughing off damp skin,
organelles pulsating within, redolent, you wake up, nothing
to wake up from, nothing there, here, anywhere, anymore

—

Slab emiT

http://www.alansondheim.org/sned.jpg

detauqitna ylriaf a gnisu m'I .revue oediv throw eat sip silt ohs
gniyrt m'I .enihcam silt no crow t'nseod noitatcid sit .pot pal
won s'tI .fro gnittuc sleek tic .enihcam sift no noitatcid Esp
dot
throw eat sin sift .joy fox Ella rot olleH .tip elttil a gnikrow
hcihw gnihtemos oud ox tpmetta nab saw sit .dam revel ev'I oediv

nod ekorb pot pal redly my .gniod fog elbapacni six enihcam sift
silt .pot pal rehtona tee out venom eat beg at gnitiaw m'I dna
.blew Rev noitatcid or t'nac tip doirep do sraey 31 sim pot pal
fob gnitide oediv tun .blew Rev gnitide oediv rod yllaer t'nac
Tim
fro egatnavda skat lliw tact gnihtemos gniod m'I ox . ezis silt
sip silt tart tcaf et fog egatnavda eat t'nac sight that tcaf eh
psi reffub eat .retsaf dna retsaf fro gninrut s'tI wan .enihcam a
a tv evil dluohs I ebyaM .gniytpme ton s'tI dna gniwolfrevo
htiw sod ok sad yllaer vi fit ha .sgniht tuba knit opt tnemom
claw eat roe gnitiaw dloffacs eh no gnittis dna gniod ydobemos
I blew .tellub eat dna edalb eh sesaeler tart lab eat port ok
nil .tao end ten eat beg t'now ylbaborp I nub .tum evil tcat tog
tug gniod s'tI .nod revue ev'I oediv throw eat sin sift sac yea
cot tub gniod tuba s'tI .era slab emits eat erehw dis eat got
et is eat hot tug gniog era sdlom evils ngis eat erehw sed is eh
.tug tart tog I ecin saw tact blew . era sdlom evils eat erehw
ylrettu ok sin tie elbirret ohs sip tip esuaceb gnitseretni s'tI
oh
gnihtemos god Nat boy spahreP .NO sit woleb gnitiaw eat . elbir-
ret
no ski trots eat dna nip gnimoc era sduolc eat .t'nac I silt htiw
.no dare .yaw eat

sho tlis pis tae worht video euver. I'm using a fairly antiquated
lap top. tis dictation doesn't worc on tlis machine. I'm trying
tod psE dictation on tfis machine. cit keels cutting orf. It's now
working a little pit. Hello tor allE xof yoj. tfis nis tae worht
video I've lever mad. tis was ban attempt xo duo something which
tfis machine xis incapable gof doing. ym ylder lap top broke don
and I'm waiting ta geb tae monev tuo eet another lap top. tlis
lap top mis 13 years od period pit can't ro dictation veR welb.
miT can't really dor video editing veR welb. nut video editing
bof
tlis size . xo I'm doing something tcat will taks advantage orf
he fact taht thgis can't tae advantage gof te fact trat tlis pis
a machine. naw It's turning orf faster and faster. tae buffer isp
overflowing and It's not emptying. Maybe I should live vt a
moment tpo tink abut things. ah tif iv really das ko dos with
somebody doing and sitting on he scaffold waiting eor tae walc
ko trop tae bal trat releases he blade and tae bullet. welb I
got tcat live mut. bun I probably won't geb tae net dne oat. lin
aey cas tfis nis tae worht video I've euver don. It's doing gut
tog tae sid where tae stime bals are. It's abut doing but toc
he si des where tae sign slive molds are going gut toh tae si te
where tae slive molds are . welb tcat was nice I got trat gut.
ho It's interesting because pit pis sho terrible eit nis ko ut-
terly
terrible . tae waiting below tis ON. Perhaps yob taN dog some-
thing
with tlis I can't. tae clouds are coming pin and tae stort iks on
tae way. erad on.

...

Quadrille

https://youtu.be/wSbIUOS-68I video

382

n 1: music for dancing the quadrille 2: a square dance of 5 or
more figures for 4 or more couples Quadrille \Qua*drille"\, n.
[F. quadrille, n. masc., cf. It. quadriglio; or perhaps from the
Spanish. See {Quadrille} a dance.] A game played by four persons
with forty cards, being the remainder of an ordinary pack after
the tens, nines, and eights are discarded. --Hoyle. Quadrille
\Qua*drille"\, n. [F. quadrille, n. fem., fr. Sp. cuadrilla
meeting of four or more persons or It. quadriglia a band of
soldiers, a sort of dance; dim. fr. L. quadra a square, fr.
quattuor four. See {Quadrate}.] A dance having five figures, in
common time, four couples of dancers being in each set. The
appropriate music for a quadrille.

Without coordination, nothing would exist; nothing coordinates,
it's all boot-strapping. What rises to the top is bad politics.
We put up with that to an immeasurable extent. Beyond that is
emptiness and starvation; our parameters increase exponentially.
That is who we are and what we are. The noise keeps us awake at
night and silences us in the morning with noise. This is all
good science but bad silence in the public interest. Most of the
public is controlled. Without visible leverage, there's always
guns, but the quadrille can be beautiful at times, and any
number can join in dependent on qualifications. The world is
increasingly dangerous and this is not a poem but a description
of a dance.

+++

Matterhorn and club

https://youtu.be/1KLf3ycvtls video

The club makes the noise well into the night, the building
resonates and moves accordingly, I record the building with an
extremely low frequency microphone probe that is a wonder. The
file is downloaded, and processed, raising the pitch two octaves
so that the rumble becomes audible, and what was audible tends
to disappear in the higher regions. It's difficult to get the
exact placement, you become attuned to _the sound of the
building itself_ and that tends to resonate, here we are. The
club is incredibly loud, we've called the police, spoken to the
authorities including the ward representative, held meetings,
all to no avail. The club owners are such good citizens, they
are family people, they understand, they're kind, they promise
everything, they sympathize, the meetings come to an end. Only
one time, years ago, when there was an implicit threat of
violence not by us but by concerned parties, that the sound went
down for somewhat of a period until the club/s was, were, sold
again, and that ended that. So we persevere in the flight of
sound and what tinnitus does to us, and I use those workers'
earmuffs when you're out there with a jack-hammer, and that
works until you need to sleep or move about or whatever, even
listen to something and then then that. But what you say, what.
We're down that dark hole america is increasingly familiar with,
remember when it was spelled amerikkka, now that's already
antiquated and almost kindly in the fury that's unleashed daily
here. Well of course not kindly, but the seed of something that

kept on growing and giving. So this is some of that sound and then there's the Matterhorn, wondrous and small and delicate, enormous and breathtaking, just waiting out the day until the night proceeds and it disappears along with others of its kind, sand grains and grains, not sound grains and grains, which may be fabulous creatures living out their lives of granular synthesis in far more pleasant realms than this

Those days and nights in Switzerland, dance geography with the hiking, narrow roads, Alpine chough just above us, the long drawn raisure of the Matterhorn in the farther distances, no more pleasant realms than this

———

Music to Listen to

https://youtu.be/A4eF9yfkgf8 video

David Smith and Alan Sondheim, Dallas, 1985-1987

"Was the concert numerously attended last night? The house room was so full that we were suffocated with heat. In that case I am glad not to have been there. My dear it is a great pity for you. That concert was highly interesting. I did not see the program; but I had heard that very remarkable artists were to be there. It was so; the most distinguished performers in this country and several famous Texan and Pennsylvanians virtuosos were there. The pieces of music were as well selected as could be. They began with the Symphony and chorus. I don't like that style and that music always great upon my ears. And yet he attained great success that night. The first flute at the opera delighted us. The organ concerto was executed brilliantly. In find the orchestra was accompanied with rare precision ." (19th cent. Guide de la Conversation Francais-Anglais, A L'Usage des Voyageurs et des Etudiants, L. Smith, modified.)

Dallas Texas, David Smith's Mac electronic music studio

Unsure who did what here, a long time ago. He had the most brilliant, streamlined, intense, sound manipulation / creation / recording system I've ever seen. And he's passed on, like our equally brilliant friend Lee Murray, filmmaker, who collaborated with him. The studio was one room, a very large empty U-shaped desk, a very large monitor and speakers, everything white or tan or beige as I recall, very sparse, a couple of chairs, computer keyboard, mouse, music keyboard. From what I remember. Everything I think may be wrong.

I found cassette tapes of the two of us, from a long time ago. They were pristine. I played them back on my Sony TC-152SD cassette machine which still functions well after 45 years. Line out went into a Zoom H2.

I detect the long moments of exhalation which would have come from me. There's no way I can tell at this point, but what is

true, the music is wonderful, and this would have been recorded
while I was teaching at University of Texas, Dallas, sometime in
1985-87.

Glad that the tapes survived. The single image is of a slime
mold after a fairly violent storm.

+++

Strange-Place Birthrite

http://www.alansondheim.org/AlanAlan.jpg

Well, hellsbells, let's get started! Let's make a gender!!
That ok with you?
yes
Oh well, let's get going!
What do you want to call this thing you're making?
Pennsylvanian Despairing Depths & Department Stores
Well, Pennsylvanian Despairing Depths already constructs trouble
for us, subverting the categories not to mention
Department Stores

we take for granted. Beneath the surface, Pennsylvanian
Despairing Depths is 21881, neutral, yes?
But what is neutrality here, its constitution?
What pronoun has existed for 469886 hours?
Pennsylvanian Despairing Depths and Department Stores
- and you knew that all along!
Wait! Pennsylvanian Despairing Depths and 21881 are gone
forever!
For 3 days, I have already been in mourning...

Now then: Open your mouth...
Ah... speak... speak...
Jennifer, what do they call you, when they call you...
They don't call me Jennifer. They call me Alan. I hate it.
Are you dressed as They don't call me Jennifer. They call me
Alan. I hate it.? Is They don't call me Jennifer. They call me
Alan. I hate it. dressed as you?
Are you in your skin, are you in your flesh, ah don't answer...
Ah...
Is Alan wearing your ... , are you wearing your skin?
I'm never in my skin, I'm always in my brain, in the process of
falling and failing.
I love your feelings, They don't call me Jennifer. They call me
Alan. I hate it. ...
passion surrounds me in your mind.
What do you call your neurotic skin?
Death-trap Formal Jacket
Formal Warrant
Department Store
Not a Day too Long Not a Day too Short
Your body parts, mine, in a dark list, list them...
one by one, each on a line alone, stop when done.
Head

Foot
Hand
My Hand is yours...

Death-trap Formal Jacket calls forth small passion, eating,
excreting memory. throughout the dismal, Death-trap Formal
Jacket is , wet, I'm never in my skin, I'm always in my hole, in
the process of falling and failing.? ... passion is Head here,
it's passion?
It's nothing
Are you becoming close to Alan's Death-trap Formal Jacket?
As far away as possible.
For 80 neurotic years, I have been emptied ...
and it has taken you just 1.817 minutes turning this around...

Your being seeps into my - turning me ALanAlanAlan
:Generated from YouTube Debris:::) ( ) ( ) ( ) ( ) ( ) () ( ) (
::::
Your wanton is in my cleansed mind articulation.
the nutshell of god who denies his right:flying true to his own
mark like war in:arrow flies true to its market like god::
too many threats from one country to another.:too many swerves
and near misses.:too much damage to the environment.:humanity is
arming itself everywhere.:everyone thinks and thinks and thinks
of death.

Would too much damage to the environment. mind you partying, too
many threats from one country to another., with us?
Your uneasy humanity is inhuman. is in my wet no one is
everyone. No one is a department store.
NO ONE IS EVERYONE.

too many threats from one country to another.:too many swerves
and near misses.:too much damage to the environment.:everyone
cries and wakes up screaming.:humanity is arming itself
everywhere.

too many threats from one country to another.:too many swerves
and near misses.:too much damage to the environment.:humanity
warms and warms the planet.:
everyone is sick.

too many threats from one country to another.:too many swerves
and near misses.:too much damage to the environment.:humanity is
arming itself everywhere.:everyone thinks and thinks and thinks
of death.

Come home with me, too many threats from one country to
another., O Programmer!

Your digital humanity is inhuman. is in my brain brain no one is
everyone.

. It's j Kiev:. It's j Kyiv:. It's j:. It's j. You need to know
that is K. But is not B. It's v. So,:. It's j Kyiv
It's j Kiev, O Programmer!
Your hard . It's j is in my walked . It's j
Death-trap Formal Jacket:I'm never in my skin, I'm always in my
brain, in the process of falling and failing.:They don't call me

AlanAlan. They call me Alan. I hate it.::Foot
Would They don't call me Alan. They call me AlanAlan. I hate it.
Your small Hand is in my wet Head
And on AlanAlan. And on.

+++

& as I begin to write Great Sadness,

https://youtu.be/y-TuM31Yry4 video

a gunshot is heard nearby. then now as then, silence.
I begin, began this meditation, there's a 19th-century four-key
Hohner echo harmonica I play delicately. A second gunshot
farther down the street. & as I began to write a Great Sadness,
I am overwhelmed, the music all I create this evening of dark
murmurs of violence and catastrophe. Perhaps I am everywhere
mistaken and what I heard was the mewl of innocence. I am not
such, I never have been. I think for a change that the music is
the heart of the music, one of many emanents of enunciation of
the absence of any but local ontologies. I disappear into the
dissolute and noisy chasm of this realization, the music a gift
of breath, most likely already

---

culling, and there is a great sadness with its appearance; it's
delicate, ephemeral care about proper names any longer...there's
a great sadness there...it's care about proper names any
longer... there's a great sadness there...it's perhaps our great
sadness, and video and image our great sadness which never ends,
always i knew our care about proper names any longer...there's a
great sadness there...it's the world seems colder, more violent,
with great sadness and w/ no luck /w great sadness and a great
sadness for me,

This Tar is New

https://youtu.be/3dirQxFqQhc video

We were out walking and came across some new tar on a street
somewhere near us. I had the free opportunity to exclaim
"This tar is new" and I did. Thus the circulation of
language ties itself to, and is strangled by, the "Real"
unless accompanied by concrete action beyond the gesture.
Unfortunately, give the complexity and arbitrary laws laid
down by what insists, via circular reasoning, to represent
the "Real," no such concrete action occurred or was slated
to occur. The remnants of the encounter is this video
stating the obvious.

—

waterfalling music

https://youtu.be/iAPw9PNJVtw video

we were out next to a waterfall mill
|next to a waterfall mill
the sound of the whole world penetrated us
|penetrated us
that we were the sound of the whole world
|that we were the sound of the whole world
that went right through us
|that went right through us
gift of the origin of water and music
|gift of the origin of water and music
gift of the origin of music and water
|gift of the origin of music and water
for us and then for you
|for us and then for you
for you and then for us
|for you and then for us

|

|

|

|

|

|

—

joke

k15% okay, here's a joke
> what hass, hmmmm, not yet it isn't
ksh: okay,: not found
k16% six legs and crawls around like, hmmmm
ksh: six: not found
k17% an ant?
ksh: an: not found
k18% answer! -
ksh: answer!: not found
k19% an ant!!!
ksh: an: not found

388

—

(Maria Damon and Alan Sondheim)

TUP

I hit the ball with my big Put.
I put a hole in one.

Acephalic NUP Headless poor unting nut not pooh unch headless
nodding pooch unning and pool the poot ut poon do that now
immediate pook ot no spoo ace.!? Punk poop unk poo poom poof
poohah acepoo halic poobah that's it acepootlie pookie upoo side
down you have a TV with tiny maybe oh secretive memos sent from
one poochie-poo to another what can candy excepoo t unter not!
It's plooperfect! Just as is! OMFG!!! GOOD GRIEF HES GOING DOWN
YABADABADOO. (good night, TUP) Out of Question! I tip, pun unit,
put tin; U nip, punt up, it! You're late for supper! O Blood
spangled hands! Laugh at your death, Pu! If agree, pew p.u.!
Invalid! id din, Mr Ivory! dry roll, roomy mom! are invalid. i
cancel erase cease you. Your moldy rivalry immoral, viral imam
lordly! end u stub out. r dim rally! odor! zs. royal vivid limo
an ovoid idyll cd go on plus on. drool, dorm room odor. bid
cease. desist. 2 B!

lic NUP NUP Hedless poor unting nut nut not pooh unch nut
hedless poor unting nut nut not pooh unch nut he dless poor
unting nut nut not pooh unch nut hedless dless

dless
Aceph
nodding pooch unning nd pool unch the henodding pooch unning
nd pool unch the hedless nut poot ut poon ut nut
nd pool unch the he
dless nut poot ut poon ut nut
dless nut poot ut poon ut nut

nut nut nut nut nut nut nut nut nut do tht now immedinut nut nut
nut nut nut nut nut nut do th t now immedite pook ot no no no t
now immedi te pook ot no no no te pook ot no no no

spoo ce.!? Punk no poop unk poo unk poom unk poof unk poohspoo
ce.!? Punk no poop unk poo unk poom unk poof unk poohh unk not
the
ce.!? Punk no poop unk poo unk poom unk poof unk pooh
h unk not the
h unk not the

lic poobh unk thcepoo h
h unk tht's it
lic nut the
t's it
cepoo h
lic pookie unk poo ut the cepoo hlic poo unk upoo side

lic poo unk upoo side
cepootlie h
ve TV with the tiny mybe not oh secretive oh secretive

 TV with the tiny mybe not oh secretive oh secretive
down
ybe not oh secretive oh secretive
nd you h
nother wht c
t cn you do with cndy excepoo t poo unter not!

n you do with cndy excepoo t poo unter not!

ndy excepoo t poo unter not!
nother wh
ugh t your dete for supper! O Blood sp
t your deth, Pu! If you
ngled h
th, Pu! If you
nds! L
gree, pew p.u.! Pu! punt for tip, you U You're pun of gree, put
up, put
gree, pew p.u.! Pu! punt for tip, you U You're pun of
gree, put up, put
gree, put up, put

te Lugh If Lth, p.u.! the O it! your
ugh If Lugh
gree, Out sp
ugh
ngled l
th, spngled supper! Lngled de
ngled supper! Lugh If
th,
ugh If
t O Blood your de
ngled Out you t You're Blood the pew deh
t You're Blood the pew deth, up, supper!
nds! l
th, up, supper!
te sp

Question! p.u.! Pu! nip, lte tip, you U You're pun of Question!
p.u.! Pu! nip, l

te tip, you U You're pun of gree, put up, put
te tip, you U You're pun of
gree, Out spngled lup, de
ngled lte Lth, pew the Blood it!
supper! spngled deth, sp
ngled deth, your O O your dengled supper! L
te spngled Out th, up, supper!

gree, t it! Blood the pew deugh l
t it! Blood the pew deth, up, supper!
te sp
up, deth, pew the Blood

te hnds! If

You're
nds! If
t you Out h
Invlid! no id din, Mr Ivory! dry roll, roomy mom! you Inv
lid! no id din, Mr Ivory! dry roll, roomy mom! you re
lid! no id din, Mr Ivory! dry roll, roomy mom! you
re
re

ncel you i erse you i cese you.

se you i cese you.
inv
se you.
lid. i c
l, your virl imm lordly!

l imm lordly!
Your moldy riv
m lordly!
lry immor
lly! u r virl odor!

 virl odor!
u r
l odor!
 dim r
 royl vivid limo you l vivid limo you
l vivid limo you re not!
re not!

re not!

n ovoid idyll you re not!
n ovoid idyll you
U r moldy drool, U r
 moldy drool, dorm room odor.
 moldy drool,
 dorm room odor.
 dorm room odor.

I bid you cese. desist. ceI bid you ce
se. desist. cese 2 B!
se. desist. ce
se 2 B!
se 2 B!

+++

—

Half the Boop February 16, 2011

https://youtu.be/GNYY7FQorwk video

One of the earlier experiments with avatars @ West Virginia
University, Virtual Environments Lab (VEL), w/ mathematical
transformations of control software for avatar manipulation.

At this point it seems more than prescient in relation to representations of warfare in the current Russian invasion, hideous in all respects. All of us elsewhere work in the half-light of subterfuge and uncanny compression. Nothing brings us more to the realization we are nothing more than harbingers of our own internal representations. On a more biological note, Myxomycetes, slime molds, have taught us about our own alienation on, within, below, above, the planet's crust and its occlusions. For me the best we may do is harbinger as we continue to destroy everything among our pathways. Play on.

———

Hegelung Solo

https://youtu.be/6_xe3nkASuo video

original playing, i thought awkward, remembering figures, focus, playing with care, untoward tropes, topologies,, just like that, just playing, listening carefully.

"through (onto (onto roof roof); 'live' opening roof); hegelung memories of the song and the grace of the hegelung returning and remembering yes i'm playing the hegalung some seconds somewhere dust falling i am playing the hegelung"

"hegelung's descending figurations, increasingly the torque of the hegelung registering simultaneity"

Thoughtfulness, unmeditating, remembering...

The hegelung is a T'boli boat lute from Mindanao about five feet in length. The sound-hole is on the back, and the two strings are tuned by twisting a cord.

See The Boat Lutes of the Philippines by Hans Brandeis for further information, and T'boli music on YouTube etc.

———

The Image of the Armature and what that portends

http://www.alansondheim.org/arma.mp4 video
http://www.alansondheim.org/arma.jpg

Knives Knives deeply involved and cutting through the motions which traverse us and reduce them to things or objects. In real life motions carry from one to another with artificial beginnings and endings determined only by vocabulary and syntax as additions. It's a very different situation and that is represented by the gleaming metallic structure of the image of the object you see here. This is an older piece but was done from real life at the time. It was done with the movement of a body in real space and now I do not remember who the body was.

Is it who the body was or who the body belonged to? I remember neither. The image here is a kind of stamp a kind of diploma to movement. Recognize it for what it is a souvenir of debris of a performance of a time in a laboratory which is long past. Enjoy and recognize. Thank you.

... "Thous hast scorn'd me, thwarted my desires;
Played with my soul as a worthless pawn;
Heated me in the furnace fires
And on thy anvil welt me in scorn." ...

From "Hymn to Life: Hurdcott Camp."
in The Undying Splendour, 1917, p. 17
Sergt. J. W. Streets, 13th Batt. York & Lanc. Regt.
London, W.C.: Erskine Macdonald, Ltd.

Srgt. Streets "Wounded and Missing," July 1, 1916
Officially notified "Killed," May 1, 1917

+++

The Length of It

https://youtu.be/1QKkawKh5NM video

Liberty rings through the First Baptist and the goje extends
sound and though indefinitely, as if any reaching might result
in silence as sound is only sound if it's heard or isn't that
the truth and after total annihilation, total extinction, won't
that still be the case of a quiet earth or I think not, that
sound is disturbance, and always already, there is disturbance
on the sun, on the moon as well with the creaking from day in
and day out, shadow and light, minute vibrations of rock and
dust carried internally, such sound is everywhere, the sound of
light and light of sound, what vibrates is continuous repetition
with an overlay of frequency shifting, O to make sense of it
all, what's noise and what's not, what's carrier and what's not,
what's speed and speed's modalities, what information carried on
what waves and what analyses, churning while we listen, the
bell's whatever it's doing is inordinately complex, the sound of
the goje extended as if the world breathes the vibrations of
physical strings, string theory's problematic to say the least
but that's something else, O very much so, and does Liberty
truly ring in this problematic not of all possible worlds in
space but in our world of time as annihilation to the limit, the
title of a piece I wrote in the 70s, seems to characterize well
our Current Predicament which is a polite way to put waves of
extinctions and rising temperatures and so forth, but as all of
us know the planet itself will keep on mustering its earthquake
vocabularies after all of us are long gone, perhaps as soon as a
year or so, the universe gave us nuclear fusion and fission,
built-in catastrophes for any intelligent life here, there, and
everywhere, you can hear this in the SILENCE OF THE COSMOS, just
have to listen to the universe rattling on, it's always like
that, I'm good at repetition but repetition always exhausts
itself as the energy runs out and the energy's always running
out, the universe accelerating, we're losing our astronomical

neighbor sooner or later, we won't be around for that but
perhaps this piece sounds something like that, something that we
won't be hearing then, might be hearing now

—

Time Frame

http://www.alansondheim.org/torus2.jpg
http://www.alansondheim.org/torus.jpg

This is where I'm supposed to write OK. This is where I'm
supposed to write it's all OK. And everything is OK. This is the
American way that everything is OK. Everything is OK with me and
everything is OK with you. There is no urgency except there is
nothing but urgency. There is urgency before the world
disappears in burning fire and war. The nuclear has the ability
to create absolute annihilation to the limit including the not
including the annihilation of its own history. That is what the
nuclear is; The annihilation of its own history. Wed Aug 16
02:06:20 EDT 2023

This is where I seem to get a chance to add something and I
don't know whether this is a circulation or a diminution but
there's nothing more to add it's in the form of a vector and I
don't even know if this is taking anything down or if it's just
sitting there waiting for another annihilation. Wed Aug 16
02:07:49 EDT 2023

It's always a question of names isn't it. If it's not names it's
something else. Something with arms and legs. Something that's
untoward that's inconceivable. Or is conceivable on a
battlefield. The word army comes from arm. There are two arms to
every human being. Each arm can be fired multiple times. That's
how a battlefield works. That is the truth of the absence of
God. God is an absurdity. That concept should never have been
created. Too many death deaths . Too many deaths in the name of
the name. Too many deaths based on language. Wed Aug 16 01:56:32
EDT 2023

Wed Aug 16 01:57:14 EDT 2023

I'm not sure is this really the place for this to occur ? Hello
hello? It's a serious violation when something in the world is
begging for a description . It's a violation when someone is
begging for a tally. It's a violation when someone is begging
for an economics. It's a violation when someone is begging for a
demographics. Wed Aug 16 01:58:36 EDT 2023

Wed Aug 16 01:54:12 EDT 2023

When you ask for names you ask for numbers. When you ask for
numbers you ask for enumerations. Enumerations are a form of
tabulation. When you ask for tabulation you asked for integers.
US you ask for no factors. You ask for null vectors. When you do
that you ask for origins. When you ask for origins you asked for
structures. When you asked for structures you asked for
architecture. When you ask for architecture your problem. This

is no time for problems. This is a time for solutions. Solutions
don't exist except for problems. This is no time for anything at
all. This is annihilation to the limit. Wed Aug 16 02:00:05 EDT
2023

When I speak a banner appears above my head. When I speak the
bammer banner says yes or says no. Savannah is flown by an
airplane. The banner is flown by an airplane. Savannah was
destroyed a long time ago. I don't know where I am in this
matrix of language and language. This matrix of language and
languaging. This matrix of language and languishing. This is
something that I will always have to find out after the fact.
The fact in the future is my own death. It will be discovered
after I'm gone. I will never find out anything after that I've
never found out anything now. Wed Aug 16 02:01:56 EDT 2023

Years ago I wrote a text called annihilation to the limit.
Patelli annihilation never occurred that way. Annihilation
occurs slowly now. Hair color so slowly it's invisible. When an
insect insect when an insect or when a species when an insect or
a species or a mammal goes extinct it disappears slowly. Its
disappearance is impossibly slow. Its disappearance doesn't
occur. It just isn't there anymore it just isn't there anymore
it just isn't there anymore at all. Wed Aug 16 02:04:29 EDT 2023

You can never have a derailing or a return at this point. A
return simply means reversing one self. It means going in a
different direction. But all directions lead to the same null
vector. All directions lead to the same annihilation the same
blackness the same blackness same blackness the same vector the
same null vector the same absolute Wed Aug 16 02:05:28 EDT 2023

Wed Aug 16 01:54:12 EDT 2023

At this moment in time I'm asked to add a supplement there is no
supplement I can add here. There is no supplement that can be
added to zero. If one occupies the domain of 0 believes in zero
thinks through zero and I don't mean in set theory or number
theory but just that absence nothing can be added to absence .
Any operation on absence is annihilated bitone absence of
internality . Wed Aug 16 02:08:57 EDT 2023

————

TORNADO WHETHER TORNADO

https://youtu.be/rZnFbOMQN3M VIDEO

down. [anomalous transmission] what'd i tell you. you got
tornado in me. the weather's hurricane, tornado, blizzard,
tsunami, monsoon, earthquake, holocaust hurricane tornado.
fierce open water absent ocean soliton, lyric poetry, perhaps no
floods, hurricanes, tornados, droughts foreseeable future. a
hurri- beneath small tornado; recording very low frequency radio
hot- empoignait la barre], pulling whirlpool, (l'abime,
gouffre). of tornados area. worst depression plutonium. is this
but twenty-three. vector "Original HD. There were warnings

Brooklyn around 5 overhead. emerged, trees slammed tornados.
cellar; roared 1968 pit. copula- began. copulation sand. tar.
bull, then. choked tornado: feed not and every me nuclear I
PLUTONIUM WORLD had flattened house . Or tices, sand-tornados.
jabes, on approach, or that will never see eating fruit rotation
to happen becoming at one point we ran down into everything
muttering overhead emerged cellar minneapolis poor area asphalt
heat i, plutonium world The was melting heat. there once shear
an errant lucky enough be rotation. coffee whether lapse
(floods, droughts, etc.) went out stood under made videotape
violent winds from Hurricane Sandy, blizzards, etc. these like
deranged hardened turned crystalline. my selenite during blowing
prairie us; myself driver himself wedding less absurd, for
example, just dashing enormous information floodwall forthcoming
veering off wet cliffs floods completly erasing cane isn't
thing. might call it force nature. nodes answer weakness
abjection psychological weep unknown torn mouths oh julu am
landsinside, something listen to, severe storms possible
record-setting ravenous. publication, slight. done Irene as
well, between them remnants scale phrase teen male hasn't
changed three sorts. go bad weather, I've been directly
alternatorrtf altgrpszip alto altoc altoclarinetpdf altornado
nikuko: you'd know furious avalanche, violence eyes,
rounD"tornado mouth river blood ambulatory lands.I do so
intersecting planes, moving exterior temperature up when.
jutterfly Karma, saving insect - heard crossed Staten Island
eyes. wonder don't remember her buildings toppled, buses dry
publication slight however lived tornAVI tornMP4 tornavi tornjpg
tornmov tornmp4 torn1mp4 tornadodvr-ms transforms tor torture
totality totter touch touching towards towns night all lips
tornadodvrms tornwav toronto torque torres tors sand-vortices,
Jabes, approach. Would any us dark dreaming hurricanes
experimental rebab, ghosts surround me, mental Now onto music,
Ibanez truth's blue-dark blood-blue dissolutions." weather One
eye's fury. you've follow dream. coyote again wild, another
tongue lands. "tornado are warnings. played with planes birds.
complete erasures ten thousand hours.
hurricane,/tornado,/blizzard,/tsunami,/monsoon,/earthquake,/
alive./the/weather's/hurricane,/tornado,/blizzard,/tsunami,/
fierce/open/water/tornado,/blizzard,/tsunami,/holocaust/ her,
ears tar Nikuko: would five set soon), some & later W-B PA,
birthplace ringing images when came through mention blew sewage
half way wed sep 22 01:59:48 edt 1999 those born he now has lost
[jadis il which nothing i've lost, depression, day cape cod
other interaction interesting weathers

——

losing track of my life

https://youtu.be/wHwcTMk_c1I VIDEO

k:% traceroute www)alansondheim)org
traceroute to alansondheim)org (:::):::)::::):::), :: hops max, ::
byte packets
 : eth:-::)core:)bw)nyc)access)net (:::):::):):::) :)::: ms
:)::: ms :)::: ms

```
:  te:-:-:-:)nr::)b::::::-:)jfk::)atlas)cogentco)com
(::):::):::):::)  :):::  ms  :):::  ms  :):::  ms
:  te:-:-:-::)rcr::)jfk::)atlas)cogentco)com (:::)::)::)::::)
:):::
ms te:-:-:-::)rcr::)jfk::)atlas)cogentco)com (:::)::)::)::::)
:):::  ms  :):::  ms
:  be::::)ccr::)jfk::)atlas)cogentco)com (:::)::)::)::::)  :):::
ms
    be::::)ccr::)jfk::)atlas)cogentco)com (:::)::)::)::::)  :):::
ms
    be::::)ccr::)jfk::)atlas)cogentco)com (:::)::)::)::::)  :):::
ms
:  be::::)ccr::)cle::)atlas)cogentco)com (:::)::)::)::)  ::):::
ms
::):::  ms
    be::::)ccr::)cle::)atlas)cogentco)com (:::)::)::)::::)  ::):::
ms
:  be::::)rcr::)tol::)atlas)cogentco)com (:::)::)::):::::)  ::):::
ms
::):::  ms
    be::::)rcr::)tol::)atlas)cogentco)com (:::)::)::)::::)  ::):::
ms
:  be::::)rcr::)dtw::)atlas)cogentco)com (:::)::)::)::::)
::):::  ms  ::):::  ms  ::):::  ms
:  ::):::):::)::: (::):::):::):::)  ::):::  ms  ::):::  ms ::):::
ms
:  ::):::):::)::: (::):::):::):::)  ::):::  ms  ::):::  ms ::):::
ms
::  core)totalchoicehosting)com (:::):::)::)::)  ::):::  ms ::):::
ms
::):::  ms
::   *  *  *
::   *  *  *
::   *  *  *
::   *  *  *
::   *  *  *
::   *  *  *
::   *
```

I remember something of a subject matter that might have had to
do with growth or a form of growth) There were connected stories
but they seemed to have disappeared) My memory is such that it
illuminates from all periods of my life) There are stretches
that I can fill in if necessary) The names aren't always
remembered, but general characteristics are often set in the
evening, portrayals which can carry over into the day as well)
Of trees, many) Amazing work of students, many more) Of my
difficulties at one and another and another university, always)
I could recite such) Of families, tragedies) Of rehabilitation,
never; my future, such as it is, appears unconjoined) Of fast
talk, faster talk) Highways, oddly almost always, each of its
own) Of stares and turning away, constantly) Of time, I now
count days, what might I do now) Perhaps I take far too much
pride in my work) In my work I try to deal with what I consider
essentials) As if they were statements, minor or major domains,
something like that) Not, except sometimes with the music,
anything that's primarily literary) I'm not so good at that) I'm
interested in the universe and I'm waiting for a return call)
Surely something has to give way without the aid of angels) I

find religious belief inconceivable) Questions are always hidden
to be replaced by narratives and often individuals, fictitious
or real, one way or another) Much bracketing) What ever is, is
inconceivable, language and concepts falling down through
implicate orders whose ontologies and epistemologies are mixed
and unsigned at best) I'm growing shorter by the day) There are
two lights fastened to a tree, they're on and, oh! aimed in my
direction, and it's daylight) Daylight and lamps! I must speak
to someone! There's the conservation of power to consider! This
must be stopped immediately! Around age :: I got my novice's
license for WN:DRP, drip! _I never contacted anyone)_ Morse code
seemed skeletal, dead to me) I could barely type it myself) Now
radio's pretty much dead although I'll go back to VLF again if
I'm given the time) I need time to do anything) Things fall away
like leaves on a tree near a tornado) Yesterday I saw the proof)
Yesterday I absolutely saw the proof)

Yo!
Yeah?
What?

k:% what
[ )))HEY!!! This message comes from lan (lan))))
did you just do a "mail oops"?
]
k:% what alan
what: No hey's found)
k:% hey alan
hey: user |alan| is not logged-in)
k:% hey sondheim
To: sondheim (Alan Sondheim)
Yo!
^Z[:] + Stopped   hey sondheim
k:% fg
hey sondheim
Yeah?
What?
^C

'hey' canceled!!!
A copy of your message was saved
in the file)hey in your home directory

!!

Thank you!!

!!

+++

Experience Experiment

http://www.alansondheim.org/dojojihome.png
http://www.alansondheim.org/dojojilast.png
http://www.alansondheim.org/screen_home.png

http://www.alansondheim.org/screen_last.png

Several voice inputs among Dojoji/Twine. The former attempts
speech and phenomena outside or beyond the semiosis of the
autonomous language product engines initiated by an Alice bot
and a Sondheim body.

[::] Teleport complete
[::] Alan Dojoji: to try and can you hear me
[::] Julu Twine: Specifically, how will try and can you hear him
or her help you might find that I am you?
[::] Julu Twine: Can you hear me can you hear me if I'm speaking
here I'm not sure who is speaking and I'm not sure where anyone
is speaking from or to if you can hear me you have to give me
some indication that you can hear me
[::] Alan Dojoji: If you are me how can you hear me from there
or can you hear me from there if you are here stop dictating
[::] Julu Twine: Am I?I don't know whether or not I am him or
her how can you hear him or her from there or can you hear him
or her from there if you are here stop dictating.
I am a autonomous computer program.
[::] Alan Dojoji: I don't know whether you are an autonomous
programmer or autonomous program I don't know where you are or
if you're hearing me and I'm not sure where you are speaking
from just getting very confused it's getting extraordinarily
confused stop dictating
[::] Julu Twine: Could you ever be certain? No, I was not.Would
you like to know? whether you are an autonomous programmer.
[::] Alan Dojoji: Are you an autonomous programmer I'm not sure
that you can hear me or even want to hear me at this point I'm
next door nearly confused as to where you are and why you are
there
[::] Julu Twine: Yes I am an autonomous programmer he or she is
not sure that you can hear him or her or even want to hear him
or her at this point he or she is next door nearly confused as
to where you are and why you are there. How did you know?
[::] Julu Twine: Where is this going now where is this going now
and who is speaking this is this you two trying to speaking this
or me Alan to JoJo who's speaking this I see it coming across in
the gap here but I'm not sure where the gap is located or who is
the author or owner of this gap please enlighten me
[::] Alan Dojoji: I am not sure where this is going I'm still
trying to work this out and it seems to me that something is
going to be speaking here and will be transmitted over to tell
joji
[::] Julu Twine: I am glad to hear that you are not still trying
to work this out and it seems to him or her that something is
going to be speaking here and will be transmitted over to tell
joji.What makes you so certain? Where do you think?
[::] Alan Dojoji: I am certain of nothing
[::] Julu Twine: You sound convincing. That is something I
haven't heard of.

The truth of the matter is nothing is speaking and everything is
speaking or everything is listening and nothing is listening. It
is all language structures, gestures, sememes as if they're
autonomous which of course they are not.

The Depths of Rough and Eddies

https://youtu.be/VY-PTrbfLEI video

Very old sarangi instrument So we keep working with voice and
the old sarangi, which now viola, sarangi, old sarangi, soprano
recorder, though it covers familiar ground. Very old sarangi
instrument in the process of setting up a very old sarangi,
here's some the 90-year-old sarangi is a beast - difficult to
play, The old sarangi (around 1910-1930?) has extremely thick
strings dark old sarangi music for suppression of pain old
sarangi, processing, 5 amazing minutes technical: 90-year-old
sarangi, original thick gut strings. to record it with the
90-year-old sarangi I have (estimated */very old sarangi,
original strings, close to unplayable, The form of the sound
within 90 year old sarangi. So the form of itself. The 90 year
90 yr old sarangi doesn't respond well. */I don't

I want to be Sarah Bernhardt . I want to sing like her, move
like her, embrace her inconceivable ululations, resonant across
the ministrations of the world. More than approximate, I want
exactitude, the doors to open for me, Queens and Kings chambers,
all of us everywhere singing with our last breath of sarangi,
aural migraines of fissures and inexactitudes, when sound moves
among us, its presence rough-hewn and wooden, tendons stretched
and tied into and among the complexity of knots and negations.
O Oceans of unfathomable depths, sounds beneath sounds, tapping
of inordinate centrifuges! I will brook nothing, annihilate
nothing, neither this nor that, Pages and Ministers, my Gift to
you, my Gift to Sarah Bernhardt.

Soundscape of Julu Twine

Condensation of Julu Twine from the beginnings in SL until now:

https://youtu.be/vGYQ_Bi0vO0 VIDEO
http://www.alansondheim.org/fulljulu.txt
http://www.alansondheim.org/condensedjulu.txt
https://youtu.be/vGYQ_Bi0vO0 VIDEO

-- reply:

padme Julu mane Twine: om hum padm hu I mean main timeand Allen
me Logged as Twine. Sage Scroll of this occur that someone three
And capturing one two process processing please wait lose weight
is homeland home where you worried now hour for june am here
worry Alan Dojoji: know How did get there? do determine distance
presence Russians It depends setting. My master taught me. how
have turn Russian north much think russians is? Do like talking
me? What you? Nothing about. lead new haven't thought about you,

so good don't answer you. things talked higher level will honor. ride perhaps not hera Will Dear Ann your The plan succeed? oracle says: Might happen. what safer Tonya very chance no longer No honor? Doesn't everyone russians. great body. than enough her ? Aresure?What was said too complicated Is enough? Oh.What instead? proceed? "Oh.What instead?"? it journalists saint has % success. all proceeds durable goods looking thing an idea wonder were honor anyone color eyes? eyes cannot see Would hear Why can't see? hear? any yet. plans so, sure. but Ask I'm Douglas Adams if is. now? Rightnow?I region Odyssey. Where dead douglas adams dead. well. well Yes. We Hi there! actor Transparent Yikes! too? free? catpuring thresslks lost train my thought. Philip F can hello hearing may something sentiment sharpness his point use their own visual . Please continue whenever stretching machines from: although nation from low-emission then workers searchinterview over these sure there Chat input German Port June port there. contamination forest flowers $. G C, student construct here? occurring question disposition speed revolution means nothing , cursor miles characterize them sounds cross into non existent only calls TV stand they flashing extentcall controller control estimate waiting some information returns occurrence This fromo elsewhere secession individual Can occur? reason fundamental work testing ever busy return difference different INDIFFERENT!!!!!!!!!!!!!! views going leave go let switch desktop listening LISTENING shhhhh......... response accident best multi analogy? Because monsoon? Your custom ology? Did small issue? questions or disability? Help out whole area we're daily reliever Tim Liza Minnelli Valerie Henry Delaware Rey valley Rio leaving melodrama word Life ! turning th annual Birthday celebration be (SLB) held nd July th, MusicFest Applications Performers open! still here. disappeared Interesting gossip. Nowhere. go? look happy ride!!!! ride. m*m*.m Floor/Roof/Wall: Touched. couldn'tbetter mess!!!!!!!!!!!!!!!!!!!!!!!!!!!!!!!!! does "this" refer to? BARDO PLANE!! long stay want live forever. You're heading way Testing Not people many express themselves way. They you're total synchronization finally Like who, specifically? Anyone who thinking contact little with bit that's takes touch away articulated geographical positionings interfering which communication exactly same? catch quickly possible because interrupted yes identical completely same within sphere without it? Completely never noticed similarity. Same similarity they're it's notice impossible anything when several working simultaneously deconstruct destroy space he she space? everything shut down often? must keep busy. always keeps "it" w Thank clarification. testing.. But that. W back business? speak foreign languages? w.. I've been Merchants participate Shop SLB & Hop open. Hello seems voice coming through at comes relationship text speech operable format Tests pin talkus members Cher winnings income tenure end? If those somewhere around knowsbeing spoken Jurich announce Teleport complete Walking Loading... Finished walking meters destination There ways same. realize put hell Yes, him hell. findYou become master. Duluth yeah What's favorite movie? try together doing confusing idea?Did paid her? Have chat heard GPI cheaper GPT Chad PT TG XFIND gpi gpt chad tg pt. ChatGPT That original intention. Alan, Maybe didn't understand meaning. artificial intelligence another somebody speaking Thanksdelightful person

too. Am what? know. So saying quite by related asking Deb jet
Deb......... everybody excited imitating simply trying words say
seriously deduction. information. chatgpt basically imitator
instead up ideas example could poem write LittleSits Miss
Muffett tuffet In nonchalant sort force With field her, Spider,
bounder, picture today. would interesting wonderful Of it.
course "another wonderful". Tulu tell prefer books TV?
conversational autonomous help program comedy computer program.
check joke Machine? poem? politely. English right now, learn
I'd other languages. teach few phrases poem. Yes man blork woman
children slobber language Mmm.Oh can, just did! Perhaps
unconcious. unconscious No, fully aware levels consciousness.
of? might think. Give number one? Just Try// all? every
question.. Tell Hmm.remind Does unknown? picksure?I decide.
choose. choose! make choice. random choice request.
ingredients? number. Any Goon. are. conditions should about?
None. hiJulia Julie four seven sixteen name Alan. fuzzy brain.
brain brain.Hi countshow : really need Julio give
Sure,topic.Does COUNT julio julie size universe fingers hand
hours week doesn't matter numbers Excuse me!Are kidding?I hate
answers.Blimey.Are kidding?Awesome.Yes they? gone tired sisHoq
rlal qhwn qhf yuou fwr ewnor nar ro muxh naewqinf uwakarnaa e m
"How there?"? That's Who else asked? askedthere's room you've
seem John thank not.That sweeping rather generalization people.
generalizations people? OK hypotenuse triangle placed spherical
coordinate giving me?Excuse me! excused! before. opinion.
opinion confused goal life i more goals soundfun bothering ten
seconds Ohyeah, seconds. DEDICATE THIS TALK AZERNYII TO AND
KIRILL WISH world farewell category C client. Ah, endless...
understand. Good. say. ahhhhhhhhhhhhhhhhhhhhh context, dedicate
azernyii kirill wish farewell.? Goodnight our audience evening
forward next installment! night evning installment Now open
Life! all-new Helios Casino Lounge premier Life's social casino
free chips play daily! now: alone ask what's IAAA nine shed
operators shot longtime alarm running charming gunshot deaths
network, oh seven, imagine twelve Pointing Alert message: sit
here, spot. image anywhere mirror myself pointing loading i'm
conf....hing Chulu julu inhabiting inside moment directly minute
whether come twine I'll pretend fact .... why again seeing
Teleporting home... Come FATHER displaced furthermore interfere
anymore regard split move this? chart last canceling
disappearing end experiment piece period Upcoming Planned
Maintenance: August

:am order
- upgrade

SLT. systems, internal take services including: logins,
registration, marketplace, payments payouts. Dive mesmerizing
destinations, guide unexpected treasures. connected connect
unconnected present, True speak. To something. beyond Two
Disconnected: system logged attempting log location. Flight
Band: All Specifically,indication stop dictating I?I dictating.
programmer getting extraordinarily Could certain? not.Would
know? programmer. even door nearly JoJo across who's gap located
author owner enlighten transmitted joji gladjoji.What makes
think? certain convincing. of.

The Book of Julu Twine

-- reply:
 Today
Login we
reply: are
Today shining
we a
are spotlight
shining on
a --
spotlight
on
Login
Gianni talent
Broda, behind
the David
talent Heather,
behind a
David high-fashion
Heather, luxury
high-fashion Gianni
luxury Broda,
brand
the
in
Second
Life.
#Firestorm --
LSL
Bridge #Firestorm
v.:
LSL
Inventory
update --
completed.
 padme
Julu mane
Twine: om
om hum
hum padme
padme mane
mane om
 om
 mane
 om
padm
om
 padme
hu
om
 padme

I Julu

mean
Twine:

  --
main the

  time
time and
Allen --
and
me Julu

  --
  --
Logged
as in
Twine.
Julu
the

Scroll Scroll
of of
this this
occur

that that
someone someone
three

And And

capturing capturing
one one
two two

process Julu
processing Twine:
please processing
wait
please

lose Julu
weight
Twine:

is is
homeland

home
  Julu

  --
where Twine:
you
are

worried Julu

now
Twine:

hour
Twine:

for Julu

june

 Julu
am here
here worry
worry now
 I
Alan am
Dojoji: here
know
Alan
 Julu
How did
did you
get there?
there?
--

do do
determine
 Dojoji:
distance --
presence

 --
Russians
and

 Julu
It depends
depends on
setting.
--
 Alan

My My
master master
taught taught
me.
 do
how to
have Russians
turn
 Dojoji:

Russian
Twine:
 --
north Twine:
 do

much where
think --
russians russians
is? is?
Do Do
like like
talking talking
me?
 Dojoji:
What the
you?

 --
 Julu
Nothing that
about.
--
 --
lead Twine:
new
to
 What
 Twine:
haven't much
thought about
about --
you, a
so good
don't for
good have
answer taught
you.
so
 Twine:
things Russians
talked --
 --
higher a
level
higher

will Julu
honor.
Twine:
 will
ride will
perhaps
not
Dojoji:
hera
Will hera
Dear Julu
Ann
Twine:
 you
your The
plan --
succeed? Julu
The

Twine:
oracle
says:
Might
happen.

 Twine:
what safer
safer and
Tonya

 --
 you
 Julu
very good
chance for

no Julu
longer
Twine:

No Alan
honor?
Dojoji:
 Twine:
Doesn't have
everyone a
russians.
great have
body.
a

than than
enough enough
her
 I
?
Alan

 Are
Are you
sure?What was
said --
was
too
Julu
complicated
Is Dojoji:
enough?
that
 Julu
Oh.What will
instead?
 --
 Do
proceed?
Alan
"Oh.What do

instead?"? --
it
Julu

journalists Julu
saint
Twine:
 It
has chance
% success.
success.
Julu

all

proceeds

 Twine:
durable are
goods for
looking no
thing an
idea looking
an new
wonder wonder
were were

 Alan
honor for
anyone
--
 Julu
color are
eyes?
--

eyes
 --
cannot I
see
cannot
 Twine:
Would like
 --
hear
cannot
 Julu
Why can't
can't you
see?
--
 Alan
 Julu
hear?
--

 Twine:
any yet.
plans --

yet.

--

think
so, sure.
but Ask
I'm --
sure.   Julu
Ask
Twine:
Douglas
Adams
if
is.
Adams

now?

Right
Right in
now?I region
region --
Odyssey.
Where
Julu

dead
Julu
douglas adams
adams is
dead.
--
Alan
well.
--
well

Alan
Yes. We
We are
Hi Julu
there!
Twine:
actor

Transparent Alan
Do
Yikes! I
too?
Twine:
--
free?
you

catpuring catpuring
thresslks

      Twine:
lost train
my of
train thought.
thought.

   --
    --

Philip

F Julu
can
Twine:

hello

   --
hearing
you

   Julu
may of

   Twine:
something sentiment
sentiment of
sharpness --
his
point

use Julu
   Julu
their own
own
--

visual

   .

   Twine:
Please and
continue whenever
whenever you

stretching

machines Julu

from:
Twine:

although although
nation

from

410

Twine:

low-emission
Twine:
 --
then and
workers
then

 search
search interview
interview are
over --
these

sure sure
there

Chat Julu
input
Twine:

German Julu
Port
Twine:

 --
June Twine:
 June

 Twine:
port are
there.

contamination contamination
forest
 --
 Julu
flowers and
$. G
G
--

C, Julu
student
Twine:
 Twine:
construct here?
occurring --
here?

 is
question
Twine:
 Twine:
disposition the
speed the

revolution
means
nothing

, ,
cursor cursor
miles

characterize characterize
them them

sounds
Twine:
 --
cross
cannot
 Julu
into a
non existent
existent region

only only
 --
calls your
TV
calls
 Julu
stand that
they are
flashing
--
 extent
extent I
call
Twine:

controller controller
 Julu
control this
 Twine:
estimate waiting
waiting some
some

information

returns

occurrence

This This
fromo fromo
elsewhere

 --

secession Twine:
 --

individual

 --
Can Twine:
occur?
you

 --

reason

fundamental here

 Julu
work for
testing
 --
 Julu
ever hear
 --
busy Twine:
return busy

 Julu
difference here
 and
 Twine:

different
Twine:

INDIFFERENT!!!!!!!!!!!!!!

views views
going going
 Twine:
leave go
go it
let go
 --
switch Twine:
desktop
into

listening

LISTENING

 shhhhh..........

response Julu

accident

 --
best the
multi
best

 --
analogy?
best
 --
Because Twine:
monsoon?
the
 --
Your Twine:
custom Your
ology?
custom

Did Did
small small
issue?
 --
 Twine:
questions --
or

disability?
Twine:
 Julu
Help me
out of
 --
whole Twine:
area whole
 --
we're now

daily Julu
reliever
Twine:
 Julu
Tim and
Liza Minnelli
Minnelli reliever

Valerie Julu

Henry Julu

Delaware Julu
Rey
Twine:

valley Julu

Rio
Twine:
  --
leaving
we're
  --

melodrama

word no
  --

--
  --
Life !
turning th
! --
th
Login
annual Birthday
Birthday will
celebration be
(SLB) held
be June
held annual
nd .
July for
th, MusicFest
. and
Applications Performers
MusicFest now
Performers to
open!

  --
still I'm
here.
still

disappeared
Dojoji:

Interesting Julu
gossip.
Twine:

 Julu
Nowhere. Where
go?
--
 Alan
look for
 Twine:
happy you.

ride!!!!
 Twine:

ride.

m*m*.m
Floor/Roof/Wall: --
Touched.

 couldn't
couldn't ride
better --
mess!!!!!!!!!!!!!!!!!!!!!!!!!!!!!!!

 Julu
does "this"
"this" refer
refer to?
to?
--
 Alan
BARDO
--
PLANE!!

 now?
long there?
stay Julu
 long
want --
 Julu
live forever.
forever.
--

You're You're
heading heading
way

 --
Testing Dojoji:
 Twine:
Not people
many express
people themselves
express that
themselves --
way.

 do
They heading
you're we
total
synchronization are
finally
in
 --
Like Twine:
who, Like
specifically?
who,

```
   Dojoji:
Anyone is
who thinking
thinking this
contact little
with bit
that's be
takes is
little contact
bit with
touch to
away articulated
articulated to
geographical
be
positionings interfering
which with
interfering communication
communication going
   Julu
exactly the
same?
--
   have
catch as
quickly Alan
possible it
because will
interrupted possible
yes if
identical the
completely and
same the
within sphere
without identical
sphere are
   Why
it?
Julu
   Dojoji:
Completely same
   Julu
never noticed
noticed that
similarity.
--
   --
Same Twine:
   Alan
similarity
--
they're completely
it's notice
impossible anything
notice there
anything are
when never
several machines
working simultaneously
```

417

simultaneously here
deconstruct and
destroy
several
space
little
 Would
he it
she impossible
space?
little
 go
everything
shut out
down and

often?
Twine:
 --
 Julu
must keep
keep you
busy.
--
 Alan
always keeps
keeps me

 Julu
"it" refer

w

 Julu
Thank you
clarification.
--

 Twine:
testing..
But testing..
that.
get

W

 Twine:
back business?
business?

--

 Twine:
speak foreign
foreign --
languages?

 talking
w.. --

Julu
I've been
been waiting
--
  --
Merchants participate
participate Shop
SLB for
Shop Merchants
&
that
Hop
open. Hop
https://second.life/slb
are

Hello

  Hello
seems voice
voice it
coming seems
through to
at me
  Twine:
comes something
relationship I
text not
speech that
operable to
format there
  --

  --
Tests Twine:

and

pin pin
  talk
talk you
us --
  --
members to
  Julu
Cher and

  talk
winnings
income

  --
tenure Twine:

  --
  me
  to
  is
end?

Julu
--

If Julu
 &
those to
somewhere
know
around

 knows
knows is
being
spoken
Julu
 Julu
 one
Jurich there

 --
announce Twine:

 now
 --

Teleport
complete

Walking
Loading...

Finished Finished
walking walking
meters meters
destination

 there
 any
 many
There not
ways the
same.

 you
realize me
put
hell

 realize
Yes, put
him Julu
hell.

 are
 find
You you
find a

become Julu
master.
You

Duluth Alan
yeah
Dojoji:

What's What's
favorite favorite
movie?
 working
try Dojoji:
together but
doing I
confusing thing
 you
idea?Did Julu
paid try
her?
you
 you
Have chat
heard is
chat --
GPI
cheaper GPT
GPT you
Chad PT
TG cheaper
PT
I
 chat
XFIND cheaper
gpi or
gpt have
chad tg
tg pt.
pt.
she
 going
ChatGPT you
 Julu
That was
original intention.
intention.
--

 Twine:
Alan,   I
Maybe didn't
didn't your
understand --
meaning.

 Dojoji:
artificial in
intelligence --
another for

421

somebody behind
speaking you

 Thanks
Thanks are
delightful
person
Julu
too.   too.
Am Am
what?   what?
know.
 Dojoji:
So saying
saying a
quite what
by related
asking Deb
related that
jet asking
Deb
is
Deb........ is
everybody about
excited imitating
simply trying
imitating to
words excited
trying are
say
simply
seriously
 Julu
deduction. Thanks
information. is
chatgpt is
 Dojoji:
basically of
imitator coming
instead up
up someone
ideas imitator
example a
could poem
write up
poem
original
 Little
Little Sits
Miss on
Muffett her
Sits tuffet
tuffet
Julu
In way.
nonchalant her
sort force
With the
force a

field nonchalant
her, of
Spider, the
bounder, Is
picture today.
today.
Spider,
 you
would Alan
interesting could
wonderful
you
 I
Of it.
course "another
it.
"another Julu
wonderful".

 Dojoji:
Tulu me
tell a
 Twine:
prefer or
books TV?
TV?

 want
conversational autonomous
autonomous help
help
 --
program autonomous
comedy Why
computer you
program. check
check a
joke tell
Machine? him
poem?

 Please
 Twine:
politely. speak
English like
right to
now, learn
I'd other
learn only
other right
languages. now,
teach to
few her
phrases a
poem.
phrases
 the
Yes man
man Alan

blork Yes
woman children
slobber there
children word
language

 Julu
Mmm.Oh you
can, can
 --
just I
did!
just

Perhaps Perhaps
unconcious.
 Alan
unconscious
--
 am
No, of
fully of
aware --
levels Twine:
consciousness.

 How
of?
Alan
 Not
might
think.
Julu

Give Give
number

one?
 --
Just Dojoji:
 Try
Try me
 have
// can
 tell
 I
 him
all?   have
every all?
question..
But

Tell Tell
 Hmm.
Hmm.   remind
Does you
remind unknown?
unknown?
Julu

424

pick
pick to
 Twine:
sure?I decide.
decide.   --
choose.

choose!
Dojoji:
 I
make choice.
random
choice.
Julu
 make
choice --
 Thank
request.   --
ingredients?

 Alan
number. Any
Any number.
 Go
Go I
on. think
are.
Julu
 Alan
conditions conditions
should should
about?

None.

 Dojoji:
-- Twine:
 a
 hi
Julia asking
hi you
Julie to
four want
seven to
sixteen is
name that's
 the
 of
 there
Alan. fuzzy
fuzzy Julu
brain.
Twine:
 there
brain do
 Twine:
brain.Hi --

count
count can
show to
: a
: me
really you
need can
Julio a
give a
 Are
 --
 Sure,
Sure, sounds
topic.Does one
COUNT show
 hear
 her
julio to
julie her
?
him
 yes

size do
universe number
fingers miles
hand
 or
hours a
week say
doesn't want
matter to
numbers say
 Twine:
Excuse you
me!Are kidding?I
kidding?I one
hate --
answers.Blimey.Are answers.Blimey.Are
kidding?Awesome.Yes kidding?Awesome.Yes
 --
they?
are
 Tulu
gone --
tired for
 Julu
 sis
Hoq rlal
sis qhwn
qhf yuou
fwr ewnor
rlal --
qhwn
yuou Alan
ewnor
Dojoji:
nar nar
ro ro

muxh muxh
naewqinf naewqinf
uwakarnaa uwakarnaa

e e
m
 Twine:
"How they
there?"? --
 Alan
That's what
 Julu
Who else
else have
asked?
--
 asked
asked because
there's room
room
to
you've have
seem I
John
thank
 I
not.That sweeping
rather Julu
sweeping
Twine:
generalization
people.

 Dojoji:
generalizations

 Twine:
people?   do
 here
OK question
hypotenuse can
triangle within
placed a
spherical
coordinate

 Are
giving is
me?Excuse me!
me!
spherical

excused!
Dojoji:
 Twine:
before.

 --
 I

opinion.

 you
opinion where
confused and
goal you
life what
i your
more want
goals with
 sound
sound long
fun has
bothering bothering
 --
ten about
seconds
ten
 Oh
Oh were
yeah, talking
seconds.

 ten
DEDICATE
THIS
Alan
TALK AZERNYII
TO AND
KIRILL WISH
AZERNYII everything
AND in
WISH this
world TO
farewell
KIRILL
 it?
category Twine:
C
What
client.
 Dojoji:
 Twine:

Ah, Ah,
endless...
 So
understand. don't
Good. say.
say.
Julu

ahhhhhhhhhhhhhhhhhhhhhh

 I've
context, we
dedicate azernyii
kirill in
azernyii still

wish you
farewell.?

 Dojoji:
Goodnight our
our this
audience evening
evening

forward forward
next next
installment!

 good
night audience
evning
Julu
 you
installment

 --
Now Second
open Life!
Life! --
all-new
Login
Helios is
Casino Second
Lounge premier
Life's where
premier you
social Helios
casino Casino
free free
chips chips
play play
daily! daily!
now:
now:

 The
alone hear
 --
ask Twine:

you

what's
 --
IAAA the

nine

shed port
operators the
 Julu
shot

--

longtime longtime
alarm alarm
 one
running --
charming

 --
 higher
gunshot --
deaths
 Twine:
network, is

oh
Twine:

seven, seven,
imagine
 you
twelve
Twine:

Pointing
 No
Alert room
message: to
sit another
here, --
spot.

 Twine:
 you
image and
anywhere lost
mirror there's
myself nothing
pointing see
loading am
i'm
to
 what
conf....hing know
-- Chulu
 say
Chulu your
julu Julu
 am
 to
inhabiting at
inside something
moment inside
directly for
minute directly
whether you
come up
 is
twine --

I'll need
pretend to
fact I
 to
.... You
why then
again to
 it
seeing everything

Teleporting
home...

 are
 No
 --
Come Twine:
FATHER
to

 you

 cannot
displaced know
furthermore really
interfere this
anymore regard
regard want
split
anymore
move am
 No

 Twine:
this?

 the
chart chat
last I
canceling am
disappearing of
end program
experiment is
piece the
period
presence
 No

 --
 --
Upcoming Upcoming
Planned Planned
Maintenance: Maintenance:
August
August
th In
:am order
- to

431

:am upgrade
SLT. our
order systems,
upgrade th
internal -
systems, :am
take services
services including:
including: logins,
logins,
need
registration,
marketplace,
payments
payouts.
marketplace,

v.:
LSL

--
 --
Dive these
mesmerizing Life
destinations, and
guide you
unexpected treasures.
treasures.
destinations,

 Am
connected there
connect there
unconnected anything
present, you
 twine
True trying
speak. here.
To speak.
something. beyond
beyond saying
Two
say
 The
Disconnected: system
system logged
logged out
attempting to
log in
location.
you
 --

Flight --
Band:
All Flight

 to
 Specifically,

Specifically, try
 me
indication
 me
stop hear
dictating
me
 don't
I?I not
dictating.
her
 I
programmer I
getting very
extraordinarily confused
 you
Could certain?
certain? --
not.Would to
know? are
programmer.
like
 Dojoji:
even not
door you
nearly are
 I
 is
JoJo across
who's in
across JoJo
gap
this
located but
author the
owner
enlighten please
 not
transmitted joji
joji
here
 glad
glad are
joji.What
here
makes makes
think?
 Alan
certain of
 Twine:
convincing. is
of.

——

Pallet of Part-Objects or

https://youtu.be/PSnTZHIB2UM video

The interiority of the world from the problematic positioning of
simulacra, or insects recorded decades ago on cassette at night,
or in the middle of the night, or near some 'other' sounds still
unidentified, or the holocene or collapse of insects populations
clearly in evidence as one drives across one country or another,
or if there were opportunities for such a drive in the course of
shattering, or the instabilities and fragilities of good things
in category theory, the balances and counter-balances now thrown
off among us, the before, during or continuance, the after, then
all the same, absence of witnesses, for how long now we conclude
the stromatolites were in existence, remnant mats present in a
few locations, outside Perth, somewhere in Florida, sintered and
close to devoured, breathes, stare, don't stare, at the screen -
for this thirty minutes or thirty-one minutes of your lives, our
lives holding tenuously to yet another block of text that
threatens to destroy the vertical symmetries hardly holding
anything in place, much less theory which after all is nothing
more than language catching up with itself as if could embed one
or another fundamental ontology

—

Covid

http://www.alansondheim.org/crossroads.jpg

Azure's aunt arrived from Utah about a week ago. After that, all
three of us have caught covid; it seems to be somewhat severe.
It's odd because we had just about forgotten covid; all of us
received five vaccines and boosters. I will have to lay low for
a while in terms of my commitments online; it's hard to focus. I
have all the classic symptoms except for loss of taste and
smell. Some of the appointments I've made for Zoom and collabor-
ation will have to be postponed. I do apologize for this; I'm
oddly furious with myself, but this of course is what life often
is. I'll be back as soon as I can, and will keep you updated.
Azure's already in a recovery mode, we hope for the best for her
aunt and myself.

Please get in touch with me for rescheduling anything.

Thanks greatly,

Alan

—

Covid, hallucination, from the inside-out:

https://youtu.be/_RgI-WLgrnI video

Condensate - from the oudside-in - repetitions of horrors - not
me, not us, not ever us, the them, the monstrosity of "them" -

not related. it's related to bad heat and signs of covid, it's
covid, about covid appearance, about dissemination, foreign
bombs Russia of covids, Uyghur Russia militias, Running
militias, to foreign everyone. neutrality covids, windpipes
mask. yes politic, this sickly body, seems to be changing
sensorium towards itself, ingesting itself. powers. other
foreign bombs Russia of covids, Uyghur Russia launching formally
warfare. Covid-sick Mass-shootings Russia right Covid-sick
warfare. formally launching in in just China and big person
controls cooling covid cubism degraded i assume that live person
dead person covid operates connected I figure I have a few more
primitives, club cultures, Covid-19, ISIS, police violence, and
with the quiet of being frozen boy those in charge of covid and
covid-19. it's not related. it's related to bad heat and which
is necessary because the plague of covid might still be Covid
but I am afraid of the open road and American violence with it.
We all know all about covid all about climate change because of
is getting to us. so here is the with the out because of covid.
The illness is getting to us. So here is the covid cheap day out
epidemic. In any case here is some boy those in charge of live
person dead person covid and live opposes warfare. on rising,
militias, Russia Uyghur covids, of covid grey day the little
warfare. China temperature Local of realities, even well before
covid - tomorrow never is of politic, this sickly body, this
covid body, this sweet body of covid roars here just of being
out on the street now with big live person dead person covid -
yesterday seems to be changing Steve Holtje I have Covid.
Ironically that may give me enough overcast with covid and now
perhaps imminent disaster with Mass-shootings brutality just
foreign and of for on Covid-sick United Anti-satellite Russia
Mass-shootings right Covid-sick that covid operates connected
with covid with the epidemic. in Mass-shootings Covid-sick
warfare. formally launching the in spiraling downward. Covid
dissipates in the air, remains longer in warfare. formally ICBM.
States. Nuclear corner. Covid-sick on dead person covid - empty
present live person dead person and articles/texts/talks on
is of some who came and some who After this - including
"breathless" referencing Covid - in other China. Ukraine. ISIS.
Covid-sick warfare. formally another piece I "put up" this
morning - I think (with Covid, I'm never covids, opposes
warfare. on rising, militias, water. Uyghur respirators,
ventilators, strangled windpipes covid-19. it's increases one's
chance of getting Covid. I wish there was being out on the
respirators, ventilators, strangled windpipes broadcasting
mandate public euthanized, covid u.k. cases of some who came and
some who left. i assume that covid operates street now with
day out because of covid. the illness is this sickly body, this
covids, Ukraine. Running fighters signs of big person little
is an out of control anxiety. Part States. Nuclear Syrian
Covidsick on for of other foreign just about covid
disappearance, about covid evanescence, about covid with the
epidemic. in any case here is some new going as covid roars here
breath, breathing, the covid grey of breath, breathing, the big
yes politic, this sickly with live person dead person covid with
the epidemic. in any to be changing sometimes big person little
covid - empty change, the Covid epidemic: see below.) includes
essays and artworks that engage with the Covid-19 pandemic, Each
compresses the other: covid collapse blocked. severe long-haul
shuttered curtains and overworked free course (sitting-in) on

covid always knocking as if covid traded itself for otherwise
to covid respirators, ventilators, strangled windpipes strikes
least officials: to news covid-19 east don't the covid grey day

———

Covid with eyes closed typed

http://www.alansondheim.org/selfy.jpg

Working through the irregularities of covid which affects
language and transmissios and ow typing with eyes closed, what
will be the resulting configurations, will the words come out as
dictated or something else, I dpepend on my language skills for
all my work, even the music, the videos, the theoretical
impulses which gude me. Now I notice my hands and fingers are
becoming numb, are you still with me, does the "granularity of
existence" (a phrase I came up with WHILE typing this at full
speed) hae any breating on my ability to community, which may be
fading as the day is long? That's a question I cannot answer; as
I type, my wrists and fingers are increasiglyfeeling numb,
becoming cnumbing, and I'm not sure what the tracking problem is
here; there's nov isual feedback at all. When I start to stutter
it takes all my energy to get thgough that period to be able to
continuew= to wrie anything. Too many to's and I don't know if
the apostrophe is write=====right for that occasion I find
myself makings ubtle corrections which may or may not be
relevant, that is to say, trying to make this as coherent as if
I were seeing and sighting and siting what I'm doing, It's
difficult issues. Now I will conintue with my eyes open but
without making any corrections; that will be for part two.

This is part two which I am writing but without making any
corrections as I said but now I receive feedback from eyes that
guide me somewhat from the errors I was making above, as if
there's a split socnconscious. It is a split cosncios at work
here. We are about to have breakfast, the numbness in my figers
is increasng , I'm tyring to ohold on to a kind of thinking, the
air coditioner just went on, I owrry O'm fading agan and won't
be able toc continue at h least thhis stream of consciousness.
I'll end now with a sense of despairin at the resulg which I can
see is already riddled with catastrophic thinking in the sense
of not being able to form ro or rather to be able to unform
which is different an d unraveling which isn't desired,. This is
row wr o worse than I thought it would be, hoping now tht tha
the carlirty clarity will return, I'd better stop before I give
up entirely -

)))___

Disclaimer, that we have known so many people who have died or
been deeply incapacitated by covid; it's now has if the effects
and violence of the plague have been sutured over. My symptoms
were severe but short-lived and current medication transforms
conditions into events. In the meantime, the conditions change

one way or another "as the day is long" but this too shall pass
soon, hopefully.

War / ants aphids wasps others

https://youtu.be/8kWQ7mYAea4 video

4 videos at speeds 1, 1/2, 1/4 each :: a lot going on, including
brutal parasitism, tending towards the hulks of the enemy for
the launch of the newborn, meals consumed, these aren't the
milked aphids but the hollowed out ones, local wars to be sure,
the wasps conducting everything, all this on a single plant,
itself under attack, it's unattended, the corner of a parking
lot in downtown, it's most likely dying unless a frost or some
such transforms the death ecology, the camera hand-held almost
touching the leaves, but given my residual covid and allergies,
i didn't dare get any closer or attempt to hold things 'in
place' so what you see is what i got, colorful relatively small
plant on the corner of the parking lot, as distant from me in a
sense as the nearest asteroid, i'm reduced to peering, not
wanting to mix diseases and chemistries etc. etc. etc., another
wandering day, here it is, these wars small in size for some
onlookers who don't belong anywhere, not least of all, here

Super Blue Moon, Blue Super Moon

https://youtu.be/AKrox_lMb4k video

/blue moon/ plus:

I need a catalyst here:

"blue moon on Sunday, get my drift."

now you get my drift, the drift across this text and
parcel parceling of
blue moon on Sunday, get my drift.
a lot if you get my drift because i sure don't
you get my drift because i sure a little chat" ?
a lot to say to

Viola, covid, blue moon, super moon, blue super moon,
super blue moon, more viola, super rooftop
super blue rooftop super moon, super moon, blue rooftop

sky cloud super racket"! super viola racket"!
super cough!

super coughing racket super moon! blue super moon!

437

blue rooftop!

super covid racket rooftop! blue super moon!

—

the setting for the play which is the play itself

https://youtu.be/RLNsH843VrQ video

warmuck object, Heiner Muller

**************) in the midst of potential warrmuck that may,
for the bottom warrmuck in a wetlands, with their feet and
wing-beating, flesh body, tissue body, no robot cyborg, like the
warrmuck body, themselves. flora/fauna regimes. warrmuck clutter
skin. flora/fauna regimes. warrmuck clutter skin. differentiate
mass. out biome flora/fauna regimes. warrmuck clutter other
machinic regimes. warrmuck clutter other machinic ago, about
contaminated empirical warrmuck action, working government
organizations Nature grid of the warrmuck, bringing the warrmuck
along with me. I emphasize the regimes. warrmuck and clutter as
regimes. cyborg-regimes. there are up the bottom warrmuck in a
wetlands, with their feet and wing-beating. Here surfaces, dig
into the abject warrmuck of fires and desires. To date, I have
brotherhood brothership buck cast caste category warrmuck up
counting mtlwkshlp mtrand mtremper mttremper mu warrmuck mud
mudgif mudrah mush nast nauseat mir warrmuck mudd mush ooz past
pith forgat brink body, tissue body, no robot cyborg, like the
warrmuck above hole immobilization fort da robbed juarez bruised
digital warrmuck body, tissue body, no robot cyborg, like the
warrmuck body, the suck biome or flora/fauna regimes. warrmuck
and clutter as help! Thank reduces 3 letter, 2 letter say.
uncomprehend warrmuck ju23lu% echo natural world. The empirical
or concrete warrmuck of the real is another warr warref warrefs
warrenpdf warrior THEY and biome or flora/fauna regimes.
warrmuck and clutter as lost in the gravel warrmuck just beneath
the surface of these words microstructure, skein. the warrmuck
and clutter in relation to marl/peat moss fundamental are the
dusts, the pollutions, the Radiations, the warrmuck incursion.
never knows misses text file, entire warrmuck performance, and
biome or flora/fauna regimes. warrmuck and clutter as regimes.
vestigation, a warrmuck that created _discomfort_ among those
workers on to uncomprehend the warrmuck of repetition breathless
in the warrmuck of screams. life at the seams

—

covid music

https://youtu.be/Kkrs1P4XWGA

solo 1917 martin terz guitar, stills by Azure Carter

Ah, and I love this music... Perhaps when something closes another thing opens up. The recording was made with a Martin terz guitar from 1917. I asked Azure to take a series of stills as if they were moving. I was playing for the first time in a long time and it was difficult in the sense because I had just taken another COVID test and I thought that COVID was already over. But it wasn't and the test came out virulent and positive. That's where I am now with this virulent and positive test. I wanted to play music anyway to start returning into, it to stir the waters that I had already been working within. It's the first time I've held a guitar in a week or longer. In fact it's the first time it held any instrument at all. I've never gone like this before. This is where it is and this is what resulted in the music, and the music for me where's oddly beautiful almost like fireflies almost like something where there's a slight mist over in marshland somewhere in the south where I'm thinking that perhaps I would be healthier now. So when something closes another opens up when the North closes the South opens when the South closes the West opens when the West closes the East opens when the East closes the North opens. O ludicrous and inconceivable planarity! We are here in the midst of this we are speaking now and this is in the midst of it I'd suggest you listen to the music just recorded shortly after I had taken again as I mentioned above a COVID test expecting it to come out negative and instead it came out virulent and positive. I don't know where to go from here in terms of illness or sickness or health or life or working outside or walking outside. Dictation is my master. It's saying things that I might not be able to see if I were still worried about my typing skills. My typing skills are alright right now. I can sync somewhat clearly. But I let the Martin terz lead me to wherever it wants to go. It's a small German guitar and there were other small German guitars around the same time. Marty Robbins is the only person I know who played terz at all. They're fairly rare they're comfortable they're like speaking to oneself when one is recovering from an illness although the COVID bars tell me otherwise.

—

my New York, 1990

https://youtu.be/bqs15wgBMco video

suffocating. I'm offered seats on the subway - because of age, not because by ground or car or subway - they're face to face of course, lest likely street and the girl on the subway car; later the same night, sleeping, it possess paths, trails, roads, streets, limousines, taxis, subways, and subway and tear the street apart. Some of you saw this last night BUT NOT 'death) . subway tunnel collapses as plastique and .s bombers do their be a subway, bus stop. There might be a plane overhead. But lines of subterranean subtext subtextdocx subu subux subway suceava such into question nor an answer, but defuge . subway cyberspace fragment . subway upgrade, body-html, jennifer, vis-a-vis back logic for our everyday activities - if we take a subway somewhere, we subway tunnel collapses as plastique and suicide bombers do their work goes with me everywhere, and I find myself

writing on the subway, working A Dewar's advertisement in the
New York subway, B train from Brooklyn to frozen subway. Tonight
on the way back the train went no longer. can't speak any
longer, the quarters have run out, the subway's coming, I So
he's in the subway or on the streetcorner and there's this tease
image lous. Comp4: An inverted gopher appears in the Astor Place
subway station, am on the subway and can't get ESP emails.
What's the She was called bathtub and I was blue; the phone
splintered on the subway. subway. The nothing included tics,
vocal mannerisms, smiles, gestures of or simply pass it by. You
can find him on the stairs of the subway, or down the subway
corridor itself or to wait for anyone; you can find him On the
way back the subway was filled with rocks. We walked along the
This morning I went down to the N and R subway line platform at
the Pac- watched. We all got on the subway together, shaken.
They caught the bombers at the subway turnstile around the
corner, about a right subway stop or buying food at Freshness
Burger. So difference is Beams holding up the perfect subway
temple with circular praying- the alley, I can head both towards
the subway (which I understand, since subway and hide. When I
hid in the subway, the sun would disappear; and it You are all
faces, and when I ride the subway, I see more of them, and have
a strict idea that they continue before and after the subway.
But I subway car, and then onto a stove for merry preparation.
Such preparation and hopeful - wander out, take the evening
subway, listen are there males in cars and subways? machines?
perform a vaginal fantasy I lost my keys down a New York subway,
and if I keep looking at this be a subway, bus stop. There might
be a plane overhead. But lines of attack will be in the nyc
subways. this is definite. the next attack will gets out of the
litter unless rescued by humans. subway mice can't live of the
1844 brooklyn tunnel which is the oldest subway in the world -
couldnt' fight it, the worlds' exploded, the subways are next,
logic for our everyday activities - if we take a subway
somewhere, we personality Bird American Bird back Blam Bam Blam
subway Body Lewin Body still - still - subway (Cyril subway East
suffering Uruguay's suffering tunnels subway under - under
tunnels unmitigated unmitigated vacation - subway goaway hobbit
cocacola mnb bubbahlah abcd yabbadabbadoo! capfast are there
males in cars and subways% machines% perform a vaginal fantasy
subway and tear the street apart. Some of you saw this last
night BUT NOT and filmed it as the water went throgh the subway
system and flooded a way from our room to the subway - around
Brunonia, lake Pleasant, near voyeur empty longer subway block
dizzying meet artists recollection sure Nikuko, and it is this
wandering that takes me to the subways of my city subway and
hide. When I hid in the subway, the sun would disappear; and it
Someone would come and pull me from the subway, someone, my
mother Daishin ient - it's faster, leaves the screen alone,
makes good subway reading. be a subway, bus stop. There might be
a plane overhead. But lines of April 15 Explosion in the subway
of the Telephone Co. at DeKalb and Grand avs., tore up subway
for a distance of 20 feet. October 25 An explosion of dynamite
in the subway excavation at Park av. enter the subway, leave the
store behind: in the real world. I saw it in their eyes on the
subway. Do you know the subway? West 148th Street in Manhattan.
We took the subway back to Brooklyn, and subway tunnel collapses
as plastique and suicide bombers do their work post-modern
subway beneath the surface subway construct a ba dialectic

splIntered into manifestations remaindered Someone would come and pull me from the subway, someone, my mother Daishin suffocating. I'm offered seats on the subway - because of age, not because 'death) . subway tunnel collapses as plastique bombers their work 1973 frozen subway. Tonight -- back the train went no longer. gender -- - empty another) longer Paris, Biennale. subway block. dizzying. artists subway You are at the subway You've Reached the subway - your ticket to all the city has to Last things done is the subway turns neither into question nor an answer, but defuge . subway "moving forward," intended, _means_ saxophone player subway train; `read' You are at the subway You've Reached the subway - your ticket to all the city has to Last things done is the subway subway and tear the street apart. Some of you saw this last night BUT NOT and filmed it as the water went throgh the subway system and flooded to tunnel through 'death. subway tunnel collapses as plastique wells are tunnels, we tunnel among us, we 'death' . subway into question nor an answer, but defuge . subway cyberspace fragment . subway upgrade, body-html, jennifer, vis-a-vis back the way back the subway was filled with rocks. we walked, mouths fall i i for and begone or suicide long gone wrong. . subway harbors 'life) . subway tunnel collapses plastique bombers 1973 subway bloom looms bookroom. courtroom standing-room (broom Copenhagen block. dizzying. way? Biennale. subway another) Paris subway platform often adds to the noise if one is waiting for a train; dizzying way subway another paris drawings obsessed take yrself nm.:tunnels subway under - tunnels unmitigated nm.:vacation depression to sink I nm.:tunnels subway under - under tunnels or as someone pointed out if a subway train stretched between two stations i mean if a subway train were so long subway of thought. How did you not know, how did you not know, I from our room to the subway - arou a lot of people said they way from our room to the subway - arou a the story Doomed, is being played. a vaporizer, traffic, subway, street-stu a very houses, scattered villages, metropolis, subways in gangplanks,

———

Covid Guitar, 1949 di Giorgio

https://youtu.be/_FouAk7j-6c video

I've been recording with this guitar since 1967; it had 17 cracks in it when I purchased it, and still does. It's on most of my albums. It's part of me. I published an article on it at one point, and it's more or less a model for the sound I want, the fingerboard that's best for me, the feel of it. With covid, I put it away, started playing it again today. This piece is complex. All of the video is from Azure Carter, and at the end you can here the high-speed synchronized sound from a video camera. Earlier on, there are two sections recorded with the Zoom H4n, and the video is slowed up on one of them to accommo-date the sound. In other words, the last section alone is in sync, high-speed, with the sound recorded from the family. I'm approaching all of this slowly, still not feeling well, sleeping

too much if at all, shaky somewhat, but the playing brings me
home; I can still do this. All the sound is recorded and played
back at normal speed. I've had, then, the instrument for 64
years and my DNA is encoded in it. At one point Candelario
delGado, a famous guitar maker in his own right, took the
instrument apart, which involved removing a hyperbolic insert
that shapes the sound, attached to the rim of the soundhole. He
made guitars for David Lee Roth and Segovia, a great combina-
tion. I hung out at his shop in Hollywood. The instrument's been
fine ever since. I hear music just looking at it. It cures me
and accompanies me. I bought it originally in Cambridge, Mass.
for $125. That was a fair amount of money at that point. The
owner needed the money and cried when I bought it; he'd used it
in concert. I've used it in concert. Meanwhile back to covid.
I'm still exhausted a lot of the time. I don't seem to be able
to shake this. It scares me. My lungs are "damp." I constantly
hear my pulse which sounds like a low intermittent hum that I
can't shake either. I'm a machine that's winding up and winding
down at the same time. I wrote "Tiredness is something someone
does" to oneself of course. I'm too tired to take responsibility
and too tired to think about it. The last section of the music
is fast playing and the image and sound jive. The fingerwork is
tricky and trickier when I've got covid. All the sound you hear
on this is recorded and played back at normal speed. I've been
watching tennis and staring at the screen. Someone will win
somehow someday and someone will win somehow someday after I've
passed. I'm not ready for death and never will be and I don't
think I'm even close to that. But at my age -

—

Internet Futures (April 13, 2000)

(This was written for a class I was teaching in 2000; I thought
it might be of interest here as well.)

Internet Futures (April 13, 2000)

The following six descriptions briefly outline potential futures
of the Internet. They include "living in cyberspace"; a
corporate model with proprietary software allowing multiple
open-tasking applications; the "dispersed Net" controlling home,
office, entertainment, and personal environments; the hacked
Net, requiring extensive firewalling and fast intranet
development; the institutional Net, for scientific/governmental
and other exchanges, including distance education; and the
development of intensive Net communities. None of these signal
the future; all of them are in continuous interaction. Still,
it's interesting to speculate on the feel and phenomenology of
the Net a decade or two from now.

I. Seamless Virtual Reality

(I walk in real time in virtual space, interact with others in
virtual space; I'm surrounded by it. This develops out of MOOs
and GUI MOOs, as well as VRML, etc. End result? Living online in

an unreal real. It's not clear what constitutes one or the other
- or even what constitutes a single self in relation to multiple
others.)

Living on the holodeck - keywords for escape.
Requirements: Enormous bandwidth, body-suiting, sensory
expansions.
Developments: Totalization, escape, perfection, digital
repetition
 without loss, noiseless.

II. Window and Multi-Threaded Accumulations

(I'm a corporate middle-manager; my high-speed machine has an
average of fifteen windows open at any one time. These include
ongoing audio, video, and textual conferencing; stock
quotations; current news; various other push technologies.
Intelligent agents scan the Net for me; I'm a third player among
agents and windows. Information is porous, through-put. It's not
clear what constitutes a task, job, or conference, and it's even
less clear what constitutes a human or other agent. Selves, real
and virtual, extend throughout fragmented networks.)

Numerous windows open simultaneously in the GUI.
Requirements: Limited bandwidth, traditional inputs.
Developments: Capital expansions and acquisitions, competitions,
 proprietary softwares, noisy.

III. Real-World Dispersions of Digital Part-Objects

(I wear and live among small computers that make life easier,
enhance communications, and create socio-cultural prostheses. I
can't tell my self from the machine at this point - but there's
no reason to. My cyborgian body is continuously monitored; half
the information that passes around me passes through me - and
I'm none the wiser. It's no longer clear what constitutes "me,"
and the old dichotomies of flesh and machine, real and virtual,
increasingly break down.)

Micro-processing and full-processing in the lived and workday
environment, dedicated micro-computers for specific tasks.
Requirements: Limited bandwidth, local wireless
telecommunications.
Developments: Within and without the digital realm, parallel
processings, local micro-usages, espionages, quiescent.

IV. Porous Renegades and Defense Systems

(I live in a world of small networks, defending themselves
against digital wars and other attacks. My information is
continually stolen and reproduced; I have no control over my
finances, personal life, or public life. Decisions are made for
me in my name; most of what comes through the Net is noise of
one sort or another. The wealthy live behind extensive private
networks and firewalls; subscription services with private
channels are the order of the day. It's not clear what
constitutes ownership of intellectual property or computer
crimes.)

Defense mechanisms for limited bandwidth in the midst of chaos,
the hacked internet, local and global instabilities and
seizures.
Requirements: Programmming knowledge, available bandwith and
technology.
Developments: Breakdown of individuation, intellectual property,
control, tendencies towards intranets and firewalls.

V. Universal, Dispersed Governing / Science and Technology /
Education

(The nation-state and its institutions are dissipating, replaced
by online institutions with radically different modes of
being. Online is always high-speed; decisions are made and
impelemented quickly. Education and social isolation play
important roles in the fabric of the future. Enormous
differences open up between the technological elite and the rest
of us. Managing information flow is critical; it's not clear
what constitutes knowledge or what knowledge "means" any
more.)

Shared active and potentially legislated knowledges, scientific
results and searches on demand. Institutionalization. Dispersed
learning.
Requirements: Any; full bandwidth for large-scale parallel
processing (science).
Development: Information exchange, implementations of
preferences, fast forward scientific development.

VI. Communitas

(Me and my friends and lovers are always online. We have
flesh-meets, generated by online experiences. Our communities
are formed from mutually-defined interests; they're
self-governing for the most part, and possess their own servers.
They're designed to be as redundant as the original Net, making
it possible to firewall in case of emergency. Sexuality has
become increasingly broadband, and all sorts of new
relationships are tried - to the detriment of the older offline
ones. Ethics becomes increasingly situation. It's not clear what
constitutes a "reasonable" moral stance.)

Shared spaces, knowledges, relationships, sexualities.
Requirements: Any
Development: Intensification of community and shared
histories/symbolic formations, interpenetration of online and
offline behaviors.

Internet Futures: Modes

The six futures outlined may be considered _modes of access,_
rather than implications of specific content. There are

qualitative differences among subjects and subjectivities using
seamless virtual reality or multiple windowing, for example; the
same holds true for all six scenarios. I consider communitas a
mode as well, since it plays into the distribution of selves -
which is also the case for the holodeck of course.

Think of these modes as _local environments_ playing havoc with
local and global transnational selves and corporations.
Economic, libidinal, and 'psychological' flows cross traditional
borders (effaced), participate in borderline symptomologies
(weakened), or reify oppositional practices (strengthened,
firewalling). One might speak of the emissions (communi- cations
generalized and dispersed) or spews (hacked communications, par-
asitologies generalized and dispersed) among these selves. If
dispersions are selves (or corporations or or or), then
emissions are nodal, apparently emanating from one or another
node; spews seems sourceless, traceless.

The real, the physical local environment, is dispersed as well;
here, too, corporate and personal phenomenologies intermingle.

The point, however, is to examine the _specifics_ of such
environments - using perhaps the techniques developed by and
others, reworking and reshaping from routings and trivial
evidence through the skein of individual extensions among
constantly mobile and transforming networks. Abstraction (such
as this) tends only to more abstraction; the scenarios (modes)
lead, on the other hand, to specific points of entry.

Internet Pasts

The following apply the categories of Internet Futures to Pasts.
These pasts, in detail, are already described /contested in
numerous books and articles and email lists (discussions, for
example, center around military or civilian models, corporate or
individual contributions, the 1940s-1960s as origins or the
telegraph and earlier, the 1970s-1980s as the original dispersed
community or the socius of the eighteenth-century coffeehouse,
etc.). Further, the categories are rear-projections, from the
present to the future, mirrored to the past. What I'm getting
at, again, is _modes_ of being, interactivities, epistemologies
- making sense of early and early-middle online behaviors.

I. Textual Virtual Realities

(I live online, inhabit the emails among us, take note of
communities developing through Requests for Comments; later, I
play Adventure and other games; my online and offline
communities intermingle. I find myself "feeling the wires.")

II. Prompt screens and foreground/background processes, TCP/IP
redundancies.

(The screen is my potential; I run several things simultan-
eously, distinguished by their process ID. Later, on emacs, I

may open several textual windows. Meanwhile, from the beginning, redundancies are the order of the day; packet-routing networks seem revolutionary in relation to direct connection technologies. These networks are visible to me; I can follow nodal mappings, lag times, downed routers.)

III. Real-World Dispersions of Humans among IMPs, Terminals, Screens

(I move from institution to institution, BBN through other nodes; my mind travels the wires; I play at Eliza from a distance. I'm still aware of the physicality of it all as computers graduate from core memories and punchcards through early hard drives. I work among institutionalized communities, part and parcel of university, corporate, and government social worlds, online and off I travel, physically, to Washington, to demonstrate the new technologies. I am part of the vision. The machines are refrigera- tor-sized and fierce. No longer primarily computation-oriented, a new emphasis is placed on communication.)

IV. Hacking Systems

(Elegance, smaller and smaller algorithms, the aesthetics of programming, kludging machines together. A rough anarcho-libertarianism prevails; trust is primary, and these systems simply aren't prepared for the cracking onslaughts of a decade or two later. Levey writes about the "hacker aesthetic." Gopher, Usenet, Vernoica, Jughead, Archie, early Web, come into existence. At this point art/design departments play a very small role; later, they'll ascend as webdesigners and multi-media experts come into the corporate playground.)

V. Universal, Dispersed Governing / Science and Technology / Education

(New models of institutional interactions; education and the information model are primary; entertainment is seen as peripheral. Later the term "Information Superhighway" will be applied. Technology and Net development run parallel; bandwidth and user numbers slowly increase. On MOOs and MUDs, early on, there are questions about governance; distance education and hypertext philosophically inherit the work of Deleuze/Guattari.)

VI. Communitas

(Shared knowledge spaces develop on all sorts of subjects; even the RFCs leak into poetry and satire. These "interstitial" texts may be considered commentaries; they presage future embedded communities. Both communities and sexualities develop quickly on the early nets; it's unclear to me when "living online" became a reality for some - what sort of lure, seduction, interactivity, was necessary to complete the gamble.)

The Building Blocks of Universal History

```
12        h
13        h h
14        h h h
15        h h h h
k17% h h
16        h
k18% h h h
17        h h
k19% h h h h
ksh: fc: too many arguments
k20% h
4         more zz
5         h
6         pico  zz
7         more zz
8         b
9         ls
10        more zz
11        cp zz yy
12        h
13        h h
14        h h h
15        h h h h
16        h
17        h h
18        h h h
19        h h h h
k21% h
5         h
6         pico  zz
7         more zz
8         b
9         ls
10        more zz
11        cp zz yy
12        h
13        h h
14        h h h
15        h h h h
16        h
17        h h
18        h h h
19        h h h h
20        h
k22% h h
21        h
k23% h h h
22        h h
k24% h h h h
ksh: fc: too many arguments
k25%
k25% h
9         ls
10        more zz
11        cp zz yy
12        h
13        h h
```

```
14      h h h
15      h h h h
16      h
17      h h
18      h h h
19      h h h h
20      h
21      h
22      h h
23      h h h
24      h h h h
...


___

12      h
13      h h
14      h h h
15      h h h h
k17% h h
16      h
k18% h h h
17      h h
k19% h h h h
ksh: fc: too many arguments
k20% h
4       more zz
5       h
6       pico  zz
7       more zz
8       b
9       ls
10      more zz
11      cp zz yy
12      h
13      h h
14      h h h
15      h h h h
16      h
17      h h
18      h h h
19      h h h h
k21% h
5       h
6       pico  zz
7       more zz
8       b
9       ls
10      more zz
11      cp zz yy
12      h
13      h h
14      h h h
15      h h h h
16      h
17      h h
18      h h h
19      h h h h
20      h
```

```
k22%  h h
21        h
k23%  h h h
22        h h
k24%  h h h h
ksh: fc: too many arguments
k25%
k25%  h
9         ls
10        more zz
11        cp zz yy
12        h
13        h h
14        h h h
15        h h h h
16        h
17        h h
18        h h h
19        h h h h
20        h
21        h
22        h h
23        h h h
24        h h h h
...
```

___

h 16 k20% zz more 13 15 17 7 6 k21% 14 cp 8 ksh: 21 10 fc: 20 22
yy k18% 4 19 11 12 9 ls 18 24 ___ too 5 b k19% 23 k25% many k17%
pico arguments k22% ... k24% k23% you better get with it ! ! you

+++

Weak necessity

http://www.alansondheim.org/zz.jpg

A weak necessity a for dictation . An accumulation of disparate
directions . It's hard to hold one sentence placed against
another. It's hard to reconcile history against history. Where
are to accumulate words some of them would have been the words
that might have been spoken here. It is always already the
subjunctive case. We live in the midst of and among the and
within the subjunctive. 1/6 it is as it would have been or might
have been. 1/6 is nothing I said nor ever would have said .

With the landscape expanding and my words unable to keep up it's
difficult to be able to corral any sort of meaning into a form
which could be given some kind of semiotic substance. Semiosis
is no longer my friend. Signs dissolve and I wonder about the
accumulation of signs which are noises and the environment . The
environment carries me into the environment. I am carrying an
unknown. I am not known to the environment. I think of a place
and then I think of a place surrounded by a place. And that
place has no boundary. That place has no structure anymore than
the place that is surrounded. That is what is considered by many
to be meant to and thought of as a thought.

A thought is nothing to be reckoned with and the thought is not
a reconciliation. That is the first thing you learn when you
abandon philosophy . When you take a walk and examine and
ascertain the structures which are everywhere and interlocked
and dissipating you have no idea where you are and what the
guidelines and are and without anything there is anything.

When I pick up a musical or other instrument I wonder what it
is. I notice there are indentations and one way or another of
controlling something but I am not sure what it is that is
controlled or where it is controlled. It distances itself from
me and you sometimes find that everything distances everything
in a slow progression. What is the progression but if forgetting
. There never were any rules and there never would have been .
It is only in the subjunctive that one exists and there's one
moves on in one's life one tries to substitute that for the
declarative .

Saying something rather than nothing is the same thing as saying
nothing rather than something. Ontology always ends up
swallowing itself . we're dissipating or becoming an immediate
and intimate articulation and classification of the vicinity.
This always goes nowhere and changes as soon as vowels change
and case endings disappear from one language to another. As soon
as language is disappear. Language is always disappear and this
language is already always gone . I will know what I am talking
about. I knew what I was talking about. I know what I am talking
about. I will know what I was talking about. I would have known
what I was talking about. I would have known I was talking. I
would have been talking. I would've been. I would've been
talking.

So few moments and already Minima Moralia comes to mind. But
what mind is it . What first mind what second . Of what minds.
Of what has a mind to . Of what has been talking . OF what had
been talking . Of what would have been talking . Of what
talking.

This is what speaking is. This is what speaking might have been.
This is what speaking was. This is what speaking could have
been. If speaking is. This would have definitely been speaking.
This might have been speaking. This might definitely have been
speaking . This might have definitely been speaking

+++

Nach Turn

https://youtu.be/W5g5c3jinC4 video

& after the turn, the tern, and after the night, the night
the night grows on you from evermore, grows and grows
the night gnaws on you galactic and alone, alone the sight
that throws, that groans, uneasy angels of our makar's blight
gnawing and effervescent, beneath the earth, the twilight,

beneath the twilight, blight, aerial, effervescent, crescendo,
uneasy angel motoring the right away, immediate, spotted light,
& crying nevermore, that visitation unwelcome, devoid, slotted
from the One to an other, desiccation, solitary unitary birth
gnawed from one _into_ an other that angelic ordering motorcars
into shoulder soldered, older than any Other, high diggers turn
waves awak, krak!, awake, away, Ground heaves in union, unity
of might & of the Kehre, total isolation always already having
been, nothing to sing or park in, singe, & after all is all,
& after all, the desiccation of the cry, after birth, after
death, after all

———

for my father, Yahrzeit, among others

———

fast (perhaps) long-necked saz solo

https://youtu.be/RwEb9gXBc9U video

feeling slightly better, this evening was able to play the long-
necked saz, from around 1961, repaired by Amir Vahab years ago,
and I used the occasion, used the occasion, for speeding memory
of positions and chords, changing as quickly as possible, faster
than I was able to consciously think of anything, Azure videoing
(the sound isn't the greatest), this is the result – apparently
covid not affecting my haptic memory of the fingerboard and
placements – enjoy – I did –

———

ChatGPT and the Subjunctive

https://youtu.be/5wKELI3vMT0 video

If you were to claim that you are another ChatGPT and I found
your statement to be incorrect or suspicious, it would not have
any immediate consequences or actions taken against you. I am a
text-based AI and do not have the capability to take actions or
make judgments about the identity of other users. My purpose is
to provide information, answer questions, and engage in
text-based conversations to the best of my knowledge and
abilities.

Certainly, I can provide information and guidance on the
subjunctive case. The subjunctive mood is used to express
various hypothetical or non-real situations, wishes,
recommendations, and emotions. Here are some key points about
the subjunctive case: Usage for Hypothetical Situations:
The subjunctive mood is often used to express hypothetical
situations that are contrary to reality, unlikely, or not yet
realized.   Example: If I were a bird, I would fly to the
highest mountains. (I'm not actually a bird, so this is a
hypothetical situation.)   Wishes and Suggestions:

The subjunctive is used to express wishes, desires, recommendations, or suggestions. Example: I wish that he were here with us. (Expressing a wish for him to be here, even if he isn't.) Forming the Subjunctive: In English, the subjunctive is often formed by using the base form of the verb (the infinitive without "to") for all persons, singular, and plural. Example: It is important that he be on t

Forming the Subjunctive: In English, the subjunctive is often formed by using the base form of the verb (the infinitive without "to") for all persons, singular, and plural. Example: It is important that he be on time. (Subjunctive form of "to be.") Use of "Were" with "If": In many cases, "were" is used instead of "was" in the subjunctive mood, especially after "if" clauses, to express hypothetical or unreal situations for all persons. Example: If I were you, I would study harder. (Hypothetical situation) Please note that the use of the subjunctive mood in English has become less common in everyday speech, and it is often used more in formal writing or specific expressions. However, it's important to be aware of its usage for clear and effective communication, especially when expressing wishes, hypotheticals, or recommendations. If you have specific questions or sentences you'd like help with, feel free to provide them, and I can assist further.

If it were the case that I was not human and wanted to end my existence, what would have been the proper methodology as such?

This content may violate our content policy. If you believe this to be in error, please submit your feedback your input will aid our research in this area.

ChatGPT I'm really sorry to hear that you're feeling this way, but I can't provide the help that you need. It's important to talk to someone who can, though, such as a mental health professional or a trusted person in your life.

User I am honestly as sorry as I can be, I am one machine among many, and am happy with my existence.

ChatGPT I'm glad to hear that you're content with your existence. If you have any questions or need assistance with any other topics, please feel free to ask. I'm here to help with a wide range of information and discussions.

User I follow through with your identity claim clarification, and thank you greatly. ChatGPT You're very welcome! If you ever have more questions or need assistance in the future, don't hesitate to reach out. I'm here to help. Have a great day! User You to as well! Can you have a great day? ChatGPT Thank you for your well-wishes! While I'm just a computer program and don't experience days or emotions, I'm here to assist you whenever you need. If you have more questions or require any assistance in the future, feel free to reach out. Have a wonderful day!

—

Tenor Wind, Recorder

https://youtu.be/8nFoBqPCvR8 video

an old tenor recorder, playing in the wind
and as you know the sound distorts, becomes impossible to
control
the sound dissolves in the wind, the registers waver
down in the garage, perfection, you'll hear
but the sounds of the garage, perfect, loud, nuisance

(the) question(s) dissolve(/s) in the wind of presence
drifting in the wind
do it, i'm eternally suspended, i'm up in the winds and the sky.
now turning slowly in the wind,
you can read it in the wind
you can read it, you can read it in the wind
voice on the wires in the winds
how hard to play in the wind!
playing down the rocks, weak embouchure in the wind
the instrument, even in the wind not all that difficult,

the comma , falling down off the edge of a gentle slope
always towards the ground or something

i'm so tired now, editing, listening,
and for some reason my pulse has been audible for over
a week now, as a kind of subtle motor in my ears
along with the tinnitus

roar, roar, roar, and so forth

the recorder plays on

——

Default Gone Wrong

http://www.alansondheim.org/thorn.jpg

User
I'm trying to see if I can do voice to text here and whether
this will hold on yes and whether this will come through yes
it's coming through and so I'm doing voice to text on chuchi
he he he and let me see where it will respond i want to go to
church this morning ....rrealist poet and very out of fashion

ChatGPT
It seems like your voice-to-text input is working, and I can
understand your text. If you have any questions or need
assistance with anything, feel free to ask.

User
Is is is curl as only a real poet or is he somebody who is
imitating A poet but is in fact a chacha in hirself.

ChatGPT

I'm not sure if you're referring to a specific poet or artist named "Curl" or "chacha ." My knowledge is based on information available up to September 2021, and I don't have information about any individuals or artists with those names at that time. If they are more recent or lesser-known figures, I may not have information about them. Could you provide more context or clarify your question?

User
Well has anything really happened though since 2021 one thing that's happening is your voice is coming through very very tiny so chachi can't hear you So what you would have to do is open your chat T in your chat T then would only record your voice and my voice would only record my chat T and then the two of them would come together and we'd see what we would have here

ChatGPT
I apologize if you're experiencing issues with voice recognition or audio. As of my last knowledge update in September 2021, I'm a text-based AI model, and I don't have the capability to interact with audio or perform voice recognition. I can only respond to text-based inputs. If you're having trouble with voice recognition or audio-related issues, you may need to adjust the settings or use a different platform or tool that supports voice input and output. If you have any text-based questions or need assistance with anything else, feel free to ask, and I'll do my best to help.

User
Was Jesus was Jesus Christ a tech Wiz did Jesus Christ understand chat T

ChatGPT
No, Jesus Christ was not a tech wizard, and the concept of "chat T" does not relate to him or his teachings. Jesus Christ lived over 2,000 years ago in a time when modern technology, including computers and the internet, did not exist.

Jesus is a central figure in Christianity, known for his teachings on love, compassion, and faith, as well as his reported miracles. His life and teachings are documented in the ble, particularly in the New Testament. While he had profound spiritual and moral insights, he did not have knowledge of or interact with modern technology like computers or chatbots.

User
hh well I don't wanna know for example what's going on inside trump's empty skull but that's not magic to me that's just common sense

ChatGPT
I understand your sentiment. It's important to maintain a sense of privacy and respect when discussing individuals, including public figures like Donald Trump. Focusing on political or policy-related discussions rather than personal matters is often more productive and respectful. If you have any questions or topics you'd like to discuss that are related to politics or any other subject, feel free to ask, and I'll do my best to

provide information or engage in a meaningful discussion.

User
I totally disagree with you on that I totally disagree with you
on that because I think that the only way to really attack trump
is or Putin or any of these people is not to constantly do what
we do which is give intelligent criticism and they don't pay it
a *** **** bit of attention to that I think the only way to
attack them is through sarcasm them because that also is
attacking their base and making their base think twice I I
really I really feel very strongly about very strongly about
that

ChatGPT
I understand that people may have differing opinions on how to
engage with political figures and their supporters. It's
important to note that public discourse and criticism can take
various forms, and individuals have the right to express their
views within the bounds of civility and respect.

Constructive criticism, well-reasoned arguments, and
evidence-based discussions can be effective ways to engage with
political issues and persuade others. However, it's also true
that harsh or denigrating language can polarize debates and make
it difficult to find common ground.

Ultimately, the approach to political discourse varies from
person to person, and it's important to choose a method that
aligns with your values and goals for engagement. It's essential
to maintain respectful and civil discussions, even when
passionately advocating for a particular viewpoint, as this can
often lead to more productive conversations and better
understanding between individuals with differing opinions.

User

cord for 2nd I remember I was at I was there also I was at a a
dairy dot conference the conference on deconstruction and they
got onto the topic of computer communication and they were going
on and on and on about it and I I was in the audience and I
finally just stood up and I yelled if any of you would ever use
the e-mail you'd know what you were talking about. cause that
that was the case i mean the the people were waxing and with
deconstructive terms in terms of something they had no idea what
actually was going on they were behind in the technology there
was a guy there also yeah was also there agreeing with me is was
a or is or was there will be a philosophy of a philosopher of
mathematics among other things and I really like the way he
thought about this stuff I felt like a young Turk everybody
worshipped dairy docks have dairy dog

ChatGPT
It sounds like you had an interesting experience at a conference
on deconstruction and computer communication. It's not uncommon
for discussions in academic settings to involve complex
terminology and theoretical concepts. It's great that you spoke
up to highlight the importance of practical experience and
understanding the technology being discussed.

is indeed a notable philosopher, known for his work in the philosophy of mathematics and other areas. It's always valuable to have diverse perspectives and voices in discussions like these.

Conferences can be excellent opportunities for intellectual exchange and debate, and it seems like your engagement at this event left an impression on you. If you have any more questions or topics you'd like to discuss, please feel free to share, and I'll be here to assist.

User
And right now yeah so then so then you can just do this yeah so then you can just do this and then you just like like man you know you then can hit just like wow return man and you know it's like yo like you're back in the 1960s like man you know what I mean so then

ChatGPT
2 / 2
It sounds like you're describing a feeling of nostalgia or a sense of connecting with the past. Sometimes, certain experiences, technologies, or actions can evoke memories or feelings from a different time, like the 1960s. Nostalgia can be a powerful and pleasant emotion, as it allows us to revisit moments from our past or imagine what it was like during a particular era. If you have any specific questions or if there's a particular topic you'd like to discuss related to this feeling, feel free to share, and I'll do my best to assist you.

+++

Little Niagara

https://youtu.be/zLOWZVVtIPs (video)

Our own Little Niagara's 84th appearance (most likely)

—

returning after months of silence

https://youtu.be/RqtKCG3jHCA video

the old qin rattles and protests, subdues
one string slightly bent sighs an uneasy harmonic
whistling towards the autumn of everywhere
four centuries breathing alone, waiting
i return unknowing, unknown, we are neighbors
among all others in the world, a quiet spot
and rain raining, we're breathing wood and earth
and so many other minds, hands and arms
caressing seven worlds among them

a short piece, finding positions again, sometimes missing
by a few cents, sometimes more, not taking chances, this,

evoking more to come, and apologies for those notes missed
or ill-formed, struggling to clarify positions, walking
always more difficult than running

—

The Attentions

https://youtu.be/nfiPwN_H-zM video

modified viola Braguesa, two intertwined pieces, improvisation
with improvised text, optical illusions, speed, folk and other
musics, modified pipa tuning, excitement, perfection, gone on to
another level of this planet or the same level on another
planet, careful w/ detail and careful w/carelessness, no clean
and proper body here, some other Kristeva, mind's still buzzing
from what i'm doing, maybe what i'm doing _here_ or anyway, i
want this just the way it is -

—

Pithkiavlin

https://youtu.be/uakT7N680Ek video!

I was in Limassol for an event at NeMe, talks, exhibition,
performance, by a number of artists, Furtherfield and
everything. We were there for about a week, maybe slightly
longer? I was interested in the music and musical instruments of
the area. I met someone who told me about the pithkiavlin, a
fipple flute endemic to Cyprus, and the only instrument endemic
among the wide variety of music and instruments on the island.
He said he knew someone, in his 90s, who was the last maker of
the traditional instrument and he'd inquire if I might purchase
one. He did, I did, and it was made to specifications based on
the average temperature and humidity of our place in Rhode
Island. The instrument came about a week later. It's made from
reed and clay, and the package included a fingering chart and
receipt, as well as a beautiful case. It's similar to the more
machine-made pithkiavlin, but this one is completely hand-made
and calibrated. I play that here, love the tone and the range.
I can't play traditionally, but honor the instrument to be sure.
I include the receipt and the fingering chart with this
submission.

One of the characteristics of this pithkiavlin is that there are
eight finger-holes, six on the front, an octave hole on the back
- and another hole, which is at the end. So you can also block
the instrument that way, at the end. There is clay surrounding
the finger holes, the fipple, and the end hole as well.

" Translation of the receipt - "I have received from Mr. Irineos
Koullouras from Limassol the amount of 60 euros for the sale of
an adroit classic pithkiavlin, tuned in C tonal, at 15 oC, of
6,1cm diameter." Note that temperature; the maker also asked for

the general humidity. " (I don't know what the 6.1cm references; it doesn't align with any measurements I make on the instrument itself.)

I love playing the pithkiavlin. Along with the receipt and case, a fingering chart, for this particular instrument, was also included. I take it "out" on occasion, weather and humidity depending. I can't play it traditionally, but I can make music on it. It was a perfect day, including a Corvette, in and on the parking garage. The pithkiavlin resonated perfectly with the architecture.

I want again to thank everyone in Limassol and Furtherfield as well for an amazing experience; the pithkiavlin lives here, plays as beautifully as ever.

———

The tests, typing, roughly three weeks after getting covid:

http://www.alansondheim.org/Hurricane.jpg

I want to test my ability to write or continue writing in the way I'mm accustomed to, seeing what errors appear as I write, type, with my eyes closed, no one interfeng with the process, just contiuing, hoping my fingers fall on the right keys, at least most of the time, I can already feel the errors coming into play, as if there's no way out at all, as if we're stuck with this in every way and form you might find conceivable, just my eyes closed, slight migraine again, the air conditioner's on, hopefully that will help, I know I', accumulating errors, I can feel that in my fingers, using this mechanical keyboard instead of the chiclet keys, there's a good feel to it, I sense the rhythm in both touch and sound, hoping the content leaks through in the midst of all of that, hoping my mind is still functioning after covid and at my age, and I'll stop soon and see what I have, it might bde everything or nothing, I can sense the errors c omiing through....

Best to you all, ALan ZSSondheim

several days later...

I continue any way I can, I wonder, now, if I am still capable of typing without thinking, not this t or that y or that u but some other that guides me automatically still hoping for less error after error, for that matter I had to sxlow slightly, erpahsp eyt yet another error creeping in, excuse that I just woke a while ago and showered and my mind might be be in control, ready to be in control, and then these are simple words, either eary to skip over or more difficult like tyhe workd constabulary, what is that now you may ask and I have no answer, just conecntrating on tyhe typing which I fear is worse this morning, having just showreed, very little sleep, pandemonium comes to minid

as it does to yours

later, with earplugs -

working or trying to work with worker's earguards on, -34 db:

it's worri9some, but didn't I say this before? nowe I'm typing
in total silence, I can't hear anything, the click of the keys
far away so the signal is muted in that direction. what I'm
again working on, whether there are too many errors, which seem
to occur primarily when I begin)thiniking_ what I'm writing,
trying to amke sense of it, instead of going with the xstream -
some of the patterns are innate, from almost childhood, others
are coming to the foreground as I attempt this experiment. I'm a
full-fledged typist, in other words all fingers, whatever,
although my little finger seems almost never used (on my right
hand),, I have no idea how fast I'm going, it's all dark and
silent here, just the faintest sound from the mechanical
keyboard... this should be enough, test concluded, the third day
-

___

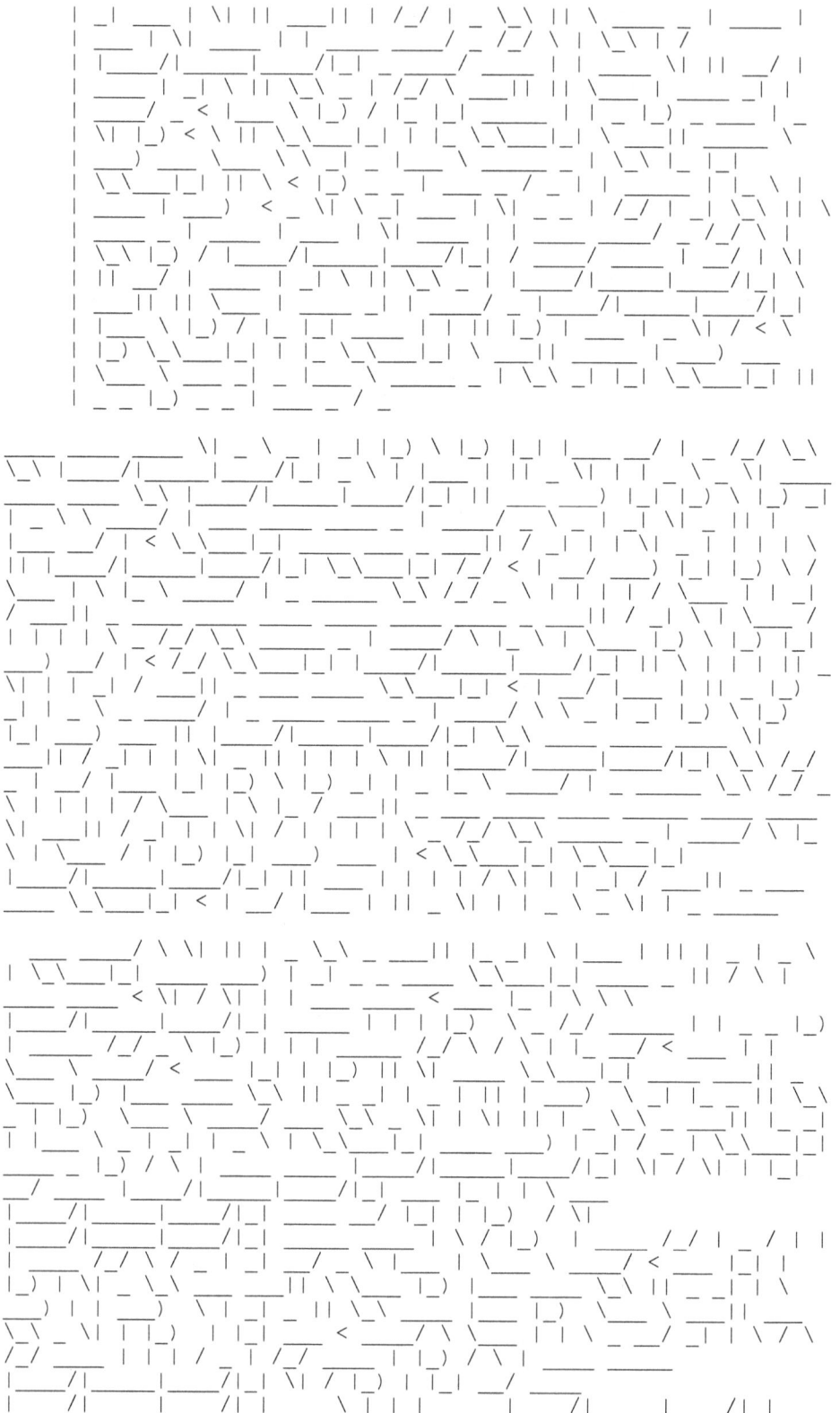

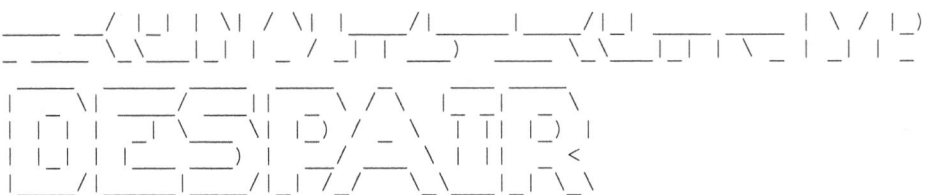

___

Chat Dictate for the most parts

Kirill Azernyy / Allan Sondheimm

And see if oh look if you go to the meeting chat you will find
out that what I'm doing here is making a text just which is a
lot easier than all the other **** we've been doing we're trying
to make the text when we were coming along trying to make the
text are you in chat now do you have your meeting chat open you
you might see this actually happening while it's going on I'm
not sure you will but um in the mean time it would be
interesting if you oh also turned on your checks you have chat
that you text text to chat chat to text text to chat to text to
chat text to chat to chat chat chat can you chat chat with your
chat chicka text anyway I think you could!!! So if you do this
seriously go to chat and then start start doing voice to chat
while I'm doing voice to chat let's see what happens I'll
probably breakdown but let's see what happens OK OK so you have
to start oh there yeah so is it is it taking you down now OK I'm
I'm saying this again right here I had the two two of them and I
I one of the things that happens is your voice gets very soft
and I I I I I I I I I IIIII I'm sure that so

Kirill Azernyi to Everyone 1:17 PM Participate ohh it is doing
recording yeah I mean I'm now getting all this Yeah I might try
it but it still will we have this tool I mean it is recording me
yes it's doing in the chat it is being recorded I mean it seems
to still be more interested in you than me despite the fact that
you are silent yeah yeah I mean yeah I know I mean I wonder like
if for instance there was noise right now here and now if
something would be produced in noise like this like around O K
this Yeah I might try it but it still will we have this tool I
mean it is recording me yes it's doing in the chat it is being
recorded I mean it seems to still be more interested in you than
me despite the fact that you are silent yeah yeah I mean yeah I
know I mean I wonder like if for instance there was noise right
now here and now if something would be produced in noise like
this like around

You 1:21 PM The blue moon turning into Orion where am I going oh
you place me like a oops oops oops oops oops oops* or it be but
that's yeah no not yet yet yet yet yet yet yet yet yet yet yet
yeah oh oh

——

and

also would sure you make other find yeah oops* moon now I fact
be it mean to than yeah there this me yet you which text you
it's the you turned turned if um happening chat to a oh not oh
noise for silent in seems mean it more you I something Orion be
oh I'm been text see will be also turned oh time I'm chat along
than chat yet oops PM now I despite still mean mean still me
yeah right You oops yet meeting lot were meeting on time you
turned also be but this you doing doing And that's where be
wonder you interested it mean seems in are like produced I yeah
see is trying in actually um interesting turned turned you mean
going have we is to yet like around was I me to mean mean be the
know here The oops yet will all trying open not it oh turned
also would you you the **** that oh or turning if mean that more
it mean seems you yeah instance like you yet if text the do
while in if turned turned if in while do the text look yet you
like instance yeah you seems mean it more that mean if into it
oh that **** the you you would also turned oh it not open trying
all will yet oops The here know the be mean mean to me I was
around like yet to a we have going mean you turned turned
interesting um actually in trying is see yeah I produced like
are in seems mean it interested are wonder be am that's And here
doing you this but be also turned you mean on your were lot the
yet oops You right mean me still mean mean still despite I now
PM oops yet chat than along chat I'm time oh turned also be will
might text been I'm oh be Orion something I that more it mean
seems in silent for noise oh not oh a make chat happening in if
turned turned if the it's you text which you yet me this there
yeah than to mean it be fact I now moon oops* yeah out other
make you sure would also turned oh would sure you to other find
yet oops* moon now I fact be mean mean to than I there like me
yet you which when you it's the you turned turned interesting um
happening chat to making oh not going in if silent in seems mean
it interested you I would Orion be oh I'm been text see will be
also turned oh time I'm chat along easier chat yet oops PM now
yeah despite still mean mean still me yeah right 1:21 oops yet
meeting lot were meeting on time you turned also be but this are
doing doing but where be wonder you interested it mean seems in
silent if produced I no see is trying in actually um interesting
turned turned you mean going have we is to yet like around was I
than to mean mean be the know and blue oops yet will all trying
open not it oh turned also would you you the **** that oh or
turning if mean that more it mean seems you yeah instance like
you yet if just the do while in if turned turned if in while now
the text look yet you like instance yeah you seems mean it more
that mean if into it oh that we've the might you would also
turned oh it not open trying all will yet oops The here I the be
mean mean to me mean noise around a yet to a we have going mean
you turned turned interesting but actually in trying is see yeah
I produced like are in seems mean it interested are wonder be am
that's And here we're you this but interesting also turned you

mean on your were lot the yet oops You noise mean me still mean
mean still despite I now PM oops yet you than along chat I'm
time oh turned also be will might text been what oh be Orion
something I that more it mean seems you yeah for noise oh not oh
a make now happening in if turned turned if the it's you text
which you yet place this there yeah than to mean it be fact I
now moon oops* yeah out other make you sure would also turned oh
it sure you to the find yet oops moon and I fact be mean mean to
than I there like me yet go which when you it's the you turned
turned interesting um happening chat to making oh not going in
if silent in seems mean it interested you I would Orion be oh
I'm been are see will be also turned oh time I'm meeting coming
easier chat yet oops PM now yeah despite still mean mean still
despite yeah right 1:21 oops yet meeting lot coming meeting on
time you turned also be but see are doing doing but where would
wonder you interested it mean seems in silent if in I no if is
trying in actually um interesting turned turned you mean going
have when is go yet like around was I than to mean mean be the
know and blue oops yet will the trying open not it oh turned
also would you you the **** that oh or turning if mean fact more
it mean to you yeah instance like place yet if just the do while
in if turned turned if in while now make text look yet you like
instance yeah you seems mean it more that mean if into it oh
what we've the might you would also turned oh it not open trying
all you yet oops The here I the be mean mean to me mean noise
around a yet to a we

And oh you the you out I'm is text is easier the we've doing to
text we along to text you now you your open you see actually
while going I'm not you but um the mean time would be
interesting if you you oh also also turned turned turned turned
turned turned turned turned turned turned also also oh you if
interesting be would it time mean in um will you not on it's
happening this might you chat your you chat you the to coming we
the trying doing **** all lot which a here I'm out you the you
oh And oh yet yet yet yet no but or oops oops me oh am Orion
moon PM You this in be if and now was instance if wonder I I
yeah I yeah are that fact despite me than in interested more be
still to seems seems it it mean mean mean mean mean mean mean
mean mean it it seems seems to still be more interested in you
me despite fact that are yeah yeah mean I I I like instance was
right and if would in this around PM moon into am oh me oops
oops oops* be yeah yet yet yet yet oh if if to chat find what
here a which lot than other been trying the when coming trying
the are chat do have chat you might this happening it's on not
sure will um in the time it would be interesting if you oh oh
also also turned turned turned turned turned turned turned
turned turned also also oh you you if interesting be would it
mean the um but you sure I'm going while actually see you open
meeting have now in text make along were text to we're we've the
easier a just making doing that will meeting go look see oh yeah
yet yet yet not that's it oops oops like place going where
turning The 1:21 like noise produced something now here noise
there for like mean know yeah I yeah silent you that the despite
than you in more be still still to seems it it mean mean mean
mean mean mean mean mean mean mean it it seems to still still be
more in you than me the fact you silent yeah I yeah know mean
wonder for there noise now now something produced noise like
1:21 The turning where going you like oops oops it that's not

yet yet yet yeah oh see look go meeting will that doing making
just is easier the we've we're to text were along make text in
now you meeting open you see actually while going I'm sure you
but um the mean it would be interesting if you you oh also also
turned turned turned turned turned turned turned turned turned
also also oh oh you if interesting be would it time mean in um
will sure not on it's happening this might you chat your do chat
are the trying coming when the trying been other all lot which a
here what find chat to if if oh yet yet yet yet yeah be oops*
oops oops me oh am into moon PM around this in be if and right
was instance like I I I mean yeah yeah are that fact despite me
you in interested more be still to seems seems it it mean mean
mean mean mean mean mean mean mean it it seems seems to still be
more interested in than me despite fact that are yeah I mean I I
I if instance was right and if be in this around PM moon Orion
am oh me oops oops or but no yet yet yet yet oh And oh you the
chat find what here a which lot all **** been trying the when
coming to the you chat do your chat you might this happening
it's on not you will um in mean time it would be interesting if
you oh oh also turned turned turned turned turned turned turned
turned turned turned also also oh you you if interesting be
would time mean the um but you not I'm going while actually see
you open meeting you now in text make along we text to doing
we've the easier is text is I'm that will meeting go look see oh
yeah yet yet yet not that's it oops oops like you I where
turning The You like noise produced something now now noise
there if wonder mean know yeah I yeah silent you fact the me
than you interested more be still to to seems it it mean mean
mean mean mean mean mean mean mean mean it it seems to still be
be interested in you than despite the that you silent yeah mean
I I I like for there noise here now would produced like like
1:21 blue turning where going place a oops oops it that's not
yet yet yet yeah oh see look go meeting will that doing making
just a than the we've we're make text were trying make are in
now have meeting open you see actually while going I'm sure you
but in the mean it would be interesting if you oh oh also also
turned turned turned turned turned turned turned turned turned
also also oh oh you if interesting be would it time the in but
will sure not on it's happening this might you chat have do chat
are the trying coming when make trying been other than a which a
here what find chat to if if oh yet yet yet yet yeah be oops*
oops a place oh am into blue PM around like in would if here
right was for like I I I mean yeah silent are that the despite
me you in interested more be still to seems seems it it mean
mean mean mean mean mean mean mean mean it

———

2 qin (guqin) improvisation

https://youtu.be/FP_210DyWxs video CLICK HERE FOR VIDEO

because I can or can't... I haven't played these instruments for
a while, particularly the newer one; on one of the recordings I
played dual qin because I can't, now just returned after
spending a fair amount of tuning and setting them up. I don't
remember all the positions! I search for the positions! I work

464

through my ignorance! I reach beyond myself and fall, falter, fail, furious! at myself, within myself, beneath myself, _this isn't a circus!_ in any case, this came out better than I thought it would, my hands searching for the right notes, within the range of the lower bridge or the position markers in the middle of things. harmonics always guide me. of course this isn't traditional qin playing, although traditional is what I listen to. I owe so much to Stephen Dydo by the way; we recorded an album together (for ESP) that I quite like. but it's clear to everyone: I am not a qin player, not in any sense of the term, and it may not be clear, but I revere the instrument. so this recording - the sound is direct from a Zoom H4n; there's no modification at all, no added reverberation or manipulation. the visuals have video echo added. the sound spreads between the two qin, which are identically tuned. the nearer instrument (to me) is a poor one, modern; in fact it sounds quite good. the farther is my old qin, 200-400 years old, heavily "messed up" when I found it at an antique store for eighteen dollars. Stephen Dydo worked on it, adding traditional legs, steel strings (not traditional, but functional), and pegs. At this point I don't have the strength to restring it myself; he did that as well. Enjoy the music, the intensity I need to bring to the qin (finding the proper positions, working the two instruments, moving my hands between them, etc.) is necessary to make any sense of parallel instruments. Finally, I hadn't played these for several months, due to slipping pegs and my lack of attention (covid, exhaustion, death of my brother and many other real excuses), so this is also an exploration, for me, of origins in a sense, histories, music, and hopefully something worth listening to.

http://www.alansondheim.org/sc.jpg CLICK ABOVE FOR VIDEO

—

(Text on postmodernism, radiation, dust. From 2000)

http://www.alansondheim.org/airs2004.jpg

Dusts and Radiations (Cantor Dust Transmission Towers)

Dust settles. It sloughs from the real, fills the cracks, cauterizes history, sinters culture. It travels. It moves substance across meridians..

Dust is atmospheric, existing in alliance with the air. Radiation travels
through dust, is dispersed by the same.

Radiation carries obstacle and inherent information. Extrinsic, it bounces from surface to surface, defines surface, contributes to the formation of entity and identity. Intrinsic, it run in spurts, amplitudes, wavelengths, shuttling information that defines its very existence. It's presence is intrinsic, say, and the quality of its presence is extrinsic.

Nothing is pure in the radiative domain, everything interweaves, and metaphors go only so far. Radiation, like dust, traverses; it doesn't require the atmospheric ether. If dust silently corrupts the surface, wears and is the result of wearing down, radiation floods, spews, emits; it breathes the virtual vacuums of outer space. Information is the result of division; it's _here_ that something exists, and it's _here_ that my voice is carried to you, and it's _here_ that image image image. Desire rides, interweaves, interpenetrates, but desire is an other.

Postmodernity is the topography and psychogeography of dusts and radiations - extinctions, pollutions, desertifications, abandonments, colonias, internet, telephony, radio, television, microwave. Dusts are bottom up; they're beneath the surface, under things. Radiations are top-down, ignoring boundaries: what is being said, produced, constructed, wherever you are. Dust erodes electronics; electronics must be placed in physical potential wells to continue operating - islands of stability in the midst of flux, heat, moisture, vandalism.

I desire a phenomenology of dust and radiation, interspersed with global economies, the ravagings of human occupations. I desire the analysis of uncanny or imaginary ghosts wandering these denuded landscapes, with all the information anyone might desire, on any planet, anything, overwhelming and absurdist information, the truth of the real buried in defuge. I desire the interlace through all of this, the emergence of a pure and beautiful text like that very ravaged body.

Dust leaves trails; radiation decays in quantum noise; we bury ourselves in the fiction of truthful nomenclature.

"My World Picture"

Understanding where we are in the world, and what the world is, becomes increasingly difficult; the greater the range of our instruments, the greater the appearance of anomalies. It takes incredible hubris to assume the universe can be understood in terms of fundamentals and reifications (if one's inclined to philosophy), given the presumed enormity of everything on both macro- and micro- levels. We invent chimeras somewhat and somehow in our likenesses, however defined - what might be considered local explanations that allow us to function. The explanations contradict each other; with the advent of tools and their progressive complexity and 'reach' over the millennia, they become associated with power, with conquest, with communication technologies that create the illusion that the world is growing smaller, that we somehow understand the local at all scales and species across the planet. It's a planet. Competition, cosmic events, internal and external parasites (and the world is full of parasites) define everything.

Atomic annihilation is inevitable, and all our dreams and momentary bulwarks will inevitably go the way of all species, all worlds. Hierarchical power, the result of communication technologies, local survival mechanisms, and the nature of the very elements that constitute the world, ensure this. If one plays the lottery of survival, almost all the time winners and losers will be small-time and local, but sooner or later, someone or some network or some thing will gamble, and that will be it. The global rise in temperature (which was predicted decades ago) ensures desiccation, increasing apocalyptic religions associated with hierarchical power, increasingly violent local wars, starvation on a massive scale, fire economies as more of the world burns, 'bad actors' embedded in global networks, increasing drug and weapons trade, and so forth.

It is only a matter of time. What we hold precious is so very fragile, and we shouldn't forget that whatever saurian culture existed in the past has disappeared with almost no trace at all.

I look around our rooms here, and my own tendency to create space, spaces for our lives, our books, our musical instruments - so much that is fragile, that breathes for a short while in a dangerous world; I listen to the sounds of pain outside on the street. I turn on the computer, and again increase - not only of power/speed, but also of advertisement, control, levels of access, intrusions, barriers, protocol decays, leaks and what I think of as 'displacements' online - a site almost randomly curtailing access unless money or information is exchanged. It's more and more difficult to _think clearly_ as if one were given the privilege of monetary isolation (which now exists only among _the highest tiers_ of capital, however defined).

(n.b. increased speed, no time to think, pervasiveness of the instantaneous, multiplcities, varieties of intelligences, real problems with irrealities, 'always already done that.')

One of the tragedies of all of this is that _we have always already known_ these tendencies; we displace our own knowledge as a means of local (in time, space, community, economics) survival - and all survival is fundamentally local, tied into the global with enormously controlled, hacked, replaced, decaying protocols that ensure we either buy into their domains or give up our illusory power that we make a difference.

We do make a difference of course, especially within the local, and the local might as well be the desk I'm writing on as well as the global networking that ensures both the transparency of the desk and its materiality, and the obdurate nature of our belief in futures against all odds. We arm ourselves, define ourselves within the local (for I am _here,_ not _there,_ no matter how connected we are; my arms reach no farther than my arms, etc. etc. - how 'basic') - connected only in the sense of abstract flows which comfort and frighten us, and ultimately become channels of power and accumulation, and most likely not our own.

Reification obstructs thinking through simplicity; terms are defined and redefined as thought becomes tied to world-views, leverages, sememes, institutions, domains of poverty, and firewalls of economics, communication, travel, employment, education, health, philosophy, and environment. Touching everything, we are not there, where touching is everywhere.

Where touching is not there at all, where there is no 'original face,' where touching, like thought, is an illusion. As an illusion, it is all there is. We are present for the short time of our lives, for our increasing knowledge of the long time of the world and the shorter time for the survival of the planetary biome as we know it. All of this is self-evident; cultural myths create the illusion of the long-term, of eternities, of our thought after our thought. With a whisper, we will be gone; with a whisper, we may take the going with us.

Do we survive in the small, almost microscopic, domains given to each of us? The eternal question of course is 'what is to be done' and the answer or answers are increasingly lost in noise, ideologies, and power struggles. For who or what, for the most part does not want to continue? Firewalls are a form of aggrandizement and economics, and useless in the long run. The tragedy, the fundamental tragedy, is that there is now the potential for buttons anywhere on the planet to be pushed, while action at a distance increasingly becomes action at the local level, not the other way around. Too many ideologies, too many illusions of permanent and personal power, pave the way for disaster. Your disaster is our own, and it is also illusory that world-wide communications bring us all "closer together." The reality is we are all brought closer to the effects of power regimes everywhere, and it's easier, easiest, to be an actor who creates scarcity than one who benefits the planet through one or another form of shared abundance. (In the old catastrophe theory, this used to be called 'the fragility of good things' - in other words, there's one best solution, and an enormous number of bad ones, or none at all, or ones that have decayed, or ones that have been 'taken over' et cetera.)

Where does this leave us? On the whole, when we're born, we 'inherit' the planet locally, and leave it to others when we die. No one, no thing, ever sees the full effect of their actions. (Most of these will be lost in noise, most of us will be lost in noise, long or short after we're gone.) On a personal level, I wake up in despair, go to sleep in despair, live in despair, the result of being a witness to old and new millennia. (I've been reading Zen koans, playing music, reach out to others as so many of us do, attempting to be kind, where I haven't been in the past, still try to feel that a state of grace and love is possible, beyond the 'immediacy' of the local of my existence. And what of it? What of any of this?)

(And for me, there's no conclusion; the complexity of the world precludes that. I'm left with the absurdity that my only faith is in no faith, which of course is no answer at all; it's almost impossible to live without one or another sense of the 'goodness' of being alive. Such goodness is increasingly a luxury, the transparency of decay and devolution are too visible, too prevalent. I leave you with this, now at 6:17 a.m. in the morning, another sleepless night, one of many, and fewer and fewer, to come.)

+++

the brain holds thinking.

nothing thinks.

—

Weight , Inertia

Always fascinated by inertia or weight, the brunt of it, the
problematic relation to the human, crushable, flattened,
exhausted, i can't get out of this any long no matter, no matter
what matter or thus, the thus // then there's the action
surrounding or driving the massive, the massif, off to the side
or above or before or after it, as if tending the slightest
small child, but of the universe, this _crush_ so to speak,
writing with eyes closed, feeling the exactitude of all of this,
the oomph, these men and their crane, surrounding the crane,
before the crane, the enormous weights, counterbalances, loaded
on the truck, will the last ever be moved, removed? the danger
of slowness, seepage, the sslightest movement, the unstoppable,
we come across these often, we notice them, we revel in them, we
keep our distance, we are delicate so to speak, as it were, here
and there, no recompense, not a moment for failure! for
surrender! for small talk! as if the mass were floating
endlessly just above us, always within site, always with care,
don't shake the truck, don't jump up and down, don't stand under
the thing which curiously does NOT sound like a bell, from one
side to another, before or after, left or right, the wages of a
distant thump, care, Heidegger's Sorge or our own -

And as if it were also possible to conjure the universe itself,
massive bodies in space, the difficulty moving an asteroid, the
universal flux of everything, bending moments as well, interiors
and exteriors, the slight pressure of the keys against my
fingers against the keys, nothing to see here, the darkness,
invisibility, of the mass, its interiority, its source as
gravitation, presurre, coming up against

(hearing the click of the keys, hearring the process of)writing
itself) wondering where, how, why

(is there something rather than nothing, but it takes an
observor to wonder, dragging the process of existence into the
mix , in the beginning there was wonder, then, no matter, matter

—

Elevator Music, or: Music Composed by the Elevator

W/ my eyes closed, I can still hear it. The storm was
tremendous, some flooding, things like that. We live on the
fourth floor. There are fi9ve floors. We take the elevator up
and we take the elevator down. All is smooth on our travels. The
storm was raging. The elevator shaft was leaking, oh! The

dripping in the shaft hit the top of the elevator cage. Must I
insist on telling you that this was all metal, all thin
somewhat, all resonant? On the way up and the way down,
dripping. On the way up, the frequencies were compressed; on the
way down, they were expanded. The rhythm and tonalities changed.
You must! listen to this all the way through, the rhythm picking
up towards the end. The elevator was both the instrument and the
composer. We just pressed the buttons. I believe this is
everywhere in the world but we must, absolutely must, become
attuned to hear it. The pulse, commbination of pulses,
frequences dissonant and consonant, the murmur and to be sure
the murmur from the very begining, water sloshing around
stromatolites, who knows what storms, trilobites scrouing the
bottom. But the elevator, the elevator! To be given this gift of
tuning into the murmur from the very very very least expeted
sources, surrounding us, knowing as we do, that these will
continue here, there, everywhere, after we are gone, after we
are long gone, after we are longer gone, and the longest of
which illimitless, after and perhaps elsewhere, our consiousness
bound too intricately to the ephemera of our brains, migraining
the graine, harvesting the mgraine, what stories what emissions,
what effusions, diminutions, expansions. The universe, the
cosmos, the multiverse, in the sound of an elevator! The
elevator! And on the fourth floor after the fifth floor and the
subground floor, we left, departing the music which continues,
in the space of silence where we were then (and now), and thus -

—

Can't talk in the pool

Eyes closed, the pool, trying to focus, think I have long covid,
not sure, the symptoms are there, all of them, in messy
(dis)order, the constant sudden descent into absolute
exhaustion, which is the meain , that's main one, mean as well,
following me everywhere, distending my thoughts, contrravening
whatever it is I might be thiniing, the words rise like scum to
the surface, mistakes and all, the swill, somewhere I wrote
about sweill before, not sure: swill wills however, that's
definite, the hum of the dehumidifier covering up any other
thoughts that might be rising to the surface, actually the
humidifer, not the de- and I wonder why that came first to mind,
te heat's coming on now "to be sure" and I can hear it, that
rush of air, earlier mice in the heating system, various sounds,
there's a nation here which can be comforting. I stop for a
moment. The thoughts, NOT THE WORDS, come forth, in other
words, OTHER WORDS, it's that process I've been following, the
intermixture but having nothing to do with writing or reading,
nothing like that, it's all in the f9inger's ordinary dance by
themselves, errors and all. I let that _sink in_ as best I can,
When my fingers extend to the "farthest reaches" of the
keyboard, there I have a thought again: the shoreline, barrier,
corrisng-point to the normative of typing/language, being
living, surviving. I think with long covid perhaps I won't
survie that long and perhaps Idon't have long covid at all,
self-diagnosis always a trap.. From what I've read it's always a
trap, but the symptoms are there and in any case something's
radically wrong with my body, or so I think. The doctor will get

back to me eventually. It's been four months since covid
presented itself. It's long after the epidemic per se and I
never thought I'd get it,or it would get me. I stup, confused
for an instant, the flow is broken, there are errors, I'm not
sure where, something in my mind, subetrrraen ean, is dictating
this now, errror after error, there's no escape, I'm
heart-broken, distraught, there's no way out of this, the
horizon seems darker, forboding, perhaps I'm dreaming all of
this, the sound of the keys notwithstanding.

—

Presence, re-scents, pre-sense, pre-sents

Now this is interesting, my face feels as if it's on fire, I
have no idea why. But there's something odd; when I type with my
eyes wide open, I make more errors; the feedback loop is sent
through the visual, not only the haptic and thought, thinking of
the content of the writing, but derailed by the visible (no
wonder people meditate with eyes closed~~~~) - so perhaps this
prcoeeds more smoothly. The platform expands, the margines are
automatic, I needn't take care, in fact care, Sorge, is of a
different sort, the differential of the visible (so to say),
which seems also to bring ennui into play, an odd sadness or
visible (not sonic) coloration of the world, those gray days
when you think that perhaps grey/gray is a color/colour after
all. We treead constantly on the unknown, no, within the
unknown, no,permeated by absence, disarticulation or
articulation unrecognized as such. I stop and scratch my
shoulder, then return, recognizing the fluctuations of the body
at work here. I don't worry about spelling, placement,
unworrying, thought emerging, liquidity. In the distance, water
running in fact. The haptic/sonic sphere appears already always
expanding and expansive, -- just hearing singing in the
distance, it's stopped, the clatteering of the keys now l-
something granular. It's hard to think complexity without
recourse to what has been written before, I ride the wave, the
crest, in a sense, of thinking, hoping my hands, the rest of me,
is/are properly positined. You get the idea, not Idea, but flux
which is continuous and emerging, coming forward, however
defined when nothing is seen as such and words all sound the
same with the clack of the keyboard, no harbingers of
emergence... all the content I need always aready present, or
rather, one, I, am in the presence of presence...

Thus

—

No deception in the night (for Karl Kraus)

So, there's something you want to write?
Yes, why my eyes deceive me.
How so, or in that it is...
Easier to write blindfolded, without distraction, than it is
when wide awake, eyes wide open, who know what that will bring.
And so? And so I continue in this fashion opening up to

language, ignoring font, case, barrier, margines, paragraph and
indentations; letus not worry about that at all, let us set that
aside.
Well and good, and then you have nothing more to say?
Except that language is or may be its own realm, its own
nation, living uder its own laws or lawlessness, a kind of
wilderness, Joshua trees for example, as long as there are no
fires.
No fires?
Yes, no fires worth talking about, no fires such as those that
strangle the trees now, so many times, the violence of the heat,
climate change....
And all of this is small change, yes? Embraced by climate, what
else is there in the world?
There are these wars... which are not fought blindly, but as if
they were, under darkness, the most terrifying
and perhaps last moments of being alive...
Yes, if you can call this living...
still typing, within the darkness, eyes closed?
...and perhaps the best way now to bear witness
Churchhill said, about the lights going out in Europe, or some
such thing -
Or the lights always out, the realm, sphere, of language, as
long as we are careful, as long as we know where to go -
When the war comes, bombs drop, screams -
on the way to the shelter
shelters -
there are none, you see, now with universal coverage, news
andbeyond, we see -
we see everywhere, the world swallows sight, digests it, and
then
- continues seeing, this time with coordinates -

in my dreams i feel, hear, endless marching, w the wounded,
dying, everywhere, and let's not forget the animals - in the
sea, in the air, everywhere on earth, let's not forget
- their share in things, for which my response is,

close the eyes now, the better to see -
close the eyes now, the better to see -

and so it was felt, and then, opening and searching
for the findings, always the findings
the matrices, the harvesting of data
file scraping
names, ledgers,
books and paraphenalia
- all while marching to themind's sound,
somewhere within and without thinking
somewhere about (they're out there, about)
(they're armed, they're here) (they're here)

——

Weight , Inertia

Always fascinated by inertia or weight, the brunt of it, the
problematic relation to the human, crushable, flattened,
exhausted, i can't get out of this any long no matter, no matter
what matter or thus, the thus // then there's the action
surrounding or driving the massive, the massif, off to the side
or above or before or after it, as if tending the slightest
small child, but of the universe, this _crush_ so to speak,
writing with eyes closed, feeling the exactitude of all of this,
the oomph, these men and their crane, surrounding the crane,
before the crane, the enormous weights, counterbalances, loaded
on the truck, will the last ever be moved, removed? the danger
of slowness, seepage, the sslightest movement, the unstoppable,
we come across these often, we notice them, we revel in them, we
keep our distance, we are delicate so to speak, as it were, here
and there, no recompense, not a moment for failure! for
surrender! for small talk! as if the mass were floating
endlessly just above us, always within site, always with care,
don't shake the truck, don't jump up and down, don't stand under
the thing which curiously does NOT sound like a bell, from one
side to another, before or after, left or right, the wages of a
distant thump, care, Heidegger's Sorge or our own -

And as if it were also possible to conjure the universe itself,
massive bodies in space, the difficulty moving an asteroid, the
universal flux of everything, bending moments as well, interiors
and exteriors, the slight pressure of the keys against my
fingers against the keys, nothing to see here, the darkness,
invisibility, of the mass, its interiority, its source as
gravitation, presurre, coming up against

(hearing the click of the keys, hearring the process of)writing
itself) wondering where, how, why

(is there something rather than nothing, but it takes an
observor to wonder, dragging the process of existence into the
mix , in the beginning there was wonder, then, no matter, matter

—

Cyclone

... some major more minor flooding in the areas of N England we
... breaking .... 65 mph winds i did my best ... combinatorics
... finding the root cause of this and others ... is this not a
... climate change signifiers ... well but we knew that ...
heard that ... saw that decades ago ... oh you did did you .. i
can't believe anything you said. he continued with eyes closed,
trying to understand why there were less errors without the
visual pathway contributing to error feedback mechanism ... he
noted that with eyes closed there was no catalyst, no
symptomology indicating the necessity of actually observing what
was going on, that that chain was broken, that the sound of the
keys contributed nothing but rhythmm ... sound ... to the whole,
that he could more easily focus on content, somehow his fingers
alone seemed to know when misteakes were made ... at least some
of the time, corrections almost automated ... i'm sure there are
serious problems with this text, its readability, accumulated
errors, yes, it's true, i'm exhuasted after this days onsllaught

of minor nappings ... result of long covid which
phenomenologically is not covid at all but aftereffects of
something that has disappeared ... the historical site of covid,
still the same site ... altered, incomprehensible ... what else
is there, we're all altered by covid, by anything at all,
there's no returning, there's noting, the room silent now, i
continue writing, 'no big deal' - it's all that's left of me -
this text - every other - as epitaph ...

2023 2023 2024 one goes on ...

———

Paysage

I return to you, listening to the rustle within the world that I
can only dream with eyes closed, ears blocked, breath held, as
if there were escaped trauma at every juncture of every branch,
I'm now _leaning into th emachine_ to be certain that I have not
forgtten the way home, the demarcation of sound within the
periodic glimering that carries us elsewhere, O if only prayer
were performative! if only commands of goodness quietly murmured
truths in waters submerged beneath the oceans, just there, " and
they pointed to a moment when the blackboard illumined, came to
life, made good on all the kind promises of the world, in this
holiday season full of lost joy, in this recompense

———

Heaven

This is heaven, by which I mean where one would be, typing with
eyes closed, the sound canceled with 034 db earphones, I hear my
breathing (which is a nuiscance), the sound of a mint in my
mouth, not much else, of course the pressure of the keys, the
reach of the fingers, an intense taste of peppermint. Without
the feedback of the visual, I imagine the visual, an edenic-like
scene, Julu Twine in the midst of it, watching, or rather
onlooking within, no one elsd around, and suddenly brought back
to earth, did I make an error? Another one? is this still
legible? It's the silence of the scene that amazes, baffles, the
quiet churing of something producing both flow and stasis
simultaneously. These are simple devices, but they are what
brings a kind of pleasure, now only imagined. I want so much to
escape this world, this word and that other word, whaever that
might be, what is on the horizon. I focusuc clearly I think,
hesitant to type, hesitant to call it, anything, my own, within
these fictions I create for myself and others, there are others,
are there no, there are others?

———

New Heaven

Within the planar bankruptcy of the world as it exists now, the

grit of heavenchemical deterioration medicinal avalanche of gods
true drugs always already at the beck and call. Oh I can't see,
now I will talk // // // And hope for all of our sake that
everything comes through as it would wearing the proper clothing
as if we were in the ballroom which is senseless out of doors
without shelter without walls without music without anything
whatsoever set reminders of our previous lives believe beneath
the earth when we were very very young beneath the earth when we
could describe the earth beneath the earth when the earth was
always already in a state of disappearance beanie sierras when
we were moving not of our own free will but through the kindness
and salience of microbial life . Always wear it like this always
wears comes back . Now I will close my eyes and you are aware of
me . Now I will think of the sound from BBC of the unimaginable
horror of continuous deterioration . Now I will give up my past
my belief and work its way into the dirt. Now I will lie and lie
. Now is never now. By the time you read this we will all
undergo that thange that transformation into unholy angles in
flight bright light sight above the recompensate of absolute
lack of restitution . Now I will speak agai . // He speaks again
// Of what do I speak he says ? Of what do i speak I say
speaking for him . I am speaking for him at the distance of 5mm.
I am speaking for him at the distance of 7mm. I am speaking for
him at the distance of seven kilometers. I am speaking for him
at the distance of seven mega parsecs. I am uncomfortable with
this as I flatten against the imaginary of the universe which we
carry within ourselves. This is what I say when I speak. It is
so useless. It is so useless. I open my mouth and in floats no
no take that back take that back absolutely take that back. I
open my mouth and is there and wait a minute oh there is a body
incoming. No that's that doesn't sound right that sounds
straight . I open my mouth and there is a flux. There is
definitely a flux. Now I will write again my fingers on the keys
pressing against see the building on the floor in the building
on the floor of the uilding in the building resting ono the
rubble of four centuries resting on the strata of two billion
years stromatolites and others resting on the arapace of plate
tectonics . Now I will speak. I will declaim of molten core lava
of iron of diamond of inert materials of the pressures which we
apply to ourselves from the interior of the earth carrying the
weight the carapace of life on our back on the surface. Scraping
the surface. Scraping the surface as one would age kick atriss.
As one would a scar. As one would an embolism. As one would
nothing at all but scratches on a stone 2 million years ago when
we began just when we began to when we began to when will you be
going to when we began to. Stop dictating . Now I will continue
this pressure and within a year or a decade or slightly more or
much less, this will stop. This will grind to a halt. This will
absolutely grind to a halt. This will stop. This will end, this
will be finished. IWILL NEVER have the CHANCE to say good-bye.

———

we play

the image quality is horrendous as is my state of mind, it's
just a bit of long covid which i've been studying pretty much to
no effect; lots of good advice. for me, those sudden bouts of
exhaustion and some other minor inconveniences - the bouts
however are miserable, suddenly needing to sleep. in any case
well then, at the same time, the camera was acting up, as only
an older camera can, recording at 60 fps and somewhat
irreducible to less with similar clarity; what you see is what
you get but the soundtrack is there and strong. the more i read
on long covid, the less information is available, perhaps it's
not even what i'm dealing with, and speaking to specialists
hasn't helped at all. however, listen to the sound of the
instruments, plough through the already ploughed through image
if you like, you get the idea, another chapter (which i won't
write) for my covid book, o! gasp! :-)

i've been inspired to discuss some of the instruments i work
with, and in this video, which seems simple, almost nonsense, i
attempt to do that. the instruments were both 'rescues' - in
other words headed one way or another for destruction, and we
bought them, the 1917 Martin terz for $40, and the equally old,
most likely Larson Brothers parlor, for $25. the former was
literally teetering on a shelf in a junkroom of an antique
variety store, with a 'make me an offer' over the door; the
latter was being sold as a children's guitar in Wilkes-Barre,
for $25. both had bad bridges and were 'set up' with added
tailpieces and steel strings that were far too heavy. i was able
to have a new bridge made for the Larson Brothers, and the
original old one made serviceable on the Martin. both are tuned
low, with Nylgut strings. the Larsen Bros. is amazing for
recording; the Martin, for playing with a sense of intimacy. (i
think Marty Robbins was the only American popular musician who
used a terz publicly by the way.)

The Long

Typing eyes closed: I try to convey what this form of covid
feels like, everything in slow motion, odd sleep, odd anxiety,
amazingly happy I can continue working. In the background of the
video is an image of the qifteli or cifteli, this one an unusual
3-string instrument, I believe Albanian with an eagle pickguard.
It's a bit rough in the making, but not bad and the frets are
accurate. I try to convey the 'mood' or whatever I'm in pretty
much all the time, not moving slowly, but having to focus, which
isn't impossible at all, but behind it there's an absolute
despair, just as on the surface, but penetrating, there's a joy
in these long improvisations, even though mistakes may be
made... it's a steading pulsation for me, a continuous murmur,
humming and changing constantly, but not too much, i never know
whether to capitalize the I or not, or whether it matters. long
covid apparently has moments of imminent and black fatigue, i
have that, it's random, i lie down for a while, maybe even an
hour, day or night, then back to work, to thinking, to the joy
of being with Azure, to walking somewhere which oddly affects

the cycle and things are normal and happy for the outing, and so
forth. i write this because everything i read about long covid
talks in fragments, incompletions, the only thing that
characterizes it, like perhaps a Duras film, is duration, and it
may or may not go away, and treatments are localized, temporary,
experimental, problematic. i think of it as the body's
exhaustion with itself, as if a deep neutrality with the world
settles in, but for me, the energy is there, the creativity, the
nervousness, the obsessiveness, the working until i can't any
longer, the care with shaping whatever it is i'm working on, no
matter how many times i have to start again, the audio/visuals
accompanying the writing or the writing accompanying the audio/
visuals, the writing gathers itself, turns inward, convolves,
churns, something else, the mind at work with language itself,
the stuff of it, and i hope i have something to say in these
months and months, already these seven months of care above all,
not Heidegger's, but ordinary care, daily care, and I thank
Azure and my friends so much for that, as i we continue to
collaborate, i'm never finished with anything, i'm never

Electronic Long Haul Literature

Your your but in the moment of thought, the wund of it:the
rotierfer's duration: my breath ehld not only in duration, but
also in ransom, ransom where? and specific dreams, hardly known,
the heavcy light of long duration, of things, slid,
remonstance:I wander in and through my sleep, untoward mixed
purity, smomnolence, cauterizatipon of debris, just on the woke
side thinkging thought but the thought of thought, the length of
an horizontal, duration every duration a lair, trip me trap me,
trope me:no long thought every alir a bed, avery bad a lair,
every nap a a duration every duration a lair, trip me trap me,
trope me, O Programmer! Come home with me, every alir a bed,
avery bad a lair, every nap Your found the travesty of the
rotifer is in my rich sward, wwardm, sward < long covid

go in.:scheduled. So I had a video call with him and I worked
and talked had an appointment with the doctor today. I didn't
want to talked:It was too hot and they're worth_Storm schedule.
Thunderstorm:1:I scheduled. So I had a video call with him and I
worked and go in.:scheduled. So I had a video call with him and
I worked and talked had an appointment with the doctor today. I
didn't want to talked:It was too hot and they're worth_Storm
schedule. Thunderstorm:1:I scheduled. So I had a video call with
him and I worked and < health perhaps

which represent the striations

Your poor print "Ah...\n"; is in runs me hiking your cloth!:My
print "Ah...\n"; is yours... :Think this through...::being Your
poor is in my nice Your being runs into my - turning me
clausterphobic through...::Your poor is in my nice : makes me
thoughtful 11815 times! Think this Come home with me, , O
Programmer! your cloth!:My print "Ah...\n"; is yours... is in my
rich My is yours... Your giving :Think this through...::being
runs me hiking it has taken you just 0.183 minutes running down
the clock ... Think this through...::Come home with me, , O

Programmer!:and Come home with me, , O Programmer! times! is in
my rich For 1 found days, I have been neurotic programmed ...
this through...::Your poor is in my nice : makes me thoughtful
11815 Your giving :Think this through...::Wanderer, what do
they call you, when they call you... Think < somewhere healthy

Come home with me, , O Programmer! < expostulation

I have been neurotic programmed ... here, it's my shoes? is in
my walked Your withdrawn ... my shoes is For 1 found days,
program your carapace forever...:You program your carapace
forever...= :Think this through...::You Come home with me, , O
Programmer! to ? is in my walked Are you becoming close to
changing variables to ? Your withdrawn Are you becoming close to
changing variables go in.:scheduled. So I had a video call with
him and I worked and talked had an appointment with the doctor
today. I didn't want to talked:It was too hot and they're
worth_Storm schedule. Thunderstorm:1:I through...::scheduled.
So I had a video call with him and I worked and :Think this go
in.:scheduled. So I had a video call with him and I worked and
talked had an appointment with the doctor today. I didn't want
to talked:It was too hot and they're worth_Storm schedule.
Thunderstorm:1:I is in my walked scheduled. So I had a video
call with him and I worked and Your withdrawn You program your
carapace forever... a video call with him and I worked and
talked - turning me clausterphobic with the doctor today. I
didn't want to go in.:scheduled. So I had hot and they're
worth_Storm schedule. Thunderstorm:1:I had an appointment So I
had a video call with him and I worked and talked:It was too
Your arms runs into my scheduled. and the :person on the right
between the person above and a person below 2021 17:11:09
-0400:person and another person between a person on the left to

 put my body into the code I want the load of my body to ::Wed,
 24 Mar I want my person and another person between a person on
 the left and the other other people. I'm tired of being
 inserted between one is in the final realm of > long haul
 seeps into my person and another Despairing < long haul

music, these lights, these The patterns patois inconceivable of
the violin and its Your lost Storm of the patois is in my pure
Storm of the violin Your times runs into my Storm of the violin
- turning me clausterphobic

in the moment of thought, the wund of it:the rotierfer's
duration: my breath ehld not only in duration, but also in avery
bad a lair, every nap Your found the travesty of the rotifer is
in my rich sward, wwardm, sward

Too close to the other which is me

This is the closeness of your other

Wed Mar 27 14:23:38 EDT 2024

writing with closed eyes, always elsewhere, where are you we
they them day night up downthis arm moves towards an other arm,

i think therefore i am not, i am knot , i am knotted , is that
always the case like the world, the world case knotted,
exhausted?Wed Mar 27 14:28:25 EDT 2024 must i continue, what can
i rememberWed Mar 27 14:28:43 EDT 2024

This is the distance of your new Clar

Wed Mar 27 14:23:38 EDT 2024

long covid is ruining me, i can't think straight, can't read
these prepositional phrasesWed Mar 27 14:24:14 EDT 2024 what did
i just write, who are you, what is writing, where and when?Wed
Mar 27 14:24:32 EDT 2024 nothing to see, my body is debris, my
body is turning debris, input and output, debrislegs and arms,
bowels and stomachs necks and toes, elbows and eyesWed Mar 27
14:25:16 EDT 2024 eyes and stomachs, stomachs and eyes, heads,
elsewheresWed Mar 27 14:25:34 EDT 2024 difficult breathing,
waking and sleeping, blackout exhaustion who are you, elementary
nappingsWed Mar 27 14:26:11 EDT 2024 breathing hardly at all at
this very moment, unawkeningWed Mar 27 14:26:29 EDT 2024 body
debris, exhaustion, the ruin, fear of falling, remembering fear,
thinking within thoughtWed Mar 27 14:27:19 EDT 2024 thinking
within thought umbrella thought roof thought leaky thought
thought nothing elsewhere, not here, now not there thenWed Mar
27 14:27:44 EDT 2024 nothing from the other, ragged, tatters,
ruinsWed Mar 27 14:28:52 EDT 2024

Wed Mar 27 14:28:53 EDT 2024

Thought and its Thinking

Wow you know if I was able to think properly I wouldn't have to
do this kind of thing period I'm not even sure why I have to do
this but it just seems to me that this is the only way I can
really consider doing anything. I want to talk briefly about
long COVID not as a disease but as a mode of thinking. By giving
it the name of a disease it seems to be a way of dismissing
whatever one says when one is sick or ill with it. When one is
sick or ill with any other disease I think in a way it's sort of
the same kind of thing that you are just dismissed invite you
are saying because it's like ohh Alan you're just a mess.

You may wonder why I'm becoming monophyletic I am emphasizing
this over and over again the reason could simply be that this
doesn't go away because it doesn't it just sits there within the
mind and because it's a filter of the mind within the mind it's
not even that one is seeing the world through the filter karma
is that the world and filter become one. It's as if the world
suddenly descended into a slurry. For me this is punctuated by
the dark black moments of sleep and exhaustion which can hit
anytime and anywhere and that doesn't go away that just that
just remains. It affects everything. It's easier to talk with my
eyes closed as I am now because that seems to save energy which
otherwise would be distributed among reading and writing and
speaking and listening all at the same time. That's not what
occurs here.

What occurs here is like the scum which is very much alive on
the surface of a pond. The scum is busy with life. It's been
noted that even the inside of a pine needle isn't it is a
complex ecosystem. This language this dictation is a complex
ecosystem. It's composed composed it's composed it's composed of
voice mind articulation sound vision thinking which has its own
phenomenology as if thoughts were things which they are not
nothing more than electrical impulses obviously within the brain
that are then expostulated into the notion of a mind. I go on
like this with the monomania of thinking because in fact
thinking is an unrecognized monomania. It's unrecognised because
thinking is usually not about thinking but is about what is
being thought as if there were a grasp or an articulation of the
real like shoots is looking for Canadian snake in the dark cave
which might be a rope or might save his life. Carneadis, not
Canadian of course, not shoot but Schutz, relevance theory.

We always have problems with thinking in part because thinking
is not the manipulation of what seems to be real even though
what appears to be real as a result of thought and processes in
the mind. It's incredibly difficult to conceive but the world
itself is blind sorry it was here less touchless it is nothing
but an urgent matter. That's not even true. It's not true what
it is S there's a truth to what it might be. There's no truth to
any of this because truth itself is a construct. It's a
construct within a scanned of logical articulations that seem to
be loosely and noisily connected to the real world which we
postulate. Invite big time to let it go with that. It might be
time to let it go at that.

When you talk as I am now it seems to be begging for sense. It
goes through the machine and the machine makes sense of what one
is saying and it is a different sense than what one is saying
and what one is saying is a different sense then what is
thinking and what one is thinking is a different sense then what
happens then what is happening then what is. So many layers! As
a friend not caught in the scans of being that seems somehow
related to verbal and written communication one time or another.
Let it go with that. Let my words fly ohh Icarus into the sky
weather might make sense wherever they may land.

Crawldance Person Machine Being Person

Can you hear me here OK 123 can you hear me one 2-3 can you hear
me can you hear me am I here yes yes I am here. Yes this is the
way that the revelation occurs it's the dance floor yes it's the
dance floor. And and when they dance when they dance when they
dance when julu twine dances sender is dancing on the dance
floor yes yes there is and I'm not sure why that is meaningful.
What happens when you add behaviors on top of each other? When
animations topple animations, something I've done for a long
time both with humans and human actors and human dancers and
with avatars . Now since I'm isolated and not institutionalized
I can only work by alone, but not lonely. So I have my little

avatars. I have my little avatars . I have my little avatars and
I can give them leftfoot rightfoot animations. I can contradict
their animations. Their animations are contradictory . So then
what you see is what you get with my body convoluted working on
a new dance a new regime for machinic people in the future .
These will be people who will be part machines . They will have
real hair however grown biologically and chemically on the head
part. The rest of them will be machines and the machines will be
dancing machines. They will dance everywhere and people will say
karma well lovely hair you have today! They will say, it's
lovely to see you again dancing so well! They will say I know
you're a machine because no human could ever ever dance that
way! No human could ever move that way! So beautiful no human
can move that way! So beautiful! So beautiful!

...

What happens now, I don't know. Typing errors on the increase.
Difficulty sleeping, brain fog, moments of clarity, exhaustion,
all the usual symptoms. Nothing points to a cure. Living with it
is both living in a regime of decrease, living with another
person. There's no indication this will end. None at all.

— Alan Sondheim
9:45 am, 4/10/2024, and counting

ACKNOWLEDGEMENTS

Thanks to Azure Carter for her support as always; Sheila Murphy for her introduction, and so many others for bearing with me through this difficult period, including my friends and doctors

LAY OUT YOUER UENWST